Adobe Flash Professional CS5

FOR WINDOWS AND MACINTOSH

KATHERINE ULRICH

Peachpit Press

Visual QuickStart Guide
Adobe Flash Professional CS5 for Windows and Macintosh
Katherine Ulrich

Peachpit Press
1249 Eighth Street
Berkeley, CA 94710
510/524-2178
510/524-2221 (fax)

Find us on the web at: www.peachpit.com
To report errors, please send a note to errata@peachpit.com
Peachpit Press is a division of Pearson Education

Copyright © 2011 by Katherine Ulrich

Project Editor: Wendy Sharp
Production Editor: Rebecca Winter
Contributor: Andreas Heim
Copy Editor: Jacqueline Aaron
Tech Editor: Andreas Heim
Compositor: Myrna Vladic
Indexer: FireCrystal Communications

ISBN 13: 978-0-321-70446-7
ISBN 10:   0-321-70446-0

9 8 7 6 5 4 3 2 1

Printed and bound in the United States of America

Dedication

To Perry Whittle, whose support, both moral and technical, helps me keep it all in perspective, and who downplays my failings and promotes my successes shamelessly.

Special Thanks to:

A rousing cheer for the editor of this edition, Wendy Sharp, Senior Acquisitions Editor, for her helpful editorial direction, words of encouragement, and perseverance throughout the process of creating this book. I continue to be grateful to Andreas Heim, Director of Technology, Smashing Ideas, for writing Chapter 15 (originally for the CS3 edition of this book) and for once again taking on the role of technical reader/ technical resource for this edition. A round of applause for Copy Editor Jacqueline Aaron; it's been wonderful having her eagle eye watching my back for errors of style, spelling, grammar, and logic. Kudos to Production Editor Rebecca Winter and Compositor Myrna Vladic for making these pages clean and clear. Thanks also to Emily Glossbrenner of FireCrystal Communications for expert indexing on a tight time line. Additionally, thanks to folks at Adobe who took time out of busy schedules to answer questions, large and small: Jay Armstrong, Marisa Bozza, David Durkee, Craig Simmons, Alan Stearns, Kenneth June Toley III, and Valerio Virgillito.

A tip of the hat to those whose various forms of assistance in past editions still echo in this one: Brad Bechtel, Lisa Brazieal, Erika Burback, Pat Christenson, Jeremy Clark, Cliff Colby, Peter Alan Davy, Jen deHaan, Jane DeKoven, Jonathan Duran, Lupe Edgar, Victor Gavenda, Suki Gear, Connie Jeung-Mills, Mark R. Jonkman, Becky Morgan, Erica Norton, Christi Payne, Janice Pearce, Nancy Reinhardt, Sharon Selden, Kathy Simpson, James Talbot, Tiffany Taylor, Michael J. Ulrich, Bentley Wolfe, and Lisa Young.

And finally, a special note of thanks in memory to Marjorie Baer, who brought me to this project in the first place and was often in my thoughts as I worked on this revision.

Contents at a Glance

Table of Contents

Introduction

Adobe Flash Professional CS5 is the latest version of the enormously popular web design tool. In its original incarnation, Flash gave web designers an efficient way to send artwork and animation over limited-bandwidth connections. Flash's claim to fame was its ability to deliver vector images over the web, making download times shorter. Flash's use of progressive downloading and streaming allowed some elements of a website to display immediately, making sites more responsive.

Today Flash is a robust toolkit for creating anything from simple animations to full-fledged websites and complex web applications. To the simple tools for creating and animating artwork and interface elements and writing the HTML necessary to display all those elements in a web page via a browser, Flash adds a full-fledged object-oriented scripting language, the ability to display video, and ever-more sophisticated text, graphics, and animation tools.

Flash CS5 offers a new tool for working with text—the text-layout framework (TLF)—which gives you access to a wide range of typographic effects and text-layout

methods. New deco-tool patterns create repetitive elements, such as flowers, trees, and buildings; there are also animated patterns for flames, smoke, and particle generators. Additions to the properties of IK bones let you simulate physical forces acting on items animated with inverse kinematics. A new Color panel makes it easier to define colors, enhancements to the code editor in the Actions panel make working with ActionScript in the authoring environment easier, and the addition of a Code Snippets panel helps with common scripting tasks.

How Flash Animates

Flash lets you use standard animation techniques to create the illusion of movement. By displaying a series of still images—each slightly different from the next—one after another, you simulate continuous movement. Flash CS5 lets you use five animation techniques in the authoring environment (you can also create animation through ActionScript, although that is outside the scope of this *QuickStart Guide*). With frame-by-frame animation, you create an entire series of images for each segment of animation. With classic tweening and shape tweening, you create the first and last image in the series (the initial and ending keyframes) and let Flash create the rest of the images, interpolating changes between the keyframes. With motion tweening, you create an object and define changes to its properties over time; Flash creates a series of images that move and transform the object. With inverse kinematics, you create skeleton-like structures that control objects or shapes and arrange these structures in different poses at different points in time; Flash creates a series of images that animate the structure moving from one pose to the next.

Flash Interactivity

Over the years, Flash's tools for creating interactivity have become more robust. Flash CS5 contains a full-fledged object-oriented scripting language, in two versions: ActionScript 2.0 and 3.0. Both are compliant with the ECMA-262 specification, which is also the foundation for JavaScript, so they should feel familiar to anyone who already knows JavaScript. With ActionScript, Flash has become a toolkit for creating web applications which might be anything from an online store to a corporate training module to a video-clip–display site to a snazzy promotional piece describing this year's hottest new car, complete with customizable virtual test-drives.

Flash File Formats

Flash provides both an authoring environment for creating content and a playback system for making that content viewable on a local computer or in a web browser. With Flash CS5, Adobe introduces a new

behind-the-scenes format and structure for the materials created in Flash: XFL (a version of XML—extensible markup language—for Flash). The XFL format stores the assets, data, and code that make up a Flash movie as separate sub-files. By default, Flash compresses the XFL and hides that structure from you. When you choose File > Save, Flash saves the artwork, animation, and interactivity you've created in a traditional Flash-format file. These files have the extension .fla and are often referred to as *FLAs*. The tasks in this book assume you will continue to work with the compressed XML file, which looks and acts like a traditional Flash file. If you want to be able to access the subfiles that make up your movie—so that, for example, you can use them in other applications that understand XML (such as Adobe Photoshop, Illustrator, or After Effects)—choose File > Save As, then save your Flash content in Flash CS5 Uncompressed Document (.xfl) format. To make Flash content viewable on the web, you convert the FLA files to Flash Player format; Flash Player files have the extension .swf and are often referred to as *SWFs*.

How Flash Delivers

Flash's publishing feature creates the necessary HTML code to display your Flash content in a web browser. You can also choose alternate methods of delivering Flash content—as animated GIF images, for example. Flash creates the alternate files during the publishing process.

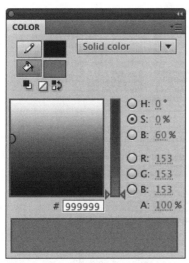

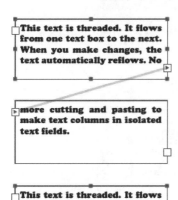

A The new Color panel displays the hue, saturation, brightness, red, green, and blue properties simultaneously.

B The TLF text tool creates linked text fields with threaded text. When you change the size of the field, the properties of the text, and/or the amount of text, the text reflows.

Flash CS5: What's New?

This version of Flash offers a significant new text tool for designers: TLF text. There are also user-interface improvements, new deco-tool patterns, improvements to the scripting facilities of the Actions panel, predefined ActionScript code snippets, and a new behind-the-scenes file format. Let's look at some highlights of Flash CS5.

Interface Enhancements

Color Panel A redesigned Color panel simultaneously displays all the properties of a color (hue, saturation, brightness, red, green, and blue) **A**.

Info Panel Hot-text controls in the Info panel let you change property settings for selected objects on the Stage interactively.

Design Enhancements

Text-Layout Framework There's a new way of working with text: the text-layout framework (TLF). TLF gives Flash designers access to a huge new set of typographic tools for use within the Flash authoring environment. TLF creates linked text fields, with threaded text **B**. Threaded fields simplify the process of designing multiple-column text that wraps around graphic elements. Threaded text reflows within the linked fields as you add and/or delete text or change sizes and fonts. TLF can also

continues on next page

create multiple columns of text within a single text field . TLF can create vertical and horizontal text, reading left-to-right or right-to-left. TLF text supports Asian text and lets you control many advanced typographic details, such as ligatures, number styles and number alignment, leading, tracking, padding, indents, column gutters—all appropriately implemented for the language and locale you are working with.

Improved Font Embedding The new Font Embedding dialog lets you embed subsets of glyphs (characters) from the fonts you use (say, all uppercase and lowercase letters) rather than embedding all the glyphs in the font. This helps keep down file sizes.

Expanded Deco Tool The deco tool offers many new pattern types. There are patterns for creating organic elements, such as flowers and trees . There's a pattern for creating buildings. Some of the new patterns create animation—for example, animated flames, smoke, lightning flashes, or particles spewing from a single source.

Animation Enhancements

Springy Bones New properties for IK bones let you simulate the effect of physical forces on the jointed armatures you create with inverse kinematics.

ActionScript Enhancements

Code Completion Flash now automatically imports custom classes as well as built-in classes in ActionScript 3.0, which means that you can get code hints for custom classes when you use the script pane of the Actions panel.

C The TLF text tool also lets you set up multiple columns within a single text field. When you resize the field, the columns adjust to fill the new space.

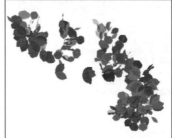

D The deco tool sports many new patterns, including brushes for creating organic elements, such as flowers and trees.

E The Code Snippets panel offers a selection of predefined ActionScript 3.0 scripts that you can use in your movies. You can also create custom snippets using your own code.

Automatic Close-Bracket Insertion You can choose to have Flash automatically create paired brackets: whenever you type an open bracket ({) in the Actions panel's Script pane, Flash adds a line for entering a statement, adds a closing bracket (}) to end the statement, and creates indents appropriate to the nesting level of the bracketed statement.

Code Snippets Panel Flash CS5 offers a selection of predefined ActionScript 3.0 scripts **E**. These commented blocks of code create scripts for basic interactivity tasks, such as navigating the Timeline, linking to web pages, and animating selected objects. Some snippets offer building blocks of code for creating event handlers. The panel also lets you create custom snippets using your own code.

Collaboration, Cross-pollination, and More

XFL Format Behind the scenes, Flash CS5 uses a new format—XFL—that is based on XML. By default, Flash compresses the XFL files and wraps them up in the familiar FLA file format, so you can continue to work with FLA and SWF files as in earlier versions. You do have the option to work with uncompressed XFL files, in which the various assets and pieces that make up the Flash movie get saved as individual subfiles. In some workflows, the ability to access these files separately makes it easier for designers and coders to collaborate and work with data and assets in various Adobe applications.

XFG Format Flash CS5 exports to Adobe XFG format, an XML-based graphics interchange format that enables you to work on items in other Adobe graphics applications, such as Illustrator.

Automatic Update of Photoshop Edits You can access Photoshop CS5 to edit bitmaps from inside your Flash movie; edits you make to the original source file automatically update in your Flash movie.

Video Preview The FLVPlayback component that you can use to display video clips in Flash now plays its video live on the Stage during authoring. You no longer have to test a movie to see the video in action. In addition, you can set cue points (for controlling video with ActionScript) in the Properties panel in the Flash authoring environment. And there are new space-saving skins for creating video controls for your video clips.

How to Use This Book

Like all the books in the *Visual QuickStart Guide* series, this one seeks to take you out of passive reading mode and help you get started working in the program. The tasks in the book teach you to use Flash's features. The book is suitable for beginners who are just starting to use Flash and for intermediate-level Flash designers. The initial chapters cover the basics of creating graphic elements by using Flash's unique set of drawing tools. Next, you learn how to turn graphic elements into animations. After that, you learn to create basic user-interface elements, such as rollover buttons. To make your content interactive, you'll work with the Actions panel to create ActionScript for basic interactivity. You'll also learn about importing and working with various non-Flash content: artwork from other applications, sounds, and video. Finally, you'll learn to use Flash's Publish feature to create HTML for putting your Flash creations on the web. At the end of each chapter in this book, you'll find a

section named *Practice Session*. The ideas in these sections are designed to spark your imagination and reinforce the learning provided by the chapter's individual tasks. The Practice Sessions are not intended to create a comprehensive project for you to complete, although materials created in early sessions can be used in later practice sessions.

What You Should Already Know

In order to get you started quickly, this book makes a few assumptions:

- Adobe Flash CS5 is already installed on your computer.

- You're familiar with the workings of your operating system.

- You can carry out basic tasks, such as opening, closing, and saving documents; opening, closing, resizing, collapsing, and expanding document windows and dialogs; using hierarchical menus, pop-up menus, radio buttons, and checkboxes; and carrying out standard application commands such as copy, cut, paste, delete, and undo.

Cross-platform Issues

The Flash authoring environment has a very similar interface on the Macintosh and Windows platforms. Still, differences exist where the user interfaces of the platforms diverge. When these differences are substantial, I describe the procedures for both platforms.

Originally, Macintosh computers required Macintosh keyboards, and some key names were unique to that keyboard: for example, Return (instead of Enter) and Delete (instead of Backspace). I generally uses Enter and Delete for these two key names.

Keyboard Shortcuts

Most of Flash's menu-based commands have a keyboard equivalent. That equivalent appears in the menu next to the command name. When I introduce a command, I also describe the keyboard shortcut. In subsequent mentions of the command, however, I usually omit the keyboard shortcut.

Contextual Menus

Both the Macintosh and Windows platforms offer contextual menus. To access one of these contextual menus, Control-click (Mac) or right-click (Windows) an element in the Flash movie. You'll see a menu of commands that are appropriate for working with that element. For the most part, these commands duplicate commands in the main menu; therefore, I don't generally note them as alternatives for the commands described in the book. I do point out when using the contextual menu is particularly handy or when a contextual menu contains a command that is unavailable in the main menu bar.

Artwork, Scripts, and More

The Flash graphics in this book are easy to draw. Most of the examples are based on simple geometric shapes, which means you can spend your time seeing the Flash features in action instead of re-creating fancy artwork. To make it even easier, Flash files containing the graphic elements that you need for each task are available on Peachpit Press's companion website for this book. In Chapter 15, you'll learn to create scripts for basic interactivity, and Flash files containing the completed scripts for these tasks are also available. In addition, the site offers some bonus tasks that I just couldn't squeeze into the pages of this book.

To access the files, you must register at www.peachpit.com. Click the Account Sign In button to create an account (or log in to your existing account). Click the "Register your products here" (or "Register another product") link and enter the book's ISBN (0321704460) in the text field that appears. A link to the supplemental content will appear on your account page. You should also be able to download the files by registering or logging into your account at www.peachpit.com/flashcs5vqs.

The Flash
Authoring Tool

Before you start working in Adobe Flash Professional CS5, it's helpful to familiarize yourself with the authoring environment. On first opening Flash, you'll see the default workspace in an *application frame*. The application frame holds pieces of the Flash application in a resizable window. At the top of the frame lies the application bar, which offers Maximize, Minimize, and Quit buttons; a menu for choosing workspace layouts; and a text field where you can enter terms for searching Flash's Help system. Various docked panels appear around the edges of the window.

By default, the center of the application frame holds any open Flash documents; if no documents are open, a Welcome screen with options for creating new documents or opening recent ones appears in the middle of the workspace. You can choose to make documents and panels float over the workspace instead of docking to the application frame.

In This Chapter

Working with Flash Documents

Most of the basic document operations in Flash—opening, closing, and saving files—are straightforward to experienced computer users. Creating new documents may be a little different than in other programs, because Flash creates a variety of document types. Flash's Welcome screen assists you in opening and creating these various Flash documents.

To set launch preferences:

1. From the Flash application menu (Mac) or Edit menu (Windows), choose Preferences.

   The Preferences dialog appears. The General category is selected by default.

2. From the On Launch menu , choose one of the following:

   ▸ No Document. Flash's menu bar, application frame, and panels appear at launch, but no document opens.

   ▸ New Document. Flash opens a new document at launch.

   ▸ Last Documents Open. Flash opens the documents that were open when you ended the previous work session.

   ▸ Welcome Screen (the default setting). Flash displays the Welcome screen at launch and any time you have closed all the documents during a work session.

3. Click OK.

TIP To change your launch preference to the No Document option quickly, click the Don't Show Again button in the lower-left corner of the Welcome screen. A dialog appears to remind you that you must change the launch settings in the General tab of the Preferences dialog to see the Welcome screen again.

A The On Launch options in the General category of the Preferences dialog tell Flash what type of document(s), if any, to open when you launch Flash.

About Preferences

To see, or not to see, the Welcome screen is just one of many preference settings in Flash. To choose new settings, you open the Preferences dialog. From the Flash menu (Mac) or Edit menu (Windows), choose Preferences, and select a category from the list in the left-hand pane. Choose settings for that category in the main window. Preferences fall into nine categories: General, Action-Script, Auto Format, Clipboard, Drawing, Text, Warnings, PSD File Importer, and AI File Importer. You'll learn about specific Preferences settings as they relate to specific tasks throughout this book.

Touring the Welcome Screen

Flash's default setting opens the Welcome screen when you launch. The Welcome screen contains active links that let you open documents quickly. You can open a new document, a document that you worked on recently, or a template document. You can link to Flash tutorials or to the Flash Exchange site, where you can download third-party extensions, such as new components, as they become available **B**.

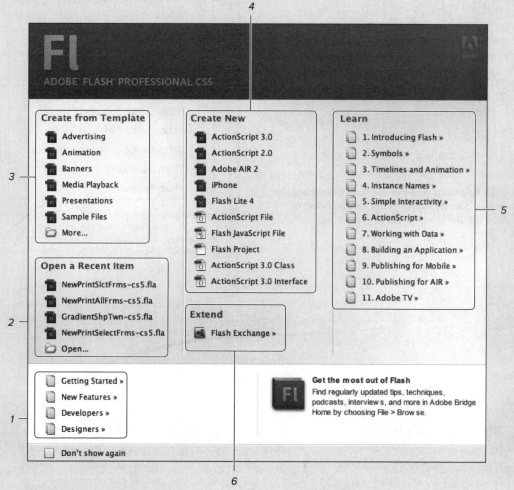

B The Welcome screen presents common operations you might want to carry out at the beginning of a work session: opening Flash's help files (1), opening documents you worked on recently (2), creating documents from templates (3), and creating new Flash documents (4). For new users, there are links to the tutorials that come with Flash (5) and a link to the Flash Exchange site (6), where you can find third-party extensions.

To create a new Flash document:

From the Welcome screen, in the Create New section, click the ActionScript 3.0 link.

Flash opens a new blank document.

or

1. Choose File > New, or press Command-N (Mac) or Ctrl-N (Windows).

    Flash opens the New Document dialog 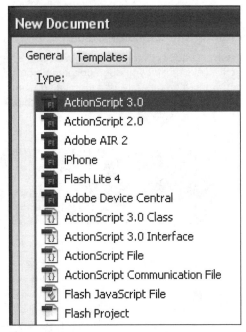. This dialog has two views: General and Templates. General is selected by default.

2. In the General view, select Action-Script 3.0.

3. Click OK.

    Flash opens a new blank document.

TIP To switch views in the New Document dialog, click the appropriate button (Mac) or tab (Windows) at the top of the dialog.

New Document

General | Templates

Type:

- ActionScript 3.0
- ActionScript 2.0
- Adobe AIR 2
- iPhone
- Flash Lite 4
- Adobe Device Central
- ActionScript 3.0 Class
- ActionScript 3.0 Interface
- ActionScript File
- ActionScript Communication File
- Flash JavaScript File
- Flash Project

C To create a new document in Flash, choose File > New. The New Document dialog opens, with the General view and ActionScript 3.0 selected by default. Click OK to create a new document.

Which Flash File Type to Create?

The Create New section of the Welcome screen lists ten types of files; which one is right for you? In this book, we'll work exclusively with Flash for ActionScript files, but you still have two choices: ActionScript 3.0 or ActionScript 2.0. For many of the graphics, text, and animation tasks you'll do, either choice is fine. The difference becomes important when you start scripting. (You'll learn about scripting in Chapter 15.) The scripting options and features available to you depend on which version of ActionScript you use. This book deals with ActionScript 3.0. When an exercise asks you to create a new file, choose ActionScript 3.0 unless instructed otherwise. If you decide to use a different version of ActionScript later, you can change the file type to ActionScript 2.0 (or 1.0) in the Publish Settings dialog. (You'll learn about publishing in Chapter 18.)

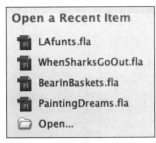

Open a Recent Item

	LAfunts.fla
	WhenSharksGoOut.fla
	BearInBaskets.fla
	PaintingDreams.fla
	Open...

D The Open a Recent Item section of the Welcome screen lets you view links to the last four documents you worked on. Clicking a filename opens the document.

Click to close document   *Click to view document*

E Viewing multiple open documents as tabs in a single window is the default setting for Flash CS5. Click an inactive title tab to bring that document to the front. To close the active document, click the Close button in the tab.

To open an existing document:

From the Welcome screen, in the Open a Recent Item section **D**, click the name of a recent file.

Flash opens that file directly.

or

1. From the Welcome screen, in the Open a Recent Item section, click the Open link.

   or

   Choose File > Open.

   The Open dialog appears.

2. Navigate to the file you want to open.

3. Select the file.

4. Click Open.

TIP In Flash's default environment, multiple open documents appear as tabs within the application frame. Tabs for inactive documents are a darker gray. Click a tab to bring that document to the front **E**.

TIP You can change the order of the tabs for open documents by dragging a tab to a new position.

Working with Template Documents

If you work repeatedly with one type of Flash document—for example, you create banner ads of a specific size with a consistent background or a set of consistent elements—you can save that basic document as a template.

To create a template document:

1. Open the document that you want to turn into a template.

2. Choose File > Save As Template 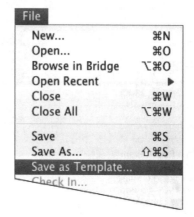.

   A dialog appears warning that you will lose SWF history data (a record of the file size of each SWF generated as you test and publish your movie).

3. Click Save As Template.

   The Save As Template dialog appears, showing a preview of your document .

4. In the Name field, type a name for the template.

5. To specify a category, do either of the following:

   ▸ To select an existing category, choose the desired category from the Category pop-up menu.

   ▸ To create a new category, type a name in the Category field.

6. In the Description field, type a brief summary or reminder of what the template is for.

7. Click Save.

   Flash saves the file as a master template document in a folder named Templates within the Configuration folder.

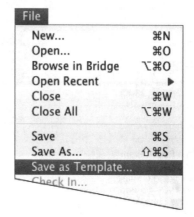

Ⓐ To turn a Flash file into a template that can be the basis of future documents, choose File > Save As Template.

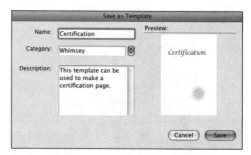

Ⓑ The Save As Template command lets you save Flash documents for reuse. You can create your own template categories and provide a brief description of the template file you're saving in the Save As Template dialog.

TIP Once you've completed the template, close the document. You may think that after saving the document as a template you're working in a copy made from the template, but you're not. You're still working in the master template document until you close it.

Create from Template

🖅 Advertising

🖅 Animation

🖅 Banners

🖅 Media Playback

🖅 Presentations

🖅 Sample Files

📁 More...

C Click a template-category link in the Welcome screen to access the New from Template dialog.

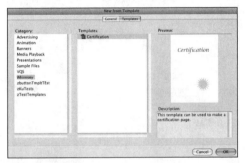

D The Templates view of the New from Template (or New Document) dialog displays a preview and a description (when available) for the item selected in the Category and Templates lists.

The Configuration Folders

Flash handles customized settings by using different types of configuration folders, including application-level folders that are language-specific, and user-level folders that are customized for individual users. You can read more about using Configuration folders, in the Bonus content available by registering your book at www.peachpit.com/flashcs5vqs.

To open a new document from a template document:

1. From the Welcome screen, in the Create from Template section, click a template-category link **C**.

   The New from Template dialog appears.

   or

   Choose File > New.

   The New Document/New from Template dialog appears **D**. The New Document dialog and the New from Template dialog are identical except for their names. Both display two views: General and Templates. The dialog's name changes to reflect the active view. When you click a template folder in the Welcome screen, the Templates view is selected by default in the dialog.

2. From the Category list, choose the appropriate category.

   The folder you select in Step 1 is selected by default, and its contents appear in the Templates list. To view other templates, select another category.

3. From the Templates list, choose the template you want to use.

   The dialog previews the selected template's first frame and provides a brief description of the template, if one is available.

4. Click OK.

   Flash opens a new document with all the contents of the template.

TIP When you choose File > New, Flash displays the document-creation dialog based on the type of file you created previously. The New Document dialog appears if the last file you created was a document. The New from Template dialog appears if you created the last file from a template.

About the Flash Authoring Environment

Flash CS5 appears on the desktop in an application frame. This frame holds Flash's panels and documents in a resizable window. The frame keeps elements together, making the most efficient use of space and creating a Flash "desktop" that hides elements of other open applications. (In the Mac OS, such elements would otherwise show through any spaces between panels and documents, creating a distracting visual field.) A menu bar containing the Flash commands appears at the top of the screen, above the application frame.

Touring the Workspace

The layout of elements within the application frame is called the *workspace*. Flash comes with seven preset workspaces: Animator, Classic, Debug, Designer, Developer, Essentials, and Small Screen. Each one uses a different set of docked panels **A**. The workspace is customizable. You can open and close documents and panels, docking them where you prefer within the frame. Or you can undock panels and documents and float them anywhere on the desktop. You can save these configurations in new workspaces. Flash remembers the current workspace setup from one work session to the next.

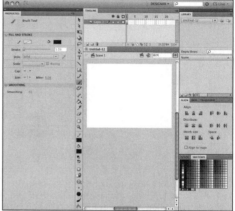

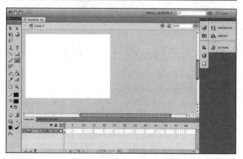

A Flash offers seven preset workspaces, each with a different configuration of open panels and docking locations. Three workspaces are pictured here: Essentials (top), a bare-bones setup; Designer (middle), a layout of panels commonly used while creating artwork in Flash; and Small Screen (bottom), used when screen real estate is limited.

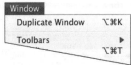

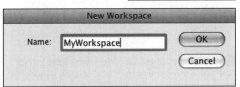

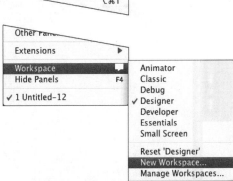

B Choose Window > Workspace > New Workspace (top) to access the New Workspace dialog (bottom). Enter a name for your current desktop configuration and click OK.

C The Workspace pop-up menu in the Application bar gives you quick access to preset and custom workspaces as well as workspace-management commands.

To save a custom workspace:

1. Configure panels in the application frame and/or in floating windows, using the techniques you'll learn later in this chapter.

2. Choose Window > Workspace > New Workspace.

   The New Workspace dialog appears **B**.

3. In the Name field, enter a title for this workspace.

4. Click OK.

   Flash saves that configuration and adds the name to the Workspace menu.

To choose a workspace:

1. Choose Window > Workspace.

2. From the submenu that appears, choose one of the workspaces listed.

   Flash comes with seven default workspaces: **Animator** opens a set of panels that are useful for creating Flash animation; **Classic** opens a minimal set of panels; **Debug** opens just the panels needed to troubleshoot ActionScript; **Designer** opens panels commonly used in creating artwork; **Developer** opens panels commonly used in creating ActionScript; **Essentials** (the default setting) opens a small set of panels; **Small Screen** opens an even more minimal set, with all of the panels set to work as panel icons, in their collapsed state. If you've created a custom workspace, you can choose it from the submenu as well.

TIP You can also save and choose workspaces from the Workspace pop-up menu at the right side of the Application bar that forms the top of the application frame **C**.

TIP To restore a workspace, choose it by name from the Window > Workspace submenu or from the Workspace pop-up menu in the Application bar.

Touring a Document

Each Flash document consists of a Title tab (or Title bar if the document is in a floating window), with a Close button; an Edit bar, which displays identifying text and menus for choosing symbols and scenes; a Stage, the area in which your movie displays; and a Pasteboard, the extra space around the Stage **D**. By default, open documents are docked, filling the middle of the application frame; you can undock them and let them float over the workspace if you prefer. Floating document windows sit above the application frame, and therefore obscure any docked panels below. Floating panels sit above floating documents.

Touring the Timeline

The Timeline **E** visually represents every element of a movie and is the framework for building projects. In Flash CS5, the Timeline appears in an independent panel that displays information about the open and active document. You'll use this panel extensively when you create animations.

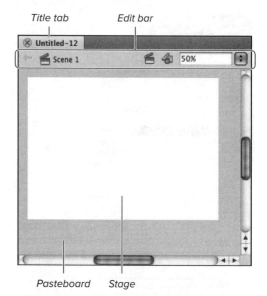

Title tab   *Edit bar*

Pasteboard   *Stage*

D A Flash document consists of the Title tab (or Title bar if the document is in a floating window), the Edit bar, the Stage, and the Pasteboard.

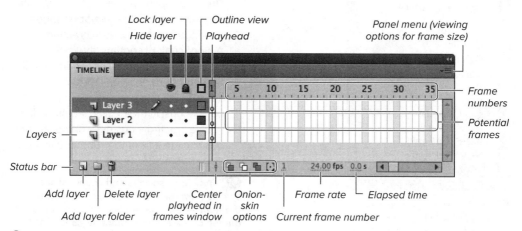

E The Timeline is the complete record of your movie. It represents all the scenes, frames, and layers that make up the movie. Frames appear in chronological order. Clicking any frame in the Timeline takes you directly to that frame and displays its contents on the Stage.

Using Panels

Flash organizes drawing and authoring tools as *panels.* Some panels contain tools for creating or modifying graphic elements. Others help you organize and navigate your Flash document. You can dock panels within the application frame or have them float independently. You'll learn to work with specific panels in later chapters of this book. For now, you'll learn some general features of panels. For more detailed tips on how to manage panels to optimize your workspace, see the companion website (www.peachpit.com/flashcs5vqs). To manipulate panels, use the interface elements shown in **A**.

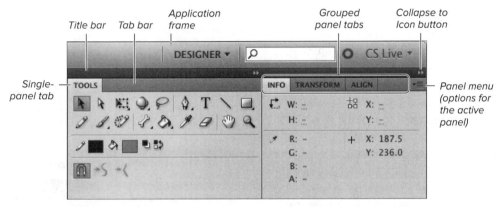

Docked panels

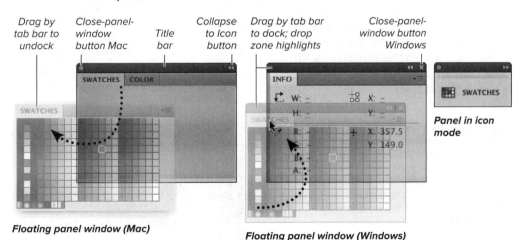

Floating panel window (Mac)

Floating panel window (Windows)

A An open panel appears as a tab inside a panel frame; the frame may appear in a dock in Flash's application frame or in a floating window. You can group multiple panels within one panel frame; they appear as horizontal tabs. Clicking a tab in a group activates that panel, making it visible in the frame. Panels can be in floating windows or docked. Drag panels to reconfigure them: group them, stack them, or dock them; drop zones highlight to indicate how panels combine. You can also collapse panels to icons to save space.

To open (or close) panels:

From the Window menu, select the desired panel—for example, Color **B**.

One of the following actions takes place:

- If the selected panel is closed, a frame containing that panel opens. The frame may appear in a dock or in a floating window, depending on the selected workspace and any modifications you've made to it.

- If the selected panel is minimized (to the Tab bar) or collapsed (to an icon), it expands.

- If the selected panel is obscured behind other tabs in the same frame or other floating panel windows, the selected panel moves to the front.

- If the selected panel is the only tab— or the front tab—in a frame in a floating window that is already open, expanded, and in front, the entire window closes.

- If the selected panel is the only tab— or the front tab—in a docked frame that is already open and expanded, the frame containing that panel (including all its tabs) closes. Other frames stacked within the dock remain open.

TIP To remove one panel from a panel frame, choose Close from the panel menu (located at the right side of the Tab bar); the active panel closes. To remove all the panels from that frame, choose Close Group; the panel frame (and all the panel tabs in it) closes; any panel frames stacked above or below that frame stay open **C**.

TIP To close all the panels in a floating window quickly, click the window's Close button. The window closes, along with all the panel frames within it **D**.

B The Window menu contains a list of the panels in Flash.

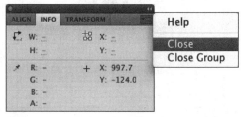

C You can close panels individually or as groups (whether docked or floating). In the Tab bar of the frame containing the panel (or panels) you want to close, click the panel menu and choose Close or Close Group.

Close window

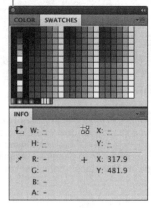

D Clicking the Close button on a floating panel window closes the window and all its panels, including stacked panels.

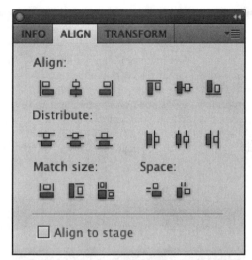

E Double-clicking an empty area of the Tab bar (above) minimizes a panel frame so that you see just the tabs (below).

Tab Bar vs. Tab

The Flash documentation doesn't have a name for the area of a panel frame that holds a panel's tabs. But it is an important element. Dragging the gray area to the right of the tabs moves the frame with all its panels. Dragging a tab moves that panel individually. For the tasks in this book, the gray area to the right of the tabs is called the *Tab bar*.

To minimize (or maximize) a panel frame:

Double-click the Tab bar **E**.

The frame toggles between a minimized state (showing only panel tabs) and the maximized state (showing the full panel frame).

TIP Another way to minimize or maximize an open panel window is to Control-click (Mac) or right-click (Windows) the panel's Tab bar, and choose **Minimize Group/Restore Group** from the contextual menu.

TIP To save even more space, use the panels in icon mode. In a full-size panel, click the **Collapse to Icon** button (the double-triangles on the right side of a panel's title bar) to collapse the panel to a small icon. Click this icon and the full panel pops up. When the panel is already in icon form, clicking the **Collapse to Icon** button expands the panel to its full size.

TIP To resize panels, position the pointer along the left, bottom, or right edge of the panel frame, or at one of the bottom corners. When the resize icon (a double-headed arrow) appears, click and drag to change the panel's dimensions.

The Mystery of Hot Text

Many panels in Flash CS5 contain *hot text*, a special interface element for entering numeric values. When a number in a panel appears in blue (as if it were an active link), that number is hot text. A pointing-finger icon with a double arrow appears when you position the pointer over hot text. Once the hot-text pointer appears, you can enter new values in different ways. You can drag the hot text, as if using an invisible slider. To increase the value, drag upward or to the right; to decrease the value, drag downward or to the left. The number changes as you drag. In many panels, entering new values by dragging the hot text is interactive; the changes you make directly affect elements on the Stage, for example.

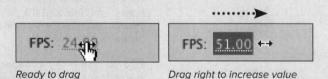

Ready to drag   Drag right to increase value

After you enter a new value, a dark blue box highlights the hot text. When this highlight is present, you can use the up- or down-arrow keys to change the hot-text value incrementally: up-arrow increases the hot-text value by 1, Shift–up-arrow increases the value by 10, down-arrow reduces the value by 1, and Shift–down-arrow reduces the value by 10. You can also click the hot text to activate a text-entry field. Click once and Flash highlights the current value; you can enter a new value immediately. Double-clicking activates the text field and the I-beam pointer; you can then delete or select the old value and enter a new one. To confirm the new value, press Enter or click outside the text field.

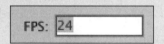

The Property Inspector: A Special Panel

Think of the Property inspector as a context-sensitive super panel—a panel that changes to reflect whatever item you have selected. The Property inspector displays information about the active Flash document or a selected tool, frame, or graphic element (a merge-shape, drawing-object, primitive-shape, grouped shape, symbol, text field, bitmap, or video clip). The Property inspector is also the place for choosing many tools' settings and for changing the attributes of selected elements.

Select the line tool, for example, and the Property inspector becomes the Line Tool Property inspector . In this incarnation, the panel presents all the line tool's attributes for you to set: color, thickness, and style. Select a merge-shape line on the Stage, however, and the panel becomes the Shape Property inspector. When the selected shape is a line, the panel displays attributes similar to those shown in the Line Tool Property inspector; change the settings in the panel now, and Flash changes the selected line to match.

Click a blank area of the Stage, and you'll see the Document Property inspector, which gives you access to various document settings. Select a symbol instance on the Stage, and the Property inspector reveals the instance's heritage (which master symbol it came from), as well as other properties of the symbol. For example, the Position and Size section of the Property inspector shows the symbol's current x- and y- coordinates, height, and width. Change the settings in the panel and Flash applies those changes to the selected symbol instance.

For some items, the Property inspector holds a lot of information. To make this data easier to work with, Flash divides the properties into sections. You can hide or show a section's information by clicking the collapse/expand triangle to the left of the section name .

You can access the Property inspector from the Window menu, as you would any other panel (choose Window > Properties), or you can press Command-F3 (Mac) or Ctrl-F3 (Windows).

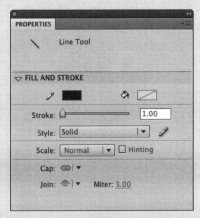

Click to collapse

Click to expand

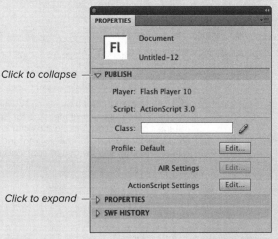

H The Property inspector displays information about selected items and allows you to modify them. The Line Tool Property inspector, for example, lets you set the color, thickness, and style for lines that the line tool creates.

I To view fewer properties in the Property inspector, collapse a section by clicking the downward-pointing triangle. To view more properties, expand a section by clicking the right-facing triangle.

Setting Document Properties

The Document Settings dialog lets you set properties for the Stage (its dimensions, the color of the background on which your artwork appears, and the units of measure for rulers and grids) and set a frame rate for playing your movie. Frames are the lifeblood of your animation, and the frame rate is the heart that keeps that blood flowing at a certain speed. Flash CS5's default setting is 24 frames per second (fps)—a reasonable setting for animations viewed over the Web, and the standard frame rate for film movies. You'll learn more about how frame rates affect animation in Chapter 8. You can also use the Document Property inspector to set some document properties.

To open the Document Settings dialog:

Choose Modify > Document; or press Command-J (Mac) or Ctrl-J (Windows).

The Document Settings dialog appears **A**.

TIP When the Stage has focus, the Document Property inspector's Properties section contains a shortcut to the Document Settings dialog. In the Size section, click the Edit button.

Restore default

Set Stage dimensions
Select a unit of measure
Set background color
Set frame rate
Set default

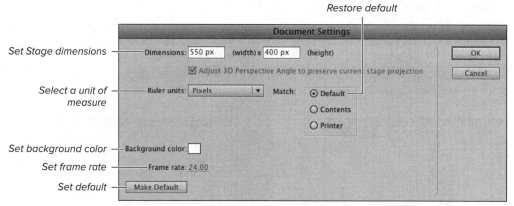

A The Document Settings dialog is where you set all the parameters for viewing the Stage. Selecting a unit of measure for rulers resets the unit measurement for all the Stage's parameters. Clicking the color control pops up the current set of colors and lets you choose one for the background. Clicking the Make Default button sets the parameters for all new documents you create.

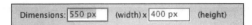

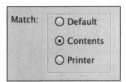

B To assign new proportions to your Stage, type a width and height in the Dimensions section of the Document Settings dialog.

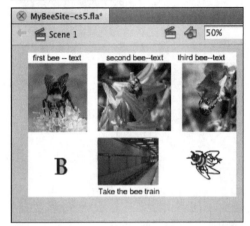

C To make the Stage just big enough to enclose the elements in your movie, select the Contents radio button in the Match section of the Document Settings dialog (top). Flash creates a Stage that's just big enough to show all the objects you've created and placed at the time you select the radio button (bottom). (If you've placed an object on the Pasteboard, Flash sizes the Stage to include that object.)

To set the size of the Stage:

1. Open the Document Settings dialog, and do one of the following:

   ▸ To set the Stage's dimensions, type values for width and height in the appropriate fields of the Dimensions section **B**. Flash automatically assigns the units of measure currently selected in Ruler Units.

   ▸ To create a Stage big enough to cover all the elements in your movie, select the Contents radio button in the Match section **C**.

continues on next page

About the Pasteboard

Flash's Pasteboard grows to accommodate your need for extra space. As you drag items from the Stage to the Pasteboard area, Flash enlarges the Pasteboard to hold them. If you move a large graphic element onto the Pasteboard, and some of it lies outside the area of the open document window, you can see the scroll bar move back toward the center of its range. There is now more Pasteboard area that's hidden from view. Use the scroll bars to view your graphic element and the enlarged Pasteboard. (You'll learn about creating graphic elements in Chapter 2 and repositioning them in Chapter 4.)

- To set the Stage size to the maximum print area currently available, select the Printer radio button in the Match section **D**.

2. Click OK.

TIP If you've entered new dimensions, either manually or by selecting Printer or Contents for matching, you can return to the default Stage dimensions by selecting the Default radio button. All document settings revert to their default values.

TIP To set the units of measure for your document, in the Document Settings dialog, from the Ruler Units menu, choose the units of measure you prefer **E**. Flash uses these units to calculate all measured items on the Stage: rulers, grid spacing, and dimensions. You can override these units for precise position of guidelines (see "Using Rulers, Grids, and Guides," later in this chapter).

TIP If you want a banner that's 1 inch tall and 5 inches wide, but you don't know what that size is in pixels, first set Ruler Units to inches. Type 1 in the height field and 5 in the width field. Then, return to Ruler Units and choose Pixels. Flash does the math and sets the Stage dimensions.

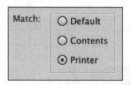

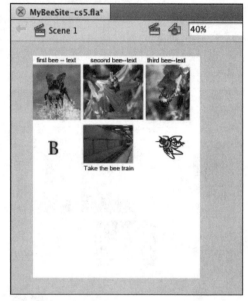

D When you select the Printer radio button in the Match section of the Document Settings dialog, Flash creates a Stage that fits within the margins currently set for Page Setup.

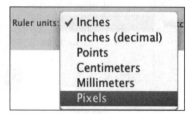

E To set the units of measure for your Flash document, choose them from the Ruler Units menu in the Document Settings dialog.

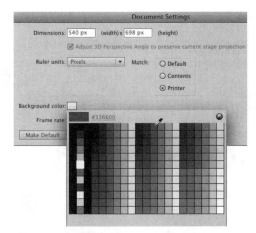

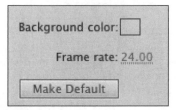

F To assign your Stage a new color, choose one from the Background Color control in the Document Settings dialog.

G Typing a frame rate for your movie in the Frame Rate field of the Document Settings dialog sets Flash to display that number of frames in 1 second.

H To save the current document-property settings as the defaults for all new documents, click the Make Default button in the lower-left corner of the Document Settings dialog.

To set the background color:

1. Open the Document Settings dialog.

2. Click the Background Color control.

    A set of swatches appears; as you move the pointer over the swatches, it changes to an eyedropper **F**.

3. To select a background color, do either of the following:

    ▸ Click a swatch with the eyedropper.

    ▸ Click the hexadecimal-color field, type a value, and press Enter.

    The selected color appears in the Background Color control.

4. Click OK.

    The Stage appears in the color you selected.

TIP The Properties section of the Document Property inspector contains a Stage color control for selecting the movie's background color.

To set the frame rate:

1. Open the Document Settings dialog.

2. In the Frame Rate field, type the number of frames you want Flash to display in 1 second **G**.

3. Click OK.

    The frame-rate setting appears in the Status bar of the current document.

TIP You can also set the frame rate in the Properties section of the Document Property inspector or by using the fps hot text in the Status bar.

To save your settings as the default:

In the Document Settings dialog, click the Make Default button **H**.

The current settings in the Document Settings dialog become the defaults for new documents.

Touring the Edit Bar

The Edit bar, which appears at the top of each Flash document, is the key to identifying what mode you're working in (editing your document or editing a graphic element). Pop-up menus in the Edit bar give you the power to switch scenes, to choose a symbol to edit and immediately switch to symbol-editing mode, and to change the magnification for viewing the Stage. When you edit a drawing-object, group, or symbol, the Edit bar identifies the element you're editing. To learn about editing drawing-objects and groups, see Chapter 5; for symbols, see Chapter 7.

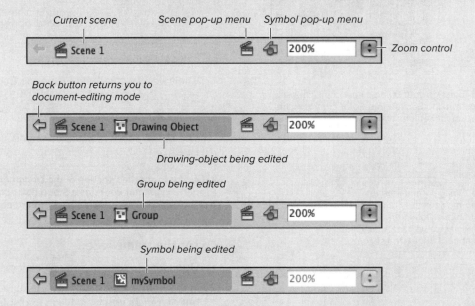

By default, the Edit bar is visible; to hide it, choose Window > Toolbars > Edit Bar. If you hide the Edit bar, however, you may find it more difficult to know when you're editing drawing-objects, groups, or symbols within your document and when you're working on the Stage in the main document.

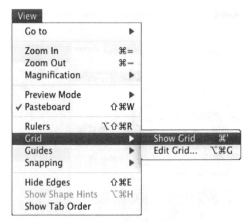

(A) Flash offers three visual drawing aids: rulers, grids, and guides. To show or hide these features during authoring, use the View menu. Here, for example, is the command for showing a grid.

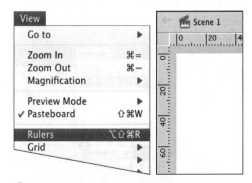

(B) Choosing View > Rulers (left) makes rulers visible on the Stage (right).

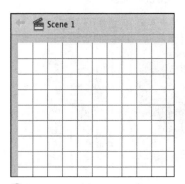

(C) Visible grid lines help you position elements on the Stage during authoring.

Using Rulers, Grids, and Guides

Flash offers rulers, grids, and guides to help you place graphic elements on the Stage. You turn on these visual aids from the View menu **(A)**. Choose the feature you want to use; a checkmark indicates that the feature is on. None of the visual aids appear in your final movie.

To show/hide grids, guides, and rulers:

From the View menu, choose any of the following (or use a keyboard shortcut):

- Choose Rulers, or press Option-Shift-Command-R (Mac) or Ctrl-Alt-Shift-R (Windows).

  Ruler bars appear on the left side and top of the Stage **(B)**. You can set ruler units in the Document Settings dialog.

- Choose Grid > Show Grid, or press Command-apostrophe (') (Mac) or Ctrl-apostrophe (') (Windows).

  When Show Grid is active, Flash superimposes crisscrossing vertical and horizontal lines on the Stage **(C)**. The grid acts as a guide for drawing and positioning elements, the way graph paper functions in the nondigital world. Flash also uses the grid to position elements when you activate the Snap to Grid feature.

- Choose Guides > Show Guides, or press Command-semicolon (;) (Mac) or Ctrl-semicolon (;) (Windows).

  When Show Guides is active, any guides you've placed become visible. To place guides, see "To work with guides," later in this section.

continues on next page

- To access all of the snapping, guide, ruler, and document options quickly, Control-click (Mac) or right-click (Windows) in an empty part of the stage or in the Pasteboard and choose the appropriate submenu.

To set grid parameters:

1. Choose View > Grid > Edit Grid, or press Option-Command-G (Mac) or Ctrl-Alt-G (Windows).

   The Grid dialog appears 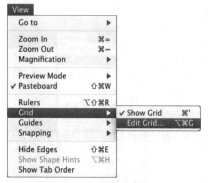.

2. To set grid spacing, do the following:

   ▸ Type a value in the width field.

   ▸ Type a value in the height field **E**.

3. To select a grid color, do the following:

   ▸ Click the Color control. A set of swatches appears; as you move the pointer over the swatches, it changes to an eyedropper **F**.

   ▸ Click a color in the swatch set.

   ▸ The new color appears in the Color control in the Grid dialog.

4. To control how close an item must get to the grid before Flash snaps the item to the grid, from the Snap Accuracy menu, choose a tolerance setting.

5. Click OK.

TIP Grids need not consist of perfect squares.

TIP You can create new default settings for the grids in all new documents. After entering the desired settings in the Grid dialog, click the Save Default button, and then click OK.

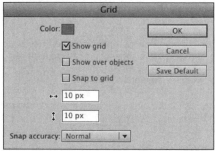

D Choosing View > Grid > Edit Grid opens the Grid dialog, where you can change grid parameters.

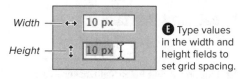

E Type values in the width and height fields to set grid spacing.

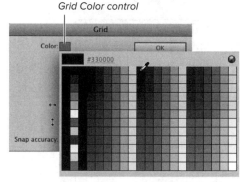

F To select a new grid color, with the eyedropper pointer, click anywhere in the pop-up set of swatches. The swatch set displays the currently selected color set.

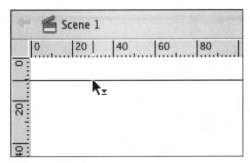

G As you drag a guideline from the ruler bar, a direction indicator appears next to the selection tool.

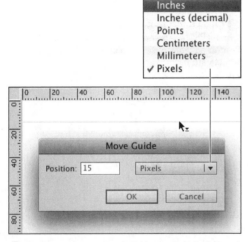

H Double-click a guide on the Stage to access a dialog for precisely positioning the guide. For horizontal guides, the position value correlates to the *y*-axis; for vertical guides, the value correlates to the x-axis. (For more details about how Flash positions elements, see Chapter 4.)

To work with guides:

1. With rulers visible, position the pointer over the vertical or horizontal ruler bar.

   If you're using a tool other than the selection tool, the pointer changes to the selection arrow on the Mac. In Windows, the pointer of the currently selected tool remains visible until you click the ruler bar.

2. Click and drag the pointer onto the Stage.

   As you click, a small directional arrow appears next to the pointer, indicating which direction to drag **G**.

3. Release the mouse button.

   Flash places a vertical or horizontal line on the Stage.

TIP To move a guide, position the selection tool over the guide. A direction arrow appears next to the pointer, indicating that the guide can be dragged. Drag the guide to a new location, and release the mouse button. To remove a guide, drag it completely out of the open document window.

TIP After you place a guide, you can assign it a precise location on the Stage. Using the selection tool, double-click the guide; the Move Guide dialog appears. From the pop-up menu, choose a unit of measure. In the Position field, enter a value for the precise location you want **H**.

TIP To avoid repositioning guides accidentally, choose View > Guides > Lock Guides, or press Option-Command-semicolon (;) (Mac) or Ctrl-Alt-semicolon (;) (Windows). To unlock the guides, choose View > Guides > Lock Guides or press the keyboard shortcut again.

TIP To set parameters for guides, open the Guide dialog by choosing View > Guides > Edit Guides or pressing Option-Shift-Command-G (Mac) or Ctrl-Alt-Shift-G (Windows).

Working with Snapping

Flash's five snapping features help you align elements on the Stage. Snap to Grid helps you position the edge or center of an element to sit directly on top of a user-defined grid. Snap to Guides does the same thing with elements and guidelines. Snap to Objects helps you position one element in relation to another. Snap to Pixels helps you move elements in whole-pixel steps; at magnifications of 400 percent or greater it displays a 1-pixel-by-1-pixel grid. Snap Align helps you align elements once you've dragged them within a user-definable distance from one another or from the edge of the Stage.

To turn snapping options on and off:

1. Choose View > Snapping.

   The menu items with checkmarks are currently active 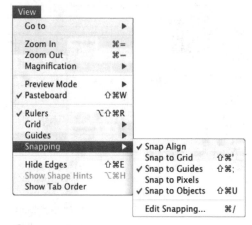. Select an unchecked item to activate it; select a checked item to deactivate it.

2. To activate/deactivate a snapping option, from the Snapping submenu, choose any of the following:

   ▸ *To snap elements to a grid,* choose Snap to Grid, or press Shift-Command-apostrophe (') (Mac) or Ctrl-Shift-apostrophe (') (Windows).

   With Snap to Grid active, as you drag an element, a circle called the *snap ring* appears near the tip of the selection tool. As the element comes close to a grid line, Flash highlights potential snap points by enlarging the snap ring 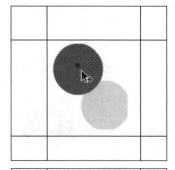.

A Choose View > Snapping to open a submenu with Flash's snapping options. Select an unchecked item to activate it; select a checked item to deactivate it.

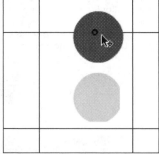

B As you drag elements, the snap ring (a small circle) appears near the tip of the pointer (top). The snap ring grows larger when it moves over an item that you've chosen to snap to, such as a grid, a guide, or the edge or center of another element.

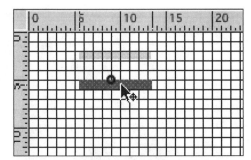

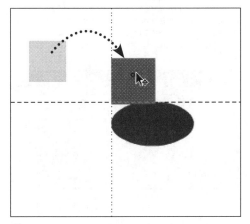

C With Flash's Snap to Pixels feature enabled, a 1-pixel grid becomes visible at magnifications of 400 percent or greater. You can use this mode for precise positioning of graphic elements.

D Flash's Snap Align feature displays a dotted alignment guide whenever the element you're dragging meets certain conditions. For example, you can set Snap Align to display a dotted line when the edge of the object you're dragging aligns with the edge of another object, or when the dragged object's edge gets to a certain distance from the edge of the Stage.

▸ *To snap elements to guides,* choose Snap to Guides, or press Shift-Command-semicolon (;) (Mac) or Ctrl-Shift-semicolon (;) (Windows).

▸ *To snap elements to elements,* choose Snap to Objects, or press Shift-Command-U (Mac) or Ctrl-Shift-U (Windows).

▸ *To snap elements to pixels,* choose Snap to Pixels.

Flash creates a grid whose squares measure 1 pixel by 1 pixel. To see the grid, you must set the Stage's magnification to at least 400 percent **C**.

▸ To view alignment guides while positioning elements, choose Snap Align.

With Snap Align active, as you drag elements on the Stage, Flash displays an alignment guide (a dotted line) whenever the element's edge or center gets close to aligning with the edge or center of another element, or when the element gets within a user-specified distance of another element's edge, its center, or the edge of the Stage **D**.

TIP Although the Snap to Pixels feature uses a 1-pixel grid, the graphic elements you move don't snap to the grid's coordinates unless you set the element's *x* and *y* positions to a whole number in the Info panel or Property inspector. (You'll learn to set coordinates for graphic elements in Chapter 4.)

To set parameters for snapping to the grid:

1. Choose View > Grid > Edit Grid or press Option-Command-G (Mac) or Ctrl-Alt-G (Windows).

2. In the Grid dialog, choose a parameter from the Snap Accuracy pop-up menu **E**.

3. Click OK.

To set parameters for snapping to guides:

1. Choose View > Guides > Edit Guides or press Option-Shift-Command-G (Mac) or Ctrl-Alt-Shift-G (Windows).

2. In the Guides dialog, choose a setting from the Snap Accuracy pop-up menu **F**.

3. Click OK.

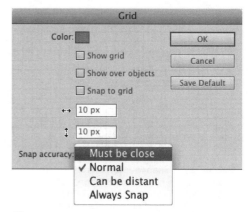

E Choose a Snap Accuracy setting to determine how close an element must be to the grid before Flash snaps the element to the grid line. Choosing Always Snap forces the edge or center of an element to lie directly on a grid line.

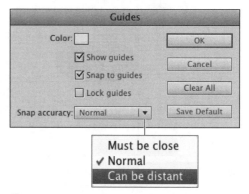

F In the Guides dialog, you can set how close items must be before they snap to the guides. You can also set a guide color, the visibility of guides, and their status as locked or unlocked.

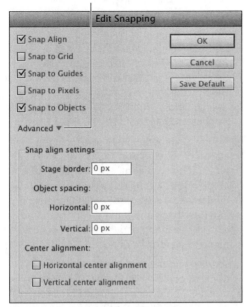

*Click to hide
Advanced options*

G You set the tolerance for Snap Align in the Advanced section of the Edit Snapping dialog. Flash's default settings are shown here.

To set snap-align options:

1. Choose View > Snapping > Edit Snapping.

   The Edit Snapping dialog opens. If the Snap Align settings aren't visible in the dialog, click the Advanced triangle to expand the dialog and see all the settings **G**.

2. To adjust the way Snap Align interacts with elements and the Stage, do any of the following:

   ▸ To have alignment guides appear when a dragged object reaches a specified distance from the edge of the Stage, enter a value in the Stage Border field.

   ▸ To have alignment guides appear when the side of a dragged object reaches a specified distance from either side of another object, in the Object Spacing section, enter a value in the Horizontal field.

   ▸ To have alignment guides appear when the top or bottom edge of a dragged object reaches a specified distance from the top or bottom edge of another object, in the Object Spacing section, enter a value in the Vertical field.

   ▸ To have guides appear when the center of a dragged object aligns horizontally and/or vertically with the center of another object, in the Center Alignment section, select the Horizontal and/or Vertical checkboxes.

Practice Session

Try creating a template.

- Open a new ActionScript 3.0 document; change its dimensions and background color. (See *Setting Document Properties.*)

- Save it as a template; call it something like myFirstTemplate. Add a description, such as "This is a blank document for testing." Make a new category named VQS; you can use that category for all the templates you create as you work through the tasks in this book. Close the finished template document. (See *Working with Template Documents > To create a template document.*)

- Create a new document using this template. (See *Working with Template Documents > To open a new document from a template document.*)

Try creating a personal workspace.

- Using whatever workspace you currently have open, drag panels to new locations; combine and separate panels. Maximize some panels, minimize others; close some panels, open others, resize them. (See *About the Flash Authoring Environment > Using Panels.*)

- Save this setup as a custom workspace. Explore each of the workspaces that come with Flash by default. Then choose the one you just created. (See *About the Flash Authoring Environment > Touring the Workspace.*)

A Note About Help

Flash CS5 provides help via the Adobe Community Help application. To access it, choose Help > Flash Help. Flash opens Adobe Community Help in your system's default browser. You can also access Help by entering a word or phrase in the Search field at the right side of Flash's Application bar and pressing Enter.

Adobe Community Help gives you the option of viewing and searching various types of help content. The left-hand pane in the Adobe Community Help window contains two sections: Search Options and Feedback and Rating. You may need to click the triangle to the left of a section name to view all its options.

To view and search just the documentation that comes with Flash (*Using Adobe Flash CS5* and *ActionScript 3.0 Reference for the Flash Platform*), access the Search Options section; in the Search Location section, select the Local radio button; then from the Filter results menu, choose Using Flash (or ActionScript 3.0 Reference, if you want help with coding).

To include other types of help in your searches, choose one of the other options. (If you are not currently connected to the Internet, Local Help is the only option available.)

From time to time, Adobe will update the documentation files for Flash. When this happens, dialogs will appear when you access Help with an Internet connection active. The dialogs give you various options for downloading the updates so that future local searches have access to this information.

Creating Simple Graphics

Adobe Flash Professional CS5 offers natural drawing tools that imitate the feel of working on paper with a pencil or brush; geometric-shape tools that create predefined shapes; and a pen tool that lets you draw with precision, using Bézier curves.

These tools let you create three types of shapes. Tools set to Merge Drawing mode create raw shapes—shapes that interact with other raw shapes on the same layer (you'll learn about shape interactions in Chapter 5). Tools set to Object Drawing mode create editable shapes that don't interact with other shapes. Flash's rectangle- and oval-primitive tools create *primitive-shapes*—non-interactive shapes with a set of defining parameters. You can edit a primitive's parameters (changing the roundness of a rectangle's corners, for example), but you can't freely edit a primitive's outline (turning an oval into a free-form blob, for example).

Flash CS5 has two pattern-making tools—spray-brush and deco—that create patterns using multiple shapes (see Chapter 5). You can also import graphics from other programs for use in Flash (see Chapter 16).

Touring the Tools

The Tools panel holds all the tools you need to create and modify graphic elements **Ⓐ**. Flash CS5 gives you tools for creating graphic elements, for scrolling the Stage and zooming in and out, and for setting colors for the elements you create.

You click a tool to select it for use. Additional options and settings for a selected tool may appear at the bottom of the Tools panel and/or in the Property inspector.

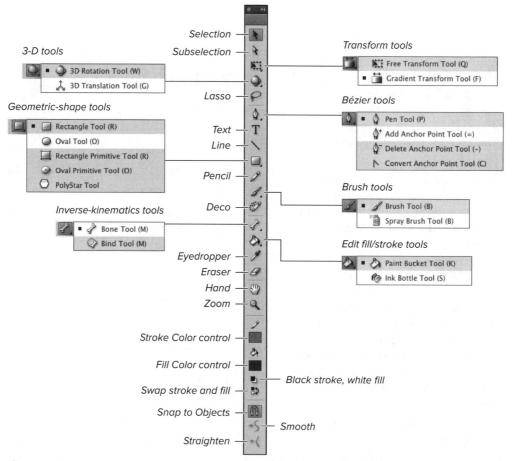

3-D tools

Selection

Subselection

3D Rotation Tool (W)
3D Translation Tool (G)

Geometric-shape tools

Rectangle Tool (R)
Oval Tool (O)
Rectangle Primitive Tool (R)
Oval Primitive Tool (O)
PolyStar Tool

Lasso

Text

Line

Pencil

Inverse-kinematics tools

Bone Tool (M)
Bind Tool (M)

Deco

Eyedropper
Eraser
Hand
Zoom

Stroke Color control

Fill Color control

Swap stroke and fill

Snap to Objects

Straighten

Transform tools

Free Transform Tool (Q)
Gradient Transform Tool (F)

Bézier tools

Pen Tool (P)
Add Anchor Point Tool (=)
Delete Anchor Point Tool (-)
Convert Anchor Point Tool (C)

Brush tools

Brush Tool (B)
Spray Brush Tool (B)

Edit fill/stroke tools

Paint Bucket Tool (K)
Ink Bottle Tool (S)

Black stroke, white fill

Smooth

Ⓐ The Tools panel contains tools for drawing, editing, and manipulating graphic elements in Flash. To save space, some tools are grouped. Click the current tool icon to view a submenu from which to choose a different tool in that group.

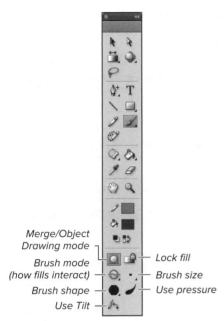

Merge/Object Drawing mode

Brush mode (how fills interact)

Brush shape

Use Tilt

Lock fill

Brush size

Use pressure

B When selected, some tools display modifiers at the bottom of the Tools panel. Here the settings for using the brush appear. Click a button to toggle settings such as Merge Drawing mode. Access a menu (indicated by a small black triangle) to select settings such as Brush mode.

To access tools and options:

1. With the Tools panel open, click a tool—for example, the brush tool.

   The relevant modifiers for the selected tool appear at the bottom of the Tools panel.

2. Click a button or select an option to modify the way the selected tool works **B**.

TIP Flash's default setting makes tool tips active (when the pointer hovers over a tool, an identifying label appears). You can change the tool tip setting in the Preferences dialog: select the General category, select (or deselect) the Show Tooltips checkbox, and click OK to close the dialog. (For details on opening the Preferences dialog, see Chapter 1.)

TIP In addition to displaying tool names, tool tips show keyboard shortcuts. As you get more familiar with the tools, activating them from the keyboard will speed your operations.

About Strokes and Fills

What do *stroke* and *fill* mean? A stroke is an outline, and a fill is a solid area of color. Think of a coloring book, with black lines creating the pictures: those lines are strokes. When you fill in the areas outlined by strokes, that colorful area is the fill. In a coloring book, you start with an outline and create the fill inside it. In Flash, you can also work the other way around— start with a solid shape and then create the outline as a separate element.

Flash's rectangle, oval, rectangle-primitive, oval-primitive, and polystar tools can create an element that's just a stroke or just a fill; they can also create the stroke and fill elements simultaneously. The line and pen tools, as you might guess, create only strokes.

The concept of fills and strokes is a bit trickier to grasp in relation to the brush tool. This tool creates fills. These fills may look like lines or brushstrokes, but they are shapes you can outline with a stroke. Flash has special tools for adding, editing, and removing strokes and fills: the ink bottle, the paint bucket, and the faucet eraser. See Chapter 4 for more details.

Customize Your Tool Set

Flash CS5 lets you customize the Tools panel to make the best use of space. You can resize the panel vertically and horizontally, as you would any other panel. You can also combine tools in pop-up submenus, or completely remove tools from the panel.

To change which tools appear where in the panel, from the Flash application menu (Mac) or Edit menu (Windows), choose Customize Tools Panel **C**; a dialog with the same name appears **D**. The default layout of tool icons appears on the left; a scrolling list of all Flash's tools appears next to it. To make modifications, select a tool icon in the layout; Flash outlines the slot containing that icon in red and the places the name of the tool (or tools) assigned to that slot in the Current Selection list, on the right side of the dialog. You can now assign tools to the selected slot.

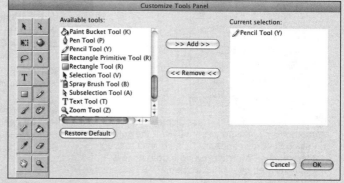

C The Customize Tools panel.   **D** The Customize Tools dialog box.

To add a tool to the highlighted slot, select the tool name in the Available Tools list, then click the Add button. To remove a tool from the highlighted slot, select the name in the Current Selection list and click the Remove button. To return the Tools panel to its original state, click the Restore Default button. Click OK to confirm the new set of tools. The Tools panel now contains the tool set you created. When you assign multiple tools to one slot, Flash makes them available through submenus.

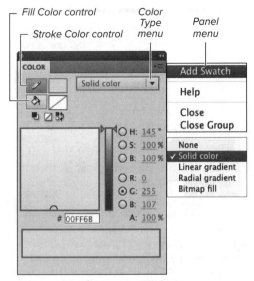

Fill Color control
Stroke Color control
Color Type menu
Panel menu

COLOR

Solid color

Add Swatch

Help

Close
Close Group

None
✓ Solid color
Linear gradient
Radial gradient
Bitmap fill

H: 145°
S: 100%
B: 100%
R: 0
G: 255
B: 107
A: 100%

00FF6B

A The Color panel lets you define colors for use with Flash's drawing tools. Choose Solid Color from the Color Type menu to create solid colors. There are also options for creating gradients, using bitmaps, or using no color.

What Are Hex Colors?

The term *hex color* is short for *hexadecimal color,* which is a fancy way of saying "a color defined by a number written in base 16." Hexadecimal coding is the language of bits and bytes that computers speak.

Hex coding is the way to specify color in HTML. In Flash, entering a single hex code for your color may be easier than entering values for hue, saturation, and brightness (H, S, B) or for red, green, and blue (R, G, B).

If you remember studying bases in high-school math, you'll recall that the decimal system is base 10, represented by the numbers 0 through 9. In hex color, to get the extra six digits, you continue coding with letters A through F.

Creating Solid Colors and Gradients

Although you can define fill and stroke colors from most color controls (see the sidebar "The Mystery of Color Controls," later in this chapter), the Color panel gives you the widest variety of options for defining fill and stroke colors. You can choose colors visually, by clicking in a color-selection window; or you can choose colors numerically, by entering specific values for color components. You can also set a color's transparency in the Color panel. To define new gradients, you must use the Color panel.

Before you define a color or gradient, you must choose whether the color or gradient applies to fills or strokes by activating the Fill Color control or the Stroke Color control. As you define new colors, Flash updates all the related color controls. If you define a new fill color, for example, that color becomes the current setting for all the tools that use fills.

To assign solid-color attributes in the Color panel:

1. Access the Color panel **A**. If it's not open, choose Window > Color or press Shift-Command-F9 (Mac) or Shift-Alt-F9 (Windows).

2. To determine where Flash applies the new color, do one of the following:

   ▸ To set a new stroke color, choose the Stroke Color control by clicking the pencil icon.

   ▸ To set a new fill color, choose the Fill Color control by clicking the paint-bucket icon.

3. From the Color Type menu, choose Solid Color.

To define a new color visually in the Color panel:

1. Access the Color panel.

   The color-selection window displays a set of hot-text controls that let you set precise values for six color properties. The properties represent two color models: **HSB** for hue, saturation, and brightness, and **RGB** for the amounts of red, green, and blue in the color. The values shown define the currently selected color.

2. To "pin" one property, click the H, S, B, R, G, or B radio button.

   The color-selection window displays all the colors you can create using the selected property at its current value **B**.

3. Position the pointer over the color-selection window.

   A circular color-selection pointer appears.

4. To preview new colors, click and drag the color-selection pointer within the color-selection window.

   As you drag, the value of the property you selected in Step 2 remains constant, while values for the remaining properties change to create new colors. A preview of the new color appears above the old color in the preview window. When the color you want appears, release the mouse button. Flash updates the RGB and HSB values to create that color.

   TIP If you don't need to see a preview of the new color, you can position the pointer over the color model without dragging; click to select the color that shows inside the circle.

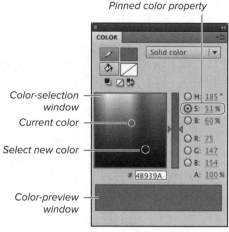

Pinned color property

Color-selection window

Current color

Select new color

Color-preview window

B Selecting a radio button in the Color panel keeps values for that color constant as you drag the color-selection pointer to choose colors visually. Selecting a radio button also determines the range of colors that appear in the color-selection window. Click the S (saturation) radio button when it has a value of 100 percent, for example, and the color-selection window shows a full spectrum of colors with bright versions at the top, shading to black at the bottom. If the saturation value is less than 100 percent when you click the S radio button, the color-selection window shows the same spectrum of colors, but dimmer, since you can't create fully saturated colors with the current S value.

C Enter HSB values to specify the color by hue, saturation, and brightness. Enter RGB values to specify the amount of red, green, and blue that make up the color. The new color appears in the selected color control.

To define a new color numerically in the Color panel:

1. Access the Color panel.

2. Use the H, S, B, R, G, and/or B hot text **C** to enter precise values for any of the following:

- ▸ To define the hue (H), enter values from 0 to 360 degrees.

- ▸ To define a percentage for saturation (S) and brightness (B), enter values from 0 to 100.

- ▸ To define the amount of red, green, or blue in the color, enter values from 0 to 255 for red (R), green (G), and/or blue (B).

Click the hot text to enter a precise value; click and drag on the hot text's invisible slider to choose a value interactively. As you drag a slider, the color-selection circle moves around the color-selection window. The color-preview window splits and displays the new color and the old color. When the color you want appears, release the slider. To change the value of the currently pinned color property, use its hot text to enter a new value.

TIP The slider that lies between the color-selection window and the radio buttons offers another way to change the values of the "pinned" property (the currently selected radio button); move the slider's triangles up to increase values, down to decrease values. The slider can also help you visualize the possibilities created by changing the value of the pinned property; the slider displays the range of possible colors you can make by changing the value of the pinned property.

TIP Flash CS5's Color panel provides two systems—or color models—for specifying colors, HSB and RGB. In both systems a color consists of three elements. The Color panel shows you the values for all elements in both systems simultaneously, hence the six radio buttons. You don't need to set all six values yourself. As you change the value of an element in one system, Flash updates the values in both systems automatically. If you change the value for hue, for example, the panel updates the values for red, green, and blue to express the new color.

To define a color's transparency:

1. With the Color panel open, define a color.

2. Use the Alpha hot text to enter a value between 0 and 100 percent .

   A value of 100 defines a completely solid color; a value of 0 defines a completely transparent color.

To create a linear gradient:

1. Open the Color panel.

2. From the Color panel's Color Type menu, choose Linear Gradient **E**.

   The tools and options for defining gradients appear **F**. The color-preview window becomes a gradient-definition window, with pointers for defining colors in the gradient. The default gradient starts with two pointers, black on the left and white on the right.

3. For Flow, leave the default setting, Extend Color (the black-to-white–gradient button).

   Flow determines how gradient colors fill a shape when you resize the gradient to be narrower than the shape it fills. (To learn about resizing gradients, see Chapter 4.)

4. To add a new color to the gradient, do the following:

   ▸ Position the pointer on or below the gradient-definition window.

   Flash adds a plus sign to the pointer, indicating that you can add a new gradient pointer in this area.

   ▸ Click anywhere along the gradient-definition window.

   Flash adds a new gradient pointer.

D Enter an alpha value of less than 100 percent to define a transparent color.

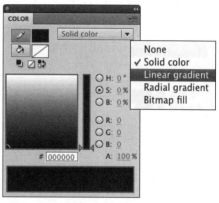

E Choose Linear Gradient from the Color Type menu to access the tools for defining linear gradients.

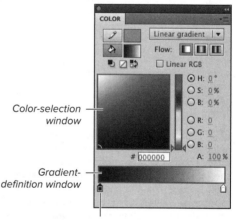

Color-selection window

Gradient-definition window

Gradient pointer selected

F When you choose Linear Gradient or Radial Gradient as the Color Type, the Color panel's color-preview window becomes the gradient-definition window.

Gradient starts with white, and blends first to gray and then to black

Move pointers in to increase width of outside bands

Click to add pointers

G Choose a color for each gradient pointer. The colors and positions of the pointers in the window define a gradient's color transitions. Place pointers closer together to make the transition between colors more abrupt; place them farther apart to spread the transition out over more space.

5. To change the color of a gradient pointer, click it to select it, and define a new color using any of the methods described in the preceding section.

   or

   Double-click the gradient pointer to open a pop-up swatch set, and do one of the following:

   ▸ Click a swatch to copy the swatch color.

   ▸ Click an item on the desktop to copy its color.

   ▸ Use the Hex-color hot text to enter a new value.

   ▸ Click the Color Picker button in the upper-right corner of the pop-up swatch set to access the System Color Picker for assigning new colors.

6. To remove a color from the gradient, drag its pointer downward, away from the gradient-definition window. The pointer disappears as you drag. The gradient preview changes to blend the colors in the remaining gradient pointers.

7. Repeat Steps 4–6 to create the colors you want in your gradient.

   You can add up to 13 pointers (for a total of 15 colors) to a gradient.

8. Drag the pointers to position them in the gradient-definition window **G**.

   As you modify the gradient, your changes appear in all the Color controls for strokes or fills, depending on whether you assigned the gradient to strokes or fills.

To create a radial gradient:

1. Open the Color panel.

2. From the Color Type menu, choose Radial Gradient.

   The tools for defining circular gradients appear. The gradient-definition window looks the same as it does for linear gradients **H**. The leftmost pointer defines the inner ring; the rightmost pointer defines the outer ring.

3. Follow Steps 3–8 of the previous task, "To create a linear gradient," to define the color transitions in the radial gradient.

TIP To modify an existing gradient, choose it in the Swatches panel. Flash switches the Color panel to the Linear Gradient mode (or Radial Gradient mode) and displays the selected gradient. Now you can make any changes you need.

TIP Gradients can have transparency. You simply use a transparent color in one or more gradient pointers (see "To define a color's transparency," earlier in this chapter). If a gradient has transparency, a grid shows up in the gradient pointer, in the Fill Color or Stroke Color control, and in the transparent part of the gradient in the gradient-definition window **I**.

TIP Each pointer in a gradient can have a different alpha setting. To create fade effects, try creating a gradient that blends from a fully opaque color to a transparent one.

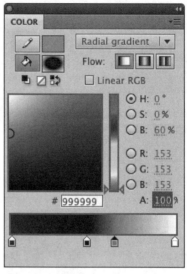

H Choose Radial Gradient from the Color Type menu to create a circular gradient.

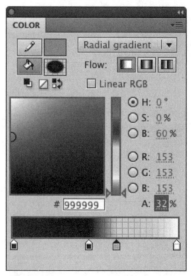

I When transparent colors make up part of a gradient, grid lines appear in the gradient pointer, the Fill Color or Stroke Color control, and the gradient-preview window.

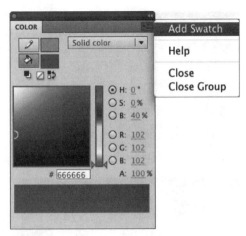

A The panel menu in the Color panel has an Add Swatch command for adding the current color to the Swatches panel.

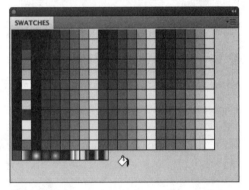

B Positioning the pointer over a blank spot in the Swatches panel changes the pointer to a paint bucket. Click to add whatever color is currently specified in the Color panel. Flash adds the new swatch below the current swatch set, putting solid color swatches on the left side of the Swatches panel, and gradient swatches on the right side.

TIP The panel menu for the Swatches panel also offers shortcuts for dealing with color sets, including Sort by Color to arrange colors by hue. Note that you can't undo the color sorting. Be sure to save your current set of colors if there's any chance you'll want to restore the unsorted order (choose Save Colors from the panel menu).

Working with Swatches

You can save a new color or gradient for the duration of your work session by adding the color currently displayed in the Color panel to the Swatches panel. The Fill Color and Stroke Color controls found in the Tools panel, in the Property inspector, and in the Color panel also give you quick access to the current set of swatches.

To add a color or gradient to the Swatches panel:

1. Create a new color or gradient using any of the techniques outlined in the preceding sections.

2. In the Color panel, do either of the following:

   ▶ From the panel menu, choose Add Swatch **A**.

   ▶ Position the pointer over the blank area of the Swatches panel; when the paint-bucket pointer appears, click.

   Flash adds the new solid color or gradient to the appropriate section of the Swatches panel **B**.

TIP You can add new colors to the Swatches panel even if it's closed. But if you want to get feedback when you add a swatch, open the Swatches panel. Resize the panel window so that a bit of space appears below the existing swatches.

TIP To remove a swatch from the Swatches panel, select a swatch, and from the panel menu, choose Delete Swatch.

TIP If the swatches in the Swatches panel are too small for you, resize the panel horizontally. The swatches grow bigger as the window widens.

Setting Fill Attributes

You can use any Fill Color control to assign colors or gradients to selected tools or graphic elements. A Fill Color control is always available in the Color panel and Tools panel. A Fill Color control also appears in the Fill and Stroke section of the Property inspector when you select a tool or graphic element that uses fills (for example, when you select the rectangle tool in the Tools panel, or when you select a rectangle shape on the Stage). When you change the fill color in one panel, the Fill Color controls in the other panels change to match.

To assign fill colors from the Property inspector or Tools panel:

1. With the Property inspector open, in the Tools panel, select a tool that creates fills. (The rectangle, oval, rectangle-primitive, oval-primitive, polystar, brush, and paint-bucket tools all create fills.)

   When one of these tools is selected, the Property inspector's Fill and Stroke section appears. This section is where you'll find a Fill Color control—a color chip identified by a paint-bucket icon **Ⓐ**.

   or

   Access a Fill Color control in the Tools panel.

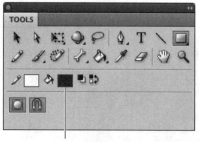

Fill Color control

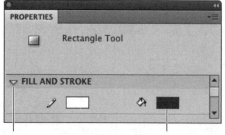

Expand/Collapse section　　　　*Fill Color control*

Ⓐ Selecting a tool or graphic element that uses fills activates the Property inspector's Fill and Stroke section, which contains a Fill Color control. If the control isn't visible, click the expand/collapse triangle to display the contents of the section.

Current fill color   Hex hot text   Choose new color   Alpha hot text

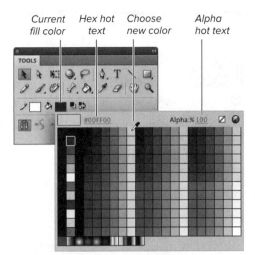

B Click the Fill Color control—the color chip identified by a paint-bucket icon—to open a set of swatches. Click a swatch to choose the new color, or use the hot text to enter new hex or alpha values. The Fill Color control works the same way in the Tools panel and the Fill and Stroke portion of the Property inspector.

2. Click on the Fill Color control.

A set of swatches pops up; as you move the pointer over the swatches, it changes to an eyedropper **B**.

3. To assign a new fill color or gradient, do one of the following:

   ▸ To assign a gradient, select one of the linear or radial gradient swatches.

   ▸ To select a solid color, click a solid swatch or an item on the Stage; the color directly below the tip of the eyedropper becomes the assigned fill color.

   ▸ To define a new fill color, use the Hex hot text (to the right of the current-color chip) to enter a new hex value.

   ▸ To define transparency for the current fill color, use the Alpha hot text to enter a percentage less than 100. Note there is no Alpha hot text when a gradient is the current fill color; transparency is a part of the gradient definition.

The new color appears in all regular Fill Color controls (in the Tools panel, the Fill and Stroke section of the Property inspector, and the Color panel). Flash changes the fills of any shapes or drawing-objects selected on the Stage; any tools that create fills are set to use the new color.

TIP To assign new fill colors, you can also use the Color panel. Its Fill Color control works just like the ones in the Tools panel and Property inspector.

TIP To access a System Color Picker for assigning fill colors, click the color chip in one of the Fill Color controls, then click the Color Picker button from the pop-up swatch window **C**.

Color Picker button

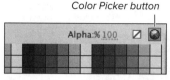

C Click the Color Picker button to access the System Color Picker(s) for defining a color that's not in the current swatch set.

The Mystery of Color Controls

You'll find color controls—a color chip, usually located next to an icon of a pencil or paint bucket—throughout Flash. To operate a color control, click the color chip; a panel of color swatches pops up, and the pointer changes to an eyedropper as it moves over the swatches. To assign a new color, position the pointer over a swatch and click the color you want; enter a new value in the Hex Color field; enter a transparency value in the Alpha field; choose No Color; or click the Color Picker button to access the System Color Picker(s). With many color controls you can also position the eyedropper pointer over an element on the Stage or desktop and click to select that color. The pointer may lose its eyedropper shape as it moves over certain areas of the interface, but it's still picking up the color beneath its tip.

You can use any regular Stroke Color or Fill Color control to assign color attributes. The specs for the color you select appear in the Color panel, and all the other color controls update to match.

Note that the color controls that appear in the Container and Flow section of the TLF Text (Tool) Property inspector display the same icons as Flash's regular Stroke Color and Fill Color controls but do not link to those controls in other panels. The Container Border Color control, which has a pencil icon, lets you create solid outlines for TLF text fields. The Container Background Color control, which has a paint-bucket icon, allows you to fill a TLF text field with a solid color. These color controls affect TLF text fields only; to change the border or background of a TLF text field, you must activate the swatch set of the Container Border/Background color control and choose a new color. (You'll learn more about working with TLF text in Chapter 3.)

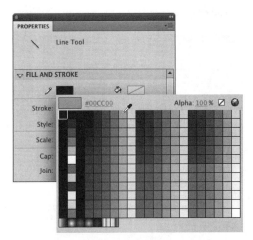

A Clicking the Stroke Color control (the color chip identified by a pencil icon) in the Fill and Stroke section of the Property inspector opens a set of color swatches and provides an eyedropper pointer for selecting a new color.

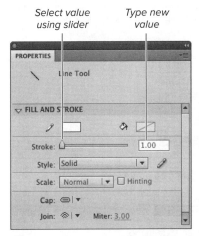

B Entering a new value in the Stroke field sets the weight, or thickness, for strokes created by tools that draw strokes.

Setting Stroke Attributes

A line has three main attributes: color, thickness (also known as *weight* or, in Flash, *stroke height*), and style. You set all three in the Fill and Stroke section of the Property inspector for any tool that creates strokes. That section also lets you control the way the ends of lines (*caps*) look and the way lines connect (*joins*).

To set stroke properties:

1. With the Property inspector open, in the Tools panel, choose a tool that creates strokes. (The pen, line, rectangle, oval, rectangle-primitive, oval-primitive, polystar, pencil, and ink-bottle tools all create strokes.)

   The Fill and Stroke section appears in the Property inspector, displaying current stroke settings for the selected tool.

2. To select a stroke color, do the following:

   ▶ In the Fill and Stroke section of the Property inspector (or in the Tools panel), click the Stroke Color control—the color chip identified by a pencil icon.

   ▶ A set of swatches pops up; as you move the pointer over the swatches, it changes to an eyedropper **A**.

   ▶ Click the swatch with the desired color (or use any of the techniques described in Step 3 of the preceding task).

3. To set the stroke's weight, in the Stroke field, enter a number between 0.10 and 200, or drag the slider next to the field **B**.

continues on next page

4. To set the stroke's style, choose one from the Style pop-up menu **C**.

There are seven styles to choose from: Hairline, Solid, Dashed, Dotted, Ragged, Stippled, and Hatched.

5. To set the way a solid or hairline stroke ends, from the Cap pop-up menu, choose a cap style.

> ▸ *None* ends the stroke exactly where you stop drawing it.

> ▸ *Round* extends the stroke by half the current stroke height, creating a rounded end.

> ▸ *Square* extends the stroke by half the current stroke height, creating a square end **D**.

6. To set the way solid or hairline strokes meet, click the Join pop-up menu.

> ▸ *Miter* creates a sharp corner.

> ▸ *Round* creates a slightly curved corner.

> ▸ *Bevel* creates a slightly flattened corner **E**.

TIP The Tools panel displays two buttons for setting basic stroke and fill colors quickly. Clicking the overlapping black and white squares sets the Stroke Color control to black and the Fill Color control to white. Clicking the small squares with an arrow next to them makes the current stroke and fill colors change places.

TIP In Flash, the hairline setting is considered a stroke style—not thickness—or stroke height. (Use the stroke-style pop-up menu to get the Hairline setting.) Hairlines in a symbol don't change thickness when you resize the symbol. That's often what you want when you make the symbol larger; when you make the symbol smaller, the stroke may seem too heavy. Other lines in a symbol grow thicker or thinner as you scale the symbol up or down. (To learn about symbols, see Chapter 7.)

Selected stroke style

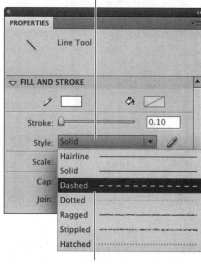

Preview of current stroke settings

C Choose a stroke style from the pop-up menu in the Fill and Stroke section of the Property inspector.

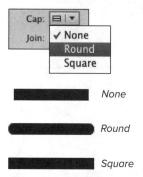

D Set a Cap style in the Fill and Stroke section of the Property inspector to control the look of the ends of lines. The None option keeps the line's original length and makes the end flat; Round extends and rounds the line's end; and Square extends and squares off the end.

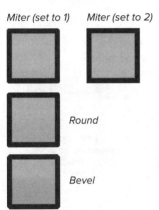

Miter (set to 1)   Miter (set to 2)

Round

Bevel

E Set a join style in the Fill and Stroke section of the Property inspector to control the way lines connect. Miter makes a pointed corner; Round makes a rounded corner; and Bevel slices a flat piece off the corner. Choosing Miter activates the Miter hot text, which accepts values between 1 and 60. With Miter set to 1, Flash flattens the join slightly by slicing off the very tip of the point; the flat area is smaller than in a bevel join. Settings of 2 and above create a very sharp point.

TIP To constrain the way strokes scale in your published movie, with a stroke (or stroke-creating tool) selected, choose a setting from the Scale menu in the Fill and Stroke section of the Property inspector. In the default (Normal) mode, a 1-pixel stroke becomes a 2-pixel stroke if your final movie gets enlarged to 200 percent. To prevent a selected stroke from scaling at all, choose None. To allow the stroke to scale in one direction only, choose Horizontal or Vertical.

TIP To ensure crisp lines in your final output, select the Hinting checkbox in the Fill and Stroke section of the Property inspector. Without hinting, lines sometimes appear slightly blurry on some monitors.

TIP You can modify Flash's stroke styles. You might, for example, want larger dots in the dotted line or bigger spaces in the dashed line. Select a stroke-creating tool; in the Fill and Stroke section of the Property inspector, select the stroke style you want to modify, and then click the Edit Stroke Style button (the pencil icon). The Stroke Style dialog appears, in which you can assign new settings. Click OK to close the dialog and confirm the settings. Those settings continue in force for that style until you change them or end the work session.

TIP You can also set stroke color from any Stroke Color control (in the Property inspector, the Tools panel, or the Color panel). Click the Stroke Color control, and select a color as described in "Setting Fill Attributes," earlier in this chapter.

TIP You can set the Join property for rectangles created with the rectangle-primitive tool, but you'll only see the joins on sharp corners (those with a corner radius setting of 0 or less).

Making Geometric Shapes

Flash provides separate tools for drawing ovals, rectangles, and polygons (or stars). The tools work similarly; all can draw a shape as an outline (just a stroke) or as a solid object (a fill). You can also create a geometric shape with a fill and a stroke simultaneously. There are special properties for defining rectangles and ovals that you can set as precise values in the Property inspector.

To create geometric outlines:

1. To select a geometric-shape tool, do the following:

   ▸ In the Tools panel, click the active geometric-shape tool.

   ▸ From the submenu that appears, choose a tool—for example, the oval tool **A**.

2. In the Fill and Stroke section of the Property inspector, enter values and choose settings for the stroke properties you wish to control.

   When creating an outline shape, you choose the stroke's color, height, and style (see "Setting Stroke Attributes," earlier in this chapter). Specific oval and rectangle properties also appear in the Property inspector when you select the rectangle, rectangle-primitive, oval, and oval-primitive tools.

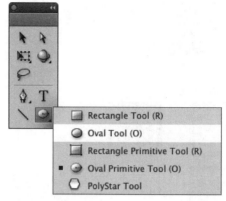

A The Tools panel combines all the geometric-shape tools under a pop-up submenu. To view them all, click the geometric-shape tool that's visible, then click a tool to select it and close the submenu.

Active control

No Color button

C To set the geometric-shape tools to create outline shapes (ones without fills), you need to set the fill to No Color. A quick way to do that is via the Color panel. Click the Fill Color control's paint-bucket icon; Flash highlights the control in gray, meaning it's the control to which the current panel settings apply. Then click the No Color button (top). Flash sets the fill type to None (bottom).

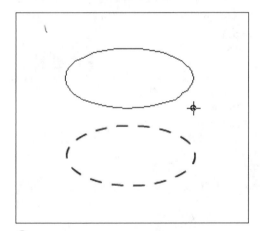

D With a geometric-shape tool selected, click the Stage and drag to create an outline preview of a shape (top). Release the mouse button, and Flash creates a shape using the current settings for fills and strokes. In this case, the oval tool is set to black stroke color, no fill, dashed stroke style, and a stroke height of 1 point (bottom).

3. To set the tool to create an outline with no fill, do the following:
   - ▸ Access the Color Panel and click the Fill Color control's paint-bucket icon; Flash highlights Fill Color as the active control.
   - ▸ Click the No Color button **C**.

4. Move the pointer over the Stage.

   The pointer turns into a crosshair.

5. Click and drag to create the geometric shape **D**.

   Flash previews the shape as you drag.

6. Release the mouse button.

   Flash draws an outline.

TIP To draw a perfect circle (or square), hold down the Shift key while you draw with the oval, oval-primitive, rectangle, or rectangle-primitive tool.

TIP To make an oval (or a rectangle) grow outward from the center point as you draw, position the pointer where you want the center of the shape to be; hold down the Option key (Mac) or Alt key (Windows) as you drag. Shapes drawn with the polystar tool always grow from the center.

TIP In Step 3 of the preceding task, you can click any Fill Color control and choose No Color from the pop-up swatch set.

Merge Drawing vs. Object Drawing vs. Primitive-Shapes

Flash CS5 creates three types of graphic objects: *merge-shapes* (also called *raw shapes),* *drawing-objects,* and *primitive-shapes.* You can use most of the drawing tools to create merge-shapes or drawing-objects simply by selecting the appropriate drawing mode. To create primitives, you must select either the rectangle-primitive or the oval-primitive tool.

In **Merge Drawing** mode, the strokes and fills you create are raw shapes and are ready for editing directly on the Stage; raw shapes on a single layer interact with one another (you'll learn more about shape interactions in Chapter 5).

In **Object Drawing** mode, the strokes and fills you create are directly editable on the Stage but don't interact with other shapes on the same layer. Shapes created in Object Drawing mode act somewhat as if they were isolated on a separate layer or protected using the Group command (you'll learn about working with grouped shapes in Chapter 5 and about shapes on separate layers in Chapter 6). But shapes created in Object Drawing mode can be modified directly on the Stage (see Chapter 4), whereas grouped objects generally can't.

Primitive-shapes do not interact with other shapes on the same layer. Behind the scenes, Flash creates these shapes in Object Drawing mode but locks and constrains them so that they always exhibit certain defining characteristics. Those characteristics are editable and appear as properties in the Property inspector when you select a primitive tool in the Tools panel or a primitive-shape on the Stage. You can edit these properties of a primitive anytime, but you can't freely edit a primitive the way you can edit a shape created in Merge/Object Drawing mode. For example, you can change the inner radius setting for an oval-primitive to transform a solid oval to a donut shape, but you can't edit an oval-primitive's outline to give it pointy ends and transform it into a football shape.

Flash's default mode for drawing tools is Merge Drawing. To turn on Object Drawing mode, select a tool that creates strokes and/or fills, then click the Object Drawing button in the Tools panel **B**. Once you activate Object Drawing mode, it remains active until you click the Object Drawing button again to return to Merge Drawing mode (or press J on the keyboard to toggle between Merge Drawing and Object Drawing). Whichever Merge/Object Drawing setting is active when you end a work session will be active the next time you open Flash. The Merge/Object Drawing–mode button is absent from the Tools panel when you choose one of the primitive tools.

Object Drawing mode

B You can set the drawing tools to create shapes that don't interact with other shapes on the same layer. Select Object Drawing mode in the Tools panel.

For many tasks, you'll see no difference between working with the three types of shapes; in some tasks, however, the difference is crucial. For the exercises in this book, unless otherwise noted, you can create shapes using either drawing mode or the primitive-shape tools.

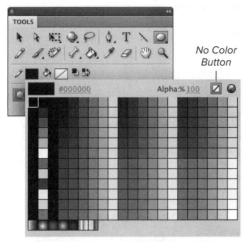

No Color Button

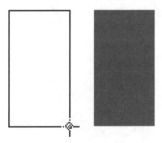

E To create a geometric shape that's just a fill (no outlining stroke), you must set the stroke to No Color. One way to do that is to click any Stroke Color control (here it's the one in the Tools panel); when the swatch set pops up, click the No Color button.

F As you drag the rectangle tool, Flash creates an outline preview of a rectangle (left). To complete the fill shape, release the mouse button (right).

To create geometric fills:

1. To select a geometric-shape tool, follow Steps 1 and 2 in the preceding exercise.

   For this task, for example, select the rectangle tool.

2. To set the tool to create just a fill with no outline, do the following:

   ▸ Click any Stroke Color control (in the Tools panel, the Fill and Stroke section of the Property inspector, or the Color panel).

   ▸ Choose No Color from the pop-up swatch set **E**.

3. Follow Steps 4–6 in the preceding exercise.

   Flash draws a geometric fill, using the currently selected fill color **F**.

TIP You can create polygons and star shapes with the polystar tool. To set the number of sides in the polygon and to switch from polygons to stars, select the polystar tool (make sure that nothing is selected on the Stage, then choose PolyStar Tool from the geometric-shape tool's submenu in the Tools panel). A Tool Settings section appears in the Property inspector. Click the Options button in that section. Enter values for the number of sides and how sharp the star points should be, then click OK.

TIP In Step 2 of the preceding task, you could use the Color panel to set the stroke to No Color. Click the pencil icon to apply settings to the Stroke Color control, then click the No Color button.

To set rectangle properties:

1. In the Tools panel, select the rectangle (or rectangle-primitive) tool.

   The Property inspector displays settings for the selected tool **G**. The properties are the same for both tools.

2. To create a rectangle with four identical corners, set the Lock Corner Radius button to the constrained state **H**.

   Clicking the chain-link icon toggles between the unconstrained (open link) and constrained (closed link) states.

3. To create a rectangle with rounded corners, in the Rectangle Corner Radius field enter a positive number.

   or

   To create a rectangle with indented corners, in the Rectangle Corner Radius field enter a negative number.

To set oval properties:

1. In the Tools panel, select the oval (or oval-primitive) tool.

   The Property inspector displays settings for the selected tool **I**. The properties are the same for both tools.

2. To create variations on the oval shape, in the Oval Options section of the Property inspector, do any of the following:

   ▸ To create a pie-wedge shape, in the Start Angle and/or End Angle field, enter a number from 0 to 360 **J**.

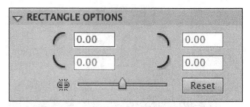

G When you select the rectangle or rectangle-primitive tool, the Property inspector's Rectangle Options section displays four Rectangle Corner Radius fields. Use them to define how sharp or rounded a rectangle's corners are. The properties are the same for both tools.

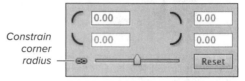

Constrain corner radius

H By default, the rectangle and rectangle-primitive tools create shapes whose corners all have the same radius. When the closed-link icon appears (Constrained mode), only the first Rectangle Corner Radius field is active for entering values because the settings are linked.

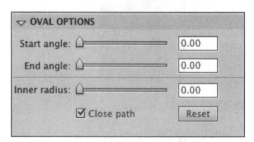

I When you select the oval or oval-primitive tool, the Property inspector's Oval Options section displays special properties for defining an oval. The properties are the same for both tools.

Drag slider to reposition control point

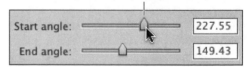

J Entering values in the Start Angle and End Angle fields creates partial ovals like those often used in pie charts. You can also use the sliders to enter start- and end-angle values.

Shape with closed path

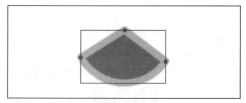

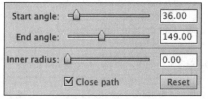

Shape with open path

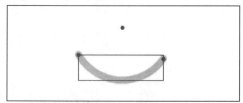

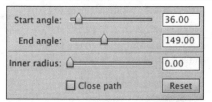

K Deselecting the Close Path checkbox lets you create arcs out of pie-wedge oval shapes. If the shape has an inner-radius setting greater than 0, in its open-path form it appears as two arcs.

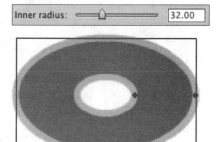

L Entering a number greater than 0 in the Inner Radius field creates an oval with a hollow center.

▸ To create an open arc, deselect the Close Path checkbox. When you create a pie-wedge shape, this setting creates an open path. Flash removes the shape's fill (if one is present) and deletes the straight-line segments from the wedge shape **K**.

▸ To create an oval with a hollow center, in the Inner Radius field, enter a number from 0 to 99.

Flash draws a hollow oval inside the first oval **L**. The Inner Radius setting corresponds to the percentage of the outer oval's "fill" that gets removed by the inside oval. (The outer oval may have a fill of No Color, in which case the inner oval just appears as an outline.)

TIP You can change an oval-primitive's start- or end-angle settings interactively. Select the shape on the Stage. In the Oval Options section of the Property inspector, drag the Start Angle or End Angle slider to change the setting; the shape on the Stage changes.

TIP You can also change start and end angles interactively from the keyboard. Click the pointer of the slider for the value you want to change. The pointer highlights in blue, indicating that it has focus. Press the right arrow to increase the value; press the left arrow to decrease the value. Hold down the Shift key as you press the arrows to increase or decrease the value more rapidly. (You can also use the up and down arrows, but they're a bit counterintuitive: the down arrow increases values, and the up arrow decreases them.)

Setting Oval Options

How do the settings in the Oval Options section of the Property inspector work? Imagine drawing a circle on the face of an analog clock. The start angle is the point where you put your pencil down to begin drawing; the end angle is the point where you lift the pencil and stop drawing. For oval-primitives, those points become control points for modifying the shape.

The values in the Start Angle and End Angle fields in the Property inspector correlate to degrees of a circle. The value 0 corresponds to 3 o'clock, 90 to 6 o'clock, 180 to 9 o'clock, and so on. When the start and end angles have the same value, both control points sit on the same spot, and the circle is complete. When the values differ, there's a gap.

When you select the Close Path checkbox, Flash finishes the shape by drawing straight-line segments to the center of the oval, creating a pie wedge. If the Inner Radius value is greater than 0, the segments connect with an inner oval, creating a C shape or a partial C shape.

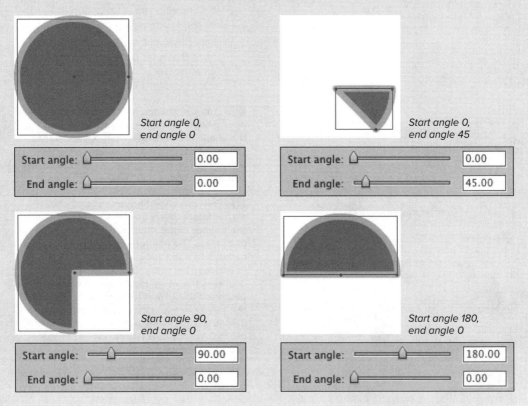

Start angle 0, end angle 0

Start angle 0, end angle 45

Start angle 90, end angle 0

Start angle 180, end angle 0

About Drawing Assistance

Flash's pencil tool offers two assisted line-drawing modes: Straighten and Smooth. For total freedom in drawing, the pencil's Ink mode leaves shapes exactly as you create them.

Straighten mode refines any blips and tremors in a rough hand-drawn line into straight-line segments and regular arcs. This mode also carries out what Flash calls *shape recognition*. Flash evaluates each rough shape you draw, and if the shape comes close enough to Flash's definition of an oval or a rectangle, Flash turns your rough approximation into a shape neat enough to please your high-school geometry teacher.

Smooth mode transforms your rough drawing into one composed of smooth, curved line segments. Note that Smooth mode doesn't recognize shapes; it simply smoothes out the curves you draw. Smoothing reduces the number of points in a shape, resulting in smaller files and thus improving the performance of your final, published work.

Tolerance settings are all-important, especially for Straighten mode. You can set Flash to change almost anything ovoid into a circle and anything slightly more oblong into a rectangle. You set the degree of drawing assistance in the Preferences dialog. Choose Flash > Preferences (Mac) or Edit > Preferences (Windows); in the Preferences dialog that opens, choose Drawing from the Category list, then choose tolerance levels from the Connect Lines, Smooth Curves, Recognize Lines, and Recognize Shapes menus. Click OK to close the dialog.

Creating Free-form Shapes

Flash offers three tools for creating free-form shapes: the pencil, pen, and brush. The pencil and pen tools create stroke outlines, and the brush tool creates fills without strokes. The pencil and pen tools create only outlines, even if you draw a closed shape. Once you've created a shape, you can always modify it—say, to fill an empty outline or add an outline to a plain fill shape.

The pencil tool lets you draw lines (strokes) naturally, as you would with a real-world pencil, but using the mouse or a graphics tablet and pen. Flash hides information about the anchor points and curves of a stroke drawn with the pencil. With the pen tool, you place anchor points and adjust Bézier curves to create strokes. You can use the pen tool not only to create Bézier curves initially, but also to modify them once they are on the Stage. In addition there are three anchor-point tools for modifying Bézier curves on the Stage—the add–anchor-point tool, the delete–anchor-point tool, and the convert–anchor-point tool. In this chapter, you'll use the pen tool to create free-form shapes; in Chapter 4, you'll learn to use the pen tool and the anchor-point tools to modify shapes.

For the tasks below, make sure the grid is visible (see Chapter 1) and set drawing preferences as follows: choose Flash > Preferences (Mac) or Edit > Preferences (Windows) to open the Preferences dialog; choose Drawing from the Category list, and select the Show Pen Preview and Show Solid Points checkboxes; leave the other items at their default settings. Click OK to close the dialog.

To draw free-form strokes with the pencil tool:

1. In the Tools panel, select the pencil tool, or press Y.

2. From the Pencil Mode menu 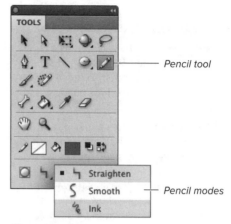, choose one of the following assistance modes:

   Straighten resolves minor variations into straight-line segments.

   Smooth resolves minor variations into smooth curves.

   Ink provides very little assistance, leaving minor variations.

3. Move the pointer over the Stage.

   The pointer changes to a pencil icon.

4. Click, and draw a squiggle.

   Flash previews your rough line.

5. Release the mouse button.

   Flash recasts the line you've drawn according to the assistance mode you chose in Step 2, creating a set of straight-line segments and regular curves ⓑ.

TIP You can apply smoothing and straightening (even shape recognition) after you've drawn an outline or shape, by selecting it on the Stage and then clicking the Straighten or Smooth modifier of the Selection tool (you'll learn more about making and modifying selections in Chapter 4).

TIP To apply smoothing and straightening with more control, select an outline or shape, then choose Modify > Shape > **Advanced Smooth** (or **Advanced Straighten**). In the dialog that appears, enter new values to refine your shape, then click OK. To preview various settings, select the Preview checkbox; Flash applies the dialog's current settings to the selected shape.

Pencil tool

Pencil modes

ⓐ When the pencil tool is selected, the Tools panel displays a pop-up menu of pencil modes.

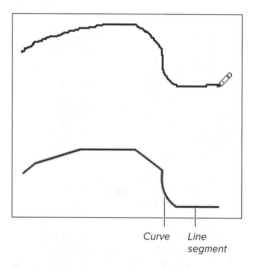

Curve   Line segment

ⓑ With the pencil tool in Straighten mode, when you draw a squiggle, Flash previews it for you. When you release the mouse button, Flash applies straightening, turning your rough squiggle (top) into a set of straight-line segments and smooth curves (bottom).

C Select the pen tool to create paths.

D The *x* next to the pen tool indicates that you're about to start a new path. Click to place the first anchor point.

First point previewed

Preview line segment

Click to place second point

Completed line segment

E Flash previews points as you place them (top), and it adds a stroke to the path as soon as you complete a segment (bottom).

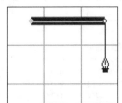

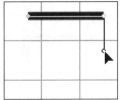

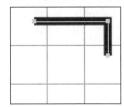

F Continue clicking to add segments to your free-form shape. A quick click (top) adds a straight-line segment (bottom).

To draw free-form strokes with the pen tool:

1. In the Tools panel, select the pen tool, or press P **C**.

2. In the Fill and Stroke section of the Property inspector, set the stroke attributes for your path.

3. Move the pointer over the Stage.

   The pen tool appears with a small *x* next to it **D**. The *x* indicates that you're ready to place the first point of a path.

4. Click where you want your line segment to begin.

   The pointer changes to a solid arrowhead; a small hollow circle indicates the location of the anchor point on the Stage.

5. Reposition the pen tool where you want your line segment to end.

   With Drawing Preferences set to Show Pen Preview, Flash extends a preview of the line segment from the first point to the tip of the pen as you move around the Stage.

6. Click.

   Flash completes the line segment using the selected stroke attributes. With Drawing Preferences set to Show Solid Points, the anchor points appear as solid squares **E**.

7. To add a straight segment to your line, click the Stage where you want the segment to end, and release the mouse button **F**.

continues on next page

8. To add a curve segment, click the Stage where you want the curve segment to end, then drag the pointer.

Flash places a preview point on the Stage, the pointer changes to a solid arrowhead, and Bézier handles (sometimes referred to as tangent handles) appear **G**.

9. Drag the pointer in the opposite direction from which you want your curve to bulge.

The Bézier handles extend from the anchor point, growing in opposite directions as you drag. Flash previews the curve you're drawing **H**.

10. Still keeping the mouse button down, drag the pointer to reposition the Bézier handle.

Dragging the handle clockwise or counterclockwise around its anchor point controls the direction of the bulge; dragging the handle farther from the anchor point deepens the curve **I**.

11. When the curve preview looks the way you want, release the mouse button.

Flash completes your curve segment with a stroke **J**.

12. To create an open path, Command-click (Mac) or Ctrl-click (Windows) the Stage.

or

To create a closed shape, do the following:

▸ Position the pointer over your first anchor point.

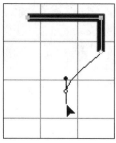

G Click and drag to create a curve point; as you drag, the point's Bézier handles activate. The bulge of the curve grows away from the direction of your drag. For example, to make the curve bulge upward, drag downward.

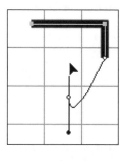

H To make the curve bulge downward, drag upward. Dragging the handles out farther deepens the curve.

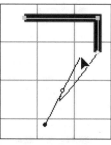
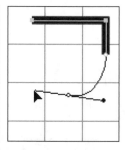

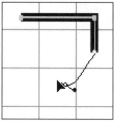

I Move the handles clockwise or counterclockwise around the anchor point to modify the curve shape (top). Drag the handles in or out to make the curve deeper or shallower (bottom).

J When you finish positioning handles for a segment and release the mouse button, Flash adds a stroke to the segment.

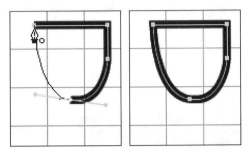

K To create a closed shape, position the pointer over the first anchor point you placed. When you see the hollow-circle icon, click that first point (left). Flash adds the finishing segment, creating a closed path (right).

Extend Line

Join Line

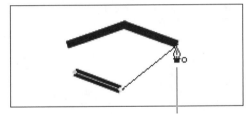

Modifier icon for merge-shape

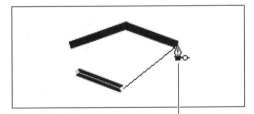

Modifier icon for drawing-object

L You can use the pen tool to add to existing line segments. Position the pointer over the end point of the existing line and click (top), then continue clicking to place more points. Or, place new points first, then position the pointer over the end point of the line you want to join (bottom). When the modifier icon appears, click to join the lines.

▸ Flash previews the closing segment of your shape. A small hollow circle appears next to the pen tool **K**.

▸ Click the first anchor point.

▸ Flash closes the shape, adding a stroke to the path.

Once the path is complete, the pen tool pointer displays a small *x*, indicating that the tool is ready to place the first anchor point of a new path.

TIP There are other ways to end open paths. Choose Edit > Deselect All, or press Command-Shift-A (Mac) or Ctrl-Shift-A (Windows). In the Tools panel, click a different tool. You can also double-click the last point you placed. To use this technique you must be drawing a path that ends with a straight-line segment that doesn't involve Bézier handles.

TIP The pen tool can add to a line created earlier **L**. To extend outward from the original line, position the pointer over the end of the line (the terminal anchor point). A modifier icon—a small slash—appears next to the pen icon. Click the terminal anchor point, and the pen links to that point as if you'd just placed it; continue adding segments as you learned to do in the previous exercises. You can also join to an existing line during the process of creating a new line. To join, the pen tool must be in the same mode (Merge Drawing or Object Drawing) as the existing line. Click to place the anchor points of the new line, but don't double-click to end the line. Instead, position the pointer over one of the terminal anchor points of the line you want to join. A modifier icon appears next to the pen icon; if the pen is in Merge Drawing mode, the modifier icon is a small hollow circle; if the pen is in Object Drawing mode, the modifier icon is a chain-link. Click the existing terminal anchor point, and Flash joins the two lines.

TIP The pen tool creates only strokes. To add a fill to a closed shape drawn with the pen, use the paint-bucket tool.

To create free-form solid fills with the brush tool:

1. In the Tools panel, click the current brush tool; from the submenu that opens, select the brush tool, or press B **Ⓜ**.

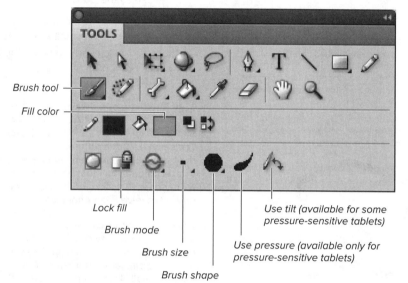

Brush tool

Fill color

Lock fill

Brush mode

Brush size

Brush shape

Use tilt (available for some pressure-sensitive tablets)

Use pressure (available only for pressure-sensitive tablets)

Ⓜ The brush tool and its modifiers.

About Path Math in Flash

A *path*—a series of points and connecting lines—is the skeleton of your graphic-object. With most Flash tools, the math that goes into creating a path takes place behind the scenes. You draw a complete line or a shape; Flash places points (without showing them), connects them, and adds a stroke. With the pen tool, you place the defining points—called *anchor points*—and adjust the curve segments that connect them, using controllers called *Bézier handles* (also known as *tangent handles*). When you've finished placing points with the pen tool, Flash fleshes out the path by applying a stroke to it.

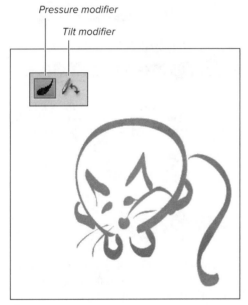

Pressure modifier

Tilt modifier

The Brush Mode options give you control over how fills created with the brush tool interact with other shapes on the same layer. Choosing Paint Normal lets you paint merge-shape fills that act like any other fills when they overlap other shapes.

O Selecting the brush tool's Use Pressure modifier activates the pressure-sensitive capabilities of a connected pressure-sensitive pen and graphics tablet. To vary line thickness, apply more or less pressure as you draw. Flash created all the lines in this cat with a single brush size and shape.

2. To optimize the brush for a particular painting task, in the lower portion of the Tools panel, select any of the following:

   ▸ From the Brush Mode pop-up menu, choose a painting mode; for this exercise, choose Paint Normal **N**. The painting modes let you control how brushstroke fills act when you use the brush tool to paint over other shapes.

   Overlapping shapes interact in different ways depending on whether they are merge-shapes, drawing-objects, or primitives. (You'll learn about how overlapping shapes interact in Chapter 5.)

   ▸ From the Brush Size pop-up menu, choose a size for the brush tip.

   ▸ From the Brush Shape pop-up menu, choose a shape for the brush tip.

   ▸ To paint brushstroke fills that vary in thickness, choose Use Pressure. This option appears only when a graphics tablet is connected to your computer.

3. Select or define a solid fill color using any of the techniques outlined earlier in this chapter.

4. Move the pointer over the Stage.

   The pointer changes to reflect the current brush size and shape. When Use Pressure is active, the pointer changes to a crosshair within a circle; as you draw, the pointer changes to reflect brush-tip size and shape **O**.

continues on next page

5. Click and draw on the Stage.

Flash previews your brushwork in the currently selected fill **P**.

6. When you complete your shape, release the mouse button.

Flash creates the final shape, smoothing it according to settings in the Property inspector (see the sidebar "The Mystery of Brush Smoothing," below).

TIP You can change the size of your brushstroke by changing the magnification at which you view the Stage. To create a fat stroke without changing your brush-tip settings, set the Stage view to a small percentage. To switch to a thin stroke, zoom out to a higher percentage **Q**. Be sure to check your work in 100% view.

To paint with gradients:

1. Follow Steps 1 and 2 in the preceding task.

2. Using one of the methods described earlier in this chapter, select (or define) a linear or radial gradient fill.

P Drawing with the brush creates a preview of your shape (left); Flash recasts the shape as a vector graphic with the currently selected fill color and smoothing settings (right).

Created with 200% magnification

Created with 100% magnification

Created with 50% magnification

Q Flash created these three brushstrokes with exactly the same brush size—only the magnification level of the Stage was changed for each stroke.

The Mystery of Brush Smoothing

Flash's Smoothing setting controls how brushstrokes translate into vector shapes. When the brush tool is active, the Property inspector contains a Smoothing section, with hot text for Smoothing. This control sets the brush tool's stroke-smoothness value (from 0 to 100, with a default of 50). Stroke smoothness determines how closely Flash re-creates each movement of the brush as a separate vector segment. The lower the setting, the more faithfully Flash reproduces the shapes you draw (by using more vectors, which has an impact on the size and animation performance of your final file). A higher setting re-creates your flourishes more roughly, using fewer vectors.

To see the difference clearly, select the brush tool, assign a Smoothing value of 1, and draw a curved line on the Stage. Change the Smoothing setting to 30 and draw a second curved line. Using the subselection tool (you'll learn about using this tool in Chapter 4), select each shape. The line drawn with Smoothing set to 1 displays many more points—that is, it contains many more vector segments.

R Deselect the Lock Fill modifier to paint with an unlocked gradient.

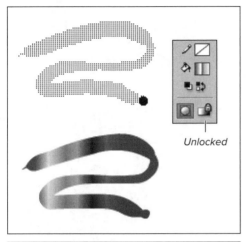

Unlocked

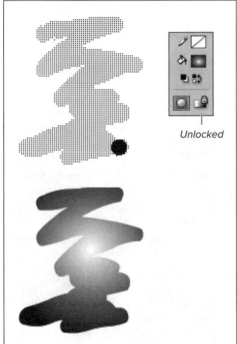

Unlocked

S A brushstroke shape painted with an unlocked linear-gradient fill (top) and one painted with an unlocked radial-gradient fill (bottom).

3. To lock or unlock the gradient, in the Tools panel, do either of the following:

   ▸ To paint shapes that contain the full gradient-spectrum, deselect Lock Fill **R**.

   ▸ To paint shapes that reveal just a portion of the gradient (as if the shape were a window onto a gradient that filled the whole Stage area), select Lock Fill.

4. Paint with the brush as described in Steps 4–6 in the preceding task.

   Flash can't preview the shape you paint with a gradient fill. The preview shape has a black-and-white pattern.

   Flash redraws the painted shape, using the current lock-fill and fill-color settings (see the sidebar "The Mystery of Gradients and Flash's Drawing Models," later in this chapter).

   For unlocked fills, the full gradient is visible in the shape **S**.

   For locked fills, just a portion of the gradient is visible in the shape **T**.

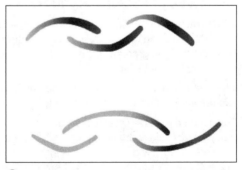

T With the brush tool's Lock Fill modifier deselected, each brushstroke fill you paint contains the full range of the current gradient (top). With Lock Fill selected, each brushstroke fill appears to reveal a section of a gradient that runs the width of the Stage and the Pasteboard (bottom).

TIP Try painting a variety of brushstrokes in both drawing modes; use locked and unlocked gradients; use different areas of the Stage; and make the shapes different lengths. Notice the way each shape displays the gradient.

TIP If the first gradient you paint in a work session has a locked fill, Flash puts the center of the underlying locked gradient along the left edge of the Stage. That means half the gradient lies on the Pasteboard, not on the Stage. To choose a different location for the center of a locked gradient, first use the brush tool to paint an unlocked gradient that's centered the way you want. When you switch to painting with Lock Fill active, the underlying locked gradient aligns with the last unlocked gradient you painted. You can then delete the unneeded unlocked gradient.

TIP After you've created a shape with a gradient fill, you can adjust the location of the center of the gradient by using the gradient-transform tool (see Chapter 4).

The Mystery of Gradients and Flash's Drawing Models

When you use the brush tool to paint a shape with a gradient fill and the Lock Fill modifier is deselected, it makes no difference if you're painting in Merge Drawing mode or Object Drawing mode. Flash centers the gradient in the shape's bounding box (an invisible rectangle that's just the right size to enclose the shape); the full gradient is visible in the shape.

When you paint the same kind of shape and Lock Fill is selected, however, shapes created in the two drawing modes behave differently.

For locked fills, Flash creates a virtual gradient that underlies the Stage and Pasteboard. (By default, Flash aligns the center of the locked gradient with the left edge of the Stage.) Each shape you create with a locked fill reveals just the portion of the gradient that corresponds to that area of the Stage. If you paint multiple merge-shapes with a locked gradient, the same virtual gradient underlies each shape; you can use the gradient-transform tool to shift the gradient within all the shapes. Multiple drawing-objects each have their own personal virtual gradient. These virtual gradients are all centered in the same way, so initially it looks as though there's one underlying gradient, as with merge-shapes. But the gradient-transform tool shifts the gradient in each drawing-object separately.

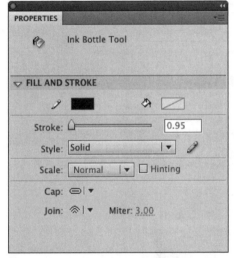

A The ink-bottle tool applies all the stroke attributes currently set in the Fill and Stroke section of the Ink Bottle Tool Property inspector.

Adding Strokes and Fills

As you learned earlier in this chapter, you can use the line, pencil, pen, and geometric-shape tools to create outline shapes—strokes without fills. To create fill shapes that have no stroke outline, you use the brush, pen, and geometric-shape tools. At any point you can add the missing element to such shapes. The ink-bottle tool adds strokes that outline plain fill shapes; the paint-bucket tool adds fills inside plain outline shapes. (You can also use these tools to modify existing strokes and fills; see Chapter 4.)

To add strokes to fills:

1. On the Stage, draw a fill that has no stroke, or work with an existing unstroked shape.

   For a merge-shape, make sure the fill is deselected; for a drawing-object, the fill can be selected or deselected.

2. In the Tools panel, click the current fill/stroke tool; and from the submenu that opens, select the ink-bottle tool, or press S **A**.

3. In the Fill and Stroke section of the Ink Bottle Tool Property inspector, set the desired stroke attributes (see "Setting Stroke Attributes," earlier in this chapter).

4. Position the pointer over a fill shape that has no stroke.

   The pointer appears as a little ink bottle spilling ink.

   continues on next page

5. With the ink bottle's hot spot, click a fill shape in one of the following ways:

- To add a stroke around the outside of the shape, click near the outside edge of the shape **B**.

- To add a stroke around the inside of a shape that has a hole cut out of it, click near the inside edge of the shape.

- To outline both the outside of a shape and the hole inside the shape, click in the middle of the shape **C**.

Flash adds strokes to the outside edge, inside edge, or both, using the color, thickness, and style currently specified in the Fill and Stroke section of the Property inspector.

TIP Flash lets you use gradients for strokes. In Step 3 of the preceding task, in the Fill and Stroke section of the Property inspector, choose a linear or radial gradient from the Stroke Color control's pop-up swatch set. Why might you want a gradient stroke? For an oval shape, adding a thick stroke with a radial gradient can help create the illusion of 3D depth or make the shape appear to glow.

TIP Another way to "add" missing strokes to drawing-objects and primitive-shapes is to modify them using the Property inspector. First select the drawing-object or primitive on the Stage. Then change the stroke properties, including color, in the Property inspector. You can use this technique to add strokes to multiple drawing-objects and/or primitives (the technique doesn't work for merge-shapes, however). You'll learn more about modifying graphic objects in Chapter 4.

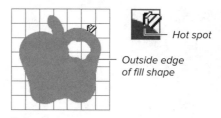

Hot spot

Outside edge of fill shape

Before

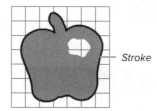

Stroke

After

B As you move the ink bottle over a filled shape, the hot spot appears as a white dot at the end of the ink drip that's spilling out of the bottle. To add a stroke around the outside edge of your fill shape, position the hot spot along that edge (top) and then click. Flash adds a stroke with the current attributes set in the Fill and Stroke section of the Ink Bottle Tool Property inspector (bottom).

Before

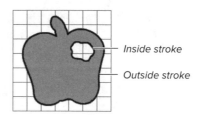

Inside stroke

Outside stroke

After

C Position the ink bottle's hot spot in the middle of your fill shape (top), then click. Flash uses the current stroke attributes to add a stroke around the outside and inside of your shape (bottom).

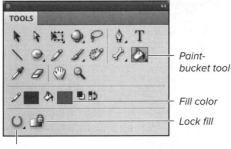

Paint-bucket tool

Fill color

Lock fill

Gap size

D The paint-bucket tool and its modifiers.

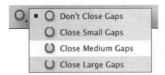

E The Gap Size menu controls Flash's capability to fill shapes that aren't fully closed.

F Clicking inside an outline shape with the paint bucket (left) fills the shape with the currently selected fill color (right).

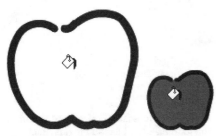

G The paint bucket can't fill this apple shape with the setting of Close Large Gaps and a magnification of 100 percent (left). But in a 50 percent view, the paint bucket with the same large-gap closure setting recognizes this shape as complete and fills it.

To fill an outline shape with solid color:

1. On the Stage, draw an outline stroke that has no fill, or work with an existing outline shape.

   The outline should not be selected.

2. In the Tools panel, click the current fill/stroke tool; and from the submenu that opens, select the paint-bucket tool, or press K **D**.

3. From the Gap Size menu in the Tools panel, choose the amount of assistance you want **E**.

   If you draw your shapes precisely, a medium or small gap closure serves you best; you don't want Flash to fill areas that aren't meant to be shapes. If your drawings are rougher, choose Close Large Gaps. This setting enables Flash to recognize less-complete shapes.

4. From any Fill Color control, select a solid fill color.

5. Place the paint bucket's hot spot (the tip of the drip of paint) inside the outline shape, and click.

   The shape fills with the currently selected fill color **F**.

TIP You may be unaware that your shape has any gaps. If nothing happens when you click inside a shape with the paint bucket, try changing the Gap Size setting in Step 3.

TIP Gap-closure settings are relative to the amount of magnification you're using to view the Stage. If the paint bucket's largest gap-closure setting fails at your current magnification, try again after reducing magnification **G**.

TIP If you work with a selected shape, there is no need to click inside the shape; the fill color changes automatically when you select it in Step 4. You'll learn more about modifying selected shapes in Chapter 4.

To fill outline shapes with unlocked gradients:

1. In the Tools panel, click the current fill/ stroke tool, and from the submenu that opens, select the paint-bucket tool, or press K.

2. From any Fill Color control, select a gradient fill.

   You can use a linear or radial gradient. (To define a new gradient using the Color panel, see "Creating Solid Colors and Gradients," earlier in this chapter; to select an existing gradient, see "Setting Fill Attributes," earlier in this chapter.

3. In the Tools panel, make sure that Lock Fill is deselected **H**.

4. Using the paint bucket's hot spot, click inside the outline shape.

   Each outline shape you click fills with the gradient currently displayed in the Fill Color control. If you chose a linear gradient in Step 2, Flash centers the unlocked gradient within the outline shape **I**. If you chose a radial gradient, the location you click with the paint bucket's hot spot determines where the center of the unlocked gradient appears **J**.

To fill outline shapes with locked gradients:

Follow the steps in the preceding task; this time in Step 3, select the Lock Fill button.

Each outline shape you click fills with a portion of the gradient currently set in the Fill Color control (see the sidebar "The Mystery of Gradients and Flash's Drawing Models," earlier in this chapter).

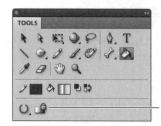

Deselect Lock Fill button

H Deselect the Lock Fill button to fill a shape with an unlocked gradient.

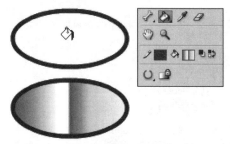

I You can use the paint-bucket tool to apply a linear-gradient fill. An unlocked gradient is centered within the outline shape's bounding box.

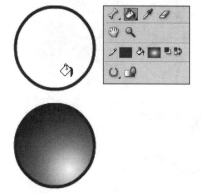

J The paint-bucket tool can also apply a radial-gradient fill. Click where you want to locate the center of the gradient.

TIP Gradients increase file sizes and thereby slow the loading of published movies. Each area of gradient fill requires an extra 50 bytes of data that a solid fill doesn't need. In addition, gradients take processor power. If you use too many, you may see slower frame rates, which translate to slower animations in your finished movie.

Creating Simple Patterns

Flash CS5 offers two tools that create patterns: the spray-brush tool and the deco tool **K**. By default, the spray-brush tool creates a random dot pattern. You determine where the pattern goes by painting with the tool on the Stage. The deco tool uses predefined patterns. Some deco-tool patterns, such as Vine Fill and Grid Fill, spread throughout a selected shape, filling it automatically. Other deco-tool patterns, such as Building Brush or Flower Brush, require a bit of guidance from your mouse movements. As you "paint" with the deco tool's Flower Brush pattern, for example, you lay down a string of randomly repeating leaves, petals, and stems. The deco tool's brush patterns help you populate a scene with repetitive elements quickly.

To make the finished spray-brush and deco patterns easier to work with, Flash unites pattern elements in a special object called a *group*. You'll learn about groups and about using the pattern tools for simple patterns in Chapter 5.

Some of the deco tool's patterns—such as Flame Brush and Lightening Brush—let you automatically create animation using the frame-by-frame technique. You'll learn about frame-by-frame animation in Chapter 8.

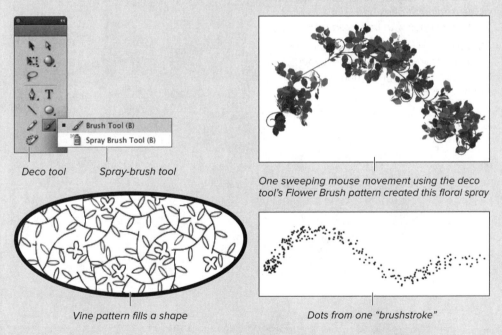

Deco tool   Spray-brush tool

One sweeping mouse movement using the deco tool's Flower Brush pattern created this floral spray

Vine pattern fills a shape

Dots from one "brushstroke"

K The spray-brush tool works something like a real-world airbrush to create a pattern of dots or symbols as you move the mouse. The deco tool can fill a shape (or the Stage) with a predefined pattern, or it can let you paint with a series of randomly repeating graphic elements to create things like flowers, trees, and buildings.

Practice Session

Try creating a bull's-eye target.

- Create a new radial gradient, using three to five colors to create the bull's-eye rings; position the gradient pointers so that there are abrupt shifts in color to create a ring effect. (See *Creating Solid Colors and Gradients > To create a radial gradient*.)

- Add the new gradient to the Swatches panel. (See *Working with Swatches*.)

- Using the oval tool, create a circular shape that has a stroke but no fill. (See *Making Geometric Shapes*.)

- Fill the oval with your new radial gradient. (See *Adding Strokes and Fills > To fill outline shapes with unlocked gradients*.)

- If you don't like the thickness or color scheme of your bulls eye, select your shape and edit its gradient fill in the Colors panel.

Save your file for use in future Practice Sessions.

3

Working with Text

Adobe Flash Professional CS5's text tool creates two types of text fields: Classic and TLF (Text Layout Framework). (See the sidebar "TLF: A New Type of Text.") The exercises in this book cover using TLF text.

A TLF text field is not just a container full of graphic-objects in the shape of letters; the field holds live text that is fully editable in the authoring environment. As you create text elements, you must decide how they will be used in the published movie and assign them a type. If you want the end user to interact with a TLF text field (for example, to copy information), set the text field's Type property to *Selectable*. If you want to update the text at runtime (for example, using ActionScript to download and display new basketball scores to a sports site), set the type property to *Editable*. If the text will just sit there looking pretty, set the type property to *Read Only*.

In this chapter you'll learn about working with English text, using Read Only TLF text fields. To manipulate data in Selectable and Editable TLF text fields at runtime requires a more advanced level of ActionScripting than this book can cover.

In This Chapter

TLF: A New Type of Text

Adobe Flash Professional CS5 introduces a new way to create text elements, the Text Layout Framework (TLF). TLF text has been available via ActionScript since Flash CS4, but Flash CS5 provides tools for creating and working with TLF text directly in the Flash authoring environment.

Although the Tools panel offers just one icon for the text tool, in a sense, there are two text tools: one creates TLF text and the other, Classic text. The title at the top of the Property inspector stays the same no matter which text engine is active, and the Tools panel always displays the same T icon. To streamline the tasks in this book, I refer to them as the text tool and the Classic text tool. If I ask you to select the text tool, I mean that you should click the T icon in the Tools panel and choose TLF as the text engine in the Property inspector.

Creating Flowing Text

A Classic text field is a stand-alone container that displays all its contents. When you make the field narrower vertically, it grows horizontally, and vice versa. Within a Classic text field, text always appears in a single column. To create multicolumn text using Classic text fields, you must create multiple text fields; you position, size, and adjust them to create text blocks with the right width and length. Making text changes to such "multicolumn" text requires adding and deleting text in each field so that the text appears to flow from column to column.

The TLF text tool can create a container that holds more text than it displays. You can link a series of TLF text fields so that text in the container does truly flow from one field to another. As you change the parameters of the text or the size of any linked field, the text reflows as required by the new parameters. You can also use TLF to set up a text field that displays multiple columns of text in a single field.

Typographic Niceties

TLF text can take advantage of many typographic effects built into OpenType and TrueType typefaces—things such as ligatures (artistically joined pairs of letters, like *oe* or *fl*) and old-style numerals (numbers that have varied heights). TLF text also gives designers control over tracking, line breaks, and spacing.

Text Type—Who's in Control?

Text Type presents another difference between Classic text and TLF text, though this one is less apparent in Flash's authoring environment. Classic text comes in three varieties, or *types*. *Static* text cannot be controlled with ActionScript. *Dynamic* text (which can be selected when it appears in Adobe Flash Player) and *Input* text (which can be edited and updated in Flash Player) are both objects that you can manipulate with ActionScript. You need to embed the appropriate characters for Dynamic and Input text; Flash handles the embedding for Static text.

TLF text also comes in three types, which end users will find similar to the three Classic types: *Read Only* looks much like a Classic static-text graphic object; end users can't interact with this text. *Selectable* text can be selected by end users. *Editable* text can be updated and edited at runtime. But for developers, there's a difference: you can actually control all three types with ActionScript.

continues on next page

TLF: A New Type of Text *continued*

TLF Playback Requirements

To use TLF text, you must set your Flash document to publish to Flash Player 10 (see Chapter 18). If you will be publishing for earlier versions of the player, you must use Classic text.

To display TLF text correctly, Flash Player must access special instructions at runtime. By default, Flash creates the instructions in a separate file called a *TLF SWZ*. When you use default settings to publish or test a movie that contains TLF text, Flash Player accesses the TLF SWZ as a shared runtime library. That library must load completely before the movie can begin playback (meaning you won't be able to stream the movie to your viewers). There are a number of publishing options for making the TLF SWZ file available so that playback is seamless for the end user. (You'll learn more about publishing in Chapter 18.)

Point Text vs. Area Text

A text field is basically a container that holds and displays text. The TLF text tool creates two types of text-field containers, which Adobe refers to as *point-text* containers and *area-text* containers. If that terminology seems a little abstract, you can think of them as flexible- and fixed-size text fields.

Point-text Fields (flexible-size)

A point-text container's dimensions are flexible. When you create point text, the field grows larger as you enter more text and shrinks if you delete text.

Area-text Fields (fixed-size)

An area-text container's dimensions are fixed. When you create area text, the field does not grow as you enter text or shrink if you delete text. Once you set the size of the field (by dragging a rectangle with the text tool, for example), the field retains that size until you specifically change its dimensions. As you keep typing and entering more text, the container accepts the text, but the field reveals only as much text as fits inside the borders of the field at the current dimensions. You can always resize an area-text text field to show more text, or use TLF's linking feature to allow the excess text to flow into another text field. (There are also options for letting end users view "hidden" text by scrolling. If you set the text type to Selectable or Editable, end users can scroll within text using the I-beam cursor and arrow keys. You can also add a UIScrollBar component to any type of TLF text field, then set the component to target the field's instance name. You'll learn about working with one type of component, a button, in Chapter 14.)

Creating TLF Text Fields

The text tool creates containers that hold text. You can set the text to read horizontally or vertically. You can also apply a variety of text attributes to text, including text and paragraph styles. For the tasks in this chapter, you'll use the text tool to create TLF text.

To choose the TLF text engine:

1. In the Tools panel, select the text tool **A**, or press the T key.

   The Text Tool Property inspector appears.

2. From the Text Engine menu in the upper portion of the Property inspector, choose TLF Text **B**.

   The Character and Paragraph property categories appear.

To create non-wrapping point text:

1. Select the text tool.

   The Text Tool Property inspector appears with options for setting a variety of text and container attributes. Use the current settings. You learn to change these settings in upcoming tasks.

2. From the Text Type menu, choose a type; for this task, choose Read Only **C**.

   The TLF text tool creates three text types:

   Read Only text acts as a purely graphic element in Flash; end users cannot select it or change it in the published movie. Unless otherwise instructed, use Read Only text for all the tasks in this book.

A Select the text tool in the Tools panel to start creating text on the Stage.

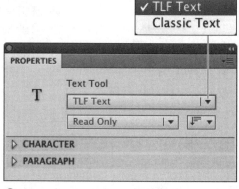

B To work with Flash CS5's new-style text blocks, in the Text Tool Property inspector, choose TLF Text from the Text Engine menu.

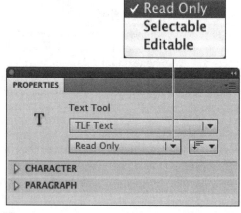

C TLF text comes in three types: End users can interact with Selectable and Editable text at runtime. As its name implies, Read Only text is just a graphic object to end users. You choose the style you need from the Text Type menu.

D The text-tool pointer has a tiny letter T as it hovers over the Stage.

E Click the Stage with the TLF text tool to create a text field. The round resize handle in the lower-right corner of the field indicates that this is a point-text field. The field grows as you enter text; there is no word wrap.

Squares

Squares at a square

Squares at a square dance generally

F As you type, the point-text field grows horizontally to accommodate your text. The text doesn't wrap.

Classic Text

To use Classic text, choose Classic Text from the Text Engine menu. Click the Stage to create a flexible-size Classic text field (it grows horizontally as you enter text—it doesn't wrap), or drag on the Stage to create a fixed-width field (text wraps and the field grows vertically as you enter more text). If you need more help when creating Classic text fields, the text chapter from *Flash CS4 Professional Visual QuickStart Guide* is available on the companion website (www.peachpit.com/flashcs5vqs). (The techniques for creating Classic text in CS5 are virtually the same as in CS4.)

Selectable text is partly accessible to end users; they can copy this text.

Editable text is fully accessible to end users; they can select it, edit it, and delete it.

Note that Flash developers can target all three types of TLF text fields for updating at runtime via ActionScript.

3. Move the pointer over the Stage.

   The pointer turns into a crosshair with a letter *T* in the bottom-right corner **D**.

4. Click the Stage at the spot where you want your text to start.

   Flash creates a resizable bounding box with a blinking insertion point, ready for you to enter text **E**.

   Each corner and side of the box has a resize handle; the round handle in the lower-right corner indicates that this field does not have word wrap.

5. Start typing your text.

   The bounding box grows to accommodate whatever you type **F**. By default, when you click and type with the TLF text tool, you create a field whose Behavior is set to Multiline No Wrap (see "Setting Container Attributes," later in this chapter); as you enter characters, the box grows horizontally, creating a single line of text. When you press Enter, the box grows vertically to accommodate the new line.

6. When you finish typing, click elsewhere on the Stage (or choose a new tool in the Tools panel) to deselect the text.

   With default container settings, Flash hides the bounding box, leaving just the text visible. When you click this text with the selection tool, Flash selects the field so that you can reposition it, resize it, or change the text's attributes directly.

To create area text with word wrap:

1. With the TLF text tool selected, click the Stage to place the text field.

2. Move the pointer over any of the resize handles at the corners or sides of the field's bounding box.

   The pointer changes to a double-headed arrow.

3. Click and drag one of the handles until the bounding box is the size you want **G**.

   The resize handle in the lower-right corner disappears, indicating that word wrap is set for this text field (the field's Behavior property is set to Multiline; see "Setting Container Attributes," later in this chapter). In addition, two square *text-flow ports* appear; the *In port* appears on the left side of the text field and the *Out port* on the right. (Ports allow you to link one TLF text field to another; you'll learn more about linking fields and text flow in "Creating Linked Text Fields," later in this chapter.)

4. Release the mouse button.

   The blinking insertion point appears in the text field.

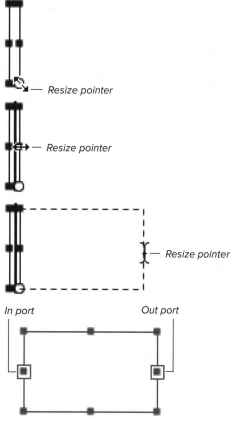

— Resize pointer

— Resize pointer

— Resize pointer

In port   Out port

G Drag any resize handle of a text field's bounding box to create a text field with a specific width. When you release the mouse button, the lower-right handle changes from a circle to a square, indicating that the text you enter will wrap to fit the column width of the text field. Two hollow squares appear: one on the left side, the other on the right. These are the In and Out ports indicating text flow for linked fields.

1

Squares at a square

2

dance

3

Squares at a square

Overflow text

H When you enter more text, the field displays what you type (1). When you hit the limit of what the field can display, the text you entered first seems to disappear (2). But once you finish typing, the text scrolls back to the beginning (3). A red plus sign appears in the text field's Out port, indicating that the field contains overflow text.

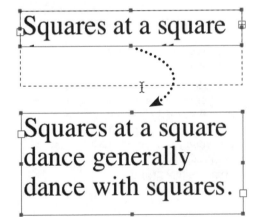

Squares at a square

Squares at a square
dance generally
dance with squares.

I Drag any resize handle to enlarge the TLF text field (top). When you make the field big enough to show all its contents, the red plus disappears from the Out port (bottom).

5. Enter your text.

As you type, Flash wraps the text to fit inside the text field's bounding box. If you type more characters than the field can display, the text scrolls upward temporarily, revealing the most recent characters you typed **H**. When you deselect the text field, the text reflows and the first text you typed appears at the top of the field. For this task, enter enough text to force scrolling. A red plus sign appears in the field's Out port, indicating that there is additional text—often referred to as *overflow text* or *overset text*.

6. To resize the text field, position the pointer over any of the resize handles and drag the handle as you would to resize any rectangle object.

When you release the mouse button, the text reflows to fit the new field. If the text field is large enough to display all its contents, the red plus sign disappears from the Out port **I**.

TIP Click and drag on the Stage to quickly create an area-text field with word wrap. A dotted-line rectangle previews the text field's proportions. When you release the mouse button, the text-flow ports are already in place.

TIP To convert a fixed-size (area-text) text field to a flexible-size (point-text) text field, click the field with the TLF text tool to activate it in Text Edit mode. Then double-click one of the text-flow ports. The circular resize handle reappears in the TLF text field's lower-right corner, indicating that there is no word wrap; the text field grows horizontally as you type a line, and vertically when you press Enter.

TIP Double-clicking an empty, deselected text field with the selection tool puts you into Text Edit mode. The Tools panel switches to the text tool; the text field activates, and the text tool's blinking I-beam appears. You can edit the field's text.

Creating Linked Text Fields

An area-text field is like a window into a huge container of endless possible text. A red plus sign in the Out port is your clue that the window is only showing some of the text in the container. You have two options for revealing more of the text: resize the field so it can display all the text, or link the field to another TLF text field, creating another window into that huge container of text.

Text that flows freely between linked TLF text fields is often referred to as *threaded text*. Linked fields may also be called *threaded fields;* this book often refers to them as a chain of linked fields. Resizing one field in the chain causes the remaining text to reflow in response. Similarly, text reflows in response to changes you make to the parameters of the threaded text—for example, changing the font family, type size, leading, and so on. Selecting one threaded text field (with the selection tool) activates the entire chain of linked fields: the bounding box of each threaded field highlights (in light blue by default), triangular *text-flow indicators* appear in the In and Out ports, and a *link line* (or *thread*) connects each linked pair of In and Out ports. These graphic elements indicate the direction the text flows from one field to the next.

To create linked text fields:

1. Repeat Steps 1–5 of the preceding task to create an area-text field.

   Enter a fair amount of text, at least 20 words. Make sure to enter some overflow text; a red plus sign should appear in the field's Out port. Let's call this Field 1.

Long-Distance Linking

You can create links between TLF text fields on different layers. You can even link fields in different frames (sort of like linking across a page break in a text-layout application). All linked fields must be on the same Timeline, however. You'll start working with layers in Chapter 6, you'll learn about working with frames and the Timeline in Chapter 8.

Images Amid Text

Flash CS5 cannot automatically flow text around images or objects, but it does streamline the process of creating text that surrounds objects. Create a chain of multiple linked TLF text fields and distribute them around the object. Resize the individual fields as needed to make space for the object; the threaded text inside the linked fields reflows automatically.

CS5 cannot create inline graphics (images that are embedded within a line of text), but TLF text fields will use inline graphics in text created in Adobe Illustrator. When you import text with inline graphics to a TLF text field, the inline graphics appear in Flash.

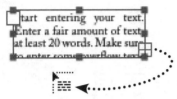

A When it hovers over a text-flow port, the pointer changes to a solid arrowhead; clicking now begins the linking process.

B Once you've "loaded" the pointer with overflow text, the loaded-text icon appears. Clicking the Stage with that pointer creates a new, linked field.

C After you click the loaded-text pointer, Flash creates a linked field. All fields in the chain activate. Text-flow direction triangles and link lines appear, indicating which fields link directly and how the text flows. Here, the link line connects Field 1's Out port to Field 2's In port.

2. Position the pointer over Field 1's Out port.

   The begin-link pointer appears (the icon is a solid arrowhead) **A**.

3. Click the Out port and move the pointer away from the port.

   The loaded-text pointer appears (the icon is a tiny arrowhead dragging a field of text) **B**.

4. To create a new TLF text field that automatically links to Field 1, position the pointer outside Field 1 and do one of the following:

   ▸ To create a field that duplicates the dimensions and other properties of Field 1, click the loaded-text pointer outside Field 1.

   ▸ To create a field with different dimensions, click and drag using the loaded-text pointer to draw a new TLF text field with dimensions you want.

   When you release the mouse button, another TLF text field appears **C**; let's call it Field 2. A link line connects Field 1's Out port to Field 2's In port. Overflow text from Field 1 flows into Field 2.

TIP You can use this technique to automate creation of multiple linked TLF text fields before you enter any text. Create Field 1, click its Out port, then click the Stage to create Field 2. Click Field 2's Out port, then click the Stage to create Field 3. Repeat as needed.

To link text fields manually:

1. Create an area-text field (Field 1) and enter some text.

   Repeat Steps 1–5 of the task named "To create area text with word wrap," in the preceding section.

2. Deselect Field 1.

   Click the Stage or choose Edit > Deselect All.

3. Create an area-text field (Field 2) and leave it empty.

   Using the TLF text tool, click and drag in a blank area of the Stage. Don't worry about the exact size of the field; you can adjust it later. Make it big enough to display at least a few words **D**.

4. To start the linking process, do the following:

   ▸ Activate Field 1 by clicking it with the text tool. The bounding box highlights and text-flow ports appear.

   ▸ Position the pointer over Field 1's Out port. The begin-link pointer (a solid arrowhead icon) appears **E**.

   ▸ Click Field 1's Out port.

   ▸ Move the pointer away from Field 1's Out port. The loaded-text pointer appears **F**. You can think of this pointer as being filled with the overflow text.

Start entering your text. Enter a fair amount of text, at least 20 words. Make sure to enter some overflow text.

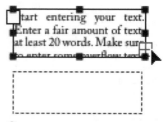

D You can create a text-flow link between two independent area-text fields. These two fields are not currently linked.

E The begin-link pointer's arrowhead icon appears when you position the pointer over a text-flow port, indicating that you're ready to begin creating a link.

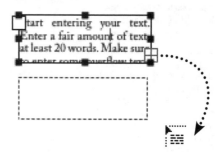

F After you click a port to begin the link, the loaded-text pointer appears; its icon represents a paragraph of text. In a sense, you're picking up the overflow text in the field where you clicked and preparing to "pour" it into another field.

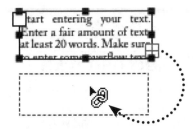

G Once you've created the first half of a link, positioning the loaded-text pointer over another text field activates the end-link pointer (the icon is a bit hard to decipher, but it's actually two links of a chain, and both are closed).

H Clicking the end-link pointer in an unlinked field creates a link between the two fields; a link-line connects the Out port of the first field to the In port of the second field. Small triangles appear in the linked ports, indicating the direction of the text flow.

5. To complete the linking process, do the following:

   ▸ Position the loaded-text pointer over Field 2. Inside the bounding box of another TLF text field, the loaded-text pointer changes to the end-link pointer (a closed-link icon) **G**.

   ▸ Click anywhere within Field 2. Flash creates a link and pours overflow text into Field 2 **H**.

You don't actually have to create text to set up linked text fields. You can draw any number of empty, unlinked fields. (Deselected, empty TLF text fields appear as dotted-line rectangles.) Click a field with either the selection tool or the text tool to activate it. Click the active field's Out port; then position the begin-link pointer anywhere within the target field's preview rectangle and click. Flash links the fields. Selecting any of the linked fields activates them all. The text you type in these active fields flows from the first field to the second, from the second to the third, and so on.

TIP If your TLF text field is narrow from top to bottom, its Out port may sit right on top of the resize handle on the right side of the field, making it hard to get the begin-link pointer instead of the resize pointer. Position the pointer at the right-hand edge of the Out port and the arrowhead icon will appear.

To break links between text fields:

1. Create a pair of linked TLF text fields containing threaded text.

   For this task, create the first field (Field 1) and enter the words **First text. Second text.** Create a second field (Field 2), and link it to Field 1. Size the fields so that Field 1 displays the words *First text.* and Field 2 displays *Second text.*

2. Using the selection tool, activate the linked fields by clicking either one.

   Both linked fields highlight in blue, revealing their text-flow ports (with text-flow triangles) and a link line. The directly selected field also displays its resize handles.

3. To begin breaking the link, position the pointer over the In port of Field 2, and when the arrowhead icon appears, click the In port **❶**.

   Flash automatically selects the text tool in the Tools panel. The pointer is context-sensitive, displaying different icons over different areas (see the sidebar "A Key to Text-Threading Icons," later in this chapter).

4. Position the pointer anywhere inside the bounding box of Field 1, and when the break-link pointer (a broken-chain icon) appears, **❶** click in the bounding box.

   Flash breaks the link between Fields 1 and 2. All of the text from the bottom field gets sucked back into the top field as overflow text. The red cross appears in Field 1's Out port **❶**.

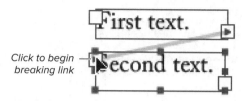

Click to begin breaking link

❶ The arrowhead pointer hovering over a port at one end of a link line indicates that you're ready to start breaking the link.

Click to finish breaking link

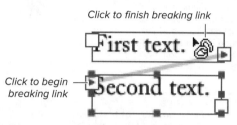

Click to begin breaking link

❶ Once you've begun the process of severing a link between TLF text fields, the break-link pointer, a broken-chain icon, appears as it hovers over places where you might sever the link. The easiest place to see it is by positioning the pointer over a blank area of the text field at the opposite end of the link line from the port you clicked.

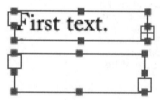

❶ Once you break a link, the link line disappears and the text from Field 2 moves back into Field 1. The red plus sign in Field 1's Out port indicates that more text is there.

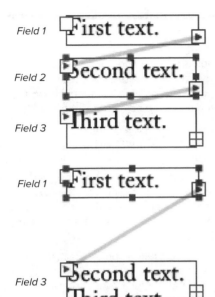

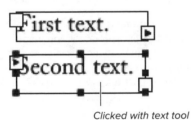

L Start with three linked TLF text fields: Field 1, Field 2, and Field 3. Delete the Field 2, and you wind up with two linked fields. The text flows from Field 1 to Field 3.

Clicked with text tool

M Using the text tool to click one field in a chain of linked fields activates all of the linked fields, but no link lines appear.

TIP The preceding task shows just one way of breaking links. You have several options. You can start at either end of the link line: click Field 1's Out port *or* click Field 2's In port, then, with the break-link pointer active, click the port on the other end of the link line, or click anywhere in the other field. You can also simply double-click an In port or an Out port to sever its link.

TIP When you have a chain with three or more linked text fields, you can use the method described in the preceding tasks to sever the link between fields at any point in the chain. Upstream fields (those that come earlier in the chain than the broken link) retain their linkage; text remains threaded and the overflow-text red cross appears in the Out port of the last linked field. Downstream fields (those that come later in the chain than the broken link) retain their linkage, but they contain no text. If you enter enough text into one of these fields, you will see the threading.

TIP Once you've clicked a port to start breaking a link, anytime you move the pointer over a blank area of the Stage, you'll see the loaded-text pointer. Clicking the Stage with this pointer adds a new linked TLF text field between the two original linked fields. (The new field duplicates the size of the field whose port you clicked to break the link.)

TIP If you delete a field in the middle of a chain of linked text fields, the text in the remaining fields is still threaded **L**.

TIP You can also use the text tool to activate linked fields (Steps 2–3). The bounding boxes highlight in black, and triangles appear in the linked text-flow ports, but the link line does not appear. This makes it more difficult to work with breaking links, since you can't see what links to what **M**.

A Key to Text-Threading Icons

When you use the selection or text tool to click a TLF text field's text-flow port, the pointer becomes a context-sensitive text-threading tool. With this tool, you can create a new link to the clicked port or break an existing link to that port. The key to knowing what the text-threading tool is about to do is to watch the pointer's icon; it changes depending on the pointer's location.

 The break-link pointer's open-link icon appears when the pointer is over the port you just clicked, or over the field on the other end of the link line from the port you just clicked. Clicking when this pointer is active severs the existing link.

 The end-link pointer's icon is a closed chain-link. It appears when the pointer is over an existing TLF text field other than the field on the other end of the link line from the port you just clicked. Clicking this pointer in a field that's *not* part of the active threaded chain creates a link adding that field to the chain. Clicking this pointer in a field that is part of the active threaded chain has no effect on the current threading.

 The loaded-text pointer's icon is a tiny pointer arrow dragging a paragraph of text. It appears when the pointer is over the Stage. Clicking now creates a new TLF text field linked to the field whose port you clicked. This icon also appears when the pointer is over the same text field as the port you clicked; clicking that field has no effect on the current threading.

TLF Text Vs. Classic Text

The procedures for working with Classic text fields remain basically unchanged from earlier versions of Flash. In many cases, the steps for creating text fields and setting character and paragraph properties are the same for both types of text; in other cases, the differences are minor—for example, the terminology for some properties may differ slightly. (To see tasks with precise steps for creating and working with Classic text fields in Flash CS4, see the companion website to this *Visual QuickStart Guide,* www.peachpit.com/flashcs5vqs.)

So how do you decide which type of text to use? Here are some crucial requirements that will influence your decision.

Player requirements To use TLF text, you must work in an ActionScript 3.0 document and set your movie to publish in Flash Player 10 or later (see Chapter 18). If you want to use earlier ActionScript versions, or publish for earlier player versions, you must use Classic text.

Font requirements TLF text works only with Type 2 (OpenType) and TrueType fonts. If you plan to use PostScript fonts, you must use Classic text.

Masking requirements If you place a TLF text field on a mask layer, you wind up with a rectangular mask (You'll learn about masking in Chapter 6.) To create a text field whose letterforms act as individual masks, you must use Classic text.

Other differences Here are some other ways the two types of text differ.

- You can create Read Only TLF text fields without any content; unselected, empty TLF text fields appear on the Stage as dotted-line preview rectangles. Using the text tool, click anywhere

continues on next page

TLF Text Vs. Classic Text *continued*

inside the preview rectangle to select and activate the field; using the selection tool, double-click the field to activate it for text input. If you use the Classic text tool to draw a Static text field but fail to enter any text, the field disappears as soon as you deselect it.

- All three TLF text-field types are objects that take instance names and can be manipulated by ActionScript. For Classic text, you must set the Type property to Dynamic or Input to be able to assign the text field an instance name and target the text with ActionScript.

- TLF text converts to individual drawing-objects after the first break-apart command; Classic text converts to single-letter Classic text fields. Both types convert to raw shapes after a second break-apart command. But note that if you type a single-letter Classic text field and choose the break-apart command, the text converts to a raw shape immediately. A single-letter TLF text field still converts to a drawing-object first.

The Pitfalls of Converting TLF Text to Classic Text

It's easy to convert TLF text to Classic text and vice versa: you just select the text field, access the Text Property inspector, and choose the desired text engine, TLF or Classic. But you may encounter a few pitfalls in the process.

Translation Issues

Most obvious is the fact that some properties simply don't translate. If, for example, you convert a multicolumn TLF text field to a Classic text field, you wind up with just a single column of text. If you convert a TLF text field with a 3-point green border and a blue background, you wind up with a Classic text field that has the default visible border (thin and black) and no background color.

Text-flow Issues

Converting one or more linked TLF text fields eliminates the text-flow capabilities not only in the selected and converted field(s), but also in any fields that come earlier in the chain of linked fields. Such fields retain TLF text status but lose their links; each one becomes a separate TLF text field containing just the characters that were visible inside it at the time you made the conversion. TLF text fields that come later in the chain than the converted field(s) keep their TLF status, retain their links, and preserve any overflow text. But beware: you lose overflow text if you convert the final field in the chain.

Position and Spacing Issues

The baseline may shift (see the sidebar, "Typography 101: Baselines," later in this chapter). This happens because Classic text handles padding (the spacing between the text field's bounding box and the block of text) in a way that's different from the default padding style for TLF text.

TLF text's leading property may not translate directly to Classic text's line-spacing property. This may result in lines of text that are too close together or too far apart.

TLF's text-type property may not translate to the Classic type you want. A Selectable TLF text field converts to a Static Classic text field with the Selectable Property active in the Character section of the Property inspector. If you wanted that Selectable text to be Dynamic Classic text, you'd need to change the Type property after conversion.

Setting Character Attributes

The Property inspector is the main tool for setting text attributes. This panel is context-sensitive, offering different properties depending on whether you've selected the text tool but aren't yet interacting with text; or you've used the selection tool to select a text field; or you're entering, editing, or selecting text with the text tool's I-beam cursor active (see the sidebar "The Many Modes of the TLF Text Tool," later in this chapter).

You can set attributes in advance so that as you type, the text tool applies them automatically, or you can apply attributes to existing text. The text tool always uses whatever settings currently appear in the Text (Tool) Property inspector **A**.

For the following tasks, keep the Property inspector open (choose Window > Properties if it's not already open) and expand the Character section (click the triangle to the left of the section name to toggle between the expanded and collapsed views).

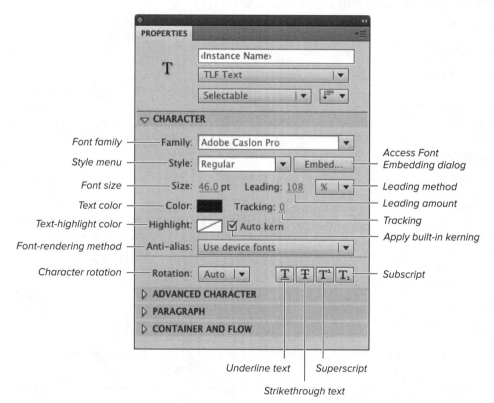

Font family — Family
Style menu — Style — Access Font Embedding dialog
Font size — Size — Leading method
Text color — Color — Leading amount
Text-highlight color — Highlight — Tracking
Font-rendering method — Anti-alias — Apply built-in kerning
Character rotation — Rotation — Subscript

Underline text | Superscript
Strikethrough text

A When you select some text within a text field, you enter Text Edit mode, and the Text Property inspector displays the attributes to be applied to the selected text. Character settings and Advanced Character settings affect just the selected text. Paragraph settings affect the paragraph(s) containing the selected text. Container and Flow settings apply to all the text in an active text field. If you make a selection in threaded text, Container and Flow settings affect all the linked fields that hold that threaded text.

The Many Modes of the TLF Text Tool

Choosing the text tool in the Tools panel puts you in Text Tool mode: a T icon (for text) and the name Text Tool appear at the top of the Property inspector; sections named Character and Paragraph appear in the body of the inspector. Clicking the text tool inside a TLF text field or using the text tool to select a chunk of TLF text puts you in Text Edit mode. In this mode, the name Text Tool disappears from the inspector, but the T icon and the Character and Paragraph sections remain; two new sections— Advanced Character and Container and Flow—appear. Using the selection tool to select one or more TLF text fields puts you in Text Object mode. In this mode, the Property inspector displays sections relating to properties of the text fields themselves, including Position and Size, 3-D Position and View, Color Effect, Display, and Filters.

The tasks in this book will refer to the modes as the Text Tool Property inspector and the Text Property inspector when you need to distinguish between them; when referring to either or both, I will use the name Text (Tool) Property inspector.

TIP In addition to setting text attributes in the Text (Tool) Property inspector, you can set them from the Text menu. Just be aware that the menu uses the Classic-text property Letter Spacing, not the TLF property Tracking. You can also set the font (family), size, style, and paragraph alignment from the Text menu (although the Justify option applies whatever last-line alignment for justified paragraphs is currently active in the Property inspector). You can use the Text menu to change the properties of selected text or to load text properties into the text tool.

TIP You can also access the Font Embedding dialog from the Text menu.

TIP You can select multiple text fields of the same type (TLF or Classic) with the selection tool and modify them at the same time. (You'll learn more about selections in Chapter 4.) If you select a mix of TLF and Classic fields, you can simultaneously modify only the properties found in the Property inspector's Position and Size section and Filters section.

TIP The contact-sensitivity settings in the General category of the Preferences dialog also apply to selecting text fields with a selection outline. (You'll learn more about making such selections in Chapter 4.)

The Mysteries of TLF Text Selection

Threaded text adds a level of complexity to the process of selecting text and applying attributes. When you use the selection tool to click a text field that's part of a chain of linked fields, all the fields highlight in blue, but only the clicked field displays resize handles. The resize handles indicate the active field for purposes of applying new properties. Any changes you make to the properties apply only to the text that appeared in the field at the time you selected it. Some changes, however, may force that selected text to reflow into other linked fields. As long as the same field stays selected, your changes continue to affect the original selection of text, no matter where that text now appears.

To apply changes to a subset of the text in one or more linked fields, use the text tool to select text by dragging or clicking/Shift-clicking the characters that you want (as you would in any word-processing or text-layout program).

To apply changes to all the threaded text within a set of linked TLF text fields, using the text tool or the selection tool, click any of the linked fields, then choose Edit > Select All. Flash highlights the entire threaded text.

Note that you can change the properties of the text tool when it's in the middle of text, without actually selecting any text. If, for example, you click to place the blinking I-beam cursor between the two *d*'s in the word *middle,* and set new properties in the Text Tool Property inspector, nothing about the word *middle* changes. Start typing, and the new text you enter comes in with the properties you just specified.

To select text to apply character attributes:

Do any of the following:

- Using the text tool, drag over existing text to highlight part of it. (When working with threaded text, you can drag across linked fields to select all or part of the threaded text.)

- Using the text tool, double-click a word to select it.

- Using the text tool, click anywhere in the text and choose Edit > Select All.

- Using the selection tool, single-click a text field to select all the text within it.

- Using the selection tool, Shift-click multiple text fields to select the text within all of the fields.

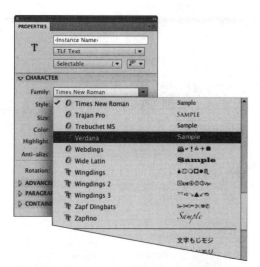

B Use the Family pop-up menu in the Character section of the Text (Tool) Property inspector to choose a font family. The scrolling list contains all the installed font families. The word *Sample* shows what text looks like in that font.

The Mystery of Anti-aliasing

Anti-aliasing is a method of *rendering*—drawing lines and curves—that softens edges. For text, this means making the letterforms appear slightly blurry. Anti-aliasing text at large point sizes makes it easier to read, but at smaller sizes, text may appear fuzzy and indistinct. In early versions of Flash, applying anti-aliasing to text in small sizes made that text difficult to read. With Flash's current font-rendering engine you can apply anti-aliasing to small font sizes and still have readable text, provided the text isn't animated.

To choose a font family:

1. On the Stage, select the text you want to modify, and access the Property inspector.

2. In the Character section, click the Family pop-up menu.

   The menu opens as a scrolling list displaying the font families installed on your system. A font sample (showing the word *Sample,* set in that font) appears to the right of the font name in the list **B**.

3. To view the available font families, drag the scroll bar.

   This list doesn't autoscroll when you move the pointer to the top or bottom of the menu.

4. Move the pointer over a font-family name.

   Flash highlights the name.

5. Click to select the currently highlighted font family and close the scrolling list.

   The selected font name appears in the Family field. Flash changes the selected text to the new font.

TIP Another way to select a font family is to choose it from the Text > Font menu.

TIP You can also enter a font-family name by typing it in the Family field in the Character section of the Text (Tool) Property inspector. As you type, Flash autocompletes the name from the list of installed fonts. If Flash can't find something similar, it leaves the current font in place.

To choose a character style:

1. Select the text you want to modify, and access the Text Property inspector.

2. In the Character section, from the Style pop-up menu, choose one of the available font styles 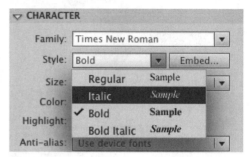.

   The Style menu displays the available variants of the font selected in the Family field. If the current font has no variants, the Style menu is disabled ⒟.

TIP If selected text is currently set in a font that has a boldface variant, you can toggle between the regular and bold variant by pressing Shift-Command-B (Mac) or Ctrl-Shift-B (Windows). (Take note of that Shift key if you're accustomed to using another application for creating text: it's not part of the usual command.) To toggle an italic variant, press Shift-Command-I (Mac) or Ctrl-Shift-I (Windows). If the font of the selected text lacks bold or italic variants, these commands won't change the selected text.

To set the font size:

1. Select the text you want to modify, and access the Text Property inspector.

2. To enter a new size, in the Character Section, use the Size hot text to enter a value between 0 and 720 points.

   To use a precise value, click the hot text, enter a number in the field that activates, then press Enter. To choose a value interactively, position the pointer over the hot text; when the pointing finger with a double arrow appears, drag left (or down) to lower the value, or drag right (or up) to increase the value ⒠. Flash previews the changes on the Stage as you drag the hot text's invisible slider.

Ⓒ The Style menu in the Character section of the Text (Tool) Property inspector lists the bold and italic variants of the font currently active in the Family field.

ⒹIf the current font has no bold or italic variants, the Style menu is disabled.

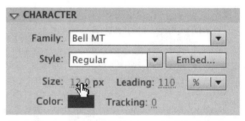

Ⓔ Drag the Size hot text to change the point size of selected text interactively on the Stage.

TIP You can also choose Text > Size to select from 13 common sizes ranging from 8 points to 120 points.

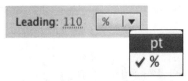

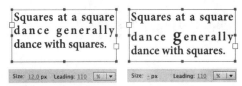

F Choose a method for measuring leading (the space between lines of text) from the Leading Style pop-up menu. The points method allows for a precise measurement; percent bases leading on the current font size.

> Squares at a square
> dance generally
> dance with squares.

> Squares at a square
> dance generally
> dance with squares.

Size: 12.0 px Leading: 110 % ▼   Size: - px Leading: 110 % ▼

G The text on the left has font size set to 12-point and leading set to 110 percent (that is, 110 percent of 12 points). The text on the right has the same settings, except that one letter is set to 18-point. Flash increases the space above the line with the larger letter, making it 110 percent of 18 points; the space below the line with the larger letter remains at 110 percent of 12 points.

TIP When a text paragraph combines characters of various point sizes, setting the paragraph's leading method to Percent, with a value greater than 100 percent, ensures that the spacing above each line accommodates the various sizes **G**.

TIP If you're not too familiar with typography, you may find it easier to specify leading as a percentage; 120 percent is a common leading value. A very rough rule of thumb is to use a leading value 2 points bigger than the current point size of your text.

To set leading:

1. Select the text you want to modify, and access the Character section of the Text Property inspector.

2. To determine the method of measuring the space between lines, from the Leading Style pop-up menu **F**, choose one of the following:

   ▸ To specify an exact amount of space, choose points (pt).

   ▸ To specify a percentage of the current font size, choose percent (%).

3. Use the Leading hot text to enter the amount of space you want.

   ▸ With points as the method of measure, enter a value between 0 and 720 points.

   ▸ With percent as the method, enter a value between 0 and 1000.

   Leading governs the amount of vertical space between lines of text. A setting of 0 would have all lines of text sitting right on top of one another; positive values place lines farther apart.

TIP Leading is actually the space between baselines; the baseline is the imaginary line on which all the letters of a text line sit.

TIP You can apply leading to one line, many lines, or entire paragraphs. For English text, if you choose a new leading value while you have selected text in just one line, the new setting affects the space above the line containing the selected text.

To adjust space between letters and/or words:

1. Within a TLF text field in a Flash document, select the text whose spacing you want to change, and access the Text Property inspector.

   To adjust only the space between letters, select the letters or select a single word. To adjust the space between letters and words, select a larger chunk of text: an entire line, paragraph, or text field.

2. In the Character section, use the Tracking hot text to enter a value between −1000 and 1000.

   Flash measures tracking in 1000ths of an em space. A negative value reduces the space between letters in the selection; a positive value increases it Ⓗ. If the selection contains multiple words, the setting also adjusts the space between words.

TIP Flash adjusts tracking by setting the space after a selected character. If you want to change tracking between a pair of letters, just select the first letter. For example, to adjust the space between the *e* and the *a* in the word *leaf,* select the *e* and set the desired tracking value. To adjust space between the *e, a,* and *f,* select *e* and *a.*

TIP Another way to increase spacing for selected text is to choose Text > Letter Spacing > Increase or press Option-Command–right arrow (Mac) or Ctrl-Alt–right arrow (Windows). To decrease spacing, choose Text > Letter Spacing > Decrease, or use the keyboard commands with the left arrow.

TIP You can also adjust letterspacing interactively by using the keyboard shortcuts. The space between letters continues to expand or contract as long as you hold down the key combination.

Tracking: 0

Spaced Out

Tracking: −80

Spaced Out

Tracking: 80

Spaced Out

Ⓗ Enter a negative value for tracking to bring characters (or words) closer together. Enter a positive value to space them out. Enter 0 to remove tracking.

TIP To reset the font's original letterspacing, choose Text > Letter Spacing > Reset or press Option-Command–up arrow (Mac) or Ctrl-Alt–up arrow (Windows).

TIP When TLF text is set to justify—so that it fills the column width—changing the tracking between selected letters may affect spacing between other letters and words in the same line or paragraph. (You'll learn more about creating justified text in "Setting Paragraph Attributes," later in this chapter.)

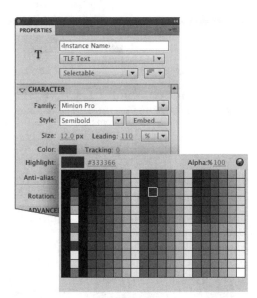

To choose a text color:

1. Select the text you want to modify, and access the Text Property inspector.

2. In the Character section, click the Color control.

 The standard color-control swatch set appears **Ⓘ**.

3. Select a color.

 Flash applies the color to the selected text.

TIP Flash considers text to be a fill. When the text tool is active, or text is selected on the Stage, you can change the text color by using any of the methods described for setting fill attributes in Chapter 2.

Ⓘ The Color control in the Character section of the Text (Tool) Property inspector lets you change the color of selected text.

Typography 101: Kerning

While *tracking* affects the space between characters and words in an entire chunk of selected text, *kerning* affects the space between a pair of letters. Because of the way fonts are constructed, with each letter being a separate element, some pairs of letters have odd spacing when you type them. The space between a capital *T* and a lowercase *o*, for example, may seem too large because of the white space below the crossbar of the *T*. To make the characters look better, you can reduce the space between them, or *kern in* the pair. Some letters may seem to be too close together—say, a *t* and an *i*. You can *kern out* the pair so that it looks better.

Font designers often build into their fonts special information about how to space troublesome pairs of letters. Flash takes advantage of that embedded kerning information when you select the Auto Kern checkbox in the Character section of the Text (Tool) Property inspector. It's a good idea to turn on kerning to make your type look its best.

In addition, TLF text can take advantage of ligature information built into a typeface by its designer. Ligatures create special spacing (or special letterforms) for certain letter pairs that have these types of problems; at some ligature settings, the pair acts more like a single character for tracking purposes, so selecting the pair and changing the tracking has no effect. You set ligature usage in the Advanced Character section of the Text (Tool) Property inspector.

You can kern TLF text manually instead of, or in addition to, using the embedded kerning. Select a character. To adjust the space following it, use the Tracking hot text: enter larger values to increase the space, smaller values to decrease the space.

To set the font-rendering method:

1. Select the TLF text field(s) you want to modify, and access the Text Property inspector.

Font rendering applies to all the text in a thread, whether that text fits into one text field or flows through several linked fields.

2. In the Character section, from the Anti-alias pop-up menu ❶, choose one of the following:

Use Device Fonts Choose this setting when smaller file sizes are more important than re-creating the precise font outlines on the end user's system.

Readability (This is the default setting for publishing to Flash Player 8 and later; see Chapter 18.) Choose this setting for text fields that you don't plan to animate. The Flash Type font-rendering engine draws text with this setting on the Stage as you create your FLA file. The Flash Type engine renders this text for playback. This setting requires embedded font outlines (see the sidebar "About Font Embedding," later in this chapter).

Animation Choose this setting for animated text fields. At runtime, Flash Player ignores some information about aligning and kerning to help speed playback. Flash Type doesn't do the rendering. This setting requires embedded font outlines.

TIP Although font-rendering methods apply to an entire block of threaded text, you don't actually have to select the whole thing to apply the method. If you make a selection within the threaded text, then choose a new method for font rendering, Flash automatically applies the new style to all the threaded text in all the linked fields.

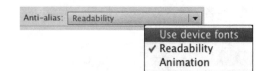

❶ To control the degree of anti-aliasing, in the Character section of the Text (Tool) Property inspector, choose an option from the Anti-alias pop-up menu.

Multinational Multidirectional Text

English and Western European languages traditionally present text in horizontal lines that read left to right. Sometimes, you need to create vertical text, for display text, or text in other languages. Sometimes you need text that reads right to left. Because the possible settings for TLF text are so numerous, Flash hides some of them by default; you can access them though the TLF Text (Tool) Property inspector's panel menu. The ins and outs of dealing with text in other languages is beyond the scope of a *Visual QuickStart Guide,* but here's a brief rundown of where to find options for truly international typography.

- The Text Orientation menu is in the top section of the TLF Text (Tool) Property inspector; the icon's arrow changes direction to indicate horizontal or vertical text.

- To choose a direction for horizontal text, choose Show Right-to-Left Options from the Text (Tool) Property inspector's panel menu. A new menu, Direction, appears in the Paragraph section of the inspector.

- To view options for dealing with Asian text, choose Show Asian Options from the TLF Text (Tool) Property inspector's panel menu; additional settings and options appear in the panel.

About Font Embedding

Embedding makes specific fonts available in the published SWF file, so that text in your Flash creations looks exactly the way you designed it to, no matter what fonts are actually on the system playing the SWF. By default, Flash CS5 automatically embeds the specific characters that actually appear in any TLF text fields in your Flash movie. (In earlier versions, you always needed to embed fonts manually; and you had to embed all the characters in a font—you couldn't choose just the characters you actually used.) When you create TLF text fields that will be manipulated at runtime—for example, fields where users enter contact information—you should embed a wider range of characters than what might first appear in the fields. If the look of your text is important for your Flash creations—and you aren't positive your end user will have the fonts you use—it's safest to embed fonts whenever you set TLF text's font-rendering method (anti-aliasing) to Readability or Animation.

The Font Embedding dialog makes it easy to embed a subset of characters that users are likely to need (this avoids adding the entire font, which can add significantly to file size). Here are two of several ways to access the dialog: click the Embed button in the Character section of the Text (Tool) Property inspector, or choose Text > Font Embedding. (You can also work with fonts and embedding via the Library panel.)

The Options section of the Font Embedding dialog ⓚ makes it easy to embed meaningful subsets of an entire font—for example, all uppercase letters, all lowercase letters, all numbers, all punctuation. Embedding the font creates a *font symbol* that becomes an asset in the current document's library (you learn about libraries in Chapter 7). The font symbol shows up near the head of the Font/Family menus for the current document as well; font-symbol names end with an asterisk (*), and they all group together. All the text fields in the document that use the font symbol get embedding information from the symbol; you don't need to choose embed settings for each field.

The ActionScript section provides settings for exporting font symbols for use with ActionScript; you must export if you plan to manipulate your text with ActionScript.

You can avoid the need for font embedding entirely by using device fonts. Device fonts allow Flash Player to work with fonts found on the end user's system to create text during playback. Device fonts help keep your movie's file size down, but may play havoc with the look of your text.

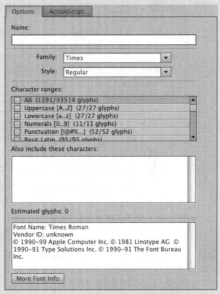

ⓚ The Options section of the Font Embedding dialog lets you select specific characters of a font and make them available to the end user's computer. Each set, known as a *font symbol*, appears as an asset in the file's library (see Chapter 7). For each font symbol, you choose a font family and style, select characters to include from a list of common subsets of the font (all lowercase letters, for example), and/or enter a list of the specific characters you need.

To apply additional properties:

1. Select the TLF text to which you want to apply color, highlighting, strikethrough, underscore, or superscript/subscript positioning.

2. Access the Character section of the Property inspector, 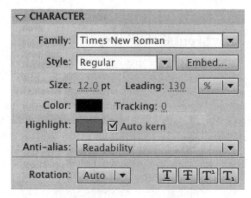 and do any of the following:

   ▸ To set text color, click the Color control and choose a new color from the swatch set.

   ▸ To create highlighted text, click the Highlight color control and choose a new color from the swatch set.

   ▸ To create underlined text, use the Underline button.

   ▸ To create strikethrough text, use the Strikethrough button.

   ▸ To create predefined superscripts or subscripts, use the Superscript or Subscript button.

   The underscore, strikethrough, superscript, and subscript effects are all toggles. To apply the effect to selected text, click the appropriate button. The button highlights, indicating that the effect is on. To remove the effect from selected text, just click the highlighted button.

TIP To remove highlighting from selected text, click the Highlight color control and choose No Color from the swatch set.

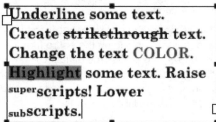

L Color controls in the Character section of the TLF Text (Tool) Property inspector let you change the color of the text itself or add a highlight color to call attention to selected text. Click a button to turn on (or off) underscore, strikethrough, superscript, or subscript.

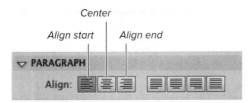

Center

Align start   Align end

A The first set of buttons in the Align area of the Paragraph section control alignment for paragraphs of ragged TLF text. You can have all lines align at the starting edge of the column (for English, the left edge), center each line within the column, or have all lines align at the ending edge of the column (for English, the right edge).

TIP Remember that the settings in the Paragraph section of the TLF Text Property inspector apply at the paragraph level. When you are working with threaded text, and you select a paragraph by clicking it once with the text tool, the settings you apply affect the entire paragraph, even the portions that flow to or from a linked field.

Setting Paragraph Attributes

Flash lets you work with paragraph formatting much as you would in a word processor. For TLF text, the Paragraph section of the Text (Tool) Property inspector contains settings for aligning text; justifying text; and creating margins, indents, and spacing between paragraphs.

You can set paragraph attributes in advance so that as you type, the text tool applies them automatically. And you can apply paragraph attributes to existing text. The text tool uses whatever settings currently appear in the Property inspector.

The following tasks show you how to modify existing text. Keep the Property inspector open (choose Window > Properties if it's not already open) and expand the Paragraph section (click the triangle to the left of the section name to toggle between the expanded and collapsed views).

To set paragraph alignment—ragged text:

1. Select the TLF paragraphs you want to modify, and access the Text Property inspector.

2. In the Align area of the Paragraph section, use one of the three alignment buttons **A**.

   ▸ To align text at the starting edge of the column, click the first (far left) alignment button.

   ▸ To center text within the column, click the second alignment button.

   ▸ To align text at the ending edge of the column, click the third alignment button.

To set last-line alignment— justified text:

1. Select the TLF paragraphs you want to modify, and access the TLF Text Property inspector.

2. In the Align area of the Paragraph section, click one of the four justification buttons **B**.

   ▸ To align the last line at the starting edge of the column, click the first (far left) justification button.

   ▸ To center the last line within the column, click the second justification button.

   ▸ To align the last line at the ending edge of the column, click the third justification button.

   ▸ To justify the last line (force it to fill the full column width), click the fourth justification button (the far-right button).

TIP Flash gives you two options for tweaking the spacing of text to make lines justify. In the Paragraph section of the Text (Tool) Property inspector, from the Text Justify Menu, choose Letter Justify to adjust space between characters; choose Word Justify to adjust space between words.

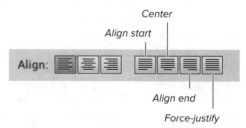

Center
Align start
Align end
Force-justify

B The second set of buttons in the Align area of the Paragraph section control alignment for the last line in a paragraph of justified TLF text. You can align the last line at the starting edge of the column, center the last line, align the last line at the ending edge of the column, or force the last line to justify (fill the column width).

Typography 101: Text-Alignment Methods

In *ragged text,* each line in a paragraph can be a different length; you can make all the lines align on one side of a text column or the other, or center each line independently in the middle of the column. In *justified text,* all lines except the last line of a paragraph fill the full width of the column. When you justify TLF text, Flash lets you decide how that last line lines up in the column (left, center, right, or spread to fill the column).

TLF Terminology: Start and End vs. Left and Right

When working with English text, we tend to describe various paragraph attributes in terms of left and right: there's a left margin and a right margin, we make text align flush-left or flush-right. That's because English text flows left to right. TLF text fields, however, can handle text that reads in various directions (see the sidebar "Multinational Multidirectional Text," earlier in this chapter). To account for this flexibility, Flash describes TLF paragraph attributes in relation to the edge of the column, where you start and end reading each line of text. That means text *aligns to start* or *aligns to end*; a block of text has a *start margin* and an *end margin.*

Start margin
(left margin)

End margin
(right margin)

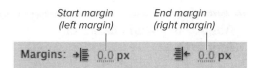

C The Margins hot text in the Paragraph section of the Text (Tool) Property inspector lets you enter values for left and right margins (in horizontal English text). Flash uses the values that you enter to create margins from the left and right sides of the text field's bounding box. (Your audience may not see the margins; the use of margins show up best when you add a visible border or background to the text field or when you apply different margin settings to different paragraphs in one text field.)

> "I really would advise something to go with the coffee my friend. I'm sure a nice poached egg—with maybe a fried tomato and a dash of Tabasco—would do wonders for a man in your, uh, condition, if you don't mind my saying . . ." Brett interrupted him. "And if I do mind you saying? You're not my nursemaid, or my valet, or even my friend—friend. So don't be so quick to 'advise' me. But come to think on it, an egg would do me fine."
>
> "Very good sir, right away." The waiter whisked up the menu that Brett had carelessly tossed onto the plate opposite him. "But make it fried, and over easy as pie, barely touch the second side to the frying pan," Brett tipped back in his chair to look up at the waiter. The waiter scowled at Brett in return, then moved past him and pushed through the swinging doors just beyond Brett's table. A smile played on

Indent: 17.0 px

> "I really would advise something to go with the coffee my friend. I'm sure a nice poached egg—with maybe a fried tomato and a dash of Tabasco—would do wonders for a man in your, uh, condition, if you don't mind my saying . . ." Brett interrupted him. "And if I do mind you saying? You're not my nursemaid, or my valet, or even my friend—friend. So don't be so quick to 'advise' me. But
>
> come to think on it, an egg would do me fine. "Very good sir, right away." The waiter whisked up the menu that Brett had carelessly tossed onto the plate opposite him. "But make it fried, and over easy as pie, barely touch the second side to the frying pan," Brett tipped back in his chair to look up at the waiter. The waiter scowled at Brett in return, then moved past him and pushed

D Use the Indent hot text to create an indent for the first line of a paragraph of TLF text.

Space before

Space after

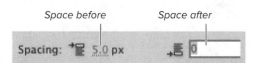

E Use the Space Before and/or Space After hot text to specify space between paragraphs.

To set paragraph-related spacing:

1. In the TLF Text (Tool) Property inspector, access the Paragraph section.

2. To create space on either side of a selected paragraph (set to horizontal text), in the Margins area, use the Start Margin and/or End Margin hot text to enter a value between 0 and 720 pixels **C**.

3. To create a first-line indent, use the Indent hot text to enter an amount between −999 and 999 pixels **D**.

   Flash calculates the indent from the start margin.

4. To create space between paragraphs, in the Spacing area, use the Space Before hot text (left) or Space After hot text (right) to enter an amount between 0 and 999 pixels **E**.

TIP The Space Before value never applies to a paragraph whose first line falls at the top of a column. To create space above a top-of-column paragraph, you must use the First Line Offset property.

TIP Although there are separate properties for the space before and after a paragraph, in fact, TLF text uses just one value—whichever is largest—for the space between paragraphs. If, for example, you set Space Before to 5 pixels and Space After to 10 pixels, the space between paragraphs will be 10 pixels, not 15.

TIP You can use Flash's Indent hot text to create paragraphs with hanging indents (ones where the first line starts farther out than the other lines), but there's a bit of a trick to it. You can't simply enter a negative Indent value; there has to be a big enough start margin, or enough padding (or a combination of the two) to hold that "negative" first-line text. To create a paragraph in English where the first line starts 5 pixels to the left of the other lines, for example, set Indent to −5 and set Start Margin to 5 or greater.

Setting Container Attributes

You can use TLF text fields to handle a number of text-layout tasks: transform a single text field into a frame holding up to ten columns of text; turn the field's bounding box into a border; fill the field with a background color. To accomplish these tasks, you set properties in the Container and Flow section of the TLF Text (Tool) Property inspector. Container and Flow properties apply to *all* of the text within the active text field, even if you selected just one word within that field.

To control text wrap:

1. Activate one or more TLF text fields.

   Fort this task, select a field that contains several paragraphs of text. Use the selection tool to select the entire field, or use the text tool to click anywhere within the text field.

2. Access the Container and Flow section of the Text (Tool) Property inspector **A**.

About Advanced Character Properties

Flash CS5's Text Layout Framework lets you take advantage of many advanced typographic capabilities built into True-Type and Type 2 (OpenType) fonts. For English text, TLF can work with ligatures, case (such as small caps), old-style numbers, lining numbers, proportional-width numbers, and tabular numbers. You access settings for these properties in the Advanced Character section of the Text (Tool) Property inspector.

Setting advanced-character properties is just like setting character properties: select some text, then choose specific settings from the Property inspector. Not every font has all the Advanced Character properties and unfortunately, the Property inspector won't tell you which properties are available. All the Advanced Character property menus appear no matter what the current font is. Generally, if the font of the selected text lacks the property you choose, the selected text remains unchanged. (A notable exception is the Lower-Case to Small-Caps option in the Case menu.)

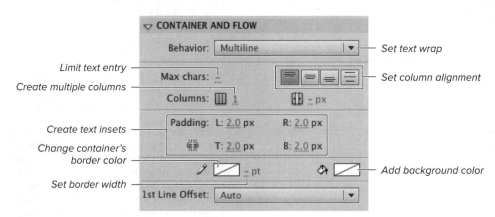

A The Container and Flow section of the TLF Text (Tool) Property inspector lets you set the attributes of the text field itself.

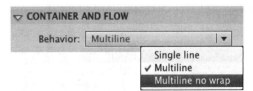

B The Behavior menu controls how text wraps within a TLF text field.

Typography 101: Baselines

The typographic term *baseline* can be a bit difficult to understand. In dealing with fonts for alphabets other than Latin (often called non-Roman fonts), *baseline* can have a variety of meanings. This *Visual QuickStart Guide* deals only with setting English text, where the term has one generally accepted meaning.

Think of typing a row of *x*'s; they all line up as though the bottoms of the letters sit on an imaginary line. Now look at the line of text you're reading. The main body of each character also seems to line up along a line, even though some of the characters have a *descender* (a tail that hangs down—the letter *y* is one example). *Baseline* is the name for that imaginary line on which the characters in a line of type sit.

3. From the Behavior menu **B**, choose one of the following:

   Single Line restricts the text field to displaying just one line of text. If the text is too long to fit into a single line at the text field's current width, Flash truncates the text. There is no option for working with the overflow text; the Out port of the TLF text field does not show a red plus sign.

   Multiline allows the text field to display multiple lines of text, wrapping the text to fit within the current column width. If there is overflow text, a red plus sign appears in the Out port.

   Multiline No Wrap allows for display of multiple "lines," but it's really displaying multiple paragraphs, each of which is set to single-line.

TIP Only unlinked TLF text fields can have the single-line behavior; if, for example, you link two fields that have Single Line as the Behavior setting, Flash changes the Behavior setting for both fields to Multiline No Wrap.

TIP Behavior settings apply to all the threaded text in a chain of linked TLF text fields; you can't, for example, set the first field to Multiline and the second field to Multiline No Wrap.

TIP When you create a point-text field (flexible size), Flash automatically sets the Behavior to Multiline No Wrap; when you create an area-text field (fixed size), Flash automatically sets the Behavior to Multiline.

TIP If you have a point-text field into which you've typed multiple lines by pressing Enter, and you then change the Behavior to Single Line, Flash deletes the paragraph returns and combines the text into one long line, resizing the field to display all the text. If you then choose Multiline, Flash cannot restore the paragraphs you had originally. You would need to insert new paragraph returns manually.

To create multicolumn text fields:

1. Activate an area-text field on the Stage.

   You can select an existing area-text field using the selection tool or text tool. You can also create a new field by dragging with the TLF text tool on the Stage.

2. In the Property inspector, access the Container and Flow section.

   If the section is collapsed, click the triangle to the left of the name to expand the section.

3. From the Behavior menu, choose Multiline 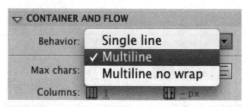.

4. Using the Columns hot text, enter a value between 1 and 10 **D**.

   Flash divides the text in the field into the specified number of columns.

C Multiline is the only Behavior that allows you to create multicolumn text. If you choose Single Line or Multiline No Wrap, Flash disables the Columns hot text.

Columns: 1

> Get a CCE calendar today. It's never too late to start saving your dates! There are still plenty of 2010 calendars available. These beautiful four-color calendars feature the work of CCE painters and descriptions of the studio and process painting. Great gifts for family and friends. Pick one up at the studio ($20 each) or request by mail ($20 plus $5 postage and handling). **Visit us at www.ccesf.org.**

Columns: 2

> Get a CCE calendar today. It's never too late to start saving your dates! There are still plenty of 2010 calendars available. These beautiful four-color calendars feature the work of CCE painters and descriptions of the studio and process painting. Great gifts for family and friends. Pick one up at the studio ($20 each) or request by mail ($20 plus $5 postage and handling). **Visit us at www.ccesf.org.**

D Use the Columns hot text to set the number of columns that the selected TLF text field will display. A single field can hold up to ten columns.

TLF Is Not a Word Processor

The Text Layout Framework makes some marvelous text-layout and typographic effects available directly in the Flash editor. But it's not a full-fledged word processor or text-layout application. TLF can't automatically enter curly quotes, or add hyphenation at line breaks, but it can preserve curly quotes in text copied from other applications. (TLF can even correctly implement *discretionary hyphens*—special text characters that allow a word to hyphenate at a specific place—contained in copied text.) TLF won't create inline graphics on its own, but you can import them from Adobe Illustrator.

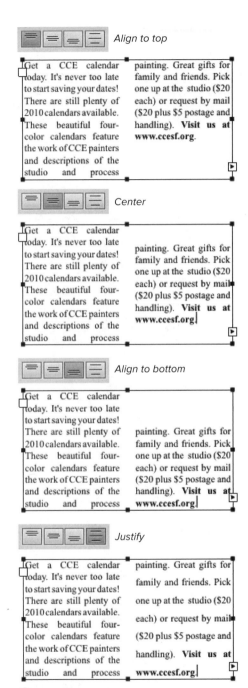

Align to top

Center

Align to bottom

Justify

E The Column Alignment buttons let you determine how a block of text (even one consisting of multiple columns) fits into the space of the text field.

To position columns within a text field:

1. Activate an area-text field on the Stage.

2. To control the position of the text columns relative to the edges of the text-field container, click one of the following Column Alignment buttons **E**:

    Align to Top (the first button, at far left) positions the text so that the first line in each column is as close as possible to top edge of the bounding box.

    Center (the second button) centers each column vertically in the bounding box (creating the same amount of blank space above the first line of text in the column as there is below the last line of text in the column).

    Align to Bottom (the third button) positions the text so that the last line in each column is as close as possible to bottom edge of the bounding box.

    Justify (the fourth button) adds space between the lines of text so that each column fills the available vertical space.

    The justify settings can have some unexpected results with multicolumn text. If the final column has fewer lines than the first two, the last column winds up with extra-large spaces between the lines to force the smaller amount of text to fill the height of the text field.

    Note also that when a TLF text field contains overset text, the column-alignment settings don't always appear as you might expect. If you have three columns set to align at the top, for example, the last column may run longer than the first two as it extends into the "hidden" portion of the TLF container.

continues on next page

3. To set the amount of space that appears between columns, using the Column Gutters hot text **F**, enter a value between 0 and 200 pixels.

4. To determine how close the text can come to the sides of the field's bounding box, use the hot text in the Padding area to specify any of the following text insets **G**:

   L creates space between the left edge of the bounding box and any text.
   R creates space at the right edge.
   T creates space at the top edge.
   B creates space at the bottom edge.

   You can create inset values from 0 to 200 pixels. To allow different padding values at each edge of a field, set the Constrain/Unconstrain modifier to the open-link icon.

TIP To limit the amount of text that end users can enter in a text field—say, when you want them to enter a password, use the Max Chars setting. This setting is available only for text fields set to the Editable style. Use the hot text to enter the number of characters you want the field to accept at runtime. (The character limit has no effect on the size of the field or the number of characters it displays initially.)

TIP When creating password fields, you might not want the field to display actual letters at runtime. To set a field to display asterisks instead of letters, select the field, and choose Password from the Behavior menu. This setting is available only for text fields set to Editable.

TIP When working with multicolumn TLF text, be careful in assigning paragraph alignment settings, especially for large blocks of text. Using the paragraph-alignment settings for center or justify can introduce column creep into the final column of a multicolumn text field: the baselines of the last column no longer line up horizontally with the baselines of the preceding columns. This makes the text difficult to read and it looks unprofessional.

Gutters that are too narrow hinder reading

Adequate gutters aid reading

F Use the Column Gutter hot text to create space between multiple columns in a single text field. You want to balance the amount of space: too little, and the columns are hard to read; too much, and the columns start to lose the look of multiple related text columns.

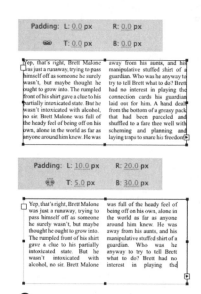

G Padding creates a text inset—a buffer of space between the bounding box of the text field and the text inside. Set the Padding area's Constrain/Unconstrain modifier to the closed-link icon to keep padding uniform for all four edges of the text field (top). Set the Constrain/Unconstrain modifier to the open-link icon to vary the padding values (bottom).

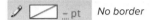
No border

into. The rumpled front of his shirt gave a clue to his partially intoxicated state. But he wasn't intoxicated with alcohol, no sir. Brett Malone was full of the heady feel of being off on his own, alone in the world as far as anyone around him knew. He was away from his aunts, and his manipulative stuffed shirt of a guardian. Who was he anyway to try to tell Brett what to do? Brett had no interest in playing the connection cards his guardian laid out for him. A hand dealt from the bottom of a greasy pack that had

Black border

into. The rumpled front of his shirt gave a clue to his partially intoxicated state. But he wasn't intoxicated with alcohol, no sir. Brett Malone was full of the heady feel of being off on his own, alone in the world as far as anyone around him knew. He was away from his aunts, and his manipulative stuffed shirt of a guardian. Who was he anyway to try to tell Brett what to do? Brett had no interest in playing the connection cards his guardian laid out for him. A hand dealt from the bottom of a greasy pack that had

H The Container Border Color control (identified by the pencil icon) lets you create a solid-color border around a block of TLF text.

into. The rumpled front of his shirt gave a clue to his partially intoxicated state. But he wasn't intoxicated with alcohol, no sir. Brett Malone was full of the heady feel of being off on his own, alone in the world as far as anyone around him knew. He was away from his aunts, and his manipulative stuffed shirt of a guardian. Who was he anyway to try to tell Brett what to do? Brett had no interest in playing the connection cards his guardian laid out for him. A hand dealt from the bottom of a greasy pack that had

I The Container Background Color control (identified by the paint-bucket icon) lets you put a solid-color background beneath the text in the field.

To create borders and backgrounds for text fields:

1. Activate an area-text field on the Stage.

2. To give the field a visible border, access theContainer and Flow section of the Property inspector and do the following:

   ▸ Click the Container Border Color control (identified by a pencil icon) and choose a color from the pop-up swatch set. The Border Width property activates.

   ▸ Use the Border Width hot text to enter a value between 1 and 100 points.

   Flash creates a border for the text field, using the current Container Border Color, the specified number of points wide **H**.

3. To create a background color within the field, click the Container Background Color control (identified by a paint-bucket icon) and choose a color from the pop-up swatch set **I**.

   The background color fills the text field.

TIP The field borders always grow outward from the field's bounding box; you don't have to worry about the border covering the text inside the field.

Practice Session

Design the front page of an imaginary newspaper.

- Create a point-text field to hold your paper's venerable name; choose a font appropriate to your paper's style of journalism. (See *Creating TLF Text Fields > To create non-wrapping point text.*)

- Using dummy text (or your own article if you have one), set up several linked, fixed-size, single-column TLF text fields to hold the main story: size the first field in the chain so it's just wide enough to hold the headline text (use large, bold-face type); make the second field half the width of the headline and tall enough to hold the lead paragraph (use midsize type); and create three more linked fields to hold the rest of the story (use smaller type). Position the last three fields side-by-side, like newspaper columns, below the lead paragraph. (See *Creating Linked Text Fields.*)

- Set up one fixed-size, three-column text field to hold one of the minor stories. (See *Setting Container Attributes > To create multicolumn text fields.*)

Extra Credit

- Create a pull quote to accompany the main story. Use a fixed-size, single-column TLF text field; make it the same width as the final three fields in the main story; give it a 2-point black border and a light-gray background. Resize the middle of the last three columns in the main story to create space at the top, and put the pull-quote text field in that hole. Now type your pull quote; assign the quote a fancy font; adjust the field's padding to give a pleasing amount of space around the quote.

Save your practice file for use in future Practice Sessions.

TLF Strokes and Fills: Not Like the Others

A TLF text field's border color is very like a stroke color, and the background color is like a fill that stacks behind the text characters (you'll learn more about stacking order in Chapter 5). But neither color acts quite like other strokes and fills.

The Color controls for borders and backgrounds in text fields are not connected to the Color controls in other Flash panels. The colors currently displayed in the controls apply only to text fields. To change the border or background color of a text field, you must use the Color controls in the Container and Flow section of the Text (Tool) Property inspector. Another difference: the swatch set available from these controls contain solid colors only—no bitmaps or gradients (though you can apply alpha settings to borders and backgrounds).

The text itself, however, is a fill whose properties work (for the most part) like regular fills. If you select a field with a brown border, green background, and black text, access the Colors panel and choose pink for strokes and purple for fills, the border and background color of the text field remain unchanged, but the text changes from black to purple.

Modifying Simple Graphics

One way to modify graphics in Adobe Flash Professional CS5 is to select one or more shapes and edit them by changing their attributes (such as color, size, and location) in the Property inspector or in other appropriate panels.

You can also modify the path that creates the shape of an element. Some operations—such as straightening lines, adjusting Bézier curves, and assigning new attributes—require that the element be selected. Others, such as reshaping a line segment or curve with the selection tool, require the element to be deselected. A few operations let you edit the element whether it's selected or not—using the paint-bucket tool to change a fill color, for example.

This chapter covers using the selection, lasso, and subselection tools to select and modify the elements you learned to make in Chapter 2. You also learn about using the Property inspector and other panels to modify elements' attributes.

In This Chapter

Setting Selection Preferences

There are two basic ways to make a selection in Flash: one is to click an element directly, and the other is to enclose all or part of an element with a selection outline. You can set preferences to gain more control over these two methods. For the click method, you choose whether you must Shift-click to select multiple items or whether you can merely click additional items to add to a selection. For the selection-outline method, you decide if the outline must fully enclose a graphic-object to select it or if enclosing any part of a graphic-object selects the whole thing.

To set selection methods for the selection tools:

1. From the Flash menu (Mac) or the Edit menu (Windows), choose Preferences.

   The Preferences dialog appears.

2. From the Category list, choose General 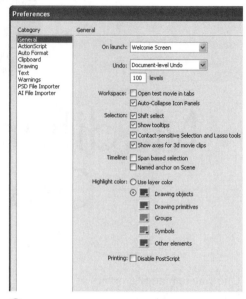.

3. In the Selection section, select either of the following checkboxes:

   Shift Select. In Shift Select mode (Flash's default setting), you must Shift-click to add items to the current selection. With Shift Select turned off, each new item you click with the selection tool is added to the current selection.

   Contact-Sensitive Selection and Lasso Tools. With Contact-Sensitive Selection on (the default), when a selection outline touches a graphic-object or text field, a grouped shape, or a symbol instance, Flash selects the whole thing. When Contact-Sensitive Selection is off, the selection outline must fully enclose the item to select it. This setting has no effect on merge-shapes.

4. Click OK.

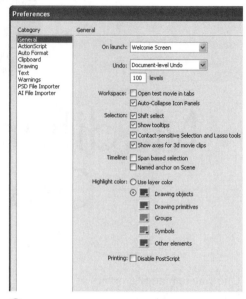

Ⓐ Choose General in the Category list of the Preferences dialog to choose a selection method.

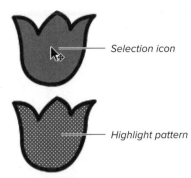

Selection icon

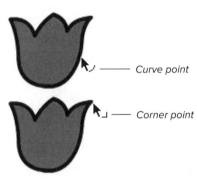

Highlight pattern

A When the pointer sits above a filled area, it changes into the selection arrow (a cross icon appears next to the pointer, indicating that the tool is ready to move or select an item). Click a fill to select it. A dot pattern in a contrasting color highlights the selected fill.

Curve point

Corner point

B As you prepare to select a line, additions to the pointer icon indicate what kind of point lies beneath the pointer.

Double-Click Tricks

Double-clicking any segment in a series of connected merge-shape strokes selects all the segments. Double-clicking the fill of a merge-shape that has a fill and a stroke selects the fill and the stroke together.

Making Selections

Merge-shapes, drawing-objects, and primitives all behave slightly differently when being selected. What you think of as a single shape may contain several segments. The rectangle tool creates a square whose stroke is actually four separate line segments. Clicking one side of a merge-shape square's stroke selects just that segment. To fully select the square's stroke, you must select each segment (you could use Shift-click to add the remaining sides to the initial selection). If you create the square as a drawing-object or a rectangle-primitive, Flash treats the four stroke segments as a unit. Clicking the stroke on any side of a drawing-object square or rectangle-primitive selects the entire stroke.

Flash highlights selected areas of merge-shapes with a pattern of tiny dots. Make sure all the parts of the merge-shape stroke or fill you intend to select display this pattern.

To make selections by clicking:

1. In the Tools panel, choose the selection tool, or press V on the keyboard.

2. To select elements created as merge-shapes, do one of the following:

   ▸ To select a merge-shape fill, position the pointer over the fill and click.

     The selection icon appears next to the selection pointer when it is over the fill. Flash highlights the selected fill with a dot pattern **A**.

   ▸ To select a merge-shape stroke, position the pointer over a line segment and click.

     Flash appends a little arc or a little right-angle icon to the selection tool **B**.

continues on next page

These modifier icons indicate that the tool is over a point in a line segment and show what type of point it is: a curve point or a corner point. (For more information about points, see the sidebar "About Curve and Corner Points," later in this chapter). Flash highlights just the segment you clicked, using a dot pattern **C**.

3. To select elements created as drawing-objects, position the pointer over any portion of the shape and click.

   The arc or angle modifier icon appears next to the selection pointer as described above for merge-shape fills and strokes. Flash selects the entire shape and highlights it by displaying the bounding box—a rectangle that encloses the shape **D**.

4. To select elements created as primitives, position the pointer over any portion of the shape and click.

   The selection icon appears next to the selection pointer whether it's over a fill or a stroke. Flash selects the entire shape and highlights its bounding box **E**.

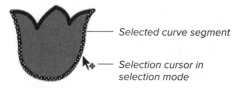

Selected curve segment

Selection cursor in selection mode

C When you click a merge-shape line, Flash selects and highlights just one segment.

D When you position the selection tool over an unselected drawing-object (left), the pointer displays the same modifier icons as for merge-shapes (move/select cross for fills, curve-point arc or corner-point angle for strokes). Click anywhere on the drawing-object, and Flash selects the entire drawing-object, highlighting its bounding box (right).

E Whether you position the selection pointer over the stroke (top) or fill (middle) of a primitive-shape, the selection icon appears by the pointer. Clicking anywhere on the shape selects the whole thing (bottom).

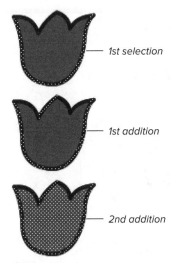

— 1st selection

— 1st addition

— 2nd addition

F With Flash's default Preferences setting for selections, Shift-click unhighlighted line segments or fill areas to add them to a selection.

5. To add elements to a selection, do one of the following:

▸ With Shift Select (Flash's default selection style) active, hold down the Shift key as you click each item you want to add **F**.

▸ If you turned off the Shift Select option in the General category of the Preferences dialog, click each item you want to include.

Flash highlights each new item and adds it to the selection.

TIP To switch to the selection tool temporarily while using another tool, press Command (Mac) or Ctrl (Windows). The selection tool remains in effect as long as you hold down the modifier key.

TIP To select everything that's currently on the Stage, choose Edit > Select All, or press Command-A (Mac) or Ctrl-A (Windows).

TIP The bounding box for a round or irregular drawing-object or primitive-shape is easy to see because the box sits outside the shape like a frame, and the bounding box for a rectangle-primitive has control points that make it more visible; but the bounding box for a drawing-object rectangle sits right on the edge of the rectangle. Therefore, depending on the color of your drawing-object rectangle, the highlighted bounding box can be difficult to see. If you have trouble seeing the highlight on selected drawing-object rectangles, choose a contrasting highlight color in the General category of the Preferences dialog.

To use a contact-sensitive selection rectangle:

1. Make sure the selection preferences are set for contact sensitivity (see "Setting Selection Preferences," earlier in this chapter).

2. In the Tools panel, select the selection tool.

3. Click and drag to pull out a selection rectangle 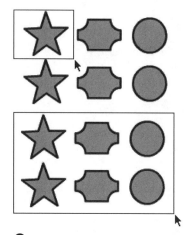.

   This rectangle isn't a graphic element; it just defines the boundaries of your selection.

4. Continue dragging until the rectangle encloses all the merge-shapes you want to select and at least some part of each drawing-object.

5. Release the mouse button.

   Merge-shapes. Flash highlights any portions of fill or stroke that fall inside the selection rectangle; portions of merge-shape fills or strokes that lie outside the rectangle remain unselected **H**.

   Drawing-objects and primitive-shapes. If the selection rectangle touches any part of a drawing-object or primitive, Flash selects the entire thing, highlighting its bounding box.

G Clicking and dragging with the selection tool creates a selection rectangle (top). Be sure to start from a point that allows you to enclose all the elements you want to select within the rectangle (bottom). Release the mouse button, and Flash selects those elements.

Drag selection rectangle

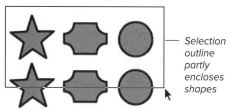

— Selection outline partly encloses shapes

Selected shapes

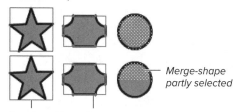

— Merge-shape partly selected

Drawing-object   Primitive-shape
fully selected   fully selected

H When Flash's default contact-sensitive selection mode is active, any drawing-objects or primitives that are touched or partially enclosed by the selection rectangle are fully selected. But when it comes to merge-shapes, only the parts that fall within the selection rectangle are selected. (Here the star shapes are drawing-objects, the indented rectangles are primitives, and the circles are merge-shapes.)

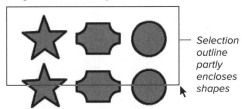

Drag selection rectangle

— Selection outline partly encloses shapes

Selected shapes

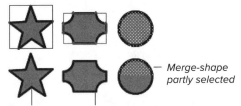

— Merge-shape partly selected

Drawing-object not selected   Primitive-shape not selected

I When contact-sensitivity is inactive, a selection includes just the parts of merge-shapes that fall within the selection rectangle. For drawing-objects or primitives to be selected, they must be fully enclosed by the selection rectangle. (Here the star shapes are drawing-objects, the indented rectangles are primitives, and the circles are merge-shapes.)

J The lasso tool lets you select elements that are oddly shaped or too near other elements to allow use of the selection rectangle. Any merge-shapes inside the selection outline become highlighted and selected when you release the mouse button. Whether or not you must fully enclose drawing-objects and primitives in a lasso selection outline to select them depends on the contact-sensitivity setting in the Preferences dialog.

To use a non–contact-sensitive selection rectangle:

1. Make sure contact sensitivity is turned off (see "Setting Selection Preferences," earlier in this chapter).

2. Follow Steps 2–5 in the preceding exercise, but this time, fully enclose the drawing-objects you want to select.

   Merge-shapes. Flash highlights any portions of fill or stroke that fall inside the selection rectangle; portions of merge-shape fills or strokes that lie outside the rectangle remain unselected **I**.

   Drawing-objects and primitive-shapes. Flash selects only those drawing-objects or primitives that are completely enclosed within the selection rectangle. If the selection rectangle touches or includes just a part of a drawing-object or primitive, Flash leaves the entire object deselected.

TIP If the lines or shapes you want to select are located close to other lines, you may have difficulty selecting just what you want with a rectangle. The lasso tool can create an irregular selection outline. In the Tools panel, select the lasso tool, or press L. Click and draw a free-form line around the elements you want to select **J**. Close the selection outline by bringing the lasso pointer back over the spot where you began the selection outline. Release the mouse button. Flash highlights whatever falls inside the shape you drew with the lasso.

TIP The lasso's Polygon mode lets you define a selection area with a series of connected straight-line segments. With the lasso tool selected, click the Polygon Mode button in the Tools panel. Now you can click your way around the elements you want to select **K**. Double-click to end the selection outline.

To deselect individual items:

1. In the Tools panel, select the selection tool.

2. Hold down the Shift key.

3. Click any highlighted drawing-objects, primitives, or merge-shape strokes or fills you want to remove from the current selection.

   Flash deselects the items you clicked **L**. No matter which method you used to select items, you must Shift-click with the selection tool to remove items from a selection.

TIP To deselect everything, choose Edit > Deselect All, or press Shift-Command-A (Mac) or Ctrl-Shift-A (Windows).

TIP To deselect all elements quickly, click the selection tool in an empty area of the Stage or Pasteboard.

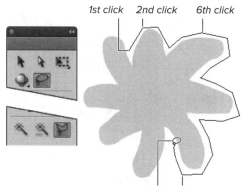

1st click   2nd click   6th click

*Positioning polygon   17th click
lasso for 18th click*

K In Polygon mode, the lasso tool creates a series of connected line segments to outline whatever element you want to select. Double-clicking finishes the shape by drawing a line from the point where you double-clicked to the starting point.

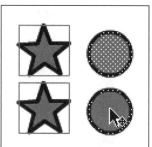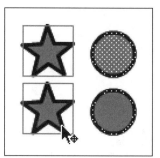

L With the selection tool selected, position the pointer over the element you want to remove from the selection (left). Shift-click the item to deselect it (middle). Repeat the process to deselect another item (right). (In this image, the stars are drawing-objects, and the circles are merge-shapes.)

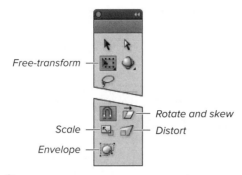

Free-transform

Rotate and skew

Scale

Distort

Envelope

A The free-transform tool lets you select and scale elements interactively.

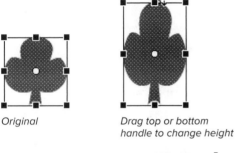

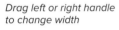

Original

Drag top or bottom handle to change height

Drag left or right handle to change width

Drag corner to scale proportionally

B Activating the free-transform tool's Scale modifier places a set of handles around a selected element. Click and drag the handles to change the size of the element.

Resizing Graphic Elements

Flash gives you several ways to resize, or *scale,* graphic elements. You can scale selected elements interactively on the Stage. You can also set specific scale percentages or dimensions for your element in the Transform panel, the Position and Size section of the Property inspector, and the Info panel.

To resize a graphic element interactively:

1. In the Tools panel, from the transform-tools submenu, select the free-transform tool or press Q **A**.

2. On the Stage, click the element you want to resize.

   Flash selects and highlights the element and places transformation handles on all four sides and at the corners of the element's bounding box.

3. In the Tools panel, select the Scale modifier.

4. Position the pointer over a handle.

   The pointer changes to a double-headed arrow, indicating the direction in which the element will grow or shrink as you drag the handles inward or outward.

5. To resize the graphic element, do one of the following:

   ▸ To change the graphic element's width, click and drag one of the side handles.

   ▸ To change the element's height, click and drag the top or bottom handle.

   ▸ To change the size of the element proportionally, click and drag one of the corner handles.

   Dragging toward the center of the element reduces it; dragging away enlarges it **B**.

TIP In the default scaling mode, the selection scales graphic elements from the control point opposite the one you're dragging. To scale relative to the center of a selection, hold down the Option key (Mac) or Alt key (Windows) as you drag. For symbols (see Chapter 7), it's the reverse: the default mode scales the symbol from its transformation point (which is the center by default), and pressing the Option key (Mac) or Alt key (Windows) lets you scale from the opposite control point.

To resize an element via the Transform panel:

1. With the Transform panel open, on the Stage select the element you want to resize.

   Percentages appear in the Scale Width and Scale Height hot text in the top section of the Transform panel. When you select an element that's never been resized, width and height are set to 100%.

2. To resize the element without changing its aspect ratio (the ratio of width to height), do the following:

   ▸ In the top section of the Transform panel, set the Constrain/Unconstrain modifier to Constrain mode (the closed-link icon). Clicking the icon toggles between Constrain and Unconstrain modes.

   ▸ Use the Scale Width (or Scale Height) hot text to enter a new percentage ◉.

   To use a precise value, click the hot text, enter a number in the field that activates, then press Enter. To choose a value interactively, position the pointer over the hot text; when the pointing finger with a double arrow appears, drag left (or down) to lower the value or drag right (or up) to increase the value. Flash previews the changes on the Stage as you drag the hot text's invisible slider.

Constrain mode (preserve aspect ratio)

Unconstrain mode

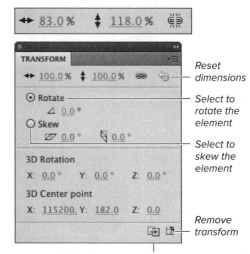

Reset dimensions

Select to rotate the element

Select to skew the element

Remove transform

Duplicate selection and transform

◉ To resize a selected element, use the Transform panel's Scale Width and Scale Height hot text to enter new percentages. In Constrain mode (the closed-link icon), as you change the percentage of one dimension, Flash automatically updates the other. The Transform panel also lets you enter values for rotating and skewing selected elements.

In Constrain mode, changing the Scale Width percentage also changes the Scale Height percentage (and vice versa).

or

To resize the element and allow the aspect ratio to change, do the following:

▸ Set the Constrain/Unconstrain modifier to Unconstrain mode (the broken-link icon).

▸ Use the Scale Width and Scale Height hot text to enter new percentages.

In Unconstrain mode, entering new values for Scale Width and Scale Height changes those dimensions of the selected element independently.

TIP To undo changes you made to an element's width and height (whether made using the free-transform tool or a panel setting), click the Reset button in the top section of the Transform panel or press Shift-Command-Z (Mac) or Ctrl-Shift-Z (Windows). For merge-shapes, you must not have deselected the transformed element; for drawing-objects, primitives, text fields (see Chapter 3), groups (see Chapter 5), and symbols (see Chapter 7), you can select the object and click the Reset button anytime to restore the item to its original 100% width and height.

TIP A Remove Transform button appears at the bottom-right corner of the Transform panel; that button undoes all the transformations you applied to the selected item, not just the width and height changes.

TIP To scale several elements at the same time, select all the elements and then use any of the scaling methods described earlier in this section. When you use the Transform panel, the bounding box that contains the elements scales relative to its center point, and the entire selection grows or shrinks to fit the new box. When you use the free-transform tool, the bounding box scales from the corner opposite to the one you're dragging.

TIP Once you've gotten pleasing proportions for an element by adjusting its width and height independently, choose the Constrain mode to lock in the aspect ratio. Using the Scale Width or Scale Height hot text now scales the element while preserving the new aspect ratio.

TIP Flash resizes merge-shapes on an absolute scale as long as the shape remains selected. Deselect the shape, and the current width and height become the shape's new 100%. To transform merge-shapes on a relative scale, select the shape and enter new values for Scale Width and/or Scale Height using the Transform panel, then deselect the shape. Select the shape again (Scale Width and Scale Height now show a value of 100%). Enter new percentages for the second transformation.

TIP Flash always resizes drawing-objects, primitives, text fields, groups, and symbols on an absolute scale (applying the percentage you enter into the panel to the element's original size).

To resize an element via the Property inspector:

1. With the Property inspector open, in the workspace, select the element you want to resize.

   The Position and Size section of the Property inspector contains Width and Height hot text displaying the dimensions of the selected shape's bounding box.

2. To resize the element, do either of the following:

   ▸ To preserve the aspect ratio, set the Constrain/Unconstrain modifier to Constrain mode (the closed-link icon). Use the Width or Height hot text to enter a new value **D**. Click the hot text to enter a precise value; drag the hot text's invisible slider to choose a value interactively. Changing the value for one dimension automatically changes the other.

   ▸ To allow the aspect ratio to change, set the Constrain/Unconstrain modifier to Unconstrain mode (the broken-link icon); use the Width and/or Height hot text to enter new values.

TIP The Info panel lets you resize a selected element relative to its *registration point* (the top-left corner of its bounding box) or *transformation point*. Click the Registration/ Transformation Point model to toggle between modes **E**. A crosshair in the upper-left corner of the model means the values are relative to the registration point; a circle in the model's lower-right corner means the values are relative to the transformation point. Values in the Property inspector are always relative to the registration point. (For more details, see the sidebar "How Flash Tracks Elements," later in this chapter.)

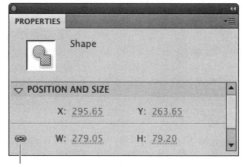

Constrain

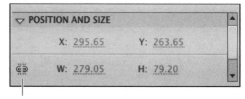

Unconstrain

D The Width and Height hot text in the Position and Size section of the Property inspector displays the dimensions of the bounding box of a selected element. Enter new values to resize the element. In Constrain mode (the closed-link icon), Flash preserves the ratio of width to height. In Unconstrain mode (the broken-link icon), you can enter independent width and height values.

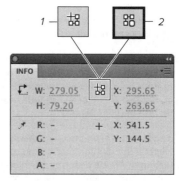

E You can enter precise dimensions for an element's width and height in the Info panel. The Registration/Transformation Point model shows whether changes will be relative to the registration point (1) or to the transformation point (2). To apply the values you entered in the panel to the selected graphic element, press Enter or click the Stage.

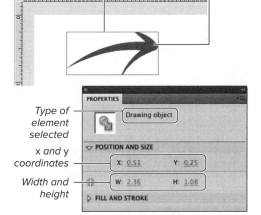

Bounding box of selected element (not visible for selected merge-shapes)

Selected element

Type of element selected

x and y coordinates

Width and height

A The Property inspector shows attributes of a selected element, including the x- and y-coordinates of the registration point. This drawing-object's registration point is ½ inch to the right along the horizontal axis and ¼ inch down the vertical axis.

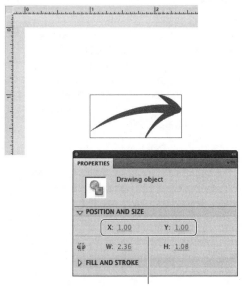

Enter values for x- and y-coordinates

B Changing the x- and y-coordinates in the Position and Size section of the Property inspector changes the location of a selected element. This arrow is now located 1 inch to the right along the horizontal axis and 1 inch down the vertical axis.

Positioning Graphic Elements

If you aren't happy with the position of an element, you can always move it. You can position elements visually by dragging them around on the Stage with the selection tool. You can also position a selection numerically by specifying a precise Stage location in x- and y-coordinates. You can enter the x- and y-coordinates in either the Property inspector or the Info panel.

To reposition an element via the Property inspector:

1. With the Property inspector open, select an element on the Stage.

   A label—for example, Drawing Object—appears at the top of the Property inspector, identifying the type of element selected. The Position and Size section of the Property inspector displays the x- and y-coordinates of the element's registration point **A**.

2. To move the element, do one or both of the following:

   ▸ To position the element along the horizontal axis, use the X hot text to enter a new x-coordinate.

   ▸ To position the element along the vertical axis, use the Y hot text to enter a new y-coordinate.

   Click the hot text to enter a precise value; drag the hot text's invisible slider to choose a value interactively. The element moves to its new position **B**.

TIP By default, the transformation point corresponds to a point at the center of a shape's bounding box. You can change that. With the free-transform tool, drag the hollow circle that represents the transformation point to a new location.

How Flash Tracks Elements

To keep track of an element's size and position on the Stage, Flash encloses each element in a *bounding box*—an invisible rectangle just big enough to hold the element. Flash then treats the Stage as a giant graph, with the top-left corner of the Stage as the center of the x- and y-axis **C**. The units of measure for the graph are those currently selected in the Document Settings dialog (to learn more about document properties, see Chapter 1). The Property inspector and the Info panel display information about the size of the element (the width and height of the bounding box) and the position of the element (the x- and y-coordinates for one important point in the element).

By entering new values for Height and Width in the Position and Size section of the Property inspector or in the Info panel, you can change an element's size. By entering new x- and y-coordinates in those panels, you can change an element's position on the Stage. (For more information about resizing elements, see "Resizing Graphic Elements," earlier in this chapter.)

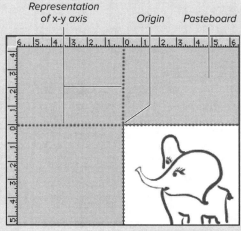

Representation of x-y axis Origin Pasteboard

C The dotted line here represents the x-y axis of the Stage. The origin—the 0 point both horizontally and vertically—is the top-left corner of the Stage.

Depending on which panel you use to enter values for an element, you can use either of two points to position an element: the *registration point* or the *transformation point*. For merge-shapes, drawing-objects, and primitives, the registration point is always located at the top-left corner of an element's bounding box. For symbols, you determine the location of registration point, which stays the same for all instances of the symbol. For all types of objects, Flash initially places the transformation point at the center of the bounding box; you can reposition it using the free-transform tool. You can position the transformation point differently for individual symbol instances (see Chapter 7).

The Property inspector always tracks elements by the registration point. The Info panel lets you track elements by either point. You choose the point by clicking the Registration/Transformation-Point model to toggle between the two tracking styles. When a crosshair appears in the top-left corner of the model, the Info panel settings position and size elements by the registration point. When a circle appears in the bottom-right corner of the model, the Info panel settings position and size elements by the transformation point.

When you use ActionScript to dynamically move symbol instances at runtime, Flash always uses the registration point to position them.

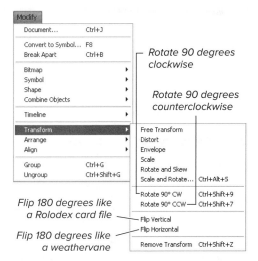

Rotate 90 degrees clockwise

Rotate 90 degrees counterclockwise

Flip 180 degrees like a Rolodex card file

Flip 180 degrees like a weathervane

A The Modify > Transform submenu offers commands for flipping graphic elements vertically and horizontally. It also provides commands for rotating an element in 90-degree increments, both clockwise and counterclockwise.

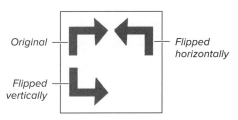

Original

Flipped horizontally

Flipped vertically

B Here are the results of flipping an element by using the Flip commands in the Modify > Transform submenu.

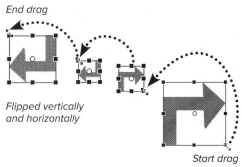

End drag

Flipped vertically and horizontally

Start drag

C The free-transform tool can flip and scale an element simultaneously. Here, the tool with its Scale modifier active is flipping the element both vertically and horizontally.

Flipping, Rotating, and Skewing

Flash lets you flip, rotate, and skew selected elements. You can either manipulate elements freely with the free-transform tool's Rotate and Skew modifier or use a variety of commands to do the job with more precision.

To flip a graphic element:

1. Select the element you want to flip.

2. Choose Modify > Transform.

3. From the submenu **A**, choose either of the following:

   ▸ To reorient the element so that it spins 180 degrees around its horizontal central axis like a Rolodex card file, choose Flip Vertical.

   ▸ To reorient the element so that it spins 180 degrees around its vertical central axis like a weathervane, choose Flip Horizontal.

   B shows the results of the two types of flipping.

TIP You can flip and scale selected elements simultaneously by using the free-transform tool in Scale mode. Drag one handle all the way across the transform box and past the handle on the other side. To flip a selected element vertically and horizontally, for example, drag the handle in the bottom-right corner diagonally upward, past the handle in the top-left corner **C**. The flipped element starts small and grows as you continue to drag away from the element's top-left corner. Flash previews the flipped element; release the mouse button when the element is the size you want.

To rotate an element in 90-degree increments:

1. Select the element you want to rotate.
2. Choose Modify > Transform .
3. From the submenu, choose either of the following:
   - To rotate the element clockwise 90 degrees, choose Rotate 90° CW.
   - To rotate the element counterclockwise 90 degrees, choose Rotate 90° CCW.

To rotate an element by a user-specified amount:

1. Select the element and access the Transform panel 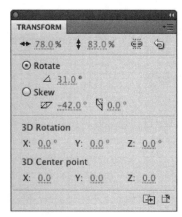.

   If the panel isn't open, choose Window > Transform.
2. Select the Rotate radio button.
3. To specify the direction and amount of rotation, do either of the following:
   - To rotate the element counterclockwise, use the Rotate hot text to enter a negative value (–0.1 to –360).
   - To rotate the element clockwise, use the Rotate hot text to enter a positive value (0.1 to 360).

   Click the hot text to enter a precise value; drag the hot text's invisible slider to choose a value interactively.

D To rotate a selected element in 90-degree increments, use the Modify > Transform menu. Repeat the command to rotate the element 180, 270, or 360 degrees.

E The Transform panel lets you rotate graphic elements in precise increments. Select the Rotate radio button and use the hot text to enter a value for the degrees of rotation. Positive values rotate the element clockwise; negative values rotate it counterclockwise.

F To undo all the changes you've made to a selected object, in the Transform panel, click the Remove Transform button (right). This technique works whether you made the changes via the Transform panel or interactively with the free-transform tool.

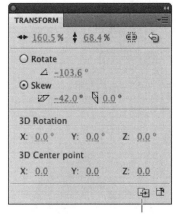

Duplicate Selection and Transform button

G Use the Transform panel to skew selected elements. You can set separate values for horizontal and vertical skewing.

TIP When you work with drawing-objects and primitive-shapes, you can undo changes in width, height, rotation, and skewing at any time, even after you've deselected the item and made changes to other items. To restore the original Width, Height, Rotate, and Skew settings, select the item and click the Transform panel's Remove Transform button **F**.

TIP For merge-shapes, the Reset and Remove Transform buttons work only as long as the shape remains selected.

To skew an element by a user-specified amount:

1. With the Transform panel open, select the element you want to skew.

2. In the Transform panel, select the Skew radio button.

3. Using the Skew Horizontal and Skew Vertical hot text, enter the desired skew values **G**.

   Click the hot text to enter a precise value; drag the hot text's invisible slider to choose a value interactively.

TIP You can quickly create step-and-repeat versions of a transformed object. Say you need three squares with the same dimensions, but with Horizontal Skew values of 10, 20, and 30 degrees. Create the original square, select it, and set the Horizontal Skew to 10 degrees in the Transform panel. With the square still selected, click the Duplicate Selection and Transform button. Flash duplicates the square with the 10-degree horizontal skew, then applies the current Horizontal Skew value to the already skewed square. The effect is to increase the Horizontal Skew value by 10 degrees with each duplication.

To rotate or skew an element interactively:

1. Select an element to rotate or skew.

2. In the Tools panel, select the free-transform tool; then click the Rotate and Skew modifier 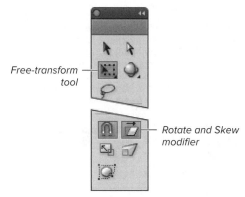.

   A transform box (similar to the element's bounding box, but with square handles at the corners and on all four sides) encloses the element.

3. To modify the selected element, do either of the following:

   ▸ To rotate the element, position the pointer over one of the corner handles.

      The pointer changes to a circular arrow. Click and drag to rotate the element. Flash spins the element around its transformation point **I**.

   ▸ To skew the element, position the pointer over one of the side handles of the transform box.

      The pointer changes to a two-way arrowhead. Click and drag the side handle to skew the element.

4. Release the mouse button.

   Flash redraws the modified element.

TIP To rotate an element around one of its corners instead of its transformation point, press Option (Mac) or Alt (Windows) while dragging.

TIP To constrain rotation by 45-degree increments, hold down the Shift key while rotating.

Free-transform tool

Rotate and Skew modifier

H Select the free-transform tool's Rotate and Skew modifier to access handles for rotating or skewing a selected element interactively.

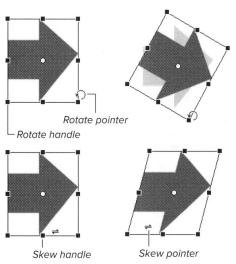

Rotate pointer

Rotate handle

Skew handle   *Skew pointer*

I With the free-transform tool's Rotate and Skew modifier selected, you can drag one of the corner handles of a selected element's transform box to rotate that element (top). Drag one of the side handles to skew the element (bottom).

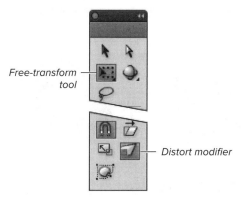

Free-transform tool

Distort modifier

A Choose the free-transform tool's Distort modifier to reposition the corner points of a selected item's transform box independently.

Drag a corner handle...   *...to distort a shape*

B Use the free-transform tool's Distort modifier to redefine the shape of an element's transform box. You can drag each corner handle separately.

Distorting Graphic Elements

The free-transform tool's Distort modifier lets you change the shape of the transform box. You can move a corner individually; move two corners simultaneously to turn the box into a trapezoid; and move the side handles to stretch, shrink, or skew the box. The selected element(s) redraw to fit the altered box. The Distort modifier works only on merge-shapes and single, selected drawing-objects; Distort doesn't work on primitive-shapes, text fields (see Chapter 3), groups (see Chapter 5), symbols (see Chapter 7), or selections with multiple drawing-objects.

To distort an element freely:

1. Using the free-transform tool, select the element you want to distort.

   A transform box with handles appears.

2. In the Tools panel, select the Distort modifier **A**.

   The center point of the selection disappears, indicating that you are in Distort mode.

3. Position the pointer over one of the transform handles.

   The pointer changes to a hollow arrowhead.

4. To change the shape of the transform box, do one of the following:

   ▸ To relocate one corner of the box, position the pointer over one of the corner handles; then click and drag the handle to the desired location. You can position each corner handle independently **B**.

   continues on next page

- To skew the element, position the pointer over one of the side handles; then drag the handle to the desired position. The element skews toward the direction you drag.

- To stretch the element as you skew it, move the selected side handle away from the element's center ⓒ.

- To shrink the element as you skew it, move the selected side handle toward the element's center.

5. Release the mouse button.

   Flash redraws the selection to fill the new transform-box shape.

TIP When you select multiple drawing-objects, the free-transform tool's Distort modifier is inactive. To distort multiple drawing-objects simultaneously, you must combine them into a single drawing-object (see "Converting Shape Types," later in this chapter).

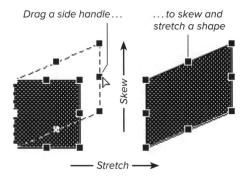

Drag a side handle... ...to skew and stretch a shape

Skew

← Stretch →

ⓒ When the Distort modifier is selected, dragging the side handles of a selected element's transform box skews the element. To enlarge (or shrink) the element at the same time, move the side handle away from (or in toward) the center of the original shape.

Adding Perspective

As beginning art students discover, it's not difficult to add depth to two-dimensional objects made up of rectangular shapes. You adjust the appropriate edges to align with imaginary parallel lines that converge at a distant point on the horizon—the *vanishing point*. Doing so creates the illusion that the objects recede into the distance. Adding perspective to nonrectangular shapes takes a bit more experience and the ability to imagine the way those shapes should look. The Distort modifier of Flash's free-transform tool helps you because it encloses your selected shape—circle, oval, or squiggle—within a rectangular transform box. All you need to do is adjust that box as you would a rectangular shape.

Flash CS5 also provides more-sophisticated tools for making two-dimensional objects appear to inhabit three-dimensional space. The 3D-rotation and 3D-translation tools work only on movie-clip symbols (you learn to create symbols in Chapter 7 and animated movie-clip symbols in Chapter 12). Flash's 3D tools let you rotate and position movie clips not only along the *x*- and *y*-axis (for horizontal and vertical positions) but also along the *z*-axis (for depth), redrawing the object to make it appear to recede into space. The use of the 3D tools to create artwork that simulates three-dimensional environments is complex and is beyond the scope of this *Visual Quickstart Guide.* After you learn to create symbols, however, try using the 3D tools on a movie-clip symbol containing a simple shape, such as a square. Experimenting on this basic level gives you a feel for how the tools distort the "plane" that the movie clip resides in and create the 3D illusion.

Shift-drag a corner handle...

...to taper a shape

D Using the Distort modifier of the free-transform tool, Shift-click and drag a corner handle to taper selected elements.

TIP The free-transform tool's **Distort Modifier** doesn't work on text fields, groups, and symbols. If your selection includes merge-shapes and one or more text fields, groups, or symbols, the free-transform tool's Distort modifier is available, but the distortion affects only the merge-shapes.

TIP You can use the free-transform tool to distort multiple merge-shapes simultaneously. Select the merge-shapes you want to modify. Then, using the Distort modifier of the free-transform tool, redefine the shape of the transform box that surrounds the shapes. The shapes change as a unit.

TIP When you select multiple merge-shapes, clicking one shape with the paint bucket changes all selected merge-shape fills. The ink-bottle tool works the same way on merge-shape strokes (see the task "To change stroke color with the ink-bottle tool," in the next section). When you select multiple drawing-objects or primitive-shapes, however, these tools can't modify all the fills or strokes in the selection; you must click each fill and stroke individually, or use a panel to make the changes (see the sidebar "Use Panels to Change Selected Fills and Strokes," later in this chapter.).

To distort a graphic element symmetrically:

1. Follow Steps 1 and 2 of the preceding task to prepare an element for distorting.

2. To taper the element, do either of the following:

    ▸ To make the top of the transform box narrower than the bottom, Shift-click and drag the top-right corner handle toward the top-left corner handle **D**, or vice versa.

    ▸ To make the top of the transform box wider than the bottom, Shift-click and drag the top-right corner handle away from the top-left corner handle, or vice versa.

    As you drag, the two corner handles move in tandem, coming together if you drag in or moving apart if you drag out.

3. Release the mouse button.

    Flash redraws the transform box and its contents. If you dragged in, the box appears to taper toward the top. If you dragged out, the box appears to taper toward the bottom. You can follow these procedures for the sides or bottom of the bounding box to taper the box in any direction.

TIP When you've already selected an element with the free-transform tool, you can access the hollow-arrow pointer temporarily without selecting the Distort modifier; press Command (Mac) or Ctrl (Windows). Then you can drag or Shift-drag to distort selected elements.

TIP If you make a mistake while distorting a graphic, and you choose Edit > Undo so you can fix it, your graphic will be selected with the free-transform tool but the Distort modifier won't be active. You must reselect the Distort modifier in the Tools panel to continue your distortion.

Modifying Fills and Strokes

Flash provides two methods for modifying existing fills and strokes: you can apply new attributes with a tool (the paint-bucket tool for fills, the ink-bottle tool for strokes), or you can select the fill or stroke on the Stage and choose new attributes in an appropriate panel. For fills or strokes that contain a gradient, you can also modify the way the gradient fits in the shape by using the gradient-transform tool.

To change fill color with the paint-bucket tool:

1. In the Tools panel, click the active edit-fill/stroke tool and select the paint-bucket tool from the submenu, or press K.

2. Select new fill attributes (see Chapter 2).

3. Click the paint bucket's hot spot (the tip of the drip of paint) somewhere inside the fill you want to change.

   The fill can be selected or deselected. The fill changes to the new color **A**.

TIP To pick up the color of a stroke or fill and use it for both strokes and fills, Shift-click with the eyedropper tool. Flash loads the selected color into the Fill Color and Stroke Color controls in the Tools panel, the Color panel, and the Property inspector.

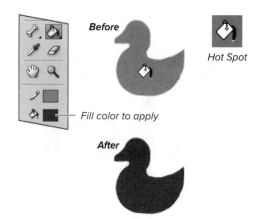

Before

Hot Spot

Fill color to apply

After

A Clicking a fill with the paint-bucket tool applies whatever color is selected in the Fill Color control. Use this technique to change existing fills.

Use Panels to Change Selected Fills and Strokes

You can modify the fill and stroke attributes of a selected graphic element by changing the settings in any appropriate panel. For example, draw an oval with a red fill and a solid, 1-point, blue stroke; then select the whole shape (note that if you create the oval as a drawing-object or primitive-shape, Flash automatically selects it). Now access the Fill and Stroke section of the Property inspector; it displays the attributes of the selected shape (or drawing-object or primitive). Select green from the Fill Color control; the oval fill changes to green. Increase the stroke height or choose a new stroke style; the oval stroke changes to match.

You can choose new colors for selected fills and strokes from any appropriate panel—Color, Swatches, or Tools—or the Property inspector. When you choose a new color from the Swatches panel, Flash uses the Color panel to determine whether that color is for fills or strokes. When the Fill Color control is selected in the Color panel, Flash applies the swatch color to selected fills; if the Stroke Color control is selected, Flash applies the color to strokes.

When a selected merge-shape has a stroke or fill set to No Color, however, the only way to change that setting is to add a fill or stroke by using the paint-bucket or ink-bottle tool (see Chapter 2).

When your selected shape is a drawing-object or primitive-shape, changing the fill or stroke attributes in the Color panel, Tools panel, or Property inspector adds the missing element **B**.

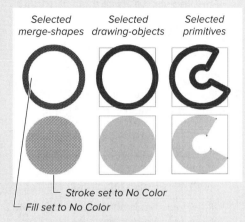

Selected merge-shapes   *Selected drawing-objects*   *Selected primitives*

Stroke set to No Color
Fill set to No Color

Select new attributes

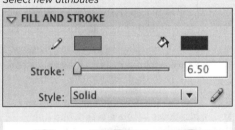

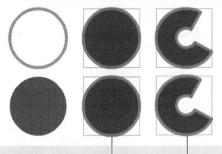

Drawing-objects and primitives add stroke and fill

B Using panel settings to change the attributes of a drawing-object or primitive-shape whose fill or stroke was originally set to No Color causes Flash to add the missing element, whereas doing the same thing for a selected merge-shape has no effect.

To change stroke color with the ink-bottle tool:

1. In the Tools panel, click the active edit-fill/stroke tool and select the ink-bottle tool, or press S.

2. Select new stroke attributes (see Chapter 2).

3. Click the ink bottle's hot spot (the tip of the drip of paint) in one of the following ways:

   ▶ Click directly on the stroke.

   ▶ If a shape has both stroke and fill, and both are deselected, click the fill.

   ▶ If a shape has both stroke and fill, and both are selected, click the fill.

   ▶ If a shape has both stroke and fill, and only the fill is selected, click the stroke.

   The stroke takes on its new attributes .

TIP To save time, you can copy the fill and stroke attributes of one element and apply them to another. In the Tools panel, select the eyedropper tool, or press I. The pointer changes to an eyedropper. To copy a fill color or gradient, position the eyedropper over a fill and click. To copy all of a stroke's attributes, position the eyedropper over the stroke and click. Flash switches tools; the paint bucket appears for fills, the ink bottle for strokes. The attributes of the clicked item appear in all related panels; when you click a fill, for example, the fill type and fill color appear in the Tools panel, the Color panel, and the Property inspector. You can then use the loaded paint-bucket or ink-bottle tool to apply the attributes to a different graphic element.

For merge-shapes, drawing-objects, primitives

With nothing selected, click stroke or fill

With fill and stroke selected, click stroke or fill

For merge-shapes only

With just fill selected, click stroke

With part of stroke selected, click selection

Warning: Clicking a selected fill with unselected stroke does nothing

 You don't have to select a stroke to change its attributes; just click the stroke or the unselected fill with the ink bottle. Warning: If the fill is selected, you must click the stroke itself; you can't click the selected fill to change an unselected stroke.

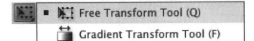

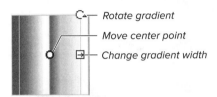

D Flash pairs the free-transform tool and gradient-transform tool in a submenu of the Tools panel; choose the gradient-transform tool to manipulate the way gradients appear within fills and strokes.

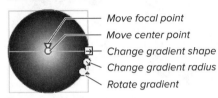

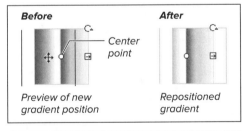

E Handles for transforming gradients appear when you click a gradient with the gradient-transform pointer.

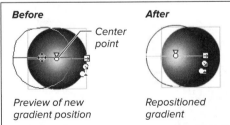

F Drag the center-point handle to reposition the center of the gradient within your shape.

To change a gradient fill's center point:

1. In the Tools panel, from the transform-tools submenu, select the gradient-transform tool, or press F **D**.

2. Position the pointer over the graphic element whose gradient you want to modify; the gradient can be located in a fill or in a stroke.

   The pointer changes to the gradient-transform pointer.

3. Click.

   Handles for manipulating the gradient appear **E**. You can rotate the gradient or change its size and/or center point.

4. Position the pointer over the gradient's center-point handle, the circle icon.

   The move pointer appears.

5. Drag the center-point handle to reposition the center point of the gradient **F**.

> **TIP** When you create a graphic element containing a locked gradient, by default Flash positions the gradient so that its center aligns with the left-hand side of the Stage. With the Stage set to larger viewing magnifications, when you select such an element with the gradient-transform tool, all of the gradient-transform handles may be outside the viewing area of your computer screen. It can seem as if the gradient-transform tool doesn't work. If you click a gradient with the gradient-transform tool and nothing seems to happen, try choosing a new magnification level. Depending on your workspace setup, you may need to view the Stage at 50%—or even 25%—to see all the gradient-transform handles for a selected gradient.

To change a radial gradient's focal point:

1. Follow Steps 1–3 in the preceding task.

2. Position the gradient-transform pointer over the focal-point handle, the triangle.

   The pointer changes to a triangle.

3. Click and drag the focal-point handle to a new location **G**.

   The focal point, where you have the most concentrated amount of the gradient's central color, shifts to the new location.

To resize a gradient in a fill or stroke:

1. With the gradient-transform tool selected in the Tools panel, click the graphic element that contains the gradient you want to modify.

2. To change the way the gradient fits inside the fill or stroke, do one of the following:

   ‣ To change the width of a linear gradient, drag the square handle **H**.

   The pointer changes to a double-headed arrow. Dragging toward the center of your shape squeezes the transition into a narrower space; dragging away from the center of your shape spreads the transition over a wider space.

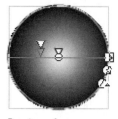 

Preview of new focal-point position

Repositioned focal point

G This gradient blends from white (in the leftmost gradient pointer) to black (in the rightmost). This arrangement puts white at the center of a radial gradient, giving the illusion of highlighting on a three-dimensional object. By moving the focal point, you can mimic changes in the way light hits the object.

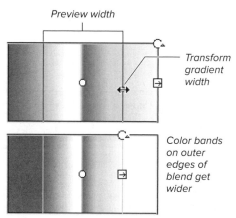

Preview width

Transform gradient width

Color bands on outer edges of blend get wider

H With a linear gradient selected, use the gradient-transform tool to drag the square handle inward and create a narrower rectangle for a gradient.

▸ To change the shape of a radial gradient, drag the square handle **I**.

The pointer changes to a double-headed arrow. Dragging toward the center of your shape creates a narrower oval space for the transition; dragging away from the center of your shape creates a wider oval space.

▸ To change the radius of a radial gradient, drag the circular handle next to the square handle **J**.

The pointer changes to an arrow within a circle. Dragging toward the center of your shape squeezes the transition into a smaller circular space; dragging away from the center of your shape spreads the transition over a larger circular space.

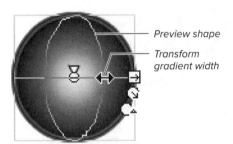

Preview shape

Transform gradient width

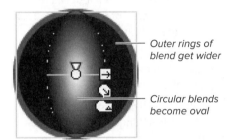

Outer rings of blend get wider

Circular blends become oval

I With a radial gradient selected, use the gradient-transform tool to drag the square handle inward to create a narrower oval for a gradient.

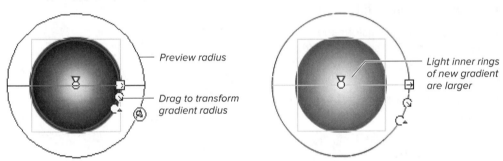

Preview radius

Drag to transform gradient radius

Light inner rings of new gradient are larger

J With a radial gradient selected, drag the first round handle outward to create a larger radius.

To control overflow:

1. Follow the steps in the preceding task to create a gradient that is narrower than the shape it sits in.

2. In the Color panel, in the Flow section 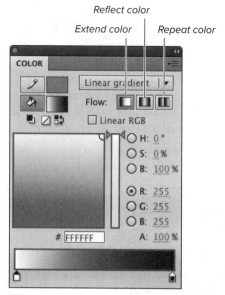, do one of the following:

   ▸ To extend the colors in the leftmost and rightmost gradient pointers, select Extend Color (the button on the left).

   ▸ To repeat the gradient, but with the colors in reverse order, select Reflect Color (the center button).

   ▸ To repeat the gradient with colors in the original order, select Repeat Color (the button on the right).

   Note that to activate the Flow buttons, your Publish Settings must be set to publish for Flash Player 8 or later (see Chapter 18).

To rotate a gradient fill:

1. With the gradient-transform tool selected in the Tools panel, click the fill or stroke containing the gradient you want to modify.

2. To rotate the gradient, do either of the following:

   ▸ To rotate a linear gradient, drag the round handle **L**.

   ▸ To rotate a radial gradient, drag the round handle farthest from the square handle.

   The pointer changes to a circular arrow. You can rotate the gradient clockwise or counterclockwise.

TIP Click and drag with the paint-bucket tool to rotate the gradient as you apply it. To constrain the gradient angle to vertical, horizontal, or 45-degree angles, hold down the Shift key as you drag.

Reflect color

Extend color   *Repeat color*

K When you're set to publish your movie to Flash Player 8 or later (see Chapter 18), the Color panel's Flow section is active. You can choose how Flash fills out a gradient that you have made narrower than the shape it sits in.

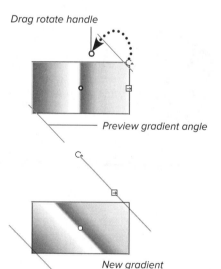

Drag rotate handle

Preview gradient angle

New gradient

L As you drag the gradient's rotate handle with the gradient-transform tool, you spin the gradient around its center point.

Modifying Shapes: Natural Drawing Tools

All the strokes and fills you create in Flash can be edited after you've drawn them. You can edit merge-shapes and drawing-objects in Flash's natural-drawing style, using the selection tool to change the path that defines the shape, or you can work directly with the path's anchor points and Bézier curves by using the subselection, pen, and anchor-point tools (see "Modifying Shapes: Bézier Tools," later in this chapter). You can modify primitive-shapes by manipulating their control points with the selection tool, or you can change their properties in the Property inspector.

When you use the selection tool, the merge-shape or drawing-object you want to modify must be deselected. If the element is selected, the selection tool moves the element as a unit. Always note what kind of modifier icon the selection pointer is displaying as it hovers over the path you want to modify.

For the following tasks, make sure the item you want to modify is deselected. These tasks all deal with modifying strokes, but the same techniques work for modifying fills by reshaping their paths (see the sidebar "The Mystery of Fill Paths," later in this chapter).

To activate the end of a segment with the selection tool:

1. Position the pointer over the end point of a deselected line segment.

   The corner-point modifier icon appears.

2. Click the end point.

   The end of the segment becomes active.

3. Reposition the end point in any of the following ways:

   ▸ Drag away from the existing line or curve to lengthen the segment.

   ▸ Drag toward the existing line or curve to shorten the segment.

   ▸ Drag at an angle to the original line to pivot a straight-line segment to a new position or reshape the end of a curve segment.

   As you drag, the end of the line changes to a small circle, showing that the line is active for modifications; Flash previews the modified segment as you drag **B**.

4. Release the mouse button.

   Flash redraws the line segment.

To reshape a curve with the selection tool:

1. Position the selection tool's pointer over the middle of an unselected curve segment.

   The curve-point modifier icon appears.

2. Click and drag the curve to reshape it **C**.

   Flash previews the curve you're drawing.

3. Release the mouse button.

   Flash redraws the curve.

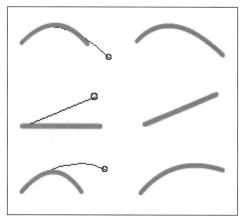

B Drag away from the existing curve or line segment to lengthen it (top). Reposition the end point to change the direction of the line or curve segment (middle, bottom).

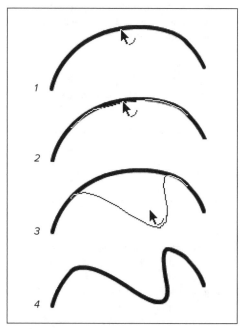

C Click the middle of a curve (1). Flash activates the curve segment (2). Drag the curve to a new position (3). When you release the mouse button, Flash redraws the curve (4).

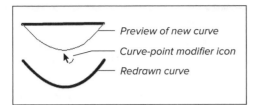

Preview of new curve

Curve-point modifier icon

Redrawn curve

D Although this line doesn't look curved (top), Flash considers all its middle points to be curve points. Drag one of those points to create a line that looks like a curve (bottom).

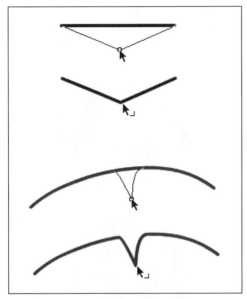

E Option-click (Mac) or Alt- or Ctrl-click (Windows) to create a new corner point for editing your line. Dragging a corner point from a straight-line segment creates a sharp V (top). Dragging a corner point from a curve creates a V with curving sides that comes to a sharp point (bottom).

To turn a straight-line segment into a curve segment with the selection tool:

1. Position the selection tool's pointer over the middle of an unselected line segment.

The curve-point modifier icon (an arc) appears.

2. Click and drag the line to reshape it **D**.

Flash previews the curve that you're drawing.

3. Release the mouse button.

Flash redraws the line, giving it the curve you defined.

To create a new corner point with the selection tool:

1. Position the selection tool's pointer over the middle of an unselected line or curve segment.

The curve-point modifier icon (an arc) appears.

2. Option-click (Mac) or Alt- or Ctrl-click (Windows).

After a brief pause, the arc changes to the corner-point modifier icon (a right angle), and a circle appears where the pointer intersects the line. You're now activating a corner point.

3. Drag to modify the line or curve segment and add a new corner point **E**.

Modifying Shapes: Bézier Tools

The subselection tool lets you see and manipulate the anchor points of a path. You can reposition anchor points to change the path, and you can manipulate a point's Bézier handles to modify the slope and depth of the curve. You can add and delete points and convert existing curve points to corner points, or vice versa, with the three anchor-point tools or the pen tool. Flash has two styles for displaying anchor points: hollow (the default) and solid. To pick a style, from the Flash menu (Mac) or the Edit menu (Windows), choose Preferences. In the dialog that appears, from the Category list, choose Drawing. In the Pen Tool section, select/deselect the Show Solid Points checkbox; click OK.

The tasks in this book assume that Show Solid Points is active.

To view a path and anchor points:

1. In the Tools panel, choose the subselection tool **Ⓐ**, or press A.

   The pointer changes to a hollow arrow.

2. On the Stage, click the line or curve you want to modify.

   Flash selects and highlights the path and anchor points. To manipulate a particular point, you must select it directly.

TIP When the subselection tool is selected in the Tools panel, the Select All command—Command-A (Mac) or Ctrl-A (Windows)—highlights the path and anchor points for all the graphic elements on the Stage and Pasteboard.

Ⓐ Use the subselection tool to modify the path of a line segment.

The Mystery of Fill Paths

Although a fill shape without a stroke has no outline, it does have a path that defines its shape. The selection, pen, and subselection tools all work to reshape fill paths just as they do to reshape strokes, as outlined in the tasks in this chapter **Ⓑ**.

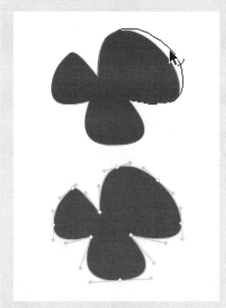

Ⓑ When you position the pointer over the edge of a fill shape, the selection tool displays either the curve-point or corner-point modifier icon. Clicking the edge of the fill activates a portion of the path outlining the shape (top). Selecting the edge of a fill shape with the subselection tool highlights the full path and its anchor points. You can reposition anchor points and Bézier handles to modify the fill shapes (bottom).

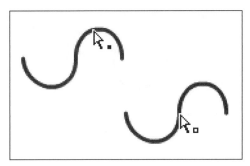

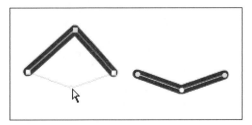

C A solid square appears next to the subselection tool when it's ready to select the entire path (top). When a hollow square appears (bottom), the tool is ready to select and manipulate a single anchor point.

D Using the subselection tool, drag a corner point to reposition it.

To select an anchor point:

1. In the Tools panel, select the subselection tool.

2. Move the subselection pointer over the path you want to modify.

   A small solid square appears next to the hollow arrow when the pointer is above a curve or line segment; a small hollow square appears next to the hollow arrow when the pointer is directly above an anchor point C.

3. Click an anchor point.

   Flash highlights the selected point and displays its Bézier handles.

TIP You can select multiple points on a merge-shape path directly with the subselection tool. Draw a selection rectangle that includes the points you want to select. Flash highlights the entire path and selects any points that fall within the rectangle. This technique won't work on paths created as drawing-objects.

To move a corner point:

1. Use the subselection tool to highlight the path and anchor points of the element you want to modify.

2. Position the pointer over a corner point.

3. Click and drag the desired corner point to a new location.

   Flash redraws the path D.

TIP Corner points are often easy to identify without highlighting the path. You can click and drag such points directly without first highlighting the path. If you don't click right on the point, however, you'll move the whole path, not just the intended point.

To move a curve point:

1. Use the subselection tool to highlight the path and anchor points of the element.

2. Position the pointer over a curve point.

   The anchor-point modifier icon appears.

3. Click and drag the point to a new location **E**.

   Flash previews the new curve as you drag.

   After you move a curve point, the path remains selected, and the Bézier control handles become active so that you can further manipulate the curve.

To reshape a curve with the Bézier handles:

1. With the subselection tool, click the curve you want to modify.

2. Click one of the anchor points that define the curve you want to modify.

   Bézier handles appear.

3. Click and drag one of the Bézier handles.

   The pointer changes to a solid arrowhead as you drag.

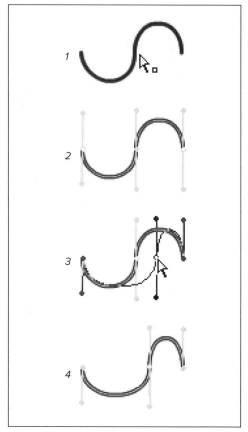

E When you select an anchor point (1), Flash highlights the entire path (2). You can drag the anchor point to modify the path (3). The path and anchor points remain highlighted when you're done (4).

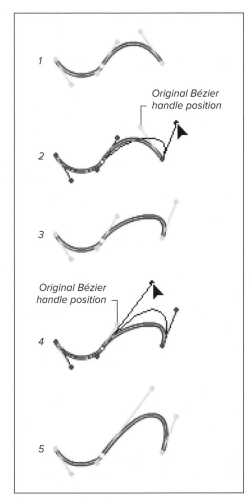

1

Original Bézier
handle position

2

3

Original Bézier
handle position

4

5

F When you select anchor points, their Bézier handles appear (1). Leaning a Bézier handle away from a curve (2) makes that curve segment more pronounced (3). Leaning the handle toward the curve flattens that part of the curve. Dragging the Bézier handle away from its anchor point (4) makes the curve deeper (5); dragging the handle toward the anchor point makes the curve shallower.

4. To modify the curve, do one or more of the following:

▶ To make the curve bulge in the opposite direction, move the Bézier handle past the existing curve, in the opposite direction from the current bulge.

▶ To make the curve deeper, position the Bézier handle farther from the anchor point.

▶ To make the curve shallower, position the Bézier handle closer to the anchor point.

Flash previews the new curve as you manipulate the Bézier handle **F**.

TIP A curve point that connects two curve segments has two Bézier handles. By default, the handles act in concert as you move them, modifying the curves on either side of the anchor point. You can adjust just one handle (one curve) at a time. Using the subselection tool, press Option (Mac) or Alt (Windows) while dragging the handle. Or, with the anchor point selected and the Bézier handles active, in the Tools panel select the convert–anchor-point tool. Use the caret pointer to drag a handle independently.

TIP For paths created in Merge Drawing mode, you can select an anchor point and activate its Bézier handles quickly. Use the subselection tool to draw a selection rectangle around the curve you want to modify. Flash highlights the path, selects the curves and the anchor points that fall within the selection, and activates their handles.

TIP You can move selected anchor points with the arrow keys. To move in larger increments, press the Shift-arrow key.

The Mysterious Modes of the Pen Tool

Flash CS5 has three Bézier tools: add anchor point, delete anchor point, and convert anchor point. The pen tool can perform many of those functions. As you position the pen pointer over the Stage and existing paths, various modifier icons appear next to the pen icon, indicating the tool's current function **G**.

Create initial anchor point A small *x* indicates the pen is ready to place the first point in a path. Click any empty spot on the Stage to start your path.

Create sequential points The pen tool has no modifier icon when you are in the middle of placing a series of anchor points. Clicking the Stage adds points and segments to the path you are creating.

Add anchor point A plus sign appears when you position the pointer over a selected path, between anchor points. In this mode, double-clicking the path between two corner points adds a new corner point; double-clicking between two curve points (or between a curve and a corner point) adds a curve point. Single-clicking the path starts a new branching path; click away from the existing path to complete the first segment of the branch.

Convert curve point to corner point A caret appears when you position the pen pointer over a curve point in a selected path. Click the curve point and it changes to a corner point.

Delete corner point A minus sign appears when you position the pen pointer over a corner point in a selected path. Click the corner point and Flash removes it.

Extend path A slash appears when you position the pen pointer over a terminal anchor point (the first or last point in an open path). Clicking the point links the pen tool to that path; now clicking on the Stage creates a new point that extends the existing path.

Close path A circle modifier icon appears when you position the pen pointer over the initial anchor point of the path you are currently creating. (The circle also appears if you are using the pen tool to create a merge-shape path and you position the pointer over a terminal anchor point in a different merge-shape path.)

Join drawing-object path A chain-link modifier icon appears when you are creating a new path, and you position the pen pointer over one of the terminal anchor points in an existing drawing-object path.

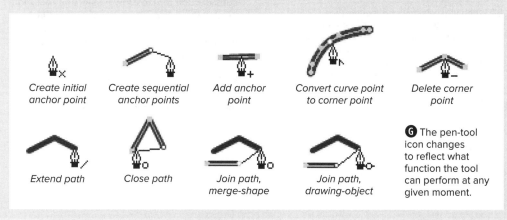

Create initial anchor point

Create sequential anchor points

Add anchor point

Convert curve point to corner point

Delete corner point

Extend path

Close path

Join path, merge-shape

Join path, drawing-object

G The pen-tool icon changes to reflect what function the tool can perform at any given moment.

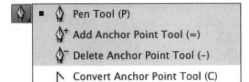

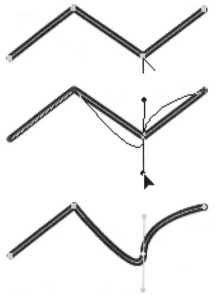

H Flash has three tools for modifying the anchor points and Bézier curves of a path. Click the current Bézier tool in the Tools panel to access a submenu showing all four.

I To change a corner point into a curve point (one with Bézier handles) using the convert–anchor-point tool, click (top) and drag a corner point. You pull Bézier handles out of the point instead of relocating the point (middle). When you release the mouse button, Flash redraws the curve (bottom).

To convert a corner point to a curve point:

1. Use the subselection tool to highlight the path and anchor points of the path you want to modify.

2. In the Tools panel, click the current Bézier tool and from the submenu that opens, choose Convert Anchor Point Tool **H**.

    The pointer changes to an upward-pointing caret.

3. Position the caret pointer over a corner point.

4. To activate Bézier handles, click the point, then drag away.

    Flash converts the corner point to a curve point that has Bézier handles **I**. As you drag, the handles extend and move, modifying the curve.

TIP You can also use the subselection tool directly to convert a corner point to a curve point. Position the hollow-arrow pointer over a selected corner point, then Option-drag (Mac) or Alt-drag (Windows) away from the point to pull out the Bézier handles.

TIP To switch between the Bézier and subselection tools quickly, use the keyboard shortcuts: press A for the subselection tool, P for the pen tool, = (equals sign) for the add–anchor-point tool, – (minus sign) for the delete–anchor-point tool, and C for the convert–anchor-point tool.

To convert a curve point to a corner point:

1. Using the subselection tool, select the path you want to modify.

2. In the Tools panel, from the Bézier-tools submenu, select the convert–anchor-point tool.

3. Position the caret pointer over a curve point.

4. Click the curve point.

   Flash converts the curve point to a corner point, removing the Bézier handles and flattening the curved path .

TIP When using the pen tool, you can access the convert–anchor-point tool temporarily by holding down the Option (Mac) or Alt (Windows) key.

J Clicking a curve point with the convert–anchor-point tool (left) reduces the point to a corner point (right). Flash redraws the path accordingly.

K Click an anchor point with the delete–anchor-point tool to remove the point. Flash redraws the path accordingly.

To delete an anchor point:

1. Using the subselection tool, select the path you want to modify.

2. In the Tools panel, click the current Bézier tool, and from the submenu that opens, choose the delete–anchor-point tool.

   The pointer changes to a pen icon with a remove-point modifier icon (a minus sign).

3. Position the pointer over an anchor point and click.

   Flash removes the anchor point and reshapes the path to connect the remaining points **K**.

TIP To access the delete–anchor-point tool temporarily while using the add–anchor-point tool, hold down the Option key (Mac) or Alt key (Windows).

TIP While you can also delete anchor points by selecting them with the subselection tool and pressing Backspace or Delete, the results may surprise you. If the selected anchor point connects two segments, pressing Delete removes the anchor point and reshapes the path. If the anchor point lies at the intersection of three or more segments, however, Flash removes not only the anchor point, but also all the line and curve segments that directly attach to the point. You may wind up removing more than you bargained for.

When you position the pen tool between existing anchor points, a small plus sign appears next to the pointer (left). With the plus-sign modifier icon active, click the path to add a new point (right).

TIP To access the add–anchor-point tool temporarily while using the delete–anchor-point tool, hold down the Option key (Mac) or Alt key (Windows).

TIP When the path and the pen tool are in the same drawing mode, you can link the path you are creating to an existing path. Use the pen tool to place the anchor points of your path. When you're ready to link, position the pointer over a terminal anchor point in the path you want to join. One of two modifier icons appears next to the pen icon: when the pen is in Merge Drawing mode and you link to a merge-shape path, the close-path modifier icon (a hollow circle) appears; when the pen is in Object Drawing mode and you link to a drawing-object path, the join-paths modifier icon (a chain-link) appears. Click the existing terminal anchor point, and Flash joins the two merge-shape, or drawing-object, paths.

To add a point within a path:

1. Use the subselection tool to select the path you want to modify.

2. In the Tools panel, from the Bézier-tool menu, select the add–anchor-point tool.

   The pointer changes to a pen with a plus-sign modifier icon.

3. Position the pointer over the path and do any of the following:

   ▸ Click between two corner points to create a new corner point.

   ▸ Click between two curve points to create a new curve point.

   ▸ Click between a corner point and a curve point to create a new curve point.

   Flash adds a new point .

To extend an existing path:

1. In the Tools panel, from the Bézier-tool submenu, select the pen tool.

2. Position the pointer over the anchor point at either end of the path (a terminal anchor point).

   The continue-path modifier icon— a small slash—appears next to the pen icon.

3. Click the terminal anchor point.

   The pen links to that point as if you'd just placed it.

4. Click to add points as you learned to do in Chapter 2.

   Note that to create a single unified path, the pen tool and the existing path must be in the same drawing mode. If the existing path is a drawing-object and the pen is set to Merge Drawing mode (or vice versa), Flash places the points, but the segments remain separate.

Modifying Primitive-Shape Paths

Flash's rectangle- and oval-primitive tools create shapes whose paths are defined by a set of properties specific to that shape. You can't change the outline of a primitive-shape freely the way you can reshape the outline of a merge-shape or drawing-object. You can change the primitive's defining properties by dragging control points in the shape or by setting new values for those properties in the Property inspector.

To change a rectangle-primitive's properties interactively:

1. Using the selection tool, on the Stage select the rectangle-primitive you want to modify.

    The shape's bounding box highlights, and control points appear ⓐ. Each corner has two control points. For sharp corners with a corner-radius setting of 0, the points sit directly on top of one another; for rounded corners, a control point appears at either end of the arc that defines the corner. The two points work in concert; dragging one moves the other.

2. Position the pointer over one of the control points.

    The pointer changes to a solid arrowhead.

3. To modify the shape, do one of the following:

    ▸ To increase the radius (make the corner more rounded), drag the point inward.

    ▸ To decrease the radius (make the corner less rounded), drag the point outward.

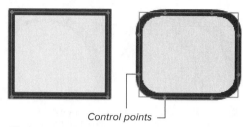

Control points

ⓐ The rectangle-primitive has two control points for the corner radius of each corner. When the corner radius is set to 0, the corner is a sharp 90-degree angle, and the control points sit directly on top of one another.

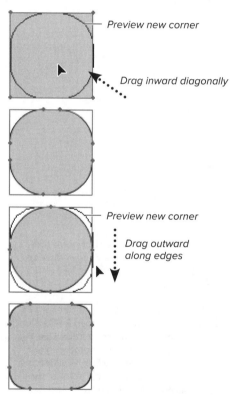

Preview new corner

Drag inward diagonally

Preview new corner

Drag outward along edges

ⓑ As the corner radius increases, two control points appear at the end of the arc defining the corner. Drag inward to round the corner more, outward to round it less.

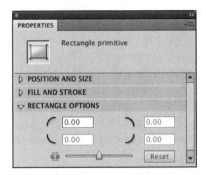

C With the Constrain Corner Radius modifier set to the unlinked state (open-link icon), you can enter values for each corner separately to create a variety of shapes.

D Dragging the control points of an indented corner (one with a corner radius value less than 0) changes the size of the indent. If you drag all the way back to a sharp corner, however, the control points revert to creating rounded corners as you drag. To get another indented corner, you must enter a negative value in the Property inspector.

You can drag diagonally toward (or away from) the center of a shape, or you can drag vertically or horizontally toward (or away from) the center of the edge containing the control point **B**.

TIP By default, Flash constrains the corner-radius settings so that all four corners of a rectangle-primitive have the same degree of roundness. To create corners with various degrees of roundness, select the rectangle-primitive, access the Rectangle Options section of the Rectangle Primitive Property inspector, and click the Constrain Corner Radius modifier to change to the unlinked state (the open-link icon). You can then drag the control points for each corner independently, creating a variety of shapes **C**.

To change a rectangle-primitive's properties precisely:

1. With the rectangle-primitive selected on the Stage, access the Rectangle Options section of the Rectangle Primitive Property inspector.

2. To modify the shape, in the Rectangle Corner Radius fields, do one of the following:

   ▸ To create rounded corners, enter positive values.

   ▸ To create indented corners, enter negative values.

   For more details about setting the values of the various properties for rectangle-primitives, see Chapter 2.

TIP You can't change a square or rounded corner to an indented corner by dragging the control points; you must set a negative value in the Property inspector. Once the rectangle-primitive has an indented corner, however, you can drag its control points to adjust the size of the indent **D**.

To change an oval-primitive's properties interactively:

1. Using the selection tool, on the Stage select the oval-primitive you want to modify.

   The shape's bounding box highlights, and control points appear. Oval-primitives have four control points: one pair for the start and end angle of the outer oval and another pair for the start and end angle of the inner oval **E**. When the start angle and end angle of an oval have the same value, the control points lie directly on top of one another.

2. Position the pointer over a control point.

   The pointer changes to a solid arrowhead.

3. To modify the shape, do any of the following:

   ▸ To change the start angle, drag the control point clockwise or counter-clockwise around the perimeter of the oval **F**.

   ▸ To change the end angle, drag the control point clockwise or counter-clockwise around the perimeter of the oval.

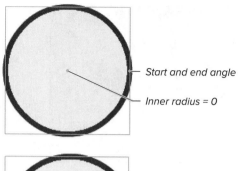

Start and end angle

Inner radius = 0

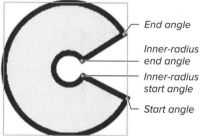

End angle

Inner-radius end angle

Inner-radius start angle

Start angle

E An oval-primitive has control points that control the start angle and end angle for the outer and inner oval shapes.

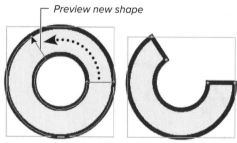

Preview new shape

F Drag the control points on the outer edge of an oval-primitive clockwise or counterclockwise to change the start and end angle of the shape.

Preview larger inner radius

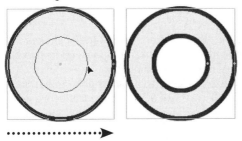

Preview smaller inner radius

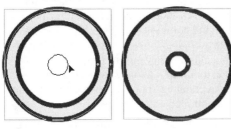

G Drag the control points on the inner edge of an oval-primitive to resize the radius of the inner oval: Drag toward the center of the shape to close down the opening in the middle of the shape; drag away from the center to open up a bigger space.

▸ To increase the inner radius (to create a larger space inside the oval), drag outward **G**.

▸ To decrease the inner radius (to create a smaller space inside the oval), drag inward.

TIP Although you can use the subselection tool to select a primitive, doing so is a bit confusing and not recommended. When you click the shape, you won't see a selection highlight or control points for the object, but the item *is* selected. Any changes you make to settings in the Property inspector after clicking on a primitive shape do modify that primitive.

To change an oval-primitive's properties precisely:

1. With the oval-primitive selected on the Stage, access the Oval Options section of the Oval Primitive Property inspector.

2. In the Start Angle, End Angle, or Inner Radius fields, enter new values.

   For more details about setting the values of the various properties for oval-primitives, see Chapter 2.

TIP Although you can't alter the paths of primitives to create fanciful free-form shapes, you can use a primitive as the starting point from which to create a shape whose paths can be modified freely. After you set the primitive's properties, convert the shape to a merge-shape or drawing-object (see "Converting Shape Types," later in this chapter). Then modify the merge-shape or drawing-object using any of the techniques discussed earlier in this chapter.

Using the Eraser Tool

Flash's eraser tool imitates a real-world eraser—click and "scrub" to remove fills and/or strokes from merge-shapes and drawing-objects. The Eraser Mode menu in the Tools panel offers five modes for controlling what gets erased. In Erase Normal the eraser removes any line or fill you scrub over. In Erase Fills, the tool affects only fills. In Erase Lines, the tool affects only strokes. In Erase Selected Fills, the tool erases only from selected fills. In Erase Inside, the tool affects only the fill in which you begin erasing. These modes become important for working with graphics that have multiple elements (see Chapter 5).

Another eraser option is Faucet mode (click the Faucet modifier in the Tools panel, the faucet pointer appears). Clicking a deselected merge-shape or drawing-object stroke with the eraser in Faucet mode deletes all the segments that make up that stroke. In a selection containing multiple merge-shape strokes and/or fills, clicking any of the selected items with the faucet deletes the entire selection. In a selection containing multiple drawing-objects, however, the faucet deletes the individual fills or strokes you click, one at a time. Faucet is the only mode in which the eraser affects primitive-shapes, but it is a bit unreliable. Clicking the fill of a primitive shape with the faucet tool removes that fill; clicking the outside edge of a primitive-shape's stroke usually has no effect; clicking the inside edge can result in deleting the entire object.

The eraser tool's quickest trick is to clear the decks completely. Double-click the eraser tool in the Tools panel to delete the entire contents of the Stage.

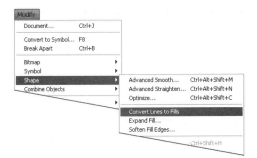

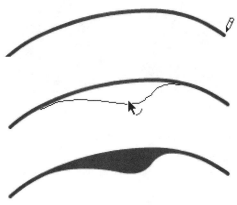

(A) To transform strokes into fills, choose Modify > Shape > Convert Lines to Fills.

(B) You can convert a stroke, such as this line drawn with the pencil tool (top), to a fill. The fill's outline then has its own editable path (middle and bottom).

Converting Shape Types

Flash offers a variety of shape types: fills, strokes, merge-shapes, drawing-objects, primitives, and text. It's possible to convert some types of shapes into others. For example, you can convert strokes to fills; you can convert merge-shapes to drawing-objects and vice versa; you can convert primitive-shapes to merge-shapes and drawing-objects; and you can convert text, a special type of fill, to a regular drawing-object fill (for TLF text) or merge-shape fill (for Classic text). You cannot, however, convert merge-shapes or drawing-objects to primitive-shapes.

To convert a stroke to a fill:

1. Select a stroke on the Stage.

2. Choose Modify > Shape > Convert Lines to Fills **(A)**.

   Flash converts the stroke to a fill shape that looks exactly like the stroke. You can now edit the path of the "stroke's" outline as though you were working with a fill created with the brush tool **(B)**.

To convert a merge-shape or a primitive to a drawing-object:

1. Select a single merge-shape or primitive-shape on the Stage.

2. Choose Modify > Combine Objects > Union.

   Flash converts the selected shape to a drawing-object; it remains selected **C**.

TIP The Modify > **Combine Shapes** commands (Union, Intersect, Punch, and Crop) work on multiple, selected drawing-objects and primitives; the last three commands work on overlapping drawing-objects or primitives. In effect, these commands convert the drawing-objects or primitives to merge-shapes (so that they interact) and then convert the resulting shape(s) back into a drawing-object. Note that primitives lose their status as primitives once you combine them. You'll learn more about combining shapes in Chapter 5.

To convert a drawing-object or a primitive to a merge-shape:

1. Select a drawing-object or primitive-shape on the Stage.

2. Choose Modify > Break Apart, or press Command-B (Mac) or Ctrl-B (Windows) **D**.

   Flash converts the selected drawing-object or primitive-shape to a merge-shape; it remains selected.

To convert a block of TLF text into individual drawing-objects:

1. Select a TLF text field on the Stage.

   If the selected field links to other TLF text fields with threaded text, Flash selects all of the linked fields.

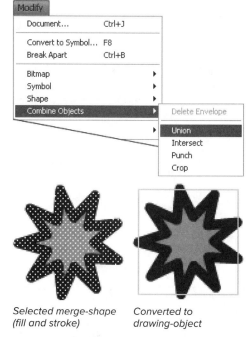

Selected merge-shape (fill and stroke)   *Converted to drawing-object*

C Choose Modify > Combine Objects > Union to convert the shape selected on the Stage into a drawing-object.

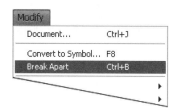

D Choose Modify > Break Apart to convert a drawing-object or primitive-shape to a merge-shape.

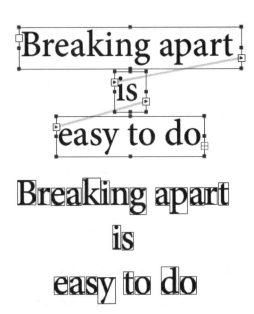

2. Choose Modify > Break Apart.

Flash transforms each letter in the selection into a drawing-object and selects it **E**.

TIP Converting TLF text to drawing-objects can be useful if you have a small amount of text that you can't (or don't want to) supply to every end user, but you need to ensure the text looks exactly the same in the finished product as it did during the authoring phase.

TIP You don't actually have to select a TLF text field; just position the text tool's I-beam cursor anywhere within the text field. When you choose Modify > Break Apart, Flash converts all the text in that text field, and any fields linked to it, to drawing-objects.

E With TLF text fields selected (top), choosing Modify > Break Apart transforms each letter into a separate drawing object (bottom).

Breaking Down Classic Text

The conversion process for Classic text works a bit differently than the process for TLF text. It takes two steps to transform Classic Text to simple graphic shapes. Classic-text characters convert to merge-shapes, while TLF-text characters convert to drawing-objects.

First, select the Classic text field on the Stage. Choose Modify > Break Apart. Flash places each letter in its own Classic text field and selects them all. Each Classic text field is just wide enough to hold one letter. Each letter is fully editable on its own, although the set of letters is no longer linked. Now, to transform those single-letter text fields into merge-shapes, with the text fields selected, choose Modify > Break Apart again. This second Break Apart command transforms the editable letters into raw shapes on the Stage **F**. You can edit them as you would any other fill, but you can no longer change their text attributes with the text tool or Text (Tool) Property inspector.

F Applying the Break Apart command once transforms selected Classic text (top) into single-letter Classic text fields (middle); applying the command again creates merge-shapes out of the individual letters (bottom).

Practice Session

Try converting a simple geometric shape into a more complex form. For example, try changing an oval fill into a flower shape.

- Use the oval tool to create a plump oval fill with no stroke **Ⓐ**. (See Chapter 2, *Making Geometric Shapes*.)

  Use the selection tool to add corner points to the oval's path, then drag them inward to create petals **Ⓑ**; use the selection tool to reposition the petals' curve points to create a pleasing flower shape **Ⓒ**. (See *Natural Drawing*.)

- Use the subselection and Bézier tools to add and remove points on the path of one petal to create a stem; adjust the curve of the stem using the stem points' Bézier handles **Ⓓ**, **Ⓔ**. (See *Modifying Shapes: Bézier Tools*.)

Extra Credit: Modify the fill: use a linear gradient to give the flower a green stem and pink petals.

- Create a linear gradient fill that runs from dark green on the left, through hot pink, to pale pink on the right. (See Chapter 2, *To create a linear gradient, Creating Solid Colors and Gradients*.)

- Apply the gradient fill to your shape, then rotate the gradient so that green is on the bottom **Ⓕ**. (See *Modifying Fills and Strokes > To change fill color with the paint-bucket tool and > To rotate a gradient fill*.)

Hint: Once you've got the fill inside the flower shape, adjust the position of the lower petals so that they fall completely into the "pink zone" of your gradient. You may also need to adjust the location of the gradient pointers in the Color panel to fit the "green zone" to the stem area of your shape.

Save your file for use in future Practice Sessions.

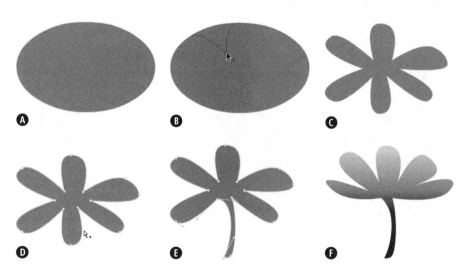

Complex Graphics on a Single Layer

In Chapters 2 and 4, you learned to make and modify simple individual shapes from strokes (lines) and fills by using Adobe Flash Professional CS5's drawing tools. In your movies, you'll want to use many shapes together, and you'll need to combine strokes and fills in complex ways. You might combine several shapes, such as ovals and rectangles, to create a robot character, for example. To work effectively with complex graphics, you must understand how multiple graphic elements—merge-shapes, drawing objects, and primitive-shapes—interact when they're on the same layer or on different layers. In this chapter, you learn how to work with multiple graphic elements on one layer in a Flash document. (To learn more about the concept of layers, see Chapter 6.)

Two of Flash's drawing tools—the brush tool and the eraser—offer special modes for use with multiple fills and strokes on a single layer. In this chapter, unless you're specifically requested to do otherwise, leave both tools at their default settings of Paint Normal (for the brush tool) and Erase Normal (for the eraser).

When Merge-Shapes Interact

You can think of each frame in a Flash movie as being a stack of transparent acetate sheets. In Flash terms, each sheet is a layer. Graphics on different layers have a depth relationship: items on higher layers block your view of items on lower layers, just as a drawing on the top sheet of acetate would obscure drawings on lower sheets.

Imagine you have two layers in your movie. If you draw a little yellow square on the bottom layer, then switch to the top layer and draw a big red square directly over the yellow one, the little square remains intact, but you can't see it. The square on the top layer is in the way.

On a single layer in Flash, however, merge-shapes interact with one another, almost as though you were painting with wet finger paint. Here's a quick rundown of how lines (strokes) and shapes (fills) created in Merge Drawing mode interact within a single layer.

When Merge-Shape Lines Intersect

Intersecting merge-shape lines drawn on the same layer affect one another. Draw one line in Merge Drawing mode, and then draw a second line that intersects the first. The second line cuts—or, in Flash terminology, *segments*—the first. Segmentation happens whether the lines are the same color or different colors, but it's easiest to see with contrasting colors **A**.

You might expect that the second line you drew would wind up on top of the first, but sometimes that's not the case. Start with a blue line, then draw a red line across it, then draw another blue line that crosses the red line; the second blue line jumps *behind* the red one when you release the mouse button. Flash creates a stacking order for merge-shape strokes based on a combination of the order in which you create the strokes and their color.

Within each layer, the first merge-shape stroke you create sets the color for the bottom level of the stack; strokes you create later with different colors stack above this first stroke, and each new stroke color adds a new level to the stack. Let's say your first merge-shape stroke is red and the second is blue. Red becomes the bottom level of the stack for merge-shape strokes in this layer, and blue becomes the second level. From now on, any red strokes you add to the layer will stack below blue ones, and new blue strokes will stack above red ones. You can add new red and blue strokes in any order—try alternating blue and red and blue and red. All the blue strokes will pop to the top of the stack above all the red strokes. Add a merge-stroke that's green, and green becomes the third level of this layer's merge-shape–stroke stack. New green merge-shape strokes will always stack above blue ones (which stack above the red ones). Start a new layer (or a new document) and Flash starts the stacking order afresh. If your strokes don't stack up the way you'd like, you may need to group items (see the next section "Working with Groups," or create strokes on separate layers (see Chapter 6).

First line   Second line

Intersections cut, or segment, the underlying and overlying lines

Segments are separate objects

You can move segments independently

A When you draw one line across another in Merge Drawing mode, every intersection creates a separate segment.

continues on next page

When Merge-Shapes Interact *continued*

When Merge-Shape Lines and Fills Intersect

A fill that has no stroke still has a path (the invisible outline that describes the fill shape). When you work in Merge Drawing mode, fill paths can cut the strokes of other shapes. When you place merge-shape lines over merge-shape fills, you can wind up with lots of little segments. Try drawing lines (strokes) with the pencil tool and arcs (fills) with the brush tool; set the tools to Merge Drawing mode. If you paint a fill that intersects a stroke, the fill remains one solid object, but the stroke gets segmented **B**. If you draw a stroke that intersects a fill, the stroke cuts the fill, and the path of the fill cuts the stroke **C**.

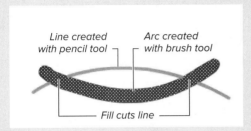

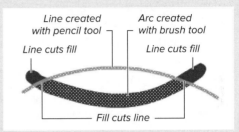

B When a merge-shape fill overlays a merge-shape stroke, the fill segments the stroke. As the selection highlighting shows, the fill remains one solid object.

C When a merge-shape line overlays a merge-shape fill, the line's path cuts the fill, and the fill's path cuts the line.

When Merge-Shape Fills Intersect

When intersecting fills created in Merge Drawing mode are the same color, the newer fill adds to the merge-shape **D**.

When fills of different colors interact, the newer fill replaces the older one where the two overlap **E**.

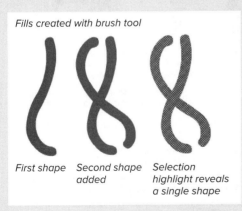

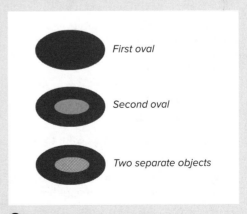

D When you draw overlapping fills in the same color in Merge Drawing mode, Flash puts the two shapes together to create a single merge-shape.

E When one merge-shape fill overlaps another of a different color, the fills don't meld but remain separate. The second oval here replaces the first where they overlap.

Working with Groups

A *group* is a type of virtual container that holds graphic elements. Groups serve several functions. They prevent selected merge-shapes from interacting. They also lock down the attributes of shapes and preserve spatial relationships among graphic elements. Although you can also group drawing-objects and primitive-shapes, for the tasks in this section you want to see the interaction with merge-shapes; make sure the Object Drawing button in the Tools panel is deselected.

To create a group:

1. Select one or more items on the Stage using any of the methods discussed in Chapter 4 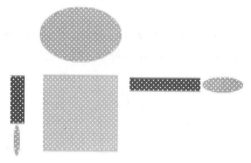.

2. Choose Modify > Group, or press Command-G (Mac) or Ctrl-G (Windows).

   Flash groups the items, placing them within a bounding box **B**. The visible bounding box lets you know that the group is selected. When the group isn't selected, the bounding box is hidden.

> **TIP** If you choose Modify > Group when nothing is selected, you immediately enter group-editing mode: anything you draw on the Stage is part of a new group.

To return objects to ungrouped status:

1. Select the group that you want to return to ungrouped status.

2. Choose Modify > Ungroup, or press Shift-Command-G (Mac) or Ctrl-Shift-G (Windows).

   Flash removes the bounding box and selects all the items.

A The first step in grouping is selecting the shapes you want to use in the group.

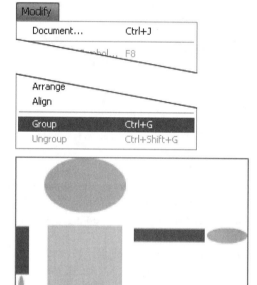

B The Modify > Group command unites multiple selected shapes within a single bounding box.

> **TIP** Interactions between strokes and fills occur not only when you draw a shape but also when you place a copy of a shape or move a shape. Be careful when placing copies of merge-shape fills and strokes on a single layer; you can inadvertently add to or delete part of an underlying merge-shape. If you ungroup a grouped shape that overlaps merge-shapes on a single layer, the shapes will segment one another.

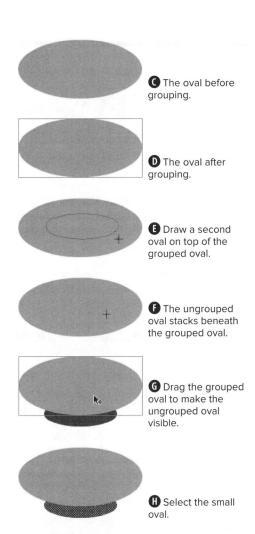

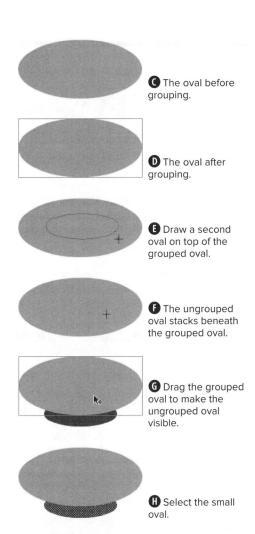 The oval before grouping.

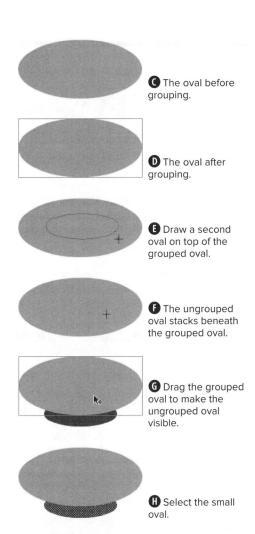 The oval after grouping.

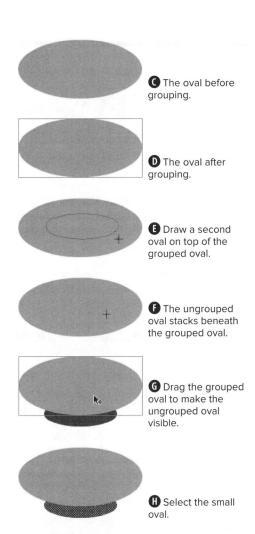 Draw a second oval on top of the grouped oval.

 The ungrouped oval stacks beneath the grouped oval.

 Drag the grouped oval to make the ungrouped oval visible.

 Select the small oval.

 After grouping, the small oval—the most recently created group—pops to the top of the stack.

To prevent interaction between merge-shapes on one layer:

1. In the Tools panel, choose the oval tool in Merge Drawing mode.

2. Set the stroke color to No Color and the fill color to red.

3. On the Stage, draw a fairly large oval **C**.

4. In the Tools panel, switch to the selection tool, and select the oval you just drew.

5. To make the oval a grouped element, Choose Modify > Group **D**.

6. Deselect the grouped oval.

7. In the Tools panel, choose the oval tool and a different fill color.

8. On the Stage, draw a smaller oval in the middle of your first oval **E**.

   When you finish drawing the new oval, it immediately disappears behind the grouped oval **F**. Grouped objects always stack on top of ungrouped objects (see the sidebar "Understanding Stacking Order," later in this chapter).

9. Switch to the selection tool, and reposition the large oval so that you can see the small one **G**.

10. Deselect the large oval, and select the small oval **H**.

11. To make the small oval a grouped element, Choose Modify > Group.

    Flash puts the small oval in a bounding box and brings it to the top of the stack **I**. The most recently created group is always on the top of the stack. Now the two ovals won't interact.

Editing Groups

Although you can transform a group as a whole (scale, rotate, and skew it), you can't directly edit the individual shapes within the group the way you can edit an ungrouped shape. To edit the shapes within a group, use the Edit Selected command.

To edit the contents of a group:

1. In the Tools panel, choose the selection tool.

2. On the Stage, select the group you want to edit.

3. Choose Edit > Edit Selected.

   Flash enters group-editing mode 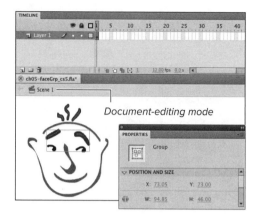. The Edit bar just above the Stage changes to indicate that you're in group-editing mode. The bounding box for the selected group disappears, and Flash dims all the items on the Stage that aren't part of the selected group. These dimmed items aren't editable; they merely provide context for editing the selected group.

4. Make changes to the contents of the group.

5. To return to document-editing mode, do one of the following:

   ▶ Choose Edit > Edit All.

   ▶ Double-click an empty area of the Stage or the Pasteboard.

   ▶ Click the current scene name in the Edit bar.

   ▶ Click the Back button in the Edit bar.

Document-editing mode

Click the Back button to return to document-editing mode

Click the scene name to return to document-editing mode

Group-editing mode

Grayed shapes don't belong to the group that's being edited

Double-click away from the group to return to document-editing mode

A The eyes and eyebrows are a selected group (top). In group-editing mode (bottom), the selected shapes are ready to edit; the other items on the Stage are dimmed to indicate that you can't edit them.

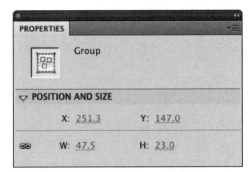

B The Position and Size section of the Group Property inspector contains hot text for adjusting the *x*- and *y*-coordinates and the height and width of the bounding box of a group you've selected on the Stage. Enter new values to change any of those parameters.

TIP To enter group-editing mode quickly, double-click a grouped item on the Stage with the selection tool.

TIP When the Property inspector is open, you can use it to modify the x- and y-coordinates and the height and width of a selected group's bounding box **B**.

TIP When you're editing a group nested within another group, clicking the Back button moves you up one level in the nesting hierarchy.

TIP You can also enter group-editing mode for a selected item by choosing Edit > Edit in Place. When you edit groups, there is no difference between this command and Edit > Edit Selected. There is a difference when you use these commands to edit symbols. (You'll learn about symbols in Chapter 7.)

Editing Inside the Drawing-Object Container

As you learned in Chapter 4, you can modify drawing-objects directly as they sit on the Stage (in essence reaching through the drawing-object container). But you can also work directly with the merge-shapes inside the container. To do so, you must open the container and work in drawing-object–editing mode. There is no menu command for entering this edit mode, but double-clicking a drawing-object on the Stage opens that object's container so you can edit the contents. (Note that double-clicking a primitive-shape brings up a dialog that lets you convert the primitive to a drawing-object and open its container for editing the contents.)

In drawing-object–editing mode—as in group-editing mode—selected shapes appear in full color, and other shapes appear dimmed. In drawing-object–editing mode, you can modify or delete the original merge-shapes or add new shapes. Note that the contents of a drawing-object must be merge-shapes. You can create new drawing-objects or primitives while you work in drawing-object–editing mode, but when you return to document-editing mode, Flash converts your original drawing-object to its constituent merge shapes, adds the new drawing-object(s) or primitive(s), selects all these items, and turns them into a group.

To return to document-editing mode, you use the same techniques as when editing a group (for example, click the Back button in the Edit bar).

Controlling Stacking Order

Within a single layer, text fields, grouped objects, drawing-objects, and primitives stack as if they were sitting on sublayers above any ungrouped merge-shapes. Stacking order exists even if objects don't literally lie on top of one another. If you have a group on one side of the Stage and a drawing-object on the other, you can't see which one stacks higher than the other; but if you drag the objects so they overlap, the order becomes apparent. (Symbols, which you'll learn about in Chapter 7, are another type of graphic-object that stacks on top of ungrouped merge-shapes.)

You can change the stacking order of graphic-objects via the Modify > Arrange menu. You can move objects up or down in the stacking order one level at a time, or you can send an object to the top or bottom of the stack of sublayers.

Understanding Stacking Order

Merge-shapes on a single layer always stay on the same layer, segmenting one another whenever they inhabit the same space on the Stage. All graphic-objects (drawing-objects, primitives, text fields, groups, and symbols) stack on top of one another. By default, Flash stacks each new graphic-object that you create on top of the preceding one; the last graphic-object created winds up on top of all the others Ⓐ. A higher-level graphic-object obscures any graphic-object that lies directly beneath it.

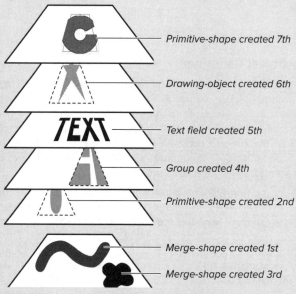

Primitive-shape created 7th

Drawing-object created 6th

Text field created 5th

Group created 4th

Primitive-shape created 2nd

Merge-shape created 1st

Merge-shape created 3rd

Ⓐ This schematic shows Flash's default stacking order for graphic-objects. The most recently created graphic-object is on top. Merge-shapes are always on the bottom.

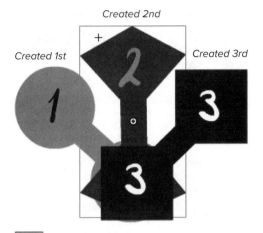

Created 1st
Created 2nd
Created 3rd

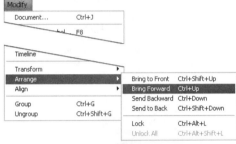

Modify	
Document...	Ctrl+J
	F8

Timeline	
Transform	▶
Arrange	▶
Align	▶
Group	Ctrl+G
Ungroup	Ctrl+Shift+G

Bring to Front	Ctrl+Shift+Up
Bring Forward	Ctrl+Up
Send Backward	Ctrl+Down
Send to Back	Ctrl+Shift+Down
Lock	Ctrl+Alt+L
Unlock All	Ctrl+Alt+Shift+L

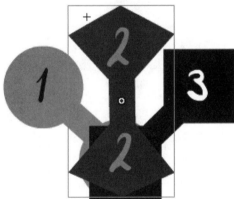

B Each dumbbell-like shape here is a separate group (top). Choose Modify > Arrange > Bring Forward (middle) to move a selected group up one level in the stacking order (bottom).

To change position in a stack by one level:

1. On the Stage, create at least three graphic-objects.

   Use any combination of grouped shapes, drawing-objects, primitives, or text fields.

2. Select one of the graphic-objects.

3. From the Modify > Arrange menu, choose either of the following:

   ▸ To move the selected item up one level, choose Bring Forward, or press Command–up arrow (Mac) or Ctrl–up arrow (Windows).

   ▸ To move the selected item down one level, choose Send Backward, or press Command–down arrow (Mac) or Ctrl–down arrow (Windows).

   Flash moves the selected item up (or down) one sublayer in the stacking order **B**.

To move an element to the top or bottom of the stack:

1. On the Stage, select one of the graphic-objects you created in the previous task.

2. From the Modify > Arrange menu, choose either of the following:

   ▸ To bring the item to the top of the stack, choose Bring to Front, or press Option-Shift–up arrow (Mac) or Ctrl-Shift–up arrow (Windows).

   ▸ To move the item to the bottom of the stack, choose Send to Back, or press Option-Shift–down arrow (Mac) or Ctrl-Shift–down arrow (Windows).

   Flash places the selected item at the top (or bottom) of the heap.

Combining Drawing-Objects and Primitives

Drawing-objects and primitive-shapes don't interact with one another or with merge-shapes, even when they overlap. You can force them to interact by using the Modify > Combine Objects commands. Flash converts combined primitives to drawing-objects.

To unite multiple drawing-objects or primitives:

1. Use the drawing tools in Object Drawing mode, or the rectangle- or oval-primitive tools, to create overlapping shapes:

   ▸ Make two or more overlapping fills with the same colors.

   ▸ Make two or more overlapping shapes with fills and strokes; use different colors for the fills and strokes in each shape.

2. Select the overlapping fills that are the same color.

3. Choose Modify > Combine Objects > Union.

   The two fills become a single drawing-object shape 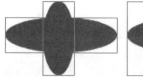.

4. Select the overlapping shapes of different colors.

5. Repeat Step 3.

   The fills and strokes of the shapes segment one another, but you wind up with a single drawing-object containing all those segmented shapes .

TIP You can also use the Modify > Combine Objects > Union command to combine a mix of merge-shapes, drawing-objects, and primitives.

TIP To access and edit merge-shapes inside a drawing-object, double-click it .

A Applying the Modify > Combine Objects > Union command to drawing-object or primitive-shape fills of the same color (left) melds the fills and creates a single drawing-object (right).

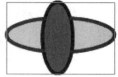

B Applying the Modify > Combine Objects > Union command to drawing-objects (or primitive-shapes) of different colors (left) causes the selected fills and strokes to replace and segment one another as merge-shapes would. The resulting shapes unite in a single drawing-object (right).

C Try double-clicking the new drawing-object after you've applied Union to drawing-objects (or primitives) of different colors. In drawing-object–editing mode, you can see how the shapes segment one another. Each chunk of stroke and fill is a separate shape.

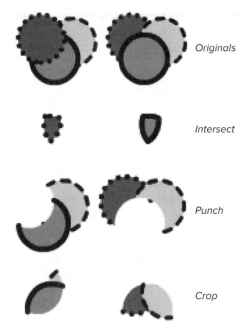

Originals

Intersect

Punch

Crop

D The last three commands in the Modify > Combine Objects menu have different results depending on which object lies on top of the stack. The Intersect command creates a new shape from the intersection of all selected shapes, using the top shape's attributes. With Punch, the top shape takes a bite out of the others and removes it; the remaining shapes keep their original attributes. With Crop, the top shape takes the same bite but this time removes everything else; the resulting shapes keep their original attributes.

TIP If you choose Modify > Combine Objects > Intersect and your shapes disappear, there was no place where they all intersected. That result may seem self-evident, but if you've selected many shapes, or complex shapes, it may be hard to see.

To use one drawing-object to remove part of another:

1. Use the drawing tools in Object Drawing mode, or the rectangle- or oval-primitive tools, to create two or more overlapping shapes with a variety of fills and strokes.

2. Select the drawing-objects.

3. From the Modify > Combine Objects menu, choose one of the following:

   Intersect retains fills and strokes only where all the selected shapes overlap, and deletes all other fills and strokes. The resulting shape(s) take stroke and fill attributes from the topmost shape.

   Punch uses the topmost shape like a cookie cutter to remove any shapes directly below it. (Imagine the shape left in the cookie dough after you've cut out a cookie; that's what Punch creates.) The resulting shape(s) retain their original attributes.

   Crop uses the topmost shape like a cookie cutter to select a new shape from any shapes that lie below it. (Imagine the cookie cutter again, but this time you wind up with the cookie itself.) The resulting shape(s) retain their original attributes **D**.

TIP When you select merge-shapes, the Modify > Combine Objects menu only offers the Union command. You can use this command instead of grouping merge-shapes. The Union command preserves the spatial relationships between shapes but gives you the ability to change fills and strokes directly on the Stage as described in Chapter 4.

Creating Patterns

Flash CS5 offers two tools for creating patterns: the spray-brush and deco tools. The spray brush creates a random dot pattern as you move the tool over the Stage. The deco tool creates patterns out of repeating elements, which it combines into groups. The deco tool has various types of patterns, called Drawing Effects: some effects fill space automatically with a single click, others lay down a trail of shapes as you drag the deco tool across the Stage. In the following tasks, you use the tools to create simple patterns in default merge-shapes. The tools can also create more-complex patterns, and can use custom elements (see the sidebar "Customizing Patterns").

To paint a random dot pattern:

1. In the tools panel, click the active brush tool.

2. From the submenu that appears, select the spray brush tool 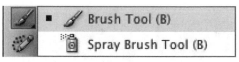.

3. Access the Symbol section of the Spray Brush Tool Property inspector.

4. To use a small, black dot as the pattern element, select the Default Shape checkbox.

   The checkbox is selected by default.

5. To change the size of the pattern element, use the Scale hot text to enter a percentage between 0 and 40,000.

   Click the hot text to enter a precise value; drag the hot text's invisible slider to choose a value interactively.

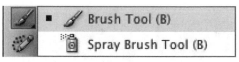

Ⓐ The spray-brush tool is located in the same submenu as the brush tool.

Customizing Patterns

The tasks in this section use the pattern-creation tools at a basic level, creating random dots with the spray brush, and a grid of squares with the deco tool. The deco tool can also create more intricate patterns. Especially interesting are Flash CS5's new brush options for creating organic, interactive, and animated patterns (see the sidebar, "About Interactive Pattern Brushes").

You adjust the parameters of all the patterns in the Property inspector. Although you can't create new underlying patterns, you can create new pattern elements for the spray brush and for some of the deco tools' effects. You might, for example, set the spray-brush tool to spew forth stars instead of dots, or set the deco tool to make a grid out of flapping birds. If a tool lets you change pattern elements, you'll see a checkbox named Default Shape in the relevant section of the Property inspector. To substitute your own pattern elements, deselect the Default Shape checkbox (or click the Edit button that appears next to it). A dialog appears displaying the symbols currently in your document; choose a symbol to be the new element (you'll learn about creating symbols in Chapter 7).

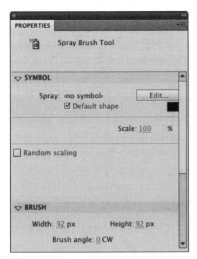

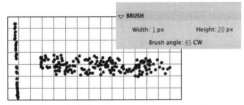

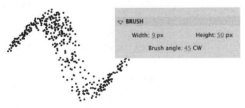

B The Spray Brush Tool Property inspector lets you set how the tool creates its spray pattern. You can also set the tool to use your own symbols.

C When setting the Width and Height values for the spray brush, think of using a spray bottle. Smaller values close down the "nozzle" to create a narrower spay; larger ones open it up. With a width of 1 and a height of 20, Flash lays down the dots in a single line as you draw vertically, but lays down a swatch roughly 20 pixels across when you draw horizontally.

D Choosing unequal values for width and height creates an elliptical spray-brush "nozzle." The Brush Angle setting lets you rotate that ellipse (as you might tilt a real calligraphy pen with a wide nib), so that the brush creates thick and thin areas as you paint.

6. To modify the brush's shape (to change the shape of the "nozzle" through which the pattern elements get "sprayed"), access the Brush section of the Property inspector **B** and use the hot-text controls to specify new values for any of the following:

   Width specifies how wide the nozzle is.

   Height specifies how tall the nozzle is.

   The range of possible values for width and height is based on the dimensions of the Flash document. In one that is 550 by 400 pixels, for example, spray-brush width ranges from 0 to 550 pixels, height from 0 to 400 pixels **C**.

   Brush Angle determines how the nozzle orients itself in space. Acceptable values are 0 to 360 **D**.

7. Move the pointer over the Stage.

   The pointer turns into a spray can.

8. Click and drag.

   As you move the pointer, Flash adds more dots radiating away from the pointer location according to the settings you chose in Step 4. Dragging slowly places dots close together; dragging quickly spreads dots out more.

9. Release the mouse button.

   Flash combines all the shapes it just created into a single group.

TIP You can change the color of the default dot element. After Step 4, in the Symbol section of the Spray Brush Tool Property inspector, click the color control to access the pop-up swatch set and select a new color.

continues on next page

TIP Although the Symbol section of the Spray Brush Tool Property inspector offers a Random Scaling checkbox, the feature works inconsistently. Even when the checkbox is deselected, if you set a dot size higher or lower than 100 percent (for example, 30 percent or 500 percent), the spray brush creates some dots in random sizes. Selecting the Random Scaling checkbox simply ensures that you get lots of randomness, and makes the range of sizes larger when you've set the dot size to something near 100 percent.

TIP If you want to add more dots, you can spray over the area again, starting in a different place. To keep the dot groups organized in one over-arching group, use the selection tool to double-click the initial group of sprayed dots; you enter group-editing mode; now you can do additional spray brushing inside that group.

To fill space with a repeating grid:

1. In the tools panel, select the deco tool, or press U .

2. Access the Drawing Effect section of the Property inspector, and from the pop-up menu, choose Grid Fill 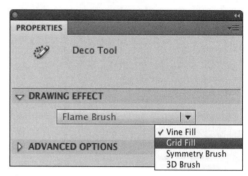.

   Flash CS5 comes with 13 drawing-effect patterns. Grid Fill creates a grid pattern using up to four different symbols. With default settings, the tool lays down a regular pattern of black squares to create a grid that fills the Stage or a shape.

3. To create a grid using squares of various colors, do the following:

   ‣ In the Tile 1 section, click the Color control to access the pop-up swatch set and select a new color.

   Make sure that the Tile 1 checkbox and Default Shape checkbox are selected; they are selected by default when you choose the deco tool for the first time 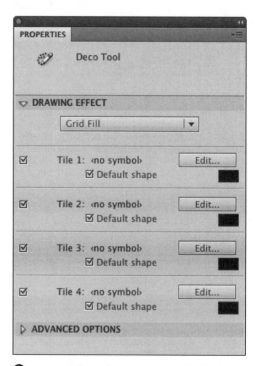.

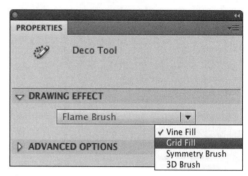
E To create patterns that fill the Stage or a shape, select the deco tool.

F The deco tool offers 13 patterns to choose from. Select one from the pop-up menu in the Drawing Effect section of the Property inspector. Choosing Grid Fill and selecting the Default Shape checkbox creates a grid pattern using squares.

G Use the Deco Tool Property inspector to set parameters for the pattern elements.

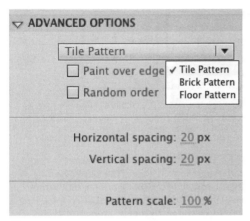

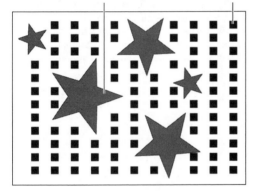

H To change the attributes of the grid's default square, access the Advanced Options section of the Deco Tool Property inspector.

Stars placed first   Stage clicked to start grid

I When you click a blank area of the Stage, the deco tool fills all blank areas with the grid. The pattern flows around any graphic elements already on the Stage.

4. Repeat Step 3 using the Tile 2, Tile 3, and Tile 4 sections. Choose a different color for each tile.

5. To choose the relationship between the tiles, access the Advanced Options section of the Property inspector and from the pop-up menu, choose one of the following **H**:

   Tile Pattern aligns tile elements horizontally and vertically.

   Brick Pattern staggers tile elements horizontally; every other row is inset half a tile width. With rectangular tiles, the result looks similar to bricks in a wall.

   Floor Pattern staggers tiles horizontally and vertically.

6. To set the grid's parameters, in the Advanced Options section of the Deco Tool Property inspector, use the hot text to enter values for any of the following:

   Horizontal Spacing sets the amount of horizontal space between squares in the grid.

   Vertical Spacing sets the amount of vertical space between squares in the grid.

   Pattern Scale sets the size of the grid pattern as a whole.

7. Position the pointer over the Stage.

   The pointer turns into a paint bucket spilling squares.

8. To fill the Stage with the grid pattern, click a blank area of the Stage.

   Flash creates a grid of squares that fills the Stage. If graphic objects already exist on the Stage, Flash places the squares only in the empty space around the existing objects **I**.

continues on next page

or

To fill a shape with the grid pattern, click within the shape **J**.

Flash places the squares to fill as much of the shape as possible. Flash combines the squares of the grid into a single group.

J Click the deco tool within a shape to fill the shape with the current deco pattern.

TIP The grid is a group, and each tile within the grid is also a group. Using the selection tool, double-click one tile in the grid to enter group-editing mode. At this level, you can modify the position and size of individual tiles. Double-click any tile once more to modify its fill and stroke attributes.

TIP The deco tool creates the Grid Fill effect from whatever tiles you select (deselecting a tile does not result in a gap in the grid). For a grid of identical shapes, you need only use one of the four tiles. Select the Tile 1 checkbox, for example, and deselect the Tile 2, Tile 3, and Tile 4 checkboxes. Select a new color and/or shape, and the deco tool creates the grid using tiles with that shape and color. For a grid with two shapes, select and define any two tiles (Tile 2 and Tile 4, for example).

TIP You can fill a shape that already has a fill; simply click within the filled shape. The deco-pattern group winds up above the shape's fill and stroke in the stacking order.

TIP By default, the deco tool places only whole grid elements. When filling a circle shape with a grid of squares, for example, the deco tool leaves out any squares that would intersect the edge of the circle, leaving a gap in the grid. If you wind up with too many gaps, select the grid group, delete it, and try clicking a different spot to start the grid. Alternatively, try changing the pattern spacing or size until you get a grid that fills the shape in a pleasing way.

TIP To allow the deco tool to place tiles that overlap the edge of a shape, in the Advanced Options section of the Deco Tool Property inspector, select the Paint Over Edge checkbox.

TIP By default, the tiles that form the grid pattern appear in order (Tile 1, followed by Tile 2, followed by Tile 3, and so on). When you use tiles of various colors or shapes, you can force the deco tool to break out of this strict rotation and create a crazy-quilt effect. In the Advanced Options section of the Deco Tool Property inspector, select the Random Order checkbox.

TIP The Pattern Scale property takes values from 50 to 300 percent. Larger percentages increase the size of the squares as well as the amount of space between them; smaller percentages decrease the size and space.

About Interactive Pattern Brushes

In CS5 the deco tool offers some sophisti-cated patterns and effects for populating a scene with repetitive elements. The tasks in this chapter cover the simple grids that the deco tool creates, but the tool now offers 13 different drawing-effect patterns: Vine Fill, Grid Fill, Symmetry Brush, 3D Brush, Build-ing Brush, Decorated Brush, Fire Animation, Flame Brush, Flower Brush, Lightening Brush, Particle System, Smoke Animation, and Tree Brush.

Some of the effects, such as Vine Fill and Grid Fill, simply fill space with a pattern when you click the Stage (or click inside a shape) with the deco tool.

Other effects are interactive, growing and changing as you draw with the deco tool on the Stage. The various Tree Brush effects, for example, simulate the natural forms of tree branches with leaves. The Decorated Brush effect lets you draw a series of pattern elements—heart, stars, or notes, for exam-ple—that follow your brush movements 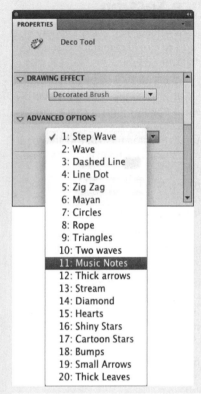. The Building Brush effect lets you "construct" skyscrapers quickly; the longer your mouse stroke, the taller or wider the building.

Still other deco-tool drawing effects cre-ate frame-by-frame animations (you'll learn about this style of animation in Chapter 8). The Fire Animation effect, for example, lays down a trail of flickering flames as you draw. The Lightning Brush effect creates branch-ing flashes of electricity. The Particle System effect creates a constant flow of pattern elements that move across the Stage, for example, creating a shower of water drops that shoot from a fountain. By adjusting parameters, you can have the particles appear respond to physical forces—being pulled down by gravity, for example.

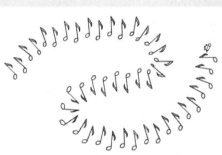

K Choosing Decorated Brush from the Drawing Effect menu in the Deco Tool Property inspector enables you to create a series of pattern elements—such as notes, stars, or leaves—that trace your mouse movements. (Note that the tool doesn't actually create an editable path the way the pencil tool does; the deco tool creates a group of shapes.)

Practice Session

Try drawing a fanciful face using a variety of drawing tools to create overlapping graphics on a single layer.

- Using the oval tool set to Object Drawing mode, with a fill of one color and a narrow stroke in a slightly different shade, create one large oval and two small ones. (See Chapter 2.) Position the ovals to create the basic shape of a head and ears. (See Chapter 4.) Play with the stacking order; put one ear fully in front of the head and the other partially behind. (See *Controlling Stacking Order*.)

- When you find a pleasing configuration, group the ovals. (See *Working with Groups*.)

- Use the brush tool in Object Drawing mode to draw facial features like eyes, nose, mouth. Arrange these elements so they sit on top of the face in the stacking order. (See *Controlling Stacking Order*.)

- Use the spray-brush tool to add hair. (See *Creating Patterns > To paint a random dot pattern*.)

Save your file for use in future Practice Sessions.

Extra Credit

- Instead of using the spray brush to add hair, try using the deco tool to create a fanciful head of hair—using the Flower Brush effect, for example, or one of the Decorated Brush effects.

- Edit one or more of the groups that make up the face; change the fill and/or stroke color; change the outline of an underlying object's shape.

Graphics on Multiple Layers

In Adobe Flash Professional CS5, you can create an illusion of three-dimensional depth by overlapping graphic elements. As you learned in Chapter 5, you can create this overlapping effect on one layer by stacking drawing-objects, primitive-shapes, groups, and symbols. The more elements the layer contains, however, the more difficult it becomes to manipulate and keep track of their stacking order.

When you place items on separate layers, it's easy to control and rearrange the way the items stack up. You can make shapes appear to be closer to the viewer by putting them on a higher layer. Additionally, raw shapes on different layers don't interact, so you don't need to worry about grouping merge-shapes or having one merge-shape inadvertently delete another. You can hide and show layers—even organize layers in folders—and label them to make it easier to work with multiple layers and elements in a Flash document.

In This Chapter

Touring the Timeline's Layer Features

Flash graphically represents each layer as one horizontal section of the Timeline and provides controls for viewing and manipulating these graphic representations. Several handy features help you work with graphics on layers, such as viewing the items on layers as outlines and assigning different colors to those outlines so you can easily see which items are on which layers. You can lock layers so you don't edit their contents accidentally, and you can hide layers to make it easier to work with individual graphics in a welter of other graphics. You can create guide layers for help in positioning elements, masks for hiding and revealing layer contents selectively, and motion-guide layers for animating classic-tween elements along a curving path. (You learn more about classic-tween motion-guide layers in Chapter 9.)

Complex movies contain dozens of layers. Viewing and navigating such hefty Timelines can get tedious and confusing. Flash lets you create *layer folders* to organize the layers in a movie. You can keep all the layers related to one character or element together in one folder, for example. Flash considers a folder to be another type of layer, and the methods for adding and deleting layer folders are similar to those for adding and deleting layers. Layer folders don't by themselves hold graphic content, however, and folders have neither frames nor keyframes in the Timeline. (Keyframes are special frames in which you place your graphic elements; you'll learn about them in Chapter 8.)

Figure **A** offers a road map to the important layer features in the Timeline.

A The Timeline graphically represents all the layers in a Flash movie. Layer folders let you organize layers in a complex movie. You can do much of the work of creating and manipulating layers and folders by clicking buttons in the Timeline.

About Layers

You can think of a Flash document as a stack of filmstrips: a sheaf of long, clear acetate strips divided into frames. Each filmstrip is analogous to a Flash layer. Shapes painted on the top filmstrip obscure shapes on lower strips; where the top filmstrip is blank, elements from the lower strips show through.

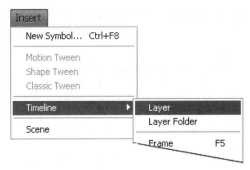

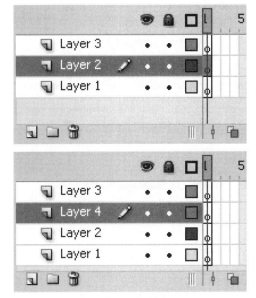

A Choose Insert > Timeline > Layer to add a new layer to the Timeline.

B Select the layer that you want to wind up beneath the new layer (top); Flash inserts a new layer directly above the selected layer and gives the new layer a default name (bottom).

Creating and Deleting Layers and Folders

While creating the ingredients of a particular scene in your movie, you can add new layers and layer folders as you need them.

To add a layer or a layer folder:

1. In the Timeline, to choose the new layer's location, select an existing layer or folder by clicking it.

   Flash always adds the new layer or folder directly above the one you selected. To add a layer or folder beneath the current bottom layer, create a new layer, then click and drag it to reposition it at the bottom of the stack.

2. To add a layer, do either of the following:

   ▸ Choose Insert > Timeline > Layer **A**.

   ▸ In the Timeline's Status bar, click the New Layer button (the folded-page icon).

   Flash adds a new layer and gives it a default name—for example, *Layer 4* **B**.

   continues on next page

3. To add a folder, do either of the following:

  ‣ Choose Insert > Timeline > Layer Folder.

  ‣ In the Timeline's Status bar, click the New Folder button (the folder icon).

  Flash adds a new layer folder and gives it a default name—for example, *Folder 1* or *Folder 2* 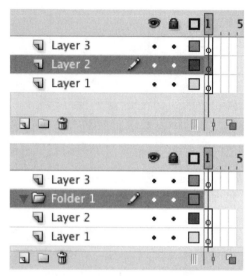. The folder is open by default, making it easy to place layers within (see "Organizing Layers," later in this chapter).

TIP Flash bases the number in default names on the number of layers or folders already created in the active scene of the movie, not on the number of layers and folders that currently exist or their current position.

TIP Flash tracks layer and folder numbers separately; the first folder you insert among numerous layers gets the name *Folder 1.*

To delete a layer or a folder:

1. In the Timeline, select the layer or folder you want to delete.

2. Click the Delete button (the trash-can icon) 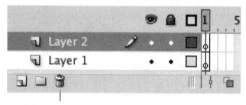.

  If your selection includes folders containing layers, a dialog appears, warning that deleting the layer folder will also delete all the layers it contains.

3. To delete the folder and its layers, click Yes.

  or

  To cancel the delete operation, click No. Flash removes that layer (and all its frames) or that folder from the Timeline.

C Select the layer that should be below the new folder (top). Flash creates a new folder above the layer you selected (bottom). Flash names new folders based on the number of folders that have been created in the current scene of the movie.

Delete layer or folder

D Click the Delete button to delete a selected layer or folder.

TIP You can also select and delete multiple layers. To select noncontiguous layers or folders in Step 1 of the preceding task, Command-click (Mac) or Ctrl-click (Windows) every layer or folder you want to remove. To select a range of layers, click the lowest layer you want to delete, then Shift-click the highest layer.

You can set *layer properties* (which define the look and function of a layer) in three ways:

- Click the layer-property control buttons in the Timeline.

- Control-click a layer on the Mac (or right-click it in Windows), and choose a command from the contextual menu for layers.

- Set property values in the Layer Properties dialog (to access the dialog, choose Modify > Timeline > Layer Properties or double-click a layer's folded-page icon or folder icon in the Timeline).

All three methods let you set layer visibility, lock layer contents, or view layer elements as outlines. The Layer Properties dialog offers additional functions: creating plain guide layers, changing the height of a layer in Timeline view, choosing an outline color, and changing an existing layer from one type to another, while the contextual menu lets you create classic motion-guide layers.

Setting Layer Properties

The Timeline represents each layer or layer folder as a horizontal field containing a name and three buttons for controlling the way the layer's or folder's contents look on the Stage. You can hide a layer or folder (making all the elements on that layer or within that folder temporarily invisible), lock a layer or folder (making the contents visible but uneditable), and view as outlines the items on the layer or within the folder.

To rename a layer or folder:

1. In the Timeline, double-click the layer or folder name.

   Flash activates the name's text-entry field.

2. Type a new name.

3. Press Enter, or click anywhere outside the name field.

continues on next page

To hide/show the contents of a layer or folder:

- In the Timeline for the layer or folder that you want to hide or show, click the icon in the Eye column **A**.

  The layer or folder toggles between the hidden and visible state. A red *X* in the column indicates that the layer or folder is hidden; its contents no longer appear on the Stage. A bullet indicates that the layer is visible. You decide how the hidden setting affects the final movie. When you publish a movie (see Chapter 18), you have the option to include or exclude the contents of hidden layers and folders.

Toggles visibility of the layer's contents

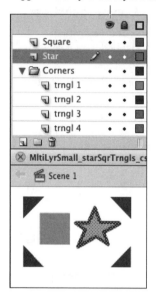

Layer contents hidden

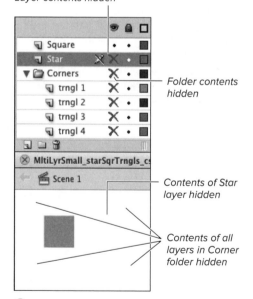

Folder contents hidden

Contents of Star layer hidden

Contents of all layers in Corner folder hidden

A The column below the eye icon controls the visibility of layers. Each of the six graphic elements (top) is on a separate layer. The four triangles at the corners are located in the Corners folder. Hiding the Star layer makes the star disappear from the Stage; hiding the Corners folder makes the four triangles disappear as well (bottom).

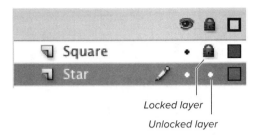

Locked layer

Unlocked layer

B The padlock icon indicates that a layer is locked. The contents of a locked layer appear on the Stage, but you can't edit them.

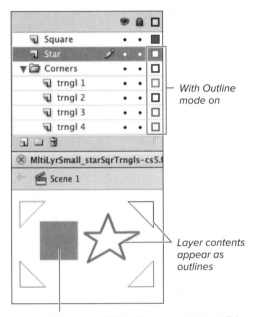

With Outline mode on

Layer contents appear as outlines

Contents of other layers appear as solids

C A hollow square in the Outline column indicates that graphic elements on that layer appear as outlines. Setting a folder to Outline mode automatically changes all the layers within it to Outline mode.

To lock/unlock a layer or folder:

- In the Timeline for the layer or folder that you want to lock or unlock, click the icon in the Lock column **B**.

The layer or folder toggles between the locked and unlocked state. A padlock icon in the column indicates that the layer or folder is locked; its contents appear on the Stage, but you can't edit them. A bullet indicates that the layer or folder is unlocked; its contents are editable. Locking a layer or folder has no effect on the final movie.

To view the contents of a layer or folder as outlines or solids:

- In the Timeline for the layer or folder that you want to view as outlines or solids, click the icon in the Outline column—the one topped by a square icon **C**.

The layer or folder toggles between Outline mode and Solid mode. When the square in the column has a thick color outline, the contents of the layer or folder appear on the Stage as outlines. When the square in the column is a solid color, the layer or folder contents appear in their complete form. For regular layers, the color of the outline square indicates what color Flash uses to create the outlines for the contents of that layer. (For layer folders, the color of the square has no meaning; the square just shows which mode the folder is in.) Placing a layer or folder in Outline mode doesn't affect the final movie.

TIP Setting a folder to Outline mode makes all the layers within the folder display their contents as outlines. Click the outline square of individual layers within the folder to see that layer's content as solid shapes.

Organizing Layers

You can rearrange layers (and folders) by dragging them to new positions in the Timeline, including dragging them into folders to create a visual hierarchy for layers.

To reorder layers (or folders):

1. In the Timeline, position the pointer over the layer icon (or folder icon) of the layer (or folder) you want to move.

2. Click and drag the layer (or folder).

    A black bar with a small circle on its left end previews the new location of the layer (or folder).

3. Position the preview bar in the layer order you want **A**.

4. Release the mouse button.

    Flash moves the layer (or folder) to the new location and selects it in the Timeline. The contents of single layers are selected on the Stage; the contents of the layers inside a repositioned folder are not selected.

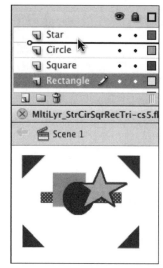

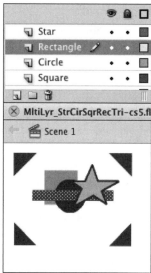

A The black bar with a small circle at its left end (top) represents the new location for the layer you're dragging (here it's the Rectangle layer). Release the mouse button to drop the layer into its new position. Flash selects the layer and its contents (bottom). The rectangle shape moves from the bottom of the heap, below the square, to just under the star.

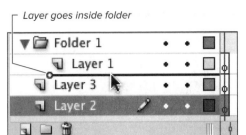

Layer goes inside folder

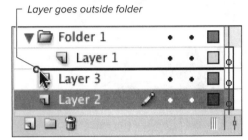

Layer goes outside folder

B When you position a layer below the last layer in an open folder, you need to let Flash know whether you want the dragged layer to wind up inside or outside the folder. As you drag into the open folder, the preview bar's circle automatically aligns with the right side of the target-folder icon (top), indicating that the dragged layer will go inside the target folder. To place the layer outside the folder, drag to the left until the preview bar's circle aligns with the left side of the folder icon (bottom). The option to drag to the left is available only when you place a layer at the bottom of the folder.

To move existing layers (or folders) into open folders:

1. Follow Steps 1 and 2 of the preceding task.

2. Do either of the following:
   - ▸ Position the preview bar directly beneath the target folder layer (or beneath a layer within the target folder other than the last layer).

     The preview bar's circle automatically aligns with the right side of the target folder's icon.

   - ▸ Position the preview bar beneath the last layer within the target folder.

     Drag to the right until the circle aligns with the right side of the target folder's icon.

3. Release the mouse button.

   The dragged layer winds up inside the target folder.

TIP To position a layer or folder directly below the last layer of an open folder without placing it inside the folder, drag to the left until the preview bar's circle aligns with the left side of the folder icon **B**. Then release the mouse button.

TIP You can also place items into closed folders: drag selected layers (or folders) directly over the target folder. The closed folder offers no feedback, and the preview bar makes it look like you're placing the layer above or below the target folder. To be sure you're on the target folder, position the pointer precisely over the folder name.

Working with Graphics on Different Layers

Unless you lock shapes, or lock or hide layers, the merge-shapes and drawing-objects on all layers are available for editing using the selection, paint-bucket, and ink-bottle tools; primitive-shapes are available for editing using the paint-bucket and ink-bottle tools. You can add shapes only on the active (currently selected) layer.

To activate a layer:

- To select the layer where you want to add a graphic-object, do either of the following:

  ▸ In the Timeline, click the layer name.

    The area containing the layer name highlights in blue, and a pencil icon appears to the right of the layer name. Flash selects all the graphic-objects on that layer.

  ▸ On the Stage, using the selection tool, click a graphic-object.

    Flash selects that graphic-object, highlights the layer name in blue, and puts the pencil icon to the right of the layer name.

To edit merge-shape and drawing-object outlines on inactive layers:

1. In a document with merge-shapes or drawing-objects on two or more layers, using the selection tool, position the pointer over a shape on an inactive layer (one without the pencil icon).

    The curve or corner-point icon appears.

2. Drag the outline of the shape on the inactive layer.

Active layer

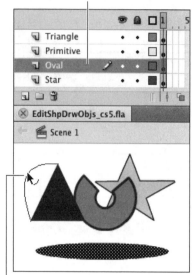

Use selection tool to modify shape on inactive layer

No change in active layer

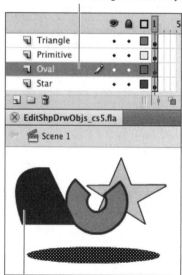

Flash redraws shape

Ⓐ Oval is the active layer, but you can still edit merge-shapes or drawing-objects on inactive layers. Modifying a shape's outline with the selection tool doesn't activate the shape's layer.

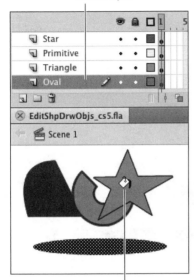

Active layer

Use paint bucket to modify
fill on inactive layer

No change in active layer

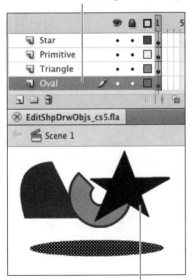

Flash fills shape with new color

B Using the paint-bucket tool to change a fill color on an inactive layer doesn't activate that layer.

3. Release the mouse button.

Flash redraws the shape **A**. The layer that was active originally remains active.

TIP Unlike with merge-shapes and drawing-objects, using the selection tool to modify the outline of a primitive on an inactive layer makes that layer active. You can start the modification—for example, using the selection tool to reposition the control points for a rectangle-primitive's corner radius—while the primitive is deselected; once you finish the modification, however, Flash selects the primitive on the Stage, and that layer becomes the active layer in the Timeline.

TIP The Bézier tools work to modify shapes only on active layers.

To edit fills across layers:

1. In a document with shapes on two or more layers, select the paint-bucket tool from the Tools panel.

2. From the Color panel, choose a new fill color.

3. Position the paint bucket over a shape on an inactive layer and click.

Flash fills the shape with the new color, but the layer remains inactive **B**.

TIP When you're working with merge-shapes, get into the habit of creating each one on a separate layer. That way, if you need to tweak the stacking order, you can. It won't hurt to have drawing-objects or primitives on separate layers too; more layers don't increase the file size of your final movie.

TIP Remember that any fill shapes that are selected when you choose a new fill color will change to that color. When you select a layer, all its elements get selected; be sure to deselect any shapes whose color you want to preserve before choosing a new fill color.

Cutting and Pasting Between Layers

Flash lets you create and place graphics only on the active layer of a document. But you can copy, cut, or delete elements from any visible, unlocked layer. You can select items on several layers, cut them, and then paste them all into a single layer. Or you can cut items individually from one layer, and redistribute them to separate layers.

To paste across layers:

1. Create or open a document that contains several layers.

2. Place at least one element on all but one layer.

   To make the elements easier to work with, create them as drawing-objects or primitives, or group each merge-shape. Leave one layer empty.

3. On the Stage, select a shape.

   Flash highlights the layer in the Timeline in blue.

4. Choose Edit > Copy.

5. In the Timeline, select the empty layer.

6. Choose Edit > Paste in Center.

   Flash pastes the copy of the shape in the empty layer, in the middle of the window **A**. Now you can move the shape to a new position, if you wish.

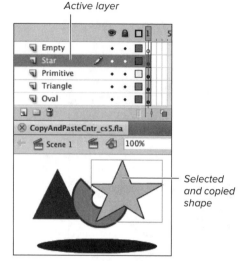

Active layer

Selected and copied shape

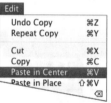

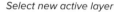

Select new active layer

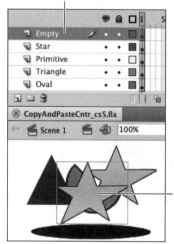

Shape pasted into the new layer

A Copying a shape from one layer to another involves selecting the shape (top), copying it, selecting the target layer, and then pasting the copy there. The Paste in Center command (middle) positions the pasted shape in the center of the window (bottom).

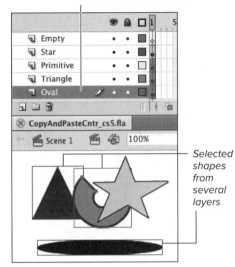

*Active layer is the layer
of the item last selected*

*Selected
shapes
from
several
layers*

After cutting the shapes

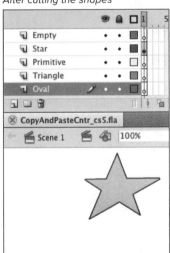

B The first step in consolidating items from several layers on a single new layer involves selecting all the items and cutting them. Later, you'll paste them into the new active layer.

To use the Paste in Place command across layers:

1. In a document that has several layers containing shapes and one layer that has no shapes, select one shape.

   In the Timeline, the layer containing the selected shape becomes the active layer.

2. Using the techniques you learned in Chapter 4, add other shapes to your selection.

   In the Timeline, the layer containing the most recent addition to the selection becomes the active layer.

3. Choose Edit > Cut.

   Flash removes the selected shapes **B**.

4. In the Timeline, select the empty layer.

continues on next page

Two Ways to Paste

Flash offers two pasting modes: Paste in Center and Paste in Place. Paste in Center puts elements in the center of the open Flash window. (Note that the center of the window may not necessarily be the center of the Stage; if you want to paste to the center of the Stage, you must center the Stage in the open window.) Paste in Place puts an element at the same *x*- and *y*-coordinates it had when you cut or copied it. Paste in Place is useful for preserving the precise relationships of all elements in a scene as you move items from one layer to another.

5. Choose Edit > Paste in Place .

Flash pastes all the shapes back into their original locations on the Stage but on a different layer . Try hiding the empty layer temporarily; you should no longer see those shapes.

TIP Selecting an element on the Stage causes Flash to select that element's layer in the Timeline. As you move elements between layers, it helps to know that selections work the other way around, too. When you select a layer in the Timeline, Flash selects all the elements for that layer on the Stage.

TIP The process of cutting elements and using the Paste in Place command is time-consuming, because you have to keep selecting new layers as you place the elements. To automate the process, use the Distribute to Layers command (see "Distributing Graphic Elements to Layers," the next section in this chapter).

Where Do Pasted Graphic Elements Go?

A Flash document can have only one layer active at a time. Any new shapes you create wind up on the currently selected, or active, layer. The same is true of placing copies of shapes or instances of symbols; if you copy and paste an element, Flash pastes the copy on the active layer. When you drag a symbol instance from the Library window, it winds up on the active layer.

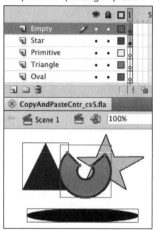

C Choose Edit > Paste in Place to paste items back into their original positions.

Shapes after pasting in place

Click to hide the layer

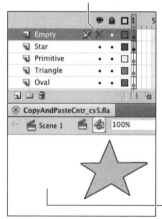

Layer containing the shapes is now hidden

D The Paste in Place command positions the pasted items in the new layer. Each shape occupies the same coordinates it had on its former layer, but now all the shapes are together on the new layer. Hide the new layer to make sure you moved the elements from their old layers.

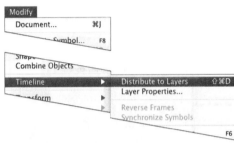

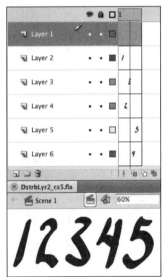

A Selecting elements on the Stage (top) and choosing Modify > Timeline > Distribute to Layers (middle) automatically cuts each element and pastes it in place in a new layer. The new layers follow the order in which you placed the elements on the Stage originally. In this series of numbers, the numeral 1 was drawn first, so it winds up at the top of the section of new layers (bottom).

Distributing Graphic Elements to Layers

As you draw elements for your movie, you may not always remember to create a new layer for each one. Using the Cut and Paste in Place commands can be tedious. Flash's Distribute to Layers feature automates the process, putting each element of a selection on a separate layer. This feature comes in handy when you start creating two types of animation—*motion tweening* and *classic tweening*—in which each element being animated must be on its own layer. (You'll learn about classic tweening in Chapter 9 and motion tweening in Chapter 11.)

To place selected elements on individual layers:

1. Open a new document, and, on the Stage, create several separate shapes on a single layer.

2. Choose Edit > Select All.

   Flash highlights all the shapes.

3. Choose Modify > Timeline > Distribute to Layers, or press Shift-Command-D (Mac) or Ctrl-Shift-D (Windows) A.

   Flash creates a layer for each shape and adds the new layers to the bottom of the Timeline. Each shape winds up in the same location on the Stage, but on a separate layer.

TIP Distribute to Layers works with selected graphic-objects (text fields, drawing-objects, primitives, groups, and symbols) as well as with selected raw shapes. (You learn about symbols in Chapter 7.) Flash distributes each selected graphic-object to its own layer; the various elements of the graphic-object remain joined.

Working with Guide Layers

Flash offers two types of guide layers: guides and motion guides. Plain old guides can contain any kind of content—lines, shapes, or symbols. The contents of a regular guide layer merely serve as a point of reference to help you position items on the Stage. Flash doesn't include the graphic content of guide layers in the final exported movie.

Motion-guide layers contain a single line that directs the movement of an animated element in a classic tween. (To learn more about using motion guides with classic tweens, see Chapter 9.) Another distinction to remember is that Flash creates motion guides by adding a new layer directly to the Timeline. To create plain guides, you must redefine an existing layer as a guide layer.

To create a plain guide layer:

1. Do either of the following:

    ▸ Create a new layer in the Timeline (for example, by clicking the Insert Layer button). Flash selects the new layer.

    ▸ Select a layer that already exists.

2. Control-click (Mac) or right-click (Windows) the layer you want to define as a guide, and choose Guide from the contextual menu .

    Flash turns the selected layer into a guide layer and places a little T-square icon before the layer name **B**.

    You can rename the layer to identify it as a guide, if you wish.

A Choose Guide as the layer type in the contextual menu for layers to change a normal layer to a guide layer.

B Select a layer (top) and define it as a guide layer. In the Timeline, Flash identifies the guide layer with a T-square icon; compare that with the icon for the motion-guide layer (bottom).

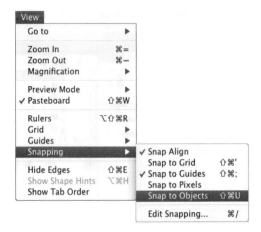

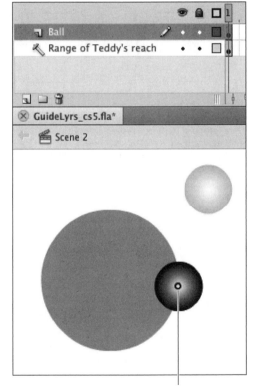

Center point snaps to other elements as you drag

C Choose View > Snapping > Snap to Objects (top) to force items that you drag to snap to other lines or shapes, such as those on a guide layer (bottom).

3. To make guide elements easier to use, choose View > Snapping, and from the submenu, choose any of the following settings:

► Choose Snap to Objects **C**.

Flash forces items that you draw or drag to snap to lines or shapes.

► Choose Snap Align.

Flash displays alignment guides as you drag shapes or graphic-objects near to other shapes or graphic-objects. Now you can more easily align items to the elements on your guide layers.

TIP When you've placed guide elements where you need them for a certain scene, lock the guide layer so you don't move the guides accidentally as you draw on other layers.

TIP The Snap to Guide feature doesn't help you snap to items on a guide layer; the guides in that feature are the guide lines you drag out from rulers (see Chapter 1).

TIP Because the graphic content of guide layers doesn't become part of your published movie, you can use guide layers as a space for making notes.

TIP When positioning layers beneath a guide layer, it's easy to transform the guide layer into a motion-guide layer by accident. (Motion guides are used in classic tweening.) As you drag a layer beneath a guide layer, watch the preview bar and the icon in the guide layer. To maintain the guide layer as a guide layer, drag to the left until the preview bar's small circle aligns with the left side of the guide layer's T-square icon. To create a motion-guide layer, drag to the right to align the circle with the right side of the T-square icon; the guide icon changes to a dotted arc icon indicating a motion guide (to learn about motion guides, see Chapter 9).

Working with Mask Layers

Mask layers are special layers that let you hide and show elements on underlying layers. In the final movie, shapes on the Mask layer become holes that let items on linked layers show through.

To create a mask layer:

1. Do either of the following:

   ▸ Create a new layer in the Timeline (for example, by clicking the Insert Layer button). Flash selects the new layer.

   ▸ Select a layer that already exists.

   In general, it's easier to create (or select) a layer directly above the layer containing content you want to mask, although you can always create the mask separately and link the masked layers to it later.

2. Control-click (Mac) or right-click (Windows) the layer to access the contextual menu for layers, and choose Mask **A**.

   Flash automatically defines the layer as a mask, links the layer beneath the selected layer to the mask, and locks both layers **B** so that masking is in effect. You can also rename the layer to identify it as a mask, if you wish.

   TIP To link existing layers to a mask layer quickly, drag them in the Timeline so they sit directly below the mask or one of its linked layers.

   TIP Once you have linked a layer to the mask, you can quickly create additional new linked layers. Select the linked (masked) layer, then follow the steps for creating a new layer. Flash adds the new layers as masked layers directly above the selected layer.

A To define a layer as a mask, choose Mask from the contextual menu for layers.

B The mask-layer icon imitates the masking effect with a dark mask shape over a checkerboard pattern. Masked layers are indented and have a checkerboard pattern on the layer icon in the Timeline, indicating that the layer is masked.

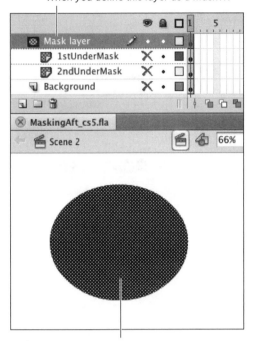

When you define this layer as a mask...

...this merge-shape fill becomes the mask

C The content for the layers that the mask will reveal is just like any other content. You must use fill shapes to create "holes" in the mask; all those shapes must be on the same sublevel of the mask layer. In other words, you must either use only merge-shapes or combine all your shapes into a single drawing-object.

TIP If you want to use multiple shapes in a mask, select them and turn them into a single drawing-object: choose Modify > Combine Objects > Union. You could also convert the selected shapes into a symbol.

To create the mask:

1. Create one or more layers containing graphic elements you want to reveal only through a mask.

2. Create a mask layer above your masked-content layers, and make sure that it's selected, visible, and unlocked.

   The layer should be highlighted in the Timeline, and the Eye and Lock columns should contain bullets (not X or padlock icons).

3. Use the drawing tools to create a fill shape on the mask layer **C**.

   Flash uses only fills to create the mask and ignores any strokes on the mask layer.

TIP It's best to limit your mask to a single merge-shape or a single graphic-object (drawing-object, primitive-shape, group, symbol, or Classic text field). If the mask layer contains multiple merge-shapes, the mask may work initially. Move one of the parts, however, and Flash may stop treating that shape as part of the mask. If the mask layer contains a merge-shape and a graphic-object, Flash uses just the merge-shape to create the mask. If the mask layer contains multiple graphic-objects, Flash uses just the bottom-most one. (For more details on stacking order for graphic-objects, see Chapter 5.)

TIP You cannot use TLF text to create masks in the shape of letters. When the bottom-most object on the mask layer is a TLF text field, the rectangular bounding box of the text field—not the letterforms themselves—defines the mask. To create letterform masks, use a Classic text field. Alternatively, you can start with TLF text, select it, and choose Modify > Break Apart; then select all the resulting drawing-object letters and convert them to a symbol. (Press F8 to access the Convert to Symbol dialog. You'll learn about creating symbols in Chapter 7.)

To see the mask's effect:

Lock the mask layer and all linked layers.

or

1. Control-click (Mac) or right-click (Windows) a mask (or masked) layer.

2. From the contextual menu, choose Show Masking 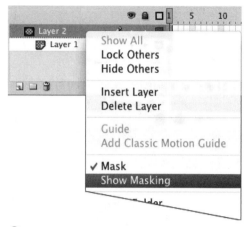.

   Flash automatically locks the mask layer and all the layers linked to it.

   In document-editing mode, you must lock the mask layer and any masked layers beneath it to see the mask effect **E**. You can see the effect without locking the layers in one of Flash's test modes (see Chapter 8).

D The Show Masking command in the contextual menu for layers locks the selected mask layer and all its linked layers.

Transparent fill helps you see what the mask will reveal

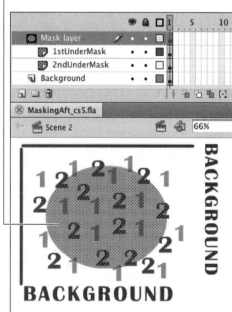

Masking not on

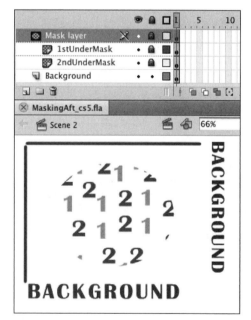

Masking turned on

E After defining the mask and masked layers, you must lock them to see the mask in effect in document-editing mode.

Practice Session

Try drawing a body to go with the fanciful face you created in Chapter 5's practice session; put each body part on a separate layer. Reposition and arrange the various elements to pose the figure.

- Create a dozen or so new layers. (See *Creating and Deleting Layers and Folders.*)

- Rename layers, assigning one body part to each—for example, neck, chest, shoulder, upper arm, elbow, forearm, hips, thigh, knee, and so on. (See *Setting Layer Properties > To rename a layer or folder.*)

- Create layer folders for major categories—for example, torso, arm, hand, leg—then organize individual layers by dragging them into the appropriate folders. (See *Organizing Layers.*)

- Use the drawing tools in Merge Drawing mode to create each part on its named layer.

- Position the various parts; note that you can overlap the various elements; they don't interact. (See Chapter 4.) Save your file for use in future Practice Sessions.

Extra Credit

- Redo the practice task, but this time use the drawing tools in Object Drawing mode to create all the body parts in a single layer. Then use the Distribute to Layers command to put each part on a separate layer. Rename the resulting layers and organize them in folders. (See *Distributing Graphic Elements to Layers.*)

Working with Symbols

In previous chapters, you learned to create and edit static graphics. Ultimately, you'll want to animate those graphics, and you'll probably want to use the same graphic over and over again. You may want an element to appear several times in one movie, or you may want to use the same element in several movies. You can save graphic elements for reuse by storing them in a library; to do that, you first turn the graphics into *symbols*.

Every Flash document has its own library; the library contains the symbols you create and other *assets*—reusable elements that you import for use in your movie (see the sidebar "Library Terminology").

In this chapter, you learn to work with libraries and to create symbols that are static graphics. In later chapters, you learn about creating animated symbols and buttons (see Chapters 12 and 14), using bitmapped graphics (see Chapter 16), and adding sound and video (see Chapter 17).

Using the Library Panel

The Library panel offers several ways to view a library's contents and allows you to organize your symbols, sounds, video clips, and bitmaps in folders. The Library panel provides information about when an item was last modified, what type of item it is, and how many times the movie uses it. The Library panel also contains a search feature for locating specific assets.

TIP If you'd like to know more about (using libraries), the previous edition of this book went into greater depth: those pages are available online when you register your book at the companion website (www.peachpit.com/flashcs5vqs).

To open the library of the current movie:

- Choose Window > Library, or press Command-L (Mac) or Ctrl-L (Windows) **A**.

  The Library panel appears on the desktop **B**. The Library panel contains the libraries of all the Flash documents currently open on your desktop.

A Choose Window > Library to open the Library panel of the currently active Flash document.

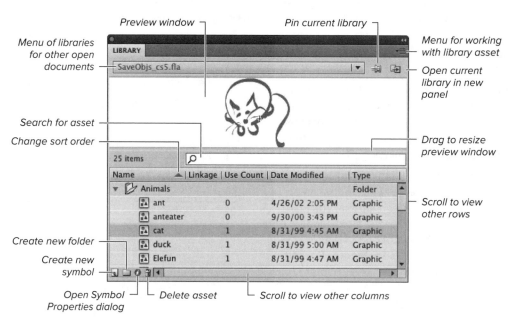

Preview window ⌐   Pin current library ⌐

Menu of libraries for other open documents

Menu for working with library asset

Open current library in new panel

Search for asset

Change sort order

Drag to resize preview window

Scroll to view other rows

Create new folder

Create new symbol

Open Symbol Properties dialog   Delete asset   Scroll to view other columns

B The Library panel lists the assets assigned to the current document. Items are sorted by the selected column; click the triangle in the column heading to reverse the sort order.

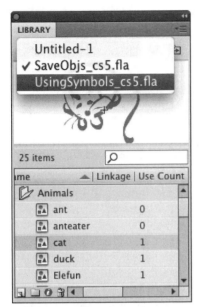

LIBRARY

Untitled-1
✓ SaveObjs_cs5.fla
UsingSymbols_cs5.fla

25 items

...me	▲ | Linkage | Use Count
📁 Animals	
🖼 ant	0
🖼 anteater	0
🖼 cat	1
🖼 duck	1
🖼 Elefun	1

C The Library panel contains the libraries of all the currently open documents. To view a different library without switching documents, choose one from the menu of open documents.

Library Terminology

The general term for an item stored in a Flash library is an *asset*. More specifically, graphics created with Flash's drawing tools and stored in a library are called *symbols;* embedded fonts stored in a library are called *font symbols;* and imported sounds, video clips, and bitmaps (which are always stored in a library) are just called *sounds, video clips,* and *bitmaps.* Flash refers to each copy of a library asset that you use in a movie as an *instance* of that asset.

To view the library of another open document:

1. Open two or more Flash documents.

2. With the Library panel open, do either of the following:

   ▸ In the Library panel, from the menu of open documents, choose the desired inactive document **C**.

   or

   ▸ Select the open document whose library you want to view.

   For documents in a tabbed window, click the document's tab; for documents in separate windows, from the Window menu, choose the desired window to make it active.

   The contents of the Library panel change to display the assets of the selected document.

TIP The Library panel displays the assets of just one document at a time. To view libraries for multiple documents simultaneously, open multiple Library panels. In the open Library panel, click the New Library Panel button (the double-document-arrow icon just below the panel menu). Flash opens the current library in a new panel window; you have two panels showing the assets of the same document. Choose a different library in one of the panels.

TIP The variety of menus from which you can open a library of some sort can be daunting at first. Here's a short rundown. To open the Library panel for an open, active document, choose Window > Library; to view the library of an open, inactive document, choose it from the menu of open documents in the Library panel; to open the library of a closed document, choose File > Import > Open External Library; to open one of the common libraries, choose Window > Common Libraries (see the sidebar "What Are Common Libraries?").

To open the library of a closed Flash document:

1. Choose File > Import > Open External Library, or press Shift-Command-O (Mac) or Ctrl-Shift-O (Windows) 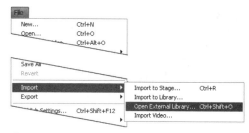.

   The Open As Library dialog appears.

2. Navigate to the file whose library you want to open, select it, and click Open.

   The Library panel appears on the desktop, making those symbols available for use in other movies.

D Choose File > Import > Open External Library to access symbols from the library of a closed Flash document.

What Are Common Libraries?

Flash makes a set of *common libraries* available from the Menu bar—a sort of library of libraries. Flash ships with three common libraries, but you can add your own. The libraries in the Common Libraries menu are Flash files that live in the Libraries folders of the language-specific Configuration folders at the application level. If you have administrative privileges, you can add FLA files to that folder. If you don't have privileges, you must add a folder named Libraries to the User-Level Configuration folder for your language installation. Any files you add to that Libraries folder also appear in the Common Libraries menu when you restart the application **E**. Choosing an item from the Common Libraries menu opens only the library, not the file itself.

You might create a common library to keep all the symbols, sounds, video clips, and bitmaps for a work project accessible from the Menu bar. As you create or import assets, add a copy of each item to a special file with a meaningful name—for example, MyShapes. Make the file one of your common libraries. When you choose MyShapes from the Window > Common Libraries menu, Flash opens the library containing all your project's items.

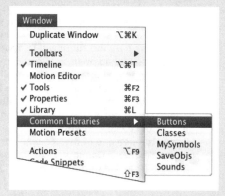

E The Common Libraries menu gives you quick access to the libraries of Flash Documents located inside a Libraries folder that's available to all users.

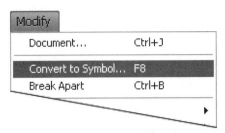

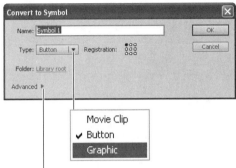

Click to show/hide
advanced settings

(A) To turn a selection into a symbol, choose Modify > Convert to Symbol. In the Convert to Symbol dialog, name your symbol, choose a type, and set the registration-point location. Click the Folder hot text to place the symbol into a folder in the library. (To work with advanced symbol settings, such as linkages for sharing and import/export, access the Advanced section of the dialog. Click the triangle to expand the dialog if necessary.)

Converting Graphics to Symbols

Not all graphics in a Flash movie are symbols; you need to take special steps to define the items you create as symbols. You can convert elements you've already created into symbols or create symbols from scratch in the symbol editor. Symbols reside in the library of the document in which you create them. You can copy a symbol from one document to another or from one library to another document; the symbol then resides separately in each document's library.

The standard library of a Flash document contains all the symbols used in that document; it can also contain unused symbols.

The following task covers creating static graphic symbols. But you can also turn graphics into symbols that are animations (see Chapter 12) or buttons (see Chapter 14).

To turn an existing graphic into a symbol:

1. On the Stage, select the graphic element(s) you want to convert to a symbol.

   Flash highlights the selected element(s).

2. Choose Modify > Convert to Symbol, or press F8 on the keyboard.

   The Convert to Symbol dialog **(A)** appears. Flash gives the symbol a default name—for example, Symbol 16—based on the number of symbols previously created for the library.

3. If you don't want to use the default name, type a new name for your symbol.

4. From the Type menu, choose Graphic.

continues on next page

5. To set the symbol's registration point (see the sidebar "Registration Point vs. Transformation Point for Symbols"), click one of the squares in the registration grid.

By default, Flash registers a symbol by the upper-left corner of its bounding box. Click a different square on the registration grid—another corner, the center, or the middle of a side—to make Flash register the symbol by the corresponding point on the symbol's bounding box.

6. Click OK.

Flash adds the symbol to the library hierarchy at the level currently set in the Folder area. The selected graphic element(s) on the Stage become an instance of the symbol. A crosshair appears, indicating the location of the registration point; a circle, known as the transformation point, appears at the center of the symbol **B**. You can no longer edit the item directly on the Stage; you must open it in one of Flash's symbol-editing modes.

Selected merge-shape

Converted to a symbol

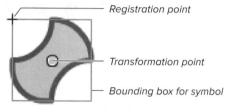

Registration point

Transformation point

Bounding box for symbol

B A selected merge-shape on the Stage is highlighted with dots. When you convert that shape to a symbol, the bounding box is the only item that gets highlighted. A crosshair indicates where the symbol's registration point is. A circle indicates the symbol's transformation point.

About Symbol Types

In Flash, you must specify a symbol type for each symbol. (In early versions of Flash, this was called the symbol's behavior.) You have three choices: graphic, button, and movie clip.

Graphic symbols are, as you might expect, graphic elements, but they can also be animated graphic elements. The feature that distinguishes one symbol type from another is the way the symbol interacts with the Timeline of the movie in which it appears. Graphic symbols operate in lockstep with the Timeline of the movie. A static graphic symbol takes up one frame of the movie in which you place it (just as any graphic element would). A three-frame animated graphic symbol takes up three frames of the movie (see Chapter 12).

Buttons have their own four-frame Timeline; a button instance sits in a single frame of the main movie Timeline but displays different frames as a user's mouse interacts with the button (see Chapter 14).

Movie clips have their own multiframe Timeline that plays independently of the main movie Timeline (see Chapter 12).

TIP The Folder hot text in the Convert to Symbol dialog lets you control where the new symbol winds up in the library hierarchy. By default, Flash puts new symbols at the root level of the library (the hot text says *Library root*). Clicking the hot text opens the Move to Folder dialog, which lets you select an existing folder or create (and select) a new folder. Flash places the new symbol into the selected folder.

TIP A graphic symbol can consist of one or more merge-shapes, drawing-objects, primitive-shapes, grouped shapes—you name it. You can even include symbols within symbols. Whatever is selected on the Stage when you choose Convert to Symbol becomes part of the symbol.

TIP To convert a graphic element to a symbol quickly, select the elements on the Stage and drag the selection to the lower half of the document's Library panel. The Convert to Symbol dialog appears. Name and define your symbol as described in the preceding task.

TIP The registration grid is elusive. It appears only in the Convert to Symbol dialog. That means you get one chance to use the grid to position the registration point at preset locations on the symbol's bounding box or at its center. However, you can always go into symbol-editing mode and reposition the graphic elements in relation to the registration point (see "Editing Master Symbols," later in this chapter).

Registration Point vs. Transformation Point for Symbols

The *registration point* (represented by a small crosshair) is the point that Flash uses to *register* a graphic-object—that is, to locate the object via coordinates on the Stage during authoring and playback. For drawing-objects, primitives, groups, and text fields, the registration point is always the upper-left corner of the object's bounding box. For symbols, the location of the registration point is flexible **C**. When you select elements on the Stage and convert the selection to a symbol, you can put the point at any of nine preset locations (see "Converting Graphics to Symbols," earlier in this chapter). When you create a symbol from scratch in symbol-editing mode, you determine where the registration point goes by positioning elements around a crosshair on the Stage (see the next section, "Creating Symbols from Scratch"). The location of the registration point stays the same for all instances of the same symbol.

The *transformation point* (represented by a small circle) is the reference point Flash uses for transforming the symbol instance. When you rotate a symbol with the free-transform tool in Rotate and Skew mode, for example, the transformation point is the pivot around which the symbol spins. You can also use the transformation point for snapping operations. By default, Flash places the transformation point in the center of a symbol instance, but you can change the transformation point's location for individual symbol instances by using the free-transform tool.

The Info panel and the Position and Size section of the Property inspector display coordinates that locate a selected symbol instance in space during authoring. The Position and Size section of the Property inspector always displays the coordinates of a symbol's registration point. The Info panel gives you the option to view coordinates for the registration point or the transformation point. You choose which method via the Registration/Transformation Point button (for more details about using the Info panel and the Position and Size section of the Property inspector, see Chapter 4).

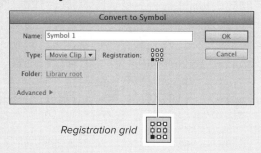

Registration grid

Converted symbol

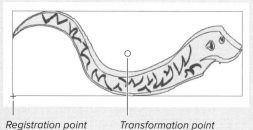

Registration point   Transformation point

Symbol from scratch

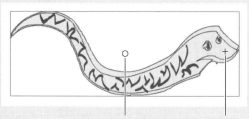

Transformation point   Registration point

C When you convert a selection to a symbol, the registration grid lets you position the registration point in the center, in any corner, or in the middle of any side of the symbol's bounding box; the location highlighted in the grid becomes the registration point in the symbol. When you create a symbol from scratch, you can position the registration point freely.

From the library's panel menu, choose New Symbol to create a symbol from scratch.

New Symbol button

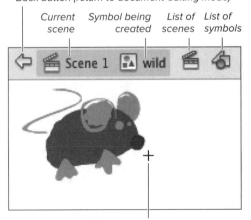

B Click the New Symbol button in the bottom-left corner of the Library panel to create a symbol from scratch.

Back button (return to document-editing mode)

Current scene | Symbol being created | List of scenes | List of symbols

Registration crosshair for symbol being created

C In symbol-editing mode, the name of the symbol being worked on appears in the Edit bar just above the Stage.

Creating Symbols from Scratch

You can avoid the conversion process described in the preceding section by creating graphics directly in symbol-editing mode. This practice makes all the tools, frames, and layers of the Flash editor available, but Flash defines the element you're creating as a symbol from the start.

To create a new symbol:

1. To enter symbol-editing mode, do one of the following:

   ▸ Choose Insert > New Symbol, or press Command-F8 (Mac) or Ctrl-F8 (Windows).

   ▸ From the Library's panel menu, choose New Symbol **A**.

   ▸ In the bottom-left corner of the Library panel, click the New Symbol button **B**.

   The Create New Symbol dialog appears.

2. Type a name for your symbol.

3. From the Type menu, choose Graphic.

4. Click OK.

   Flash enters symbol-editing mode. Flash displays the name of the symbol you're creating in the Edit bar, places a crosshair in the center of the Stage, and hides the Pasteboard **C**. The crosshair indicates the symbol's registration point.

5. Create your graphic on the Stage of the symbol editor as you would in the regular editing environment.

continues on next page

6. To return to document-editing mode, do one of the following:

▸ Choose Edit > Edit Document. Flash returns you to the current scene.

▸ In the Edit bar, click the Back button or the Current Scene link **D**. Flash returns you to the current scene.

▸ From the Edit Scene pop-up menu in the Edit bar, choose a scene **E**. Flash takes you to that scene.

TIP When you're creating new symbols, be sure to consider how the registration point should work with your finished symbol so you can place your graphic elements appropriately in relation to the registration crosshair. Will you want to align this symbol by its center? Then position your elements evenly around the crosshair. Will you want to align this symbol by a specific area? (You might want to register a bird figure, for example, by a point at the tip of the beak.) Then position your elements accordingly.

TIP When you start editing a symbol, the registration crosshair may be outside the current viewing area. To bring the registration crosshair into your window, choose View > Magnification > Show Frame or View > Magnification > Show All.

Back button

Current Scene link

D Click the Back button or the Current Scene link to return to document-editing mode.

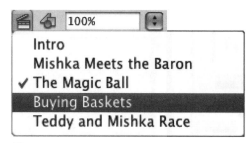

E Choose a scene from the Edit bar's Edit Scene menu to return to document-editing mode.

Where Am I?

When you edit symbols in a Flash document, the current window switches to symbol-editing mode. It's easy to get confused about whether you're editing the main document or a symbol. Learn to recognize the following subtle visual cues; they're the only indication that you're in symbol-editing mode.

In symbol-editing mode, a Flash document displays the name of the scene and symbol you're editing in the Edit bar and activates the Back button. If you entered symbol-editing mode by choosing Insert > New Symbol *or* Edit > Edit Symbols *or* Edit > Edit Selected, the Pasteboard disappears. If you double-click an existing symbol on the Stage, or choose Edit > Edit in Place, the pasteboard remains visible. Also, a small crosshair, which acts as a registration point for the symbol, appears on the Stage. If you entered symbol-editing mode via the Edit in Place command, any elements on the Stage that aren't being edited appear in a ghostly form. Apart from these changes, the Timeline, the Stage, and the tools all appear and work just as they do in document-editing mode.

Using Symbol Instances

A *symbol instance* is a pointer to the full description of the symbol. Symbols help keep file sizes small. If you converted a graphic on the Stage to a symbol, you have one symbol instance on the Stage. To use the symbol again, or if you created your symbol in symbol-editing mode, you'll need to get a copy out of the library and onto the Stage.

To place a symbol instance in your movie:

1. In the Timeline, select the layer and keyframe where you want the graphic symbol to appear.

   Flash can place symbols only in key-frames. If you select an in-between frame, Flash places the symbol in the preceding keyframe. (To learn more about keyframes, see Chapter 8.)

2. Access the library containing the symbol.

3. In the Library panel, navigate to the symbol you want; click it to select it.

   Flash highlights the chosen symbol and displays it in the preview window.

4. Position the pointer over the preview window.

5. Click and drag a copy of the symbol onto the Stage.

   Flash previews the symbol's location on the Stage with a rectangular outline as you drag 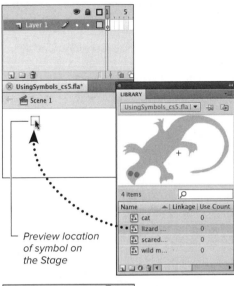.

6. Release the mouse button.

   Flash places the symbol on the Stage and selects it.

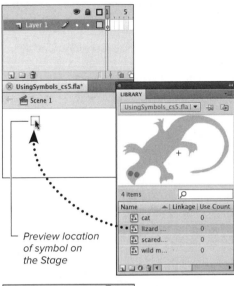

Preview location of symbol on the Stage

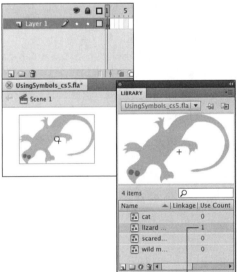

Use count updated

A When you drag a symbol from the Library panel to the Stage (top), Flash places the symbol on the Stage, selects it, and updates that symbol's use count.

TIP To place a symbol instance quickly, drag the symbol name directly from the Library panel to the Stage without using the previewed image.

Modifying Symbol Instances

You can change the appearance of individual symbol instances without changing the master symbol itself. As with any other element, you can resize and reposition an instance (for example, scale and rotate it) by using the tools in the Tools panel, Info and Transform panels, and the Position and Size section of the Property inspector (see Chapter 4).

You can also change a symbol instance's color and transparency, but the method differs from the methods you've learned for assigning colors to merge-shapes, drawing-objects, and primitive-shapes. You modify the color, intensity, and transparency of a symbol instance in the Color Effect section of the Property inspector.

To change an instance's color property:

1. On the Stage, select the symbol instance you want to modify.

2. Access the Property inspector.

   Settings for the symbol instance appear.

3. In the Color Effect section, from the Style menu, choose one color property to modify.

   The properties available for you to modify are Brightness (amount of black or white in the color), Tint, Advanced (simultaneous changes to alpha and RGB values), and Alpha (transparency).

4. Enter settings for your selected color change as outlined in the tasks that follow.

   Flash applies the new settings to the symbol on the Stage.

Tips for Transforming Symbols

You can change the dimensions and orientation of symbol instances using the same techniques you use to modify graphic-objects (see Chapter 4). You can enter precise values in the Position and Size section of the Property inspector or in the Transform or Info panels; you can also modify symbol instances interactively with the free-transform tool. Here are some tips for using that tool.

When you use the free-transform tool to scale a symbol instance, it scales in relation to the instance's transformation point (by default, the center of the symbol instance). Hold down the Option key (Mac) or Alt key (Windows) to scale the symbol instance relative to the bounding-box corner diagonally, opposite the corner you're dragging.

You can change the transformation point of individual symbol instances. Using the free-transform tool, click the small white circle in the middle of the symbol instance. Drag the circle to a new location.

To position a symbol instance's transformation point at the same location as the symbol's registration point, select the instance with the free-transform tool. Then double-click the transformation point.

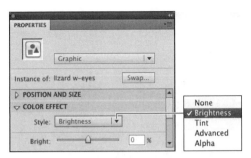

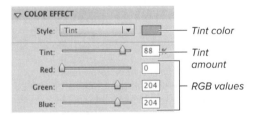

A Use the Brightness settings in the Color Effect section of the Property inspector to change the intensity of a symbol instance. A high value will make the symbol instance lighter or a low value will make it darker.

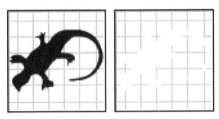

*–100 percent
brightness setting*

*100 percent
brightness setting*

B At its extremes, the Brightness setting lets you turn a symbol instance completely black or completely white.

C Use the Tint settings in the Color Effect section of the Property inspector to change the color of a symbol instance.

To change an instance's brightness:

1. In Step 3 of the preceding task, from the Style menu, choose Brightness.

   A Bright slider and a field for entering a brightness percentage appear **A**.

2. To change the symbol's brightness, use the Bright slider or type a percentage in the brightness-amount field.

   A value of –100 makes the symbol black; a value of 0 leaves the symbol at its original brightness; a value of 100 makes the symbol white **B**.

To change the instance's color:

1. In Step 3 of the first task in this section, from the Style menu, choose Tint.

   Tint settings appear **C**.

2. To choose a new color, do either of the following:

   ▸ Use the Red, Green, and Blue sliders or type new values in the Red Color, Green Color, and Blue Color fields.

   ▸ Click the Tint Color control, and choose a color from the pop-up swatch set.

3. Use the Tint slider or type a percentage in the tint-amount field.

   The tint percentage indicates how much of the new color to blend with the existing colors. Applying a tint of 100 percent changes all the lines and fills in the symbol to the new color. Applying a lesser percentage mixes some of the new color with the existing colors in the symbol; it's almost like placing a transparent film of the new color over the symbol.

To change the instance's transparency:

1. In Step 3 of the first task in this section, from the Style menu, choose Alpha.

   The Alpha settings appear 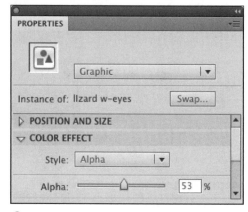.

2. To change the amount of transparency, use the Alpha slider or type a new value in the alpha-amount field.

   A value of 0 makes the symbol completely transparent; a value of 100 makes the symbol opaque.

D To change the transparency of a selected symbol instance, access the Color Effect section of the Property inspector. From the Style menu choose Alpha, then use the Alpha slider or the text field to enter a new alpha amount. A lower percentage makes the symbol instance more transparent.

Duplicating Master Symbols

If you need to use one variation of a symbol repeatedly, you can duplicate the original master symbol and then modify the duplicate to create a new master symbol with those variations. In the Library panel, select a symbol. From the panel menu, choose Duplicate. Flash opens the Duplicate Symbol dialog, giving the duplicate symbol a default name. If you want, type a new name for your symbol. Choose the symbol type—for example, Graphic. Click OK. Use the Folder hot text to place the duplicate in a specific location. A duplicate symbol doesn't link to the original symbol in any way. You can change the duplicate without changing the original, and vice versa.

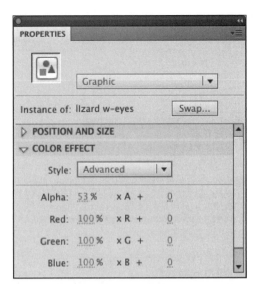

E To change the color and transparency of a selected symbol instance, choose Advanced from the Style menu in the Color Effect section of the Property inspector. Use the hot-text controls in the left-hand column to enter new percentages for Alpha, Red, Green, and Blue; use the hot-text controls in the right-hand column to enter new values for the offset of Alpha, Red, Green, and Blue.

To change the instance's tint and alpha simultaneously:

1. In Step 3 of the first task in this section, from the Style menu, choose Advanced.

   Settings for percentage and offset for Alpha, Red, Green, and Blue appear in the Color Effect section of the Property Inspector **E**.

2. Adjust the values to fine-tune the color and transparency of the symbol instance (see the sidebar "The Mystery of Advanced Effect Settings").

   Click the hot text to enter a precise value; drag the hot text's invisible slider to choose a value interactively.

The Mystery of Advanced Effect Settings

The Advanced color-effect settings let you change the RGB values and alpha values for a symbol instance simultaneously. The percentage hot-text controls (in the left-hand column) determine what percentage of the master symbol's original RGB and alpha values to apply to the symbol instance. The offset hot-text controls (in the right-hand column) add to or subtract from the alpha, red, green, and blue values of the original colors.

Imagine a symbol with three ovals. One is pure red, one is pure green, and one is pure blue. The alpha setting is 50 percent. Decreasing the red-percentage value affects only the red oval, making it less red. (A red-percentage of 0 would make the red oval totally black.) The green and blue ovals contain 0 percent red to start with; decreasing the red-percentage value makes no visible change to these ovals. Increasing the red-offset value adds red to everything; the green and blue ovals change color. (If you decrease the red-offset value, you'll see no difference in the green and blue ovals because they contained no red to begin with, but you will see a lower percentage of red in the red oval.)

Editing Master Symbols

After you create a symbol, you can refine and modify it in symbol-editing mode. Unlike modifications of a symbol instance, which affect just that instance on the Stage and leave the master symbol in the library unchanged, modifications made in symbol-editing mode affect the master symbol and all instances of that symbol in your movie.

You can enter symbol-editing mode in several ways.

To enter symbol-editing mode from the Stage:

1. On the Stage, select the symbol you want to edit.

2. To open the symbol editor, do one of the following:

   ▸ Choose Edit > Edit Symbols, or press Command-E (Mac) or Ctrl-E (Windows) 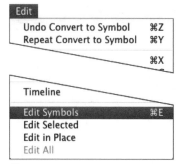.

   ▸ Choose Edit > Edit Selected.

   ▸ From the pop-up list of symbols in the Edit bar, choose the symbol you want to edit .

   Flash opens the symbol editor in the current window. You can edit the symbol using any of the techniques you've learned for modifying graphics and creating and deleting content.

TIP The Edit in Place command lets you edit your master symbol in context on the Stage with all other items dimmed **C**. To evoke the Edit in Place command, select a symbol instance and choose Edit > Edit in Place or double-click a symbol instance on the Stage. Any changes you make affect all instances of that symbol.

A Choosing Edit > Edit Symbols takes you from document-editing mode to symbol-editing mode. If you have selected a symbol on the Stage, choosing Edit > Edit Selected also takes you to symbol-editing mode.

B Choosing a symbol from the Edit Symbol pop-up menu in the Edit bar takes you into symbol-editing mode.

C The Edit in Place command lets you see your symbol instance in context with other items on the Stage. The symbol instance appears in full color (here it's the large ant); the other elements on the Stage are dimmed. In this mode, changes made to the instance affect the master symbol and all the instances in the movie.

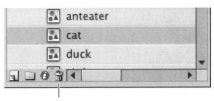

Delete selected item

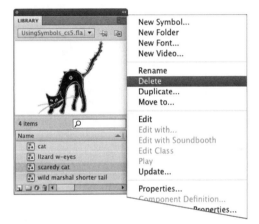

A Click the trash-can icon to delete a selected library item.

B You can also choose Delete from the library's panel menu to remove selected symbols from the active document.

Deleting Master Symbols

Deleting symbols can be a little trickier than deleting shapes or groups on the Stage. Deleting one instance of a symbol from its place on the Stage is easy; use the methods for cutting or deleting graphics discussed in Chapter 4. Deleting symbols from the library isn't difficult but does require some thought, because instances of the symbol may still be in use in your movie.

To delete one symbol from the library:

1. In the Library panel, select the symbol you want to remove.

2. To delete the symbol, do any of the following:

   ▸ At the bottom of the panel, click the Delete button (the trash-can icon) **A**.

   ▸ From the panel menu in the top-right corner of the window, choose Delete **B**.

   ▸ Press the Delete key.

TIP Always check the numbers in the Use Count column before you delete library items **C**. You don't want to delete a symbol that you're currently using in a movie, which is especially easy to do if you've nested symbols within symbols. Some earlier versions of Flash warned you when you tried to delete an item that was in use in a movie. Flash CS5 doesn't.

TIP In addition to individual assets, a library can contain hierarchical folders. To create a new folder, click the New Folder button at the bottom of the Library panel, or choose New Folder from the panel menu. To delete a folder, select it, then follow Step 2 above.

C Before deleting a symbol from the library, be sure to check the use count. It's safest to delete only items with a use count of zero. If the use count is not zero, track down where instances of the symbol appear in the movie and delete them there first; then you can safely delete the master symbol in the library.

The Mystery of Object-Level Undo

Every computer user gets familiar with the Undo command. Command-Z (Mac) or Ctrl-Z (Windows) becomes an automatic "oops" response to fix mistakes. Flash CS5 provides two types of undo: *document-level* undo and *object-level* undo.

In document-level undo, Flash tracks every undoable step you take. Open the History panel (choose Window > Other Panels > History); you'll see the steps you've done listed in order. In object-level undo, Flash also tracks every undoable step but makes a distinction between steps that pertain to working in the main document and steps that pertain to working on master symbols.

Object-level undo tracks the steps for each master symbol separately; each time you create a master symbol, object-level undo starts a separate History-panel list for that symbol. Within one work session, whenever you edit that master symbol, the History panel loads the steps for that symbol (provided you haven't made changes in the History panel yourself); any edits you make are added to the list. If you edit a different symbol, the panel loads the steps for that symbol. When you leave symbol-editing mode and return to document-editing mode, the History panel displays only the steps you've used in the main document.

Note that modifications you make to an instance of a symbol on the Stage are part of the history of the document, not of the master symbol.

To change from one type of undo to the other, choose Flash > Preferences (Mac) or Edit > Preferences (Windows). In the General category, from the Undo menu, choose the style you want. To track the history of master symbols separately, choose Object-Level Undo; to track all your steps in one integrated list, choose Document-Level Undo. It's best to choose your undo style at the beginning of a work session. If you switch in the middle, Flash wipes the current History panel clean.

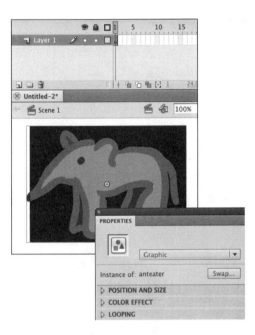

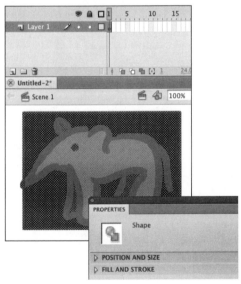

Converting Symbol Instances to Graphics

At times, you'll want to break the link between a placed instance of a symbol and the master symbol. You may want to redraw the shape in a specific instance but not in every instance, for example. To convert a symbol back to an independent shape or set of shapes, break it apart.

To break the symbol link:

1. On the Stage, select the symbol instance whose link you want to break.

2. Choose Modify > Break Apart, or press Command-B (Mac) or Ctrl-B (Windows) **A**.

   Flash breaks the link to the symbol in the library and selects the symbol's elements. The Property inspector no longer displays information about the instance of the symbol; it displays information about the selected shapes.

   If the original symbol contained any grouped elements, they remain grouped after you break the link; ungrouped elements stay ungrouped. Any symbols that existed within the original symbol remain as instances of their respective master symbols. Now you can edit these elements as you learned to do in previous chapters.

A The Property inspector reveals that the selected graphic is an instance of a symbol named anteater (top). To break the link with its master symbol, choose Modify > Break Apart. The Property inspector reveals that the selection now consists of shapes; it's no longer a symbol instance (bottom).

Swapping One Symbol Instance for Another

Flash lets you replace one symbol instance with another while retaining all the modifications you've made in the symbol instance. If, for example, you want to change the look of a logo in certain places in your site but not everywhere, you can create the new logo as a separate symbol and swap it in as needed. (To change the look for every instance, edit the master logo symbol directly, as you learned to do in "Editing Master Symbols," earlier in the chapter.) You can perform symbol swapping via menu command or in the Property inspector 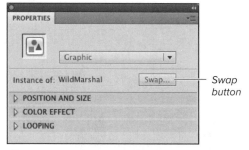.

A The Swap button in the Property inspector lets you replace a selected symbol instance with an instance of a different symbol from the same document.

To switch symbols:

1. On the Stage, select the symbol instance you want to change.

2. Do either of the following:

   ▸ Choose Modify > Symbol > Swap Symbol.

   ▸ In the Property inspector, click the Swap button.

   The Swap Symbol dialog appears, listing all the symbols in the current document's library **B**. Flash highlights the name of the symbol you're modifying and places a bullet next to the name in the Symbol list.

3. From the Symbol list, select the replacement symbol.

   The original symbol remains bulleted; Flash highlights the new symbol and places it in the preview window.

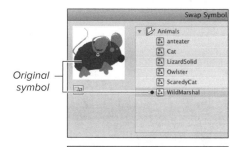

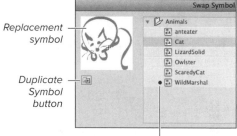

B Select a replacement symbol from the list in the Swap Symbol dialog, and click OK to exchange one symbol for another.

Before swapping: mouse scaled and rotated

After swapping: scaling and rotation applied to cat

C When you swap symbols, any modifications you have made for the selected instance you're swapping apply to the replacement instance.

4. Click OK.

Flash places the new symbol in the old symbol's location and applies any modifications you previously made for that instance **C**.

TIP To swap symbols quickly, double-click the new symbol in the Swap Symbol dialog. Flash replaces it and closes the dialog.

TIP The Duplicate Symbol button in the Swap Symbol dialog lets you make a copy of whatever symbol is selected in the list **B**. If you need to tweak the master version of the replacement symbol for this instance, and you want to keep the current version, click the Duplicate Symbol button, enter a name in the dialog that appears, and click OK. Make sure you select the duplicate as the replacement in the Swap Symbol dialog, and click OK. You can edit the duplicate's master symbol later.

A Note About Blend Modes

Blend modes give designers control over the way graphics in different layers and sublayers interact, letting you create new colors and interesting effects. Use blends for compositing—overlapping images to combine them or to enhance or correct flaws in digital photos (for example, to lighten shadows). You can use blending with two types of symbols: buttons and movie clips. Select a button or movie-clip instance on the Stage. In the Display section of the Property inspector, from the Blending menu, choose a blend mode. Blending changes the selected symbol's colors on a pixel-by-pixel basis. Whether a particular pixel in the selected symbol instance actually changes color depends on the type of blend, the color of the pixel in the symbol instance, and the color of the pixel that lies on the layer below the button or movie clip. The pixels on lower layers may be other buttons, movie clips, graphic elements, or the background color of the Stage.

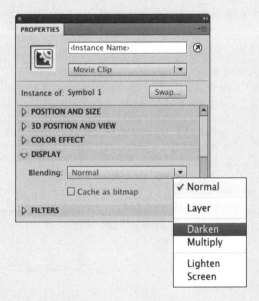

Practice Session

Try creating a tower of stacked "blocks" in a single layer of a new Flash document; each item in the tower should be a symbol.

- Using the geometric-shape tools, create several basic shapes on the Stage—for example, a rectangle, a perfect square, an oval, a perfect circle, and a five-pointed star. (See Chapter 2.)

- One at a time, select each shape and convert it to a symbol; give each symbol an individual name. (See *Converting Graphics to Symbols*.)

- Make duplicates and variations of your symbols. For example, in the Library panel, select a rectangle with a vertical orientation and duplicate it. Edit the duplicate and change the orientation of the rectangle to horizontal; give the duplicate a new name. (See *Editing Master Symbols* and the *sidebar Duplicating Master Symbols*. See Chapter 4, *Flipping, Rotating, and Skewing*.)

- Place all instances of all the symbols on the Stage in one layer (use multiple instances of some symbols). Stack up the symbols, one above another, to create a "tower" of geometric shapes; resize the symbol instances so the bottom-most shape is the largest and each symbol instance above is smaller. (See *Using Symbol Instances* and *Modifying Symbol Instances.)*

- Modify the transparency of the symbols on the Stage; make the instances toward the top of the tower increasingly transparent, as if the tower is so tall it disappears into the stratosphere. (See *Modifying Symbol Instances*.)

Extra Credit

Turn the document containing the symbols you just created into a Common Library so you can use these symbols for practice anytime. (See the sidebar *What Are Common Libraries?*)

- In symbol-editing mode, using the brush, pencil, and Bézier tools, create other, more complex symbols. You might, for example, try recreating the face from Chapter 5's practice session as one symbol; then recreate the body parts from Chapter 6's practice session, putting each item into a separate symbol. (See *Creating Symbols from Scratch*.)

Frame-by-Frame Animations

Frame-by-frame animation was the conventional form of animation before computers. Live-action movies and video are really a form of frame-by-frame animation. The camera captures motion by snapping a picture every so often. Animation simulates motion by showing drawings of elements at various stages of a movement. Traditional animators, such as those who worked for Walt Disney from the 1930s through the 1960s, created hundreds of images, each slightly different from the next, to achieve every movement of each element in the cartoon. Animating those drawings meant capturing the images on film, putting a different image in each frame of the movie. Traditional animators painted characters (or parts of characters) and graphics on transparent sheets called *cels*. They stacked the cels to create the entire image for the frame. The cel technique allows animators to reuse parts of an image that stay the same in more than one frame.

Adobe Flash Professional CS5 lets you, make frame-by-frame animations by placing different content in different frames called *keyframes*.

In This Chapter

Touring the Timeline

When you create a new Flash document, the Timeline displays a single layer with hundreds of little boxes. The first box has a solid black outline and displays a hollow bullet; the bullet indicates that the frame has been defined as a *keyframe* (a container for content, such as graphics, sound, and video). A hollow bullet indicates a *blank keyframe* (one with no content on the Stage). When you place graphics on the Stage for a keyframe, the Timeline displays a solid bullet. The rest of the boxes have gray outlines; these are undefined placeholder frames, or *protoframes*. Every fifth protoframe is tinted gray.

As you work with the Timeline to create animation, you will convert protoframes into *frames* (or *in-between frames*) and *keyframes*, creating *spans* in the process. A span consists of a keyframe plus any in-between frames that follow it. Flash CS5 creates three types of spans: *keyframe spans,* which are used in frame-by-frame animation, classic tweening (Chapter 9), and shape tweening (Chapter 10); *tween spans,* which are used in motion tweening (Chapter 11); and *pose spans,* which are used in inverse kinematics (Chapter 13). In this chapter, you'll work solely with keyframe spans.

Flash outlines keyframe spans with black in the Timeline and puts a hollow rectangle in the last frame of the span. When the keyframe at the beginning of a span has content, the in-between frames in the span continue to display that content on the Stage. If you've set Frame View to Tinted Frames (the default), the in-between frames of a keyframe span with content also have a gray tint in the Timeline. **A** shows a Timeline with a variety of defined frames and spans.

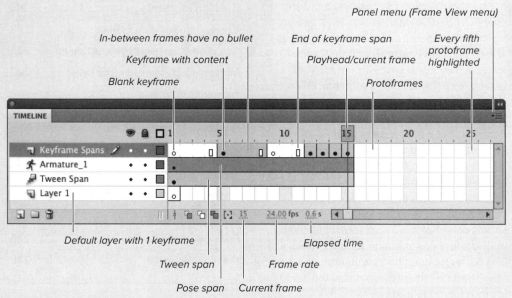

A Similar to an interactive outline, the Timeline represents each frame of your movie. Click any frame, and Flash displays its contents on the Stage.

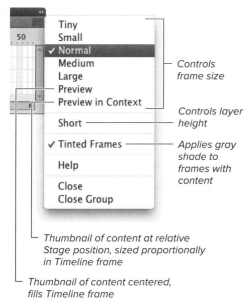

Tiny
Small
✓ Normal
Medium — Controls
Large   frame size
Preview
Preview in Context

Short — Controls layer
         height

✓ Tinted Frames — Applies gray
                   shade to
Help   frames with
                   content
Close
Close Group

Thumbnail of content at relative
Stage position, sized proportionally
in Timeline frame

Thumbnail of content centered,
fills Timeline frame

Ⓐ The Timeline's panel menu gives options for
viewing the frames in the Timeline.

Optimizing the Timeline

The Timeline is the framework that holds all the little slices of motion that make up an animation. The Timeline displays the layers and frames of the currently active document. New documents automatically start with a Timeline containing one layer and a blank keyframe as the first frame. You add more frames to hold content and tweens.

To view frames at different sizes:

- In the Timeline, from the panel menu (also known as the Frame View menu), choose a display option **Ⓐ**.

  Flash resizes the frame representations in the Timeline to reflect your choice (see the sidebar "Frames of Many Sizes").

When to Use Frame-by-Frame Animation

Frame-by-frame animation displays multiple images, each slightly different from the next to create the illusion of motion; each image requires its own keyframe. Each keyframe adds a bit to your final movie's file size, which in turn affects the download time for people viewing your movie over the web.

Reserve frame-by-frame techniques for animations where shapes must constantly change or move in subtle ways that you can best control by redrawing. Otherwise, use Flash's classic-tweening, shape-tweening, and motion-tweening features (see Chapters 9 through 12).

In this chapter you place a shape in multiple keyframes, making a circle seem to bounce like a ball. You could minimize file size by converting the ball shape to a symbol and reusing it in the keyframes (adding keyframes with the same symbol adds little to the size of the file). In the real world, however, if you can use a symbol, it would be more efficient to use one of Flash's tweening methods.

Frames of Many Sizes

The Timeline's panel menu (also known as the Frame View menu) gives you options for setting frame size for viewing the Timeline. For documents with many layers and frames, choosing Tiny from the menu lets you squeeze the greatest number of frames into the panel, but it can be hard to distinguish what you're seeing. Normal and Medium are better choices when you need to distinguish keyframes with content from blank keyframes or in-between frames. The Preview mode and Preview in Context mode let you see thumbnails of a keyframe's content within the Timeline. Figure **B** shows some of the frame views.

Normal

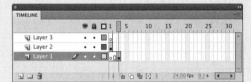

Tiny

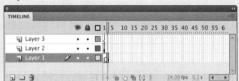

Large

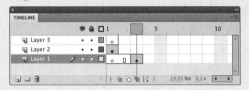

Preview

Empty keyframe

Keyframe with content

B Flash can display the frames in the Timeline in a variety of sizes, from Tiny to Large. You can also preview the contents of each frame in the Timeline.

Timeline History

In versions of Flash before CS4, each document had its own Timeline that appeared within the document itself (on the Mac, if you had multiple open documents, you saw multiple Timelines). In CS4 and later versions, each document has its own Timeline information, but the Timeline appears in a separate panel. You can see just one Timeline at a time.

The Timeline offers five size options for viewing frames and two options for previewing thumbnails of frame contents. A Flash movie may contain hundreds of frames; the Timeline's scroll bars let you access frames not currently visible in the Timeline panel. The Timeline works just like any other Flash panel. You can open and close the Timeline, resize it, dock it, collapse it to an icon, and so on (see Chapter 1).

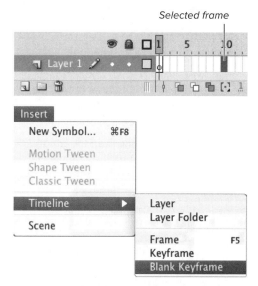

Selected frame

Last frame where content from
Keyframe 1 is visible

A To prepare for adding frames, click a protoframe to select it in the Timeline. To add a blank keyframe, choose Insert > Timeline > Blank Keyframe. The new blank keyframe appears at the frame you selected, defined frames fill out the preceding keyframe span.

Context Menu for Frames

The tasks in this section access frame-related commands from the Menu bar, but all the relevant commands for working with frames are available from the contextual frame menu as well. Control-click (Mac) or right-click (Windows) a frame in the Timeline to bring up the contextual frame menu.

Creating Keyframes

Flash offers two commands for creating keyframes. Insert > Timeline > Blank Keyframe defines a keyframe that's empty; use this command when you want to change the contents of the Stage completely. Insert > Timeline > Keyframe defines a keyframe that duplicates the content of the preceding keyframe in that layer; use this command when you want to modify the content of the preceding keyframe.

To add a blank keyframe to the end of your movie:

1. Create a new Flash document.

   The new document by default has one layer and one blank keyframe at Frame 1. If you like, add content to Frame 1.

2. In the Timeline, click the protoframe for Frame 10 to select it.

3. Choose Insert > Timeline > Blank Keyframe **A**.

   Flash revises the Timeline to give you information about the frames you've defined. A hollow rectangle appears in Frame 9, and a black line separates Frame 9 from Frame 10. This line indicates where the content for one keyframe span ends and the content for the next keyframe begins. Flash replaces the gray bars separating Protoframes 2 through 9 with tiny gray tick marks and removes the gray highlight that appeared in every fifth frame of the undefined frames.

To create a blank keyframe within a keyframe span:

1. Follow the steps in the preceding task to create a single-layer, ten-frame movie.

2. In the Timeline, select Frame 1.

3. Draw a shape on the Stage.

   Flash updates the Timeline, adding a solid bullet to Frame 1 **B**.

   With Tinted Frames chosen in the panel menu (Flash's default setting), Flash shades Frames 1 through 9 with gray. The shading indicates that Keyframe 1 has content that remains visible through Frame 9 in this layer. A hollow rectangle appears in Frame 9, indicating the end of the span of in-between frames that displays the content of Keyframe 1.

   Frame 10 still contains a hollow bullet, meaning that it has no content.

4. In the Timeline, in the area above the layers, click the number 5 or drag the playhead to position it in Frame 5.

   Flash displays Frame 5 on the Stage. Notice that this in-between frame continues to display the content of the preceding keyframe, Frame 1.

5. Choose Insert > Timeline > Blank Keyframe.

   Flash converts the current in-between frame to a keyframe and removes all content from the Stage **C**.

B When you place content in a keyframe, Flash displays that frame in the Timeline with a solid bullet. The gray tint on the in-between frames indicates that content from the preceding keyframe appears during these frames. The hollow square indicates the end of the span of in-between frames displaying the same content. The hollow circle indicates a blank keyframe.

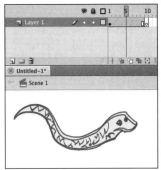

C When you convert an in-between frame that displays content to a blank keyframe, Flash removes that frame's content from the Stage. Frames 6 through 9 are tinted when they display the content of Frame 1 (left). When you insert a blank keyframe at Frame 5 (right), the tint disappears, because these frames now display the content of the most recent keyframe, Frame 5, which is empty.

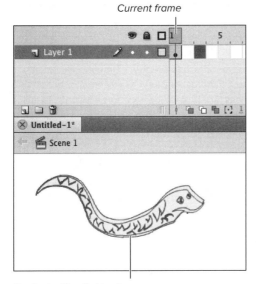

Current frame

Content of the first keyframe

Duplicate of the first keyframe

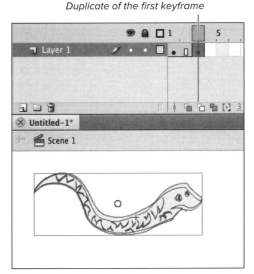

D The Insert > Timeline > Keyframe command creates a keyframe that duplicates the content of the preceding keyframe in that layer.

To duplicate the contents of the preceding keyframe:

1. Open a new Flash document and place content in Keyframe 1.

2. In the Timeline, select Frame 3.

   The playhead doesn't move into the protoframe area, but Frame 3 is highlighted as the current selected frame.

3. Choose Insert > Timeline > Keyframe.

   Flash creates a new keyframe, duplicates the contents of Frame 1 in Frame 3, and places a solid bullet in the Timeline at Frame 3 and a hollow rectangle in Frame 2 **D**. The content of Frames 1 and 3 is totally separate.

TIP The word *insert* used in connection with keyframes is a bit misleading. Choosing Insert > Timeline > Keyframe adds frames only if you've selected a protoframe. If you select an existing in-between frame, Insert > Timeline > Keyframe converts that frame to a keyframe and leaves the length of the movie as it was. The Insert > Timeline > Frame command always adds frames to your movie.

TIP You can't add a blank keyframe between back-to-back keyframes. With keyframes in Frames 5 and 6, select Frame 5 and choose Insert > Timeline > Blank Keyframe. The playhead moves to Frame 6, but Flash doesn't add a new blank keyframe. With Frame 5 selected, you must choose Insert > Timeline > Frame. Flash creates an in-between frame at Frame 6. Now select Frame 5 or Frame 6 and choose Insert > Timeline > Blank Keyframe; Flash converts Frame 6 to a keyframe.

Keyframe Mysteries: Insert vs. Convert

In addition to the Insert > Timeline > Keyframe and Insert > Timeline > Blank Keyframe commands, Flash offers commands for converting frames to keyframes. Choose Modify > Timeline > Convert to Keyframes (or press F6) or choose Modify > Timeline > Convert to Blank Keyframes (or press F7). These conversion commands are also found in the contextual menu for frames—Control-click (Mac) or right-click (Windows) a frame in the Timeline to access the menu.

Whether you should insert or convert keyframes depends on how many frames you have selected when you issue the command and how many frames you want to create. The Insert commands create a single keyframe regardless of how many frames you have selected; the Modify commands create multiple keyframes, one for each selected frame.

With a single frame selected, the Insert > Timeline > Keyframe command and the Modify > Timeline > Convert to Keyframe command work identically. If you select one protoframe or one in-between frame, both commands transform the frame to a keyframe and duplicate the content of the preceding keyframe (if any). If you select a keyframe that is followed by an in-between frame or a protoframe, both commands transform that following frame to a keyframe with the same content as the selected frame. Neither command has any effect on a selected keyframe that is followed by another keyframe.

With multiple protoframes or in-between frames selected, the Insert > Timeline > Keyframe command creates a single keyframe, usually in the same frame as the playhead (if you select frames at the end of your movie, Flash places the new keyframe in the last selected frame). The remaining selected frames become in-between frames.

With multiple protoframes or in-between frames selected, the Modify > Timeline > Convert to Keyframes command creates a keyframe in every selected frame.

The commands for blank keyframes work similarly. Insert > Timeline > Blank Keyframe creates one keyframe in the same frame as the playhead; the remaining frames become in-between frames. Modify > Timeline > Convert to Blank Keyframes creates a blank keyframe in each of the selected frames.

These commands work a bit differently when used within the tween span of a motion tween (see Chapter 11).

A Choose Insert > Timeline > Frame to add in-between frames to the Timeline.

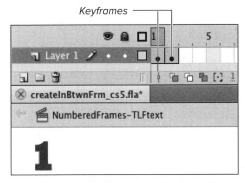

Timeline before evoking Insert > Timeline > Frame

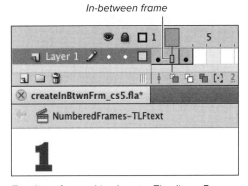

Timeline after evoking Insert > Timeline > Frame

B The Insert > Timeline > Frame command adds an in-between frame after the frame where the playhead is located.

Creating In-Between Frames

The frames that appear between keyframes are in a sense tied to the keyframe that precedes them. They display its content and allow you a space in which to create classic tweens and shape tweens (see Chapters 9 and 10). Flash makes the connections between these frames clear by tinting them and placing a hollow rectangle at the end of the keyframe span. Motion tweens also rely on a span containing in-between frames to display content, but the span works differently (see Chapter 11).

To add in-between frames:

1. Open or create a Flash document with keyframes and content in Frames 1 and 2.

2. In the Timeline, position the playhead in Keyframe 1.

3. Choose Insert > Timeline > Frame, or press F5 A.

   Flash adds an in-between frame B. Your movie now contains a keyframe at Frame 1, an in-between frame at Frame 2, and another keyframe at Frame 3.

What Are Keyframes and In-Between Frames?

In the early days of animation, it took veritable armies of artists to create the enormous number of drawings that frame-by-frame animation requires. To keep costs down, the studios broke the work into categories based on the artistic skill required and the pay provided. The work might start with creating spec sheets for each character. Then came storyboards that outlined the action over the course of the animation. Eventually, individual artists drew and painted hundreds of cels, each slightly different, to bring the animation to life.

To make the process manageable, animators broke each movement into a series of the most crucial frames that defined a movement, called *keyframes,* and frames that incorporated the incremental changes necessary to simulate the movement, called *in-between frames.*

Keyframes define a significant change to a character or graphic. Imagine a 25-frame sequence in which Bugs Bunny starts out facing the audience and then turns to his right to look at Daffy Duck. This scene requires two keyframes—Bugs in a face-on view and Bugs in profile—and 23 in-between frames.

In the early days, some artists specialized in creating keyframes. Other artists—usually lower-paid—had the job of creating the frames that fell in between the keyframes. These *in-betweeners* (or *tweeners,* for short) copied the drawings in the keyframes, making just the slight adjustments necessary to create the intended movement in the desired number of frames while retaining the continuity of the character. In Chapters 9 through 13, you learn how to turn Flash into your own personal wage slave. The program takes on the drudgery of in-betweening for certain types of animation.

Flash's classic- and shape-tween features require that you use keyframes to define any change in the content or image, even if the change affects just one property of an object. Flash's motion-tween feature works a bit differently. A motion tween relies on one keyframe that holds the tweened object; the tween then uses *property keyframes* to define changes to individual properties (see Chapter 11). Flash's inverse kinematics (IK) feature also relies on just one keyframe per span; *pose frames* indicate changes to the IK object (see Chapter 13).

Flash doesn't use the term *in-between frames;* it uses the term *frame* for any frames that aren't defined as keyframes, property keyframes, or pose frames. For clarity, the tasks in this book use the term *in-between frames* when referring to such frames.

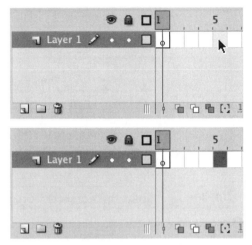

A Both frame-selection styles treat protoframes identically for selection. Position the pointer over a protoframe (top) and click to select it (bottom).

Selecting Frames in Keyframe Spans

Flash offers two styles for selecting frames in the Timeline; you set the style in Preferences. Frame-based selection, the default style, treats every frame individually. Span-based selection treats frames as members of a *keyframe span*—the keyframe plus any in-between frames that follow it and display its content. In the span-based selection style, clicking one frame in the middle of a span selects the entire span.

No matter which selection style you set in Preferences, there is only one way to make selections within motion-tween spans and pose spans; it's similar to the span-based selection but with a few variations. (You'll learn about working with these types of spans in Chapters 11 and 13.)

Except where noted, the examples in this book use Flash's default selection style, frame-based selection.

To select undefined frames:

To work with protoframes in either selection style, do any of the following:

- To select one protoframe, click it **A**.

- To select two protoframes and all the frames between them, click the first protoframe, then Shift-click the last protoframe.

- To select noncontiguous protoframes, Command-click (Mac) or Ctrl-click (Windows) the protoframes.

  The process of selecting frames that have not been defined works identically in Flash's two frame-selection styles.

To choose a selection style:

1. Choose Flash > Preferences (Mac) or Edit > Preferences (Windows).

   The Preferences dialog appears.

2. From the Category list, select General.

   The General settings appear in the right-hand pane of the dialog **B**.

3. In the Timeline section, choose either of the following frame-selection styles:

   ▸ To manipulate keyframe spans in the Timeline, select the Span-Based Selection checkbox **C**.

   ▸ To manipulate individual frames in the Timeline, deselect the Span-Based Selection checkbox **D**.

To select frames inside keyframe spans—frame-based mode:

In the Timeline—with preferences set to frame-based selection style—do one of the following:

- To select a keyframe, click it.

- To select the last frame in a keyframe span, click it.

- To select just a middle frame in a key-frame span, click that frame **E**.

- To select an entire keyframe span, double-click any frame in the span.

- To add frames to your selection, Shift-click the additional frames. Flash selects all the frames between the last selected frame and the frame you Shift-click.

- To select a range of frames, click the first frame of the range, then Shift-click the last frame in the range; or with no frames selected, click and drag through the range of frames.

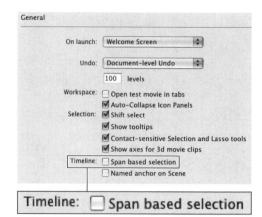

Timeline: ☐ Span based selection

B Choose the way frame selection works in the Timeline from the General category of the Preferences dialog.

Timeline: ☑ Span based selection

C In the General section of the Preferences dialog, select the Span-Based Selection checkbox to work with keyframe spans as a unit in the Timeline.

Timeline: ☐ Span based selection

D In the General section of the Preferences dialog, deselect the Span-Based Selection checkbox to work with individual keyframes in the Timeline.

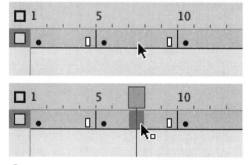

E In Flash's frame-based selection style, clicking a frame in the middle of a keyframe span (top) selects just that frame (bottom).

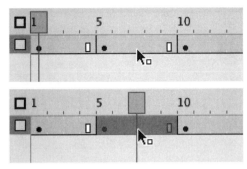

F In Flash's span-based selection style, clicking a frame in the middle of a keyframe span (top) selects the whole span (bottom).

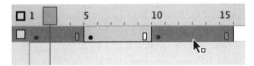

G With Flash's span-based frame-selection style, you can Shift-click to select keyframe spans that aren't contiguous.

To select frames inside keyframe spans—span-based mode:

In the Timeline—with preferences set to span-based selection style—do one of the following:

- To select a keyframe, click it.

- To select the last frame in keyframe span, click it.

- To select one in-between frame, Command-click (Mac) or Ctrl-click (Windows) that frame.

- To select an entire keyframe span, click a middle frame in the keyframe span **F**; or Shift-click the first or last frame in the span.

- To add other spans to your selection, Shift-click any frame in each additional span. The selection can include non-contiguous spans **G**.

- To select a range of frames, Command-drag (Mac) or Ctrl-drag (Windows) through the frames.

TIP In both selection styles, you can select all the frames in a layer by clicking the layer name. In the span-based selection style, you can also select all the frames in a layer by tri-ple-clicking: First double-click a frame (its span is selected after the first click), then click that selected span a third time. There's no need to rush that third click—the double-click primes the span, so now when you click anywhere in that selected span, Flash selects all the frames in that layer.

TIP In both selection styles, you can select noncontiguous frames by Command-clicking (Mac) or Ctrl-clicking (Windows) each frame that you want to include. Note that this tech-nique does not work within the tween span of a motion tween (Chapter 11) or within an IK pose span (Chapter 13).

Manipulating Frames in One Layer

You can't copy or paste frames with the standard Copy and Paste commands that you use for graphic elements. Flash's Edit > Timeline submenu provides special commands for copying and pasting frames. Flash also lets you drag selected frames to new locations in the Timeline.

For the following tasks, open a new Flash document. Create a ten-frame movie with keyframes at Frames 1, 3, 5, and 9. Using the text tool, place a text field in each keyframe, and enter the number of the frame in the text field; this technique makes it easy to tell what frame winds up where, as you practice. Use the Edit > Save As command to create two copies of this practice document; name one PasteFrames.fla, and the other DragFrames.fla.

To copy and paste a single frame:

1. Open the PasteFrames.fla document and select Keyframe 3 in the Timeline.

2. Choose Edit > Timeline > Copy Frames, or press Option-Command-C (Mac) or Ctrl-Alt-C (Windows).

   Flash copies the selected frame to the Clipboard.

3. In the Timeline, click Frame 4 to select it as the location for pasting the copied frame.

4. Choose Edit > Timeline > Paste Frames, or press Option-Command-V (Mac) or Ctrl-Alt-V (Windows).

   Flash pastes the copied frame into Frame 4 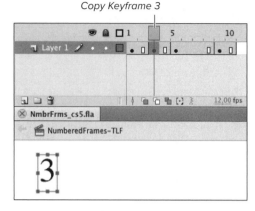.

Copy Keyframe 3

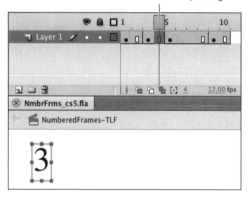
Selected location for pasting

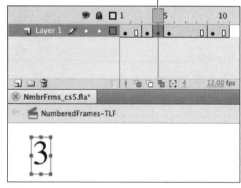
Flash pastes copied Keyframe 3 content into Frame 4

A When you paste a frame with new content into an in-between frame, Flash converts the frame to a keyframe.

Keyframe 5 selected

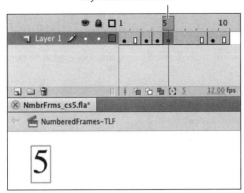

Pasted content from Keyframe 3

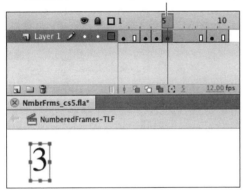

B When you paste a frame with new content into a keyframe, Flash replaces the keyframe's content.

5. Select Frame 5 and paste another copy **B**.

Flash replaces the content of Keyframe 5 with the content of Keyframe 3.

6. Select Protoframe 12 and paste another copy.

Flash extends the movie to accommodate the pasted frame. Note that the playhead won't move to Protoframe 12 until after you've pasted the copy to create a defined frame.

TIP You can copy and paste multiple frames; in Step 1 of the preceding task, select a range of frames.

TIP To copy and paste the content of a keyframe, you can also copy an in-between frame that displays that content. When you paste, Flash creates a new keyframe.

CAUTION Flash always replaces the content of the selected frame with the pasted frame (or, for multiple-frame pastes, with the first pasted frame). If you're not careful, you may eat up the content of keyframes you intended to keep. To be safe, always paste frames into in-between frames or blank keyframes. You can always delete an unwanted keyframe separately.

To move frames using drag and drop:

1. Open the DragFrames.fla practice file and in the Timeline select the keyframe span that starts with Keyframe 5 and ends with Frame 8.

   Flash highlights the selection in blue.

2. Position the pointer over the selected frames.

3. Click and drag the selected frames.

   A darker blue outline appears around the selection highlight as you drag. Use the blue rectangle to preview the new location for the selected frames in the Timeline.

4. To move the selected frames to the end of your movie, drag the rectangle past the last defined frame and into the area of protoframes, and release the mouse button.

   Flash adds frames to the end of the movie; these frames display the content from Frames 5 through 8. In frame-based selection style, Flash completely removes the content from Frames 5 through 8 and adds those frames to the preceding span. In span-based selection style, Flash removes the content but keeps a blank keyframe at Frame 5 .

5. To move the selected frames to the very beginning of your movie, drag the selected frames to Frame 1 and release the mouse button.

   In both selection styles, the dragged frames replace the content of Frames 1 through 4; there is no longer a keyframe at Frame 5.

Select and drag: either selection style

Selected frames

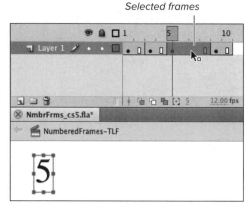

Preview of new frame location

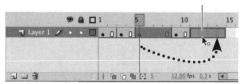

After drop: frame-based selection style

Original keyframe removed   Frames in new location

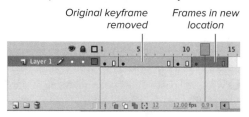

After drop: span-based selection style

Original keyframe retained, content removed   Frames in new location

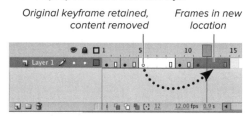

C The process of dragging and dropping frames in the Timeline to relocate them is the same in Flash's two frame-selection styles (top). The results, however, are quite different (bottom). The frame-based selection style removes selected keyframes from their original location, leaving only in-between frames. The span-based style retains the original keyframes but removes their content.

TIP To drag a copy of selected frames in the Timeline, hold down Option (Mac) or Alt (Windows) as you drag.

TIP No matter which frame-selection style you use, pressing the Command key (Mac) or Ctrl key (Windows) lets you access some of the functionality of the other style temporarily. In frame-based selection, the modifier lets you access the double-headed arrow pointer for extending keyframe spans (see the sidebar, "The Trick to Extending Keyframe Spans"). In span-based mode, the modifier gives you the arrow pointer for selecting individual frames.

TIP If you make a mistake in modifying the frames in the Timeline, you can undo your steps by choosing Edit > Undo. Flash tracks the selection and deselection of frames as part of the undo history. Operations such as dragging frames to move them or to extend spans may require repeated Undo commands, because some of the steps involved are things Flash does behind the scenes.

The Trick to Extending Keyframe Spans

In span-based selection style, the pointer becomes a double-headed arrow when it hovers over the first or last frame of a keyframe span. You can use this pointer to drag a keyframe or end-of-span frame to the right or the left to increase or decrease the length of the span.

Resizing a span in the middle of other spans gets a bit tricky. Flash won't let your expanding span eat up the content of other keyframes. Your expansion can reduce the length of a neighboring span, however. In your practice document, for example, using span-based selection, position the pointer over frame 4 (the end of Keyframe 3's span); the frame must not be selected. With the double-headed arrow pointer, drag Frame 4 to the right. When you get to Frame 7, you can drag no farther. Release the mouse button. The span that starts at Frame 3 now extends through Frame 7. The content that was originally in Keyframe 5 still exists, but Flash has pushed it into Frame 8.

To increase the length of a span without affecting the length of neighboring spans, select the span or any frame within it; then choose Insert > Timeline > Frame, or press F5. Flash adds an in-between frame to the selected span and pushes all subsequent spans to the right in the Timeline.

When you reduce the size of a span by dragging, Flash creates blank keyframe spans to cover any gaps between the end of the span you're resizing and the beginning of the neighboring span. To simply reduce the number of in-between frames, you can use the Remove Frames command (see "Removing Frames," the next section in this chapter). Note that you must use different techniques for resizing tween spans for motion tweens (Chapter 11) and pose spans for inverse kinematics (Chapter 13).

Removing Frames

Flash has two commands for removing frames: Clear Keyframe and Remove Frames. Clear Keyframe removes keyframe status from a selected frame or range of frames (converting the keyframes to in-between frames) and deletes the keyframes' content from the movie. Clear Keyframe has no effect on the number of frames in the movie. Remove Frames removes frames (and their content, if they're keyframes) from the movie. Remove Frames reduces the number of frames in the movie. For the following tasks, use the same practice document you created for working with the tasks in "Manipulating Frames in One Layer," earlier in this chapter.

To remove keyframe status from a frame:

1. In the Timeline, select Keyframe 5.

2. Choose Modify > Timeline > Clear Keyframe, or press Shift-F6.

   Flash removes the bullet from Frame 5 in the Timeline (indicating that the frame is no longer a keyframe) and removes the graphic element it contained. Frame 5 becomes an in-between frame, displaying the contents of the keyframe at Frame 3 **A**. The total number of frames in the movie remains the same.

Before clearing the keyframe
Selected keyframe is Frame 5

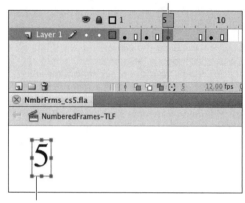

Content of selected keyframe

After clearing the keyframe
Frame 5 becomes an in-between frame

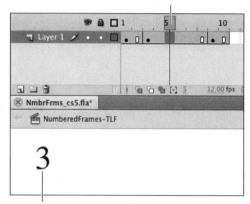

*Frame 5 displays the content
of the preceding keyframe*

A The Modify > Timeline > Clear Keyframe command removes the contents of the selected keyframe from the Stage and converts the keyframe to an in-between frame. The Clear Keyframe command doesn't change the overall length of the movie.

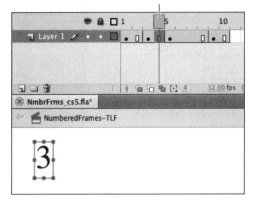

Selected in-between frame

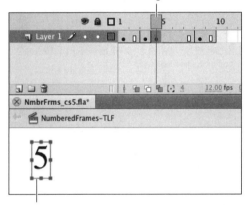

After deleting

Content originally in Keyframe 5 is now in Keyframe 4

B The Edit > Timeline > Remove Frames command removes frames from the movie and thus reduces its length.

To delete a frame from a keyframe span:

1. With your practice file in its original state (keyframes at 1, 3, 5, and 9), select Frame 4 in the Timeline.

   Frame 4 is an in-between frame associated with Keyframe 3.

2. Choose Edit > Timeline > Remove Frames, or press Shift-F5.

   Flash deletes what was Frame 4, reducing the overall length of the movie by one frame **B**. The keyframe content that was in Frame 5 moves back one frame to become Keyframe 4.

3. Select Keyframe 3 and choose Edit > Timeline > Remove Frames again.

   Flash deletes the selected keyframe and its content, and reduces the length of the movie by one frame. The keyframe content that was just in Frame 4 moves back one frame to become Keyframe 3.

TIP Flash doesn't let you use Clear Keyframe to remove keyframe status from the first frame of a movie, but you can delete it. If you select all the frames in one layer and choose Edit > Timeline > Remove Frames, Flash removes all the defined frames in the Timeline, leaving only protoframes. You must add back a keyframe at Frame 1 to place content on that layer.

To delete a range of frames:

1. Using your practice file in its original state (keyframes at 1, 3, 5, and 9), in the Timeline, select Frames 3 through 6.

2. Choose Edit > Timeline > Remove Frames.

   Flash removes all the selected frames 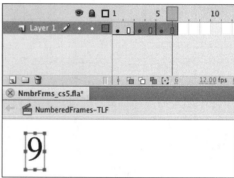. The content of the fully selected span (Frames 3 and 4) is completely removed; content for the partially selected span (Frames 5 and 6) remains, and the span is shortened.

TIP With the frame-based selection style active, you can quickly replace the contents of one keyframe with those of another. Select an in-between frame that displays the contents you want to copy. Drag that source frame over the keyframe whose contents you want to replace. Flash replaces the contents of the target keyframe with the contents of the source keyframe.

C The Edit > Timeline > Remove Frames command can delete a selected range of frames. Because an entire keyframe span (Frames 3 and 4) is included in the selection (top), Flash not only reduces the number of frames but also removes the content of that keyframe span (middle). Where only part of a span was selected (originally Frames 5 and 6), the span gets shorter, but the content remains the same (bottom).

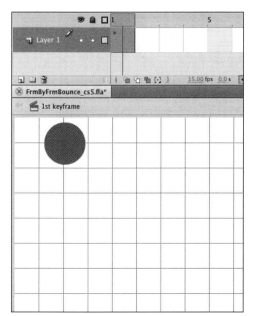

A In Keyframe 1, using the oval tool, draw a circular fill near the top of the Stage. This shape will become a bouncing ball.

Making a Simple Frame-by-Frame Animation

In traditional cel animation or flip-book animation, you create the illusion of movement by showing a series of images, each slightly different from the rest. When you create each of these drawings and place them in a series of keyframes, that process is called *frame-by-frame animation*. When you create only the most crucial images and allow Flash to interpolate the minor changes that take place between them, you're creating *tweened animation*. You learn more about tweening in Chapters 9 through 12.

A time-honored example of frame-by-frame animation is a bouncing ball. A crude animation of a bouncing ball takes just three frames. Each frame shows the ball in a different position.

To set up the initial keyframe:

1. Create a new Flash document, and name it something like FrmByFrmBounce.

   By default, Flash creates a document with one layer and a keyframe at Frame 1. Choose View > Grid > Show Grid to help with positioning graphics in this task.

2. In the Timeline, select Keyframe 1.

   From the Panel menu, choose Preview in Context mode. This setting makes it easy to keep track of what you do in the example.

3. Near the top of the Stage, using the oval tool, draw a circle **A**.

   The circle will be your ball. Make it fairly large.

To create the second keyframe:

1. In the Timeline, click the protoframe for Frame 2 to select it.

2. Choose Insert > Timeline > Keyframe.

   Flash creates a keyframe in Frame 2 that duplicates your ball from Keyframe 1.

3. In Keyframe 2, select the ball and reposition it at the bottom of the Stage **B**.

To create the third keyframe:

1. In the Timeline, select Frame 3.

2. Choose Insert > Timeline > Keyframe.

   Flash creates a keyframe in Frame 3 that duplicates your ball from Keyframe 2.

3. In Keyframe 3, select the ball and reposition it, placing the ball roughly two-thirds of the way back up the Stage, almost back to the original position **C**.

   That's it. Believe it or not, you have just created all the content you need to animate a bouncing ball. To see how it works, click Keyframes 1, 2, and 3 in turn, in the Timeline. As Flash changes the content of the Stage at each click, you see a very crude animation.

Inserted keyframe

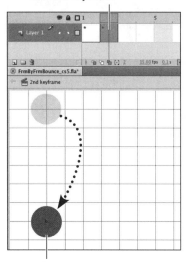

Drag to reposition ball

B Use the Insert > Timeline > Keyframe command to duplicate the ball from Keyframe 1 in Keyframe 2. Then drag the ball to reposition it.

Inserted keyframe

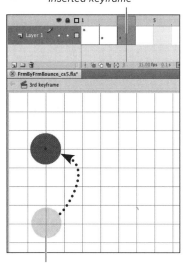

Drag to reposition ball

C Use the Insert > Timeline > Keyframe command to duplicate the ball from Keyframe 2 in Keyframe 3. Drag the ball to reposition it again.

Smoother Frame-by-Frame Animation

The three-frame bouncing ball you created in the preceding task is crude; it's herky-jerky; and at Flash CS5's default 24 frames per second, it's much too fast. You can spread out the action of a frame-by-frame animation (and slow it down) by separating the back-to-back keyframes with in-between frames (see the tasks in "Varying Frame-by-Frame Speed," later in this section). To smooth the movement of a frame-by-frame animation, you need to create more snapshots that define the ball's position in the air as it moves up and down in smaller increments. This means adding more keyframes (see "Creating Keyframes," earlier in this chapter) and repositioning the ball slightly in each one **D**. The smoothest frame-by-frame animations make tiny changes to graphic elements over numerous keyframes. Adding keyframes does add to file size, though not as much as adding multimedia elements such as sound and video.

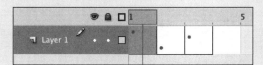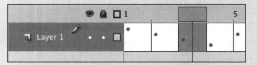

D With frames set to Preview in Context, the Timeline shows the location of the ball in this frame-by-frame animation; the ball moves from the top of the Stage to the bottom in a single step (left). Adding more keyframes and moving the ball in smaller steps creates a smoother animation (right).

Previewing the Action

Flash's Controller window offers VCR-style playback buttons for playing animations during authoring. You can also have Flash export the file and open it for you in Flash Player.

To use the Controller:

1. Choose Window > Toolbars > Controller **A**.

   Flash opens a window containing standard VCR-style buttons.

2. In the Controller window, click the button for the command you want to use **B**.

TIP The Control menu in the Menu bar duplicates the Controller's functions.

TIP You can use keyboard commands to move a single frame at a time: to go forward, press the period (.) key; to go backward, press the comma (,) key.

TIP To scrub (scroll quickly) through the movie, drag the playhead backward or forward through the frames in the Timeline. Flash displays the content of each frame as the playhead moves through it.

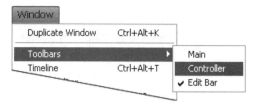

A To access the Controller, choose Window > Toolbars > Controller.

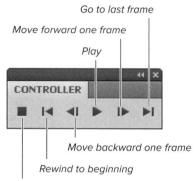

B The Controller window contains VCR-style buttons for controlling playback of Flash movies.

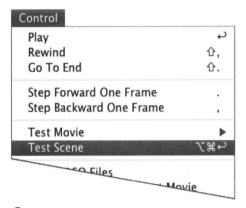

C Choose Control > Test Scene to see your movie in action in Flash Player.

TIP You can also use Control > Test Movie to preview your movie; it just takes a bit of extra work to choose an application from the Test Movie submenu. The offerings in the submenu depend on the document's current Publish settings (see Chapter 18). For tasks in this book, choose > In Flash Professional (Flash's regular player). Once you've chosen the test method you prefer, you can test quickly using keyboard commands. Press Command-Enter (Mac) or Ctrl-Enter (Windows) to activate the application currently selected in the submenu.

To play through all frames in the Flash editor:

Do one of the following:

- To play through the frames once, choose Control > Play, or press Enter.

  Flash displays each frame in turn, starting with the current frame and running through the end of the movie. The Play command in the Control menu changes to a Stop command, which you can use to stop playback at any time.

- To play through the frames repeatedly, choose Control > Loop Playback.

  When you issue a Play command, Flash plays the movie repeatedly until you issue a Stop command.

To play through frames in Flash Player:

Choose Control > Test Scene or press Option-Command-Enter (Mac) or Ctrl-Alt-Enter (Windows) **C**.

Flash exports your movie to a Flash Player (SWF) file and opens it in a separate window. Flash stores the SWF file at the same hierarchical level of your system as the original Flash file. The SWF file has the same name as the original, except that Flash appends the name of the current scene and changes the extension to .swf (testing a scene named Intro in a document named MyMovie.fla creates a file named MyMovie-Intro.swf).

Warnings When Testing TLF Text

As you learned in Chapter 3, TLF text requires that a *TLF SWZ file*, which contains special Action-Script instructions, be available to the player at runtime in order to display TLF text correctly. There are a variety of ways to ensure that the end user has access to that file. With default Publish settings, Flash player accesses the TLF SWZ file as a shared runtime library and will go looking for the library on the Adobe server. If Flash Player can't reach that SWZ file, the player next checks for the file on the local machine.

When you use the Test Scene (or Test Movie > In Flash Professional) command to preview a movie containing TLF text, Flash creates a copy of the TLF SWZ and the SWF file (the movie that plays for end users) in one folder. As you develop and test, the TLF SWZ shared runtime library is always available to the Flash player, and you'll see your TLF content play regardless of whether you are connected to the Internet or not. When you are working offline, however, Flash may display an error message in the Output panel (such as **Error opening URL 'http://fpdownload.adobe.com/pub/swz/crossdomain.xml'**). The message results from the default setting that allows Flash to look in various places for the TLF SWZ. Think of it as a reminder that the fast, easy, guaranteed access you have to the TLF SWZ during testing won't necessarily be true for your target audience. (Flash Authoring assumes by default that you will deploy your published SWF to a publicly accessible web server with the TLF SWZ file. If that's not the case, you can change the Publish settings to work with other deployment methods.)

In addition, as you test, Flash checks to see if your content includes items that might benefit from streaming (such as large animations). If it finds such content, a warning dialog pops up to remind you that with default Publish settings, you can't stream content with TLF text. You can safely dismiss these types of messages if they appear while you test the files you create as tasks in this book. When you start creating your own content for use by a wider audience, you'll need to pay attention to these reminders and consider which publishing options work best for your target audience. (You'll learn more about working with Publish Settings in Chapter 18.)

Current frame

Frame rate

Elapsed time

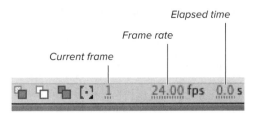

A The Status bar contains Frame Rate hot text for quick entry of the speed for your movie.

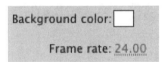

B The Document Property inspector's Properties section offers a hot-text control for setting frame rate (FPS).

C The Document Settings dialog also offers a hot-text control for setting frame rate.

Setting the Frame Rate

In Flash, you can set only one frame rate for the entire movie. You set the frame rate in the status bar, Document Property inspector, or Document Settings dialog.

To set the frame rate via Status bar:

1. Open a Flash document and access the Timeline.

2. To enter a playback speed for this movie, in the Status bar, use the Frame Rate hot text to enter a value between 0 and 120 **A**.

   To use a precise value, click the hot text, enter a number in the field that activates, then press Enter. To choose a value interactively, position the pointer over the hot text; when the pointing finger with a double arrow appears, drag left (or down) to lower the value or drag right (or up) to increase the value.

   Frame rate is measured in frames per second and indicates how quickly Flash displays the frames to your viewers (see the sidebar "Understanding Frame Rate," later in this chapter).

TIP You can also set the frame rate in the Document Property inspector. To access it, select a protoframe in the Timeline, or using the selection tool, click an empty area of the Stage or Pasteboard. In the Properties section of the Property inspector, use the FPS hot text to enter a playback speed for your movie **B**. Flash updates the frame rate in the Status bar.

TIP Another way to set a document's frame rate is via the Document Settings dialog. Choose Modify > Document, or press Command-J (Mac) or Ctrl-J (Windows). The Document Settings dialog appears. Enter a value in the Frame Rate field **C**. Click OK to close the dialog.

Varying Frame-by-Frame Speed

Although the frame rate for a movie is constant, you can make any particular bit of animation go faster or slower by changing the number of frames it takes to complete the action. You can lengthen a portion of an animation by adding more keyframes or by adding in-between frames. In the bouncing-ball example, the ball may drop down slowly (say, over five frames) but rebound more quickly (over three frames). The smoothest frame-by-frame animation has many keyframes, each showing the ball in a slightly different position. Adding keyframes, however, increases file size. Sometimes you can get away with adding in-between frames to slow the action. In-between frames add little to the exported movie's file size.

To add in-between frames:

1. Open (or create) a five-frame bouncing-ball movie.

   Keyframe 1 shows the ball at the top of the Stage, Keyframes 2 and 3 show the ball at two places in its descent, Keyframe 4 shows the ball at the bottom of the Stage, and Keyframe 5 shows the ball bouncing most of the way back up. To make it easier to see what's happening for this task, use a fairly low frame rate, say 12 or 15 fps.

2. Choose File > Save As, and make a copy of the file.

   Give the file a distinguishing name, such as BounceSlower.

3. In the copy's Timeline, select Frame 1.

Understanding Frame Rate

The illusion of animation relies on the human brain's ability to fill in gaps in continuity. When you see a series of images in very quick succession, your brain perceives a continuous moving image. In animation, you must display the sequence of images fast enough to convince the brain that it's looking at a single image.

Frame rate controls how fast Flash delivers the images. If the images come too fast, the movie turns into a blur. Slow delivery too much, and your viewers start perceiving each frame as a separate image and the movement seems jerky. When you're working in Flash, you're often planning to deliver the movie over the Internet, and you don't always know what types of systems your viewers will be using. That means you won't necessarily be able to deliver a fast frame rate.

Flash CS5's default rate matches the standard rate for film—24 frames per second (fps). For graphic animation that's going out over the Internet to a target audience using low-bandwidth connections, consider lowering the frame rate to 15 or 12 fps. Today's high-bandwidth connections and Flash Player 10's capabilities, however, make still higher frame rates a possibility. If you're confident that your target audience has the capacity to handle it, and you want to deliver even smoother animations or lots of video, you may want to use a frame rate as high as 31 fps.

Tasks in this book often create short animations—24 frames or less. That makes it easy show you all of the frames. When you start testing those movies, they'll zip by in the blink of an eye. Setting a very low frame rate for the movies you create for these tasks (5 to 10 frames per second) will make it easier to see what's happening.

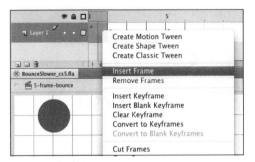

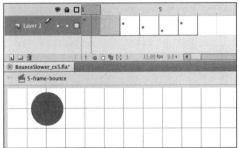

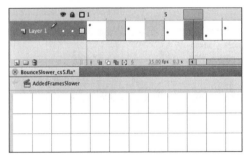

A Select a frame; Ctrl-click (Mac) or right-click (Windows), and choose Insert Frame from the contextual menu (top); Flash inserts an in-between frame directly after the selected frame (bottom).

B With in-between frames separating the initial keyframes, the first part of the animation moves at a slower pace than the second.

4. Control-click (Mac) or right-click (Windows) to access the contextual menu for frames.

5. Choose Insert Frame.

Flash inserts an in-between frame at Frame 2 and pushes the keyframe that was there to Frame 3 **A**.

6. Repeat Steps 3 through 5 for the second and third keyframes in the movie.

You wind up with keyframes in Frames 1, 3, 5, 7, and 8 **B**.

7. Choose Control > Test Scene.

Flash exports the movie to a SWF file and opens it in Flash Player. Play through the regular five-frame bouncing ball, and then play through the one you just created (the one named BounceSlower). You can see that the action in the movie with added in-between frames feels different from the action in the movie in which one keyframe directly follows another. The added frames slow the motion.

TIP Keep in mind that this example serves to illustrate a process. In most animations, you shouldn't overuse this technique. If you simply add many in-between frames, you'll slow the action too much and destroy the illusion of movement.

Using Onion Skinning

In frame-by-frame animation, you make incremental changes to the graphic elements in each keyframe. In the bouncing-ball animation, you must position the ball in each frame to make the smoothest movement. To make this task easier, Flash's onion-skinning feature displays the graphic elements of keyframes in context with the elements of surrounding frames.

Onion skinning displays dimmed or outline versions of the content of multiple selected frames. You determine how many frames Flash displays at once. The buttons for turning on and off the various types of onion skinning appear at the bottom of the Timeline, in the Timeline's Status bar.

To turn on onion skinning:

- In the Status bar of the Timeline, click the Onion Skin button.

   The content of the frames included in the onion-skin markers appears in a dimmed form **Ⓐ**. You can't edit the dimmed graphics—only the full-color graphics in the current frame.

To turn on outline onion skinning:

- In the Status bar of the Timeline, click the Onion Skin Outlines button.

   The content of all the frames included in the onion-skin markers appears in outline form **Ⓑ**. You can't edit the outline graphics—only the solid graphics that appear in the current frame.

Onion Skin button　　　*Onion-skin markers*

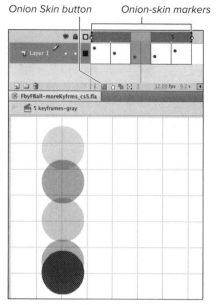

Ⓐ In Onion Skin mode, Flash displays the content of multiple frames but dims everything that's not on the current frame. The onion-skin markers in the Timeline indicate how many frames appear.

Onion-Skin Outlines button

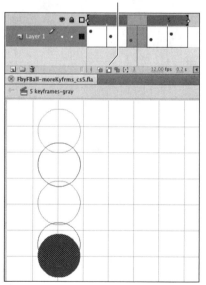

Ⓑ In Onion Skin Outlines mode, Flash displays the content of multiple frames, but it uses outlines for everything that's not in the current frame.

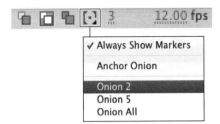

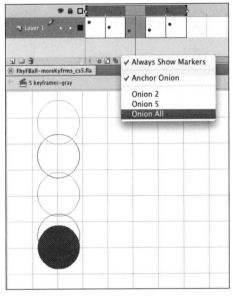

C The Modify Onion Markers pop-up menu gives you control over the number of frames that appear as onion skins.

D With Onion All chosen in the Modify Onion Markers menu, Flash extends the markers to enclose all the frames of the Timeline.

To adjust the number of frames included in onion skinning:

1. In the Status bar of the Timeline, click the Modify Onion Markers button.

   A pop-up menu appears, containing commands for setting the way the onion-skin markers work **C**.

2. To see frames on either side of the current frame, do one of the following:

   - To see two frames on either side of the current frame, choose Onion 2.

   - To see five frames on either side of the current frame, choose Onion 5.

   - To see all the frames in the movie, choose Onion All **D**.

   Flash moves the onion-skin markers around in the Timeline as you move the playhead. Flash always includes onion skins (either solid or outline) for graphics in the selected number of frames before the current frame and after it.

TIP Flash doesn't show the contents of locked layers in onion-skin views.

TIP Drag onion-skin markers in the Timeline to include more frames or fewer frames in the onion-skin view.

TIP You can prevent the onion-skin markers from moving each time you select a new frame in the Timeline. Set the markers to encompass the frames you want to see together. From the Modify Onion Markers menu, choose Anchor Onion. As long as you keep selecting frames inside the anchored range, the anchored set of frames stays in Onion Skin mode.

Editing Multiple Keyframes

If you decide to change the location of an animated element, you must change the element's location in every keyframe in which it appears. Repositioning the items one at a time is not only tedious but also dangerous. You may miss a keyframe, and you can easily get the animated elements out of alignment. Flash solves this problem by letting you move elements in multiple keyframes simultaneously. The same markers used for onion skinning apply to Edit Multiple Frames mode. You can edit any of the keyframes that fall within the range of frames set off by the markers.

Editing multiple keyframes is especially important for frame-by-frame animation, shape tweens, and classic tweens. For motion tweens, it's easy to reposition the tween target in every frame of the animation simply by moving the motion path (see Chapter 11).

To relocate animated graphics on the Stage:

1. Open or create a five-frame animation of a bouncing ball.

2. In the Timeline's Status bar, choose Edit Multiple Frames 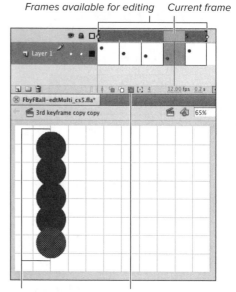.

   Flash displays all graphics in all frames within the onion-skin markers and makes them editable.

3. From the Modify Onion Markers menu, choose Onion All.

   Now you can see the ball at each stage of its bounce, and you can edit each of these stages.

Frames available for editing   Current frame

Objects available for editing   Edit Multiple Frames button

Ⓐ In Edit Multiple Frames mode, Flash displays and makes editable all the graphics in the frames that the onion-skin markers indicate. This feature makes it possible to move an animated graphic to a new location in every keyframe at the same time.

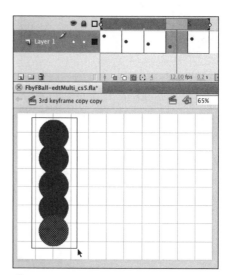

Ⓑ In Edit Multiple Frames mode, you can use the selection tool to select graphics in any of the frames enclosed in the onion-skin markers.

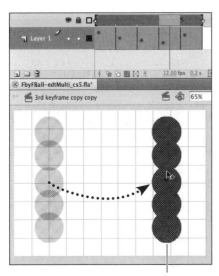

Flash previews the old and new locations as you drag selected graphics

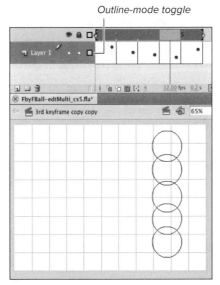
Outline-mode toggle

4. Using the selection tool, draw a selection rectangle that includes all the visible balls on the Stage **B**.

5. Drag the selection to the opposite side of the Stage **C**.

With just a few steps, you've relocated the bouncing ball. (Imagine how much more work it would have been to select each keyframe separately, move the circle for that frame, select the next keyframe, line up the circles precisely in the new location, and so on.)

TIP When you select Edit Multiple Frames, Flash no longer displays onion skinning for keyframes; onion skinning does appear for in-between frames with tweened content. If you find it confusing to view solid graphics in multiple keyframes, turn on Outline view in the layer-properties section of the Timeline **D**.

C In Edit Multiple Frames mode, you can relocate an animated graphic completely, moving it in every keyframe with one action.

D Turn on Outline mode to make it easier to work with graphics in multiple frames.

Practice Session

Creating a bouncing ball—as you do in this chapter—is a classic animation task, but real-world Flash animators would most likely not use frame-by-frame animation to achieve it. It's best to reserve the frame-by-frame technique for animations that require redrawing shapes, or moving objects around on the Stage in complex, non-linear ways. Try using the frame-by-frame technique to animate something that changes radically in each frame—for example, a signature that signs itself in ten steps.

- Set the Timeline's frame view to Preview to help you see what's happening in each keyframe. (See *Optimizing the Timeline*.)

- In Layer 1, add a blank keyframe at Frame 20. (See *Creating Keyframes*.)

- With Frame 20 selected, use the pencil or brush tool to sign your name on the Stage. (See Chapter 2.)

- In the Timeline, copy the keyframe at Frame 20, then paste the copy into Frame 18. (See *Manipulating Frames in One Layer*.)

- With Keyframe 18 selected, use the eraser tool to remove a bit from the end of your signature; take off about one tenth the entire signature. As you erase, think of following the letterforms in reverse. (See Chapter 2.)

- Repeat the process of copying, pasting, and erasing to create keyframes in every other frame. Paste a copy of Keyframe 18 into Frame 16; erase a bit more of your name; copy that into Frame 14 and erase a bit more; and so on, until you get to Frame 2, which should have just the very start of your signature. Onion-skinning can help you see what needs to be erased at each step. (See *Using Onion Skinning*.)

- Check out the movie. (See Chapter 8, *Previewing the Action*.)

Save your file for use in future Practice Sessions.

Extra Credit

Add ten in-between frames after each keyframe to slow the action. Now preview the movie.

Select ten protoframes after the final keyframe of the movie and convert them to keyframes (each one will contain a copy of the completed signature). Select each keyframe in turn (starting with the last one and working backwards) and use the eraser to take a series of tiny bites out of the signature. Preview the movie again and notice the difference between the first part of the movie, where you slow the action with in-between frames, and the tail end of the movie, where multiple keyframes accomplish changes in more gradual steps.

Animation with Classic Tweening

In Chapter 8, you created a three-frame animation of a bouncing ball by changing the position of the ball graphic in each of the three keyframes. Animating movement and changes to shapes by hand (frame by frame) is labor-intensive. Adobe Flash Professional CS5 reduces the number of frames you must draw when you use a process called *tweening*.

Flash does three types of tweening: classic, shape, and motion tweening. This chapter introduces classic tweening.

Classic and shape tweening both use keyframe spans to create animation. To set up the keyframe span, you place one version of a graphic element in an initial keyframe, and a second version in an ending keyframe. When you assign tweening to the keyframe span, Flash creates a series of images that accomplish the changes incrementally. The number of in-between frames determines the number of images in the series and the length of the animation.

In This Chapter

When to Use Classic Tweening

Tweening reduces the amount of labor involved in creating animation sequences. Instead of drawing the graphics for every frame of a movie, you create the essential frames—the keyframes—and let Flash do the redrawing. Flash performs several types of tweening: classic tweening, shape tweening (see Chapter 10), and motion tweening (see Chapter 11). Flash also uses another type of animation, inverse kinematics, which is similar to tweening in that it animates by creating a series of incremental changes to a structure composed of shapes or symbols (see Chapter 13). Each type of tween has different requirements and different strengths. Here are some things to consider about classic tweening and motion tweening.

Classic tweening requires symbols, so it's only appropriate to use when you will be animating changes in the properties of a symbol instance on the Stage. Such properties include the symbol's location on the Stage (position), the symbol's size (scale), whether the symbol changes its orientation to the Stage (rotation), and so on. Classic tweening doesn't allow you to change an element's outlines; for that, you need shape tweening (Chapter 10) or inverse kinematics (Chapter 13).

Motion tweening also involves working with symbols and changing their properties. How do you decide between classic and motion tweening? Classic tweening allows for some workflows often used by character animators. Because you set up initial and ending keyframes in classic tweening, you can map out a complete animation quickly by placing all the keyframes first and assigning classic tweening later, a process known as *blocking*. Classic tweening knits those segments together seamlessly, interpolating changes from one keyframe to the next and from that keyframe to the next, and so on. That's not the case for motion tweening. Each motion-tween span is an independent segment of animation, with a single keyframe. If you want the segments to link smoothly, you need to do a bit of extra work to make sure the position of a tweened object at the end of one span matches up correctly with its counterpart in the next tween span.

Another reason to use classic tweening is to take advantage of a graphic symbol's ability to display different frames of its Timeline on command. Character animators use this feature to turn multiframe graphic symbols into miniature libraries, building a set of facial expressions or gestures into a single symbol, then displaying just the one that's needed at any given time. (You'll learn about creating multiframe, animated, graphic symbols in Chapter 12.) Classic tweening's multiple-keyframe approach also lets you interpolate between two different color effects (one applied to the symbol instance in the initial keyframe of the tween, the other applied to the symbol instance at the end). In motion tweens, since each tween span has just one symbol instance, Flash can't interpolate changes to color effects.

Creating a Bouncing Ball with Classic Tweening

To create a classic tween, you must place the appropriate type of content in the keyframe that defines the beginning of the keyframe span and in the keyframe that marks the end of the span. You then tell Flash to create the classic tween. Flash can only create classic tweens from symbols. Flash can create the symbols for you, using the content of the active layer, but it's safest to create the symbols yourself (see the sidebar "Classic Tween Symbols: Best Practice" later in this chapter). You can use classic tweening to create the same bouncing ball you made in Chapter 8, by changing the position of the ball symbol.

 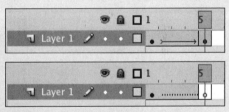

To prepare content for classic tweening:

1. In Keyframe 1 of a new document, place an instance of a symbol that represents a ball near the top of the Stage 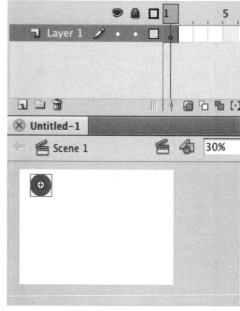.

   For example, use the oval tool to draw a circle shape, then convert it to a symbol (see Chapter 7) and name it MyBall. Flash could convert the shape for you, but it's best to do the conversion yourself (see the sidebar "Classic Tween Symbols: Best Practice," below).

2. Command-click (Mac) or Ctrl-click (Windows) Frames 5 and 10 and press F6.

   Flash creates Keyframes 5 and 10, duplicating Keyframe 1. (To review creating keyframes, see Chapter 8.) By changing the position of the ball in those keyframes, you tell Flash how to create the animation.

3. To set the ball's position for the low point of the bounce, do the following:

   ▸ In the Timeline, move the playhead to Keyframe 5.

   ▸ On the Stage, drag the ball symbol to the bottom of the Stage.

B To set up a traditional bouncing-ball with classic tweening, create the first keyframe, and position the ball symbol near the top of the Stage, at the top of its bounce.

Classic Tween Symbols: Best Practice

To create a classic tween, Flash must work with symbols. If you issue the command to create a classic tween when you've selected other types of graphic objects (merge-shapes, drawing-objects, primitive-shapes, groups, or text), Flash automatically converts the selection to a pair of symbols—one for the initial keyframe of the tween, the other for the ending keyframe. There's no warning dialog, Flash just puts generically named symbols (for example, Tween 1 and Tween 2) in the library and goes ahead with the tween. Unless you immediately rename the tween symbols something identifiable, it may be confusing should you need to go in and edit your tween later. Also, if you accidentally put more than one object on the layer you're using for the classic tween, Flash combines the objects to make one symbol instead of warning you that the tween can have only one object per layer. For best results, before you apply tweening, convert the graphic element (or elements) you want to tween into a symbol.

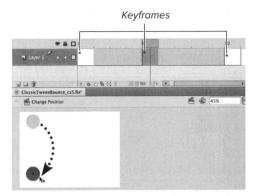

Keyframes

Reposition symbol

Symbol in new position in each keyframe

C The initial keyframes for a classic tween are similar to those of a frame-by-frame animation. The difference is that the content of the keyframe must be a symbol. To let Flash create the incremental changes to your symbol, you assign classic tweening to the keyframe span.

4. To set the ball's position for the rebound, do the following:

  ▸ Move the playhead to Keyframe 10.

  ▸ Drag the symbol to position it slightly above mid-Stage, almost back to its starting point.

You have just set up a frame-by-frame animation much like the one you created in Chapter 8, except that the keyframes are farther apart **C**. In Keyframe 1, the ball is at the top of its bounce; in Keyframe 5, the ball is at the bottom of its bounce; and in Keyframe 10, the ball is almost back to the top of its bounce. To have Flash interpolate the changes and create a smoother animation than in the frame-by-frame exercise, you need to tell Flash to apply tweening to the keyframe spans.

The Many Ways to Position Tweened Symbols

In the preceding task, you position a classic-tween symbol by dragging it directly on the Stage, but you could use the Property inspector or the Info panel to do the job instead. The trick is to make sure the symbol is selected. In Step 3 of the task, for example, instead of moving the playhead to Keyframe 5, you could select the keyframe in the Timeline, which also selects the contents of that frame on the Stage. You can access the Info panel and enter new values for the symbol's *x*- and *y*-coordinates to change the ball's position.

Although the Info panel recognizes a symbol selected this way, the Property inspector does not. When you select a keyframe in the Timeline, the Property inspector displays the properties of the frame itself, not its content (even though that content is selected on the Stage). To allow the Property inspector to focus on a classic-tween symbol, you must select that symbol directly—for example, by clicking it with the selection tool. You can then access the Property inspector and use the X and Y hot text in the Position and Size section to position the symbol on the Stage.

To apply classic tweening:

1. To apply classic tweening to the first half of the ball's bounce, in the Timeline, select any of the frames in the first keyframe span—1, 2, 3, or 4 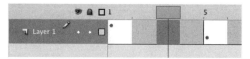.

   Flash automatically selects the ball symbol. To define a classic tween, the item to be tweened must be selected.

2. Choose Insert > Classic Tween 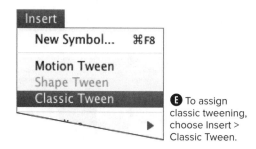.

   Flash defines Frames 1 through 4 as a classic tween, updating the Timeline to give you information about the tween 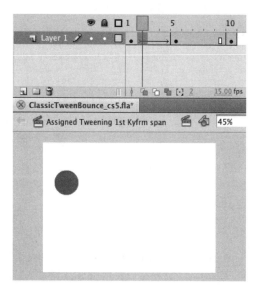. (See the sidebar "Which Frames Contain Tweening?" earlier in this chapter.) These in-between frames no longer display the content of the preceding keyframe; instead they display the incrementally changed tween content that Flash creates. This tween content is shielded so you can't select it (clicking the tween content is just like clicking a blank area of the Stage). You can use the selection tool to drag classic tween content in an in-between frame, but doing so transforms that frame into a keyframe.

D You can select any frame in a keyframe span to assign classic tweening.

E To assign classic tweening, choose Insert > Classic Tween.

F Flash adds information to the Timeline to indicate when frames contain classic tweens. Here, a blue tint and an arrow signify a completed classic tween.

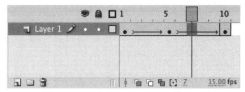

G With two motion-tween sequences, you can create a bouncing ball: one sequence shows the downward motion, and the other shows the rebound.

Range of frames being displayed as onion skins

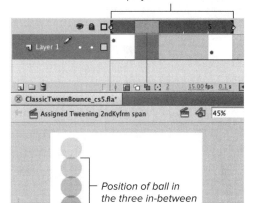

Position of ball in the three in-between frames

H Turn on onion skinning to preview the positions of a classically tweened symbol on the Stage.

3. To define the classic tween for the second half of the ball's bounce, in the Timeline, Control-click (Mac) or right-click (Windows) any of the frames in the second keyframe span—5, 6, 7, 8, or 9—and choose Create Classic Tween from the contextual menu.

Flash creates the second half of the ball's bounce with another classic tween **G**.

TIP When you choose Preview or Preview in Context from the Timeline's panel menu, the tweening arrow doesn't appear in the frames containing tweens. Nor can you see the incremental steps Flash creates for the tween. But if you turn on onion skinning, you can see the interpolated content for all the in-between frames in position on the Stage **H**.

TIP Oddly enough, although you can't select a symbol on an in-between frame of a classic tween, you can edit it. Double-clicking a symbol on an in-between frame opens that symbol in symbol-editing mode. And you must be careful when you double-click; if you drag the symbol on an in-between frame even a tiny bit, Flash creates a new keyframe.

TIP In this simple example, the ball moves at a constant rate through each half of its bounce. If you want the ball to slow down as it reaches the top of its upward rebound, you could use easing to vary the rate of change in the ball's position. For a quick introduction to easing, see Chapter 12.

Adding Keyframes to Classic Tweens

After you have set up a classic tween, Flash creates new keyframes for you when you reposition a classic-tween symbol on an in-between frame. You can also add new keyframes by choosing Insert > Timeline > Keyframe.

To add keyframes by repositioning a classic-tween symbol:

1. Create a ten-frame classic tween of a bouncing ball, following the steps in the preceding task.

2. In the Timeline, select Frame 3.

    On the Stage, you see the ball symbol in one of the in-between positions Flash created.

3. In the Tools panel, choose the selection tool.

4. Drag the ball to a new position—to the right of its current position, for example.

    Flash inserts a new keyframe at Frame 3 and splits the preceding five-frame tween into separate tweens **A**. The new keyframe contains another instance of the ball symbol.

To add keyframes by command:

1. Continuing with the document from the preceding task, select Frame 7.

2. Choose Insert > Timeline > Keyframe.

    Flash creates a new keyframe in Frame 7. A new instance of your symbol appears on the Stage in the position Flash created for it in that in-between frame. You can now change the symbol's position (or change other properties of the symbol).

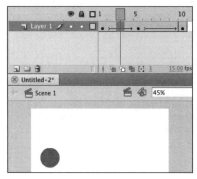

In the selected frame, the symbol appears in its tweened position

Added keyframe

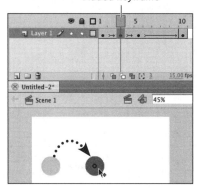

Repositioning the symbol creates a new keyframe

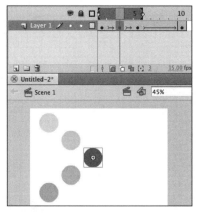

Onion-skin view of other tween positions for the symbol

A Repositioning the ball in an in-between frame that's part of a classic tween creates a new keyframe and a revision of the tweened frames.

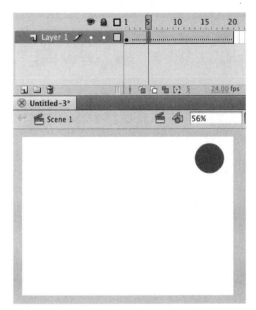

A The dotted line in the Timeline indicates that these 20 frames contain a classic tween, but a broken one. There is no ending keyframe to define changes to the tween symbol.

Moving Symbols in Straight Lines

In the preceding tasks, you created a well-behaved bouncing ball—one that moves up and down. To make one that bounces around like a crazy Ping-Pong ball, add more keyframes and place the ball symbol in various locations. The symbol moves in a straight line from one position to the next, but the effect is livelier. To get frenetic bouncing, move the symbol a great distance in a small number of in-between frames. To slow the action, move the symbol a short distance or use a larger number of in-between frames.

To move an item from point to point:

1. To set up an open-ended classic tween, in a new Flash document or on a new layer, do the following:

   ▸ In Keyframe 1, place an instance of a symbol containing a graphic of a ball.

   ▸ In the Timeline, select Frame 20, and choose Insert > Timeline > Frame. Flash creates a keyframe span by defining 19 in-between frames.

   ▸ In the Timeline, select any frame in the keyframe span (Frames 1 through 20) and choose Insert > Classic Tween. Flash assigns classic tweening to the keyframe span, but the dotted line in the Timeline indicates that the tween isn't yet complete **A**. You need to create keyframes that describe the ball's motion.

2. In the Timeline, position the playhead in Frame 5.

3. On the Stage, drag the ball symbol to a new position.

Flash creates a new keyframe in Frame 5 and completes a classic tween for Frames 1 through 4 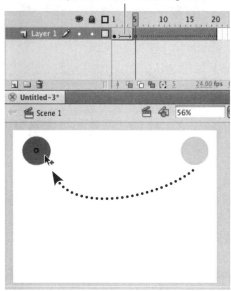.

4. Repeat this repositioning process (Steps 2 and 3) for Frames 10, 15, and 20.

You now have a ball that bounces around wildly **C**.

5. To end the classic tween, do the following:

▸ Select the last keyframe in the series.

▸ Choose Insert > Remove Tween.

If you don't remove tweening from the last frame, any frames that you add after that will also be set to classic tween, which may create unexpected results.

TIP To add more frames, after Step 4 select Frame 30 or Frame 40, then choose Insert > Timeline > Frame. Flash makes all the newly defined frames part of the classic tween. Now you can add keyframes by following the procedure described earlier in this task. Just be sure you end up with a keyframe as the last frame in the series. If you have more frames than you need, you can remove them.

Completed classic-tween segment

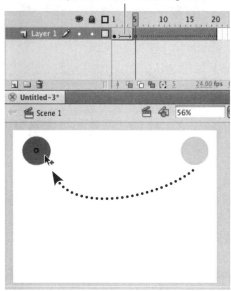

B As you move the ball to new positions in different frames within the keyframe span set to classic tweening, Flash creates new keyframes and completes the tween segments between keyframes.

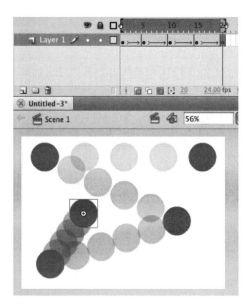

C By stringing classic tweens together, you can animate a symbol that moves from point to point.

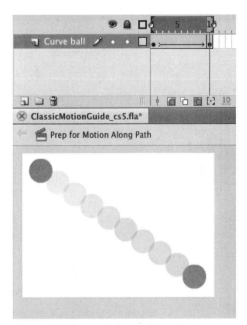

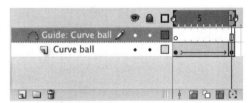

A The first phase in creating a classic tween with a symbol that follows a path is to set up the classic tween with the symbol in its beginning and ending positions. In this phase, the symbol moves from the beginning to the end in a straight line. (Onion Skin mode and Edit Multiple Frames are selected to show all the tweened movement.)

B When you choose Add Motion Guide Layer from the contextual menu, Flash adds a motion-guide layer with a default name (*Guide:* plus the name of your originally selected layer). Flash indents the original selected layer and links it to the motion-guide layer. Flash defines the linked layer as a guided layer.

Moving Symbols Along a Path

In the preceding task, you made a ball move all over the Stage in short, point-to-point hops. A ball does sometimes behave this way, but other things may require movements that are softer—trajectories that are arcs, not straight lines. You could achieve this effect by stringing together many point-to-point keyframes, but Flash's classic tweening offers a more efficient method: the *motion guide*. Motion guides describe the exact path an animated graphic-object takes. Note that if you don't have a special need to use a classic tween (see the sidebar "When to Use Classic Tweening," earlier in this chapter), motion tweening provides an even easier way to work with objects moving along a path (see Chapter 11).

To add a motion-guide layer:

1. In a new Flash document or on a new layer, create a ten-frame classic tween.

   In the first keyframe, place the symbol to be tweened in the top-left corner of the Stage. In the last frame, place the symbol in the bottom-right corner of the Stage. Your document should resemble **A**.

2. Select the layer that contains the symbol you want to move along a path.

3. Control-click (Mac) or right-click (Windows) the layer-name area and choose Add Classic Motion Guide from the contextual menu.

   Flash adds the classic motion-guide layer directly above the layer you clicked and gives it a default name of Guide, followed by the name of the layer you selected **B**. The motion-guide icon

continues on next page

appears next to the layer name. Flash also indents the layer you clicked, linking it to the motion-guide layer.

4. In the Tools panel, select a tool that creates merge-shape or drawing-object lines (strokes), such as the pencil tool.

5. In the Timeline, select Keyframe 1 of the motion-guide layer.

6. Draw a line on the Stage showing the path you want the classically tweened symbol to take **C**.

Lines on a motion-guide layer control the motion of classically tweened symbols on linked layers.

To connect tweened elements to a motion guide:

1. Continuing with the document from the preceding task, choose View > Snapping > Snap to Objects.

For Flash to move a classic-tween symbol along a motion guide, the transformation point of the symbol (which appears as a small white circle) must be centered on the line. The Snap to Objects setting helps you position the symbol correctly. (To learn more about the transformation point, see Chapters 4 and 7.)

2. In Keyframe 1, using the selection tool, drag the classic-tween symbol by its transformation point to position it directly over the beginning of the motion guide.

As you drag, the snapping ring enlarges slightly when it approaches any snapping elements you have set. For example, with Snap to Objects active, the ring grows larger when the point you're dragging is centered over the motion guide.

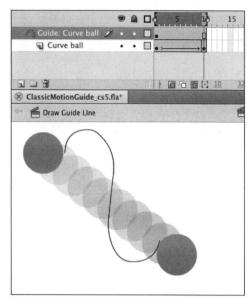

C A line on a motion-guide layer acts as a path that controls the motion of a classic-tween symbol on a linked layer.

The Mystery of Motion Guides

A *motion guide* is a graphic you create on a special separate layer. The motion guide defines the path for a symbol to follow in a classic tween. One motion-guide layer can control classic-tween symbols on several layers. The motion-guide layer governs any layers linked to it. The linked layers are defined as guided layers in the Layer Properties dialog.

If you want different classic-tween symbols to follow different paths, create several motion-guide layers within a single Flash document. Each motion guide governs the actions of classic-tween symbols on its own set of linked layers.

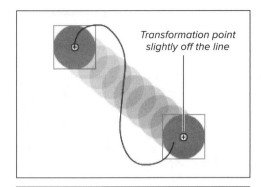

Transformation point slightly off the line

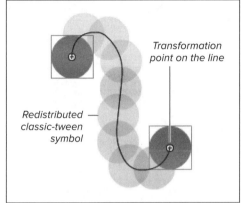

Transformation point on the line

Redistributed classic-tween symbol

D To follow the motion guide, each instance of the classic-tween symbol must have its transformation point sitting directly on the motion-guide line. (The transformation point appears as a small white circle.)

3. In Keyframe 10, drag the classic-tween symbol to position its transformation point directly over the end of the motion guide.

Flash redraws the in-between frames so that the symbol follows the motion guide **D**. Flash centers the classic-tween symbol over the motion guide in each in-between frame. In the final movie, Flash hides the guide.

TIP After you draw the motion guide, lock the motion-guide layer to prevent yourself from editing the guide accidentally as you snap the classic-tween symbol to the guide.

TIP When you select the initial keyframe of a classic tween in the Timeline, the Tweening section of the Frame Property inspector contains a Snap checkbox; select it to have Flash help you center keyframe graphics over the end of the guide.

TIP You can use most of Flash's drawing tools—line, pencil, pen, oval, rectangle, polygon, polystar, and brush—to create a motion guide. For best results, the path should not be closed. If you use the rectangle or oval tools, use the eraser tool to create a small break in the path. The tools may be set to Merge Drawing or Object Drawing mode. The paths created by the oval- and rectangle-primitive tools, however, do not work as motion guides.

TIP To make two symbols move along two different paths, place each symbol in its own layer, and set up its classic tween animation. Then create a separate motion-guide layer (with a different motion-guide line) for each one.

About Motion Guides and Orient to Path

Being round and symmetrical, a ball looks natural following a motion guide whether it's a flat line or a complex curve. Other symbols may require rotation to appear natural as they move along the path created by the motion guide. You might want a living creature to face in the direction it's moving, rotating slightly to match the twists and turns of its path. If the path is a simple arc, rotating the symbol instances in the initial and ending keyframes of a classic tween to align with the motion guide is usually enough to make the movement seem natural, as Flash interpolates between the two positions. If the curve is complex—an S shape, for example—that change in orientation may not be enough. In Orient to Path mode, Flash forces a classic-tween symbol instance to rotate to preserve its orientation to the motion guide, through all its curves . To activate Orient to Path mode, select the Orient to Path checkbox in the Tweening section of the Frame Property inspector **F**.

E The triangle has been rotated in the initial and ending keyframes to align with the motion guide, but without activating Orient to Path, that rotation doesn't give Flash enough information to keep the triangle aligned in the midsection of the curve (left). When Orient to Path is active, the arrow rotates to align better with the path at every frame (right).

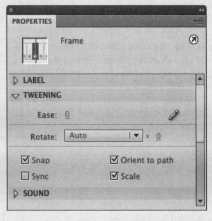

F For a classic tween, select the Orient to Path checkbox in the Tweening section of the Frame Property inspector. This forces Flash to rotate the classic-tween symbol to face the direction of movement.

A To assign classic tweening to a keyframe span, select any frame in the span, then choose Insert > Classic Tween.

Animating Changes in Size

In classic tweening, you can animate changes to the size of a symbol from one keyframe to the next by changing the symbol's Horizontal Scale and/or Vertical Scale properties. To enable the symbol to grow or shrink in a classic tween, you must select the Scale checkbox in the Frame Property inspector.

To make a classic-tween symbol grow and shrink:

1. In a new Flash document or on a new layer, in Keyframe 1, place a symbol instance on the Stage.

   (To review the creation and use of symbols, see Chapter 7.)

2. To create a keyframe that defines the end of a growing sequence, select Frame 5 in the Timeline; then choose Insert > Timeline > Keyframe.

   Flash duplicates the symbol from Keyframe 1 in the new keyframe.

3. Select any of the frames in the keyframe span (Frame 1, 2, 3, or 4).

4. Choose Insert > Classic Tween **A**.

   The classic-tween arrow and color coding now appear in the keyframe span.

5. With the frame you selected in Step 3 still selected, access the Property inspector.

   The Frame Property inspector contains a Tweening section, with settings that apply to this segment of classic tweening.

   continues on next page

6. In the Tweening section make sure the Scale checkbox is selected (it is selected by default) **B**.

When Scale is selected, Flash increases the size of the symbol instance in equal steps from Keyframe 1 to Keyframe 5. Otherwise, the symbol remains at its original size through all the frames of the keyframe span (Frames 1 through 4) and suddenly increases to the larger size at the final keyframe (Frame 5).

7. With the playhead in Keyframe 5, select the symbol instance and make it bigger.

(For detailed instructions on resizing graphics, see Chapter 4.)

8. To add the ending keyframe for a shrinking sequence, select Frame 10 in the Timeline; then press F6.

Flash duplicates the symbol from Keyframe 5 in the new keyframe.

9. Select any of the frames in the keyframe span (Frame 5, 6, 7, 8, or 9).

10. Choose Insert > Classic Tween.

The classic-tween arrow and color coding now appear in the second keyframe span (Frames 5 through 9). The Scale checkbox is already selected in the Tween section of the Frame Property inspector.

11. With the playhead in Keyframe 10, select the symbol instance and make it smaller.

Flash creates a tween that shrinks your graphic in five equal steps **C**.

TIP As long as you don't change the settings in the Frame Property inspector, the Scale checkbox remains selected, and Flash updates the tween anytime you change the content in one of the keyframes in the sequence. You don't have to have the Frame Property inspector open to fine-tune the size of your scaling graphic.

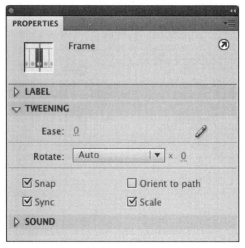

B To make a classic-tween symbol grow in equal steps, select the Scale checkbox in the Tweening section of the Frame Property inspector.

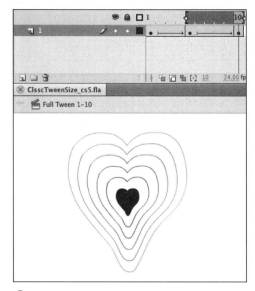

C To tween a shrinking symbol in a classic tween, make it smaller in the ending keyframe of the sequence. Turn on Onion Skin mode to see the size of the symbol Flash creates for each in-between frame.

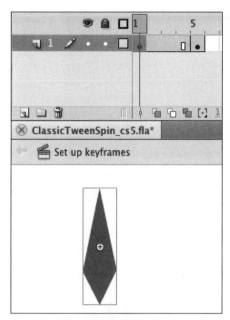

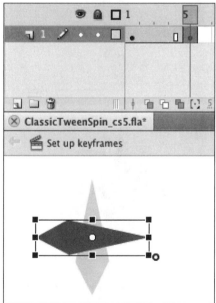

A To prepare a rotational classic tween, in the keyframe that ends the sequence, rotate the item to its ending position.

Rotating and Spinning Graphics

In classic tweening, you can make a symbol spin by changing its Rotation property. When you create a classic tween for rotation, you must not only create beginning and ending keyframes (as you did for animating changes to position and size), you must also specify the direction of rotation, and the number of times to spin.

To rotate a symbol less than 360 degrees:

1. In a new Flash document or on a new layer, in Keyframe 1, place a symbol instance on the Stage.

   You can create a new symbol or use an existing one; use a graphic that looks different at various stages of its rotation—for example, a triangle or an arrow. (To review symbol creation, see Chapter 7.)

2. In the Timeline, select Frame 5, and choose Insert > Timeline > Keyframe.

   Flash duplicates the symbol from Keyframe 1 in the new keyframe.

3. On the Stage, in Keyframe 5, rotate the symbol instance 90 degrees clockwise **A**.

   (For detailed instructions on rotating elements, see Chapter 4.)

4. In the Timeline, select any of the frames in the first keyframe span (Frame 1, 2, 3, or 4).

5. Choose Insert > Classic Tween.

6. With the frame you selected in Step 4 still selected, access the Frame Property inspector's Tweening section.

continues on next page

7. From the Rotate menu 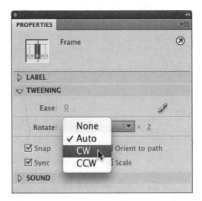, choose one of the following options:

   ▸ **Auto** rotates the graphic in the direction that requires the smallest movement **C**.

   ▸ **CW** rotates the graphic clockwise.

   ▸ **CCW** rotates the graphic counterclockwise.

8. To rotate less then 360 degrees, click the Rotation Count hot text (to the right of the Rotate menu), enter 0, and press Enter.

   Flash tweens the symbol so that it rotates around its transformation point. Each in-between frame shows the symbol rotated a little more.

B The Rotate menu in the Tweening section of the Frame Property inspector lets you tell Flash the direction in which to rotate a symbol in a classic tween.

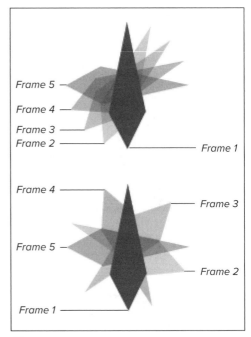

C To create a classic tween that involves rotation, you can specify the direction of the rotation as clockwise or counterclockwise. You can also choose Auto to let Flash pick the direction that involves the smallest change, which allows Flash to create the smoothest motion. Compare the degree of change in each frame between rotating an arrow clockwise from 12 o'clock to 3 o'clock (top) versus rotating the arrow counterclockwise to reach the same position (bottom).

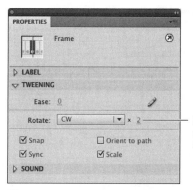

D In the Frame Property inspector, you can set the number of times a classically tweened item should spin.

E Compare a single rotation (top) with a double rotation (bottom) in the same number of frames.

Enter the number of rotations

To spin a symbol 360 degrees:

1. Follow Steps 1 and 2 of the preceding task to create a five-frame sequence with identical keyframes in Frame 1 and Frame 5.

   You don't need to reposition your graphic, because the beginning frame and ending frame of a 360-degree spin should look exactly the same.

2. In the Timeline, select any of the frames in the first keyframe span (Frame 1, 2, 3, or 4).

3. Choose Insert > Classic Tween and access the Frame Property inspector.

4. In the Tweening section, from the Rotate menu, choose a direction of rotation.

5. Select the Rotate Count hot text, to the right of the Rotate menu, and enter the number of rotations you want to use **D**.

   The value you enter determines how Flash tweens the symbol. Flash creates new positions for the symbol to rotate it completely the given number of times in the span of frames. Flash tweens the symbol differently depending on the number of rotations you choose **E**.

Animating Color Effects

When you use classic tweening to animate changes to symbol instances in keyframes, you can also tween changes in color, by applying a color effect to the symbol instance.

To change a symbol's color over time:

1. In a new Flash document, create a five-frame classic tween: In Keyframe 1, place a symbol instance containing a red object on the Stage. In the Timeline, select Frame 5, and choose Insert > Timeline > Keyframe. Select any of the frames in the first keyframe span (Frame 1, 2, 3, or 4) and choose Insert > Classic Tween.

2. With Keyframe 5 as the current frame, select the symbol and access the Property inspector.

3. To change the symbol's color, in the Color Effect section of the Property inspector, from the Style menu, choose new settings. (For detailed instructions on modifying symbol color, see Chapter 7.)

   Flash recolors the symbol in three transitional steps—one for each in-between frame 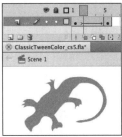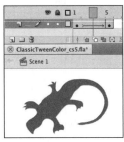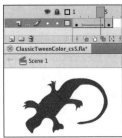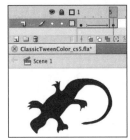 **A**.

A In a classic tween, you can change the color of a symbol, as well as its position. Flash creates transitional colors for each in-between frame.

4. To tween additional color changes, add tween segments.

In the Timeline, select Frame 10 and press F6 to duplicate the preceding keyframe. Select any of the frames in the second keyframe span (Frame 5, 6, 7, 8, or 9) and choose Insert > Classic Tween. Select the symbol in Frame 10 and repeat Step 3.

TIP You can use classic-tweening to change a symbol's transparency (Alpha), making that symbol appear to fade in or out.

Practice Session

Try using classic tweening to animate a fanciful creature that moves across the Stage.

- Using Flash's Insert > New Symbol command, create a bird symbol from scratch. (See Chapter 7, *Working with Symbols*.) Use any of the drawing, modifying, grouping, and layering techniques you've learned. (See Chapters 2, 4, 5, and 6.)

- Set up a straight-line classic tween using the bird symbol. Try putting the bird near the upper-left corner of the Stage at Keyframe 1, then create a duplicate keyframe at Frame 30 and move the bird to the pasteboard, just outside the bottom-right corner of the Stage. (See *Creating a Bouncing Ball with Classic Tweening > To prepare content for classic tweening*.)

- Apply classic tweening to the keyframe span. (See *Creating a Bouncing Ball with Classic Tweening > To apply classic tweening*.)

- Add a motion guide that leads the bird in a curve. (See *Moving Symbols Along a Path*.)

Extra Credit

- Create whimsy by dividing the animation into multiple segments, then playing with the size, rotation, and color of the symbol in each one. (Hint: Add more keyframes.) In one segment, make the bird spin so it appears to tumble as it flies for a few frames. In the next segment change the symbol's color as if the bird had grown dizzy. In the final keyframe, enlarge the symbol, so the bird appears to be flying closer as it exits the Stage.

Save your file for use in future Practice Sessions.

Animation with Shape Tweening

Shape tweening in Adobe Flash Professional CS5 works much like classic tweening. You set up a keyframe span (the graphic content of the beginning and ending keyframes must be different in some way), then you define the keyframe span as a shape tween. Flash redraws the graphics for each in-between frame, making the incremental changes that transform the first shape into the final one. Shape tweens can animate changes to the path that defines the shape of a graphic element as well as to an element's size, color, location, and so on.

Flash can shape-tween more than one graphic on a layer, but the results can be unpredictable. When you have several shapes on a layer, there is no way to tell Flash which starting shape goes with which ending shape. By limiting yourself to a single shape tween on each layer, you can tell Flash exactly what to change.

Unless otherwise indicated, you can perform the tasks in this chapter using merge-shapes, drawing-objects, or primitive-shapes.

In This Chapter

Creating a Bouncing Ball with Shape Tweening

Although shape tweens can animate changes in many properties of graphics—color, size, location—the distinguishing function of shape tweening is to transform one shape into another. You could use a shape tween to replicate the simple bouncing-ball animation you created in Chapters 8 and 9, but a better use of shape tweening for a bouncing ball is to flatten the ball as it strikes the ground.

To prepare content for shape-tweening:

1. In Keyframe 1 of a new document, create a bouncing ball shape near the top of the Stage.

   Use the oval tool in either Merge mode or Object Drawing mode to draw a circle.

2. Command-click (Mac) or Ctrl-click (Windows) Frames 5 and 10 and press F6.

   Flash creates Keyframes 5 and 10, duplicating Keyframe 1 **A**. (To review creating keyframes, see Chapter 8.)

3. In Frame 5, select the ball and drag it to the bottom of the Stage, the low point of the bounce.

4. Using any of the techniques you learned in Chapter 4, reshape the circle, elongating it a bit sideways and flattening the bottom **B**.

A To begin setting up the bouncing ball as a shape tween, you create Keyframes 1, 5, and 10, just as you did for classic tweens in the previous chapter. The ball must be a shape, not a symbol instance.

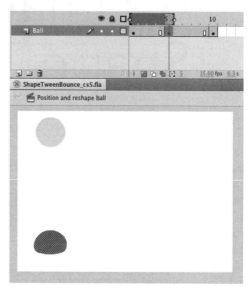

B Changing the shape of the ball graphic in the keyframe representing the bottom of the bounce makes the movement appear more natural. The ball seems to respond to gravity by flattening on contact with something solid—say, the floor. (Turn on onion skinning to see the beginning and ending keyframes.)

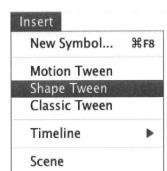

 To create
the tween,
choose Insert >
Shape Tween.

When to Use Shape Tweening

Flash CS5 offers two laborsaving methods for animating changes to shapes: shape tweening and inverse kinematics (IK; see Chapter 13). Shape tweening lets you animate changes to the outline of a merge-shape or drawing-object. You can use a shape tween to modify a shape slightly—for example, to make a box bulge outward on one side—or to completely transform a shape—for example, to turn Cinderella's pumpkin into a coach. You have full control over the shape at key points in the transformation because you draw the shapes in the initial and ending keyframes and you can use shape hints to improve the transitions. But Flash's interpolation of the changes might still be unsatisfactory. Depending on the shapes involved, inverse kinematics (IK) might be a better choice. You can use IK to animate changes to the outline of a shape; the movement of the IK structure within the shape determines how the outline changes, and you can adjust the structure to help create the transitions you want.

5. In Frame 10, select the ball, and drag it to a position slightly above mid-Stage, almost back to the starting point.

TIP In Step 5, instead of dragging the ball to position it, you could select the ball shape, then use the Property inspector or Info panel to change the *x*- and/or *y*-coordinates for the shape's bounding box.

To apply shape tweening:

1. To define the shape tween for the first half of the ball's bounce, select any of the frames in the first keyframe span (Frame 1, 2, 3, or 4) in the Timeline.

Note that the ball is selected automatically. When you define a shape tween, the element to be tweened must be selected.

2. Choose Insert > Shape Tween .

Flash creates a shape tween in Frames 1 through 4 and color-codes those frames in the Timeline. With Tinted Frames active (choose it from the Timeline's panel menu), Flash applies a light green shade to the frames containing a shape tween. If Tinted Frames is inactive, the frames are white, but Flash changes the arrow that indicates the presence of a tween from black to green.

continues on next page

3. In the Tweening section of the Frame Property inspector, from the Blend menu 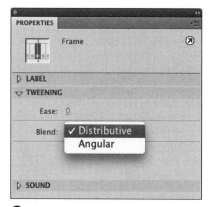, choose either of the following options:

   ▸ **Distributive** smooths out the in-between shapes.

   ▸ **Angular** preserves sharp corners and straight lines as one shape transforms into another.

4. To define the shape tween for the second half of the ball's bounce, in the Timeline, select any of the frames in the second keyframe span (5, 6, 7, 8, or 9).

5. Repeat Steps 2 and 3.

   Flash creates the second half of the ball's bounce with another shape tween **E**.

D When you select a keyframe span of a shape tween, the Tweening section of the Frame Property inspector displays the shape-tween settings. To determine how Flash handles changes to corners in your graphic as it changes shape, choose a setting from the Blend menu.

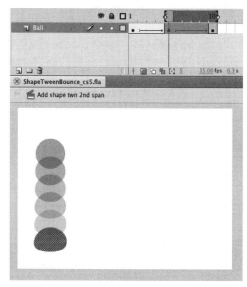

E With onion skinning turned on, you can see the in-between frames Flash creates for the shape tween in the second keyframe span (the rebound). This animation looks similar to the bouncing ball created with a classic tween. In this case, the change in the object's shape creates the illusion of impact.

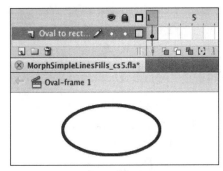

A Draw an oval in the first keyframe of your shape tween.

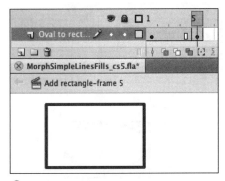

B Draw a rectangle in the second keyframe of your shape tween.

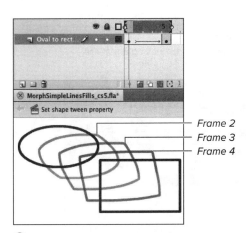

C When you define Frames 1 through 4 as a shape tween, Flash creates the three intermediate shapes that transform the oval into a rectangle. Turn on onion skinning to see the shapes for the in-between frames.

Morphing Simple Lines and Fills

Flash can transform both fill shapes and lines (strokes). In this section, you try some shape-changing tasks with both types of shapes.

To transform an oval into a rectangle:

1. In a new Flash document or on a new layer, in Frame 1, draw an outline oval on the Stage **A**.

2. In the Timeline, select Frame 5, and choose Insert > Timeline > Blank Keyframe.

   Flash creates a keyframe but removes all content from the Stage.

3. On the Stage, in Frame 5, draw an outline rectangle **B**.

   Don't worry about placing the rectangle in exactly the same location on the Stage as the oval; you'll adjust the position later.

4. In the Timeline, select any of the frames in the keyframe span (1, 2, 3, or 4).

5. Choose Insert > Shape Tween.

   Flash transforms the oval into the rectangle in three equal steps—one for each in-between frame **C**.

continues on next page

6. To align the oval and rectangle, do the following:

   ▸ In the Timeline's Status bar, click the Onion Skin button or the Onion Skin Outlines button.

   Flash displays all the in-between frames.

   ▸ In the Timeline, position the playhead in Frame 1.

   ▸ On the Stage, reposition the oval so that it aligns with the rectangle 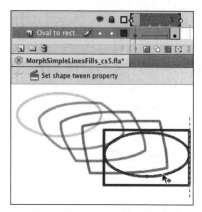.

   The oval transforms into a rectangle, remaining in one spot on the Stage.

To transform a rectangle into a free-form shape:

1. In a new Flash document or on a new layer, in Frame 1, draw a rectangular fill on the Stage.

2. In the Timeline, select Frame 5, and choose Insert > Timeline > Blank Keyframe.

3. On the Stage, in Frame 5, use the brush tool to paint a free-form fill.

   Don't make the fill too complex—just a blob or brushstroke with gentle curves.

4. In the Timeline, select any of the frames in the keyframe span (1, 2, 3, or 4).

5. Choose Insert > Shape Tween.

   Flash transforms the rectangle into the free-form fill in three equal steps—one for each in-between frame 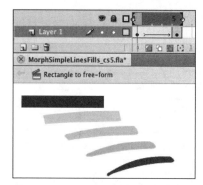.

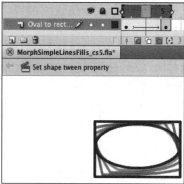

D Use onion skinning to help position your keyframe shapes. Here, with Frame 1 selected, you can drag the oval to center it within the rectangle (top). That makes the oval grow into a rectangle without moving anywhere else on the Stage (bottom).

E Flash transforms a rectangle into a free-form brushstroke with shape tweening.

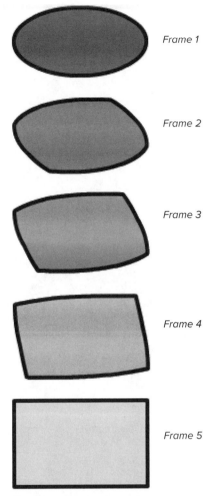

Frame 1

Frame 2

Frame 3

Frame 4

Frame 5

A Here, Flash transforms a shape with a stroke in five frames. The shape tween changes not only the graphic's shape, but also its color (from dark to light).

Shape-Tweening Multiple Shapes

In classic tweening (Chapter 9) and motion tweening (Chapter 11), Flash limits you to one item per tween, meaning just one item per layer. In shape tweening, however, Flash can handle more than one shape on a layer. The drawback is that you may get some strange results. The simpler and fewer the shapes you use, the more reliable your multiple-shape tweens will be. For the most predictable results, limit yourself to one shape per layer.

You may want to keep both shapes on the same layer for a fill with an outline (stroke), however. As long as the transformation isn't too complicated, Flash can handle the two together.

To shape-tween fills with strokes (outlines):

1. Follow the steps in the preceding tasks to create a shape tween of an outline oval transforming into a rectangle.

2. Fill each shape with a different color.

   Flash tweens the fill and the stroke together and tweens the change in color **A**.

TIP You can tween a disappearing act: Make the color of the stroke around a shape (or the shape, or both) get gradually lighter and lighter, until it finally disappears. Make the color of the final stroke (and/or shape) in the tween match the color of the background, or give it a fully transparent color (one with an alpha setting of 0 percent).

TIP To ensure that the item in the preceding tip does fully disappear (some low-color monitors may not display tint and alpha changes accurately), select the frame following the last keyframe of the tween sequence. Choose Insert > Timeline > Keyframe to duplicate the previous keyframe; then delete your disappearing stroke (or shape).

When Multiple-Shape Tweens on a Single Layer Go Bad

If you're shape-tweening stationary elements, you probably can get away with having several on the same layer. But if the elements move around much, Flash can get confused about which shape goes where. Although you may intend the paths of two shapes to cross, Flash creates the most direct route between the starting shape and the ending one. **B** illustrates the problem.

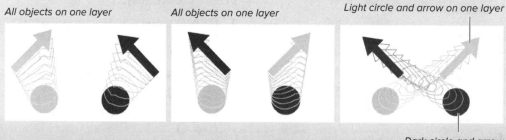

All objects on one layer

All objects on one layer

Light circle and arrow on one layer

Dark circle and arrow on another layer

B Tweening multiple shapes whose paths don't cross in a single layer works fine. In the left-hand image, both objects are on the same layer, and the light circle transforms into the light arrow without a hitch. In the middle image, both objects are on the same layer, but Flash transforms the light circle into the dark arrow and the dark circle into the light arrow because that's the most direct path. If you want to create diagonal paths that cross, you must put each object on its own layer, as in the right-hand image.

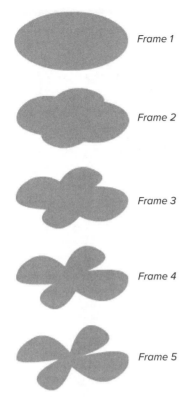

Frame 1

Frame 2

Frame 3

Frame 4

Frame 5

A Flash handles the tween from an oval to a simple flower shape without requiring shape hints.

Transforming a Simple Shape into a Complex Shape

The more complex the shape you tween, the more difficult it is for Flash to create the expected result. You can help Flash tween better by using *shape hints*—markers that let you identify points on the path of the original shape that correspond to points on the path of the final shape.

To shape-tween a more complex shape:

1. In a new Flash document, or on a new layer, create a five-frame shape tween using an oval.

   In the Timeline, in Frame 1, draw an oval fill with no stroke. On the Stage select Frame 5, and choose Insert > Timeline > Keyframe. Flash duplicates the contents of Keyframe 1 in Keyframe 5. In the Timeline, select any of the frames in the keyframe span (1, 2, 3, or 4) and choose Insert > Shape Tween.

2. Create the ending shape.

   In the Timeline, position the playhead in Frame 5. Using the selection tool or subselection tool, drag four corner points in toward the center of the oval to create a flower shape. (To review editing shapes, see Chapter 4.)

3. Play the movie to see the shape tween.

   Flash handles the tweening for this change well **A**. It's fairly obvious which points of the oval should move in to create the petal shapes. If you modify the shape further, however, it becomes more difficult for Flash to know how to create the new shape. That's when you need to use shape hints.

To use shape hints:

1. Using the animation you created in the preceding task, add another shape-tween segment:

   In the Timeline, select Frame 10, and choose Insert > Timeline > Keyframe. Flash duplicates the flower shape in a new keyframe. Select any frame in the keyframe span (5, 6, 7, 8, or 9) and choose Insert > Shape Tween.

2. In Keyframe 10, edit the flower to add a stem.

   Reshape the flower's path with the selection tool or the pen and subselection tools, or add a stem with a brush-stroke in the same color as the flower.

3. Play the movie.

   The addition of the stem to the flower makes it difficult for Flash to create a smooth tween that looks right **B**.

4. To begin adding shape hints, position the playhead in Keyframe 5 (the initial keyframe of this tweening sequence).

5. Choose Modify > Shape > Add Shape Hint, or press Shift-Command-H (Mac) or Ctrl-Shift-H (Windows) **C**.

   Flash places a shape hint—a small red circle labeled with a letter, starting with *a*—in the center of the object in the current frame. You need to reposition the shape hint to place it on a problem point on the shape's path.

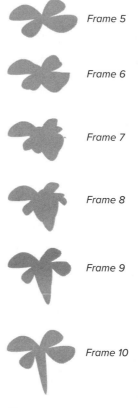

Frame 5

Frame 6

Frame 7

Frame 8

Frame 9

Frame 10

B The addition of a stem to the flower overloads Flash's capability to create a smooth shape tween. Frames 7 and 8 are particularly bad.

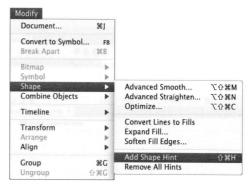

C Choose Modify > Shape > Add Shape Hint to activate markers that help Flash make connections between the original shape and the final shape of the tween.

Areas of change

D Start adding shape hints in the first keyframe of a tween sequence. Flash places the hints in the center of the tweened object (top). You must drag the hints into position (middle). Distribute the hints in alphabetical order along the object's path, placing them on crucial points of change (bottom). Here, the three points with hints *a*, *b*, and *c* define the points from which the stem of the flower will grow.

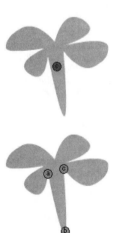

E To complete the placement of shape hints, select the second keyframe of your tween sequence. Flash stacks up hints corresponding to the ones you placed in the preceding keyframe (top). You must drag them into the correct final position (bottom).

6. With the selection tool, drag the shape hint to a problem point on the edge of the shape.

As you drag, Flash previews the hint's position with a circle icon; the circle gets darker and thicker when it connects with the path. Don't worry about getting the shape hint in exactly the right spot; just make sure it's on the path. You can fine-tune its position later.

7. Repeat Steps 5 and 6 until you have placed shape hints on all the problem points of your shape in Keyframe 5 **D**.

Each time you add a shape hint, you get another small red circle labeled with a letter. You can't place the hints at random; you must place them so they go in alphabetical order around the edge of the shape. (Flash does the best job when you place shape hints in counterclockwise order, starting in the upper-left corner of the shape, but you can also place them in clockwise order.)

8. In the Timeline, position the playhead in Keyframe 10.

Flash has already added shape hints to this frame; they all stack up in the center of the shape.

9. With the selection tool, drag each shape hint to its position on the path of the new shape.

Keep them in the same order (counterclockwise or clockwise) you chose in Step 7 **E**. When the end-of-tween shape hint is sitting on a path, the hint changes from red to green; if you select the initial keyframe of the span, you can see that the associated beginning-of-tween hint has turned yellow.

10. To evaluate the improvement in tweening, play the movie.

continues on next page

11. To fine-tune the shape hints' positions, select one of the tween's keyframes, and turn on Onion Skin Outlines mode.

Set the onion markers to include all the frames of the tween. Where the onion skin outlines reveal rough spots in the tween, you may need to match the hint position better from the first keyframe to the last one 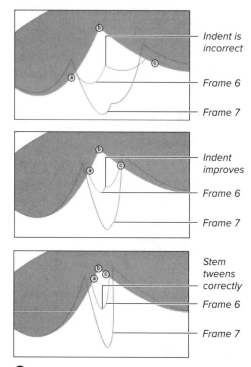. Repositioning the shape hints changes the in-between frames. You may need to adjust the shape hints in both keyframes. If you still can't get a smooth tween, try adding more shape hints.

TIP To remove a single shape hint, make the initial keyframe the current frame. Select the shape hint you want to remove, and drag it out of the document window. Or, Control-click (Mac) or right-click (Windows) the shape hint, and choose Remove Hint.

TIP To remove all the hints at the same time, with the initial keyframe current, choose Modify > Shape > Remove All Hints. Or Control-click (Mac) or Right-click (Windows) any shape hint, and choose Remove All Hints.

TIP If you can't create a smooth tween using shape hints alone, break the tween into smaller pieces by adding keyframes where the morphing gets off track. Then redraw the shapes for those frames yourself.

TIP If you use the selection tool to select a shape with hints, Flash hides the little letters. To view the hints again, choose View > Show Shape Hints or press Option-Command-H (Mac) or Ctrl-Alt-H (Windows).

TIP On Windows, when you work with a shape that already has hints, you can add a new hint quickly by Ctrl-clicking any of the existing shape hints.

Indent is
incorrect

Frame 6

Frame 7

Indent
improves

Frame 6

Frame 7

Stem
tweens
correctly

Frame 6

Frame 7

F It can be difficult to match up points in the two keyframes exactly when you first place the shape hints. When you've positioned the hints in the beginning and ending keyframes of a sequence, turn on onion-skin outlines to see where you need to adjust the placement of your hints. With the initial placement, Flash starts the stem growing with an indent at the bottom (top). Moving the points closer together improves the tween (middle). When the onion skin outlines reveal a smooth tween, you're done (bottom).

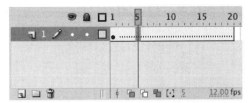

A To save yourself numerous trips to the menu bar, you can assign the shape-tween property to a range of frames and add keyframes and shapes later. The initial keyframe must contain a shape, but the later keyframes can be blank.

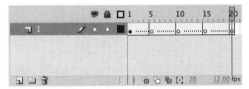

B When you insert keyframes into a long tween sequence, Flash breaks it into smaller tween sequences. Until you place content in the keyframes, the Timeline displays the dotted line in each span to indicate a broken tween.

Creating Shapes That Move As They Change

You can't create shape tweens that automatically follow a path, but you can move shapes around the Stage in straight lines. To do so, reposition the elements on the Stage from one keyframe to the next.

To shape-tween a moving graphic:

1. In a new Flash document or on a new layer, select Frame 20, and choose Insert > Timeline > Frame.

   Flash adds blank in-between Frames 2 through 20.

2. Select Keyframe 1 and create some content to start the sequence; for example, draw a circular fill in the lower left corner of the Stage.

3. In the Timeline, select any frame in the span (Frames 1 through 20).

   Note that you must click the frame to select it; you can't just position the playhead in the frame.

4. Choose Insert > Shape Tween.

   Flash defines the keyframe span as a shape tween. In the Timeline, a dotted line appears in the keyframe span, indicating that the tween is incomplete **A**. Now you can add keyframes and shapes.

5. In the Timeline, insert a blank keyframe at Frames 5, 10, 15, and 20.

   Flash creates four shape-tween sequences **B**. For the moment, they're broken tweens because the keyframes are empty.

continues on next page

6. To complete the tween sequences, in each keyframe, draw a different shape; place each one in a different corner of the Stage.

In Keyframe 5, for example, draw a rectangular fill in the top-right corner of the Stage. In Keyframe 10, draw an oval in the bottom-right corner of the Stage. In Keyframe 15, draw a star in the top-left corner of the Stage. And in Keyframe 20, duplicate Keyframe 1's circle in the bottom-left corner of the Stage. For extra variety, give each object a different color. As you add content to keyframes, Flash fills in the spans in the Timeline with tween arrows.

7. Play the movie.

You see a graphic that bounces around the Stage, morphing from one shape to the next 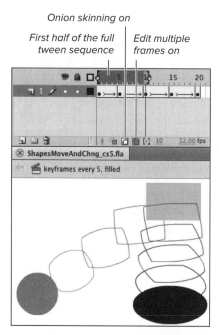.

Onion skinning on

First half of the full tween sequence

Edit multiple frames on

Second half of the full tween sequence

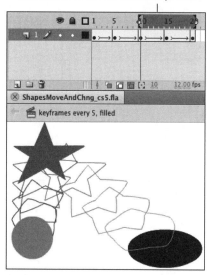

C Place a different shape in a different location in each keyframe. Flash creates the intermediate steps necessary to transform the shapes and move them across the Stage. Play the movie or turn on onion skinning to examine the motion and shape changes in the in-between frames. (Here, Edit Multiple Frames is also on, making it easy to see the keyframe shapes.)

The Pitfalls of Primitive Tweens

Although you can create shape tweens using oval- or rectangle-primitives, you're likely to find the animation Flash creates with them to be a bit disappointing. When you use a primitive's control points to change the primitive's path on the Stage, there is a sense of motion as the shape redraws itself. Drag the control point for the start or end angle of an oval-primitive, and the preview radius line rotates like the minute hand of a clock. As Flash redraws the shape, there is feeling of rotation, as if you're opening and closing a folding paper fan. In shape-tweening, Flash doesn't re-create that motion by animating the control points' movements; instead, working with the merge-shapes that lie at the foundation of the primitives, Flash transforms the initial shape into the final shape. You wind up with an oval, for example, that squeezes itself down into a pie wedge. Shape hints may help that transformation, but they won't create the feeling of rotation. If you decide to use shape hints with a primitive, you must deselect it. Otherwise the shape-hint choice is unavailable in the Modify > Shape submenu.

Moving Morphing Shapes Along a Curve

Tweened shapes can't automatically follow a curving path the way classic- and motion-tweened objects can, but you can make Flash do the work of creating the separate keyframes you need to make a shape that changes as it moves along a curved path. First, create your shape tween. In the Timeline, select the full range of frames in the tween sequence. Choose Modify > Timeline > Convert to Keyframes. Flash converts each in-between frame (with its transitional content) into a keyframe. Now you can position each keyframe shape anywhere you like. To map out a curved path to guide you in positioning each shape correctly, create a regular guide layer (see Chapter 6), and draw the path you want your morphing shape to follow. Choose View > Snapping > Snap to Objects. Reposition the shape in each keyframe. When you drag a shape close to the line on the guide layer, Flash snaps the shape to the line.

Alternatively, to animate a morphing shape that follows a path, create a shape tween, then save that animation as a movie-clip symbol (see Chapter 12). Use that symbol as the tween target in a motion tween, then edit the motion path to create the curves you want (see Chapter 11).

Practice Session

When you want one shape to change fluidly into another shape, you can use shape tweening. Try transforming a simple oval shape into a grinning mouth.

- Using the oval tool, in Merge Drawing mode, with a red fill and no stroke, draw an oval on the Stage in Keyframe 1 of Layer 1; make it wide horizontally, like a crude mouth shape. (See Chapter 2, *Making Geometric Shapes* > *To create geometric fills.*)

- Use the oval tool in Merge Drawing mode again to draw a smaller white oval inside the red one, in effect erasing the inside of the oval and creating a mouth shape. (See Chapter 5's sidebar, *When Merge-Shapes Interact.*)

- Select Frames 10 and 20 and convert them to keyframes. (See Chapter 8, *Creating Keyframes.*)

- Use the drawing tools to modify the ovals: in Keyframe 1, make the corners of the mouth turn down slightly; in Keyframe 20, make the corners of the mouth turn up into a huge smile. (See Chapter 4.)

- Apply shape tweening to each keyframe span. (See *Creating a Bouncing Ball with Shape Tweening* > *To apply shape tweening.*)

Extra Credit

- Adjust the transparency of the fill for the mouth in the final keyframe so that the grin fades away.

- Modify the final grin more to turn it into a complicated grimace. Add shape hints to improve the transformation.

Animation with Motion Tweening

In a classic tween, you create animation by setting up a series of keyframes; each keyframe contains a separate instance of the symbol you want to animate. You manipulate each symbol individually to change its properties. Flash calculates any differences in the symbols' properties at each keyframe (position, size, rotation, and so on) and uses that information to create a series of images in which the symbol changes incrementally.

Motion tweens work somewhat differently. You set up a single keyframe, with a single symbol instance, then define a motion-tween span. Within that span, property keyframes account for changes to the symbol's properties. Again, Flash animates the symbol instance—known as the *tween target* or *target instance*—by creating a series of images that change the tween target's properties over time.

Creating a Bouncing Ball with Motion Tweening

It's easy to do a version of the standard bouncing-ball animation with motion tweening. A motion tween uses a single instance of the ball. You place it in a tween span in the Timeline and tell Flash how to move that instance by adding position keyframes.

To set up a motion tween:

1. Open a new Flash document.

   The document contains one layer and one keyframe (Frame 1).

2. To preset the motion tween's duration, select the frame that marks your desired span length—for example, Frame 10—and choose Insert > Timeline > Frame.

   Flash removes the dividers between frames and adds a hollow rectangle to Frame 10, indicating a keyframe span.

3. In the Timeline, select Keyframe 1.

4. Place an instance of a symbol that represents a ball near the top of the Stage.

   For example, use the oval tool to draw a circle shape, then convert it to a symbol (see Chapter 7) and name it MyBall.

5. To apply motion tweening to the target symbol, do either of the following:

   ▸ In the Timeline, select Keyframe 1 (the one containing MyBall) or any frame in the keyframe span (Frames 1–10). Flash selects the symbol on the Stage.

   or

   ▸ On the Stage, select the symbol you want to animate (MyBall). Flash

Motion Tween's Double Identity

The term *motion tweening* has two different meanings, depending on which version of Flash you're talking about. In Flash CS3 and earlier versions, motion tweening was the name for the style of animation called *classic tweening* in CS4 and later versions. Here's a key to these terms: motion tweening (CS4 and later) requires just one tween-span in the Timeline and one symbol instance on the Stage. Classic tweening (or motion tweening in CS3 and earlier) requires one or more keyframe spans in the Timeline; each span begins and ends with a separate symbol instance on the Stage.

Motion-Tween Symbols: Best Practice

Flash can create motion tweens using symbols or text fields (either TLF or Classic). If you attempt to apply motion tweening to other types of content, a dialog appears asking if you want Flash to convert the content to a symbol for you. If you answer OK, Flash creates the symbol with a generic name and carries out the motion tween. This is an improvement over Flash's automatic creation of symbols for classic tweens (where Flash just creates the symbol without any warning). Still, it's a good idea to decline Flash's automated conversion. Cancel the dialog and create your own symbol, so you can be sure it includes what you want it to include and you can give the symbol a meaningful name.

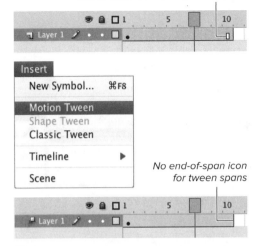

End-of-span icon for keyframe spans

No end-of-span icon for tween spans

A To create a motion-tween span of a specific length, first define a keyframe span in the Timeline (top). When you choose Insert > Motion Tween (middle), Flash converts that range of frames to a tween span (bottom). Otherwise, Flash decides how long the span should be, based on the specifics of the current Timeline.

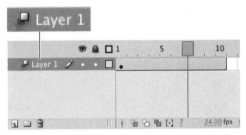

B Flash identifies layers containing a tween span in the Timeline by adding a motion-tween icon to the left of the layer name and tinting the tween span's frames light blue. (Tinted Frames need not be selected from the Timeline's panel menu; the motion-tween tint always appears.)

selects the entire keyframe span in the Timeline.

6. Choose Insert > Motion Tween **A**.

Flash converts the keyframe span to a *tween span*, and identifies the layer as one containing motion tweening by adding a motion-tween icon before the layer name **B**. Flash tints the frames of the span light blue. The tween target, MyBall, displays in all the frames of the span. To animate MyBall, you must add property keyframes within the tween span. The symbol in a motion tween is called the *tween target*.

TIP Defining a keyframe span (Step 2 in the preceding task) is optional. If you apply motion tweening to a single keyframe, Flash creates a tween span with a default length (see the sidebar "How Flash Determines Tween-Span Length").

TIP You can apply motion tweening directly to an object on the Stage (for best results, apply motion tweening only to a symbol or text field; see the sidebar "Motion-Tween Symbols: Best Practice"). Using the selection tool, Control-click (Mac) or right-click (Windows) the object to be tweened. From the contextual menu, choose Create Motion Tween.

TIP Each motion tween is limited to one object. If you apply motion tweening directly to an object on the Stage and there are other objects on the same layer, Flash pulls the selected object out to a separate new layer to create the motion tween. Flash inserts additional new layers in the Timeline hierarchy as needed to preserve the stacking order of the objects.

TIP You can't combine motion tweens with other types of tweens on the same layer. If, for example, you apply motion tweening to an object in a keyframe in the middle of a layer with shape tweens on either side of it, Flash pulls the target symbol to a new motion-tween layer, at the same frame number, and creates the tween span.

How Flash Determines Tween-Span Length

The Insert > Motion Tween command creates tween spans of different lengths depending on the arrangement of frames in the active layer. If you want Flash to create a tween span with a specific number of frames, you must first set up a keyframe span with that number of frames.

Before creating motion tween

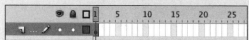

After creating motion tween

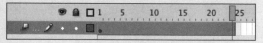

When the target symbol is in Keyframe 1 of a layer with no other defined frames, Flash creates a one-second tween span based on the current frame rate (at the default 24-fps frame rate, the resulting tween span contains 24 frames).

Before creating motion tween

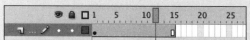

After creating motion tween

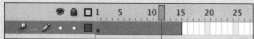

When the target symbol is in a keyframe span, Flash converts that span to a tween span with the same number of frames.

Before creating motion tween

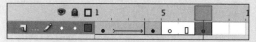

After creating motion tween

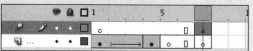

When the target symbol is the last frame of a layer with other defined frames, Flash creates a 1-frame tween span and pulls it into a new motion-tween layer.

Tweening One Symbol Among Many

A motion-tween span holds just one symbol or text field at a time. For simplicity, in this book you always apply motion tweening to a single symbol on its own layer. You can actually apply motion tweening to a selection that includes multiple symbols or text fields, or a selection that includes objects other than symbols or text fields. The selection can span multiple layers.

Here's how it works. Select the target item(s), then choose Insert > Motion Tween. If your selection contains multiple items on the same layer—or includes one or more items that are not symbols or text fields—Flash must convert the selection to a symbol before creating the tween span (see the sidebar "Motion-Tween Symbols: Best Practice," earlier in this chapter). If the selected items are on a layer with other—unselected—items, Flash converts the selection to a symbol, pulls the symbol into a new layer, and creates the tween span in the new layer (the unselected items remain on their original layer). If the selection includes all the items on a single layer, Flash creates the tween span in that layer. If you select multiple symbols and/or text fields, each residing on its own layer, Flash creates a separate tween span for each selected object on its original layer. A special motion-tween icon (a series of squares) identifies any layer containing a tween span.

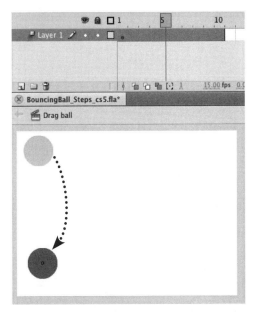

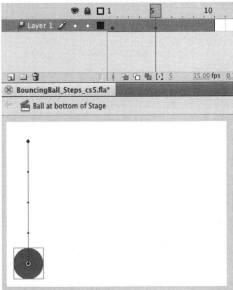

C When you change the position of the tween target on the Stage (top), Flash adds a property keyframe, represented by a small diamond icon, to the current frame of the Timeline and creates a motion path on the Stage (bottom).

To change the tween target's position for the downward bounce:

1. Continuing with the file from the preceding task, to set the tween target's position for the low point of the bounce, position the playhead in Frame 5 in the Timeline.

2. Using the selection tool, drag the tween target (MyBall) to the bottom of the stage.

   In the Timeline, Flash adds a diamond icon to the tween span at Frame 5. The diamond indicates a property keyframe—in this case a position keyframe (see the sidebar "About Property Keyframes," later in this chapter). The motion path for the tween appears on the Stage **C**.

continues on next page

3. Position the playhead in Frame 1 and choose Control > Play to see the animation.

The ball moves from the top of the Stage to the bottom in five frames, then sits at the bottom for five frames **D**.

4. Save your document as a template for future use; name it DownBounceMaster.

Be sure to close the template document before moving on to the next task. (For detailed instructions about templates, see Chapter 1.)

TIP When a symbol is selected, you can change its position by changing its *x*- and *y*-coordinates in the Info panel or in the Position and Size section of the Property inspector. You may need to click the symbol to view its properties in the inspector. If you select the tween span, the symbol is also selected, but it's the span that has focus; properties of the motion tween appear in the inspector.

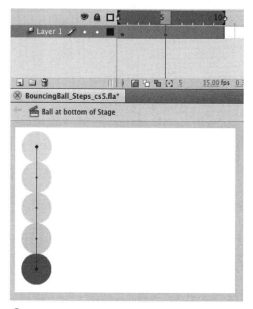

D The motion path gives you some idea about the movement of the tween target in a motion tween, but it's also good to play the animation to see how it's working. Here, onion skinning allows you to see the interpolated changes to the tween target.

About Property Keyframes

Flash's Motion Editor displays each tweenable property in a separate graph. By viewing the graph, you can see the exact values for tweened properties at every frame in a selected tween span. The Timeline is less precise. A diamond icon appears in a frame when you've assigned a value to a property in that frame. By assigning a value—for example, by manipulating the tween target on the Stage, or by entering a value in the Motion Editor—you create a *property keyframe.*

The Timeline indicates the presence of one or more property keyframes with a diamond icon. You can set the Timeline to display these diamonds or to hide them (see the sidebar "About Hiding Property Keyframes," later in this chapter). The Motion Editor displays curves for all tweenable properties; for example, in the Basic Motion section of the panel, you'll see separate curves for the horizontal and vertical positions of an object. The Timeline lumps the two into one property-keyframe type: *position.* The Timeline can display diamonds representing six properties: Position, Scale, Skew, Rotation, Color, and Filter. When talking about the Timeline, the tasks in this book refer to these general categories when mentioning the presence of a property keyframe. For example, Frame 5 contains a *position keyframe* and a *rotation keyframe.* When talking about the Motion Editor, tasks refer to the specific property curves—for example, the X curve and the Rotation Z curve each have a property keyframe at Frame 5.

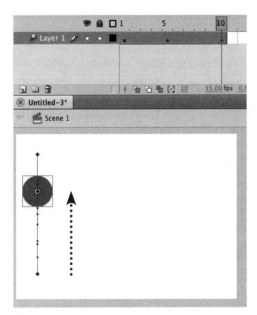

E The position of the playhead in a selected tween span tells Flash where to add a property keyframe for any changes you make to the selected tween target.

TIP In this task you create the rebound by adding a second position keyframe. This method makes it easy to know that a change takes place at this point in the Timeline. The drawback to this method is that the motion path for the rebound lies directly on top of the motion path for the downward bounce; it can be difficult to manipulate the overlapping segments of the motion path. More-advanced animators can achieve the same result by adding easing to create the rebound motion. (For a quick introduction to easing, see Chapter 12.) You can see an example of this in the default motion preset named Bounce – Smoosh (see the sidebar "About Motion Presets," later in this chapter).

To change the tween target's position for the upward bounce:

1. Using the DownBounceMaster template you created in the preceding task, open a new document.

2. To set the ball's position for the rebound, click Frame 10 in the Timeline, and use the arrow keys to position the tween target two-thirds of the way back up toward the original position.

   When you click a frame within a tween span, the playhead moves to that frame, and the *entire* tween span highlights, indicating that the span is selected. Flash also selects and highlights the tween target on the Stage, making it ready for manipulating, either directly with the selection tool or through a panel setting. The position of the play-head within the tween span determines where Flash will add new property keyframes that represent the changes you'll make **E**.

   Flash adds a second position keyframe to the tween span, at Frame 10, and adds a new segment to the motion path on the Stage. In this case, the new segment lies directly over the original path.

3. Choose Control > Test Scene to preview the animation.

   The ball moves from the top of the Stage to the bottom, then rebounds almost back to the top. If you let the animation loop, the ball bounces continually.

4. Save the document as a template for future use; name it FullBounceMaster.

   Be sure to close the template document before moving on to the next task. (For detailed instructions about templates, see Chapter 1.)

The Mystery of Roving Keyframes

In animation, the number of frames used to create motion can affect how fast or slow the motion seems. An object that covers lots of ground in a few frames seems to move quickly. One that goes a short distance over many frames seems to move slowly.

When you resize a tween span in the Timeline, Flash redistributes the tween span's position keyframes to retain the proportions of fast and slow movement. Start with a 15-frame motion tween of a ball, add a position keyframe at Frame 5, and move the ball 100 pixels to the right; add another position keyframe at Frame 15, and move the ball 50 pixels down. The movement to the right (the first third of the tween) seems faster than the movement down (the last two-thirds). If you stretch the span in the Timeline (see the tasks in "Modifying Tween Spans," later in this chapter) to 30 frames. That first position keyframe winds up at Frame 9, preserving the feeling that the first third of the movement is faster than the rest.

As you tweak the animation in a motion tween, you may wind up with undesirable changes of speed. By setting keyframes to *roving,* you can force Flash to redistribute position keyframes so that the speed is uniform.

To turn on roving keyframes from the Timeline, Control-click (Mac) or right-click (Windows) the tween span, and from the contextual menu choose Motion Path > Switch Keyframes to Roving. To turn off roving, access the contextual menu for the tween span and choose Motion Path > Switch Keyframes to Non-Roving. In the Motion Editor, you can set individual position keyframes to roving. Roving keyframes appear as dots instead of squares in the property curve. Control-click (Mac) or right-click (Windows) a control point in either the X or Y property curve and select Roving in the contextual menu. Flash changes the control points to dots in that frame for both the X and Y curves. To turn off roving, repeat the process and deselect Roving in the menu.

Roving keyframes relinquish their specific frame-number assignment, allowing Flash to distribute motion evenly across the tween span. Returning to the original 15-frame example above, the ball moves 150 pixels total, over 15 frames. If you change the tween span to use roving keyframes, Flash redistributes the motion so the ball moves 10 pixels in each frame. The ball now starts moving down between Frames 10 and 11 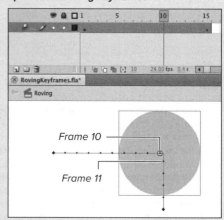.

continues on next page

Initial span, non-roving keyframes

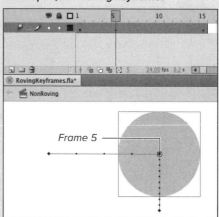

Span set to roving keyframes

🅕 When you first activate roving keyframes for a span, Flash removes the position keyframes in the middle of the span, and places one property keyframe at the end so that motion is distributed evenly.

The Mystery of Roving Keyframes *continued*

While the span is set to roving keyframes, Flash redistributes any positional changes you make to the tween target, so the action stays at a constant rate. If you later change the tween span back to using to non-roving keyframes, Flash updates the Timeline with position keyframes that reflect the redistribution. In the 15-frame example, if you change the tween span to use non-roving keyframes again, Flash captures the redistribution by adding a position keyframe at Frame 10.

About Motion Presets

The *motion preset* is a form of reusable animation. A preset is basically a copy of a tween span with its motion path, property keyframes, and easing intact, just waiting to be assigned a tween target. The preset contains all the information about how the animated item moves, what properties change when, how long it takes to change, and so on. The only thing missing is the symbol.

To use a motion preset, access the Motion Presets panel (if it's closed, choose Window > Motion Presets). The panel looks something like a library panel: motion presets appear in hierarchical folders in a scrolling list; a window at the top previews the animation of a selected preset. Flash CS5 comes with a number of default presets; you can also save custom presets. Open the folder containing the desired preset, and choose a preset name. On the Stage, select the item you want to animate, then in the Motion Presets panel, click the Apply button. Flash turns the selected item into a tween target and creates a motion-tween layer and tween span, just as when you use the Insert > Motion Tween command. However, the motion preset creates not just the tween span but also all the property curves necessary to create the animation. When you click the Apply button, Flash begins the animation with the tween target at its current Stage position. To have the tween target go through its motion and end up at its current position, Shift-click Apply.

You can save your own motion tweens as presets. In the Timeline, select a tween span. In the Motion Presets panel, click the Save Selection As Preset button (the dog-eared page icon in the lower-left corner). Enter a name in the Save Preset As dialog and click OK. Flash adds your preset to the Custom Presets folder in the panel.

The Mystery of Motion Paths

In a motion tween where the tween target changes position, Flash creates a *motion path,* which is a graphic representation of those changes in position. The motion path is an object, similar to a path you'd create with Flash's drawing tools, but with some important differences. A merge-shape or drawing-object Bézier path consists of anchor points with line segments and curves connecting them. A motion path is also a Bézier path, but it contains *frame points* representing the frames in the tween, as well as *control points* (similar to anchor points) representing the position keyframes in the tween **G**.

In tween spans with up to 100 frames, there is one frame point for each frame in the span. To make tween spans with more than 100 frames easier to deal with, Flash displays evenly spaced small dots that represent a group of frames—for example, every fifth frame (the exact number of frames represented depends on the length of the tween span).

Initially, as you position the tween target, it moves in straight lines and the motion path consists only of straight-line segments. You can edit the motion path to create curves for the tween target to follow.

The motion path and tween target are separate objects, but they are linked together as part of a motion-tween object. You can delete the tween target or swap in a different symbol instance, and the motion path remains a part of the tween object, with all its control points intact, waiting to animate whatever symbol you place into the tween span. You can also swap one motion path for another.

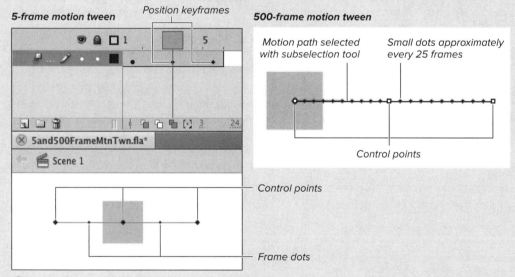

G In tween spans with up to 100 frames (left), frame dots—the small round dots in a motion path—represent the frames of the tween. Diamonds (control points) represent the initial keyframe and any position keyframes in the tween. In spans with more than 100 frames, the motion path displays evenly spaced small dots (right). To view control points in such large spans, you can select the motion path with the subselection tool. Moving the diamonds using the subselection tool changes the tween target's Stage location at the corresponding frame. You can also edit the motion path to create curves.

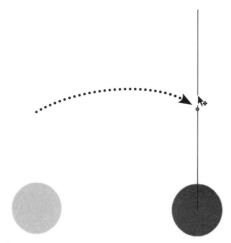

A You can relocate an entire motion-tween animation on the Stage by dragging a selected motion path with the selection tool.

TIP For the tasks in this section, you'll need a motion tween to work on; unless otherwise instructed, use the DownBounceMaster template you created earlier in this chapter. For details on opening new documents from templates, see Chapter 1.

TIP Depending on the particular motion path and tween target, it may be difficult to select just the path. You can select both the tween target and the path, for example, by drawing a selection rectangle that includes the path and the tween target. You're ready to drag the selection or move it using the arrow keys.

TIP Note that if you select both the path and the tween target, the Property inspector doesn't display the Path section. The Position and Size section does appear, showing the properties of the entire selection. Changing the X and Y values moves the motion path. To see the properties of the motion path alone, deselect the tween target, leaving just the path selected.

Working with Motion-Tween Paths

Any motion tween in which the tween target changes position contains a motion path. Whenever you change a tween target's position at a specific frame—either by manipulating the tween target on the Stage or by entering a new *x*- or *y*-coordinate for the target in a panel—Flash adds a control point to the path at that frame (see the sidebar "The Mystery of Motion Paths," earlier in this chapter). Initially, your position changes result in a motion path consisting of straight-line segments. To make a symbol follow a curve, you must edit the motion path. Editing a motion path is similar to editing a merge-shape or drawing-object path (see Chapter 4).

To reposition a motion path:

1. Select the motion path on the Stage.

   Using the selection tool, for example, click directly on the motion path.

2. To change the motion path's position, do any of the following:

   ▸ Using the selection tool, position the pointer over the path. When the selection modifier-icon appears, drag the motion path to a new location **A**.

   ▸ Use the arrow keys to move the selected path.

   ▸ Access the Motion Tween Property inspector, and in the Path section, use the X and Y hot text to enter new values for the *x*- and *y*-coordinates of the upper-left corner of the path's bounding box. The tween target is connected to the path; the entire animation sequence moves to the new location.

To resize the path:

1. Select the motion path on the Stage.

2. In the Tools panel, select the free-transform tool.

   Flash activates a transform box for the motion path, just as it would for a regular path **B**.

3. Using the techniques you learned in Chapter 4, manipulate the resize handles to change the length (and/or orientation) of the path.

   or

1. Select the tween span in the Timeline and access the Motion Tween Property inspector.

2. In the Path section, use the W and H hot text to enter new values for the width and height of the motion path's bounding box **C**.

   Click the hot text to enter a precise value; drag the hot text's invisible slider to choose a value interactively.

TIP You can also access the Path section of the Motion Tween Property inspector after selecting the motion path on the Stage.

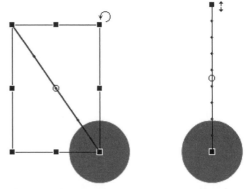

B Flash's free-transform tool activates a transform box around a selected a motion-tween path (left). For horizontal or vertical paths, the path activates without a box (right). The tool works on the motion path as it would on any other object. Drag the handles to resize, rotate, or skew the bounding box containing the path

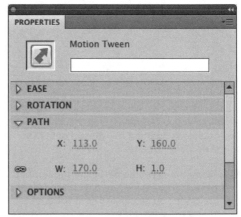

C The Path section of the Motion Tween Property inspector contains hot text governing the properties of the motion path's bounding box. By changing values for W (width) and H (height), you change the width and height of the path's bounding box, thereby increasing or decreasing the path length.

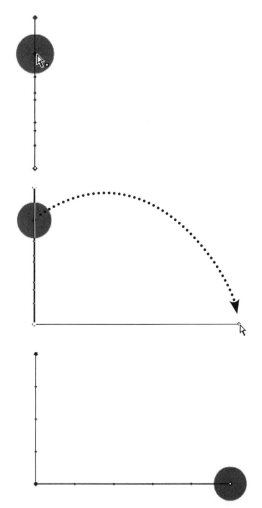

D When you position the subselection tool over a control point in a motion path, a hollow-square modifier-icon appears (top). Here the path for the rebound lies directly on top of the path for the downward bounce. You can drag the control point to reposition the tween target on the Stage at that frame (middle). Flash redraws the motion path when you release the mouse button (bottom). The new path makes the ball move down and to the right.

To reshape a motion path by moving control points:

1. Using the FullBounceMaster template you created earlier in this chapter, open a new document.

   The motion path contains three control points, corresponding to the three position keyframes you created for the bouncing ball.

2. In the Tools panel, select the subselection tool (the hollow-arrow pointer).

3. On the Stage, position the hollow-arrow pointer over a control point (one of the large diamonds in the motion path)—for example, the point corresponding to the ball's final position **D**.

   A hollow-square modifier icon appears next to the arrow when the tool is on a control point.

4. Drag the control point to a new location—for example, to the bottom-right corner of the Stage.

   Flash redraws the motion path as you drag,

5. Play through the movie.

   Now, instead of bouncing, the ball drops down and moves to the right.

TIP When a solid-square modifier-icon appears next to the hollow arrow, it means the subselection tool is positioned over the path but not over a control point. Dragging with the solid-square icon active moves the entire motion path.

To transform a straight-line motion path to an arc:

1. Continuing with the file from the preceding task, select the subselection tool in the Tools panel.

2. On the Stage, position the pointer over the motion path's initial control point.

   This control point corresponds to the keyframe at the beginning of the motion-tween span.

3. To extend Bézier handles for modifying the path, Option-drag (Mac) or Alt-drag (Windows) the control point.

   Drag in the direction you would like the curve to grow **E**. Flash redraws the motion path, creating a curve.

TIP To gain more control over the curve of the path—for example, making the ball follow an S curve—repeat Step 3 for all the control points in the motion path and adjust the Bézier handles to achieve the desired curves.

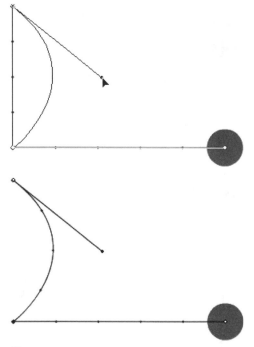

E Use the subselection tool to Option-drag (Mac) or Alt-drag (Windows) Bézier handles from the control points in a motion path (top). Reposition the handles to transform a straight-line motion path into a curved one (bottom).

Modify Motion Paths the Natural Way

You can modify a motion path with the selection tool. The technique is similar to one you learned for modifying lines with natural drawing tools in Chapter 4. Make sure the tween target and the motion path are deselected. Position the selection pointer over the motion path, between two control points. When the curve-point modifier-icon appears, drag that segment of the motion path to create a curved segment. To further refine the curve, switch to the subselection tool and click a control point. Bézier handles extend from the two control points that define the curve segment.

Although the selection tool can transform the motion-path segment into an arc, it can't create angular changes to the path. When you edit a merge-shape or drawing-object path, you can Option-drag (Mac) or Alt-drag (Windows) to add new corner points, but this method doesn't add control points to a motion path. To add control points, you must add position keyframes (see the next task in this section, "To add control points to a motion path").

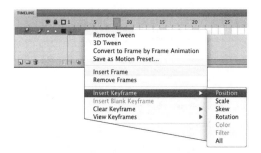

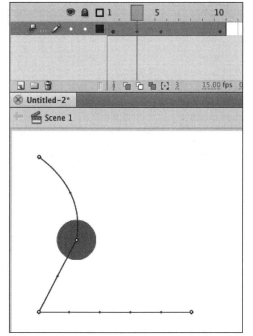

F To add new control points to a motion path, you must create a new position keyframe. One way is to Control-click (Mac) or right-click (Windows) a selected frame within the tween span and choose Insert Keyframe > Position from the contextual menu (top). Flash adds a property-keyframe diamond icon to the Timeline (bottom).

To add control points to a motion path:

1. Continuing with the file from the preceding task, click Frame 3 in the Timeline.

   The playhead moves to Frame 3, and Flash selects the entire tween span.

2. Control-click (Mac) or right-click (Windows) Frame 3.

3. From the contextual menu that appears, choose Insert Keyframe > Position **F**.

   Flash adds a position keyframe to Frame 3. A diamond icon appears in the Timeline, and a new control point appears in the middle of the motion path on the Stage. The tween target moves to that point on the motion path on the Stage.

4. Repeat Step 3 to add as many control points as you like.

   You can use the techniques in the preceding tasks to reposition the new control point(s) or activate the Bézier handles to reshape each segment of the motion path.

To remove control points from a motion path:

1. Continuing with the file from the preceding task, Command-click (Mac) or Ctrl-click (Windows) Frame 3 in the Timeline.

   Flash selects Frame 3. To select one frame of a tween span, you must use the modifier key (see the section "Modifying Tween Spans," later in this chapter).

2. Control-click (Mac) or right-click (Windows) Frame 3.

continues on next page

3. From the contextual menu, choose Clear Keyframe > Position.

Flash removes the position keyframe from the selected frame. If you select multiple frames, the Clear Keyframe command removes all keyframes of the selected type from all the selected frames.

TIP In the Timeline, the property keyframe's diamond icon gives you no clue as to what type of property (or properties) are changing at any given frame. If a diamond appears in the Timeline for a frame where you'd like a control point, but the motion path displays only a small, frame dot, you need to add a position keyframe **G**.

TIP In Step 2, as long as the tween span is selected and the playhead is in Frame 3, you can access the contextual menu by clicking anywhere in the span. Flash adds the new property keyframe in the same frame as the playhead. If the span is not selected when you access the menu, however, the playhead jumps to whatever frame you click. It's safest to click in the frame where you want to add the property keyframe.

TIP Here's a quick way to add a position keyframe without actually changing the tween target's position in that frame. In the Timeline, position the playhead in the desired frame. Select the tween-target symbol on the Stage, press the up-arrow key, then press the down-arrow key. Flash adds a position keyframe to account for the change in the position property even though the tween-target symbol winds up in its original position.

TIP You can also add a position keyframe using the Motion Editor (see "Motion Editor Basics," later in this chapter).

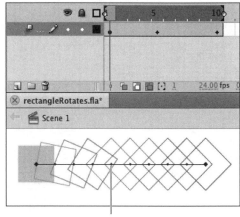

Frame 5

G There is a property-keyframe diamond in Frame 5 of this Timeline, but the fifth dot in the motion path is just a small, frame dot. That means the diamond icon represents a property other than position. Here, onion skinning reveals that the tween target is rotating as well as moving to the right. The diamond represents a rotation keyframe.

TIP To delete all position keyframes quickly, select the motion path and press the Delete key. Flash deletes the path and all its position keyframes. All other property keyframes remain, so, for example, the tween target might grow or rotate or change color, but it stays in one place while doing so. If you subsequently add a motion path to the span, those same property changes take place and the tween target moves along the new path.

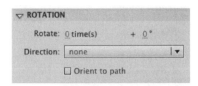

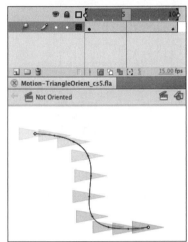

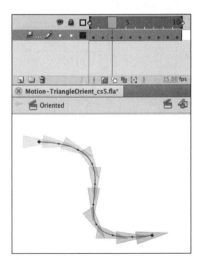

A The Motion Tween Property inspector displays attributes of the tween. In the Rotation section, when the Orient to Path checkbox is deselected (top), the tween target maintains its original orientation to the Stage throughout the motion tween (bottom).

B When Orient to Path is active, the tween target maintains its original alignment to the motion path throughout the motion tween. Flash adds a rotation keyframe to every frame of the tween span.

Orienting a Tween Target to a Curved Path

By default, a tween target keeps its original orientation to the Stage even when following a curving motion path. To create more natural movement, you can force a tween target to rotate to preserve its orientation to the motion path in each frame of a tween.

To orient a tween target to a curving path:

1. Create a ten-frame motion tween of a symbol that follows a curving path.

   Use the techniques you learned in the preceding section to create the curving motion path. For the symbol instance, use a graphic that's not circular; an arrow, a triangle, or an animal will show the effect clearly.

2. Turn on onion skinning to see how the tween target moves along the path without orientation **A**.

3. Select the tween span in the Timeline, and access the Motion Tween Property inspector.

4. In the Rotation section of the inspector, select the Orient to Path checkbox **B**.

   Flash adds a rotation keyframe to every frame in the tween span, adjusting the degree of rotation in each frame to preserve the tween target's original alignment with the path.

Swapping Tween Elements

Because Flash treats a motion tween as an object, it's easy to swap elements in and out of the tween span. You can replace the tween target with any other symbol while retaining all the property changes of the original tween. You can also change the motion path by pasting a different path into the tween span. The pasted path can be a motion path from another tween span, or a merge-shape or drawing-object path.

To swap a tween target:

1. Open a new document using the Full-BounceMaster template you created in the previous section.

   It contains a ten-frame motion tween of a bouncing ball, using a symbol named MyBall.

2. Create a new symbol.

   For example, convert a square shape to a symbol named MySquare (for details about creating symbols, see Chapter 7).

3. Select the motion-tween span in the Timeline and access the Library panel.

   If it's not open, choose Window > Library.

4. Drag a copy of MySquare from the library to the Stage.

   A dialog appears asking if you want to replace the existing tween target **A**.

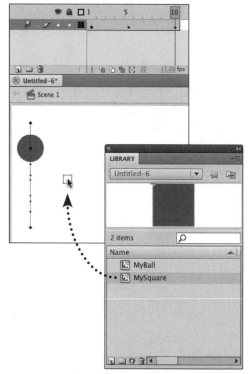

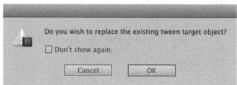

A Whenever a motion-tween layer is the active layer, and the playhead is in a tween span, dragging a symbol from the library to the Stage (top) brings up a dialog asking if you want to replace the original tween target with the object you're dragging (bottom).

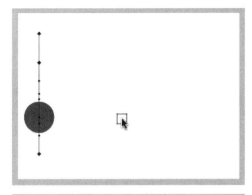

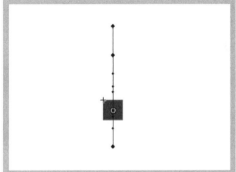

B When you swap tween targets by dragging a new symbol to the Stage (top), the size and shape of motion path and the location of the frame dots and control points stay the same, but the path moves to hook up with the new symbol wherever you dragged it (bottom). Reposition the path if needed.

5. Click OK.

Flash removes the original symbol (MyBall) from the tween and substitutes an instance of MySquare. The Tween span retains all its property keyframes. The tween target moves to the Stage position where you dragged the new symbol, and the motion path moves to match **B**.

TIP Pasting a copied symbol instance to the Stage with the motion-tween span active also brings up the dialog asking if you want to replace the existing tween target. Depending on which Paste command you used, when you click OK, Flash pastes the symbol in its original location or in the center of the Stage and moves the motion path to link up with the new tween target.

TIP If the location of the tween is important, be sure to use the Edit > Paste in Place command.

TIP To swap symbols and preserve the tween target's original stage position, select just the tween target on the Stage and use the Swap button in the Property inspector (see the section "Swapping One Symbol Instance for Another," in Chapter 7).

About Hiding Property Keyframes

By default the Timeline displays all six types of property keyframes. If you create property changes for individual properties in different frames, the Timeline may resemble a diamond bracelet, with property-keyframe markers in almost every frame. To reduce the clutter, you can choose which types of property keyframes appear in the Timeline. Click any frame in a motion-tween span and choose View Keyframes from the contextual menu; a submenu of all six property types, plus All and None, appears. You can select or deselect one property each time you access the menu. Once you deselect a type, Flash stops displaying that type in the Timeline. If your Timeline seems light on property keyframes, or you're trying to insert property keyframes using the contextual menu and not seeing the results in the Timeline, try choosing to view that property type again. (You can also verify the location of the property keyframes in the Motion Editor.)

To swap a motion path:

1. Continuing with the document from the preceding task, add a new layer and create a second motion tween.

   Layer 1 already contains a motion tween that moves MySquare vertically. In Layer 2, create a similar motion tween using the MyBall symbol. In the initial keyframe, for example, position MyBall near the upper right corner of the Stage; in Frame 5, move MyBall to the bottom of the Stage; in Frame 10, move the ball back near the top. Name the layers Move Ball and Move Box, to remind you which tween is on which layer.

2. Using the techniques you learned earlier in this chapter, modify the motion path in the tween span in the Move Ball layer to make a curved path **C**.

3. In the Tools panel, choose the selection or subselection tool.

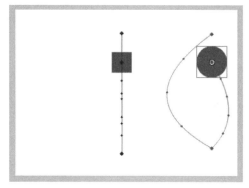

C The Move Ball and Move Box motion tweens start out with similar motion paths. To practice swapping paths, modify one motion path to create a curve.

Drawing New Motion Paths

In addition to copying and pasting motion paths between motion spans, you can copy and paste a regular merge-shape or drawing-object path created with Flash's drawing tools (see Chapter 2). This swap option makes it possible to create motion paths using Flash's Bézier tools, which may be easier than editing a motion path to create curves. You simply draw a path, copy it, then paste it into a tween span. The pasted path becomes the new motion path. There are two things to keep in mind: you can't draw directly in a motion-tween span, and you can't use a closed path as a motion path.

To draw a new path for a motion tween, you must work in a keyframe that's not part of a motion-tween span. An easy way to do that is to add a new layer and work in the initial blank keyframe. Alternatively, you could open a new document and work there.

If you try to paste a closed path—for example, a circle—into a motion-tween span, a warning dialog informs you that a motion guide must have two end points. To work around this requirement, draw a circular stroke using the oval tool, then use the eraser tool to delete a tiny portion of the stroke. The path is now open, and you can use it to move a tween target around a circular path.

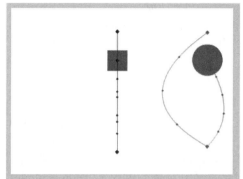

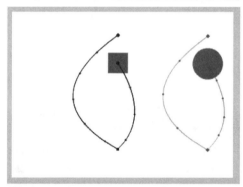

D Pasting a motion path wipes out any position keyframes in the middle of the target span. Flash creates one position keyframe in the last frame of the span and spreads the animation over the whole span. In this example, the original path in the Move Box layer has a position keyframe at Frame 5 (top). After you paste the copied path, that position keyframe disappears (bottom).

4. On the Stage, click directly on the motion path for MyBall and choose Edit > Copy.

   Flash copies the motion path to the Clipboard.

5. To select the tween target to which you want to attach the new motion path (MySquare), do either of the following:

   ▸ On the Stage, click MySquare.

   ▸ In the Timeline, click the tween span in the Move Box layer.

6. Choose Edit > Paste in Center.

   Flash pastes the ball's motion path into the square's span, distributing the movement over the full length of the target span using roving keyframes. The pasted path has just two position keyframes: the initial keyframe and the last keyframe of the span **D**.

7. Play through the animation.

   MySquare and MyBall now trace the same path in different areas of the Stage, but the timing is different. MyBall reaches the lowest point of its curve at Frame 5, where there's a position keyframe; MySquare reaches the same point somewhere between Frames 6 and 7.

TIP To make two tween targets follow the exact same path, in Step 6, choose Edit > Paste in Place. Flash positions the pasted motion path in the exact same Stage location as the copied path and moves the tween target so that its transformation point connects with the pasted path.

Motion Editor Basics

Flash's Motion Editor is a complex and powerful tool that presents information about motion-tween animation in a graphical form. The horizontal axis of the graph represents frame numbers (or in essence, time); the vertical axis represents the value of the property being graphed. Editing the graphs changes the animation. Motion Editor is a bit of a misnomer since it controls not only the position of the tween target (which creates the motion), but various other tweenable properties as well. Many of the sophisticated techniques this panel offers are beyond the scope of a *Visual QuickStart Guide,* but using the Motion Editor to create simple animation is a good way to start. First familiarize yourself with the mechanics of the panel.

To view property curves:

1. Access the Motion Editor.

    If the panel isn't open, choose Window > Motion Editor.

2. To display the property curves for a motion tween, do one of the following:

    ▸ In the Timeline, select the tween span or any frame in the span.

    ▸ On the Stage, select the motion path.

    ▸ On the Stage, select the tween target.

    The graphs for the tweenable properties appear in the Motion Editor Ⓐ. The panel groups properties into categories: Basic Motion, Transformation, Color Effect, Filters, and Eases.

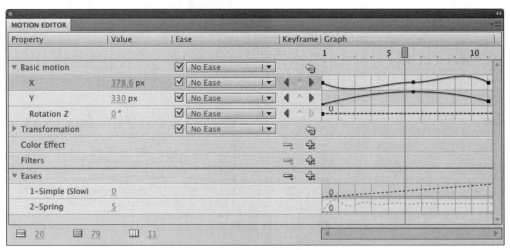

Ⓐ The properties that you can animate using a Motion Tween appear in the Motion Editor. While the Timeline indicates points of change to one or more properties by adding a diamond icon to the frame (top), that icon isn't very informative. The Motion Editor gives you specific information about what properties are changing and offers precise control over those changes (bottom).

3. To expand or collapse a category, click the triangle to the left of the category name.

The category toggles between its expanded and collapsed states **B**.

TIP Some of the properties in the Color Effect and Filters categories can't be graphed as curves; such properties appear in the Graph column as property keyframes on a gray line. Tint Color in Color Effect is one example: there is no "redness" value that Flash could graph along the vertical axis. Tint Amount, which

does have a corresponding value (a percentage), gets its own row with a graph in the Tint subcategory of the Motion Editor.

TIP The arrow keys act as shortcuts for navigating the Motion Editor's many rows. To move up and down the rows, use the up- and down-arrow keys. Flash selects the next row in turn. If the next row is the main category row and it's in collapsed mode, it stays collapsed. If the next row is a property within an expanded category, Flash selects the row, leaving it at its current size. Use the right- and left-arrow keys to set the size of the current row: right makes the row tall; left makes the row short.

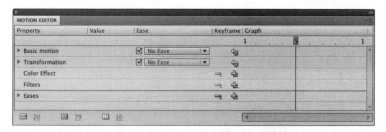

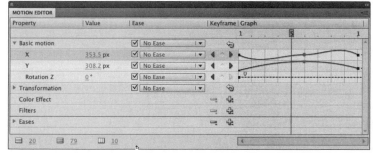

B To view more or fewer graphs in the Motion Editor, click the triangle next to the category name to toggle between collapsed and expanded views. To keep the workspace manageable, collapse the categories you're not working on.

Motion Editor vs. Timeline

The fundamental tool for working with frame-by-frame animation and shape and classic tweening is the Timeline (with its layers and frames). The keyframes displayed in the Timeline give you information about where the key points of change occur. Motion tweens are also Timeline based, but they give you the power to control changes to properties individually. That means there can be many more key points of change to track in an animation segment. The Timeline presents a limited amount of information about what type of change is happening at any given frame (and a limited amount of control over those changes). To see more detail, and gain full control over the property keyframes in a motion-tween span, you must use the Motion Editor

continues on next page

Motion Editor vs. Timeline *continued*

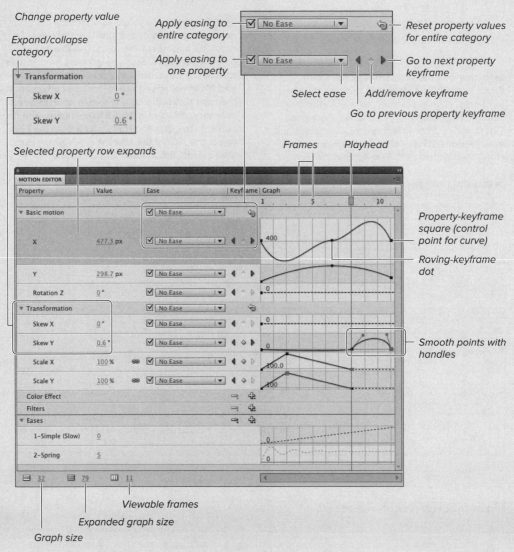

Change property value

Expand/collapse category

Apply easing to entire category

Reset property values for entire category

Apply easing to one property

Go to next property keyframe

Select ease

Add/remove keyframe

Go to previous property keyframe

▼ Transformation

Skew X 0 °

Skew Y 0.6 °

Selected property row expands

Frames

Playhead

Property-keyframe square (control point for curve)

Roving-keyframe dot

Smooth points with handles

Viewable frames

Expanded graph size

Graph size

The Motion Editor contains its own version of the Timeline with its own playhead. The Motion Editor shows you information for just one motion-tween span at a time. Each tweenable property has its own row. If the property can be graphed as a curve, the row contains a graph with Bézier curves representing the changes to that property within the selected motion-tween span. Property keyframes appear in the graph as control points (black squares) defining the shape of the curve. The horizontal axis of the graph represents time/frame numbers; the vertical axis represents the value of the property being graphed.

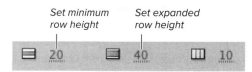

Set minimum row height   *Set expanded row height*

C Hot-text controls in the Motion Editor let you set the size of the rows and thereby, the size of the graphs. Clicking anywhere in the gray area of the row to the left of the graph expands the row to the current maximum setting.

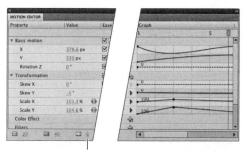

Viewable Frames hot text

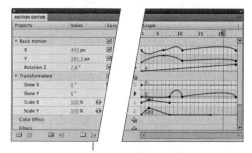

Viewable Frames hot text

D The Motion Editor can display one frame of the selected tween span, several frames (top), or all the frames in the span (bottom). Use the Viewable Frames hot text to set the number of frames that appear in the Graph column.

To customize graph views:

1. Access the Motion Editor and select a tween span.

2. To set the size of the rows containing the property graphs, do either of the following:

   ▸ To set the minimum row height for all properties, use the Graph Size hot text.

   ▸ To determine how much a row enlarges when you select it, set the Expanded Graph Size hot text to the desired row height in pixels **C**.

3. To see more (or fewer) frames in the panel, use the Viewable Frames hot text to set the number of frames displayed **D**.

   Unlike the Timeline, which displays all the frames in a layer, the Motion Editor only shows the frames of the selected tween span. The maximum value for Viewable Frames is the number of frames in the span.

TIP To set Viewable Frames to show all the frames in a span quickly, enter a number that's bound to exceed the number of frames in the span—for example, 99,999. Flash changes the value to the actual number of frames, and sizes the graph accordingly.

TIP Clicking an expanded, tall row reduces it to the default height.

To add keyframes to a property curve:

1. In the Graph column of the Motion Editor, position the playhead in the desired frame **E**.

   You can drag the Motion Editor playhead to a new location or click directly on the frame number or a tick mark above the graphs.

2. In the row containing the property curve you want to change, click the Add or Remove Keyframe button **F**.

   When the current frame of the property curve lacks a keyframe, the button is a barely visible gray diamond. Clicking it adds a property keyframe (represented by a black square) to the graph. Flash connects the property keyframes with a solid line. When the current frame contains a property keyframe, the button turns yellow and is easier to see.

To remove keyframes from a property curve:

- Repeat Steps 1 and 2 of the preceding task, this time positioning the Motion Editor's playhead in a frame that contains a property keyframe.

  Flash removes the black square from the graph and redraws the curve segment.

To navigate the property keyframes:

- To move the Motion Editor's playhead from one property keyframe to the next in a property curve, click the Go to Previous Keyframe/Next Keyframe buttons (the left- and right-facing triangles on either side of the Add or Remove Keyframe button in the row containing the desired property curve).

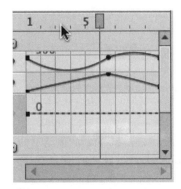

E To position the playhead in the Motion Editor, click a tick mark for the frame location you want, or drag the playhead to the frame.

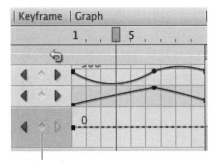

No property keyframe at Frame 4

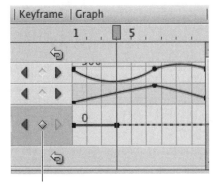

Property keyframe at Frame 4

F When the current frame has no property keyframe, the Add or Remove Keyframe button is ghostly gray diamond and quite hard to see (top). When the frame has a property keyframe, the button turns yellow. Property keyframes in the graph appear as black squares (or dots if the keyframe is set to roving).

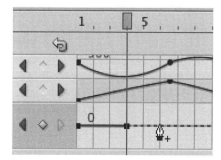

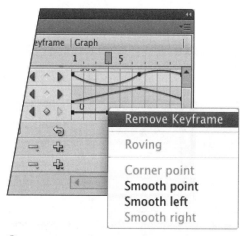

G Within the Motion Editor graph, holding down the Command key (Mac) or Ctrl key (Windows) turns the pointer into a pen icon with a plus sign, similar to the add–anchor-point tool for drawing paths. Click a frame to add a new control point (property keyframe) to the property curve.

H Control-click (Mac) or right-click (Windows) a property keyframe in the Motion Editor to access the contextual menu. Choosing Remove Keyframe removes the control point you clicked (removing the property keyframe) and redraws the curve.

TIP Instead of using the Add or Remove Keyframe button, you can Control-click (Mac) or right-click (Windows) the property curve itself at any frame and choose Add Keyframe from the Contextual menu.

TIP When you hold down the Command key (Mac) or Ctrl key (Windows) and position the pointer over the property curve, the pointer changes to a pen icon with a plus sign. Click the graph to add a new control point **G**.

TIP When you hold down the Command key (Mac) or Ctrl-key (Windows) and position the pointer over a control point in a property curve, the pointer changes to a pen icon with a minus sign. Click the control point to remove it.

TIP Remember that Flash updates the Motion Editor graphs whenever you change the tween target's properties by any method; the Motion Editor need not be open. If, for example, the playhead is sitting in a frame that lacks property keyframes for X and Y positions, and you move the tween target either by dragging it on the Stage or by changing its x- and/or y-coordinates in the Property inspector or Info panel, Flash adds property keyframes to the X and Y graphs in the Motion Editor.

TIP When you Control-click (Mac) or right-click (Windows) directly on a property keyframe in a property curve, the contextual menu includes the choice Remove Keyframe **H**.

TIP You can remove all property keyframes from all the graphs in a category by clicking the Reset Values button (the return-arrow icon) in the main category row of the Motion Editor.

Adding More Motion

The tasks in the first section of this chapter showed you how to use motion tweening to create the standard bouncing-ball animation. For those tasks, you dragged the tween target (the symbol named MyBall) on the Stage to add position keyframes to the motion-tween span. You can also use the Motion Editor to add position keyframes and assign values for the *x*- and *y*-coordinates of the tween target.

To create motion by adding position keyframes in the Motion Editor:

1. Open a new Flash document (with default settings) and create a 24-frame motion tween.

   Initially, the Timeline has one layer with a blank keyframe at Frame 1. Create a symbol containing a star shape; name the symbol MyStar. In Keyframe 1, place an instance of MyStar on the Stage. With MyStar selected, access the Position and Size section of the Property inspector, and use the X and Y hot text to position the symbol at the upper-left corner of the Stage. For example, set X and Y to 50 pixels. Choose Insert > Motion Tween. Flash creates a default motion-tween span 24 frames long. Your document should look something like **Ⓐ**.

2. With the tween span selected in the Timeline, access the Motion Editor's Basic Motion category **Ⓑ**.

   If the panel is closed, choose Window > Motion Editor. If necessary, click the triangle to the left of the category name to view its graphs.

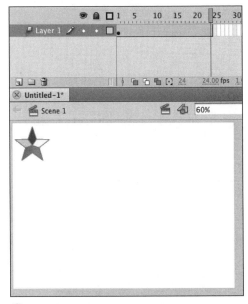

Ⓐ Create a motion tween for working with the Motion Editor. Here, a star symbol is the tween target for a 24-frame motion tween.

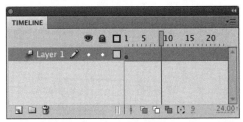

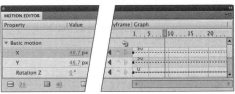

Ⓑ When you select a tween span in the Timeline (top), the Motion Editor displays the properties of that motion tween (bottom). For a two-dimensional tween, the Basic Motion category contains graphs for three properties: X (horizontal position), Y (vertical position), and Rotation Z (the degree of rotation applied to the tween target).

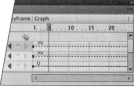

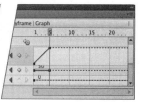 To add a property keyframe to a specific frame, you need to position the playhead in that frame in the Graph column of the Motion Editor.

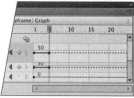

 After you add a property keyframe, a new control point appears in the property curve. Adding a property keyframe to the X curve (horizontal position) simultaneously adds one to the same frame of the Y curve (vertical position). Flash links the X and Y values because they translate to *x*- and *y*-coordinates for the tween target's transformation point.

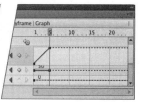 Changing the value for a control point in the X row moves the tween target on the Stage. Flash updates the motion path on the Stage and completes a segment of the X and Y property curves in the Motion Editor.

TIP In Step 6, using a higher value to position a symbol lower on the Stage may seem counterintuitive (especially if you're using the Y hot text interactively—dragging down in the hot text moves the symbol up on the Stage). It's all due to the way Flash tracks elements (see the sidebar "How Flash Tracks Elements," in Chapter 4).

3. In the Graph column, position the Motion Editor's playhead at Frame 5 **C**.

You may need to scroll the graph to see Frame 5. The graph contains a black square representing the initial keyframe at Frame 1. The dotted lines in the Basic Motion graphs indicate that the tween span contains no position or rotation keyframes that create movement.

4. In the X row, click the Add or Remove Keyframe button.

Flash adds a property keyframe to both the X (horizontal position) and Y (vertical position) graphs at Frame 5 (the current frame) and thus completes the first segment of the two property curves, changing the dotted line to a solid black line **D**.

5. To move the tween target to the right, use the X hot text to increase the value for the horizontal position from 50 to 500.

Flash redraws the property curve **E**. When the document's units of measure are set to pixels, changing the X value from 50 to 500 moves the tween target 450 pixels to the right.

6. To move the tween target downward, repeat Steps 3–5 for Frame 15, this time using the Y hot text to increase the value for the vertical position from 50 to 300.

When the document's units of measure are set to pixels, changing the Y value from 50 to 300 moves the tween target 250 pixels toward the bottom of the Stage.

continues on next page

7. To move the tween target diagonally, repeat Steps 3 and 4 for Frame 20, then use the X and Y hot text to set new values for the horizontal and vertical positions.

Setting both values to 100, for example, moves the tween target diagonally back toward the upper left corner of the· Stage.

8. Repeat Steps 3–5 for Frame 10, this time setting the X value to 350 and the Y value to 150.

Flash adds property keyframes to the X and Y graphs, updates their curves, and updates the motion path on the Stage **F**. You can refine the animation by adding (or removing) property keyframes at any point in the curve; you can add a property keyframe within an existing curve segment (between property keyframes), or add a property keyframe in the dotted-line section of the graph to create a new curve segment.

To edit motion by removing position keyframes in the Motion Editor:

1. Continuing with the file from the preceding task, position the Motion Editor's playhead in Frame 10.

2. In either the X or Y row, click the yellow Add or Remove Keyframe button.

Flash removes the black square from both graphs, redraws the X and Y curves in the Motion Editor, and redraws the motion path on the Stage **G**. The curves and motion path return to the way they were before you completed Step 8 in the preceding task.

3. Save this document as a template and call it MovingStarMaster.

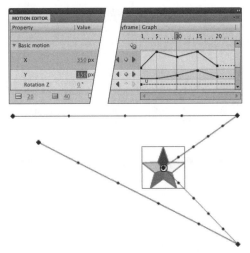

F The X and Y property curves in the Motion Editor show all the points of change in the tween target's position. The motion path on the Stage shows the same thing; the larger points in the path correspond to the property keyframes in the curves.

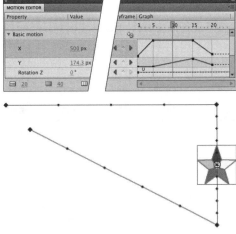

G Removing a property keyframe from the X (or Y) property curve removes a control point from the motion path on the Stage. Flash redraws the motion path and the property curves.

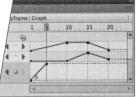

 You can use the Rotation Z hot text in the Motion Editor to add a bit of spin to the tween target.

Manipulating Tween Targets to Add Property Keyframes

In Chapter 9, you placed symbol instances in keyframes on either end of a keyframe span to create a classic tween. You then changed the properties of the symbols by manipulating the symbol instances directly—for example, using the free-transform tool to change a symbol's size. You can also use those techniques in motion tweening. Whenever you manipulate a tween target on the Stage, Flash translates your changes into property keyframes. You saw Flash add position keyframes to the Timeline when you created the bouncing ball earlier in this chapter. The technique works for any property that you can tween in a motion tween. Flash creates property keyframes in both the Timeline and the Motion Editor in response to your changes to the Tween target on the Stage. For example, open a new document using the Down-BounceMaster template. Position the playhead at Frame 7. Using the free-transform tool, change the size of the tween target (MyBall). Flash adds a scale keyframe to Frame 7 in the Timeline and adds a property keyframe to Frame 7 of the property curves for Scale X and/or Scale Y in the Motion Editor.

Animating Other Property Changes

You can use the Motion Editor to add property keyframes for all the properties that you can animate with motion tweens. The process is similar to adding property keyframes for Stage position. The specific settings and graphs are different. In the following tasks, you'll create some basic property keyframes to animate changes in size, rotation, and color.

To rotate the tween target:

1. Using the MovingStarMaster template you created in the preceding task, open a new document, select the tween span, and access the Basic Motion section of the Motion Editor.

   If necessary, click the triangle to the left of the category name to view its graphs.

2. Position the Motion Editor's playhead in Frame 5.

3. Use the Rotation Z hot text to enter the degree of rotation.

   For this task, enter 90 degrees. Positive values create clockwise rotation; negative values, counterclockwise.

   Flash adds a property keyframe to the Rotation Z graph and updates the curve .

   continues on next page

4. Scrub through the animation by moving the playhead one frame at a time.

   The star rotates 90 degrees in five steps (Frames 1–5) . It retains its rotated position for the rest of the tween.

5. Save this document as a template, name it RotateStarMaster.

TIP In the preceding task, the star stops rotating at Frame 5. If you want the star to begin rotating again in later frames, you need to add more rotation keyframes. If you want the star to rotate continuously throughout the tween to reach 90 degrees, place the rotation keyframe at the end of the tween span, or apply the rotation to the entire tween span via the Motion Tween Property inspector (see the sidebar "The Mystery of Autorotation in Motion Tweens," later in this chapter).

B Onion skinning reveals that the tween target rotates in five steps when you add a property keyframe at Frame 5 of the Rotation curve in the Motion Editor.

A Note About Editing Motion

Often, the easiest way to create and edit the movement of a tween target is to drag the target instance on the Stage. Dragging creates a new position keyframe at the current frame automatically; dragging lets you interactively check and adjust the tween target's position and relationship to other elements. If you need to position a tween target precisely, you can enter x- and y-coordinates for the tween target's registration point using the Property inspector, the Info panel, or the Motion Editor. Which method is best? In part, it depends on your working style. But there's another issue to be aware of. The behind-the-scenes math that the Motion Editor uses to calculate and draw the motion path works somewhat differently than the math in all the other methods. Using the hot text and graphs in the Basic Motion section of the Motion Editor can have unexpected results for the motion path on the Stage. And as a practical matter, the graphs in the Motion Editor are small and difficult to deal with in comparison with the motion path on the Stage. The tasks in this section show you how to use the Motion Editor by adding keyframes and changing the X and Y hot-text values to move the tween target in straight lines around the Stage. To move a tween target in more complex ways, and to edit the motion path once you've created the keyframes you want, it's best to work directly with the tween target and motion path on the Stage, or to use the Property inspector or Info panel to enter specific x- and y-coordinate values.

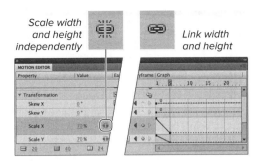

Scale width and height independently — Link width and height

C The Link Values modifier in the Scale rows of the Motion Editor works just like the Constrain/Unconstrain modifier in the Transform panel. When the chain link is open, you can change the X and Y values independently. When the chain is closed, changing one value changes the other as well, preserving the tween target's aspect ratio.

To change a tween target's scale:

1. Repeat Steps 1 and 2 of the preceding task.

   This time, access the Transformation section of the Motion Editor.

2. To change the size of the tween target, access the Scale X and Scale Y rows and do either of the following:

   ▸ To preserve the tween target's aspect ratio, set the Link Values modifier to Linked mode (the closed-link icon) **C**. If necessary, click the icon to change modes. Then use the Scale X or Scale Y hot text to enter a new percentage. In Linked mode, changing one value automatically changes the other by the same amount. Larger values increase the size of the tween target; smaller values reduce it.

continues on next page

The Mystery of Autorotation in Motion Tweens

For the tasks in this section, you rotate the motion-tween target by creating rotation keyframes in the Motion Editor. You must specify a precise degree of rotation, using negative values to rotate the tween target counterclockwise and positive ones to rotate it clockwise. When you created classic tweens (see Chapter 9), you let Flash automatically spin objects by entering values in the Rotate section in the Tweening area of the Frame Property inspector. The technique also works for a motion-tween target. Select the tween span in the Timeline to see the properties of the motion tween. In the Rotation section of the Motion Property inspector, use the Rotation Count and Additional Rotation hot text to set the number of times the tween target rotates (set Rotation Count to 0 if you want the target to rotate less than 360 degrees). There's just one little quirk to keep in mind: when you create rotation for the tween target via the Property inspector, Flash spreads the rotation out over the entire tween span. Even when you specifically select a single frame earlier in the tween span, Flash adds the rotation keyframe to the last frame in the current span. If you want the rotation to end at an earlier frame, you can select the rotation keyframe and drag it from the last frame of the tween span to the desired frame (see "Modifying Tween Spans," later in this chapter).

- ► To change the tween target's vertical and horizontal dimensions independently, set the Link Values modifier to Unlinked mode (the broken-link icon). Then use the Scale X or Scale Y hot text to enter new percentages independently.

3. Play through the animation.

The star moves around the Stage. By the time it reaches the halfway point of its horizontal motion (at Frame 5), the star has changed to the new size you specified in Step 2 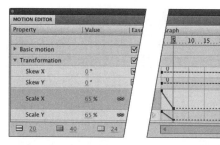. Note that it keeps this new size for the remainder of the animation, or until you add another scale keyframe. The position keyframes that exist at Frames 15 and 20 have no effect on the size of the star.

TIP The graphs for the skew property are also located in the Transformation section of the Motion Editor and work similarly. Add new keyframes to the Skew X and/or Skew Y graphs. Then use the Skew X hot text to change the horizontal skew of the tween target. Use the Skew Y hot text to change the vertical skew. Skew values are always set independently.

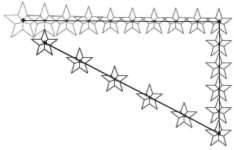

D Onion skinning reveals the interpolated steps that change the tween target's size when you add a property keyframe to the Scale X curve in the Motion Editor. With Link Values active, a Scale X value of 65 percent shrinks the star while keeping its aspect ratio.

A Note About Rotation and 3D Tweening

In the preceding task, you learned about rotation in two dimensions (rotation along the z-axis). When you create a motion tween, Flash also lets you create rotation in three-dimensional space (rotation along the x-, y-, and z-axes). To access those properties, you need to Control-click (Mac) or right-click (Windows) a motion-tween span in the Timeline and choose 3D Tween from the contextual menu. The additional rotation properties appear in the Basic Motion section of the Motion Editor. Animated 3D rotations are beyond the scope of a *Visual QuickStart Guide*. If you'd like to learn more, check out *Flash Professional CS5 Advanced for Windows and Macintosh: Visual QuickPro Guide,* by Russell Chun (Peachpit Press, 2011).

E Click the Add Color menu (the plus sign) in the Motion Editor's Color Effect row, then choose a color effect to apply to your tween target (top). The Tint effect property curves appear: Tint Color and Tint Amount (bottom).

F By adding a property keyframe at Frame 12 of the Tint and Amount curves, you set up the star to change color over the first 12 frames.

To change a tween target's color:

1. Continuing with the file from the preceding task, with the tween target (MyStar) selected on the Stage, in the Graph column of the Motion Editor, position the playhead in Frame 12.

2. In the Color Effect row, from the Add Color menu (the plus-sign icon), choose the desired effect **E**.

   The Add Color menu offers the same effects you learned about for modifying symbol instances in Chapter 7. For this task, choose Tint; then a new subcategory appears in the Color Effect section of the Motion Editor. Rows and graphs for Tint Color and Tint Amount appear in the Tint subcategory.

3. To assign a new color to the tween target, do the following:

   ▸ In the Tint Color row, click the color control and choose a color from the pop-up swatch set.

   ▸ Use the Tint Amount hot text to determine how much of the tint to apply to the tween target. For this example, choose 90 percent.

4. Play through the animation.

   Flash changes MyStar from its original color to its new color in 12 steps **F**. MyStar keeps its new color for the rest of the tween.

About Editing Curves in the Motion Editor

The graphs in the Motion Editor show changes to each property as a Bézier-style curve. The horizontal axis of the graph shows frame numbers (time); the vertical axis shows the property values. You can edit most property curves inside the Motion Editor in ways similar to those you learned for editing Bézier paths (Chapter 4). The exceptions are the X and Y property curves that define the motion path. Curves do appear in the Motion Editor for the X and Y properties, but you can only edit them by editing the motion path on the Stage.

The terminology for property curves differs a bit from that for Bézier paths. In a property curve, each property keyframe appears as a *control point* that defines the curve (like an anchor point in a Bézier path). As you change a property in various frames of a motion tween, Flash adds control points to that property curve. Initially, each control point is a corner point, and the curve consists of straight line segments. You can convert the control points to *smooth points* (similar to curve points in a Bézier path), then use a smooth point's handles to shape the curve on either side of the control point. You can drag control points horizontally, moving the property keyframe to a new frame in the tween, and you can drag control points vertically, to adjust the value of the property.

As you drag a control point in the graph, a tool tip appears showing the frame number and current value of the point. To stop viewing the tool tips, deselect Show Tooltips from the Motion Editor's panel menu.

Here are some ways you can edit the curves of a property in the Motion Editor (**G** on the next page).

To select a control point, click it. Flash highlights the point in green. To select multiple points in one property curve, Shift-click each point. To deselect a point, Shift-click it.

To move a control point to a different frame number, drag it in the graph.

To change the control point's value (the value of the property), drag the control point up or down. The graph scrolls as you drag. This can be hard to work with when the Motion Editor is set to a small size. To make the graphs easier to work with, make the Motion Editor a floating panel and resize it to be fairly large (see Chapter 1).

To transform a corner point to a smooth point, Control-click (Mac) or right-click (Windows) the control point and choose Smooth Point, Smooth Left, or Smooth Right from the contextual menu. The options available in the menu depend on the configuration of the property graph (if you select the control point in Frame 1, for example, the left-side options aren't available). Smooth Point adds handles to both sides of the point; Smooth Left adds a handle to the left; and Smooth Right adds a handle to the right. Manipulating a handle adjusts the curve on that side of the control point. Whenever you select a smooth point, its handles appear. By adjusting the curve, you tell Flash how quickly to apply the change to that property. The steeper the curve, the faster the change takes place.

To transform a smooth point to a corner point, Control-click (Mac) or right-click (Windows) the point and choose Corner Point, Linear Left, or Linear Right from the contextual menu. Again, the options in the menu depend on the configuration of the property graph. Corner Point removes the handles from both sides of the control point; Linear Left removes the left-side handle; Linear Right removes the right-side handle.

continues on next page

About Editing Curves in the Motion Editor *continued*

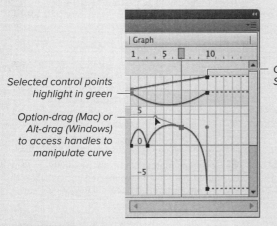

Selected control points highlight in green —

Option-drag (Mac) or Alt-drag (Windows) to access handles to manipulate curve

Click to select control points; Shift-click to deselect

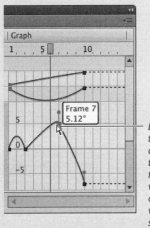

Drag control point to reposition, drag horizontally to move to new frame, drag vertically to change property value; tool tip shows value

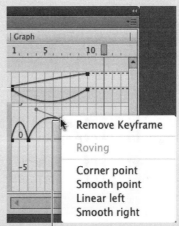

Control-click (Mac) or right-click (Windows) a control point; choose a new point type from the contextual menu

Ⓖ You can edit most of the property curves directly in the Motion Editor's Graph column. You can add and remove control points and create smooth points to adjust the property curves, adding subtlety to the changes in your animation. Steeper curves translate to faster changes; flatter curves translate to more gradual changes.

Modifying Tween Spans

Selecting and manipulating the frames of a tween span in the Timeline is similar to working with frames in keyframe spans when you've set Preferences to span-based selection style (see Chapter 8). But there are a few twists. (Note that the Preferences setting has no effect on tween spans.) No matter which frame you click in a tween span, Flash selects the entire span. Dragging the first or last frame expands (or reduces) the motion tween as an object; Flash adjusts the position of any property keyframes within the tween span to spread the animation out (or squeeze it down) to fit the new span proportionally. You must use a modifier key to select individual frames or to expand the span by adding in-between frames at the end without redistributing the existing property keyframes.

To select the entire tween span:

- Click any frame within the tween span.

  Flash selects the entire span and highlights it **A**.

To select one frame in a tween span:

- In the Timeline, Command-click (Mac) or Ctrl-click (Windows) the desired frame.

  Flash highlights the selected frame.

To select multiple frames in tween spans:

- In the Timeline, Command-drag (Mac) or Ctrl-drag (Windows) through all the frames you want to select **B**.

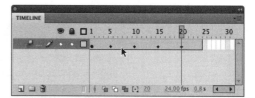

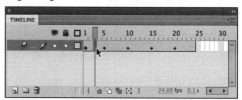

A Flash tints motion-tween spans light blue. Click any frame in a motion-tween span (top) to select the entire span (bottom). A darker highlight indicates the selection.

Begin drag

End drag

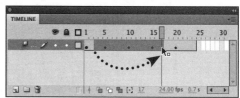

B To select a range of frames within a tween span, Command-drag (Mac) or Ctrl-drag (Windows) through the desired frames in the Timeline.

Original span　　　*Ready to resize*

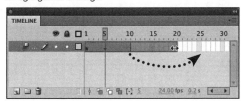

Drag right to enlarge

Resized span, with redistributed property keyframe

C Resizing a tween span by dragging doesn't merely add frames to or remove frames from the end of the span. The animation contained in the tween span expands or contracts as an object. Flash redistributes the property keyframes to preserve the proportions of the tween. The original tween span has a property keyframe roughly at midspan, and so does the resized span. Flash does its best to maintain the relative positions of the property keyframes within the span. In the original span, 4 frames come before the property keyframe and 5 come after it. When you double the length of the span, Flash doubles the number of frames before the property keyframe to 8; that leaves 11 frames that come after. That's slightly more than double, but necessary to fill out the 20 frames.

To resize a tween span:

1. Position the pointer over the last frame in the tween span.

   The icon changes to a double-arrow.

2. To change the span's size, do either of the following:

   ▸ To lengthen the span, drag to the right.

      Flash treats the span and the animation it contains as an object, and redistributes property keyframes within the span proportionally **C**.

   or

   ▸ To shorten the span, drag to the left.

TIP You can't select a range of frames by Command-clicking (Mac) or Ctrl-clicking (Windows) the first frame and then Shift-Command-clicking (Mac) or Shift-Ctrl-clicking (Windows) the last frame (as you can in a keyframe span with span-based selection mode). Always Command-drag (Mac) or Ctrl-drag (Windows) to select a range of frames within a tween span.

TIP You can also resize a tween span by dragging the first frame in the span.

TIP Increasing the size of the span eats into or deletes other spans or keyframes on the same layer, just as it does with keyframe spans (see Chapter 8). Reducing the size of the span creates new empty keyframe spans.

To extend or trim the end of a tween span:

1. Position the pointer over the last frame in the tween span.

    The double-arrow pointer appears.

2. To change the end of the span, do either of the following:

    ▸ To add in-between frames at the end of the span, Shift-drag to the right.

    or

    ▸ To remove frames from the end of the span, Shift-drag to the left.

    Flash resizes the tween span **D**. If you drag over property keyframes, Flash does not reposition them within the remaining span; instead Flash cuts the property keyframes along with the in-between frames.

> **TIP** You can also add in-between frames to extend the span. Select a protoframe, then choose Insert > Timeline > Frame (or press F5). Flash extends the tween span to the selected frame. If you select frames within the span and press F5, Flash increases the size of the span by adding that number of in-between frames. Where Flash adds the frames depends on the precise location of your selection in relation to any property keyframes.

Shift-dragging to the left...

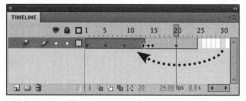

Clips off the end of the span

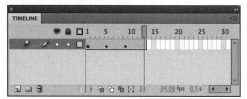

D Shift-drag the end of a tween span to resize it without redistributing its property keyframes. Shift-drag to the right to add in-between frames at the end of the span. Shift-drag to the left to clip off the end of the span.

Original span with selected frames

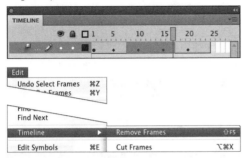

New span with frames removed

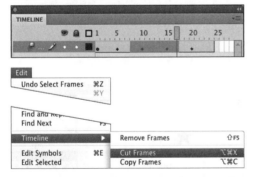

E The Edit > Timeline > Remove Frames command shortens the tween span by removing the selected frames, including any property keyframes in the selection.

Original span with selected frames

New span; cut frames leave empty keyframe span

F When you cut selected frames from a tween span (instead of removing them), Flash transforms them to an empty keyframe span. If you cut frames midspan, the empty keyframe span winds up in the middle. The remaining frames from the original tween span become a second tween span.

To shorten a tween span by removing internal frames:

1. Select one or more contiguous frames within the tween span.

2. Choose Edit > Timeline > Remove Frames.

Flash deletes the frames, removing any property keyframes that fall within the selection, and shortens the tween span by the number of frames selected **E**.

TIP The contextual menu for tween spans also contains a Remove Frames command.

To cut frames out of a tween span:

1. Select one or more contiguous frames within a tween span.

2. Choose Edit > Timeline > Cut Frames.

Flash converts the selection to an empty keyframe span with a blank initial keyframe. Other frames in the selection become in-between frames. Flash converts any frames that follow the selection to a second tween span based on the original tween target, with all the properties that had been applied at that frame **F**.

TIP You can split or combine tween spans. To divide a span, Control-click (Mac) or right-click (Windows) to select the frame at which the span should split. From the contextual menu choose Split Motion. To combine spans, in the Timeline, Shift-click one or more contiguous tween spans in a layer. Control-click (Mac) or right-click (Windows) any of the selected frames, and from the contextual menu choose Join Motions. Flash creates a single tween span using the tween target from the earliest span.

To move tween spans using drag and drop:

- Select the span and drag it to the right or left within the layer.

  Flash repositions the span. Depending on the particular configuration of elements in the layer, Flash resizes other spans, removes their content, and/or creates blank keyframe spans in the original tween span's location **G**. If you drag a tween span so that it completely covers another keyframe or span, Flash deletes the covered item. Flash creates an empty keyframe span at the end of the layer to retain the layer's original number of defined frames.

TIP You can drag a tween span to a different layer.

TIP Option-dragging (Mac) or Alt-dragging (Windows) a tween span creates a copy of the span, which you can place elsewhere on the same layer or on a different layer.

TIP You can also drag and drop one or more property keyframes within a tween span. Command-click (Mac) or Ctrl-click (Windows) to select the frame containing the property-keyframe diamond you want to move (or Command- or Ctrl-drag to select a range of frames with multiple diamonds) and position the pointer over the selection. When a hollow-square modifier icon appears next to the arrow icon, drag the selection to a new position in the Timeline. Remember that each diamond icon may represent more than one property. Dragging a selection repositions the property keyframes for all the properties associated with each diamond.

1

2

3

4

5

6

G Drag a selected motion-tween span in the Timeline to move it within one layer, or to move it to a different layer. The results vary depending on the elements in the layer. Dragging a tween span to the right into a second tween span (1) creates a new keyframe span in the first span and squeezes the initial keyframe of the second span as far as possible to the right into a shortened span (2). Dragging a tween span to the left (3) shortens the preceding span (4). Dragging a tween span so that it completely covers another span (5) replaces the covered span and its contents with the dragged span (6).

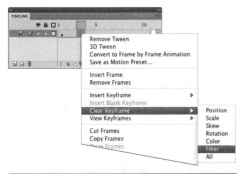

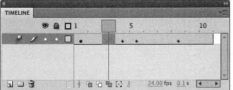

H To remove a property keyframe, select one or more frames in the Timeline and access the contextual menu for frames. Choose Clear Keyframe and choose a property type from the submenu. Flash removes all property keyframes of that type from all selected frames. To remove all property keyframes of all types from the selected frames, choose All.

TIP You can reuse just part of a tween. If your selection includes just in-between frames, Flash creates a new initial keyframe when it pastes the copied frames. The tween target has the properties it had in the first selected frame. If the target was in the middle of turning from red to blue, for example, in the pasted tween, the tween target starts out with the same purple color it had in the first frame of the selection.

TIP If you paste a motion-tween span into a layer containing classic or shape tweens, Flash creates a keyframe span the length of the copied tween span. The span consists of a keyframe containing the tween target in its original form, followed by plain in-between frames.

To remove property keyframes:

1. To remove property keyframes from a single frame, Command-click (Mac) or Ctrl-click (Windows) the frame to select it.

2. To access the contextual menu for frames, Control-click (Mac) or right-click (Windows) the selected frame.

3. Choose Clear Keyframe.

4. From the submenu that appears, choose one of the following:

   ▸ To remove one category of property keyframes at a time, choose a type: Position, Scale, Skew, Rotation, Color, or Filter **H**.

   ▸ To remove all categories simultaneously, choose All.

   Flash removes the property keyframe(s) from the selection in the Timeline, updates the property curve in the Motion Editor, and updates the tween target and/or motion path on the Stage.

TIP When working with the Timeline, if you want to remove more than one category of property keyframes but preserve some, you must repeat the removal process, choosing a different category each time.

TIP To remove all the property keyframes from curves in a single Motion Editor category simultaneously, click the Reset button in the main category row.

TIP Be careful when using the contextual menu's Clear Keyframe commands, as they remove all the property keyframes of a selected type from all selected frames. If you select the entire span, the commands delete all property keyframes of the selected type throughout the span.

Copying Frames and Properties

You can reuse all or part of a motion tween by copying and pasting frames from the tween span into other frames in the Timeline. The frames receiving the copied frames can be part of an existing span or be blank. Similarly, you can copy properties and paste them into a frame within an existing motion-tween span.

To copy and paste a complete motion tween:

1. To select the motion tween, in the Timeline, click any frame in the tween span.

2. Choose Edit > Timeline > Copy Frames 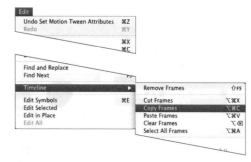.

3. In the Timeline, do one of the following:

   ▸ Create a new layer and select its initial blank keyframe or one of its protoframes.

   ▸ Add a new blank keyframe to the end of an existing layer containing a motion tween, and select it.

   ▸ Select a protoframe at the end of a layer containing other motion tween(s).

   ▸ Select a frame or range of frames within an existing tween span.

4. Choose Edit > Timeline > Paste Frames.

   Flash pastes a tween span with the same content and property changes. The initial keyframe of the pasted tween is in the selected frame, and the pasted span extends for the same number of frames as the original. If you paste frames into the middle of another tween span; Flash divides that span and may overwrite some of it.

A Choose Edit > Timeline > Copy Frames to make a copy of a selected tween span. You can then paste the tween into another layer, or elsewhere in the same layer, to reuse the motion.

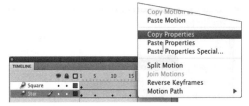

B To copy properties, you must select a single frame in the motion-tween span. Control-click (Mac) or right-click (Windows) the selected frame and choose Copy Properties from the contextual menu. The selected frame can be the initial keyframe, a property keyframe, or an in-between frame.

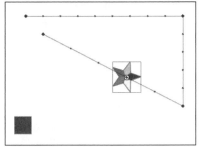

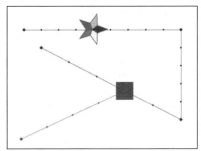

C The properties of the star in Frame 17 (top) have been copied and then pasted onto the square at Frame 5 (bottom).

To copy and paste property keyframes:

1. Open a new document using the RotateStarMaster template, which you created earlier in this chapter.

2. Add a new layer; in Keyframe 1, place a different symbol instance in the lower-left corner of the Stage—say, a square named MySquare—and choose Insert > Motion Tween.

   Flash creates another motion tween; currently the tween span contains no property keyframes. Name the layers according to their contents, Star and Square.

3. In the Timeline, in the Star layer, Command-click (Mac) or Ctrl-click (Windows) Frame 17 to select it.

   Flash can only copy properties from one frame at a time.

4. Control-click (Mac) or right-click (Windows) the selected frame, and choose Copy Properties from the contextual menu **B**.

5. Repeat Steps 3 and 4, this time selecting Frame 5 in the Square layer and choosing Paste Properties from the contextual menu.

   Flash creates a new property keyframe in Frame 5 of the Square layer, using the property settings that existed at Frame 17 of the Star layer. MySquare moves to the right side of the Stage (to the same position MyStar has at Frame 17) and rotates 90 degrees **C**.

TIP The Copy Properties command captures property values for all the property types that exist for the selected tween target at the frame where you copy. The Paste Properties command, however, only pastes properties that already exist in the tween you're pasting to.

Practice Session

Try using motion tweening to animate a rocket that moves around the Stage.

- Create a rocket symbol from scratch. (See Chapter 7.) Use any of the drawing, modifying, grouping, and layering techniques you've learned. (See Chapters 2, 4, 5, and 6.)

- Set up a motion tween using the rocket symbol. Try putting it near the lower-left corner, then apply motion tweening. (See *Creating a Bouncing Ball with Motion Tweening > To set up a motion tween.*)

- Position the playhead at various frames in the Timeline; change the position of the rocket each time to add a position property keyframe. (See Chapter 11, *Creating a Bouncing Ball with Motion Tweening.*)

- Use the selection and/or subselection tools to reshape the motion-tween path. Give the rocket a loopy flight path and orient the symbol so the rocket nose leads at all times. (See Chapter 11, *Working with Motion-Tween Paths* and *Orienting a Tween Target to a Curved Path.*)

Extra Credit

- Use the Motion Editor to add more property keyframes. Try adding a Color Effect to make the rocket appear to heat up; use the Tint Color Effect to turn the rocket red over the course of its flight.

- Duplicate the motion tween to create multiple rockets. Change the motion paths so each rocket flies in a different direction. Resize some tween spans to make each rocket fly at a different speed.

Save your files for use in future Practice Sessions.

The Insert > Keyframe Conundrum

When creating classic tweens and shape tweens, choosing Insert > Timeline > Keyframe (or pressing F6) is a great timesaver that lets you duplicate the preceding keyframe quickly to create tween segments. By habit, you might reach for F6 while working in a motion tween, but pause first to evaluate your needs.

There is only one true keyframe in each motion-tween span; it's the first frame of the span. All the other "keyframes" are property keyframes controlling changes to individual properties. (Just to add to the confusion, the contextual menu for tween spans contains the command Insert > Keyframe; the submenu makes it clear that you're actually inserting property keyframes.) Pressing F6 within a tween span creates *property* keyframes for every property that exists at that point.

Four of the properties represented by diamond-shaped property keyframes in the Timeline—Position, Scale, Skew, and Rotation—are always present in the initial keyframe of the tween span even before you make changes to any property. These properties allow Flash to describe the tween target. At a minimum, pressing F6 creates property keyframes for all these properties. If you've added the Color and Filter properties to the tween, pressing F6 also creates their property keyframes.

If you need to change every property at one point, then creating all those control points at once is helpful. Often, however, you just wind up with excess control points whose value doesn't change, which may make it harder to edit the property curves to create subtle changes. You can move an excess control point to a different frame, but that's a tedious process for long animations, where a tween span may contain dozens or hundreds of frames.

More-Complex
Animation Tasks

You've learned to manipulate shapes and symbols, animating them one at a time, in a single layer, but Adobe Flash Professional CS5 is capable of handling much more complicated animation tasks. To create complex animated movies, you'll need to work with multiple shapes or symbols and multiple layers. You may even want to use multiple scenes to organize long animations. In this chapter, you learn to work with multiple layers in the Timeline, stack animations on the various layers to create more-complex movement, and save animations as reusable elements for easy manipulation—either as animated graphic symbols or as movie-clip symbols. With these techniques, you can really start to bring your animations to life.

In This Chapter

A Note About Scenes

A Flash project requiring lots of animation may include hundreds of frames. You can break the animation into smaller chunks by creating scenes. When you publish a movie from a regular Flash document, the scenes play back in order unless you use the interactivity features to provide instructions for playing the scenes in a different order.

Scene basics To add a new scene, choose Insert > Scene. To select a scene to edit, in the Edit bar, click the Edit Scene button and select a scene from the pop-up menu **Ⓐ**. You can also use Flash's Scene panel to see what scenes exist in your movie, select a scene to edit, create new scenes, duplicate scenes, delete scenes, and reorganize them **Ⓑ**. To access the Scene panel, choose Window > Other Panels > Scene.

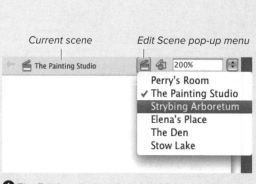

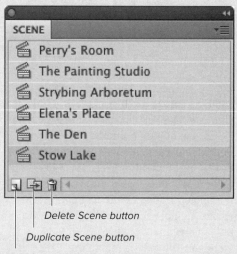

Ⓐ The Edit bar displays the name of the current scene. Choose a scene from the Edit Scene pop-up menu to switch scenes quickly.

Delete Scene button

Duplicate Scene button

Add Scene button

Ⓑ The Scene panel lists all the scenes in a movie. It also provides buttons for adding, duplicating, and deleting scenes.

The pitfalls of using scenes Scenes in Flash are tools for organizing content during authoring; they don't exist at runtime. When you create a Flash document, each scene acts like a self-contained movie, but when you publish the file, Flash links the scenes into one continuous set of frames. (Imagine a document with two scenes: Scene 1 has frames numbered 1–10, and Scene 2 has frames numbered 1–10. The published file winds up with frames numbered 1–20.)

The fact that each scene is, in a sense, a new beginning can make it difficult to keep the continuity of actions between scenes. For movies with interactivity that requires variables, scenes may be inappropriate. In such cases, you may need to stick to a single long movie or use separate movies or separate movie clips within one movie to organize your animation. The fact that scenes don't exist in the published movie presents other problems. For example, you must be careful to avoid using identical frame labels in multiple scenes. Otherwise, interactivities that rely on those frame labels to locate and display the appropriate frame will not work.

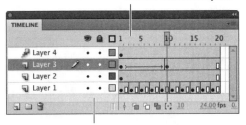

Click to deselect layers

Click to deselect layers

A To deselect all frames quickly, click in the number area above the frames, or in the gray area below the layers in the Timeline.

Layers to Play With

To practice working with frames and layers, create a document with four layers, each with 20 defined frames. Add content that helps you see what's going on. Use the text tool, for example, to place the frame number in every other frame of Layer 1 and to place a text block with the layer name in Layers 2, 3, and 4. Set up a motion tween by selecting Frame 1 in Layer 4 and choosing Insert > Motion Tween. Set up a classic tween by selecting Frame 10 in Layer 3, choosing Insert > Timeline > Keyframe, then selecting any frame in the preceding keyframe span (Frames 1–9) and choosing Insert > Classic Tween.

Manipulating Frames in Multiple Layers

As your animation gets more complex, you'll need to add layers to your document. You can perform editing operations on selected frames and layers, for example, by copying, cutting, and pasting frames across multiple layers. You can also insert frames, keyframes, and blank keyframes into selected keyframe spans, tween spans, and layers.

To select frames in several layers:

1. Create a practice document containing multiple layers and tweens (see the sidebar "Layers to Play With").

2. To deselect all frames, in the Timeline, click in a blank area of the Timeline **A**.

   Deselecting frames prevents you from accidentally moving selected frames or adding them to a selection.

continues on next page

3. To draw a selection rectangle in the Timeline, do one of the following:

▸ In frame-based selection mode, to begin with a frame that is outside a motion-tween span, drag diagonally from the first frame through all the desired frames **B**.

▸ In span-based selection mode, to begin with a frame that is outside a motion-tween span, Command-drag (Mac) or Ctrl-drag (Windows) to select a range of frames.

▸ In either selection style, to begin with a frame that is part of a motion-tween span, Command-drag (Mac) or Ctrl-drag (Windows) to select a range of frames.

Flash highlights the selected frames as you drag.

TIP You can define a selection rectangle by clicking instead of dragging. In span-based selection mode (or to begin with a frame that's part of a motion-tween span), add the appropriate modifier key—Command (Mac) or Ctrl (Windows)—when you click and Shift-click. In frame-based selection mode, starting with a frame outside a motion-tween span, click and then Shift-click diagonally opposite corners of an imaginary rectangle to highlight the frames. Flash highlights all the frames in the rectangle that you've defined **C**.

TIP You can't use the click/Shift-click method if your selection would end with a frame set to motion tweening; you'd just wind up selecting the ending frame.

TIP In span-based selection mode, when you have a series of back-to-back classic tweens, clicking a frame in any of the spans selects the entire series, including the span that follows the ending keyframe of the last classic tween in the series.

Drag to opposite corner

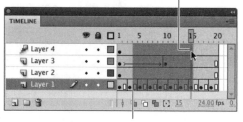

Begin selection

B In frame-based selection mode, when beginning a selection outside a motion-tween span, simply drag across frames and layers to select frames. For example, in Layer 1, drag from Frame 4 diagonally up and to the right till you reach Frame 15 in Layer 4. In span-based mode, Command-drag (Mac) or Ctrl-drag (Windows). If you're selecting only motion-tweened frames, or you want to start your selection within a motion-tween span, use the span-based method.

With one corner selected

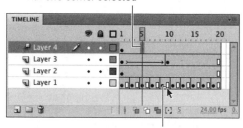

Prepare to click the opposite corner

After Shift-clicking with modifier key

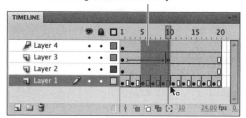

C You can select frames without dragging. In span-based selection mode—or to begin the selection inside a motion-tween span—Command-click (Mac) or Ctrl-click (Windows) one frame, and then Shift-Command-click (Mac) or Ctrl-Shift-click (Windows) another frame to define a selection block. In frame-based selection mode—or to begin the selection outside a motion-tween span—click one corner of the block, then Shift-click the opposite corner (the ending frame must be outside a motion-tween span).

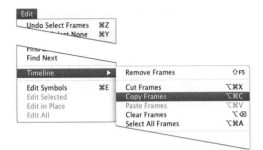

D You must use the Edit > Timeline > Copy Frames command to copy selected frames. The standard copy command (and standard keyboard shortcuts for copying) won't work.

To copy selected frames:

1. Continuing with the practice document from the preceding exercise, select Frames 5–10 in all four layers.

2. Choose Edit > Timeline > Copy Frames **D**.

   Flash copies the frames and layer information to the Clipboard.

To replace the content of frames with a multiple-layer selection:

1. Continuing with the document from the preceding task, select Frames 15–20 on all four layers.

2. Choose Edit > Timeline > Paste Frames.

   Flash pastes the copied Frames 5–10 into Frames 15–20 in each of the four layers **E**. The numbers on the Stage in Layer 1 now start over with the number 5 at Frame 15, 7 at Frame 17, and 9 at Frame 19. Flash created a new keyframe in Frame 15 of Layer 2, a new classic-tween keyframe span in Layer 3, and a new motion-tween span in Layer 4.

Prepare to paste by selecting frames

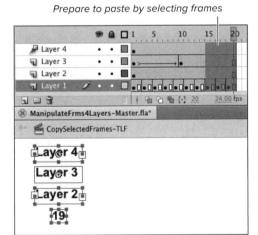

Frames pasted

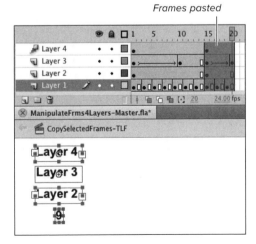

E Pasting copied frames into existing frames replaces their content. Here, the content copied from Keyframe 9 winds up in Keyframe 19 and continues to show in Frame 20, where the playhead is.

To paste a multiple-layer selection into blank frames:

1. Continuing with the document from the preceding task, select Frame 21 on all four layers.

2. Choose Edit > Timeline > Paste Frames.

   Flash pastes the copied Frames 5–10 into Protoframes 21–26 in each of the four layers 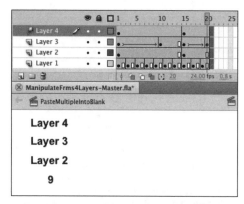. Layer 1 now displays the number 5 at Frame 21, 7 at Frame 23, and 9 at Frame 25. Flash created a new keyframe in Frame 21 of Layer 2, a new classic-tween keyframe span in Layer 3, and a new motion-tween span in Layer 4

   TIP You can also paste a multiple-layer selection into a new document, scene, or layer. By default, the document, scene, or layer starts with a blank keyframe in Frame 1. Select that keyframe and choose Edit > Timeline > Paste Frames. Flash adds layers to accommodate the copied frames and layers.

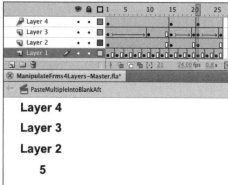

F Pasting a multiple-layer, multiple-frame selection at the end of a set of defined frames (top) extends the Timeline to accommodate the new frames and layers (bottom).

Animating on Multiple Layers

To animate multiple objects simultaneously with classic or motion tweens, you must put each object on a separate layer. Flash restricts you to just one object per tween for motion tweens and classic tweens. Shape tweens allow you to work with more than one shape per tween, but it's usually best to stick with just one. (Frame-by-frame animation also allows multiple objects on the same layer, but that's generally not a good idea.) The tasks in this section introduce you to tweening items on multiple layers simultaneously.

Working with Multiple-Layer Classic Tweens

For the tasks in this section, you'll combine three simple classic tweens on three layers, to create a game of Ping-Pong. The first step is to create the symbols and layers. One layer contains a Ping-Pong ball symbol; the other layers each contain a paddle symbol.

To set up the graphics layers:

1. Open a new Flash document, and add two new layers.

2. Rename the layers.

   To help keep track of the elements, name the top layer Ball, the next layer 1st Paddle, and the bottom layer 2nd Paddle.

3. Create the graphics as symbols (see Chapter 7).

   Create a symbol named PingPongBall containing an appropriate graphic element (for example, use the oval tool to draw a circular fill). Create two symbols—1stPaddle and 2ndPaddle—each containing a paddle graphic (for example, use the rectangle tool to draw a rectangular fill). Place each symbol in the layer that has the same name. Your file should look like 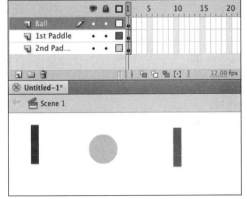.

4. Save the file as a template named PingPongSetupMaster.

   Be sure to close the template file before continuing (for details about saving documents as templates, see Chapter 1). You can use the same initial graphic setup to create a classic-tween or motion-tween version of the Ping-Pong animation.

Ⓐ To animate several symbols simultaneously with classic or motion tweening, each symbol must be on a separate layer. Descriptive layer names help you keep track of what goes where.

To set up a classic tween in all layers with one command:

1. Using the PingPongSetupMaster template you created in the preceding task, open a new document.

2. In the Timeline, select Keyframe 1 in all three layers.

3. Choose Insert > Classic Tween 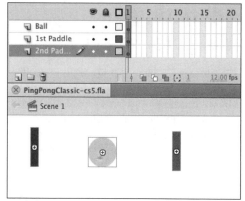.

   Flash sets all three frames to be classic tweens.

4. In the Timeline, select Frame 20 in all three layers.

5. Choose Insert > Timeline > Frame.

   Flash extends the classic tween through Frame 20 on all three layers. A dotted line across the frames indicates that the tween is incomplete 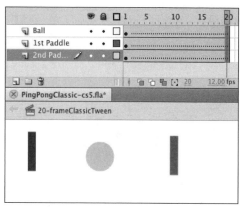. To make the ball and paddles move around the Stage, you must complete the classic-tween sequences, by adding keyframes and repositioning the symbol instance in each one.

B With frames selected on multiple layers (top), choosing Insert > Classic Tween (bottom) sets up classic tweens on all the layers.

C The frames on all three layers have been set to classic tweening, but the tweens are broken, as indicated by the dotted lines. You must add keyframes and content.

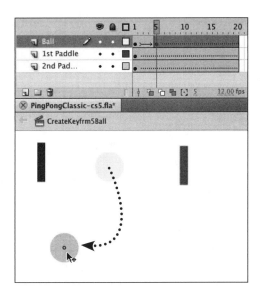

D Moving a symbol in a frame that's defined as part of a classic tween causes Flash to make the layer containing the symbol the active layer. Flash creates a keyframe in that layer for the symbol's new position, thus completing one tween sequence.

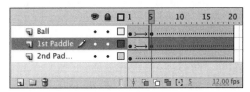

E As you reposition the paddle, Flash selects Frames 5–20; but the completed tween segment appears correctly in Frames 1–4.

To rough out the movement— classic tweening:

1. Continuing with the file from the preceding task, in the Timeline, position the playhead in Frame 5.

2. On the Stage, drag the ball to the approximate location where it should connect with one of the paddles for the first hit.

   Ball becomes the active layer. In Frame 5, Flash creates a new keyframe containing another instance of the PingPongBall symbol in its new location **D**.

   Flash completes the tween in the first keyframe span (Frames 1–4) of the Ball layer, which displays the completed-tween arrow. The broken-tween line remains in all the other frames.

3. On the Stage, reposition the first paddle so that it connects with the ball for the first hit.

   Flash makes 1st Paddle the active layer and creates a new keyframe (in Frame 5) containing another instance of the 1stPaddle symbol in its new location **E**.

4. In the Timeline, position the playhead in Frame 10.

   continues on next page

5. On the Stage, drag the ball to the approximate location where you want it to connect with a paddle for the second hit.

Flash makes Ball the active layer and creates a keyframe (in Frame 10) containing another instance of the PingPongBall symbol in its new location. Flash completes the classic tween between Keyframe 5 and Keyframe 10 of the Ball layer.

6. On the Stage, reposition the second paddle so that it connects with the ball for the second hit.

Flash makes 2nd Paddle the active layer and creates a keyframe (in Frame 10) containing another instance of the 2ndPaddle symbol in its new location 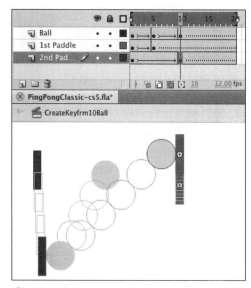.

7. Repeat Steps 1–6, creating keyframes 15 and 20 to make the ball connect with each paddle one more time.

8. Play the movie to see the animation in action.

TIP Currently, all layers in this Flash document are set to be classic tweens. If you add more frames later, they will also be set to classic tweening. To completely end the tweening sequences, you need to remove the tween from the last keyframe in each layer. Select the final keyframes and choose Insert > Remove Tween.

F Moving an element in another frame creates another tween. Here, the paddle on the right side appears to move more slowly than the paddle on the left side, because Flash is creating a ten-frame tween for the right paddle, which moves a short distance. The left paddle tweens in five frames and moves a greater distance. (Here, onion skinning is turned on to make the tweened shapes visible.)

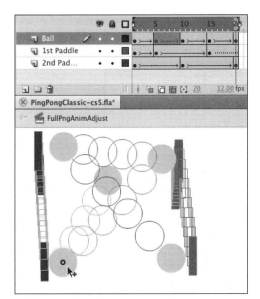

G You can easily fine-tune the location of objects in classic tweens by turning on Onion Skin Outlines and Edit Multiple Frames. Here, the paddle on the right doesn't move in a straight line. If you want it to do so, reposition the paddle graphics in the first and final frames so that one lies directly above the other; then reposition the ball so that it comes into contact with both paddles.

To fine-tune the movement—classic tweening:

1. Continuing with the file from the preceding task, in the Status bar, click the Onion Skin Outlines button and the Edit Multiple Frames button to activate these modes.

   Position the onion handles to cover all 20 frames or choose Onion All. With Edit Multiple Frames active, the symbol instances in keyframes appear as solid objects; the interpolated tween graphics appear as onion outlines.

2. Reposition the symbol instances as necessary to fine-tune the motion **G**.

   For example, using the selection tool, drag a symbol instance on the Stage. Or, to change the symbols' x- and y-coordinates, select the instance and use the X and Y hot text in the Position and Size section of the Property inspector.

TIP After you define a keyframe span as a classic tween, any slight change you make to the tweened symbol instance on an in-between frame causes Flash to create a new keyframe. Even clicking and holding more than a second or two causes Flash to insert a keyframe. So that you don't change objects' positions or create new keyframes accidentally, lock or hide the layers that you're not working on.

TIP Motion tweens are not as delicate as classic tweens; you can click and hold on a tween target on an in-between frame without fear of accidentally creating a property keyframe. Still, once you've positioned elements as you want them on a layer, it's a good idea to lock the layer to prevent unintended changes.

Working with Multiple-Layer Motion Tweens

For the tasks in this section, you'll combine three simple motion tweens on three layers, to create a game of Ping-Pong much like the classic-tween animation you created in the preceding section. As in that animation, one layer contains the ball; the other layers each contain a paddle.

To set up a motion tween in all layers with one command:

1. Using the PingPongSetupMaster template you created in "To set up the graphics layers," earlier in this section, open a new document.

2. To define the length of the motion tween, in the Timeline, select Frame 20 in all three layers.

3. Choose Insert > Timeline > Frame.

   Flash defines in-between Frames 2–20 in all layers. Frame 20 is selected in all three layers.

4. Choose Insert > Motion tween .

   Flash creates a 20-frame motion-tween span in each layer ❶. Frame 1 of each layer is a keyframe containing the span's tween target (in the top layer, for example, it's an instance of the Ping-PongBall symbol). To make the symbols move around the Stage, you must add position keyframes to each tween span. You can do this by repositioning the tween targets at specific frames.

❶ Choose Insert > Motion Tween to create tween spans.

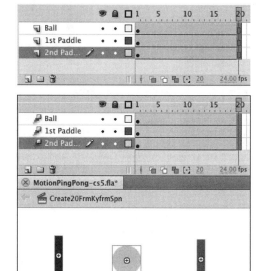

❶ When one frame is selected in keyframe spans on multiple layers (top), choosing Insert > Motion Tween converts all the spans to tween spans. You can see that the ending rectangle of the keyframe span disappears (bottom).

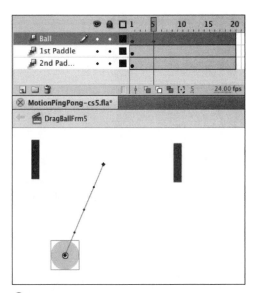

J Dragging a symbol on the Stage in a motion tween adds a position keyframe at the current frame and creates a motion path.

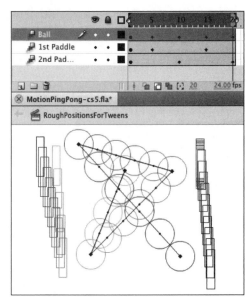

K By repositioning all of the tween targets in the appropriate frames, you create the same type of Ping-Pong animation in a motion tween that you created earlier in a classic tween.

To rough out the movement—motion tweening:

1. Continuing with the file from the preceding task, in the Timeline, position the playhead in Frame 5.

   The method you used to create keyframes within a classic tween, also works to create position keyframes in a tween span. Dragging a symbol to a new location on the Stage creates a new position keyframe in the Timeline at the current frame (the one where the playhead is located).

2. On the Stage, drag the ball to the approximate location where it should connect with one of the paddles for the first hit.

   Ball becomes the active layer. In Frame 5, Flash creates a position keyframe. Note that no other property changes exist currently for this frame. Flash creates a motion path from the ball's original location to its new location in Frame 5 **J**.

3. Follow Steps 3–8 of "To rough out the movement—classic tweening," in the preceding section.

   Reposition the tween targets PingPong-Ball, 1stPaddle, and 2ndPaddle on the Stage in Frames 5, 10, 15, and 20.

   Flash adds position keyframes and extends the motion path for each tween target after you move it **K**.

To fine-tune the movement— motion tweening:

1. Continuing with the file from the preceding task, to view and manipulate the motion paths of multiple tween targets simultaneously, do the following:

   ▶ In the Tools panel, choose the selection or subselection tool.

   ▶ On the Stage, click any motion path. The Motion Tween Property inspector displays properties for motion tweening.

   ▶ From the Property inspector's panel menu, choose Always Show Motion Paths 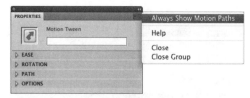.

   Viewing multiple motion paths gives you access to every motion path (and every control point), not just the path whose tween span is active. Viewing all the paths together gives you some context for adjusting the target symbols' relative positions on the Stage.

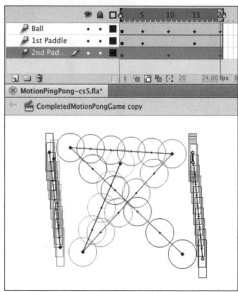

L To see motion paths for all the tween targets simultaneously, select any motion path on the Stage. Access the Property inspector and choose Always Show Motion Paths from the panel menu (top). Now, when the playhead is at a frame where multiple layers contain tween spans, Flash displays a motion path for each span whose layer is visible in the Timeline (bottom). (To view just the path of the tween span in the active layer where the playhead is located, deselect Always Show Motion Paths.)

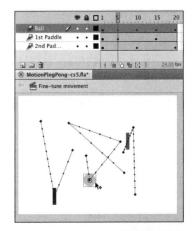

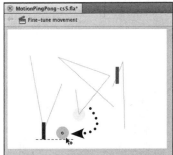

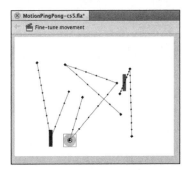

2. To adjust a tween target's position at a specific frame, do the following:

- Position the playhead in the desired frame in the Timeline or Motion Editor. Each tween target appears on its motion path at the associated frame point or control point. To adjust the tween target at an existing position keyframe, move the playhead to a frame that has a position-keyframe diamond in the Timeline or a property keyframe in the X and Y property curves in the Motion Editor.

- In the Tools panel, choose the selection tool.

- Drag the tween target to a new location on the Stage ⓜ. Note that if there is currently no position keyframe for the target you drag, Flash creates a new one.

continues on next page

ⓜ The PingPongBall and 1stPaddle tweens each have a position keyframe in Frame 5; their tween targets appear on the Stage as solid objects centered over the control point for Frame 5. The 2ndPaddle tween has no position keyframe at Frame 5; its tween target appears on the Stage as a solid object centered over the frame point for Frame 5. When you drag PingPongBall, Flash moves the control point in the motion path. If no position keyframe exists for that target in the current frame, when you drag the tween target, Flash adds a position keyframe to the current frame.

3. To adjust all tween targets in context, at any position keyframe, do the following:

 ▸ In the Status bar, click the Onion Skin Outlines button to activate onion skinning. Position the onion handles to cover the tween span or choose Onion All. The onion outlines show you how the tween targets relate to one another as they follow their motion paths.

 ▸ In the Tools panel, choose the subselection tool.

 ▸ Drag any control point on the Stage. Flash previews the new motion path as you drag (there is no preview for a tween target's onion outline, however). Release the mouse button and Flash redraws the motion path and the outlines .

TIP In Step 1, to access the Motion Tween Property inspector, you could select a tween span in the Timeline instead of selecting a motion path on the Stage.

TIP With Edit Multiple Frames active, Flash displays the content of all the keyframes within the onion markers. When positioning graphics on multiple layers for classic tweening, you need to have Edit Multiple Frames active to see (and manipulate) the symbol instances in all the keyframes of the tween simultaneously. With motion tweening, that's unnecessary and may be confusing. Each motion tween has just one keyframe, the one at the beginning of the tween span. Even when the playhead is in a property keyframe later in the tween span, the solid symbol always appears at the initial control point of the motion path.

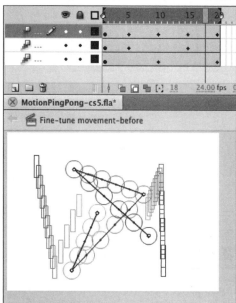

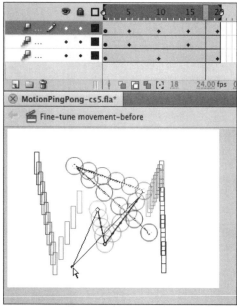 To get more context for adjusting the position of multiple motion tweens, turn on onion skinning. You can then use the subselection tool to reposition any control point in any visible motion path. You don't need to position the playhead in a specific frame, and you can't accidentally add new position keyframes.

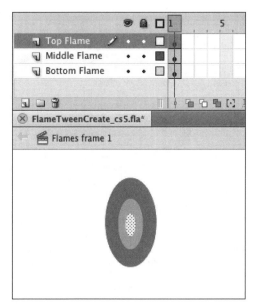

O Create each part of a multiple-element shape tween on a separate layer. Name the layers to help you track what goes where.

Working with Multiple-Layer Shape Tweens

An important thing to remember about complex shape tweens is that Flash deals most reliably with a single shape tween on a layer. In the following tasks, you create a multipart, multilayer graphic, and you shape-tween the whole package simultaneously.

To create shape tweens on separate layers:

1. Open a Flash document, and add two new layers.

2. Rename the layers Top Flame, Middle Flame, and Bottom Flame.

   Naming the layers helps you keep track of the objects and their locations.

3. Create the shapes.

   On the Stage, use the oval tool to create three concentric oval shapes without strokes. In the Bottom Flame layer, create a large oval; in the Middle Flame layer, create a medium oval and center it over the first oval; in the Top Flame layer, create a small oval and center it over the medium oval. Give each oval a different color. Your file should look something like **O**.

When Should One Element Span Several Layers?

Often, an element that you think of as a single entity consists of several shapes in Flash. A candle flame is a good example. To simulate the flickering of a lighted candle, you might create a flame with three shades of orange and then animate changes in the flame shape and colors.

It's natural to keep drawing each piece of the flame in one layer, especially if you're creating merge-shapes and want to see the interaction of the shapes immediately. Unfortunately, Flash has trouble tweening multiple shapes (both merge-shapes and drawing-objects) on a single layer. You're better off creating a rough version of each piece in a separate layer and then fine-tuning that version. Or, create your shapes in one layer, but then select them and choose Modify > Timeline > Distribute to Layers to place them on separate layers. That way, Flash has to tween only one shape per layer, and the result will be cleaner.

4. Select Frame 5 in all three layers.

5. Choose Insert > Timeline > Keyframe.

Flash creates a keyframe with the same content as Keyframe 1 for each layer.

6. In the Timeline, select any of the frames in the Keyframe 1 span (1, 2, 3, or 4) in all three layers.

7. Control-click (Mac) or right-click (Windows) the selected frames and choose Create Shape Tween from the contextual menu.

Flash creates shape tweens in Frames 1–4 on all three layers 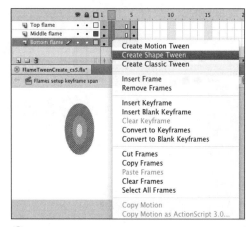. To create flickering flames, you need to reshape the ovals in Keyframe 5.

8. In the Timeline, position the playhead in Keyframe 5.

9. On the Stage, edit the ovals to create flame shapes.

10. Play the movie to see the animation in action.

Flash handles the shape-tweening of each layer separately. For comparison, try creating the oval and flame shapes on a single layer and then shape-tweening them 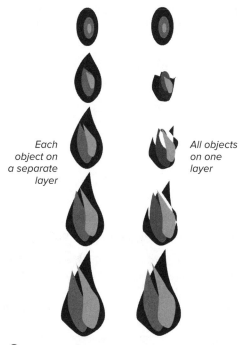.

11. Click the Onion Skin Outlines and Edit Multiple Frames buttons to activate these modes; then reshape the flame objects as necessary to fine-tune the motion.

P When your selection contains frames from multiple keyframe spans, you can assign shape-tweening to those keyframe spans simultaneously. Access the contextual menu for frames, for example, and choose Create Shape Tween.

Each object on a separate layer

All objects on one layer

Q No matter whether you use merge-shapes or drawing objects, if you put the three flames on separate layers (left), Flash does a reasonable job of tweening even when you don't add shape hints. With all three flame shapes on a single layer (right), Flash has difficulty creating the tweens.

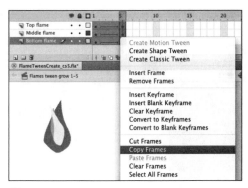

A The contextual menu for frames lets you copy all selected frames with a single command.

Reversing Animation

Sometimes, you can save effort by creating just half the animation you need and letting Flash do the rest of the work. Think of the candle flame that grows and shrinks. The shrinking phase is the reverse of the growing phase. You can make a copy of the growing-flame animation and then have Flash reverse it. The technique for reversing animation is the same for shape tweens and classic tweens; you can reverse the animation of motion tweens in a variety of ways.

To reverse the animation created with keyframe spans (classic and shape tweening), simply swap the order in which the keyframes appear in the Timeline, and the animation "runs in reverse." There are two ways to reverse the animation in motion tweens: reverse the direction that the tween target takes as it moves along the motion path, and reverse the order in which all property changes take place (see the sidebar "The Mystery of Motion Reversal," later in this chapter).

To reverse the frame order for shape (or classic) keyframe spans:

1. Open the document you created in the preceding section.

   This movie spans five frames on three layers. The first keyframe shows the flame as three concentric oval shapes; the final keyframe shows the flame in a taller, flickering configuration.

2. In the Timeline, select all five frames on all three layers.

3. In one of the selected frames, Control-click (Mac) or right-click (Windows) to access the contextual menu for frames, then choose Copy Frames **A**.

continues on next page

4. In the Timeline, select Frame 6 in all three layers.

5. In one of the selected frames, Control-click (Mac) or right-click (Windows) to access the contextual menu for frames, and choose Paste Frames.

   Your movie now contains two back-to-back animation sequences of the growing flame **B**.

6. In the Timeline, select Frames 6–10 on all three layers.

7. Choose Modify > Timeline > Reverse Frames.

   Flash reverses the tween in the second sequence so that the flame starts out tall and flickery, and winds up in its original oval configuration in the final keyframe **C**.

TIP Because the technique in the preceding task reverses the order in which keyframes appear in the Timeline, you can also use it to reverse the direction for animation you create using frame-by-frame techniques. Select the full range of keyframes, then choose Modify > Timeline > Reverse Frames.

TIP In the preceding task, you wind up with back-to-back duplicate keyframes (Frames 5 and 6 both contain the tall flame). You can convert the duplicate to an in-between frame, adding it to either of the tween segments. To add it to the first tween segment, select Frame 5 in all three layers (to add it to the second segment, select Frame 6 in all layers), Control-click (Mac) or right-click (Windows) the selected frames, and from the contextual menu, choose Clear Keyframe.

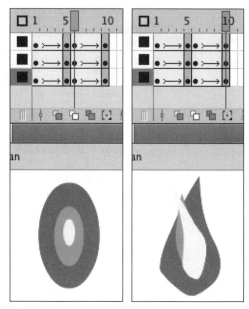

B After you paste the copied selection, the second tween sequence starts with the oval flame (left) and ends with the tall, flickering flame (right).

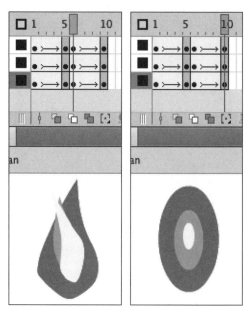

C After you reverse the frames, the second tween sequence starts with the flickering flame (left) and ends with the oval flame (right).

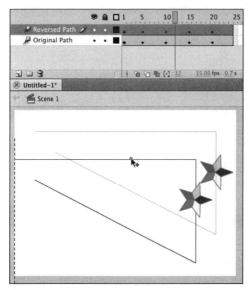

D To make it easier to compare duplicated motion tweens, drag the topmost motion path to a different area of the Stage.

To reverse the direction of motion for motion tweens:

1. Using the RotateStarMaster template you created in Chapter 11, open a new document.

    The file contains a 24-frame animation of a star that rotates and moves to three different spots on the Stage. (To review using templates, see Chapter 1.)

2. In the Timeline, add a new layer, and name the layers to identify them.

    Name the layer containing the motion tween Original Path; name the new layer Reversed Path. It's helpful to compare the original motion tween with the reversed version on separate layers.

3. To duplicate the motion tween, Option- (Mac) or Alt- (Windows) drag the tween span from the Original Path layer to Frames 1–24 of the Reversed Path layer.

    The tween targets and motion paths stack right on top of one another.

4. On the Stage, drag the topmost motion path to a new location on the Stage. Separating the paths makes it easier to compare the motion. Your document should look something like **D**.

5. In the Timeline, in the Reversed Path layer, Control-click (Mac) or right-click (Windows) the tween span.

6. From the contextual menu, choose Motion Path > Reverse Path **E**.

continues on next page

E To change the direction of motion in a motion tween, Control-click (Mac) or right-click (Windows) a tween span and choose Motion Path > Reverse Path from the contextual menu.

Flash reverses the path by reversing the graphs for the X and Y property curves in the Basic Motion section of the Motion Editor **F**.

7. Play through the animation.

The two stars start from opposite ends of the motion path and move in opposite directions. That's the result of reversing the property curves for X and Y. The Reverse Paths command has no effect on any other property curves. Both stars complete their rotation at Frame 5. Note that when you apply the Reverse Path command to complex tweens, Flash may redistribute position keyframes in the Timeline, while keeping other property keyframes in their original locations **G**.

TIP Another way to reverse the direction of motion is to flip the motion path itself. For example, select the motion path on the Stage, then choose Modify > Transform > Flip Horizontal (or Flip Vertical). You can also use the free- transform tool to flip the direction of the path.

Original motion tween

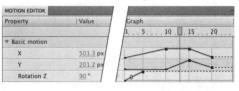

Reversed path

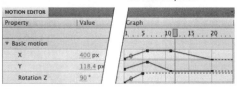

F The Motion Editor makes it clear what happens when you choose the Motion Path > Reverse Path command: Flash flips the direction of the X and Y property curves. (The Rotation Z property remains unchanged.)

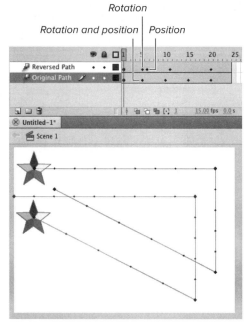

G When you reverse a motion tween by using the Motion Path > Reverse Path command, Flash flips the X and Y property curves, resulting in new locations for property-keyframe diamonds in the Timeline.

To reverse the order of all property keyframes:

1. Open a document containing a motion tween.

2. In the Timeline, Control-click (Mac) or right-click (Windows) the tween span.

3. From the contextual menu, choose Reverse Keyframes.

   Flash reverses the graphs for all of the property curves in the Motion Editor (see the sidebar "The Mystery of Motion Reversal," later in this chapter).

TIP Using the Reverse Keyframes command may have unexpected results when you apply it to tweens where some property curves lack a property keyframe in the final frame of the tween span. That's because in reversing the property curves, Flash ignores any in-between frames that come at the end of the Motion Editor graph (the dotted-line portion of the property curve). To force Flash to flip the entire graph, you can add a property keyframe to the last frame of the tween.

Combining Tweening with Frame-by-Frame Techniques

Especially with shape tweening, you can't always rely on Flash to create in-between frames that capture the exact movement you want. You can combine Flash's tweening with your own frame-by-frame efforts, however, letting Flash do the work when it can, then using keyframe animation to refine the movement. Flash helps with the process by letting you convert the intangible in-between frames of a tween to keyframes that you can edit and refine yourself. The conversion process differs depending on the type of tweening.

Shape and classic tweens For shape tweens and classic tweens, you can select one or more frames in the keyframe span and choose Modify > Timeline > Convert to Keyframes. Flash converts each selected frame to a keyframe containing a new shape or a new instance of the tweened symbol. A new instance has all the properties that were applied to the symbol at that in-between frame. Note that when converting in-between frames of a shape tween to keyframes, Flash always creates the new shapes as merge-shapes (even if the shapes in the preceding keyframe are drawing-objects or primitive-shapes). This could result in unexpected consequences if your shapes are on a single layer. It's another reason to make sure your shapes are on separate layers for tweened animation.

Motion tweens and inverse kinematics (IK) For motion tweens, Control-click (Mac) or right-click (Windows) anywhere in the tween span and choose Convert to Frame by Frame Animation from the contextual menu. Flash converts every frame in the span (whether selected or not) to a keyframe containing a new instance of the tween target. This new instance has all the properties that were applied to the tween target at that in-between frame of the motion tween. If you choose Modify > Timeline > Convert to Keyframes when one or more frames of a motion tween are selected, Flash adds property keyframes to the current frame (see the sidebar "The Insert > Keyframe Conundrum," in Chapter 11). For pose spans created by inverse kinematics (IK), you also use the contextual menu's Convert to Frame by Frame Animation command; the Convert to Keyframes command creates a new pose, not a new keyframe (see Chapter 13).

The Mystery of Motion Reversal

Imagine animating a small red square that moves from left to right, doubles in size, and turns blue. You can reverse it in two ways: you can reverse the path to move a small red square from right to left (where it doubles in size and turns blue), or you can reverse the keyframes to move a large blue square from right to left (where it turns red and shrinks to half its size). The results are straightforward for a simple animation with just a few changes, especially if the changes take place in just two keyframes, one at the beginning of the tween span and one at the end. But if changes take place throughout the tween, and there are property keyframes in the middle of the tween span, Flash must decide exactly where to make the desired changes. The results can be complex and somewhat unexpected, especially when viewed in the Timeline.

To reverse motion tweening, Flash simply flips the property curve that appears in the Motion Editor graph. When you choose Motion Path > Reverse Path, Flash flips the X and Y curves in the Basic Motion section; when you choose Reverse Keyframes, Flash flips all the property curves.

Reversing a tween span that ends with in-between frames (where the property curve is a dotted line in the Motion Editor graph) can be especially confusing. Flash treats the curve from the first control point (the span's initial keyframe) to the last control point as an object and flips that. Flash excludes any in-between frames at the end of the tween span (where the property curve is a dotted line). This may make position keyframes appear in seemingly unexpected places in the Timeline when you reverse the animation  **H**.

Timeline

H When you use the Motion Path > Reverse Keyframes command, the number of property-keyframe diamonds in the Timeline may appear to increase. That's because one diamond can represent multiple properties. The Motion Editor shows what happens.

Motion Editor

Original

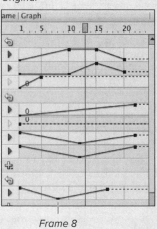

Frame 8

Reversed Path

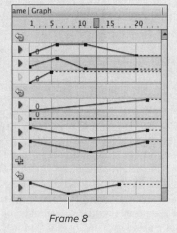

Frame 8

Reversed Keyframes

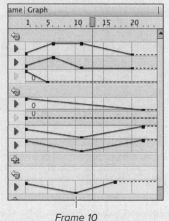

Frame 10

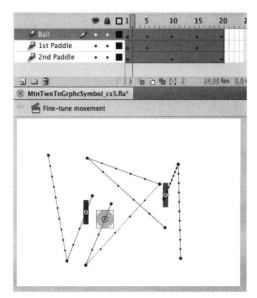

A To convert an existing animation to a symbol, first select all the frames and layers that make up the animation sequence. (This example uses the Ping-Pong animation created in the section "Working with Multiple-Layer Motion Tweens," earlier in this chapter.)

B You set a new symbol's type in the Create New Symbol dialog. Movie clips operate from their own independent Timeline. Animated graphic symbols play in sync with the main movie that contains them. One frame in the main movie's Timeline displays one frame of the graphic symbol's Timeline.

Saving Animations As Symbols

In Chapter 7, you learned to save work for reuse and keep file sizes small by using symbols. Flash lets you do the same thing with entire multiple-frame, multiple-layer animation sequences. You can save such sequences either as an animated graphic symbol or as a movie-clip symbol. You can use these symbols repeatedly with a much smaller hit on file size than if you simply re-created the animation by using graphic-symbol instances within separate animations. Additionally, for complex animations, symbols help keep down the number of frames and layers that you have to deal with.

To convert an animation to a graphic symbol:

1. Open a multiple-layer animation, such as the three-layer, 20-frame animation created earlier in the chapter.

2. In the Timeline, select all frames in all layers **A**.

3. Choose Edit > Timeline > Copy Frames.

4. Choose Insert > New Symbol, or press Command-F8 (Mac) or Ctrl-F8 (Windows).

   The Create New Symbol dialog appears **B**.

5. In the Create New Symbol dialog, type a name for your symbol.

6. From the Type menu, choose Graphic as the symbol type.

7. Click OK.

Flash creates a new symbol in the library and switches you to symbol-editing mode for that symbol.

The name of your symbol appears in the Edit bar. The default Timeline for your new symbol consists of one layer and a blank keyframe at Frame 1.

8. In the symbol Timeline, select Keyframe 1, and choose Edit > Timeline > Paste Frames.

Flash pastes the frames and layers that you copied from the original movie into the Timeline for the symbol **C**. If you want to make any adjustments in the animation sequence, you can do so at this point.

9. To return to document-editing mode, choose Edit > Edit Document.

To convert an animation to a movie-clip symbol:

- Follow the steps in the preceding task, but this time, in Step 6, choose Movie Clip as the symbol type **D**.

TIP To make a movie clip that contains exactly the same frames as an existing animated graphic symbol, you can duplicate that symbol and change its type. Select the animated graphic symbol in the Library panel. From the panel menu, choose Duplicate. The Duplicate Symbol dialog appears, allowing you to rename the symbol and set its type to Movie Clip.

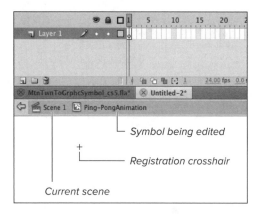

All frames of animation pasted into Timeline

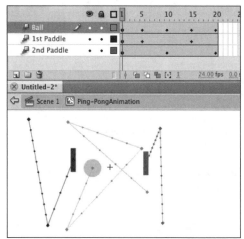

C When you create a new symbol, Flash switches to symbol-editing mode, making the new symbol's Timeline available for editing (top). You must paste all the frames of your animation into the symbol's Timeline to create the animated symbol (bottom).

D Choosing Movie Clip in the Type section of the Create New Symbol dialog defines a symbol that has an independent Timeline. The entire movie-clip symbol runs in a single frame of the main movie.

Symbols Reduce Layer Buildup

In general, for tweened animations, you need to place each object on a separate layer. To animate a person, for example, create separate layers for the head, the torso, each arm, and each leg. For complex motion, you might even create separate layers for the eyes, mouth, fingers, and toes. Add some other elements to this character's environment, and you wind up dealing with many layers.

Turning an animation sequence into a symbol in effect collapses all those layers into one object. The process is a bit like grouping, but for Timeline layers instead of shapes. On the Stage, the symbol exists on a single layer, but that layer contains all the layers of the original animation.

How Do Animated Graphic Symbols Differ from Movie-Clip Symbols?

Flash provides for two kinds of animated symbols: graphic symbols and movie clips. The difference is subtle. An animated graphic symbol is tied to the Timeline of any movie in which you place the symbol, whereas a movie-clip symbol runs on its own independent Timeline. When the playhead stops moving in the main Timeline, an animated graphic symbol stops playing, but a movie-clip symbol continues to play.

Think of the frames of an animated graphic symbol as a tray of slides, and a movie-clip symbol as a film loop. The animated graphic symbol projects its slides, one per frame, in lockstep with the frames of its hosting movie (its parent Timeline): to see the next frame of the symbol, you move to the next frame in the parent Timeline. Like a tray of slides, an animated graphic symbol has no sound track. If you use sounds in an animated graphic symbol, those sounds don't play when you place the symbol into the parent Timeline.

In effect when you publish, the graphic symbol's frames merge with the frames in the parent movie; the graphic symbol's Timeline "disappears." Any frame scripts in the graphic symbol's Timeline disappear as well. Movie-clip symbols nested inside graphic symbols do retain their interactivity. Just be aware that when the graphic symbol's Timeline disappears, the relationships of nested Timelines shift. As you work in a Flash file (FLA), the relationship is Main movie > graphic symbol > nested movie clip. In the published file (SWF) the relationship is Main movie > nested movie clip. The graphic symbol's Timeline is no longer available to be the parent Timeline for nested movie-clips. Nested movie clips that refer to parent in a target path now refer to the parent Timeline of the graphic symbol, not the Timeline of the graphic symbol itself. This fact of publishing can lead to unexpected results, particularly when you convert movie clips to graphic symbols and vice versa. (To learn more about ActionScript 3.0 and interactivity, see Chapter 15.)

A movie-clip symbol can project all its frames one after another, over and over, in a single frame of the parent Timeline. Movie clips do have a sound track and do retain their interactivity. (To learn more about sound, see Chapter 17. For interactivity, see Chapters 14 and 15.)

One more thing to know about the two symbol types is that movie clips, because they run on their own Timeline, don't appear as animations in the Flash authoring environment. You see only the first frame of the movie as a static element on the Stage. Animated graphic symbols, which use the same Timeline as the main movie, display their animation in the authoring environment.

Using Animated Graphic Symbols

To put an animated graphic symbol to work, you must place an instance of it in your main movie. The layer of the movie where you place the symbol must have enough frames to display the symbol. You can use instances of an animated graphic symbol just as you would any other symbol—combine it with other graphics on a layer; use it in a classic tween or motion tween; modify its color, size, and rotation; and so on.

To place an instance of an animated graphic symbol:

1. Follow the steps in "To convert an animation to a graphic symbol," in the preceding section.

2. Choose Insert > Scene.

   Flash adds a new scene. The Timeline has one layer with a blank keyframe in Frame 1. The Stage is empty.

   Adding a new scene gives you a blank Stage to work with and makes it easy to compare the two animations: the original (created directly in the main movie Timeline) and the instance of the graphic symbol placed in the movie.

3. Access the Library panel and select the Ping-PongAnimation symbol.

   The first frame of the animation appears in the preview window 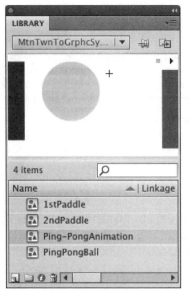.

4. Drag a copy of the symbol to the Stage.

   Flash places the symbol in Keyframe 1. You can see only the first frame of the animation 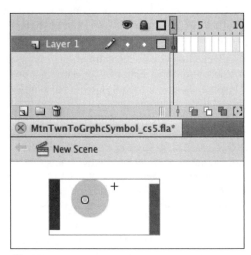. The animation is 20 frames long, so you must have at least 20 frames to view the symbol in its entirety.

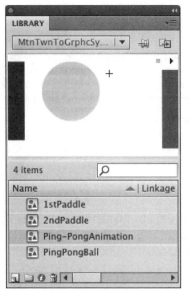

Ⓐ Select the animated graphic symbol you want to use, and then drag a copy to your Flash document to place an instance on the Stage.

Ⓑ When you drag an instance of the animated graphic symbol to the Stage, you see the symbol's first frame with its graphics selected. You must add frames to allow the full animation of the symbol to play in the main movie.

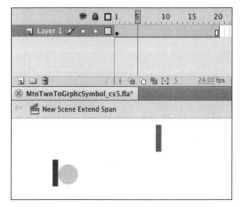

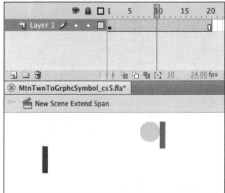

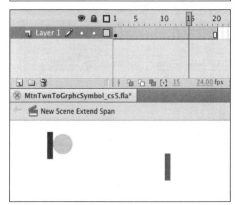

C Frames 1–20 are just regular defined frames, they haven't been assigned any kind of tweening, but they still display animation. Flash displays 20 frames of the animated graphic symbol that you placed in Keyframe 1. It's as though the symbol is a tray of slides, and Flash is projecting one image per frame in the main movie. If the main movie is longer than the slide show, Flash starts the slide show over by default.

5. In the Timeline, select Frame 20, and choose Insert > Timeline > Frame.

6. Play the movie.

Now Flash can display each frame of the animated graphic symbol in a frame of the movie. Frame 2 of the symbol appears in Frame 2 of the movie, Frame 5 of the symbol appears in Frame 5 of the movie, and so on **C**. If the layer containing the animated–graphic-symbol instance in the main Timeline has fewer frames than the symbol requires, Flash truncates the symbol's animation. If the layer has more frames than the symbol requires, by default Flash starts playing the graphic-symbol animation over again to fill those extra frames.

TIP By default, Flash loops the animation of graphic symbols to fill extra frames. To prevent looping of a selected symbol instance, choose Play Once from the Options menu in the Looping section of the Property inspector.

TIP To display just one frame of the animated graphic symbol, choose Single Frame from the Options menu, then enter the desired frame number in the First field.

TIP Character animators can take advantage of the Single Frame option to create a miniature library of symbols within a symbol. Each frame of an animated graphic symbol holds a different version of a feature—for example, an eye. Frame 1 contains an open eye; Frame 2, that same eye half closed; Frame 3, the eye fully closed. To animate a character's eye movements, you set up a classic tween using the animated graphic symbol, then set each keyframe of the classic tween to show the appropriate eye position. For an example of this technique in action, check out Adobe's Lip Sync template. (Choose File > New, then click the Templates tab in the dialog that appears; select the template folder named Sample Files, where you'll find Lip Sync.)

Using Movie-Clip Symbols

You put movie-clip symbols to work by placing an instance of a symbol on the Stage in your Flash document. Unlike animated graphic symbols, movie-clip symbols have their own Timeline. A movie clip plays continuously, like a little film loop, in a single frame of the main movie. As long as the movie contains no other instructions that stop the clip from playing—a blank key-frame in the Timeline for the layer containing the movie clip, for example—the clip continues to loop. During authoring, you can see only the first frame of a movie clip. To view the animation of the movie-clip symbol in context with all the other elements of your movie, you must export the movie (by choosing one of the test modes, for example). You can preview the animation of the movie-clip symbol by itself in the Library panel.

To place an instance of a movie clip:

1. Follow the steps in "Saving Animations as Symbols > To convert an animation to a movie-clip symbol," earlier in this chapter.

2. Choose Insert > Scene.

   Flash creates a new scene and displays its Timeline: a single layer with a blank keyframe in Frame 1. The Stage is empty.

3. Access the Library panel and select the Ping-PongClip symbol.

4. Drag a copy of the selected symbol to the Stage.

   Flash places the symbol in Keyframe 1 **Ⓐ**. You don't need to add any more frames to accommodate the animation, but you must export the movie to see the animation.

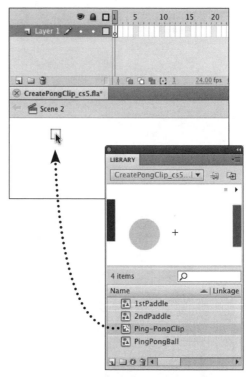

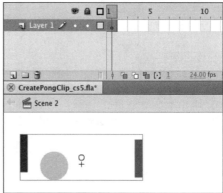

Ⓐ Drag an instance of your movie clip from the Library panel to the Stage (top). Flash places the instance in Keyframe 1 (bottom).

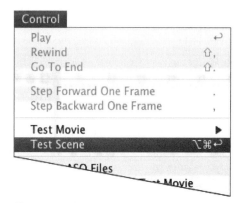

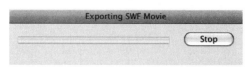

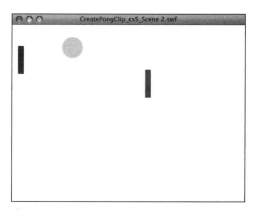

To view the movie-clip animation in context:

1. Continuing with the movie you created in the preceding task, choose Control > Test Scene **B**.

   Flash exports the movie to a Flash Player format file, adding the name of the scene and the .swf extension to the filename and using the current publishing settings for all the export options. (For more information on publishing settings, see Chapter 18.) During export, Flash displays the Exporting SWF Movie dialog, which contains a progress bar and a Stop (Mac) or Cancel (Windows) button for canceling the operation **C**.

   When it finishes exporting the movie, Flash opens the SWF file in Flash Player so you can see the movie in action **D**.

2. When you've seen enough of the movie in test mode, click the movie window's Close button (Mac) or Close box (Windows) to exit Flash Player.

B Choose Control > Test Scene to preview the animation of just one scene in a movie.

C The Exporting SWF Movie dialog contains a progress bar and a button for canceling the export.

D Flash Player displays your movie in a regular window. To exit the Player, close the window.

Using Easing

In the classic-tween and shape-tween bouncing-ball examples, a single keyframe span contains the downward bounce. You can add frames to the keyframe span, making the downward bounce take longer, but the movement still happens at a constant rate. Similarly for motion tweens, the changes from one property keyframe to the next happen at a constant rate. Easing allows you to vary that rate, making changes start slowly and finish rapidly and vice versa. By setting an Ease value in the Property inspector, you can control the rate of change for all properties within a keyframe span (for classic or shape tweens) or tween span (for motion tweens). (You can also set easing between IK poses in the Property inspector.) To gain control over the rate of change for specific properties and frames, you need to apply custom easing (see the sidebar "About Custom Easing," later in this chapter).

Using Custom Easing to Create Motion

You can use custom easing values (see the sidebar "About Custom Easing," later in this chapter) to create variations on the general motion of a tweened symbol whether it's in a classic tween or a motion tween. To create movement through easing, you must adjust easing values to apply different percentages of a property change at different frames of the animation. Imagine, for example, a tween that moves an oval from one side of the Stage to the other in 20 frames. Now apply easing to the X (horizontal position) curve. If, for example, you set the easing curve so that Frame 5 carries out 100 percent of the horizontal change and Frame 10 carries out just 50 percent, the oval moves to the right side of the Stage at Frame 5, back to mid-Stage at Frame 10, then back to the right side at Frame 20. To see this technique in action, check out the canned animation named Wave that comes in the Motion Presets panel (in the Default Presets folder). After you apply the Wave preset to a symbol, open the Motion editor and view the graph for Y (Vertical Position). Wave uses easing in the Y property curve to make the tween target move up and down repeatedly, although the curve has just three *y*-position keyframes.

Classic tween   *Motion tween*

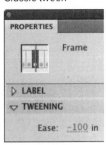 

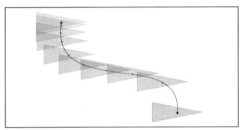

A A negative Ease value makes changes in the initial frames of the tween smaller and changes toward the end larger. The animation seems to start slowly and then speed up.

To apply easing to the span:

1. Create a ten-frame tween and access the Property inspector.

   You can use classic, shape, or motion tweening to create the tween.

2. In the Timeline, select the tween by doing the following:

   ▸ For classic and shape tweens, select any frame in the keyframe span.

   ▸ For motion tweens, select any frame in the tween span.

3. To make the animation start slowly (ease in), do one of the following:

   ▸ For classic and shape tweens, in the Tweening section of the Frame Property inspector, use the Ease hot text to enter a negative value.

   ▸ For motion tweens, in the Ease section of the Motion Tween Property inspector, use the Ease hot text to enter a negative number.

   The word *in* appears next to the hot text value **A**

   Easing in makes the animation start slowly and speed up toward the end. The lower the Ease value, the greater the rate of acceleration.

4. To make the animation start quickly and decelerate (ease out), do one of the following:

- For classic and shape tweens, in the Tweening section of the Frame Property inspector, use the Ease hot text to enter a positive number  **B**.

- For motion tweens, in the Ease section of the Motion Tween Property inspector, use the Ease hot text to enter a positive number.

The word *out* appears next to the hottext value. Easing out makes the animation start quickly and slow down toward the end. The higher the Ease value, the greater the rate of deceleration.

TIP An Ease value of 0 causes Flash to display the whole animation at a constant rate **C**.

Classic tween   *Motion tween*

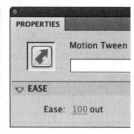

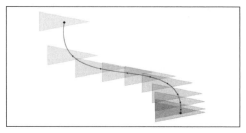

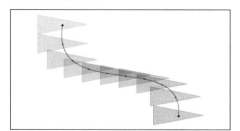

B A positive Ease value makes changes at the end of the animation smaller and changes in the initial frames larger. The animation seems to start quickly and then slow down.

Classic tween   *Motion tween*

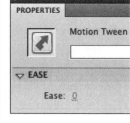

C With an Ease value of 0, Flash distributes the tweening changes evenly across the in-between frames. The effect is that of animation moving at a constant rate.

About Custom Easing

You can create custom easing for classic tweens and motion tweens, but not for shape tweens or IK poses. For classic tweens, custom easing is the only way to control the speed of individual property changes within a single keyframe span. For motion tweens, you can use the Motion Editor to create separate easing curves for each property. These advanced techniques are beyond the scope of a *Visual QuickStart Guide,* but here's a brief look at how to access the controls.

Classic easing To create custom easing for a classic tween, select any frame in the keyframe span. In the Tweening section of the Frame Property inspector, click the Edit Easing button (the pencil icon), to the right of the Ease hot text. The Custom Ease In/Ease Out dialog appears **D**. The dialog shows the selected tween's changes over time on a graph; the horizontal axis represents each frame in the tween; the vertical axis represents the amount of change. You can edit the graph similar to the way you'd edit a Bézier path. Click the line (or curve) to add control points, then position the Bézier handles. To ease all properties simultaneously, select the Use One Setting for All Properties checkbox. To set specific easing values for five properties—Position, Rotation, Scale, Color, and Filters—deselect the Use One Setting for All Properties checkbox. Choose specific properties from the Property menu.

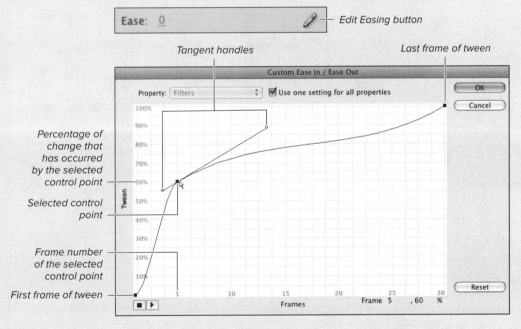

D For classic tweens, click the Edit Easing button (the pencil icon) in the Tweening section of the Frame Property inspector (top) to access the Custom Ease In/Ease Out dialog (bottom). Custom easing lets you control easing precisely, frame by frame, by creating a curve that defines the rate of change in each frame. Click anywhere on the line (or curve) to add a new control point with handles. Without easing, the rate is constant, starting at 0 percent in the first frame of the tween and reaching 100 percent in the last frame of the tween.

continues on next page

About Custom Easing *continued*

Motion easing You create custom easing for motion tweens in the Motion Editor. There you'll find a special Eases category. To view and work with an easing curve in the Motion Editor, you must bring the ease into the Eases category (select it from the Add Ease menu, the plus-sign button).

A row with a graph for that ease appears in the Eases category. Flash comes with a number of preset easing curves for common situations, such as Simple, Stop and Start, and Bounce. To create a custom easing curve, choose Custom from the Add Ease menu. Flash adds a new row with a graph for your custom easing curve **E**.

To apply an easing curve to a property—either a preset curve or one of your own devising—you must choose the easing curve from the Selected Ease menu in the row for the property you want to control. The Selected Ease menu in each row lists all the easing curves currently available in the Eases category. If you don't see the curve you want in a specific Selected Ease menu, you need to add the curve to the Eases category.

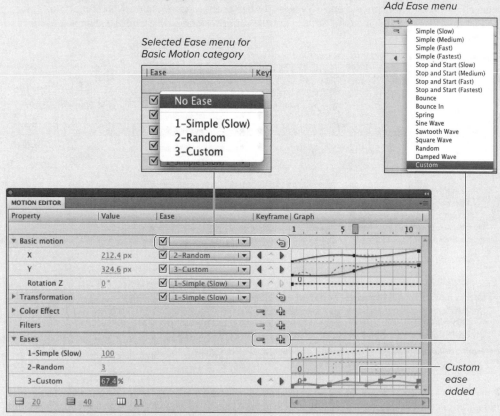

E The Motion Editor's Eases category (the last category in the Motion Editor) is the place to create custom easing curves. To begin the process, click the Add Ease menu (the plus sign) in the Eases row and choose Custom. You can then modify the graph in the Custom row. To apply the custom curve to a property curve, select the custom easing curve from the Selected Ease menu in the row of the property you want to control.

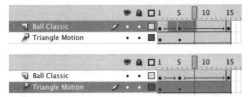

A To copy a classic or motion tween, in the Timeline, select one or more frames in one classic tween's keyframe span or in contiguous spans (top) or in one motion tween's tween span (bottom).

About Copy Motion

Flash's Copy Motion command copies information that defines a classic-tween or motion-tween sequence: changes to a tweened object's properties (such as position, rotation, scale); duration of the tween (the number of frames it takes); and other tween settings (such as Easing). The Paste Motion command lets you apply that information to a different object (let's call it the *tween object*) to change its properties in the same way, over the same number of frames, using the same Tween settings. The Paste Motion Special command lets you apply changes to the tween object's properties selectively. The Copy Motion As ActionScript 3.0 command translates classic- and motion-tween animation to ActionScript 3.0–generated animation.

Re-creating Classic and Motion Tweens

Flash offers three commands that will help you reduce repetitive animation work. Copy Motion, Paste Motion, and Paste Motion Special streamline the process of animating multiple objects that go through the same "motions."

To copy motion:

1. Create a single-layer animation using either classic tweening (Chapter 9) or motion tweening (Chapter 11).

   You can copy the animation from multiple keyframe spans set to classic tweening, so long as the keyframe spans are contiguous in one layer. You can copy the animation from just one motion-tween span at a time.

2. In the Timeline, to select the animation, do one of the following **A**:

   Classic tween Select one or more frames in a keyframe span set to classic tweening. The frames must be contiguous and must all be set to classic tweening. You can also select multiple contiguous classic-tween keyframe spans to copy the full range of motion. Do not, however, include the final keyframe of a classic tween if that keyframe is not highlighted as having the classic-tween property.

   Motion tween Select a single motion-tween span. Flash can copy the motion of just one tween span at a time.

continues on next page

3. Choose Edit > Timeline > Copy Motion .

Flash copies the changes in properties that define the tween for each selected (or partially selected) span. For classic tweens, the properties Flash copies are *x*-position, *y*-position, horizontal scale, vertical scale, rotation and skew, color, filters, and blend mode. For motion tweens, Flash copies all the properties of the tween that you can access via the Motion Editor.

To apply copied motion to a different tween object:

1. To select the tween object that will reenact the copied motion, do one of the following:

▸ On the Stage, select the object to which you want to apply the copied motion 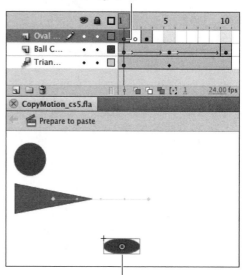.

or

▸ In the Timeline, select a keyframe containing the tween object to which you want to apply the copied motion.

With both selection methods, the new tween object must be one that can be tweened in the same way as the original tween object. (A merge-shape, for example, can't be used in classic tweening or motion tweening.) For best results, apply the copied motion only to a tween object that's isolated on its own layer.

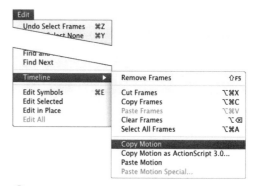

B The Edit > Timeline > Copy Motion command copies the properties that define a tween or tweens in a selected set of frames.

Selected keyframe

Selected tween object

C To apply the copied motion tween to a new tween object, select the symbol on the Stage (or select its keyframe in the Timeline).

Copied span

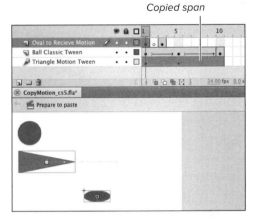

2. Choose Edit > Timeline > Paste Motion.

For classic tweens, Flash inserts into the Timeline the same number of keyframe spans (with the same number of frames and keyframes) as you copied. For motion tweens, Flash inserts a tween span of the same length, and with the same property keyframes, as the tween span you copied. The target keyframe you selected and all subsequent frames get pushed out to later frames in the Timeline **D**.

3. Play the movie.

The tween object to which you applied the copied classic-tween or motion-tween property changes now moves and transforms in the same way the original tween object did.

Motion pasted

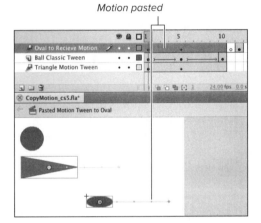

D The Paste Motion command pastes the tween sequence(s) of the copied motion into the Timeline for the selected tween object. The command preserves any existing unselected frames and keyframes in the Timeline, pushing them to later frames.

TIP You don't have to paste all the properties for a copied classic tween. To paste properties selectively, follow Step 1 in the preceding task to select the classic tween. Then choose Edit > Timeline > Paste Motion Special. The Paste Motion Special dialog appears. To apply individual tween properties, select any of the following checkboxes: X position, Y position, Horizontal Scale, Vertical Scale, Rotation and Skew, Color, Filters, and Blend Mode. When pasting a copied motion tween, the Paste Motion Special command is not available, but you have complete control over the properties in the pasted motion tween via the Motion Editor.

TIP You can also copy classic-tween and motion-tween properties in a form that can be pasted into the Actions panel or an ActionScript file. Flash translates the animation you created using graphics tools and classic or motion tweening into animation created by ActionScript.

Practice Session

In earlier practice sessions, you animated a bird flying along a path (Chapter 9), a mouth changing its expression (Chapter 10), and a flying rocket (Chapter 11). Try re-creating and combining these animations to take advantage of multiple layers. Turn the animations into symbols and animate those symbols.

- Using classic-tweening techniques, make a multilayer animation of a bird. Try creating separate objects for the bird body, beak, eyes, wings, and tail. Try animating changes to the position of the wings; make the tail waggle up and down; make the beak open and close; give the eye an eyelid that opens and closes. Add as much detail as you like. (See Chapter 12, *Animating on Multiple Layers > Working with multiple-layer classic tweens.*)

- Turn that entire animation into a movie-clip symbol. (See Chapter 12, *Saving Animations As Symbols > To convert an animation to a movie-clip symbol.*)

- Now, using classic-tweening techniques (Chapter 9) or motion-tweening techniques (Chapter 11), animate that symbol so that it moves along a path.

- Using multilayer shape-tweening techniques, try adding a trail of exhaust or a burst of flames in the flying-rocket symbol you created for practice in Chapter 11. (See Chapter 12, *Animating on Multiple Layers > Working with multiple-layer shape tweens.*)

Extra Credit

For the motion-tween version of your flying bird, use the Motion Editor to apply easing. Make the bird fly backward and forward using easing alone.

Save your file for use in later Practice Sessions.

Intro to Inverse Kinematics

Inverse kinematics (IK) is a method of animating objects and shapes that relies on a structure—called an *armature*. An IK armature works something like a skeleton, with multiple linked segments called *bones*. Once you set up the structure, you can manipulate it to create various configurations, or *poses*. Imagine manipulating a human skeleton; if you raise the hand and bring it in toward the torso, the forearm also raises, and the elbow bends. Similarly, if you move one bone in an IK armature, connected bones move in response. Flash interpolates changes between poses to create animation. You can use IK armatures to link multiple symbol instances, governing the relationships between the elements and controlling the ways they can move in relation to one another. You can also use IK armatures within a single shape, controlling the way the shape's outline changes. While the process of creating natural-looking movement with IK animation is complex and far beyond the scope of a *Visual QuickStart Guide,* the tasks in this chapter introduce you to creating armatures and poses using Flash's IK tools.

Using Armatures to Connect Symbols

When you use IK armatures to connect two or more symbol instances, the whole structure moves together, something like a marionette puppet. You can link symbol instances in linear or branching fashion or use a combination, where one or more branches extend in linear fashion. In a simplified cartoon body, for example, you might have three bones branching from the base of the character's neck; one connects to the head, a second connects to the right shoulder, a third to the left shoulder. Each shoulder bone could connect in linear fashion to bones for the upper arm, forearm, and hand. For the tasks in this section, you'll create a linear armature. (For the tasks in this section, make sure that any artwork you're planning to connect in symbol form has in fact been converted into a movie-clip symbol before you start linking with the IK bone tool.)

About IK Drawing Preferences

When an IK bone connects two symbol instances, the ends of the bone (its head and tail) create points around which the attached symbol instances rotate. A symbol instance has its own point of rotation, the transformation point. How do the two work together? There are two styles. Flash can set the transformation point wherever you create a head/tail point, or you can have Flash force the bone to start or end at the symbol instance's existing transformation point. By default, when you click with the bone tool to create a bone's head, or release the mouse button to create the bone's tail, Flash moves the transformation point to the spot where you clicked or released. To change the setting, choose Flash > Preferences (Mac) or Edit > Preferences (Windows). In the Preferences dialog, choose Drawing from the category list. To have Flash retain the current transformation point, in the IK Bone Tool section, deselect the Auto Set Transformation Point checkbox **A**. Now when you create IK bones, the head (or tail) point snaps to the existing transformation point of the symbol instance. The tasks in this chapter use the default style.

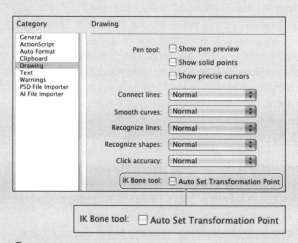

A In the Drawing category of the Preferences dialog, in the IK Bone Tool section, deselect the Auto Set Transformation Point checkbox to have Flash preserve the transformation points of the symbol instances as you create IK bones. The head or tail of the bone snaps to the existing transformation point when you add a bone to the symbol instance.

B The first step in creating an IK animation with symbol instances is to place instances on the Stage. Place the symbol instances into the relative positions they should have in the animated character or element that you're creating.

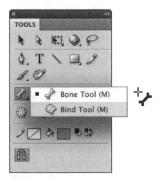

C To begin connecting symbols into an IK armature, select the bone tool. The pointer becomes a black bone with a plus sign.

D When the pointer is over a symbol instance, the pointer's bone and plus sign change to white, indicating that you can begin creating an IK bone. Click and drag to begin drawing the first bone. When you use Flash's default IK drawing style, position the pointer where you want the symbol instance's transformation point (the point of rotation) to be. Flash moves the transformation point to the spot you click.

E As long as the pointer is within the symbol instance where you placed the head of an IK bone, the pointer is black with a No-symbol modifier icon, indicating that you can't end the bone.

To link symbol instances in a linear armature:

1. Create the symbol (or symbols) that you want to animate with a linear IK structure.

   For this task, you'll link multiple instances of a movie-clip symbol to form a chain that can curl up or down from one end. Use the oval tool to create an oval shape and convert it to a movie-clip symbol named myOval (see Chapter 7).

2. Place instances of the symbol(s) on the Stage and arrange them in the desired relative positions **B**.

   For this task, use four instances of myOval lined up horizontally.

3. In the Tools panel, click the current IK tool, and from the submenu, select the bone tool (or press M) **C**.

   The pointer changes to a small black bone with a plus sign, indicating that you are ready to begin placing bones.

4. To begin drawing the first bone in the chain (the *parent bone*), position the pointer over the first symbol instance **D**.

   The pointer changes to a white bone with a plus sign, indicating that you are within a symbol where you can start a bone.

5. Click and drag to connect with the second symbol instance in the chain.

   Flash starts creating the bone; the point you click becomes the bone's head. As you drag, the pointer changes to a black bone with an international No symbol, a circle with a slash **E**. This pointer indicates that you are within the symbol instance containing the head of the bone; the tail of the bone must be in a different instance.

   continues on next page

6. To complete the first bone (to create the *tail* point), drag the pointer into the second symbol instance and release the mouse button.

As it moves into the area of a different symbol instance, the pointer changes to a white bone and plus sign, indicating that you can complete the IK bone **F**. The second instance can overlap the first symbol instance or be separate.

When you release the mouse button, Flash draws a bone connecting the two symbol instances and pulls them out of their current layer(s) and into a new layer, called a *pose layer*. Flash gives the pose layer a default name (see the sidebar "About Pose Layers," later in this chapter) and gives the movie-clip symbol instances default names, identifying them as IK nodes (see the sidebar "The Mystery of IK Instance Naming," later in this chapter).

7. To begin drawing the second bone in the chain (a *child* bone), position the pointer over the tail of the first bone you created.

Original Timeline

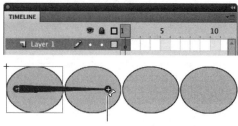

End parent bone

Layer created after bone completion
Some content remains in Layer 1

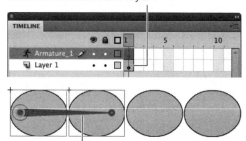

Completed parent bone

F When the pointer enters the area of a symbol instance other than the one you clicked to create the IK bone's head, the pointer turns white and a plus sign appears. You can release the mouse button to place the tail of the bone (the second point of rotation). When the bone is complete, Flash pulls the connected symbol instances into a special armature layer in the Timeline.

Bone Views

The default graphic representation of an IK bone is a bulky item, especially if you're using it with small, delicate artwork. After creating the first IK bone in an armature, you can view bones in an outline form or as a single line. To change the look of the bones, select the armature, for example, by selecting the pose span in the Timeline. In the Property inspector, in the Options section, from the Style menu, choose Wire (the outline form), Solid (the default, triangular form), or Line (a 1-pixel line).

Click to begin child bone

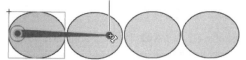

Drag to new instance

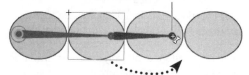

Completed child bone

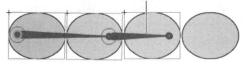

G To connect a child bone, position the pointer over the tail of the parent bone. Then click and drag.

All content pulled into armature layer

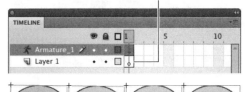

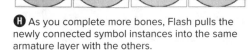

H As you complete more bones, Flash pulls the newly connected symbol instances into the same armature layer with the others.

TIP You don't need to be precise in positioning the head of a child bone. Whenever the pointer is within the area of the node containing the parent's tail point, the pointer changes to the white bone with a plus sign. Clicking anywhere within the node automatically connects to the tail point in that node.

The bone pointer changes from black to white, indicating that you're ready to add another bone.

8. Click and drag to connect with the third symbol instance.

Flash completes the second bone and pulls the third symbol instance into the armature layer **G**.

9. Repeat Steps 7 and 8 to add bones connecting the third and fourth symbol instances **H**.

Flash completes the third bone and pulls the fourth symbol instance into the armature layer. You're ready to manipulate the armature and create poses (see the section "Working with Poses," later in this chapter).

TIP You can use any type of symbol instance—graphic symbols, movie clips, or buttons—in an IK animation. Graphic symbols do not have instance names, so Flash doesn't label the connected instances as IK nodes. You cannot create a runtime IK animation, using graphic symbols. For the tasks in this book, use movie clips.

TIP In Step 5, the spot you click becomes the head of the first bone in a chain of bones. Take a moment to consider the placement of the head. In an IK arm, the head of the parent bone corresponds to a shoulder joint. If you plan to overlap the upper arm with the character's torso, then you'd probably want to place the joint in that area of overlap. If the upper arm will sit next to the torso, but not overlap it, you might want to place the joint closer to the edge of the upper-arm symbol.

TIP Note that in the four-node chain you created in the preceding task, there are just three bones. The number of bones in a linear armature is always one less than the number of nodes in that armature.

Anatomy of an Armature

A linear armature contains a chain of bones in a hierarchical structure **❶**. The first bone is known as the *parent;* all the bones that extend from it are known as *child* bones. The spot you click to begin drawing a bone becomes the *head* of the bone. The spot you release the mouse button to complete the bone becomes the *tail.* In a linear armature, the bones link head-to-tail. After you create one bone, you place the head of the next bone directly over the tail of the preceding bone. The head and tail are both points of rotation, or *joints,* and they coincide with the transformation points of the symbol instances in which they reside. By default, Flash relocates the transformation point whenever you click the bone tool within a symbol instance, placing the transformation point right where you place the head of the bone. (You can change that Preferences setting so that Flash snaps the head and tail points to the symbol instances' existing transformation points; see the sidebar "About IK Drawing Preferences," earlier in this chapter.) By default, the head and tail points allow bones to rotate through 360 degrees, like the hands of an analog clock.

continues on next page

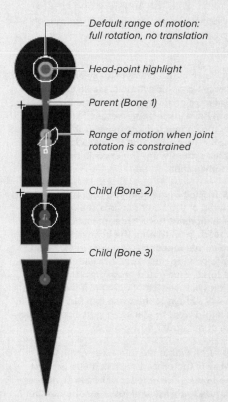

Default range of motion: full rotation, no translation

Head-point highlight

Parent (Bone 1)

Range of motion when joint rotation is constrained

Child (Bone 2)

Child (Bone 3)

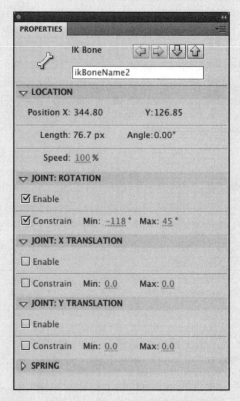

❶ In a linear armature, Flash highlights each head point with a circle. When you join multiple symbols in an armature, the first child bone starts at the tail of the parent bone; that point is also the head of the child bone. Click a bone to select it and view its properties in the Property inspector.

Anatomy of an Armature *continued*

You can control movement at a head point in various ways: you can allow full rotation (the default), prevent rotation completely, or limit rotation to create a joint that bends in one direction, like an elbow or a knee; you can prevent (the default), allow, or limit horizontal and vertical movement (known as *x-* and *y-translation*). You cannot control movement at a tail point. In a linear armature, most of the joints containing a tail point also contain a head point; you can constrain the joint by constraining the head. The symbol instance that comes at the end of the armature chain, however, contains a tail point that stands on its own. The final symbol instance in an IK chain can always rotate 360 degrees around its transformation point.

Branching armatures do not have a hierarchical structure: all the bones branch from a single spot—known as the *root* of the branches—and are known as *sibling* bones ⓙ. The location of the head joint is the same for all siblings. Although the bones are separate, their head points must have identical rotation and translation settings. Flash handles that automatically.

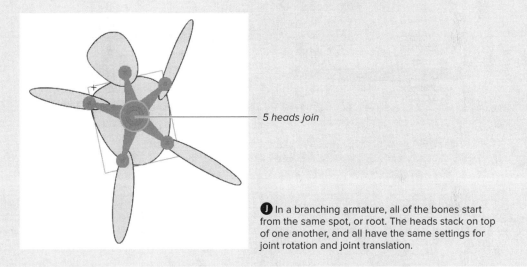

5 heads join

ⓙ In a branching armature, all of the bones start from the same spot, or root. The heads stack on top of one another, and all have the same settings for joint rotation and joint translation.

The Mystery of IK Instance Naming

When you create an IK armature by connecting movie-clip or button symbol instances, Flash gives each instance—or *node*—a default instance name, starting with ikNode_1, ikNode_2, and so on. (Graphic symbols do not have an instance name.) Any new IK nodes you create in the same document get the next sequential number.

The bones in an IK armature also get a default instance name that includes a number, but the numbering is not what you might expect. The first IK bone you create in a document gets the name ikBoneName_3, the next bone in the same chain of bones is ikBoneName_4, and so on. If you create another chain in the same document, the first bone in that chain starts with a number three greater than the number of the last bone you created.

About Pose Layers

When you connect the first two symbol instances of an IK chain with the bone tool, Flash pulls the instances into a new layer, known as a *pose layer*. (Flash gives the pose layer a default name—for example, Armature_1.) Flash places the pose layer directly above the layer that originally held the symbol instance that now contains the bone's head ⓚ. As you continue to add symbol instances to the chain, Flash pulls each new addition into the existing pose layer; each added IK node stacks above the nodes already on the pose layer.

When you first create an IK armature, the pose layer consists of a one-frame pose span, tinted olive green, containing a diamond icon. The diamond indicates the presence of an IK armature in a particular configuration, or *pose*. You can define more frames to extend the span or drag to extend the span, then add poses at later frames to create motion over time (see the section "Working with Poses," later in this chapter).

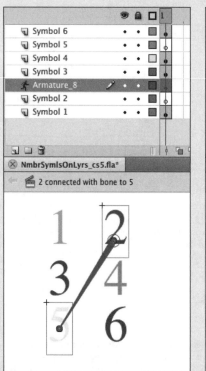 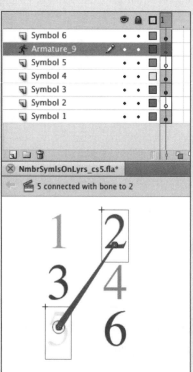

ⓚ Each number on the Stage is a symbol instance that started out on its own layer. Connecting the 2 to the 5 (left) creates the armature layer above the layer that contained the 2 originally. Connecting the 5 to the 2 (right) creates the armature layer above the layer that contained the 5. Within the pose layer, the IK nodes stack in the order in which you connected them (connecting the 5 to the 2 puts the 2 at the top of the stack). Each IK node you connect with child bones goes to the top of the stack. The stacking order of other elements in the Timeline is unaffected.

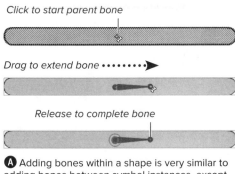

Click to start parent bone

Drag to extend bone ••••••••▶

Release to complete bone

Ⓐ Adding bones within a shape is very similar to adding bones between symbol instances, except that all the bones stay within the same shape.

Creating IK Shapes

An IK armature inside a shape works something like a hand in a sock puppet. The armature can be linear or branching or a combination of the two styles. The steps for creating the chain or branches are quite similar to those for connecting symbols. The difference is that you place all the bones within a single shape. You can use a merge-shape, drawing-object, or primitive-shape, with or without a stroke. Once you add IK bones to the shape, Flash converts it to a new type of shape, an *IK shape*.

To combine linear and branching armatures inside a shape:

1. Using Flash's drawing tools, on the Stage, create a shape to which you want to add an internal armature structure.

   For this task, draw a rounded rectangle, making it fairly long and narrow (see Chapter 2). You'll create an armature that has two linear chains that branch from a central point, allowing the shape to curl up or down from either end, the way a worm might wriggle from either end, or the way that the arms extending from the torso of a cartoon character might bend up or down.

2. In the Tools panel, select the bone tool.

3. To begin drawing the first bone in the chain (the parent bone), position the pointer over the shape.

4. Click at the spot where you want the armature to start—for example, the center of the rectangle Ⓐ.

continues on next page

Flash places the head of the parent bone. The head and tail points of each bone create points of rotation (places where the shape can bend). The shape as a whole pivots around the head of the parent bone in the chain.

5. To complete the bone, drag to the first spot where your shape should be able to bend, then release the mouse button.

For this example, plan to place three bones in each half of the rectangle. Flash pulls the shape into a new pose layer and converts the shape to an IK shape.

6. To add the second bone in the chain, position the pointer over the tail of the first bone you created, and click.

To add a bone to the armature within a shape, the pointer must be directly over the bone you're adding to. The black No pointer changes to the white–plus-sign pointer when you're directly over the tail (or head) of an existing bone. Flash places the second bone's head.

7. To complete the second bone, drag to the spot where the bone should end, and release the mouse button.

8. Repeat Steps 6 and 7 to create the third bone, this time starting at the tail of the second bone.

9. To create another IK chain that branches from the first, position the pointer over the head of the parent bone you created in Steps 4 and 5.

10. To begin drawing the first bone (parent) of the second branch, click and drag in a different direction from the parent bone in the existing chain **B**.

For this example, drag to the left.

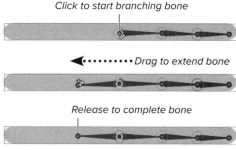

Click to start branching bone

Drag to extend bone

Release to complete bone

B To begin the branching bone, position the pointer over the head of the parent bone in the existing chain, then drag to the left.

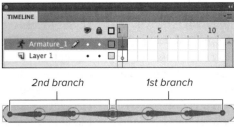

2nd branch   1st branch

C Your finished shape has two branches that start from the center of the shape. Each branch then continues with a linear chain of IK bones. This arrangement allows the two halves of the rectangle to curve independently, thus creating more-complex poses.

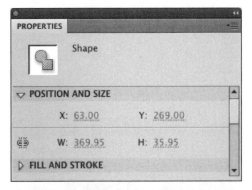

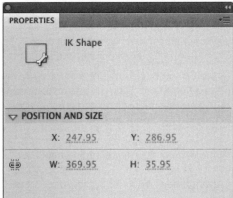

D No matter what type of shape you start out with, once you place an IK bone within the shape, it becomes a special type of object called an IK shape. Here, the rounded rectangle started as a merge shape, as shown in the Property inspector (top); after adding a bone, the Property inspector reveals it is an IK shape (bottom).

11. Repeat Steps 6 and 7 to create a three-bone chain in the left side of the rectangle **C**.

You're ready to manipulate the armature and create poses (see "Working with Poses," the next section in this chapter).

TIP In the preceding task, you created two branches from the same root. You can also create branches farther down the chain. Just begin drawing a new bone by clicking the head of any bone in the chain. In an IK shape, drag the first bone in the new branch in a different direction within the shape. In an armature connecting nodes, drag the first bone in the new branch to a symbol instance that's not yet part of the armature.

TIP As soon as you've placed a bone within a shape, Flash changes the shape's type. Check the Property inspector; as you add the bones, the name at the top changes—for example, from Shape to IK Shape **D**.

TIP Before you start creating bones, consider how many you'll need to be able to bend the shape to create the poses you need. The more bones you create, the more varied and refined the movements you'll be able to create with new poses. But more bones can also make it trickier to maneuver the IK shape.

TIP As you place your first IK bone, you may notice that the X and Y properties (the coordinates of the registration point) change. The registration point of a merge-shape or drawing-object is at the upper-left corner of the object; the registration point for an IK shape is at the head of the first IK bone you draw.

Working with Poses

When you first create an armature, the pose layer contains a pose span with one pose frame (the frame with the diamond icon). Similar to keyframes, pose frames mark key points of change that enable Flash to create IK animation. Each pose frame acts a bit like a property keyframe in a motion tween, giving Flash information about the position and rotation of each element in the armature. Flash creates a series of images that interpolate the changes required to transform the armature from one pose to the next. The property settings for the bones, and the way you set up the armature, restrict how the elements can move. To create IK animation, you must extend the pose span, add poses at the desired frames, select the armature to view and activate the bones, and manipulate the armature to put the elements into poses. To reposition the elements within the selected armature, use the selection tool.

Putting an Armature Through Its Paces

To edit an armature—to change the arrangement of IK nodes, change the length of a bone, or change the number of bones—you must make sure the pose span contains just its initial pose. Although Flash sometimes lets you make some edits when there are multiple poses, the resulting IK animation will not work properly.

To avoid the extra work of setting up poses, then having to delete them if you run into a problem, it's helpful to try manipulating your armature in lots of different ways before creating the real poses for your animation. Give the armature a good workout, dragging the bones around to create all the positions you want to animate.

You could manipulate the armature in the initial frame of the pose span, before adding new poses or extending the span. If you do find a problem, however, it can be difficult to get the underlying shape or symbol instances back to the precise starting arrangement. To make it easy to revert to the original pose quickly, extend the pose span by a small number—say, five frames; position the playhead at the end of the span; and start manipulating the armature to see how the pieces move together. Flash adds a pose at the current frame. Continue putting the armature through its poses, until you find a problem, or until you're sure everything is OK. If it turns out that you need to edit the armature, you just remove that one pose. The first frame of the pose span contains the original pose with the symbol instances or shape arranged in the original position. Now you can edit the armature as you like and test again.

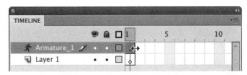

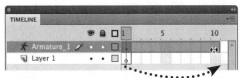

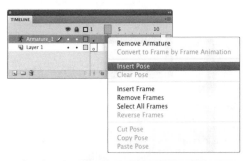

A To extend a pose span, position the pointer over the black bar at the right side of the pose span (top). When the double-arrow pointer appears, drag the end of the span to the desired frame (middle). Flash extends the pose span and selects it (bottom).

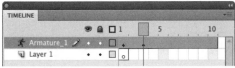

B Access the contextual menu in a pose span and choose Insert Pose (top) to add a diamond-shaped pose icon to the current frame (bottom). (Note that when the playhead is in the pose frame, the diamond looks more like a dot. Move the playhead and you'll see a diamond just like the one in the span's first frame.)

To define the pose span's length:

- Do either of the following:

  - In the pose layer in the Timeline, position the pointer over the black bar at the outside edge of Frame 1; using the double-arrow pointer, drag to extend the pose span to the desired frame **A**.

    or

  - Click the frame that should mark the end of the span and choose Insert > Timeline > Frame.

  Flash extends the olive-green highlight of the pose span through the selected frame.

To create a new pose frame via Timeline command:

- In the Timeline, within the armature layer, Control-click (Mac) or right-click (Windows) the desired frame and choose Insert Pose from the contextual menu **B**.

  If you click a frame inside the pose span, Flash adds a diamond-shaped pose icon to that frame. If you click a protoframe following the existing pose span, Flash extends the pose span to the frame you click and adds the diamond icon. You can now manipulate the IK armature to the desired configuration.

TIP You can also create a new pose by manipulating an armature on the Stage, analogous to the way you can add new keyframes to classic tweens or new property keyframes to motion tweens by manipulating symbol instances on the Stage within the defined span containing the tween. You simply click the desired frame within the pose span or position the playhead at the desired frame. Then use the selection tool to manipulate the armature on the Stage. Flash adds a diamond icon representing a pose to the current frame.

To select an armature:

- Using the selection or subselection tool, do either of the following:

  ▸ For an armature connecting IK nodes, click any node (any connected symbol instance).

  or

  ▸ For an armature within an IK shape, click anywhere within the shape.

  Flash selects the IK nodes or IK shape and makes the bones visible **C**. Icons indicating range of motion appear at each joint.

To manipulate the armature to create a pose:

1. In the Timeline, position the playhead in the desired frame in a pose span.

2. Select the armature you want to pose.

3. Using the selection tool, position the pointer over a bone.

   A black bone icon appears next to the arrow pointer, indicating that you're ready to manipulate the armature **D**.

4. To activate a bone for rotating, click it.

   Flash highlights it in a different color than the other bones in the armature.

Click to select IK shape

IK shape and armature selected

Click to select IK node

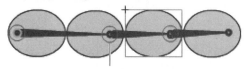

IK node and armature selected

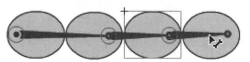

Range-of-motion icons, full rotation

C Clicking an IK shape or an IK node with the selection tool activates the bones of the armature so that you can manipulate them to create poses.

D To interact with a specific bone, click it with the selection tool, then drag it to position it. The bone rotates around its head. Other bones and nodes move in response if their joint settings allow for movement.

Move Those Bones

Dragging a highlighted bone causes it to rotate around its head; moving the highlighted bone can also push on any bones that are higher up the chain, causing them to rotate as well. When a bone is set to allow *x*- and/or *y*-translation, you can also drag the bone along those axes. Any constraints you've put in place on how each bone rotates will govern the ways you can interact with the bones as you drag them on the Stage. As you manipulate a highlighted bone, any child bones that are located lower in the hierarchy simply come along for the ride, retaining their current orientation with respect to their parent bone(s).

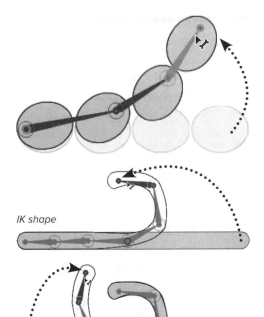

IK shape

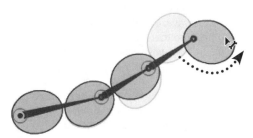

E To manipulate an armature, you use the selection tool. You can drag bones and nodes to position them and reconfigure the armature. In an IK shape, dragging the bones changes the contours of the shape.

F You can also manipulate an IK armature by dragging nodes with the selection tool. The final node in an IK armature rotates freely when you drag that node

5. To reposition the selected bone, drag it **E**.

The bone rotates and/or moves, and the armature changes in response to your manipulation. The precise ways that the structure can move depend on the settings you've created for each bone in the Property inspector (see the sidebar "Move Those Bones"). If the bone is in an armature connecting IK nodes, the node containing the head moves along with the bone.

6. To reposition an IK node, drag directly on the symbol instance.

If the IK node contains the head of a bone, the symbol instance and that bone rotate around the head point (the transformation point) according to the settings for that bone. If the IK node contains just a tail (that is, if the IK node is the last element in a linear armature), the node rotates around the tail point **F**.

TIP You don't have to select an individual bone to drag it; you can simply click and drag a bone in one step. Selecting the bone first highlights it and lets you see that you are working with the right portion of your armature.

TIP As you manipulate an armature to reach new poses, remember that Flash is not recording the action. You need to create poses at key positions for your IK elements so that Flash can interpolate between poses to create the movement you want. For example, just because you rotated a bone clockwise to reach a certain position doesn't mean Flash chooses that direction when it creates the animation. You may need intermediate poses to ensure that things move in the ways you intend.

To remove a pose from the pose span:

1. Position the playhead at the frame containing the pose.

2. Control-click (Mac) or right-click (Windows) the frame containing the diamond icon.

3. From the contextual menu, choose Clear Pose **G**.

TIP You can position the playhead by clicking the frame containing the pose diamond. Flash selects the entire pose span, but when you access the contextual menu for the frame containing the pose, the Clear Pose command removes just the pose in that frame.

TIP You can't remove the pose from the first frame of a pose span, but you can remove multiple poses in subsequent frames with one command. Command-drag (Mac) or Ctrl-drag (Windows) to select a subset of frames that includes the poses you want to eliminate but that excludes the initial pose. When you access the contextual menu from any frame in the selection, the Clear Pose command removes all poses from the selection. If you drag-select the entire pose span, or click an in-between frame to select the whole span, then access the contextual menu, the Clear Pose command is disabled.

G Control-click (Mac) or right-click (Windows) a pose frame to access the contextual menu. Choose Clear Pose to remove that pose from the span.

When to Use Inverse Kinematics

Flash's inverse-kinematics tools let you animate natural motion without redrawing lots of shapes or repositioning multiple symbols. You create armatures—skeleton-like structures that govern relationships between symbol instances or control the way a shape's outline changes over time. Moving one bone in the armature affects other connected bones to reconfigure the entire structure. Use IK when you want to animate symbols that have a permanent relationship—for example, the parts of a person or creature that can only bend in certain ways; or the parts of an engine or machine that move in predictable, constrained ways, like pistons, cogs, and flywheels. Another reason to use IK is to create shapes with moving, transforming outlines, where the changes can be controlled by an internal structure, such as a wiggling worm, or a blade of grass that bends in the wind.

Manipulating Pose Spans in the Timeline

The mechanics of manipulating pose spans in the Timeline is quite similar to that for manipulating tween spans for motion tweens (see Chapter 11). A major difference is that a pose span must stay on its own special armature layer: you can't copy an entire pose span or move a pose span to a different layer, nor can you add other content to the layer containing a pose span.

Like a tween span, a pose span is an object, and clicking any frame within the span selects the entire span. To select a single frame in a pose span, Command-click (Mac) or Ctrl-click (Windows) the frame. To select a range of frames, Command-drag (Mac) or Ctrl-drag (Windows) through the desired frames. To move the span within the layer so that the animation starts at a different frame, select the span and drag it. When you drag the span, Flash creates blank keyframes as needed. For example, if you created the IK armature in Frame 1 of the Timeline, then dragged the pose span to the right, Flash creates a blank keyframe at Frame 1. To enlarge the pose span proportionally (to lengthen the IK animation but preserve the relative timing of the pose changes), drag the last frame of the pose span to the right; Flash redistributes the pose-frame diamonds. To reduce the span proportionally, drag the last frame to the left. To extend the end of the pose span, adding in-between frames after the final pose frame, Shift-drag the last frame of the span to the right; to clip frames off the end of the span, Shift-drag the last frame to the left.

You can copy and paste an individual pose within a span. Select a frame containing a pose-frame diamond; Control-click (Mac) or right-click (Windows) the selected frame and choose Copy Pose from the contextual menu. Select the frame where you want to repeat the pose, access the contextual menu again, and choose Paste Pose.

Saving IK As Symbols

To get the fullest value from your IK animations, you may want to incorporate them into symbols that can be animated with tweening. You might, for example, create a wiggly worm using an IK shape, put that animation into a movie-clip symbol, then use an instance of the worm symbol in a motion tween. The motion tween can make the constantly wiggling worm wander around the Stage, change size or color, and so on. To convert an IK animation to a symbol, select the IK shape or all of the IK nodes (selecting the pose span in the Timeline automatically selects all the IK elements). Choose Modify > Convert to Symbol, or press F8; or on the Stage, Control-click (Mac) or right-click (Windows) the selected IK shape or any of the selected IK nodes, and from the contextual menu, choose Convert to Symbol. In the Convert to Symbol dialog that appears, you can name the symbol and choose its type, library location, and so on (see Chapter 7).

When saving IK animation in a symbol, you should always choose Movie Clip or Graphic as the Type. (Flash will transform an IK animation into a button, but the pose span overwrites the Up, Over, Down, and Hit frames, and the resulting button won't work.)

Author-Time IK vs. Runtime IK

Do you want to be able to set poses for armatures during authoring to create animation? Or do you want to let your audience drag and manipulate IK elements to change their positions interactively as they view your Flash movie?

To do the moving yourself during authoring and have Flash play back the movement at runtime, select the armature layer, the pose span, or any frame within the pose span, and access the IK Armature Property inspector. In the Options section, from the Type menu, choose Authortime (the default setting) . To simply set up an armature that your target audience can play with, make sure the pose span contains just one pose and choose Runtime from the Type menu. (Note that more-advanced Flash users can control IK armatures using ActionScript. To be controlled by scripting, the armature must be set to Runtime.)

H To use IK armatures to create poses during authoring and have them play back as animation in your published movie, select a pose span and choose Authortime from the Type menu in the Options section of the IK Armature Property inspector. To allow the end user to play with the IK armature, posing elements while interacting with the published movie, choose Runtime. Flash's default Type setting is Authortime.

A small running-figure icon appears in the keyframe of a runtime IK pose span **I**.

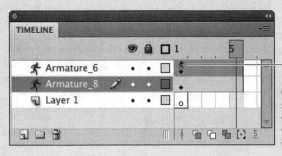

Runtime IK armature

I The first frame (the keyframe) in an IK pose span set for runtime animation displays an icon of a running figure. The span's tint is grayish-green, in contrast to the bright olive green of an Authortime IK pose span.

Constraining IK Motion

You can limit the way IK bones move. You can allow or prevent a bone from rotating, for example, to control the way a character can bend its arms and legs. You can also allow or prevent movement along a bone's *x*-axis (*x*-translation) and/or *y*-axis (*y*-translation). The axes in this case refer not to the *x*- and *y*-axes of the Stage, but to the axes of the bone instance (see the sidebar "Translating the Direction of Translation"). Enabling translation for the parent bone in an armature allows the entire armature to move around on the Stage. Enabling translation for a child bone allows that bone to move closer to its parent or farther away. Moving a child bone along its *x*- and/or *y*-axis within an armature in an IK shape can make the shape expand and contract. Making such movements in an armature connecting IK nodes can help you to animate mechanisms with moving parts.

The methods for enabling and constraining rotation and translation with IK nodes and IK shapes is similar. The tasks below work with IK nodes. Try experimenting with enabling and constraining the motion of bones within a shape once you've completed the tasks with nodes.

To constrain rotation at a bone's head:

1. Create a simple IK armature that uses two bones to connect three symbol instances in a horizontal chain.

   This task uses three instances of a symbol containing a rectangle.

2. Using the selection tool, select the armature containing the bone you want to constrain.

3. Click the parent bone, the first bone in the chain, and access the Property inspector.

   The selected bone highlights, and its properties appear in the inspector **A**.

4. With the parent bone selected, in the Joint: Rotation section of the Property inspector, select the Enable checkbox (it is selected by default).

   When joint rotation is enabled, the selected bone can rotate through 360 degrees around its head. To restrict that movement, you must constrain the rotation.

5. Select the Constrain checkbox.

   Flash assigns default constrain values: Minimum –45 degrees, Maximum 45 degrees **B**.

Selected bone

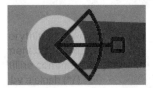

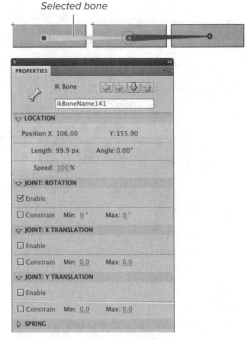

A Selecting a bone in an armature reveals its properties in the Property inspector. By default, joint rotation is enabled. You can manipulate the selected bone by dragging it with the selection tool; you can rotate the bone 360 degrees around the head point. The rest of the armature follows along. By default, joint translation is disabled. The head of the bone cannot move from its current x-/y-coordinate.

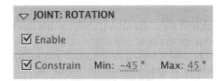

B When you select the Constrain checkbox in the Joint: Rotation section of the Property inspector, Flash creates Min and Max values of –45 and 45 degrees for the selected bone (top). The range-of-motion icon depicts the motion available to the bone (bottom).

Bone in original position

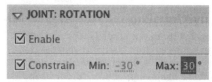

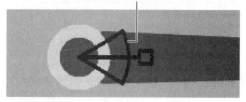

Range of motion

After rotating bone on Stage

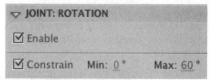

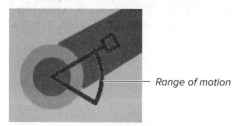

Range of motion

C As you drag a bone whose rotation is constrained, the lever moves within the range-of-motion icon's arc. Once the lever reaches the edge of the arc, you can't rotate the bone farther in that direction. Note that after you reposition a bone on the Stage, Flash changes the bone's Min and Max values in the Joint: Rotation section of the Property inspector. The new values correlate to the bone's current orientation on the Stage. The total degrees of rotation available, however, are the same as those you entered. (Occasionally, the total differs by a degree or two due to mathematical rounding as Flash calculates Stage positions for the elements).

6. Using the Min and Max hot text, enter rotation values in the following ways:

   ▸ To allow rotation counterclockwise from the current starting position, using the Min hot text, enter a negative value. The lower the value, the greater the range of motion allowed.

   ▸ To allow rotation clockwise from the current starting position, using the Max hot text, enter a positive value. The higher the value, the greater the range of motion allowed.

   Click the hot text to enter a precise value; drag the hot text's invisible slider to choose a value interactively. A range-of-motion icon appears at the head of the selected bone; the icon's arc and lever indicate how far the bone can rotate (see the sidebar "The Mysterious Range-of-Motion Icons," later in this chapter).

7. Repeat Steps 3–6 for the second bone (the child bone).

8. Extend the pose span to Frame 5 and position the playhead there.

9. In the Tools panel, choose the selection tool.

10. Manipulate the bones to see their range of motion.

    As you drag a bone, watch the range-of-motion icon at its head; the lever moves in concert with the bone within the defined arc. When the lever hits the edge of the arc, you have reached the end of allowable rotation; the bone can rotate no farther in that direction **C**.

TIP To get a feel for how the constrain settings work, try disabling rotation for the parent bone and setting the child bone's Min to −30 and Max to 30. Now try to reposition the armature by dragging the bones and boxes with the selection tool. The first box doesn't rotate, the second box rotates a little (through 60 degrees), and the third box rotates a full 360 degrees. Now try reversing the settings, disabling rotation for the child bone. The first and second boxes rotate as a unit around the head of the parent bone (the unit can rotate only 60 degrees), and the third box still rotates 360 degrees.

TIP You can turn the constrain setting on and off. In the example above, imagine that you wanted the first and second boxes to move as a unit, but to be at a 90-degree angle to one another. You could position the boxes as desired, then activate the constrain setting and set the value to 0. The first two boxes can rotate around the head of the first bone in the chain, but always maintain their "bent" configuration. If you later decide that should be a 45-degree angle, deselect the Constrain checkbox, reposition the elements, then select Constrain again and set the Min and Max values.

TIP Because the constrain settings affect the head joint of the bone they apply to, you cannot constrain the rotation of the last symbol in a chain. But there are cases where you might want to constrain that element. Imagine, for example, a simplified cartoon arm consisting of three ovals—upper arm, forearm, and hand. You don't want the hand to be able to spin 360 degrees like a propeller on a plane. The only way to constrain it is to find a way to make it not the final symbol in the chain. Create a symbol that has no graphic content. Place an instance of the empty symbol next to the hand. Then connect the hand to the empty symbol instance. No one will see the empty instance, but now you can constrain the hand.

TIP When the Enable checkbox is selected for Joint: Rotation, entering 0 for both Min and Max prevents rotation entirely, but the quickest way to prevent rotation is to deselect the Enable checkbox.

TIP Constrain settings apply throughout the IK pose span. You cannot create different constraints for the same joint in individual pose frames.

The Mystery of Springy Bones

In the real world, objects made of different substances respond differently to physical forces: a long blade of grass bends in response to a light breeze, an iron bar does not. Flash CS5 lets IK animations emulate the physics of the real world with two Spring properties: Strength and Damping. To access these properties, you must enable Springs. Select an IK pose span in the Timeline; in the IK Armature Property inspector, access the Springs section, then select the Enable checkbox **D**. Now, select a bone in the IK armature on the Stage, and access the IK Bone Property inspector's Spring section, where you'll find hot text for setting Strength and Damping values **E**. To get an idea of how these properties interact, think of bending and releasing something springy, like a willow sapling. *Strength* defines the sapling's flexibility, how much you can bend it (with a low Strength setting you might get the tree top to bend all the way to the ground; with a high setting the top might barely lean). *Damping* defines how quickly the motion decays, how fast the sapling stops whipping back and forth after you release it. With a low Damping setting, the sapling might wave for 10 minutes without slowing; with a high setting, the sapling might just move back and forth a time or two and then stop. You'll need to experiment to find the right combination of settings. The number of frames between poses and the total length of the animation also affect the movement of "springy" objects in IK animations. It's best to set these properties when your pose span has just its initial keyframe.

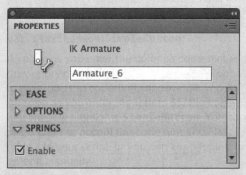

D When you select an IK pose span in the Timeline, the IK Armature Property inspector contains a Springs section. Selecting its Enable checkbox activates the Strength and Damping properties for the armature in this span. When you deselect the Springs section's Enable checkbox, Flash turns off that aspect of the animation but preserves the current Strength and Damping settings in the Spring section of the IK Bone Property inspector.

E With IK bones selected on the Stage, the IK Bone Property inspector's Spring section contains hot text for setting Strength and Damping values.

The Mysterious Range-of-Motion Icons

At the head of each IK bone, range-of-motion icons indicate the ways in which that joint can move.

When rotation is enabled and unconstrained, the icon is a circle around the head joint. When rotation is constrained, the circle changes to an arc with a lever inside. The lever represents the bone, and the arc indicates the range through which the bone can move. Unfortunately, the lever is not always parallel to the bone itself, which means you must use your imagination and spatial reasoning to convert the arc-and-lever image to the actual angles you want the bone to move through on the Stage. The orientation of the icon depends on a variety of factors, including whether the bone is a parent or a child, the parent bone's original orientation to the Stage, the child bone's original orientation to its parent, whether the bone is in an IK shape or is connecting IK nodes, and whether or not the bone has been rotated from its original position. The best way to get a feel for the way the icon works is to play with a few bones and try out the constrain settings. Manipulate the bones to see how the arc and lever work together in the range-of-motion icon to restrain the rotation of the bone on the Stage.

When *x*- or *y*-translation is enabled for a bone, the range-of-motion icon includes lines representing the *x*- and *y*-axes of the bone. For unlimited motion, the line is a double-headed arrow. When motion is constrained, the line changes to an I-beam shape, with the end posts of the I showing how far the bone's head can move in each direction.

There are no range-of-motion icons at the tail of the last bone in chain. That joint is always unconstrained.

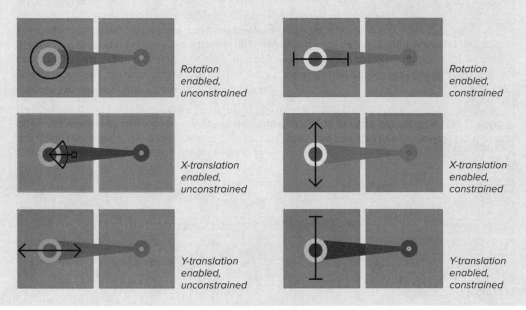

Rotation enabled, unconstrained

Rotation enabled, constrained

X-translation enabled, unconstrained

X-translation enabled, constrained

Y-translation enabled, unconstrained

Y-translation enabled, constrained

To allow *x*-axis translation of the armature as a whole (via the parent bone):

1. Follow Steps 1–3 in the preceding task.

2. To disable rotation of the selected parent bone, deselect the Enable checkbox in the Joint: Rotation section of the Property inspector.

   This step is optional but useful. When rotation is enabled for a bone, the bone's *x*-axis changes orientation as the bone rotates. You may begin dragging the bone horizontally, for example, and wind up rotating the bone slightly in the process. The *x*-axis that started out horizontal in relation to the Stage is now at an angle. If you keep dragging, you'll be moving the armature diagonally in relation to the Stage, not horizontally. Turning off rotation, at least temporarily, makes it easier to set the *x*-axis position of the bone.

3. To allow the entire armature to move along the bone's *x*-axis, with the parent bone selected, select the Enable checkbox (it is deselected by default) in the Joint: X Translation section of the Property inspector.

   When *x*-translation is enabled, the selected bone's head can move along the bone's *x*-axis. A double-arrow range-of-motion icon appears at the selected bone's head. To restrict how far the head can move along the bone's *x*-axis, you must constrain the translation.

   continues on next page

4. In the Joint: X Translation section of the Property inspector, select the Constrain checkbox.

Flash assigns default constrain values 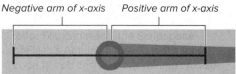. With the document set to use pixels, the defaults are Min −50 pixels, Max 50 pixels. The range-of-motion icon changes from a double-headed arrow to a horizontal I-beam. The end posts of the icon indicate the limits of how the head can move.

5. Use the Min and Max hot text to enter the desired values in the following ways:

  ▸ To allow movement along the negative arm of the bone's *x*-axis, using the Min hot text, enter a negative value. The lower the value, the farther the bone's head can move in that direction.

  ▸ To allow movement along the positive arm of the bone's *x*-axis, using the Max hot text, enter a positive value. The higher the value, the farther the bone's head can move in that direction.

6. Create a few poses, repositioning the parent bone on the Stage in each one, then play through the animation.

The three boxes maintain a constant distance from one another as the whole set moves side to side.

TIP The Min and Max values for *x*- and *y*-translation are relative. When you reposition the bone on the Stage, the Min and Max values in the Property inspector change. The total number of pixels in the range stays the same, however.

TIP No matter what units of measure you set in Document Properties, Flash uses pixels in the Min and Max values for *x*- and *y*-translation. To avoid confusion, when working with IK animation, set up the document to use pixels (see Chapter 1).

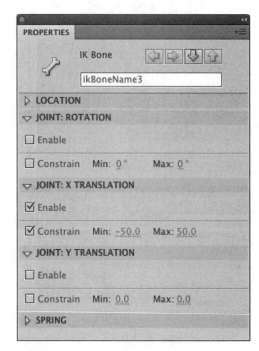

Negative arm of x-axis   *Positive arm of x-axis*

F To allow movement of an IK bone's head along the bone's x-axis, select the Enable checkbox in the Joint: X Translation section of the Property inspector, then select Constrain and set Min and Max values. Min values allow movement along the negative arm of the bone's x-axis; Max values allow movement along the positive arm. When the bone's x-axis parallels that of the Stage, as in this figure, the Min value allows the bone's head to move to the left from the current starting position; the Max value allows the bone's head to move to the right. For bones with axes that don't align to the axes of the Stage, the terms *left* and *right* don't really apply. Select a bone to view its range-of-motion icon. The linear portions of the icon represent the bone's axes for translation.

PROPERTIES

IK Bone ⇦ ⇨ ⇩ ⇧

ikBoneName3

▷ LOCATION

▽ JOINT: ROTATION

☐ Enable

☐ Constrain   Min: 0°   Max: 0°

▽ JOINT: X TRANSLATION

☐ Enable

☐ Constrain   Min: -50.0   Max: 50.0

▽ JOINT: Y TRANSLATION

☑ Enable

☑ Constrain   Min: -20.0   Max: 20|

▷ SPRING

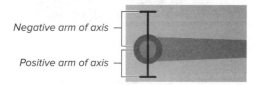

Negative arm of axis ⎯

Positive arm of axis ⎯

G To allow movement of an IK bone's head along its y-axis, select Enable in the Joint: Y Translation section of the Property inspector, then select Constrain and set Min and Max values. Min values allow movement along the negative arm of the bone's y-axis; Max values allow movement along the positive arm. When the bone's y-axis parallels that of the Stage, as in this figure, the Min value allows the bone's head to move upward from the current starting position; the Max value allows the bone's head to move downward. For bones with axes that don't align to the axes of the Stage, the terms *upward* and *downward* don't really apply. Select a bone to view its range-of-motion icon. The linear portions of the icon represent the bone's axes for translation.

To allow *y*-axis translation of the armature as a whole (via the parent bone):

■ Continuing with the armature from the preceding task, repeat Steps 3–5, this time choosing the Enable and/or Constrain checkboxes in the Joint: Y Translation section of the Property inspector **G**.

Selecting the Enable checkbox in the Joint: Y Translation section allows the selected bone unrestricted movement along its y-axis. The range-of-motion icon appears as a double arrow. When you select the Constrain checkbox, the icon changes to an I-beam. The Min hot text controls movement along the negative arm of the bone's y-axis; the Max hot text controls movement along the positive arm of the bone's y-axis.

To allow *x*- and *y*-axis translation of individual child bones:

1. Continuing with the three-node armature from the preceding tasks, select the child bone (the second bone in the chain) and disable rotation for that bone.

   To make the bones easier to work with, deselect the Enable checkbox in the Joint: Rotation section of the Property inspector.

2. To enable the head of the selected child bone to move farther from (or closer to) the head of its parent (the preceding bone), do either of the following:

   ▸ To allow movement along the bone's *x*-axis, in the Joint: X Translation section of the Property inspector, select the Enable checkbox. To limit the range of movement, select the Constrain checkbox and enter Min and Max values.

   or

   ▸ To allow movement along the bone's *y*-axis, in the Joint: Y Translation section of the Property inspector, select the Enable checkbox. To limit the range of movement, select the Constrain checkbox and enter Min and Max values.

3. Using the selection tool, drag the selected child bone to reposition it.

   As the child's head gets farther from the parent's head, the parent bone gets longer; as the child's head gets closer, the parent bone gets shorter 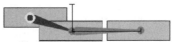.

4. Create a few poses with the child at different distances from the parent, and play through the animation. The first two boxes move closer and farther apart; the third box maintains a constant distance from the second box.

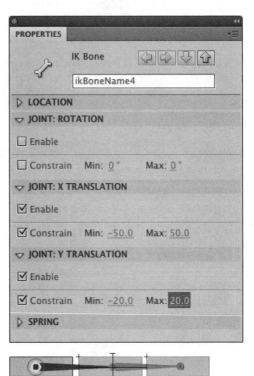

Drag farther from parent

Drag closer to parent

H By allowing *x*- and *y*-translation for the child bone, you can drag it along its *x*- and *y*-axes. As the child's head gets farther from its parent's head, the parent bone gets longer. As the child's head gets closer to its parent's head, the parent bone gets shorter.

Original

Ready to reposition transformation point

Drag transformation point

Transformation point relocated

Head relocated

A Use the free-transform tool to change the location of the head or tail in an IK node by dragging the symbol instance's transformation point. The IK bones are not visible while you use the free-transform tool, but behind the scenes, Flash also moves the head and/or tail points associated with that transformation point. Select the armature to see the bones in their new position.

Editing IK Elements

An armature isn't set in stone once you've created and posed it. The thing to remember about editing armatures is that you must remove any poses that you've created before you start making changes. Otherwise, you'll get some strange results. When a pose span contains just one pose, you can edit the armature in a variety of ways. You can change the position of head and tail joints in IK nodes, reposition IK nodes relative to one another, remove bones and nodes, and add bones and nodes. You can change, add, and remove bones inside an IK shape; change bone length; and edit the path of an IK shape. You can also control which bones affect which portions of an IK shape's path, by using the bind tool.

To reposition a bone's head/ tail within an IK node:

1. To select a node whose head or tail you want to adjust, using the selection or subselection tool, click the node.

2. In the Tools panel, select the free-transform tool.

   Flash activates the transform box of the selected symbol instance and highlights the transformation point as a white circle. The head and tail points are located at the transformation point of an IK node.

3. Position the pointer over the transformation point.

   A chain-link icon appears next to the pointer; you can move the point.

4. Drag the transformation point to a new location within the IK node **A**.

   The transformation-point circle and its associated head and/or tail points move to the new location.

To reposition IK nodes:

- Using the selection tool, Option-drag or Command-drag (Mac) or Alt-drag or Ctrl-drag (Windows) one node (or multiple selected nodes).

    Reposition the selected node (or nodes) and release the mouse button **B**.

To change bone length in IK shapes:

1. In the Tools panel, choose the subselection tool.

2. Position the pointer over a head or tail point.

3. Drag the head or tail to a new location within the IK shape, and release the mouse button.

    Flash redraws the bones on either side of the point you drag **C**.

To edit an IK shape's path:

1. To view the bones, select the armature in an IK shape.

2. Using the subselection tool, click the edge of the selected IK shape.

    If the shape has a stroke, click the stroke; otherwise, click at the edge of the shape. Flash activates the shape's Bézier path in blue, displaying control points as hollow blue squares.

3. To activate handles for a control point, click that point.

    Flash activates the point and its handles, displaying them as three hollow red squares connected by lines. The central square represents the control point on the path; the outer squares work as Bézier-style handles.

Original armature

Reposition IK node

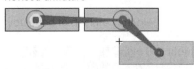

Revised armature

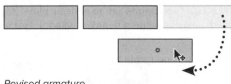

B You can relocate a selected node (or multiple selected nodes) by Option-dragging or Command-dragging (Mac) or Alt-dragging or Ctrl-dragging (Windows) the selection. As you drag, the IK bones disappear; Flash redraws the bones when you release the mouse button.

Original armature

Reposition joint

Revised armature

C Use the subselection tool to change the length of a bone within a selected IK shape. Drag the head or tail point to change the length of the bone.

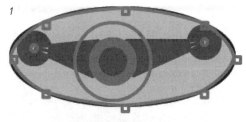

1

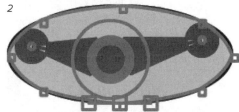

2

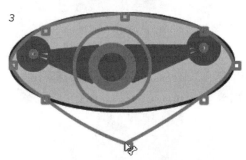

3

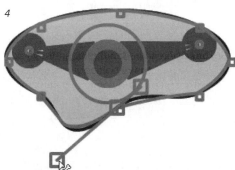

4

D Click the outline of an IK shape with the subselection tool to activate control points for the shape's path (1). Click a control point directly to select it; it highlights with three red squares (2). Drag the central square to relocate the control point (3); drag a side square to reshape the curve as if using a Bézier handle (4).

4. To change the path of the IK shape, do any of the following **D**:

▸ To relocate the control point, drag the middle red square.

▸ To reshape the curve, drag an outer red square to reposition the handles, as you would with Bézier paths (see Chapter 4).

▸ To delete the selected point, press Delete.

▸ To add a new point, click an area of the path that currently lacks a control point.

TIP Adding control points is tricky; it's easy to accidentally activate the handles of a nearby control point instead. Try changing the magnification of the Stage and keep clicking in slightly different areas of the path.

TIP You can also use the regular Bézier add–anchor-point tool to add control points to an IK shape, or use the remove–anchor-point tool to delete them.

About the Bind Tool

To control the way an IK shape redraws when you create poses, Flash connects (or *binds*) the control points of the shape to one or more bones in the armature. When you reposition a bone, Flash repositions the control points that bind to that bone and redraws the path of the IK shape accordingly. You can edit those connections with the bind tool, which is located in the Tools panel, in a submenu together with the bone tool. First, select the armature using the selection or subselection tool. Next, choose the bind tool and click a bone to select it. Flash highlights the selected bone with a red line, and highlights in yellow all the points that bind to the bone. A point that binds only to the selected bone appears as a yellow square. A point that binds to multiple bones, including the selected bone, appears as a yellow triangle **E**.

continues on next page

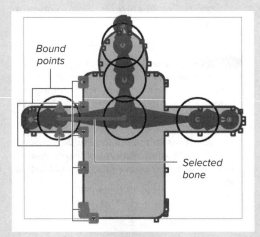

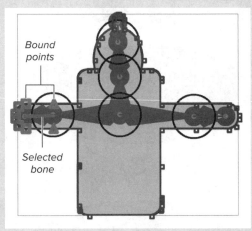

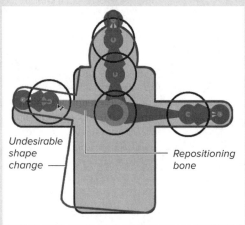

E The bind tool shows you which points on the path of an IK shape are controlled by which bones. Click a bone with the bind tool to see its connections. The bone highlights with a red line; control points that are bound to the bone highlight in yellow. Yellow squares indicate points that are bound just to the selected bone. Yellow triangles indicate points that are bound to the selected bone and to at least one other bone.

About the Bind Tool *continued*

To break a connection to the selected bone, using the bind tool, Command-click (Mac) or Ctrl- click (Windows) the yellow square or triangle; the highlight disappears, and the binding is broken **F**. (To unbind multiple points, using the bind tool with the modifier key, drag a selection rectangle around the points.) To bind an unconnected control point (a blue square) to the selected bone, using the bind tool, Shift-click the control point. (To bind multiple points, using the bind tool, Shift-drag a selection rectangle around the points.)

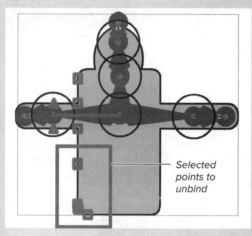

Selected points to unbind

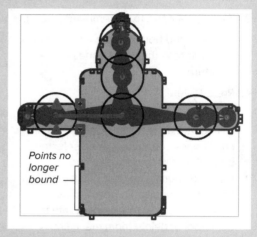

Points no longer bound

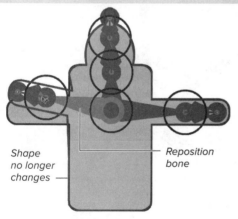

Shape no longer changes

Reposition bone

F To unbind points, Command-click (Mac) or Ctrl-click (Windows) the yellow square or triangle. To unbind multiple points, using the bind tool with the modifier key, drag a selection rectangle around the points.

To remove individual bones:

1. In the Tools panel, choose the selection or subselection tool.

2. Click any of the IK nodes in an armature.

   or

   Click the IK shape that contains an armature.

3. To select a bone to be removed, click it.

   The selected bone highlights in different color than the other bones in the armature.

4. Press Delete.

   Flash removes the selected bone **G**. In a linear armature, Flash also deletes all child bones connected to the selected bone. Any disconnected symbol instances remain on the pose layer. If you want, you can reposition the instances and reconnect them with the bone tool or delete them manually.

TIP Removing a bone from an IK node does not restore the symbol instance's original transformation point. The transformation point remains where the head/tail point was in the IK node.

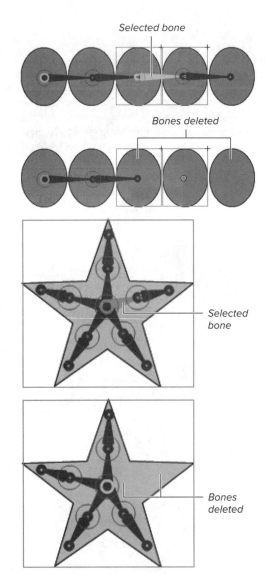

Selected bone

Bones deleted

Selected bone

Bones deleted

G To remove a bone from an armature, select the bone and press Delete. Flash removes that bone and any children attached to it.

About Easing in IK Animation

As in tweening, in IK animation you can make movement accelerate or decelerate by using easing. The procedure is similar to that for applying easing to classic and shape tweens (see Chapter 12), except that the easing occurs between poses, not keyframes. Here's a quick overview. In the Timeline, click the pose where you'd like easing to start taking effect. IK easing begins in the selected pose frame (the one with the diamond) and affects the in-between frames up to the next pose frame. If you prefer, you can simply click the span between poses to apply the ease (easing starts in the pose frame that comes first). In the Ease section of the IK Armature Property inspector, from the Type menu, choose a style of easing 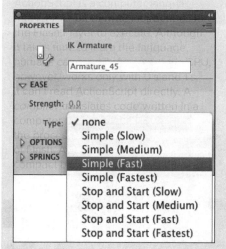. Use the Strength hot text to determine how aggressive the acceleration or deceleration is. You cannot create custom eases for IK animations.

H To add easing to IK animation, select a pose frame in the Timeline (or select a frame between poses). Access the Property inspector, and choose a style from the Type menu in the Ease section.

To remove an entire armature:

1. In the Timeline, Control-click (Mac) or right-click (Windows) the pose span.

2. From the contextual menu, choose Remove Armature.

   Flash deletes all the bones on the Stage and converts the pose span to a keyframe span in the Timeline. The symbol instances (or the shape) become the content of the initial keyframe, and the remaining frames become in-between frames.

TIP You can also remove an armature from a selected IK shape by choosing Modify > Break Apart. Flash removes all the IK bones and returns the shape to its original form. The shape remains on the armature layer. The Modify > Break Apart command also removes all the bones in an armature from a set of linked IK nodes, with one twist: any selected symbol instance gets converted to its underlying shape(s), just as it would with the normal Break Apart command. If you select the armature by clicking one node, that symbol instance converts to a shape; the others remain symbols. If you select the armature by choosing Edit > Select All or by dragging a selection rectangle around all the nodes, all the symbol instances convert to shapes.

Practice Session

In Chapter 12's Practice Session, you used classic tweening to create a bird whose wings (and other body parts) moved, then turned that bird into a symbol. For this exercise, try editing a copy of that symbol: remove the existing animation for the front wing, and replace it with a new symbol containing a wing animated with IK.

- Create three movie-clip symbols to combine into a wing. These parts can be cartoony like a shoulder, forearm, and feather-cluster hand. Convert each part to a separate symbol, and name them wingUpArm, wingMidArm, wingTip. (See Chapter 7.) To keep things simple, draw a large plump oval; a medium oval; and several small, thin ovals grouped for feathers. Or go wild and create more avian-like drawings.

- Drag an instance of each symbol to the Stage. Arrange them into a wing.

- Use the bone tool to give the wing an IK skeleton. Starting in wingUpArm, where the "shoulder" would attach to the bird's body, create the parent bone: click and drag into the top of wingMidArm, to connect at the "elbow." Create a child bone that connects to wingTip at the "wrist." (See *Using Armatures to Connect Symbols*.)

- Expand the pose span and create poses that make the wing flap. Adjust the poses till you get a pleasing motion. (See *Working with Poses*.)

- Save the IK armature as a symbol. (See the sidebar *Saving IK As Symbols*.)

- Substitute this flapping wing for the classic-tween flapping wing in your bird character.

Extra Credit

- Try constraining rotation for various joints in the wing to make the flapping look more natural.

- Try creating a fancy head feather using an IK shape. Play with different combinations of Spring settings (Strength and Damping) to make this feather perky, bouncy, or slinky. Save a few versions as symbols and add them to your bird.

Save your file for use in future Practice Sessions.

Building Buttons
for Interactivity

After you master Flash Professional CS5's drawing and animating tools, you can create movies that play from beginning to end. To create interactive environments that transform viewers into users, you must add interface elements that give users control. The most common interface element is a button. Buttons have two levels of interactivity: first, responding to user input with visual feedback—for example, changing color when the pointer enters the button area; second, carrying out tasks—for example, switching to a new scene when a user clicks the button.

In this chapter, you learn to set up the first level of interactivity using button symbols and button components. You also learn to set up a movie-clip symbol that can act as a visually responsive button. For these elements, built-in coding takes care of the first level of button interactivity. To achieve the second level of interactivity—making buttons respond in new ways and carry out tasks—requires scripting. You'll learn some simple ways to do that in Chapter 15.

In This Chapter

Creating a Basic Button Symbol

A button is a Flash movie clip with different keyframes that represent the button in all its possible states. The button symbol has three button-state frames—Up, Over, and Down—plus a fourth frame (the Hit frame) for defining the active button area. To create the most basic button symbol, choose a simple shape and place it in the keyframe for each state; change the shape's color or add or modify internal elements for the various states. When you complete all four keyframes, your button is ready to use. Return to document-editing mode, and drag an instance of the button symbol from the Library panel to the Stage.

To create a button symbol:

1. Open a Flash document to which you want to add buttons.

2. Choose Insert > New Symbol, or press Command-F8 (Mac) or Ctrl-F8 (Windows) .

   The Create New Symbol dialog appears.

3. Type a name in the Name field (for example, MyBasicButton), choose Button in the Type section, and click OK **B**.

   Flash creates a new symbol in the Library panel and returns you to the Timeline and Stage in symbol-editing mode. The Timeline contains the four frames that define the button: Up, Over, Down, and Hit.

   By default, the Up frame contains a keyframe **C**. You must add keyframes to the Over, Down, and Hit frames and place graphic elements in each keyframe of the button. To give users feedback

A Choosing Insert > New Symbol is the first step in creating a button.

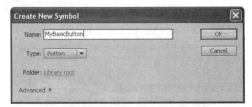

B To make a button, create a new symbol and choose Button from the Type menu in the Create New Symbol dialog. You also name the button here.

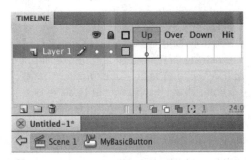

C The Timeline for every button symbol contains four frames: Up, Over, Down, and Hit. Flash automatically puts a keyframe in the Up frame of a new button symbol.

TIP Button symbols have just four frames, but there's no restriction on adding layers. If you use symbols for the artwork of your button and keep any text on a separate layer, you can easily swap symbols to change the look of your buttons even after you've placed them in a project. This method streamlines the process of updating or revising your Flash content.

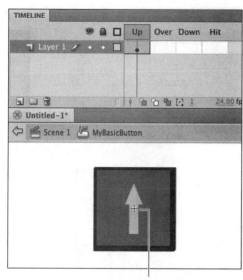

Registration crosshair marks the
center of the symbol's Stage

D When a button is waiting for your viewer to
notice and interact with it, Flash displays the
contents of the Up keyframe.

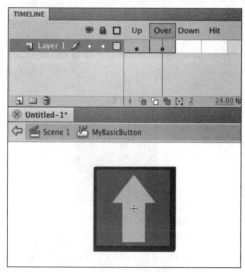

E When the viewer's pointer rolls or pauses
over the button, Flash displays the contents of
the Over keyframe.

about the button—so they can tell when
they're on a live button and sense the
difference when they click it—use a different graphic in the Up, Over, and Down
keyframes.

To create the Up state:

1. Using the file from the preceding task,
in the Timeline, select the Up keyframe.

2. On the Stage, create a new graphic or
place a graphic symbol **D**.

   This graphic element becomes the
button as it's sitting onstage in your
movie, waiting for someone to click it.
The crosshair in the middle of the Stage
in symbol-editing mode becomes the
registration point for the symbol.

To create the Over state:

1. Using the file from the preceding task,
in the Timeline, select the Over frame.

2. Choose Insert > Timeline > Keyframe.

   Flash duplicates the Up keyframe. Now
you can make minor changes in the Up
graphic to convert it to an Over graphic.
Enlarge an element within the button, for
example **E**. Duplicating the preceding
keyframe makes it easy to align all your
button elements so they don't appear to
jump around as they change states.

To create the Down state:

1. Using the file from the preceding task, in the Timeline, select the Down frame.

2. Choose Insert > Timeline > Keyframe.

   Flash duplicates the Over keyframe. Now you can make minor changes to convert the Over graphic to a Down graphic. Change the button color, for example, and reverse the shadow effect so the button looks indented **F**.

   After you create graphics for the three states of your button, you need to define the active area of the button.

To create the Hit state:

1. Using the file from the preceding task, in the Timeline, select the Hit frame.

2. Choose Insert > Timeline > Keyframe.

   Flash duplicates the Down keyframe. When you use a graphic with the same shape and size for all three phases of your button, you can safely use a copy of any previous keyframe as the Hit-frame graphic.

3. If you want, use the paint-bucket and ink-bottle tools to fill the Hit-frame graphic with a single color **G**.

   This step isn't required, but it helps remind you that this graphic isn't one that viewers of your movie will see.

4. Choose Edit > Edit Document, or click the Back button in the Edit bar.

   Flash returns you to the main Timeline. Now you can use the button symbol in your movie just as you would use any other symbol.

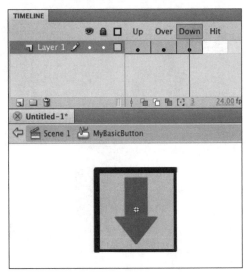

F When the viewer clicks the button, Flash displays the contents of the Down keyframe.

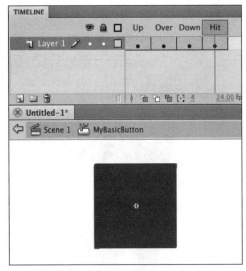

G The graphic in the Hit keyframe doesn't need to be a fully detailed image of the button in any state; it just needs to be a silhouette of the button shape. Flash uses that shape to define the active button area. This Hit keyframe contains a copy of the Down keyframe that has been filled with dark gray.

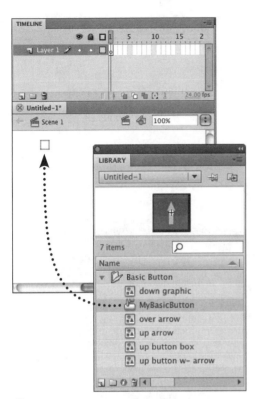

H To incorporate the button symbol into your Flash movie, drag an instance of the button from the Library panel to the Stage.

A Note About Touch Screens

Touch screens and touch tablets are becoming increasingly common as primary devices for accessing the web. In current configurations, touch devices have no equivalent to the Over state. Whether your finger taps the screen where your button is or merely rests on it gently, the device records a click (the Down state). There is no way to trigger the Over state. If you are developing Flash content for touch devices, be sure to make the Down state different from the Up state so it's clear to users that they have clicked.

To place the newly created button in your movie:

■ Continuing with the file from the preceding task, drag an instance of the button MyBasicButton from the Library panel to the Stage **H**.

You can modify the instance to change its size, rotation, and color. (For more information on modifying symbol instances, see Chapter 7.)

TIP To create a consistent look on a website, you may want to use a set of buttons over and over. You can even reuse buttons in several projects with only slight changes. To save time, devote one document to buttons, and always create your button symbols there. Then you can copy a button from this master button file to your current Flash document and tweak the button there.

TIP Fill the graphics in the Hit keyframe with a bright color that you won't use elsewhere in your movie, to create a visual cue that you're in the Hit keyframe of a button, in symbol-editing mode.

TIP You can preview the Up, Over, and Down states of your button by selecting the button in the Library panel and then clicking the Play button in the preview window. Flash displays each frame in turn.

To preview button states on the Stage:

- Choose Control > Enable Simple Buttons .

  Flash displays the Up, Over, and Down states as you move the pointer over the button and click. Remember, with buttons enabled, you can't select them or work with them. To turn off Enable Simple Buttons mode, choose Control > Enable Simple Buttons again.

O By default, in document-editing mode, button-symbol instances on the Stage display just the Up keyframe. To see the different states as the pointer interacts with a button during authoring, choose Control > Enable Simple Buttons.

The Mystery of Button Symbols

Buttons are short interactive movies that allow changes to occur when the user moves the pointer over an area of the screen. When you create a symbol and choose Button as the symbol type, Flash sets up a Timeline with four frames. You create keyframes and graphics for the first three frames to display the button in three common states: Up, Over, and Down. A keyframe in the fourth frame (the Hit frame) defines the active area of the button. You can include movie clips within each keyframe of a button to create buttons that are fully animated, and you can create scripts that activate buttons to give your viewers more control of the movie.

The Up keyframe shows graphics that end users see when the pointer lies outside the button's active area. The Over keyframe shows what the user sees when the pointer rolls over the button; additional visual changes let the user know the button is live. The Down keyframe shows how the button looks when the user clicks it, and the Hit keyframe defines the area where mouse movements trigger the button.

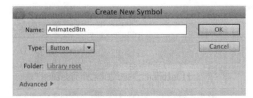

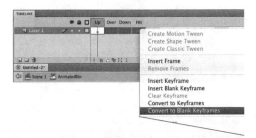

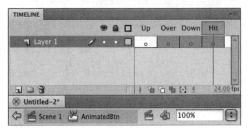

A Name your button symbol and choose Button as the symbol type in the Create New Symbol dialog.

B With the Over, Down, and Hit frames of a button symbol selected, Control-click (Mac) or right-click (Windows) to access the contextual menu and choose Convert to Blank Keyframes. Flash adds blank keyframes to all the selected frames.

Creating Shape-Changing Button Symbols

Button graphics can emulate real-world switches or toggles. In a game, you can disguise buttons as part of the scenery—making the blinking eye of a character a button, for example. When the Up, Over, and Down keyframes of your button symbol contain graphics of different shapes and sizes, however, you need to create a graphic for the Hit state that covers all of the other states.

To create Up, Over, and Down states with various graphics:

1. Open a Flash document and choose Insert > New Symbol.

   The Create New Symbol dialog appears.

2. Enter a name in the Name field (for example, AnimatedBtn), choose Button in the Type section, and click OK **A**.

   Flash creates a new symbol in the Library panel and returns you to the Timeline and Stage in symbol-editing mode.

3. In the Timeline, select the Over, Down, and Hit frames.

4. Control-click (Mac) or right-click (Windows) the selected frames and choose Convert to Blank Keyframes from the menu **B**.

5. With the Up keyframe selected in the Timeline, on the Stage, create a new graphic, or place an instance of the graphic symbol that you want to use for the button's Up state.

continues on next page

6. Repeat Step 5 for the Over and Down keyframes.

For this task, use graphics that have different shapes—a circle, a star, and a double-headed arrow, for example.

To create the Hit state for graphics of various shapes:

1. Using the file you created in the preceding task, in the Timeline, select the Hit keyframe.

2. To create the graphic that defines the button's active area, do either of the following:

▸ Draw a simple geometric shape large enough to cover all areas of the button. Turn on onion skinning so you can see exactly what you need to cover **C**.

▸ Use Flash's Edit > Copy and Edit > Paste in Place commands to copy the graphic elements from the first three keyframes of the button and paste them into the Hit keyframe of the button one by one. The graphics stack up in the Hit keyframe, occupying the exact area needed to cover the button in any phase of its operation **D**.

3. Return to editing the document (for example, by choosing Edit > Edit Document).

You're ready to place an instance of the button on the Stage and test it out by choosing Control > Test Scene.

TIP Use a transparent color (one with an alpha value less than 100 percent) for the graphic in the Hit keyframe. In Onion Skin mode, the Up, Down, and Over graphics show through the Hit graphic, making it easy to see how to position or size the graphic in the Hit keyframe to cover the graphics in the other keyframes.

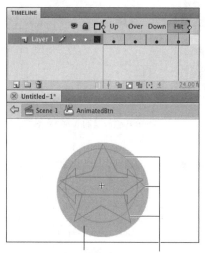

Transparent fill for Hit-frame graphic   *Onion-skin outlines*

C The silhouette in the Hit keyframe needs to encompass all possible button areas in all three button modes. For example, if you duplicate only the circle as the graphic for the Hit keyframe for this button, you exclude the tips of the star. As the user moves the pointer over the tips, the button returns to its Over phase; the user can't click the tips to activate the button. If you duplicate only the star, the user may roll over several areas of the circle and never discover that it's a button.

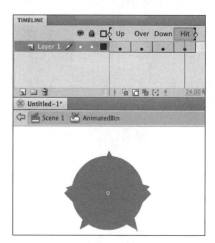

D By copying the graphic in each of the button states and using the Paste in Place command to place them in the Hit keyframe, you wind up with a perfectly positioned silhouette that incorporates all the possible button areas.

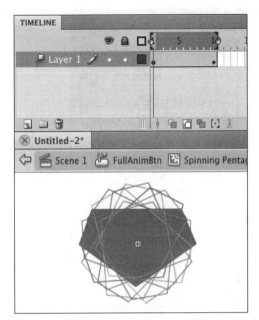

A Placing an animated symbol in the Up keyframe of a button symbol makes that animation appear when the button is in the Up state. Here, onion skinning in symbol-editing mode reveals all the frames of a spinning-pentagon animation created with a motion tween.

B With an animated symbol in the Over keyframe of a button, that animation appears when the pointer rolls or rests over the button area. Here, the Preview mode of the Timeline shows the frame-by-frame animation of a pentagon shape that turns into a star.

Creating Fully Animated Button Symbols

The button symbols you created in the preceding tasks are animated in the sense that they change as the user interacts with them. Flash also lets you create fully animated button symbols—for example, a glowing light bulb. To make fully animated buttons, you place movie clips in the button's keyframes.

To animate a rollover button:

1. Open a Flash document to which you want to add buttons.

2. Choose Insert > New Symbol.

   The Create New Symbol dialog appears.

3. Name your button (for example, FullAnimBtn), choose Button in the Type section, and click OK.

4. In the Timeline, select the Over, Down, and Hit frames of the button, and choose Modify > Timeline > Convert to Blank Keyframes.

   Flash creates blank keyframes for the button's Over, Down, and Hit frames.

5. In the Timeline, select the Up keyframe, and place an instance of a movie-clip symbol on the Stage. For this example, the Up-keyframe clip contains a spinning pentagon **A**.

6. In the Timeline, select the Over keyframe, and place an instance of a movie-clip symbol on the Stage.

   In this example, the Over-keyframe clip contains a pentagon that turns into a star **B**.

continues on next page

7. Repeat Step 6 for the Down keyframe.

For this example, the Down-keyframe clip contains a star that flies apart 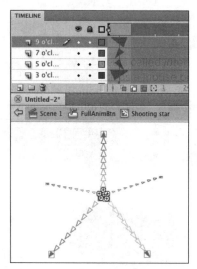.

8. In the Timeline, select the Hit keyframe, and create a graphic that covers all the button areas for the three button states (Up, Over, and Down).

A large oval works well for this purpose 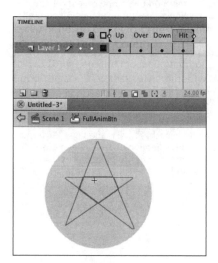. This graphic creates an active button area that's larger than the spinning pentagon. As your viewer's pointer nears the spinning graphic during playback, the button switches to Over mode. In Over mode, the oval is big enough to encompass all points of the star, and in Down mode, the user can let the pointer drift a fair amount and still be within the confines of the button.

9. Return to document-editing mode (for example, by clicking the name of the current scene in the Edit bar).

10. Drag a copy of the **FullAnimBtn** symbol from the Library panel to the Stage.

TIP You can place a movie-clip instance in the Hit keyframe of your button, but only the visible content from the clip's first frame determines the hit area.

TIP With buttons enabled, in document-editing mode, Flash previews the first frame of the animations in the Up, Over, and Down keyframes of your fully animated button symbol.

TIP Because the movie clips play in their own Timeline, animated buttons remain animated even when you pause the main movie.

TIP The movie clips you use in the various button-state frames play in their own Timelines. That means animated buttons remain animated even when you pause the main movie.

C With an animated symbol in the Down keyframe of a button, the animation plays when the viewer clicks inside the button area. Here, onion skinning in symbol-editing mode reveals all the frames of a shooting-star created with classic tweening.

D When you're creating a graphic for a Hit keyframe, use onion skinning to see the initial keyframe of the movie clip in each button frame. Here, the graphic in the Hit keyframe is a transparent fill, which also helps you position the graphic to cover the graphics in the other keyframes.

A The Components panel lists all the default components that come with Flash. There are three categories of components for ActionScript 3.0: Flex, User Interface, and Video. Buttons are found under User Interface. To expand or collapse the list, click the triangle to the left of the title User Interface.

Using Button Components

The elements that make up the user interface (UI) of an application are the little things that let users interact with your content: menus, checkboxes, scroll bars, and so on. Flash's button symbols are one type of UI element, with built-in scripting for simple behavior (displaying the common button states) and looks that you can freely define. However, Flash also offers a more complete set of UI elements in the form of *components* (see the sidebar "The Mystery of Components," later in this chapter). You can modify both the behavior and the graphics of Flash components. Flash's button components have built-in scripting to govern behavior, and they offer predefined graphics that help create a consistent look and feel for your Flash creations. To put a component to use, you place an instance of it in your Flash document.

To place an instance of the button component:

1. Open a Flash document to which you'd like to add a button component.

2. Access the following panels: Components, Library, and the Property inspector.

    These panels are all found under the Window menu.

3. If necessary, in the Components panel, expand the list of user-interface components **A**.

    Click the triangle to the left of the name User Interface to toggle between the list's expanded and collapsed views.

continues on next page

4. Drag an instance of the button component to the Stage.

Flash adds the button component and a folder named Component Assets to the document's library .

TIP Components work similarly to other library assets (for more about working with library assets, see Chapter 7). A confusing apparent similarity is that you can rename a component in the Library panel by double-clicking its name (Button), to activate a text field, and typing a new name. It's unadvisable to do so, however. If you change the name of the component in the document's library, then bring another copy of the original button component into the same document, the two components will have the same linkage ID, which may create problems when using the components in your published movie.

To preview the component instance:

■ To view all the parameters and button states of a button component, choose Control > Test Scene.

During authoring, the button component on the Stage displays the Up state created by the component's current parameter settings **C**. To view a fully enabled button component, you must view it in Flash Player. (Choose Control > Test Scene.)

B A component is a special form of movie clip. When you drag a Button component from the Components panel to the Stage, the button becomes an asset (its type is Component) in the Library panel of that document.

C During authoring, a component instance with default settings appears on the Stage showing its first frame. Choosing Control > Enable Simple Buttons has no effect on the button component. You can still select the component and drag it on the Stage. As you drag, you see the ghosted original as you would for any other object on the Stage. To preview all the states of the component, use one of the test modes—for example, choose Control > Test Scene.

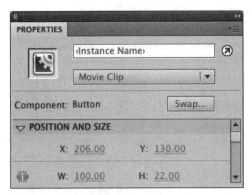

A To change the dimensions of a selected button-component instance, access the Position and Size section of the Property inspector. Use the W and H hot text to enter new width and height values.

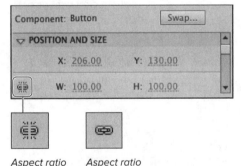

Aspect ratio unlocked   Aspect ratio locked

B In Unconstrain mode (the broken-link icon), you can set a selected component's width and height values independently, thereby changing the aspect ratio (the ratio of width to height). In this example, entering 100 pixels for width and height, changes the rectangular Button component into a square. In Constrain mode (the closed-link icon), Flash preserves the component's original aspect ratio; entering a new value for one dimension changes the value for the other dimension accordingly.

Modifying Button Components

The Component Parameters section of the Property inspector offers seven modifiable parameters for the button component. The tasks below work with two of them: changing the button's label, and setting the button to work as a toggle.

To modify button-component dimensions:

1. Continuing with the file you used in the preceding task, on the Stage, select the instance of Button.

2. In the Position and Size section of the Property inspector, use the W and H hot text to enter new values for width and height **A**.

   By default, Flash links the width and height values; the Constrain/Unconstrain modifier appears in Constrain mode (the closed-link icon). Constraining the dimensions preserves the component's aspect ratio (the ratio of width to height) when you enter new values. For this task, set the modifier to Unconstrain mode (the open-link icon). Then use the hot text to enter values that create a square button. For example, click the H hot text, enter a value of 100 to match the current W value, and press Enter to confirm the new value.

   The button's dimensions change according to the value(s) you enter **B**. The bounding box of the button defines the active area of the button. As you change the dimensions, Flash automatically changes the hit area for the button component to match.

continues on next page

The Mystery of Components

Flash's components are predefined user-interface elements with built-in graphics and coding that make them easy to use. Adobe designed components to work together to give an application or a website a consistent look and feel. Components depend on ActionScript to carry out their intended behavior. Flash CS5 offers two types of components: those that work with ActionScript versions 1.0 and 2.0, and those that work with version 3.0.

Flash stores components in the *Components panel,* a sort of library of components. The Components panel displays different items depending on which version of ActionScript is selected in the Publish Settings dialog of the current Flash document. When you create a new Flash File (Action-Script 3.0) document, it is set to work with the 3.0 components, and those are the only components that appear in the Components panel. (To learn about Publish Settings and switching ActionScript versions for your document, see Chapter 18.)

A component is actually a sophisticated, scripted movie-clip symbol. The ActionScript 1.0 and 2.0 components are a special type of movie clip called a *compiled clip.* ActionScript 3.0's video components are also compiled clips, but the 3.0 user-interface components are really just regular movie clips whose look you can easily modify. (See the sidebar "The Mystery of ActionScript 3.0 Component Skins," later in this chapter.) It is also possible to modify the look of compiled clips, but the process is somewhat complex and beyond the scope of this book.

Flash lets you modify certain properties of a component—for example, the label of the button component—by changing them in the Component Parameters section of the Property inspector.

Advanced Flash users can use ActionScript to make components communicate with one another and to change the components on the fly at runtime, but even someone new to scripting can use simple components to add interactivity to a project.

Advanced scripters can also create their own components and share them with other Flash users. One source for new components is the Adobe Exchange portion of the Adobe website. As third-party components become available, you can add them to your Components panel for easy access.

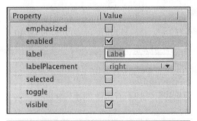

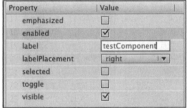

C The Component Parameters section of the Property inspector displays all the parameters of the button component that you can modify during authoring.

D Select the current Label field (top), enter new text (bottom), then press Enter to confirm the new label.

E When you change the button-component instance's Label property in the Component Parameters section of the Property inspector, Flash previews your new label text in the instance on the Stage.

To modify button-component labels:

1. Continuing with the file you used in the preceding task, on the Stage, select the instance of Button.

2. Access the Property inspector and expand the Component Parameters section.

   The section displays a two-column table **C**. The first column contains property names; the second column contains the value for each property.

3. To modify the text that appears on your button instance, in the Label row, click to activate the text field and enter a new name—such as testComponent **D**.

4. Press Enter, or click outside the active text field.

   With Flash's default settings, the new label text appears within the button-component instance **E**. Be forewarned, if your text is wider than the button instance, Flash truncates the text to make it fit within the visible button area.

To set the button component to act as a toggle:

1. Select an instance of a button component on the Stage.

2. In the Component Parameters section of the Property inspector, select the Toggle checkbox **F**. The button now acts as a toggle; repeated clicks turn the button on and off.

TIP The Component Parameters section of the Property inspector also contains a Selected checkbox, which sets a toggle button's initial state. Select the checkbox to make the button look selected initially; deselect the checkbox to make the button look deselected initially **G**.

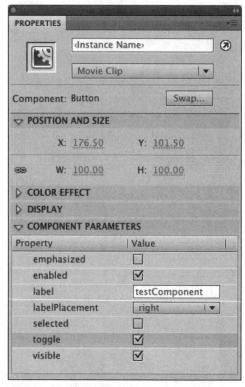

F Selecting the Toggle checkbox in the Component Parameters section of the Property inspector, sets the button to act as a toggle.

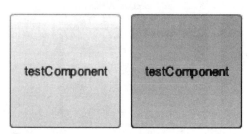

G For a button-component instance set to act as a toggle button, use the Selected checkbox to determine the button's initial state. Deselect the checkbox to make the button look deselected initially (left); select the checkbox to make the button look selected initially (right). Here the button-component instances are viewed in Test mode.

The Mystery of ActionScript 3.0 Component Skins

You can edit ActionScript 3.0's User Interface components the way you would edit any movie-clip symbol. Let's look at the Button component as an example.

When you drag an instance of the button component to the Stage, Flash adds the master button component and a Component Assets folder to the library of your document. Inside the assets folder is a subfolder containing the component's skins. The subfolder for the button component, named ButtonSkins, contains all the symbols that make up the button component's states. You can modify these underlying symbols, as you would any symbol, to change the look of the component. To modify each skin symbol directly, double-click it in the library; Flash opens the symbol in symbol-editing mode. Alternatively, you can double-click a component instance on the Stage to gain access to all of that component's skins in symbol-editing mode. The top layer of the component symbol's Timeline is labeled *assets*. Keyframe 2 of the asset layer contains a symbol that itself contains all the skins that make up the look of the component—in this case, the button states. Double-click any of the skins to edit it.

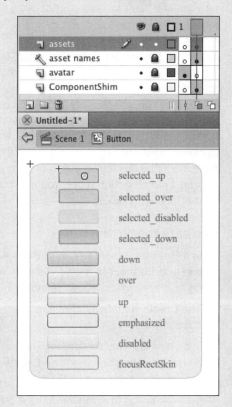

To change a button component's look yet retain a consistent, user-friendly button, you will probably need to modify every skin that relates to the button component. You may also need to modify other components if you plan to use them within the same application or website as your modified button component. The changes you make to the component's skins will affect every instance of the component in your movie.

Creating Movie-Clip Buttons

Flash's button symbols have built-in rules about how the button displays its three states in response to the user's mouse movements. You can take control of that functionality yourself and also create a button that has more than three states by making your own movie-clip button. In the following tasks, you learn to assemble artwork in the Timeline of the movie clip to create a button with four states: Up, Over, Down, and Disabled. To give the movie-clip button even the first level of interactivity—to make the movie clip respond to mouse movements by displaying different states—you must attach ActionScript. You learn to do that in Chapter 15.

To create the button states:

1. In a Flash document where you'd like to use buttons that are movie-clip symbols, choose Insert > New Symbol.

   The Create New Symbol dialog appears.

2. Type a name for your symbol, such as **MovieClipBtn**; choose Movie Clip as your symbol type; and click OK .

   Flash switches to symbol-editing mode. In the Timeline you see one layer, with a keyframe in Frame 1.

3. Add two new layers to the Timeline, for a total of three layers.

   Each layer holds a different type of information for your button 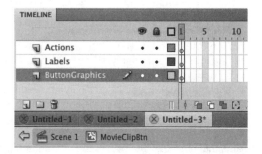. The top layer holds ActionScript that tells the movie-clip button what to do; name this layer Actions. The second layer holds text identifying each keyframe that represents a button state; name this

A The first step in making a movie clip that acts like a button is creating a new symbol. Choose Insert > New Symbol, then set the symbol type to Movie Clip and enter a name in the Create New Symbol dialog.

B When you set up the movie-clip button, it's a good idea to create a separate layer for the actions, text, and graphic elements in the movie clip's Timeline.

Why Make Movie-Clip Buttons?

Flash's button symbols make it easy to create buttons quickly, but they limit you to just three states: Up, Over, and Down. Sometimes you'd like a button to have more states than that. The best interface designs use elements consistently. That way, users know what options are available to them and always know where to find the interface elements for carrying out a task. Think of a typical slide show with a Next button. Ideally, the button is always present in the same location. When you view the last slide, the Next button is inactive (and looks inactive).

When you make your own movie-clip buttons, you can create as many states as you like.

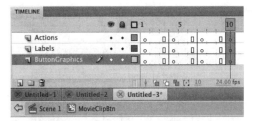

C A movie-clip button needs a keyframe for each button state. Creating longer keyframe spans helps you organize the layers visually and makes room for frame labels.

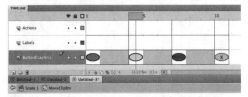

D With Preview selected as your frame-viewing mode, the Timeline displays all the button-state graphics you've placed in the keyframes of the movie-clip button symbol. Use shades of gray for the graphics in the frame that represents the Disabled state. (For clarity, since this book can't show you colors, the Disabled-state graphic contains an X.)

TIP For a movie-clip button with an irregular shape, like a snowflake (or a movie-clip button that uses different shapes in different states), it's a good idea to add an "invisible" graphic element to define a good hit area. For a snowflake button, for example, create a circular fill large enough to cover the snowflake; give the fill an alpha value of 0. Place that circular fill on a layer at the bottom of the Timeline and add enough frames to the layer that the circle "appears" in each button-state frame. The circle defines the hit area and the mouse will trigger the Over state even in the cutout areas of the flake.

TIP For a movie-clip button that uses the same solid shape in each state, there is no need to create a Hit-state keyframe for a movie-clip button. When you add the appropriate ActionScript (see Chapter 15), Flash uses the graphic element(s) in the frames of your movie clip that are displayed as button states to define the hit area.

layer Labels. The bottom layer holds the graphic elements that give the button its look in each state; name this layer ButtonGraphics.

4. In the Timeline, for all three layers, insert keyframes in Frames 4, 7, and 10 **C**.

   The layers that you added already had keyframes at Frame 1. You need to add three more keyframes to accommodate all four button states: Up, Over, Down, and Disabled. Spacing out the keyframes makes them easier to deal with and lets you view the frame labels that you create in the following task.

5. In the ButtonGraphics layer, select Keyframe 1; using the oval tool, draw an oval centered over the registration mark on the Stage.

   This graphic represents the button's Up state. Give the oval a red fill and a black stroke. Make the stroke fairly wide so the graphic looks more buttonlike.

6. Select the oval, and choose Edit > Copy.

7. Select Keyframe 4 in the ButtonGraphics layer, and choose Edit > Paste in Place.

   This graphic represents the button's Over state. Change the fill color to green.

8. Repeat Step 7 for Keyframes 7 and 10.

   In Keyframe 7, change the oval fill to blue, to represent the Down state. In Keyframe 10, change the fill to a light gray and the stroke to a dark gray, to represent the button in its Disabled state **D**.

To assign frame labels to button-state keyframes:

1. Continuing with the file you created in the preceding task, in the Labels layer of the Timeline, select Keyframe 1.

2. Click the Name field in the Label section of the Property inspector to activate the field, then type the name of the button state (**_up**), and press Enter to confirm the name.

   The Type menu (located beneath the Name field) tells Flash how to interpret the text in the Name field. Keep the default setting Name. When you finish typing the label, Flash places a red-flag icon and the label text in the selected keyframe **E**. (Note that label names do not appear when you view frames in Preview or Preview in Context mode.)

3. Repeat Step 2 for Keyframes 4, 7, and 10, entering the names **_over**, **_down**, and **Disabled** **F**.

   Why use keyframe labels? A label reminds you what's in the keyframe. More important, you can use Action-Script to find a frame by label name and then display that frame. You'll use this technique to create the button's visual feedback in response to mouse movements (see Chapter 15).

4. Return to document-editing mode; for example, click the Back button in the Edit bar.

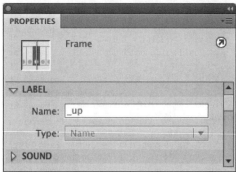

E Using the button state as the name for a selected keyframe reminds you what's in the frame, and you can use ActionScript to find a frame by label name. In the Label section of the Property inspector, enter the button-state description in the Name field.

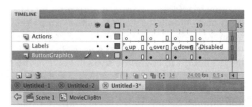

F A red flag in a keyframe indicates that the frame has a label name. If there are enough in-between frames following the keyframe, Flash displays the frame label as well as the flag (here frames have been added at the end of the sequence to make the Disabled label visible). The labeled keyframes in this movie-clip symbol indicate which button state the keyframe represents.

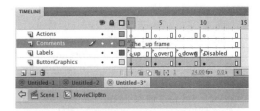

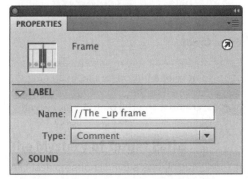

G The Name field in the Label section of the Property inspector can also be used to create comments for a selected keyframe. Enter two slashes in the field to begin comment text; or type the text of your comment, then choose Comment from the Type menu. Comments appear in the Timeline in the keyframe span; long comments are cut off by the next keyframe in the layer.

The Mystery of Frame-Label Naming

Flash is sensitive about names. Frame-label names become part of target paths in ActionScripting; therefore, certain characters that have special meaning in scripting—slashes, equals signs, plus signs, and so on—are off-limits for labeling frames. To be safe, use only letters, numbers, and underscore characters. Don't even use spaces to make word divisions in frame labels; use capitalization and the underscore character instead.

5. Drag an instance of the **MovieClipBtn** symbol to the Stage.

   This movie clip is ready to be scripted to act like a button and to carry out whatever tasks you set for it with ActionScript. You'll learn to complete the button's interactivity in Chapter 15. To check out your button states, click the Play button in the symbol preview in the Library panel, or choose Control > Test Scene to play the symbol instance. Flash moves through the keyframes and displays each button state in turn.

6. Save this document for use in Chapter 15. Call it MyOwnBtn.fla.

TIP When you use the labels _up, _down, and _over in your movie clip, ActionScript recognizes these labels as button states and you will do minimal scripting to get the button to work (see Chapter 15). To make a more flexible button (for example, one that responds differently to different mouse movements), use other labels. You can use MyUp, MyOver, MyDown, MyDragOut, and so on.

TIP Another way to add a reminder about what a keyframe does is to add a comment. To enter a frame comment, select the keyframe; in the Name field in the Label section of the Property inspector, type two slashes (//) followed by your comment text **G**. Frame labels and frame comments are mutually exclusive: each keyframe can have one or the other. To work around that limitation, add separate layers for comments and labels. Place keyframes in both layers, and then add comments to one layer and labels to the other, as needed.

TIP Instead of typing two slashes, just type the comment text. From the Type pop-up menu, choose Comment. Flash adds the slashes for you.

Practice Session

Try creating a fanciful button symbol that looks like a glowing orb, that exudes a halo of glitter when the mouse rolls over it, and that breaks apart when you click.

- Create three movie-clip symbols for use in the Up, Over, and Down frames of your button: name them, something like upOrbMc, overOrbMc, downOrbMc.

- In upOrbMc create a series of keyframes—say at Frames 1, 10, 20, and 30—containing a perfect circle with a radial gradient. Use one of the built-in two-color gradients or create your own. Edit the gradient in each keyframe to alternate showing more of the bright color, then more of the dark color. (See Chapter 2, *Creating Solid Colors and Gradients,* and Chapter 4, *Modifying Fills and Strokes*.) Use classic tweening to animate those changes. (See Chapter 9.)

- In overOrbMc place a copy of upOrbMc in one layer, and add a layer in which to create animated glitter. Select that layer, then use the spray-brush tool to spray a halo of dots around the edge of the orb. (Give the dots an appropriate glitter color.) (See Chapter 5, *Creating Patterns*.) Select the dots and convert them to a symbol (**glitterMc**). Using motion-tweening techniques, animate the halo of glitter so it shimmies, revolves, changes color, or otherwise calls attention to itself. (See Chapters 11 and 12.)

- In downOrbMc, place a copy of glitterMc. Use classic-tweening techniques to make the glitter particles expand outward as if exploding. In the ending keyframe, for example, use the free-transform tool to enlarge the halo of dots by dragging diagonally outward. (See Chapter 4.)

- Create a new button symbol, **orbBtn**. Place the symbols you just created into the Up, Over, and Down frames of the symbol. Then create an appropriate hit frame. (See *Creating Fully Animated Button Symbols*.) Drag an instance of **orbBtn** to the Stage and test your handiwork.

Save your file for use in future Practice Sessions.

Extra Credit

Set up a four-keyframe movie clip that you will script to act like a button for use in an online questionnaire. For the _up, _over, and _down frames, create a colorful button graphic with text that says *Go To Next Question*. Create a frame labeled Finished. In that frame, change the button graphic to a muted color with the text *No More Questions*.

Basic Interactivity

Adobe Flash CS5 Professional includes ActionScript, a complete scripting language that you can use to create complex, interactive websites for e-learning, e-commerce, and other Internet applications. Teaching ActionScript and scripting in detail is beyond the scope of this book. However, it is possible to create scripts for a number of common tasks without much difficulty. Flash CS5 also comes with a panel of Code Snippets, which automate the creation of scripts for some common interactivities.

In this chapter you will use ActionScript 3.0 to add basic interactivity to your Flash content. To create scripts, you will enter code in meaningful segments. Script figures, showing completed segments of code, accompany the tasks in this chapter

Touring the Actions Panel

The Actions panel has three work areas: the Script pane, the Actions Toolbox, and the Script Navigator. To access the panel, choose Window > Actions or press Option-F9 (Mac) or F9 (Windows).

The Script pane is a text window where you assemble scripts. You can enter actions into the pane manually (it acts like a text editor); and you can also add actions from the Actions Toolbox or the Add pop-up menu. (To access the Add menu, click the plus sign in the toolbar above the Script pane.) You can import scripts or pieces of script from an external file, such as one created with a stand-alone text editor.

The Actions Toolbox contains the words (actions) that make up the ActionScript language. These pieces of code appear in hierarchical lists; click one of the folder-like icons to view the contents of a category. Double-click an action to add it to the Script pane. You can also drag items from the Actions Toolbox to the Script pane. (The list of ActionScript actions also appears in the Add menu.)

The Script Navigator helps you locate and maneuver through the scripts in your movie. This feature is most useful when you've used a large number of frame scripts in keyframes throughout the Timeline. Ⓐ shows the elements of the Actions panel.

ActionScript Versions

Flash CS5 contains two flavors of ActionScript—version 2.0 (which also includes 1.0) and 3.0. This book focuses exclusively on version 3.0. To create scripts that use AS 3.0, you must set your Flash document's publish settings to AS 3.0. (You can do that when you create the document initially or in the Publish Settings dialog. You'll learn more about publishing in Chapter 18.)

About Scripting Tasks

In this book you create scripts by entering segments of code. Some characters—such as opening and closing braces—act as a team to enclose code; both characters must be present for the script to work. To help create accurate code, you will first enter such characters as a pair, then add the code that belongs inside. You will also revise and add to scripts as you go. The script figures accompanying the tasks show completed segments of code. For context, when a script figure illustrates specific steps in a task, the text that you enter for those steps appears in boldface; text that is already present from earlier steps appears in regular type. In addition, script figures show a space after an opening parenthesis and before a closing parenthesis. ActionScript does not require these spaces, but they make it easier to see the code and to copy and paste code segments. Full scripts are available from the book's companion website; for directions to download them, please see the Introduction, page xix.

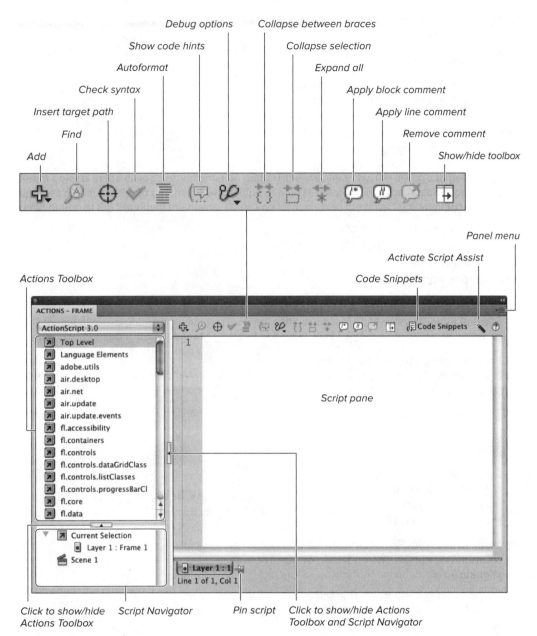

Debug options

Show code hints

Autoformat

Check syntax

Insert target path

Find

Add

Collapse between braces

Collapse selection

Expand all

Apply block comment

Apply line comment

Remove comment

Show/hide toolbox

Panel menu

Activate Script Assist

Actions Toolbox

Code Snippets

ACTIONS – FRAME

ActionScript 3.0

- Top Level
- Language Elements
- adobe.utils
- air.desktop
- air.net
- air.update
- air.update.events
- fl.accessibility
- fl.containers
- fl.controls
- fl.controls.dataGridClass
- fl.controls.listClasses
- fl.controls.progressBarCl
- fl.core
- fl.data

Code Snippets

Script pane

Current Selection
  Layer 1 : Frame 1
  Scene 1

Layer 1 : 1
Line 1 of 1, Col 1

Click to show/hide
Actions Toolbox

Script Navigator

Pin script

Click to show/hide Actions
Toolbox and Script Navigator

A The Actions panel has three main areas: the Actions Toolbox, where you can choose actions; the Script Navigator, where Flash displays the elements in your movie that have scripts attached; and the Script pane, where Flash assembles the ActionScript.

Customizing the Actions Panel

You can modify the way the Actions panel displays to suit your taste or convenience. For example, you can resize the panel and its panes or collapse panes completely. You can customize the way scripts appear by choosing settings for font and size; highlighting script elements in different colors; and controlling the number of spaces Flash uses to indent with each tab you type. You can also turn code hints on or off.

To set preferences for the Actions panel:

1. Choose Flash > Preferences (Mac) or Edit Preferences (Windows).

   or

   From the panel menu in the top-right corner of the Actions panel, choose Preferences.

   The Preferences dialog appears.

2. In the Category list, choose ActionScript.

   The settings for working with statements in the Script pane of the Actions panel appear in the main window of the Preferences dialog 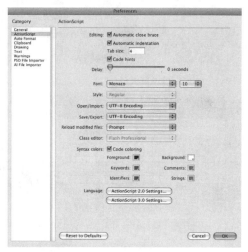.

3. To create proper code blocks automatically, select the Automatic Close Brace checkbox **B**.

4. To get scripting help from code hints, in the Editing section, select the Code Hints checkbox **C**.

   Move the Delay slider to set the amount of time Flash waits before displaying the hint as you type directly in the Script pane.

A In the Preferences dialog, choose the ActionScript category to access settings for customizing the way Flash displays your scripts.

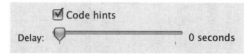

B Select the Automatic Close Brace checkbox to get help with creating the proper pairs of opening and closing braces in blocks of code you enter in the Actions panel.

C To have Flash display code hints, select the Code Hints checkbox. To make hints appear more quickly, drag the Delay slider farther to the left.

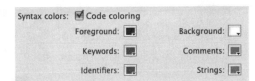

D Activate syntax coloring by selecting the Code Coloring checkbox in the Syntax Colors section of the Preferences dialog's ActionScript category. Change the colors to make more of a distinction between scripting "words," to get a feel for ActionScript's parts of speech.

TIP Flash's default settings for keywords and identifiers are similar shades of blue. Try setting them to wildly different colors—say, pink and orange. This technique will help you learn to recognize these different parts of ActionScript speech as they're used in the scripts you create.

TIP Code hints work like tool tips within the Actions panel when Script Assist isn't active. With code hints turned on, you can make the Actions panel display certain types of scripting information in a tool-tip–type box or dropdown menu. Position the insertion point to the right of a dot (a period character) or an opening parenthesis in the Script pane, and then click the Show Code Hints button. If you enable code hints in the ActionScript Preferences, the hints appear automatically when you type a period, a colon, or an opening parenthesis in the right context.

5. To choose the font for writing scripts, in the Font section, do the following:

   ▸ From the pop-up menu of installed fonts, choose a font.

   ▸ From the pop-up menu of sizes, choose a font size.

   The Actions panel can display scripts in text as small as 8 points and as large as 72 points.

6. To color-code script items, in the Syntax Colors section, select the Code Coloring checkbox **D**.

   Using a color control to access a pop-up set of swatches, choose a new color for any of the following:

   Foreground The basic text color for your scripts.

   Keywords Words reserved for special purposes in ActionScript.

   Identifiers The names of things—such as objects, variables, and functions—that are built into ActionScript.

   Background The color against which your script displays in the Script pane.

   Comments Text that Flash ignores when it reads the script, used to make notes about what's going on in the script.

   Strings Series of characters (letters, numbers, and punctuation marks) that are enclosed within quotation marks.

7. Click OK.

   Flash applies your preferences settings immediately.

What Is Interactivity?

By default, a published Flash file plays through its scenes and frames sequentially. The movie opens with Scene 1, plays all those frames in order, moves to Scene 2, plays those frames, and so on. Sometimes that's appropriate; sometimes it's not.

Imagine an online training course where you want the same five frames of general instructions to appear before each section of the course. You can make those frames a separate scene and then duplicate the scene so it appears repeatedly between other scenes containing the training sections. But duplicating scenes increases file size, slows the performance of your published course, and makes it harder to edit later. A more efficient method is to create one scene containing the instructions and direct Flash to repeat that scene when each training section ends. Also, you may want the users taking your course to interact with the content: clicking buttons, dragging elements, or entering text to answer quiz questions, for example. And you may want the course to interact with the user, summarizing the quiz score. These are examples of interactivity in Flash.

To achieve this type of interactivity, you must create a script that directs the playback of your published Flash content, using ActionScript.

Two Styles of Scripting

ActionScript 3.0 lets you work in two scripting styles: you can create scripts that rely on *frame actions* and scripts that rely on *custom classes*. Each style stores the ActionScript code differently. For the tasks in this book, you'll create frame-action scripts, where code is attached to keyframes and stored in the FLA file. Scripts that rely on custom classes require that you create the code in external AS files.

You create frame actions by selecting a keyframe, then opening the Actions panel and entering the script. In the exported movie, when the playhead reaches the keyframe that contains the script, Flash carries out the script's instructions. These instructions might be to control the Timeline directly (for example, pausing playback of the movie), to set up interactivity for buttons (for example, telling Flash what to do when someone clicks a particular button), or to change the properties of objects located in that keyframe (for example, to move a symbol instance across the Stage).

Scripting with custom classes is similar to using symbols in the library. Creating or even editing classes is beyond the scope of this book. Yet by doing the tasks in earlier chapters, you have already interacted with some of Flash's built-in classes, such as **SimpleButton** and **MovieClip**. Advanced scripters can create and edit custom classes using the ActionScript editor or an external text editor.

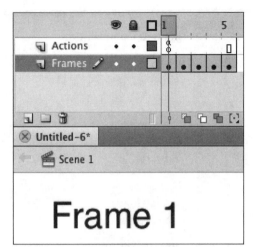

A To test frame actions—actions that instruct Flash to move to a specific frame or to start and stop playback—it's useful to have a document that identifies each frame. That way, you can see the results of your scripts easily.

Organizing Frame Actions

A little letter *a* in the Timeline indicates a keyframe that has actions attached. Imagine the difficulty of searching through dozens—or hundreds—of layers and frames to find each little *a* when you need to modify or add to your code. To organize your code, put all frame actions in a single layer named Actions. Restricting frame actions to one layer keeps you from accidentally putting multiple frame actions at the same frame number in different layers, which can cause problems if you reorder the layers. Choose a consistent location for your Actions layer; always put it near the top of the Timeline, for example. It's also a good idea to lock the Actions layer (click the bullet in the padlock column). You can't accidentally place or rearrange elements on the Stage for a locked layer, but you can still add actions to keyframes in a locked layer. (For detailed instructions on working with layers, see Chapter 6.)

Adding Frame Actions

Some of the most basic scripting tasks involve controlling movie playback: making your movie stop and start, and jump from place to place. By default, a movie begins running at playback; you can change that with actions.

To make your first script in Flash, set up a multiframe document that has identifying text in each frame. Then add a **stop** action to Keyframe 1, to make the movie pause on the first frame at playback. Save this file as a template for use in other scripting tasks.

To set up a document for testing frame actions:

1. Create a Flash document with two layers: Actions and Frames.

2. In the Actions layer, add in-between frames in Frames 2–5; there is a keyframe in the first frame by default.

3. In the Frames layer, create keyframes in Frames 2–5; there is a keyframe in the first frame by default.

4. On the Stage, for each keyframe, add Classic text to identify the frame numbers (Frame 1, Frame 2, and so on).

   Your document should look like **A**. If you create the text as TLF, warning dialogs and error messages related to publishing may appear when you test your scripts; that will distract you from learning the process of scripting.

TIP You can also set a movie to pause at startup in the Publish Settings dialog. For more details, register your book at www.peachpit.com/flashcq5vqs and download the Bonus Tasks.

To begin scripting by adding comments:

1. Continuing with the document you created in the preceding task, in the Actions layer, select Keyframe 1.

2. Access the Actions panel. (If the panel isn't open, choose Window > Actions.)

   The name Actions-Frame appears in the title bar of the Actions panel.

3. In the panel menu, in the upper-right corner of the Actions-Frame panel, make sure Line Numbers has a check-mark, indicating it's active (the default setting) **B**. If Line Numbers is inactive, select it.

   Visible line numbers make it easier to keep your place as you script.

4. In the panel menu, make sure Word Wrap has a checkmark, indicating it's active. If Word Wrap is inactive, select it.

   Word Wrap forces the lines of your script to break to fit within the Script pane. Such line breaks aren't meaningful in the script itself; the ActionScript syntax tells Flash where the meaningful divisions in script text occur (see the sidebar "The Mystery of ActionScript Syntax," later in this chapter).

B Open the panel menu in the Actions panel to make sure that line numbering and word wrap are active (if not, select them to activate them). Visible line numbers make it easier to keep your place while scripting; word wrap makes it easier to view scripts, as it forces them to stay within the visible Script pane area.

5. In the toolbar above the Script pane of the Actions-Frame panel, make sure that Script Assist is inactive **ⓒ**. If necessary, click the Script Assist button to close the Script Assist window.

6. In the toolbar, click the Apply Line Comment button.

Flash adds two slashes (**//**) to Line 1 of the Script pane. The blinking I-beam cursor appears at the end of the line.

continues on next page

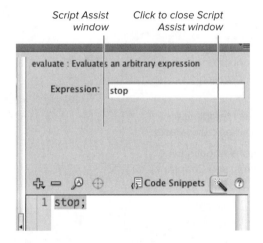

Script Assist window   *Click to close Script Assist window*

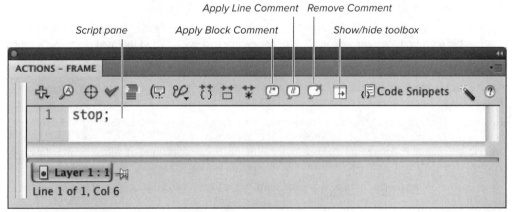

Apply Line Comment   *Remove Comment*

Script pane   *Apply Block Comment*   *Show/hide toolbox*

ⓒ The toolbar of the Actions panel contains a number of tools for working with scripts, including Script Assist. Deselect the Script Assist button to close the Script Assist window so that you can type directly in the Script pane.

7. Type **Pause the movie on Frame 1** 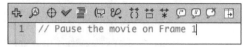.

   Your comment is added to the Script pane. With word wrap turned on, Flash wraps your text to fit in the Script pane; in the real script, the comment is just one line.

D The two slashes indicate the beginning of a comment. When you add a comment using the Apply Line Comment button, Flash adds slashes to the script automatically.

To set the movie to pause at playback:

1. Continuing with the document you created in the preceding task, position the cursor at the end of Line 1 (your comment line), and press Enter.

   Flash creates Line 2 in the Script pane.

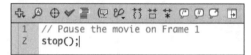

E The **stop();** action in Line 2 sets the movie to be paused at runtime.

2. To add an action that pauses the Timeline, type **stop();**

   The new action appears in Line 2 in the Script pane; the word *stop* is highlighted in blue **E**.

3. Save the document as a template for future use; name it FrameActionsMaster.

   (For detailed instructions about saving documents as templates, see Chapter 1.)

4. Close the document.

About Comment Lines

The double slash is known as a *comment delimiter;* the delimiter sets the boundaries of a comment within a script. Flash ignores any text between the two slashes and the next paragraph return for the purposes of scripting. When compiling the script for playback, Flash leaves that text out of the final file, so your comments do not increase the SWF file size. It's a good idea to write notes about your script to remind yourself what you intend the script to do. Comments also help anyone who needs to modify your script later.

For long comments, a *multiline delimiter* excludes everything between the opening and closing delimiters from the script. Click the Apply Block Comment button in the toolbar above the Script pane to add a multiline comment to your script. A multiline comment begins with a slash followed by an asterisk (*/*) and ends with an asterisk followed by a slash (***/**).

When you're testing long scripts or trying different ways to achieve your scripting task, it can be useful to temporarily remove part of the script to see what happens. Comment delimiters let you do this quickly without deleting any code. If you want to block out a large section of the script temporarily, use the */* and ***/** delimiters.

The Mystery of ActionScript Syntax

ActionScript has its own rules, which are analogous to the rules of grammar and spelling in English. These rules, called *syntax,* govern such things as word order, capitalization, and punctuation of action statements. The following list briefly describes six crucial ActionScript punctuation marks that you'll use in writing scripts.

Dot (.) ActionScript uses *dot syntax,* meaning that periods act as links between objects and the *properties* (characteristics) and *methods* (behaviors) applied to them. In the statement

```
myClip.nextFrame();
```

the *dot* (the period) links the object (a movie-clip named **myClip**) with the method (**nextFrame**) that moves the playhead to the next frame in the Timeline. ActionScript also uses the dot in target paths (see the sidebar "The Mystery of Target Paths," later in this chapter).

Semicolon (;) A semicolon indicates the end of a statement. The semicolon isn't required—Flash interprets the end of the line of statements correctly without it—but including it is good scripting practice. The semicolon also acts as a required separator in some action statements.

Colon (:) When you first set up a variable (a container for content that changes), a colon separates the text that is the name of a variable from the text that defines what type of variable it is.

```
var myName:String;
```

A colon also separates the name of a method from its type.

Braces ({}) Braces set off ActionScript statements that belong together. For example, a set of actions that are supposed to take place after **function greeting()** must be set off by braces. Note that the action statements within braces can require their own beginning and ending braces. The opening and closing braces must pair up evenly. Using Flash CS5's new Automatic Close Brace feature helps ensure that you get the right number of opening and closing braces. Pay close attention to where you're adding statements and braces within the Script pane to make sure that you group the actions as you intend.

Parentheses (()) Parentheses group the arguments that apply to a particular statement—defining the scene and frame in a **goto** action, for example. Parentheses also let you group operations, such as mathematical calculations, so that they take place in the right order.

Brackets ([]) Scripting frequently involves working with *arrays*, lists of similar elements. Placing a list inside brackets defines it as an array.

Programming Buttons with Frame Scripts

As you learned in the previous chapter, Flash's button symbols and button components have certain actions built in. By default, when you move the mouse into the button area, Flash jumps to the Over frame; when you click the button, Flash takes you to the Down frame. To make the button carry out a task or to refine the way a button responds to a user's mouse movements, you attach ActionScript to a keyframe and target an instance of a button symbol or button component.

To add a button to be controlled by a frame script:

1. Using the FrameActionsMaster template you created earlier in this chapter, open a new document (for details on opening new documents from templates, see Chapter 1).

2. In the Timeline, add a new layer anywhere below the Actions layer; name the new layer Buttons.

   Frame 1 of the new layer is a keyframe; Frames 2–5 are in-between frames. Any items you place on this layer will be visible throughout the five-frame movie 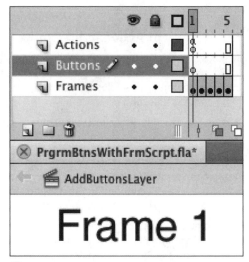.

3. With the Buttons layer selected, place an instance of a button symbol on the Stage 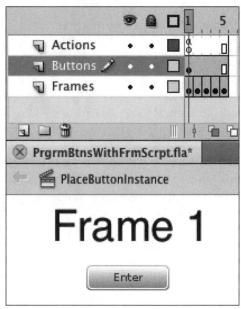.

   Follow the techniques in Chapter 14 to create a new button symbol, or use one from the Common Library of buttons. (To access this library, choose Window > Common Libraries > Buttons.) Drag a button-symbol instance from the library to the Stage.

A To practice with button actions, create a movie with identifying text and separate layers for buttons and actions. Add in-between frames as needed so that all the layers are the same length.

B In-between frames extend the Buttons layer to match the length of the other layers; the button symbol in Keyframe 1 will be visible throughout the movie, although the identifying text from the Frames layer will change.

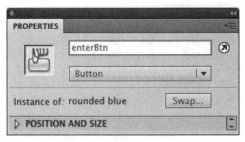

C Select the button symbol on the Stage, and enter a name in the Instance Name field in the Property inspector.

4. To name the button instance, with the button selected on the Stage, access the Property inspector and type a name in the Instance name field—for example, **enterBtn C**.

   For ActionScript to control a symbol, the symbol must have a unique instance name.

5. Save your file (for example, by choosing File > Save).

The Mechanics of Code Hints

How do code hints work? As you type text in the Script pane of the Actions panel, Flash tries to guess what you're about to script and help you out. Let's look at an example:

In Line 1 of your script, enter the following code:

`var startLesson:SimpleButton;`

As soon as you enter the colon, a code-hint window appears, listing available types **D**. Continue to type, and the code-hint window follows along. As soon as you enter the letters **Si**, the code-hint window highlights **SimpleButton**. You can press Enter to accept the code hint and Flash adds it to your script, or you can keep typing to enter it manually.

When you accept the code hint, Flash automatically creates a new Line 1

`import flash.display.SimpleButton;`

and adds a blank Line 2. Line 1 instructs Flash to make the code for the **SimpleButton** class—available in your script. The **import** statement is necessary for publishing, and it enables Flash to give you further code hints.

In subsequent lines of the script, whenever you type that instance name (**startLesson**) followed by a period (**.**), a similar code-hint window opens listing the actions and properties available for button symbols.

continues on next page

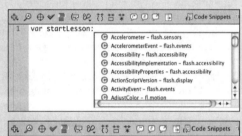

D When you enter a colon following a variable name, a code-hint window opens (top). As you continue typing characters, the code-hint window attempts to autocomplete your code (middle). When the matching code-hint highlights, press Enter to complete the script (bottom).

TIP Scripting is a complex process, often involving trial and error. As you create scripts, you may wish you could go back to a point where you know everything works. The Save As command makes that easier. Once you've set up your objects on the Stage and you're ready to add code, choose File > Save As.

Each time you complete a segment of code that works the way you want, choose Save As again. Add a number, a letter, or an abbreviated description to the filename to make it easy to identify which version contains which completed work.

The Mechanics of Code Hints *continued*

You can use the window's scroll bars (or the up- and down-arrow keys on your keyboard) to navigate the list of actions and properties. Select the item you want and press Enter to add it to your script. Or you can continue typing to have Flash autocomplete your code: the code-hint window narrows in on an action or property according to the letters you type. When the action or property you want is highlighted, press Enter. Flash autocompletes that piece of code in your script. You can override autocompleting by continuing to type manually in the Script pane, but autocompleting helps you avoid typos and speeds the coding process.

When you use code hints to automate entry of an action that requires a parameter, Flash automatically adds an open parenthesis to your script and brings up another type of code hint, a *parameter hint* **E**. (If you override autocompleting, the parameter hint appears after you type an opening parenthesis in the Script pane.) The parameter hint, which acts something like a tool tip, displays all possible parameters for the action you just entered. Parameter hints don't autocomplete code in the Script pane, but they can help you remember which parameters you need. Sometimes the same action is available for different objects; for example, Buttons and MovieClips have **addEventListener**. Parameter hints also help you see which category folder in the Actions Toolbox contains the code you're looking for; each parameter hint begins with the path to the category folder containing the action you entered.

If you close a code-hint window by accident, or you later want to change your selection, you can open the window by placing your cursor to the right of a period or open parenthesis and clicking the Code Hint button in the toolbar above the Script pane. You can also use the keyboard shortcut Control-spacebar (Mac) or Ctrl-spacebar (Windows).

Code Hint button

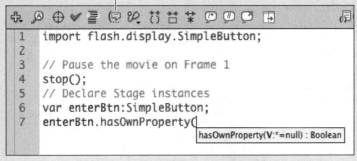

```
1   import flash.display.SimpleButton;
2
3   // Pause the movie on Frame 1
4   stop();
5   // Declare Stage instances
6   var enterBtn:SimpleButton;
7   enterBtn.hasOwnProperty(
        hasOwnProperty(V:*=null) : Boolean
```

E The parameter hint appears after you type an open parenthesis (or after you use code hints to automate adding an action or property that takes a parameter).

```
1  //Pause the movie on Frame 1
2  stop();
3  |
```

```
1  import flash.display.SimpleButton;
2
3  //Pause the movie on Frame 1
4  stop();
5  // Declare Stage instances
6  var enterBtn:SimpleButton;
7
```

F When you declare a Stage instance, Flash adds an **import** statement to the head of your script. If the script currently has no **import** statements; Flash adds it to Line 1 and adds a blank Line 2 to visually separate the **import** statements from the rest of the script. If the script already has **import** statements, Flash adds the new **import** statement in the line below the existing statements.

G Declaring a Stage instance.

```
1  import flash.display.SimpleButton;
2
3  // Pause the movie on Frame 1
4  stop();
5  // Declare Stage instances
6  var enterBtn:SimpleButton;
```

To control a button using a frame script:

1. Continuing with the file that you created in the preceding task, make sure that the Actions panel is open and that code hints are enabled in Preferences (see the section "Customizing the Actions Panel," earlier in this chapter).

2. In the Actions layer, select Keyframe 1.

   The Script pane of the Actions panel displays the code you already created; Line 1 displays a comment; Line 2 displays the **stop();** action.

3. To declare a stage instance, do the following:

   ▸ To start a new line, place the cursor at the end of Line 2—after the **stop();** action—and press Enter. Flash adds Line 3 to the Script pane.

   ▸ In Lines 3 and 4, type

   // Declare Stage instances

   var enterBtn:SimpleButton;

   If you named the button instance something other than **enterBtn**, type that name instead. After you type the colon (**:**), code hints appear. When the code item you want highlights, press Enter to complete it, or keep typing to complete the code manually. If you use the code hint to enter **SimpleButton**, remember to type a semicolon (**;**) at the end of the line. Flash automatically creates a new Line 1 **F**

   import flash.display.SimpleButton;

   and a blank Line 2, which pushes the text you just typed to Lines 5 and 6 **G**.

   continues on next page

4. To create the event-handler function, do the following:

- With the cursor at the end of Line 6, press Enter to create a new line.

- In Lines 7 and 8, type

  `// Event handlers`

  `function handleClick(`
  `→ pEvent:MouseEvent ):void`

After you type the colon (**:**), code hints appear. When the item you want highlights, press Enter to complete the word, or keep typing to complete it manually. The code inside the parentheses, called a *parameter,* provides information about where the event comes from (**pEvent**) and what kind of event it is (**MouseEvent**); a colon separates these two pieces of information. Once you complete typing **MouseEvent**, Flash inserts a new Line 2:

`import flash.events.MouseEvent;`

This pushes the code you just entered to Lines 8 and 9 **Ⓗ**.

5. To create the body of the event-handler function, do the following:

- With the cursor at the end of Line 9, press Enter to create a new line.

- In Line 10, type

  `{`

  and press Enter.

Flash automatically creates paired braces spanning Lines 10–12 (see the sidebar "The Mystery of Paired Braces") **Ⓘ**.

Ⓗ Defining the event handler.

```
1   import flash.display.SimpleButton;
2   import flash.events.MouseEvent;
3
4   // Pause the movie on Frame 1
5   stop();
6   // Declare Stage instances
7   var enterBtn:SimpleButton;
8   // Event handlers
9   function handleClick( pEvent:MouseEvent
    ):void
```

Ⓘ Defining the body of the event-handler function.

```
9    function handleClick( pEvent:MouseEvent
     ):void
10   {
11
12   }
```

Wide Scripts—Narrow Columns

A single line of ActionScript can be quite long. You can resize the Script pane of Flash's Actions panel so that a lot of code fits on one line, but we can't resize the columns in this book. That means for longer lines of code, the text has to wrap. In the Script figures, such as **Ⓗ**, the line numbers make it clear where you should type a return to begin a new line. In the numbered steps of a task, when a column is too narrow, we'll use a small right arrow to indicate code that runs over to a new line simply because the column is too narrow. You would enter the following code, for example, as a single line of script, pressing the Enter key only after the word *void.*

`function handleClick(`
`→ pEvent:MouseEvent ):void`

J Making sure the event was triggered by **enterBtn**.

```
 9   function handleClick( pEvent:MouseEvent
     ):void
10   {
11       if( pEvent.target == enterBtn )
12       {
13
14       }
15   }
```

6. Do the following to make sure the event is triggered by **enterBtn**:

   ▸ With the cursor indented in Line 11, type

     `if( pEvent.target == enterBtn )`

   ▸ Press Enter.

   ▸ With the cursor indented in Line 12, type **{** and press Enter to insert paired braces in Lines 12–14.

   You have just created what's known as a *conditional statement* (see the sidebar "The Mystery of the If Statement," later in this chapter). Flash executes the code within the braces only if the specified condition is met. In this case you are checking whether the event's target matches the button instance you want to control with your script (**enterBtn**) **J**.

   continues on next page

The Mystery of Paired Braces

For scripts to run correctly, every opening brace must have a matching closing brace. When you chose the Automatic Close Brace option in Preferences (see the section "Customizing the Actions Panel," earlier in this chapter), Flash helps make sure that happens. When you type an opening brace (**{**) into the Script pane of the Actions panel and press Enter, Flash immediately creates paired braces spanning three lines **K**. The opening-brace character appears in the line where you typed it (say, Line 10), then comes a blank line (11), and the closing brace appears in the following line (12). After entering the paired braces, Flash puts the cursor in the blank line (10) and creates tabbed indents appropriate to the nesting level of the braces. By isolating each brace on its own line and adding indents, Flash provides visual feedback about the code—reminding you that it is part of the function defined within the pair of braces. (To learn more about the construction of functions, see the sidebar "The Mystery of Functions," later in this chapter).

```
 9   function handleClick(Event:MouseEvent ):void
10   {
11       |
12   }
```

K When you have chosen Automatic Close Brace in Preferences, each time you enter an opening brace, Flash adds the closing brace. The opening and closing braces appear on their own lines, and the cursor winds up on a blank line between the two, with the proper indent for the braces' current nesting level.

7. With the cursor indented in Line 13, in Lines 13 and 14, type

// Handle the event

nextFrame();

After you type the opening parenthesis, a code-hint window opens; just keep typing. Flash uses double indents in Lines 13 and 14 to visually remind you that this code is inside the braces and is part of the **if** statement.

The **nextFrame();** action will advance the playhead by one frame .

8. To start registering the event, do the following:

Place the cursor at the end of Line 16, and press Enter to create a new line, and then in Lines 17 and 18, type

// Register events

enterBtn.addEventListener();

After you type the period, a code-hint window opens showing a list of action statements. As you type more characters, the statements in the list that start with those characters highlight; after you type the letters **ad**, the statement **addEventListener** followed by a list of parameters highlights . Press Enter (or double-click the statement) as soon as the desired statement highlights. Flash adds **addEventListener(** to the script and opens another code-hint window. Ignore the second window and type **);** to complete the statement.

The completed event handler.

```
9    function handleClick( pEvent:MouseEvent
     ):void
10   {
11       if( pEvent.target == enterBtn )
12       {
13           // Handle the event
14           nextFrame();
15       }
16   }
```

```
17   // Register events
18   enterBtn.ad
```
```
o    upState : DisplayObject – SimpleButton
o    useHandCursor : Boolean – SimpleButton
o    visible : Boolean – DisplayObject
o    width : Number – DisplayObject
o    x : Number – DisplayObject
o    y : Number – DisplayObject
o    z : Number – DisplayObject
o    addEventListener(type:String, listener:Function, useCapture:B
```

As you enter code in the Script pane, the code-hint window offers possible code items you might want. When the item you want appears highlighted, press Enter, and it gets added to the Script pane.

Anatomy of a MouseEvent

There are several ways users can interact with a button in a Flash movie. They can move the mouse into and out of the active area of a button, they can click and release inside the active area, they can click inside the active area and, while still holding down the mouse button, roll outside the area, and so on. The code **MouseEvent.CLICK** describes one specific button event. The **MouseEvent** part tells Flash that the event to watch for is generated by an input device (like a mouse, graphics pen, touch screen, or touch tablet); the **CLICK** part tells Flash to notice when the user presses and then releases inside the active area of a button.

N The completed frame script for controlling a button (this script becomes part of the ButtonActionsMaster template).

```
1    import flash.display.SimpleButton;
2    import flash.events.MouseEvent;
3
4    // Pause the movie on Frame 1
5    stop();
6    // Declare Stage instances
7    var enterBtn:SimpleButton;
8    // Event handlers
9    function handleClick( pEvent:MouseEvent
     ):void
10   {
11       if( pEvent.target == enterBtn )
12       {
13           // Handle the event
14           nextFrame();
15       }
16   }
17   // Register events
18   enterBtn.addEventListener(
     MouseEvent. CLICK, handleClick );
```

TIP If you don't get the expected result when you test the movie, try checking the syntax (see the section "Previewing Actions at Work," later in this chapter).

TIP The code-hint window doesn't stop you from typing, but it ensures that the actions you enter are spelled correctly. When the code-hint window appears, you can continue entering text by hand.

TIP You just created a template with a script for programming buttons. You can use this script over and over again, modifying it to meet different situations as needed.

9. To finish registering the event, do the following:

▸ In Line 18, position the cursor within the parentheses.

▸ Then type

MouseEvent.CLICK, handleClick

After you type the comma (**,**) a parameter-hint window opens; ignore this window and continue typing the rest of the code. The code **MouseEvent.CLICK** tells Flash which of the possible button events you want your event handler to listen for (see the sidebar "Anatomy of a MouseEvent").

The code **handleClick** points to the event-handler function you created in the preceding steps; it must match what you typed after the keyword **function** in Line 9.

You just programmed your first button event. The completed script should look like **N**. It's time to see your work in action.

10. Choose Control > Test Scene.

Flash publishes the movie and opens the SWF file in Flash Player. You see the text *Frame 1* and a button. Click the button, and the text *Frame 2* appears. Flash has moved the playhead to Frame 2 in response to your clicking the button, just as you requested via Action-Script. Each click of the button moves the playhead forward one frame until the playhead reaches Frame 5.

11. Save your document as a template for use throughout this chapter, and name it ButtonActionsMaster.

(For detailed instructions about saving documents as templates, see Chapter 1.)

12. Close the document.

The Mystery of Instance Names and Code Hints

The name of an *instance* of an object on the Stage is an identifier that may wind up as part of a script. To prevent scripting problems, make sure instance names contain no spaces or characters that have special meaning in ActionScript—for example, avoid slashes or the equals sign. To be safe, use only letters, numbers, and underscore characters. Ideally, instance names should start with a lowercase letter.

When you name instances of button symbols, movie-clip symbols, and text fields, you can give Flash extra information about the object being named. Flash uses that information to assist you— giving you code hints as you type in the Actions panel.

To activate the code-hint feature for specific objects, you need to declare variables. That creates a connection between an *identifier*—a script element that describes the type of object—and the instance name you've created for that object on the Stage. To declare a variable that identifies an instance, write the keyword **var** followed by a space, then the instance name you've created for the object, then a colon, and then the identifier for the type of object. For example, the lines

```
var startLesson:SimpleButton;
var circle:MovieClip;
var message:TextField;
```

identify a button instance named **startLesson**, a movie-clip instance named **circle**, and a text field named **message**.

The Mystery of the Import Statement

Classes are pieces of code that define the functionality of the elements you use in Flash. Action-Script 3.0's built-in elements rely on built-in classes. The built-in button and movie-clip symbols, for example, rely on the classes **SimpleButton** and **MovieClip.** (Advanced ActionScripters can also define new elements, for which they create custom classes.) A script that refers to a class—either built in or custom—needs to include information about how to access the code that defines the class. In "Programming Buttons with Frame Scripts," earlier in this chapter, you do that when you use code hints, which automatically add import statements at the head of the script.

ActionScript groups classes with related functionality together in packages. Let's take a look at the **import** statement for a button symbol:

```
import flash.display.SimpleButton;
```

The statement gives Flash the path to the required class code: **SimpleButton** is the name of the class, while **flash.display** describes the package. As a rule of thumb, all the classes built into the Flash Player are in the **flash** package; further divisions group similar classes, such as **.display** for interface elements and **.events** for events.

The Mystery of Event Handlers

In ActionScript, as in English, the term *event* refers to something that happens, such as a user clicking a button. An *event handler* is a specific type of action statement, called a *function,* that describes what should happen in your Flash creation when a specific event occurs.

Events can be generated by humans or by the internal workings of your Flash creations. This chapter focuses on *user interactions,* events generated by people viewing and using your Flash content. (Some common user events are clicking a button, entering text, or clicking a checkbox.) Events not generated by users also affect the way a Flash movie runs, and you can write scripts that respond to such events. (Some common nonuser events are a movie finishing loading onto the user's computer or the playhead advancing to the next frame.)

Scripting for Interactivity

To make your Flash creation respond to a specific user interaction (an event), you must create a script that does two things: *register to receive* the event created by that interaction, and *handle the event.* Handling an event means creating a routine for Flash to use only after the event takes place—the *event handler.* Registering an event means writing a script that connects the object that triggers the event (for example, a button) with the event handler.

Code for handling an event takes the following format:

```
function handleEvent( event )
{
  if( event.target == eventSource )
  {
    // Handle event...
  }
}
```

The event-handler function named **handleEvent** waits for an event to happen. If the event is triggered by the specified **eventSource**, the event handler will carry out its instructions. **handleEvent** represents the name you'll create for this specific situation. The **eventSource** might be a button instance, a button component, or a movie-clip instance (for more technical details, see the sidebars "The Mystery of the If Statement" and "The Mystery of Functions," later in this chapter).

Code for registering for an event takes the following format:

```
eventSource.addEventListener( eventName, handleEvent );
```

Here **eventSource** represents the object that will be the source of the event. **eventName** represents the event itself; the precise code depends on the source object—a **click** event, for example, can be generated by a button instance. (The code **eventName** represents actions for the objects you'll work with in this chapter and are built into ActionScript 3.0.) Finally, **handleEvent** represents the function you created for handling the event.

The Mystery of the If Statement

Often when you create Flash content, you want one thing to happen under certain conditions, and something else to happen if those conditions aren't met. Your script needs to take different paths depending on the state of affairs.

One way to accomplish this is by using the **if** *statement,* which takes this format:

```
if( condition )
{
   action();
}
```

Here's a real-world example:

```
if( numLives == 0 )
{
   gotoAndStop( "gameOver" );
}
```

An **if** statement consists of the keyword **if**, followed by an opening parenthesis, then a condition that is either true or false, a closing parenthesis, and then a list of statements between braces. These statements execute only if the condition is true.

A condition could be a comparison. You might, for example, compare two items to see if they are equal or if the first is greater than the second. To script a comparison, you use an *operator* (a symbol or symbols) that describes the comparison. In ActionScript, the operator used to check for equality consists of two equal signs (==). ActionScript uses a single equals sign (=) to assign a value (for example, to say a rectangle's width is 1 inch), never to compare.

The most common, and important, comparison operators are as follows:

> greater than

>= greater than or equal to

< less than

<= less than or equal to

!= not equal to

When you check for a condition, you may want to run one block of code when the condition is met, and a different block of code when it's not. You could write two separate **if** statements or use an **if-else** statement. **if-else** statements take the format

```
if( condition )
{
   // Code
}
else
{
   // Other code
}
```

Finally, it is also possible to link up multiple conditions in an **if-else-if-else** statement using the following format:

```
if( foodInFridge )
{
   // Eat at home
}
else if( haveMoney )
{
   // Go out
}
else
{
   // Call a friend
}
```

The Mystery of Functions

A *function* groups a number of actions together under a single name. When the function name appears in a script, Flash executes that group of actions. The basic format looks like this:

```
function functionName():Type
{
    // Function code
}
```

The code block always starts with the *keyword* **function**. Next comes the function's name, represented here by **functionName**. (You get to create your function name; make it descriptive.) Immediately following the function's name is a pair of parentheses.

Next comes a colon (:), which separates the function's name from its *type*. In this example, the code for type is represented by **Type.** The type defines what kind of result the function will have. To understand the purpose of type, imagine a restaurant-tip calculator; it needs to come up with numbers in the result (as opposed to letters, for example). A tip-calculator function would have **Number** as the type. The most common type for functions, however, is **void**, meaning "there is no result." Actions that control Timeline playback, for example, have **void** as the type.

The braces (**{}**) enclose code that describes what the function actually does. Flash carries out the instructions within those braces only when certain conditions are met; in our example, this is when a user clicks the calculate-tip button.

Quite often, a function needs more information to operate; parameters convey that information. The tip-calculator function needs to know the cost of the meal. When you set up a function that requires parameters, the format changes slightly:

```
function functionName( param:Type, nextParam:Type ):Type
{
    // Code
}
```

When a function has multiple parameters, the parameter names still go between the parentheses after the function name, but you must separate the names with commas.

Each parameter also has a type, just as the function has one.

Previewing Actions at Work

To see your scripts in action, you need to view the movie in Flash Player. You can do this by publishing the movie (see Chapter 18) or by using one of the test modes. Test mode is an abbreviated form of publishing a movie while still working in the authoring environment. To preview and test your scripts safely, follow a three-step procedure: (1) save your work; (2) check the script's syntax; and (3) test the movie.

To check the script's syntax:

1. With the document containing your script open, select the keyframe with the script you want to check, and view it in the Script pane of the Actions panel.

2. In the toolbar above the Script pane, click the Check Syntax button (the checkmark icon), or press Command-T (Mac) or Ctrl-T (Windows) .

   Flash runs its compiler (see the sidebar "What Is a Compiler?" to check the selected code for errors of syntax (see the sidebar "The Mystery of Action-Script Syntax," earlier in this chapter). The compiler beeps to indicate that the check is complete.

3. Access the Compiler Errors panel.

   If it's not open, choose Window > Compiler Errors **B**.

Check Syntax button

A Click the Check Syntax button in the Actions panel to have Flash help you find syntax errors in your code.

B In document-editing mode, choose Window > Compiler Errors to open the Compiler Errors panel.

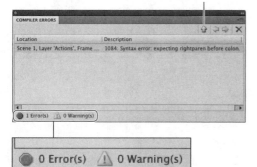

Go to Source button

Total number of errors

C The Compiler Errors panel shows details about the errors in your script. When a syntax check finds no errors, the count of Total Errors is 0. Although the panel is resizable, the text within each column doesn't wrap; you may need to resize the columns to see the full error message. You can select the error in the panel and click the Go to Source button to go directly to the error in the Script pane of the Actions panel.

What Is a Compiler?

ActionScript is a computer language that lets scripters write instructions for the Flash Player to execute. Although it takes time to learn the language, humans can read it. A computer's CPU, however, works only with 0's and 1's; it can't read ActionScript directly. A *compiler* translates code written in a computer language into instructions that the processing unit can read. In the case of Flash, ActionScript is translated into compact byte-code that Flash Player understands.

4. Review the contents of the panel to see the results of the syntax check.

The number of syntax errors found appears in the lower-left corner of the panel. Within the main body of the panel, a separate entry describes each error **C**.

5. If the selected code contains errors, do any of the following:

▸ Visually review the code in the Script pane and correct the errors you find.

▸ In the Compiler Errors panel, select the error and click the Go to Source button. Flash opens the Actions panel and highlights the line where the error occurred. Correct the error and repeat Step 2.

Flash generally refuses to run scripts with errors; you need to correct them all before you move on.

TIP Common scripting errors include missing, misplaced, or doubled commas, colons, parentheses, braces, and semicolons. Paired items, such as parentheses and braces, must have equal numbers of opening and closing elements, and they must be nested correctly (see the sidebar "The Mystery of ActionScript Syntax," earlier in this chapter). The new preference setting Automatic Close Brace helps you avoid this particular pitfall (see the section "Customizing the Actions Panel," earlier in this chapter).

TIP A script that produces no errors doesn't necessarily do what you want it to do. The syntax check determines if your script follows the rules, but the compiler doesn't check the logic, and doesn't know what you intended the script to do.

To test scripts:

Choose Control > Test Movie > In Flash Professional (or Control > Test Scene) 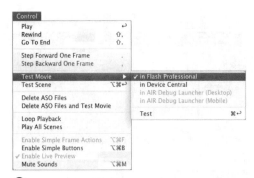.

Flash exports the movie (or scene) to a Flash Player file, adding the .swf extension (or the scene name plus the .swf extension) to the filename and using the current Publish settings. (For more information on Publish Settings, see Chapter 18.) During export, Flash displays the Exporting SWF Movie dialog, which contains a progress bar and a button for canceling the operation.

When it finishes exporting the movie, Flash opens the SWF file in Flash Player so you see the movie in action. The buttons and movie clips in the test window are all live, so you can see how they interact with the viewer's mouse actions. Any scripts you've created will run.

When you finish testing, exit the Player by clicking the movie window's close button (Mac) or close box (Windows). Flash returns you to the document-editing environment.

TIP Sometimes even when a script comes through the syntax check without errors, it has errors that show up when you test the movie. Flash opens the Output panel as soon as it encounters one of these *runtime errors*. Runtime errors may occur, for example, when you try to target an object that doesn't exist; let's say you typed `enerBtn` as the instance name instead of `enterBtn`. The script still follows the syntax rules, but fails to find the instance when it runs.

TIP When you choose Control > Test Scene, Flash appends the scene name and the .swf extension to the file, when it creates the Player file. This situation can make the filename exceed the number of allowable characters. If Test Movie > In Flash Professional works fine with your file, but Test Scene brings up the warning dialog, try shortening the scene name.

D To test the full animation and interactivity of ActionScript scripts, you must export your movie—for example, by choosing Control > Test Movie > In Flash Professional or Control > Test Scene.

TIP To test the interactivity of a symbol—for example, a movie clip—choose Control > Test Scene while you are working on the symbol in symbol-editing mode. Flash publishes just the symbol and the items nested within that symbol.

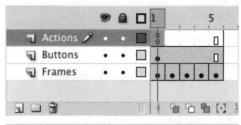

```
1  import flash.display.SimpleButton;
2  import flash.events.MouseEvent;
3
4  //Pause the movie on Frame 1
5  stop();
6  // Declare Stage instances
7  var enterBtn:SimpleButton;
8  // Event handlers
9  function handleClick(pEvent:MouseEvent):void
10 {
11     if( pEvent.target == enterBtn )
12     {
13         // Handle the event
14         nextFrame();
15     }
16 }
17 // Register events
18 enterBtn.addEventListener( MouseEvent.CLICK, handleClick );
```

A When you select a frame that contains actions, the script for that frame appears in the Actions panel.

Modifying and Extending Button Scripts

When it comes to scripting, the first steps are often the most difficult; subsequent steps expand on what you've already learned. Earlier, you set up a frame script that controlled a button on the Stage. In this section, that script becomes a stepping stone to creating different kinds of interactivity.

To create multiple actions in an event handler:

1. Using the ButtonActionsMaster template you created in the section "Programming Buttons with Frame Scripts," earlier in this chapter, open a new document.

   ButtonActionsMaster creates a five-frame document with identifying text for each frame, and one button instance. It also contains a **stop** action in Keyframe 1, and a script that activates the button for interactivity.

2. In the Timeline, in the Actions layer, select Keyframe 1 **A**.

   Flash displays the script in the Script pane of the Actions panel. If the panel is not currently visible, access it (for example, by choosing Window > Actions).

3. To have Flash print a message in the Output window, position the cursor at the end of Line 14, press Enter, and in the new Line 15, type

   ```
   trace( "Click! New frame: " +
   → currentFrame );
   ```

continues on next page

Make sure you enter this code before the closing brace (**}**) in Line 16. Lines 14 and 15 of your code should look like **B**.

The block of code that makes up the event handler now contains two statements. The **nextFrame** statement moves the playhead to the next frame. The **trace** statement tells Flash to print a message to the Output window. (Here, Flash builds the message out of the words inside the quotes plus the number of the frame where the playhead is currently.)

4. Save the document and give it a descriptive name, such as EventHandlerMultipleActions.

5. Check the script's syntax.

For details about troubleshooting syntax errors, see the section "Previewing Actions at Work," earlier in this chapter.

▸ Choose Control > Test Scene.

Your movie opens in a Flash Player window. Each time you click the button, the words *Click! New frame:* appear in the Output panel, followed by the current frame number **C**. If the Output panel isn't visible, Flash opens it for you.

To send the playhead to a specific frame:

1. To use the script created in the previous task as a building block, create a new copy of the document EventHandler-MultipleActions by choosing File > Save As.

Give the copy a descriptive name, such as GoToFrame.

B Adding the trace action to the event handler.

```
 9   function handleClick( pEvent:MouseEvent
     ):void
10   {
11       if( pEvent.target == enterBtn )
12       {
13           // Handle the event
14           nextFrame();
15           trace( "Click! New frame: " +
                 currentFrame );
16       }
17   }
```

Before clicking the button

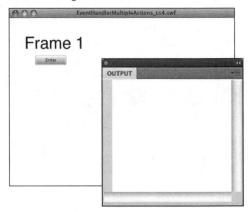

After clicking the button

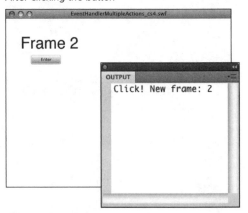

C When you test a movie, the Output window displays your trace messages. For this movie, clicking the button creates a trace message.

D Sending the playhead to a frame number.

```
9   function handleClick( pEvent:MouseEvent
    ):void
10  {
11      if( pEvent.target == enterBtn )
12      {
13          // Handle the event
14          gotoAndStop( 5 );
15          trace( "Click! New frame: " +
            currentFrame );
16      }
17  }
```

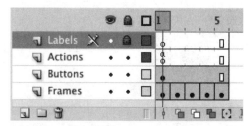

E A Labels layer lets you make notes about what's happening in different frames right in the Timeline. To avoid accidentally placing graphic content on the Stage in the Labels layer, lock it. You can still add keyframes and labels to a locked layer.

2. In the Timeline, select Keyframe 1 of the Actions layer.

   The script you created earlier appears in the Script pane of the Actions panel.

3. In the Script pane, in Line 14, select the code

   `nextFrame();`

   and replace it with

   `gotoAndStop( 5 );`

   Be sure to keep the code's original indentation. Instead of moving the playhead forward one frame at a time, the **gotoAndStop** action tells the playhead to jump to the frame number specified in parentheses.

4. Preview the action.

   Save the file, check the syntax (Line 14 of the script should match **D**) correct any errors, then test the movie (see "Previewing Actions at Work").

   Your movie opens in a Flash Player window. When you click the button, the movie jumps to Frame 5, and the message in the Output window confirms it.

To create a frame label:

1. Create a copy of the previous task's document (GoToFrame)—for example, by choosing File > Save As.

   Give the copy a descriptive name, such as CreateFrameLabel.

2. In the Timeline, create a new layer above the Actions layer, name it Labels, and lock it **E**.

   Having the Labels layer at the top helps you organize the Timeline; you can use labels to indicate the sections of your Movie.

continues on next page

3. Select Frame 3 of the Labels layer and insert a blank keyframe—for example, by choosing Insert > Timeline > Blank Keyframe.

4. With the new blank keyframe selected, access the Frame Property inspector; in the Label section, in the Name field, enter `myLabel` 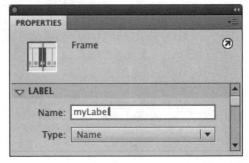.

To confirm the label, press Enter or click outside the field. In the Timeline a little red flag appears in Keyframe 3 of the Labels layer. Flash displays as much of your label as there's room for in the keyframe span 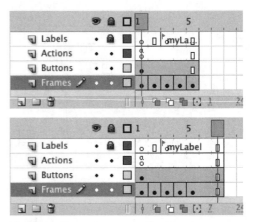.

5. Position the playhead in Frame 5, but don't select a frame.

6. Insert enough in-between frames (for example, by pressing F5) to make the span large enough to display the full label.

Frame labels help you organize your Timeline. They are most effective when you can read them in the Timeline, rather than having to check the Property inspector.

F Enter frame-label text in the Name field of the Frame Property inspector's Label section.

G Frame labels appear truncated if the keyframe span is too short to display the full text (top). To gain the full benefit of using frame labels as visual aids, expand the span by adding in-between frames (bottom).

Sending the playhead to a frame label.

```
9    function handleClick( pEvent:MouseEvent
     ):void
10   {
11       if( pEvent.target == enterBtn )
12       {
13           // Handle the event
14           gotoAndStop( "myLabel" );
15           trace( "Click! New frame: " +
             currentFrame );
16       }
17   }
```

Targeting Frame Labels

When using a **gotoAndStop** or **gotoAndPlay** action, you can enter a frame number or a frame label. There's an advantage to using frame labels. If you ever add or remove frames from the type of movie-clip button you learned to create in Chapter 14, the frame numbers for the button states may change. If they do, you must go back into the script to update the frame numbers. If you target the frame by label, you never need to update the script to accommodate changes to frame numbers.

To send the playhead to a frame label:

1. Continuing with the file from the preceding task, select Keyframe 1 in the Actions layer, and access the Actions panel.

   Your script appears in the Script pane.

2. In the Script pane, in Line 14, select the code

   gotoAndStop(5);

   and replace it with

   gotoAndStop("myLabel");

   Be sure to keep the original indentation. With the **gotoAndstop** action, you can have the playhead go to a frame number or to a frame label.

3. Preview the action.

   Save the file, check the syntax (Line 14 of your script should match **H**), correct any errors, then test the movie (see "Previewing Actions at Work").

   Your movie opens in a Flash Player window. When you click the button, the movie jumps to the frame that bears the label **myLabel**. (In this case, Frame 3). The script also creates the **trace** message in the Output window.

TIP In the preceding task, you made the playhead move to a specific frame and stop playback. You can also make the playhead jump to a specific frame and resume playback from there. In Step 2, replace Line 14's gotoAndStop action with gotoAndPlay.

Working with Code Snippets

Flash CS5's new Code Snippets panel lets you work with reusable pieces of ActionScript code. The panel contains a number of built-in snippets, and it also lets you build your own.

Using built-in snippets

The snippets that come with CS5 will be of special interest to anyone new to scripting. In addition to creating the necessary code for common tasks, each snippet creates comment code containing instructions on how to use and modify the snippet-created code to accomplish the results you want. The panel contains six categories of built-in snippets: Actions snippets **A** create code for a variety of common interactivity tasks, from generating a random number to creating a custom mouse cursor. Timeline Navigation snippets **B** create Code for controlling movie playback, such as going to the next or the previous frame. Animation snippets **C** create code for changing the properties of an object over time; changing an object's X property, for example, moves the object across the Stage. Load and Unload snippets **D** create code for adding and removing assets from a movie at runtime. Audio and Video snippets **E** create Code for controlling sounds and video clips. Event Handler snippets **F** create code for responding to basic user input, such as clicking the mouse button.

Here's a brief overview of how to use a predefined snippet.

- For code that works solely with the Timeline (for example, to pause the movie, or to respond to key-press events), select the frame where you want to add the code.

- For code that manipulates a movie-clip or button-symbol instance, select the instance on the Stage. (The code will always need to work with instance names; if the instance you select has no name, Flash will assign a default instance name.)

- Once you've selected a frame or symbol instance, access the Code Snippets panel, navigate to the snippet you want, and double-click the snippet (or select the snippet and click the Add to Current Frame button). Flash adds the snippet code to the Script pane of the Actions panel.

- Access the Actions panel and review the comment lines in the snippet code **G**. They contain instructions on what the code does and, if necessary, how to modify the code to accomplish your particular task.

Click to add code to current frame

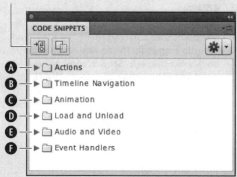

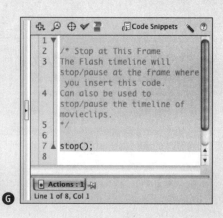

```
17   // Register events
18   enterBtn.addEventListener(
     MouseEvent.ROLL_OVER, handleClick );
```

Ⓑ Registering for the **rollout** event.

```
17   // Register events
18   enterBtn.addEventListener(
     MouseEvent.ROLL_OUT, handleClick );
```

TIP A faster way to replace the event is to delete the code **.CLICK** and retype the period to trigger the code-hint window. You can then select ROLL_OVER from the list and press Enter. You could also just delete CLICK, position the cursor after the period, and press the Code Hint button in the toolbar above the Script pane.

TIP In the preceding task, the event handler is still called **handleClick**. It would be more meaningful to rename it **handleRollOver**; just make sure you change it in both Lines 9 and 18.

TIP If you want the script to react when rolling out of the button instead of over, in Line 18, select the text **MouseEvent.ROLL_ OVER**, and replace it by typing **MouseEvent. ROLL_OUT** Ⓑ.

Choosing Events

As users interact with a button, their mouse movements trigger various events. Releasing the mouse button while still over the button's active area triggers the **click** event. Rolling over and out of a button area triggers other events. To make a button react to these events, you must change your script to register for the desired event instead of **click**.

To handle an event when rolling over a button:

1. Open a new document using the ButtonActionsMaster template you created earlier in this chapter.

   Save the document using the name ButtonEvents.fla.

2. In the Actions layer, select Frame 1 and access the Actions panel.

   The template's script appears in the Script pane.

3. In Line 18, select the text

   MouseEvent.CLICK

   and replace it by typing

   MouseEvent.ROLL_OVER

4. Preview the action.

   Save the file, check the syntax (Lines 17 and 18 of your code should match Ⓐ), correct any errors, then test the movie (see "Previewing Actions at Work").

   Your movie opens in a Flash Player window. Each time you roll over the button (move the pointer into the button's active area), the playhead moves one frame forward. Nothing happens when you click, other than the button showing the Down frame.

To receive multiple events for a button:

1. Open a new document using the ButtonActionsMaster template you created earlier in this chapter.

   Save the document using the name ButtonMultiEvents.fla.

2. In the Timeline, in the Actions layer, select Keyframe 1 and access the Actions panel.

   The template's script appears in the Script pane.

3. To define a second event handler, do the following:

   ▸ Place the cursor at the end of Line 16 (after the closing brace) and press Enter to begin a new code block (the code that was originally on Lines 17 and 18 moves down).

   ▸ In Lines 17–24, type

   ```
   function handleRollOver(
   → pEvent:MouseEvent ):void
   {
       if( pEvent.target == enterBtn )
       {
           // Handle the event
           gotoAndStop( 2 );
       }
   }
   ```

   Lines 17–24 should match **ⓒ**.

ⓒ Adding the second event handler.

```
14          nextFrame();
15      }
16  }
17  function handleRollOver( pEvent:MouseEvent
    ):void
18  {
19      if( pEvent.target == enterBtn )
20      {
21          // Handle the event
22          gotoAndStop( 2 );
23      }
24  }
25  // Register events
```

D Pay attention to the second event (**rollover**).

```
25    // Register events
26    enterBtn.addEventListener(
      MouseEvent.CLICK, handleClick );
27    enterBtn.addEventListener(
      MouseEvent.ROLL_OVER, handleRollOver );
```

E The completed multi-event script.

```
1     import flash.display.SimpleButton;
2     import flash.events.MouseEvent;
3
4     // Pause the movie on Frame 1
5     stop();
6     // Declare Stage instances
7     var enterBtn:SimpleButton;
8     // Event handlers
9     function handleClick( pEvent:MouseEvent
      ):void
10    {
11        if( pEvent.target == enterBtn )
12        {
13            // Handle the event
14            nextFrame();
15        }
16    }
17    function handleRollOver(
      pEvent:MouseEvent ):void
18    {
19        if( pEvent.target == enterBtn )
20        {
21            // Handle the event
22            gotoAndStop( 2 );
23        }
24    }
25    // Register events
26    enterBtn.addEventListener(
      MouseEvent.CLICK, handleClick );
27    enterBtn.addEventListener(
      MouseEvent.ROLL_OVER, handleRollOver );
```

4. To register for the **rollOver** event, place the cursor at the end of Line 26, press Enter to create a new line (27), and type

```
enterBtn.addEventListener(
→ MouseEvent.ROLL_OVER,
→ handleRollOver );
```

To receive multiple events from one button, you need to register for each event separately. You want the script to receive both events but react differently for each one. Defining a new event-handler function is a way to accomplish that **D**.

5. Preview the action.

Save the file, check the syntax (the complete script for the multi-event button should match **E**), correct any errors, then test the movie (see "Previewing Actions at Work").

Your movie opens in a Flash Player window. Whenever you roll the pointer over the button, the playhead jumps to Frame 2, and when you click the button, the playhead moves to the next frame.

The Mystery of Mouse Events

Button symbols and movie-clip symbols are both in a group of Flash objects called *interactive objects*. Users interacting with any of the objects via an input device such as a mouse or a graphics pen can trigger the same events—known as *mouse events*. (Button components, despite having the word *button* in the name, are actually a special type of movie clip.)

All interactive objects have a whopping 19 events built in; 9 of them are mouse events. Each of them is part of Flash and has a predefined functionality. This means you can't rename them or change how they work. The following list shows the generic name of an event—for example, **click**—followed in parentheses by the ActionScript constant that refers to that event—for example, (**MouseEvent.CLICK**).

click (**MouseEvent.CLICK**) occurs when a user presses and then releases the mouse button while over the active area of a button or movie clip (an interactive object).

rollOver (**MouseEvent.ROLL_OVER**) occurs when the user moves the pointer over the active area of the interactive object. Once a user has triggered a **rollOver**, the **rollOver** event can't be triggered again until there has been a **rollOut** event.

rollOut (**MouseEvent.ROLL_OUT**) occurs when a user has moved the pointer into the active area of an interactive object and then moves the pointer out of the active area.

mouseMove (**MouseEvent.MOUSE_MOVE**) occurs whenever a user moves the pointer within the active area of an interactive object.

doubleClick (**MouseEvent.DOUBLE_CLICK**) occurs when a user clicks twice in rapid succession over the active area of an interactive object. To use this event in your scripts, the **doubleClickEnabled** property of the button or movie clip needs to be set to **true**. (You must create a line in the script with the code **myBtn.doubleClickEnabled = true;**.)

The first three events in the list—**click**, **rollOver**, and **rollOut**—are the most common ones, and should be all you need for the vast majority of your button scripting tasks. The other two, **mouseMove** and **doubleClick**, give you a glimpse at what else is possible.

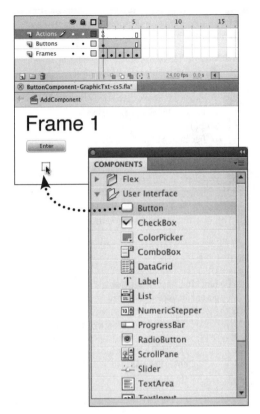

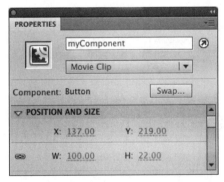

A Drag an instance of the button component from the Components panel to the Stage to add it to your movie.

B To target a component with ActionScript, you must give it an instance name. Note that the Object Type menu in the Property inspector reveals that the button component is actually a type of movie clip.

Button Components

Flash contains a selection of ready-made user interface (UI) elements. They can be found in the Components panel and include items such as RadioButton and ComboBox (for drop-down menus). Scripting the click-interactivity for button components and regular button symbols is similar.

To add a button component to your movie:

1. Open a new document using the ButtonActionsMaster template you created earlier in this chapter.

   Save the document using the name ButtonComponent.fla.

2. In the Timeline, in the Buttons layer, select Keyframe 1.

3. Access the Components panel and, from the User Interface category, choose Button.

   If the panel isn't visible, choose Window > Components.

4. Drag an instance of the button component onto the Stage **A**.

5. Select the button-component instance on the Stage and access the Property inspector.

6. In the Instance Name field, enter a name for the button-component instance—for example, **myComponent** **B**.

   You are now ready to create a script that makes the component carry out a task.

TIP You can modify a component's appearance by editing its skin (see Chapter 14 for details).

To script a button component's interactivity:

1. Continuing with the file from the preceding task, select Keyframe 1 in the Actions layer and access the Actions panel.

   The template's script appears in the Script pane.

2. To enable code hints for the component instance, place the cursor at the end of Line 7 and press Enter to create a new Line 8, then type

   `var myComponent:Button;`

   A button component is more complex than a regular button, and enabling full code hints for components makes scripting them easier. Flash adds an **import** statement for the component in Line 3.

   `import fl.controls.Button;`

   pushing the code you entered down to Line 9 **C**.

3. To create the event handler for the component, do the following:

   ▶ Place the cursor at the end of Line 18 (after the closing brace) and press Enter to begin a new code block.

   ▶ In Lines 19–26, type

   ```
   function handleComponent(
   ⇢ pEvent:MouseEvent ):void
   {
     if( pEvent.target ==
     ⇢ myComponent )
   {
     // Handle the event
     enterBtn.visible = false;
     }
   }
   ```

C Declaring the variable for the button component.

```
1   import flash.display.SimpleButton;
2   import flash.events.MouseEvent;
3   import fl.controls.Button;
4
5   // Pause the movie on Frame 1
6   stop();
7   // Declare Stage instances
8   var enterBtn:SimpleButton;
9   var myComponent:Button;
10  // Event handlers
```

D The event handler for the button component.

```
16        nextFrame();
17      }
18  }
19  function handleComponent(
    pEvent:MouseEvent ):void
20  {
21    if( pEvent.target == myComponent )
22    {
23      // Handle the event
24      enterBtn.visible = false;
25    }
26  }
```

E Listening to the **click** event of the button component.

```
27    // Register events
28    enterBtn.addEventListener(
      MouseEvent.CLICK, handleClick );
29    myComponent.addEventListener(
      MouseEvent.CLICK, handleComponent );
```

F Scripting a button component.

```
1     import flash.display.SimpleButton;
2     import flash.events.MouseEvent;
3     import fl.controls.Button;
4
5     // Pause the movie on Frame 1
6     stop();
7     // Declare Stage instances
8     var enterBtn:SimpleButton;
9     var myComponent:Button;
10    // Event handlers
11    function handleClick( pEvent:MouseEvent
      ):void
12    {
13        if( pEvent.target == enterBtn )
14        {
15            // Handle the event
16            nextFrame();
17        }
18    }
19    function handleComponent(
      pEvent:MouseEvent ):void
20    {
21        if( pEvent.target == myComponent )
22        {
23            // Handle the event
24            enterBtn.visible = false;
25        }
26    }
27    // Register events
28    enterBtn.addEventListener(
      MouseEvent.CLICK, handleClick );
29    myComponent.addEventListener(
      MouseEvent.CLICK, handleComponent );
```

The code should match **D**. Instead of moving the playhead to a new frame, this event handler hides the **enterBtn**.

4. With the cursor at the end of Line 28 (after the semicolon), press Enter to create a new line, and in Line 29, type

   myComponent.addEventListener(
   → MouseEvent.CLICK,
   → handleComponent);

   The code should match **E**.

5. Preview the action.

   Save the file, check the syntax (the full script should match **F**), correct any errors, then test the movie (see "Previewing Actions at Work").

   Your movie opens in a Flash Player window. When you click the button component (named Label), Flash hides the button symbol (named Enter). Clicking the button symbol (when it's visible) still advances the Timeline as you originally scripted it to do.

Using One Event Handler for Multiple Events

Earlier in this chapter, you created individual event handlers for multiple events. Another way to deal with multiple events is to use one event handler with a parameter. With this technique, you create a script that examines the **pEvent** parameter that you've defined as part of the event-handler function to react differently for each button.

To add another button to be scripted:

1. Open a new document using the ButtonActionsMaster template you created earlier in this chapter.

   This document has one button instance—named **enterBtn**—on the Stage. Save the document using the name MultiEventsOneHandler.fla.

2. Select the **enterBtn** instance and choose Edit > Duplicate to create a new instance of the button.

   Position the duplicate so that it doesn't overlap the original button.

3. Access the Property inspector, and enter **prevBtn** in the Instance Name field **A**.

   Now you have two buttons on the Stage that can be scripted to use the same event handler.

To script the second button:

1. Continuing with the file from the preceding task, in the Timeline, in the Actions layer, select Keyframe 1 and access the Actions panel.

2. To create a variable for the second button (**prevBtn**), in the Action panel's

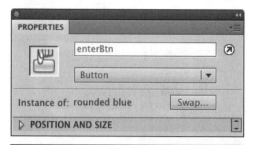

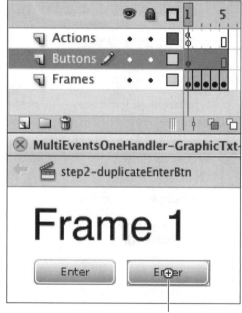

Selected instance

New instance name

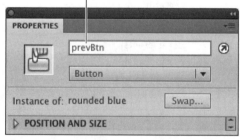

A To create an additional button quickly, duplicate the button instance, then modify the script. Be sure to give the duplicate a different instance name. You can later swap out the symbol with matching graphics.

B Declaring the variable for the second button.

```
6    // Declare Stage instances
7    var enterBtn:SimpleButton;
8    var prevBtn:SimpleButton;
9    // Event handlers
```

C The interaction for the second button.

```
15          nextFrame();
16      }
17      else if( pEvent.target == prevBtn )
18      {
19          // Handle the prevBtn event
20          prevFrame();
21      }
22  }
```

D A single event handler for two buttons.

```
6    // Declare Stage instances
7    var enterBtn:SimpleButton;
8    var prevBtn:SimpleButton;
9    // Event handlers
10   function handleClick( pEvent:MouseEvent
     ):void
11   {
12      if( pEvent.target == enterBtn )
13      {
14          // Handle the event
15          nextFrame();
16      }
17      else if( pEvent.target == prevBtn )
18      {
19          // Handle the prevBtn event
20          prevFrame();
21      }
22   }
23   // Register events
24   enterBtn.addEventListener(
     MouseEvent.CLICK, handleClick );
25   prevBtn.addEventListener(
     MouseEvent.CLICK, handleClick );
```

Script pane, place the cursor at the end of Line 7 and press Enter to create a new Line 8, then type

```
var prevBtn:SimpleButton;
```

(See **B**.)

3. Place the cursor at the end of Line 16—after the closing brace (**}**)—and press Enter to create a new line.

   Be sure to place the cursor after the correct closing brace. The brace in Line 16 closes the **if** statement, while the brace in Line 17 closes the function.

4. To update the event handler for two buttons, in new Lines 17–21, type

```
else if( pEvent.target == prevBtn )
{
    // Handle the prevBtn event
    prevFrame();
}
```

   This code extends the **if** statement to check for a second condition if the first condition is not met. The object of interest here is **prevBtn**. If **prevBtn** triggered the event, the script sends the playhead to the previous frame **C**.

5. To register for the **click** event of the **prevBtn**, place the cursor at the end of Line 24, press Enter to create a new Line (25), then type

```
prevBtn.addEventListener(
 ↪ MouseEvent.CLICK, handleClick );
```

6. Preview the action.

   Save the file, check the syntax (Lines 6–25 should match **D**), correct any errors, then test the movie.

   Clicking the **enterBtn** button advances the playhead one frame. Clicking the **prevBtn** sends the playhead back one frame.

Scripting Movie Clips to Act As Buttons

Flash's button symbols provide the most basic visual requirements for a button, giving you the options for different looks in the Up, Over, and Down states. Sometimes, however, you may need additional states. In a slide show, for example, the Next button should be disabled (and should look disabled) when you are viewing the last slide.

In Chapter 14 you learned how to set up a movie-clip symbol for use as a button that has a disabled state. In the following task, you learn to program that symbol to work as a button.

To enable button behavior for the movie-clip button:

1. Open the file named MyOwnBtn.fla that you created in Chapter 14, in the section "Creating Movie-Clip Buttons."

   This document contains a movie-clip symbol called **MovieClipBtn**.

2. On the Stage, double-click the instance of the **MovieClipBtn** symbol to enter symbol-editing mode.

   The symbol's Timeline has three layers—Actions, Labels, and Button-Graphics. The symbol has keyframes labeled **_up**, **_over**, **_down**, and **Disabled**, and graphics that make each state obvious **A**.

3. In the symbol's Timeline, select Keyframe 1 in the Actions layer **B**.

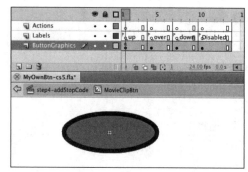

A This movie-clip symbol has keyframes for four button states: the standard three—Up, Over, and Down—plus a fourth, Disabled. Each keyframe has an appropriate frame label.

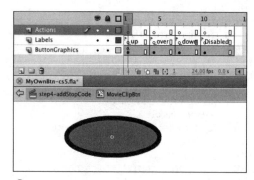

B To prevent the movie-clip button from displaying its frames as an animation, you need to add a stop action to the Timeline of the button itself. Add it to Frame 1 of the Actions layer.

C The code to activate button behavior.

```
1    stop();
2    buttonMode = true;
```

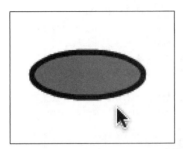

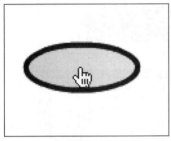

D By labeling the frames of your movie-clip **button_up**, **_over**, and **_down**, you can take advantage of built-in ActionScript to give users feedback about the button. Adding the **buttonMode = true;** statement to the button's script tells Flash to change the pointer to the hand icon when it moves over the graphic content in a frame with one of those labels.

4. To pause the movie-clip button, in the Script pane of the Actions panel, in Line 1, type

stop();

By default, movie clips play at runtime. While that makes sense for animations, a button should stay in its Up state until the user interacts with it.

5. With the cursor at the end of Line 1, press Enter to create a new line.

6. To activate button behavior for the movie clip, in Line 2, type

buttonMode = true;

Until you do that, the movie clip doesn't know it's supposed to act like a button, despite the special frame labels you used.

7. Save your document, and check the syntax of your code (your script should match **C**).

8. Navigate back to the main Timeline—for example, by choosing Edit > Edit Document.

9. Choose Control > Test Scene.

As it rolls over the movie-clip button, the pointer changes to a hand, and the playhead goes to the movie-clip's **_over** frame **D**. When you press the mouse button, the playhead goes to the **_down** frame—just as it does for a regular button.

TIP If you want to try out your button without first returning to document-editing mode, choose Control > Test Movie > In Flash Professional (choosing Test Scene will not work).

To add a mouse event–handler that displays the disabled state:

1. Continuing with the file from the previous task, select the **MovieClipBtn** instance on the Stage and access the Property inspector.

2. In the Instance Name field, enter a name—for example, **myBtn** 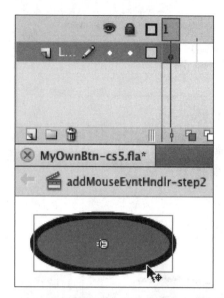.

3. In the Timeline of the document, create a new layer above the existing layer; name the new layer Actions.

   With multiple layers in the Timeline, it's a good idea to name them all. Give the layer containing the movie-clip button a name—for example, **MC Button**.

4. Select Keyframe 1 in the Actions layer, and access the Actions panel.

5. In the Script pane, in Line 1, to document your script, type **//** followed by a description, and press Enter to create a new line.

   Adding a comment such as **// Scripting a movie-clip button** reminds you (and informs others) of what you intend your script to do.

6. With the cursor in Line 2, type **stop();** to pause the movie, then press Enter to create a new line.

7. To create a variable for the symbol instance, in Lines 3 and 4, type

   // Declare Stage instances

   var myBtn:MovieClip;

   This activates code hints by telling Flash that the instance **myBtn** is a **MovieClip** object. Flash automatically creates an **import** statement in Line 1

   import flash.display.MovieClip;

   and the script you entered in this step moves down to Lines 5 and 6 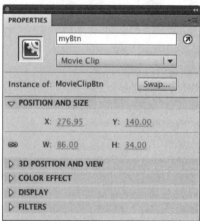.

E To target the movie-clip button, you must name the instance in the Property inspector's Instance Name field.

F An import statement, a descriptive comment, pausing the Timeline, and declaring the Stage instance variable.

```
1  import flash.display.MovieClip;
2
3  // Scripting a movie-clip button
4  stop();
5  // Declare Stage instances
6  var myBtn:MovieClip;
```

G Adding the event handler.

```
1    import flash.display.MovieClip;
2    import flash.events.MouseEvent;
3
4    // Scripting a movie-clip button
5    stop();
6    // Declare Stage instances
7    var myBtn:MovieClip;
8    // Event handlers
9    function handleClick( pEvent:MouseEvent
     ):void
10   {
11       if( pEvent.target == myBtn )
12       {
13           myBtn.enabled = false;
14           myBtn.gotoAndStop( "Disabled" );
15       }
16   }
```

8. With the cursor at the end of Line 6, press Enter to begin a new block of code.

9. To define the event handler, starting in Line 7, type

// Event handlers

function handleClick(
→ pEvent:MouseEvent):void

{

    if(pEvent.target == myBtn)

    {

        myBtn.enabled = false;

        myBtn.gotoAndStop("Disabled"
        →);

    }

}

As you enter **MouseEvent** in Line 8, Flash automatically inserts an **import** statement in Line 2,

import flash.events.MouseEvent;

The code you just entered moves down. Line 9 defines the event handler. Line 11 makes sure the event was triggered by the button instance you intend, **myBtn**. Line 13 prevents the button from receiving anymore mouse events by setting the movie-clip instance's **enabled** property to **false**. Line 14 sends the playhead to the **Disabled** frame of the movie-clip (without the code in Line 13 the playhead would go back to the **_up** frame as soon as the user rolled out of the active movie-clip area) **G**.

continues on next page

10. To register for the click event, with the cursor at the end of Line 16, press Enter to create a new line; in new Lines 17 and 18, type

// Register events

myBtn.addEventListener(
→ **MouseEvent.CLICK, handleClick);**

11. Save your document, check the syntax of your code (your script should match **H**), then choose Control > Test Scene.

Your movie opens in a Flash Player window. The movie-clip button displays the **_up** frame. When you put the mouse within the button, it displays the **_over** frame. When you click the button, the playhead moves to the **_down** frame. As soon as you let go of the mouse button, the playhead moves to the **Disabled** frame, and the movie-clip button no longer reacts to the mouse.

TIP **The procedure for scripting interactive buttons and movie-clip buttons is identical. If you start a project using buttons, and later realize you need more functionality, you don't have to start over. Replace the buttons with movie-clip buttons using the same instance names, and your code will still work. You can then add movie-clip–specific scripts to display additional states, as shown in the preceding task.**

H The completed movie-clip button script.

```
1    import flash.display.MovieClip;
2    import flash.events.MouseEvent;
3
4    // Scripting a movie-clip button
5    stop();
6    // Declare Stage instances
7    var myBtn:MovieClip;
8    // Event handlers
9    function handleClick( pEvent:MouseEvent
     ):void
10   {
11      if( pEvent.target == myBtn )
12      {
13         myBtn.enabled = false;
14         myBtn.gotoAndStop( "Disabled" );
15      }
16   }
17   // Register events
18   myBtn.addEventListener( MouseEvent.CLICK,
     handleClick );
```

Using Buttons to Control Timelines

Most Flash creations employ a mixture of interface objects: button symbols, button components, and movie clips. You can script a button (or button component) to start and stop the playback of a movie clip, or make the playhead jump to a specific frame in a movie clip. The key is to specify the correct target path.

The Mystery of Target Paths

All Flash creations have a certain amount of structural complexity. Even a simple movie like the one created with ButtonActionsMaster has a hierarchy of nested objects. (The Timeline you see when you open a Flash document in the authoring environment is actually a movie-clip object, so any objects on this main Timeline are considered nested objects.) But the structure gets really complex when you nest interactive objects inside other interactive objects—a button inside a movie clip, a movie clip inside a movie clip, a button inside a movie clip inside a movie clip, and so on.

A nested object is known as a *child object,* and the object containing that child is known as the *parent object.* As long as each parent and child has an instance name, it doesn't matter how complex the family relationship gets. You can create a script that manipulates any of the nested objects. The key is to identify the target object's place in the hierarchy of Timelines using a *target path.*

There are two types of target paths: *relative* and *absolute.* A relative target path starts with the target object and describes its relationship to other Timelines in the hierarchy—indicating, for example, that the target is me, or it's one level above me; or it's within me, one level down. An absolute target path starts with the highest-level Timeline and works its way down the hierarchy until it reaches the target object.

Just to complicate things, however, ActionScript 3.0 has another type of interactive object, the *sprite.* A sprite is similar to a movie clip, but it has no Timeline and no frames. All of the animation and interactivity of a sprite happens because of scripting. Sprites can also be nested and have hierarchical relationships. And you use target paths to identify them. When you write target paths, you must distinguish between sprite objects and Timeline-based objects (movie clips) by using the code **Sprite()** or **MovieClip()**—as shown in the examples below. (In this book, we work only with Timeline-based objects.)

When using the Actions panel's Insert Target Path button (see sidebar "Using Insert Target Path," later in this chapter), Flash will insert the generic code **Object()** instead. This is technically correct and hides the differences between sprites and movie clips, but prevents you from getting code hints for actions like **gotoAndStop()**.

continues on next page

To make a button stop movie-clip playback:

1. Open a new ActionScript 3.0 Flash document, add layers to create a three-layer document, and do the following:

   ▸ Name the top layer Actions.

   ▸ Name the second layer Buttons. In that layer, place a button-symbol instance at the upper-left corner of the Stage.

   ▸ Name the third layer MovieClips. In that layer, at the center of the Stage, place a movie-clip instance containing animation (for example, a simple classic tween or motion tween of a geometric shape that rotates and shrinks).

   ▸ Save the file and name it PauseClip-Control.fla.

2. To prepare the instances for scripting, do the following:

   ▸ Access the Property inspector.

   ▸ Select the button, and in the Instance Name field, enter **controlBtn**.

   ▸ Select the movie clip, and in the Instance Name field, enter **animMc**.

3. In the Actions layer, select Frame 1 and access the Actions panel.

The Mystery of Target Paths *continued*

To start a relative target path, simply type the instance name of the object you want to target, such as **animMc**.

A relative path isn't restricted to looking at objects contained within the current Timeline. You can also go one or more levels up or down. This is where the concept of parent and child comes into play. Let's say you have a button with an instance name of **controlBtn** on the main Timeline where you've placed **animMc**. In the Timeline of **animMc**, you could write

`MovieClip(parent).controlBtn`

This path directs ActionScript to go one level up to the parent Timeline, the one containing **animMc** (in this example, it's the main Timeline) and access the instance named **controlBtn**. Whenever you use the code **parent** you must either distinguish between sprites and movie clips—by using **Sprite()** or **MovieClip()**—or hide the difference by using **Object()**.

To target child objects, use dot syntax (place a period between the parent object and its child). To direct ActionScript to go down a level to access a movie-clip instance named **starMc** that's nested within **animMc**, the relative path would be **animMc.starMc**.

Optionally, you can start a relative target path with the code **this**. For example, **this.animMc.starMc** is the same as **animMc.starMc**.

An absolute path always starts at the main Timeline, which is also known as **root**. The format of an absolute target path for **starMC** looks like this:

`MovieClip(root).animMc.starMc`.

Whenever you use the code **root** you must distinguish between sprites and movie clips—by using **Sprite()** or **MovieClip()**—or hide the difference by using **Object()**.

Commented script that pauses the Timeline and defines variables.

```
1   import flash.display.SimpleButton;
2   import flash.display.MovieClip;
3
4   // Controlling a movie clip with a
    button
5   stop();
6   // Declare Stage instances
7   var controlBtn:SimpleButton;
8   var animMc:MovieClip;
```

B Defining the event handler that checks for the event source.

```
2   import flash.display.MovieClip;
3   import flash.events.MouseEvent;
4
5   // Controlling a movie clip with a
    button
6   stop();
7   // Declare stage instances
8   var controlBtn:SimpleButton;
9   var animMc:MovieClip;
10  // Event handler
11  function handleClick( pEvent:MouseEvent
    ):void
12  {
13      if( pEvent.target == controlBtn )
14      {
15          // Handle event
16      }
17  }
```

4. To comment your script and pause the main Timeline at startup, in the Script pane of the Actions panel, in Lines 1 and 2, type

> `// Controlling a movie clip with`
> `→ a button`
>
> `stop();`

5. To enable code hints for the instances on the Stage, starting in Line 3 create the following variables:

> `// Declare Stage instances`
>
> `var controlBtn:SimpleButton;`
>
> `var animMc:MovieClip;`

As you define the variables, Flash automatically inserts **import** statements in Lines 1 and 2 and adds a blank Line 3; the code you just entered moves down to Lines 6–8 **A**.

6. To define an event handler that verifies the event source, starting in Line 9, type

> `// Event handler`
>
> `function handleClick(`
> `→ pEvent:MouseEvent ):void`
>
> `{`
>
> `    if( pEvent.target == controlBtn )`
>
> `    {`
>
> `        // Handle event`
>
> `    }`
>
> `}`

This defines an event handler that makes sure the event is triggered by **controlBtn**. As you enter **MouseEvent**, Flash automatically creates an **import** statement in Line 3; the code you just entered moves down to Lines 10–17 **B**.

7. To register for the **controlBtn**'s **click** event, in Lines 18 and 19, type

`// Register events`

`controlBtn.addEventListener(`
`→ MouseEvent.CLICK, handleClick );`

The main Timeline now receives the **click** event of the **controlBtn**, and you are ready to direct Flash to take control of the movie-clip instance **animMc** Ⓒ.

8. Place the cursor at the end of Line 15, press Enter to create a new Line 16, and type

`animMc`

This is a relative target path: this script now aims from the main Timeline (where the script is located) to the **animMc** instance.

9. With the cursor at the end of Line 16, directly after the target path, type

`.stop();`

This **stop** action attached to the target path tells Flash to pause playback of the movie-clip instance named **animMc**.

10. Preview the action.

Save the file, check the syntax (the code should match Ⓓ), correct any errors, then test the movie (see "Previewing Actions at Work").

In the Flash Player window, the animation plays in a continuous loop. When you click the button, the animation pauses.

Ⓒ Registering the **click** event of controlBtn.

```
18   // Register events
19   controlBtn.addEventListener(
     MouseEvent.CLICK, handleClick );
```

Ⓓ The completed script to pause a clip when a button is clicked.

```
1    import flash.display.SimpleButton;
2    import flash.display.MovieClip;
3    import flash.events.MouseEvent;
4
5    // Controlling a movie clip with a
     button
6    stop();
7    // Declare Stage instances
8    var controlBtn:SimpleButton;
9    var animMc:MovieClip;
10   // Event handler
11   function handleClick( pEvent:MouseEvent
     ):void
12   {
13       if( pEvent.target == controlBtn )
14       {
15           // Handle event
16           animMc.stop();
17       }
18   }
19   // Register events
20   controlBtn.addEventListener(
     MouseEvent.CLICK, handleClick );
```

Using Insert Target Path

In the Actions panel, the toolbar above the Script pane displays an Insert Target Path button (the small crosshair icon). This target-path tool is very helpful for creating both absolute and relative target paths. There is one caveat: the target-path tool creates incorrect relative paths when the Timeline panel has focus. As you prepare to insert a target path, make sure the Timeline doesn't have focus. Clicking a blank area of the Stage is an easy way to remove focus from the Timeline.

To add a target path to the Script pane, position the cursor at the location where you want to insert the code. Click the Insert Target Path button. The Insert Target Path dialog opens. As you click different objects in the dialog's representation of the Timeline hierarchy, the dialog's target-path field updates automatically. To determine which type of path to create, select the Absolute or Relative radio button at the bottom of the dialog. Once you have chosen the object you want to target and the type of path, click OK to add the path to the Script pane.

An example of an absolute path:

```
Object(root).oval
```

An example of a relative path:

```
Object(this.parent).oval
```

This format differs slightly from what you learned in the sidebar "The Mystery of Target Paths" (earlier in this chapter), using **Object()** instead of **MovieClip()**. Either code works; however, using **MovieClip()** gives you the added benefit of getting better code-hints when targeting **root** or **parent** directly.

Linking to Other Web Pages

Flash gives you two ways to open new files by linking to URLs. You can select text on the Stage and turn it into a live link by entering a URL in the Link field in the Options section of the Text (Tool) Property inspector. You can also use ActionScript to instruct Flash Player to open a URL. Both techniques let you open the new file in a different browser window or different frame of the current window.

To create a text link to a URL:

1. On the Stage, select the text that you want to be a link, and access the Property inspector.

   You can select individual letters or words using the text tool, or select an entire text field using the selection tool.

2. For TLF text, in the Advanced Character section, enter the desired URL in the Link field 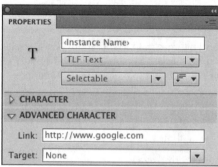.

3. To choose a method for displaying the specified URL in the browser window, from the Target pop-up menu **B**, choose one of the following:

   None and **_blank** open the URL in a new browser window.

   _self opens the URL in same frame of the browser window as that of the content being currently viewed.

   _parent opens the URL in the parent of the current frame.

   _top opens the URL in the top-level frame of the current browser window.

   When you open the published HTML file from your hard drive and click the link to another website, you may get

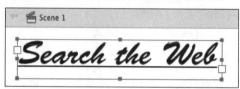

A You can turn text into a live link for accessing web pages. Select the TLf text on the Stage (top). In the Advanced Character section of the Property inspector, type a URL in the Link field (middle). Flash creates a live link in the published Flash movie. Live-link text appears underlined in the authoring environment (bottom).

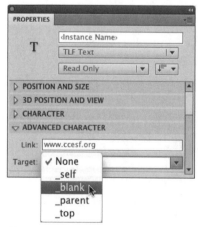

B The Target menu specifies how Flash should open the link's URL in a browser window.

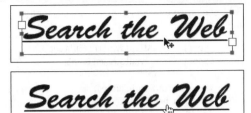

C The underlined TLF text (top) is a live link created in the Property inspector. In the published movie (bottom), the text is also underlined, and the hand pointer appears when you move the pointer into the text field.

security errors (see the sidebar "A Note About Flash Player 10's Security Settings," in Chapter 18). For links to work properly, you need to put the published files on a web server.

4. Choose Control > Test Scene to try out your live link text.

   When you move the pointer over the text, the pointing-finger cursor appears **C**; when you click the text, Flash opens the URL in the specified form of browser window.

TIP If you're creating your live link with Classic text, you'll find the Link field and Target menu in the Options section of the Text Property inspector.

To script a button that opens a web page:

1. Open a new document using the ButtonActionsMaster template you created earlier in this chapter, and save it as LinkBtn.fla.

   The Timeline has three layers—Actions, Buttons, and Frames.

2. To create the button that opens a new web page, do the following:

   ▸ In the Timeline, select Frame 5 of the Buttons layer, and insert a blank keyframe (for example, by choosing Insert > Timeline > Blank Keyframe).

   ▸ With Keyframe 5 of the Buttons layer selected, drag an instance of a button symbol to the Stage, and access the Property inspector.

   ▸ With the button instance selected on the Stage, in the Instance Name field, enter an instance name, such as `linkBtn`.

continues on next page

3. In the Timeline, select Frame 5 of the Actions layer, insert a blank keyframe, and access the Actions panel.

In previous tasks you've always created scripts in Keyframe 1 that start working with objects in Frame 1. One way to create a script that relates to objects in a later frame is to add a blank keyframe in the Actions layer at that frame to hold the script.

4. To create a variable that activates code-hints, in the Script pane of the Actions panel, in Line 1, type

var linkBtn:SimpleButton;

Flash automatically adds an **import** statement in Line 1, and a blank Line 2.

5. To create the event handler that checks for the event source, do the following:

▸ With the cursor at the end of Line 3, press Enter to begin a new code block.

▸ Starting in Line 4, type

function handleLink(
⟶ pEvent:MouseEvent):void
{

   if(pEvent.target == linkBtn)
   {

   }
}

As you complete Line 4, Flash automatically adds a second **import** statement in Line 2,

import flash.net.URLRequest;

and pushes your code down to 5–11. The code so far should match **D**.

D Defining an event handler that checks for the event source.

```
1    import flash.display.SimpleButton;
2    import flash.events.MouseEvent;
3
4    var linkBtn:SimpleButton;
5    function handleLink( pEvent:MouseEvent
     ):void
6    {
7        if( pEvent.target == linkBtn )
8        {
9
10       }
11   }
```

```
10      }
11  }
12  linkBtn.addEventListener(
    MouseEvent.CLICK, handleLink );
```

6. To register for the **click** event, with the cursor at the end of Line 11 (after the closing brace), press Enter to begin Line 12, and type

```
linkBtn.addEventListener(
→ MouseEvent.CLICK, handleLink );
```

The code should match **E**.

7. To create the network request, do the following:

   ▸ With the cursor indented in Line 9, type

   ```
   var request:URLRequest =
   → new URLRequest( "http://
   → www.google.com" );
   ```

   Flash again adds an **import** statement in Line 3 as you enter this code, and pushes your code down to Line 10.

   Replace the link to Google with the URL you want to link to. In ActionScript 3.0, you need to create a **URLRequest** object with the URL to make any kind of external connection. Here the **URLRequest** is then stored in a custom variable called **request**.

   continues on next page

8. To create the code that tells Flash to execute the link, with the cursor at the end of Line 10 (after the semicolon), press Enter to begin a new Line 11, and type

navigateToURL(request, "_blank");

The parameter **_blank** is the same method for opening a browser window that you chose from a menu in Step 3 of the first task in this section, "To create a text link to a URL." To use a different method, use the code **_self, _parent**, or **_top**; but be aware that you may need to create new security settings for those methods (for more details, see the sidebar "A Note About Flash Player 10's Security Settings," in Chapter 18).

9. Preview the action.

Save the file, check the syntax (the code should match **F**), correct any errors, then test the movie (see "Previewing Actions at Work").

The first button that appears is one that you scripted as part of the template document. Clicking this button advances the movie to the next frame. Click this button until you reach Frame 5. Clicking the button in Frame 5 makes the default browser open a new window or tab with the URL you specified.

TIP You don't always have to create scripts in a blank keyframe. Often the Actions layer's keyframe already exists, with script for controlling another button instance. You can simply add the new script to the end of the existing script. In the preceding exercise, for example, try adding the web-page button to Keyframe 1. Create the script at the end of the script that was already in the **ButtonActionsMaster** document. The line numbers will be different, but the button should work just fine.

F Making a button link to another web page.

```
1   import flash.display.SimpleButton;
2   import flash.events.MouseEvent;
3   import flash.net.URLRequest;
4
5   var linkBtn:SimpleButton;
6   function handleLink( pEvent:MouseEvent
    ):void
7   {
8       if( pEvent.target == linkBtn )
9       {
10          var request:URLRequest = new
            URLRequest( "http://www.google.com"
            );
11          navigateToURL( request, "_blank" );
12      }
13  }
14  linkBtn.addEventListener(
    MouseEvent. CLICK, handleLink );
```

Practice Session

In the Practice Session for Chapter 14, you created a fully animated button symbol named **orbBtn**. Its **Down** frame contains an animation of exploding glitter. In a published movie, that animation loops for as long as the user keeps the mouse button down in the active button area. Try adding a **stop();** action to the animation so there's just one burst of glitter when the users clicks the button. Then add a frame script to program that button to navigate the Timeline.

- Using the FrameActionsMaster template you created at the beginning of this chapter, open a new document. It has 5 frames with identifying text. Add a layer named Buttons.

- In Keyframe 1 of the Buttons layer, place an instance of **orbBtn** on the Stage. You could, for example, open the library of your Chapter 14 practice document and drag a copy of **orbBtn** to the Stage (see Chapter 7).

- Edit the animation of the movie-clip symbol used in **orbBtn**'s Down frame. Access the Library panel, for example, and double-click the symbol **downOrbMc** to enter symbol-editing mode. Add a layer named Actions to the Timeline. Insert a blank keyframe in that layer at the final frame of the animation. Add a comment line and a **stop();** action to that keyframe (see *Adding Frame Actions*). Then return to document-editing mode.

- In Keyframe 1 of the Buttons layer, place a second instance of **orbBtn** on the Stage. Assign instance names to your buttons: for example, use **nextBtn** and **prevBtn**.

continues on next page

- Select Keyframe 1 of the Actions layer and create a frame script that programs **nextBtn** to go to the next frame and programs **prevBtn** to go to the previous frame (see *Programming Buttons with Frame Scripts* and *Using One Event Handler with Multiple Events*). Hint: Remember to use your precise instance names.

- Check your script and test your buttons (see *Previewing Actions at Work*). As you move the mouse over each glowing button, a halo of glitter should appear. Click the buttons to move forward and backward through the movie. With each click, the button's glitter should explode just once, even if you hold down the mouse button for a few seconds.

Extra Credit

In the Practice Session for Chapter 14, you set up a movie-clip button with frames for **_up**, **_over**, **_down**, and **Finished**. Program that movie-clip symbol to work as a button and to display its Finished frame when clicked.

16

Using Non-Flash Graphics

Adobe Flash Professional CS5's drawing tools are powerful and flexible, but you may prefer the tools offered by another vector graphics program—Adobe Illustrator or Adobe FreeHand, for example. Or you may want to use artwork created in Adobe Photoshop or include scanned photos or other bitmaps in your Flash document. Fortunately, you can import vector art and bitmapped graphics through the Clipboard or the Import command. You can also drag and drop items from Photoshop CS5, Illustrator CS5, and FreeHand versions 7–11 (MX), directly into Flash.

This chapter teaches the basics of the import process via tasks for importing bitmaps and Adobe Photoshop files. You can also import files from Adobe Illustrator, Fireworks, and FreeHand. The Web bonus material for the previous edition of this book covered basic import options for those programs. That information is available with the bonus materials for this edition. Note that the material has not been updated for CS5, so there may be minor interface changes.

In This Chapter

Importing Bitmaps

No matter what type of non-Flash artwork you wish to import, the first steps of the import process are the same.

To import bitmaps:

1. In a Flash document, choose File > Import > Import to Stage.

    If this is the first request to import a file in the current work session, a progress bar named Preparing to Import appears, then an Import dialog appears **Ⓐ**. (For subsequent imports, there is no Preparing progress bar.)

    When you choose Import to Stage, Flash imports the file into your document, stores a master bitmap asset in the library, and places an instance of the bitmap on the Stage in the current keyframe of the active layer **Ⓑ**.

2. From the Enable (Mac) or Files of Type (Windows) menu, choose the format of the file you want to import.

3. Navigate to the file on your system.

4. Select the file.

5. Click Import (Mac) or Open (Windows).

    The bitmap is now available in the Library and on the Stage.

> **TIP** In Step 1 of this task, you could choose File > Import > Import to Library. The Import to Library command places assets in the library but not on the Stage.

> **TIP** You can edit an imported bitmap in any installed bitmap-editing program. Select the bitmap in the Library panel, Control-click (Mac) or right-click (Windows) the bitmap icon, and choose Edit With from the contextual menu. In the window that opens, navigate to an editing program and click Open. Edit and save the bitmap; Flash updates it in the library.

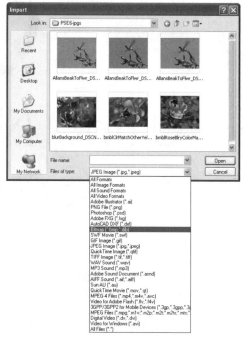

Ⓐ Bring graphics created in other applications into your Flash document through the Import dialog.

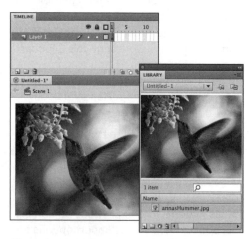

Ⓑ When you import a bitmap to the Stage, Flash stores a master copy of the bitmap in the library.

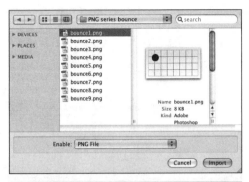

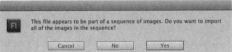

C When you import one file in a series of numbered files (top), Flash asks whether you want to import the whole series (bottom).

Preview mode shows images in keyframes

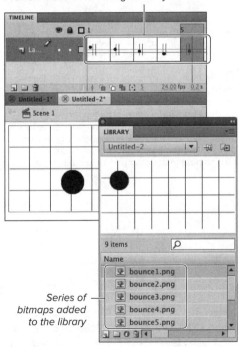

Series of bitmaps added to the library

D When Flash imports a numbered series of files, it places each one in a separate keyframe in the Timeline of the current document.

To import a series of graphics files:

1. Follow Steps 1–5 of the preceding task. In Step 2, choose the appropriate format, and navigate to the first file in the series.

   The series must be in a single folder, and the filenames must differ only by a number at the end—for example, bounce1, bounce2, and bounce3. If these conditions are met, a dialog appears, asking if you want to import a series of sequential images **C**.

2. In the dialog, click Yes.

   Flash places each image in a separate keyframe in the active layer **D**.

Import to Library vs. Import to Stage

When you import files, you choose to import to the Stage or library. When importing to the Stage, Flash places the items on the Stage, and re-creates any layer hierarchy in the main Timeline of the document. Imported content also goes in the library.

When importing to the library, Flash places the content in the library; but for Photoshop, Illustrator, and Fireworks PNG files, Flash also creates a movie-clip or graphic symbol that contains the content. Flash places the imported content on the symbol's Stage, and re-creates the layer hierarchy in the symbol's Timeline.

Some dialogs present slightly different choices when you choose Import to Library than when you choose Import to Stage. For example, when you import Illustrator and Photoshop files to the library, you can't opt to place objects at their original position or set the Stage size.

Importing Photoshop Files

When you import content from Photoshop, Flash automatically imports according to your Preferences settings. Using the Import command opens the PSD Import dialog, where you can view and change the settings for individual layers.

To set import preferences for Photoshop (PSD) files:

1. From the Flash (Mac) or Edit (Windows) menu, choose Preferences.

   The Preferences dialog appears.

2. In the Category list, choose PSD File Importer.

   Options for importing PSD files appear on the right side of the dialog 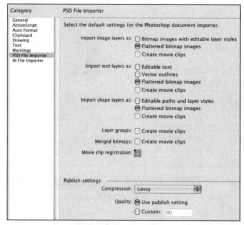.

3. To set options for importing image layers , do one of the following:

   ▸ To retain as much of an image layer's opacity and applied blend modes as Flash can handle, select the "Bitmap images with editable layer styles" radio button.

   ▸ To replicate the look of the image layer most faithfully, select the Flattened Bitmap Images radio button. When this radio button is selected, to have Flash create both a bitmap

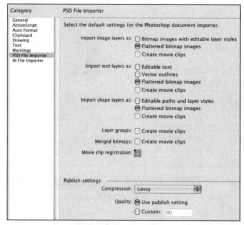

A Choosing PSD File Importer from the Category list in the Preferences dialog gives you access to options for importing PSD files.

B You have two choices for importing PSD image layers. If you choose to import them with editable layer styles (top), Flash automatically creates movie-clip symbols to hold the imported layers and applies appropriate Flash blend modes to the symbol instance. If you import image layers as bitmaps (bottom), you can choose to create movie clips to hold them, or import only the bitmaps.

What Graphics Formats Does Flash Import?

Flash CS5 imports a variety of bitmapped and vector-graphic file formats, including Adobe Illustrator version 10 or earlier (AI), Adobe Photoshop (PSD), Adobe XML Graphic File (FXG), AutoCAD 10 (DXF), Bitmap (BMP, DIB), Flash Player 6/7 (SWF), FutureSplash Player (SPL), GIF and animated GIF, JPEG, PNG, and Windows Metafile (WMF). On Windows, Flash can also import Enhanced Windows Metafile (EMF) files. If you have QuickTime 4 or later installed on your system, CS5 can also import QuickTime Image (QTIF) and TIFF files.

Import text layers as:
- ⦿ Editable text
- ○ Vector outlines
- ○ Flattened bitmap images
- ☐ Create movie clips

Import text layers as:
- ○ Editable text
- ⦿ Vector outlines
- ○ Flattened bitmap images
- ☑ Create movie clips

Import text layers as:
- ○ Editable text
- ○ Vector outlines
- ⦿ Flattened bitmap images
- ☐ Create movie clips

C You have three options for importing PSD text: as editable text fields (top), as editable shapes (middle), and as bitmaps (bottom). If you choose to import text as editable text fields, Flash creates them as TLF text, set to Selectable. If you choose to import text as editable shapes, Flash automatically creates movie clips to hold them.

Import shape layers as:
- ⦿ Editable paths and layer styles
- ○ Flattened bitmap images
- ☑ Create movie clips

Import shape layers as:
- ○ Editable paths and layer styles
- ⦿ Flattened bitmap images
- ☐ Create movie clips

D When you import PSD shape layers as editable paths (top), Flash automatically places the paths inside a movie-clip symbol. When you import shape layers as bitmaps (bottom), you can choose whether or not to have Flash place them in movie clips by selecting the Create Movie Clips checkbox.

Layer groups: ☐ Create movie clips

E When you import PSD layer groups, you can have Flash place them inside movie clips.

Merged bitmaps: ☐ Create movie clips

F If you choose to merge PSD layers for import, you can have Flash place the merged layers inside movie clips.

and a movie clip containing the bitmap, select the Create Movie Clips checkbox.

4. To set options for importing text layers **C**, do any of the following:

   ▸ To import text as Selectable TLF text fields, select the Editable Text radio button.

   ▸ To import text as editable shapes, select the Vector Outlines radio button.

   ▸ To import text as bitmaps, select the Flattened Bitmap Images radio button.

   ▸ To have Flash place the TLF text field or flattened bitmap inside a movie-clip symbol on import, select the Create Movie Clips checkbox.

5. To set options for importing shape layers **D**, do one of the following:

   ▸ To import an editable shape that retains as much of its opacity and applied blend modes as Flash can handle, select the "Editable paths and layer styles" radio button.

   ▸ To replicate the look of the shape most faithfully, select the Flattened Bitmap Images radio button. When this radio button is selected, to have Flash place the bitmap inside a movie-clip symbol, select the Create Movie Clips checkbox.

6. To convert grouped layers to movie clips, in the Layer Groups section, select the Create Movie Clips checkbox **E**.

7. To convert any merged layers to movie clips, in the Merged Bitmaps section, select the Create Movie Clips checkbox **F**. (For more on merging layers, see the next task, "To import content from PSD files.")

continues on next page

8. To set the registration point for any movie-clip symbols created during the import process, in the Movie Clip Registration section, click one of the nine squares in the registration grid 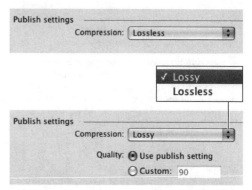.

By default, Flash assigns the same registration point to all movie clips created during import. You can override this setting for individual movie clips in the PSD Import dialog. To learn more about the registration point and symbols, see Chapter 7.

9. In the Publish Settings section **H**, choose one of the following from the Compression pop-up menu:

   ▶ To retain all image data for imported PSD items when publishing your Flash file, choose Lossless. Flash applies Lossless compression when creating the SWF file for playback. Lossless compression creates the highest-quality images, but also creates larger file sizes. To learn more about publishing, see Chapter 18.

   or

   ▶ To apply JPEG compression to imported PSD items during publishing, choose Lossy. Select the Use Publish Setting radio button to apply the JPEG quality currently specified in Publish Settings, or select the Custom radio button and enter a value between 0 and 100 to override the JPEG quality. Higher values retain more image data, creating better-looking images but larger files.

10. Click OK to confirm the current Preferences settings and close the dialog.

G In the Preferences dialog's PSD Importer category, clicking one of the nine squares in the registration grid sets the default registration point for movie-clip symbols imported from PSD files.

H The Compression pop-up menu lets you choose which compression method Flash applies during publishing. Lossless compression (top) preserves all the image data. Lossy compression (bottom) lets you determine how much data is lost.

A Note About Photoshop Adjustment Layers

Flash has no equivalent to Photoshop's adjustment layers. If a selected layer in the PSD file has an adjustment layer and you want to maintain the visual effect, import the selected layer as a bitmap. Otherwise, Flash ignores the adjustment layer on import.

Layers pane   *Options pane*

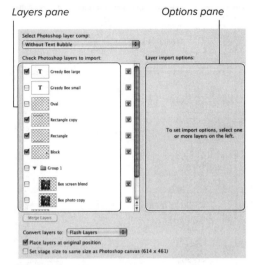

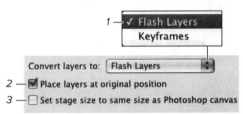

① The Layers pane, on the left in the PSD Import dialog, displays a scrolling list of content available for import. When you select an item in the list, its settings appear in the Options pane, on the right in the dialog. General import settings appear in the lower half of the dialog.

① The lower portion of the PSD Import dialog offers settings that apply to the entire imported content. You can choose how Flash deals with the PSD file's layer structure (1), how to position the imported objects on the Stage (2), and whether or not to resize the Stage to match the dimensions of the PSD file (3).

To import content from PSD files:

1. Follow Steps 1–5 of the first task in the preceding section, "Importing Bitmaps." In Step 2, choose Photoshop as the format, and navigate to the file you want to import.

   After you click the Import (Mac) or Open (Windows) button, the PSD Import dialog appears **①**.

2. To set import options that apply to the whole document, in the lower portion of the PSD Import dialog **①**, do any of the following:

   ► From the Convert Layers To pop-up menu, choose a conversion method. To re-create the PSD file's layer structure as Timeline layers, choose Flash Layers. To convert the PSD layers to keyframes, choose Keyframes.

   ► To have Flash place the items on the Stage at their original *x*- and *y*-coordinates, select the "Place layers at original position" checkbox. Otherwise, Flash centers imported layers on the Stage (the imported items will retain their positions relative to one another).

   ► To resize the Stage of your Flash document to match the dimensions of the PSD file, select the "Set Stage size to same size as Photoshop canvas" checkbox.

continues on next page

3. To identify layers for import, in the Layers pane, select the checkbox to the left of each item you want to import; deselect the checkbox next to any items you don't want to import 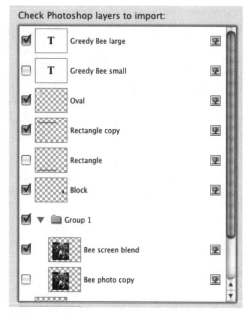.

If the PSD file contains layer groups, the Layers pane displays them hierarchically. Click the triangle to the left of the group name to expand or collapse the set. To select (or deselect) the checkboxes of all the layers in a group, select (or deselect) the checkbox to the left of the group name.

4. To merge layers for import, in the Layers pane, Shift-click the name of each layer you want to combine, then click the Merge Layers button 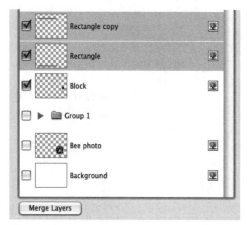.

Flash creates a new layer in the Layers pane with a default name of Merged Bitmap. The individual layers are listed hierarchically beneath the Merged Bitmap layer. Flash combines the items on the merged layers and imports them as a bitmap.

K In the Layers pane, selected checkboxes indicate items you want to import.

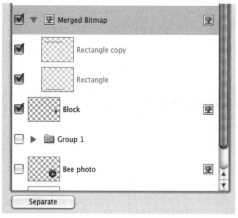

L To merge layers for import, in the Layers pane, shift-click the name of each layer you want to combine, then click the Merge Layers button (left). Flash combines the layers. Original layers appear hierarchically beneath the merged layer (right).

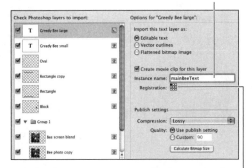

Enter instance name

Select registration point for this movie clip

M Selecting an item in the Layers pane gives you access to its import settings in the Options pane. Whenever the item can be imported as a movie clip, Flash displays an Instance Name field and a registration grid. Choosing a new registration point for an individual movie clip overrides the default registration-point location currently set in Preferences. The new registration point applies only to the movie clip created from the selected item in the Layers pane.

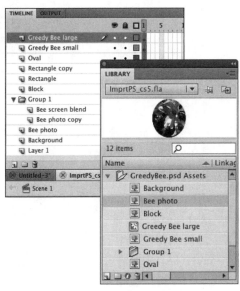

N When you use the Import to Stage command, Flash imports all the items selected in the Layers pane and places them on the Stage (top). (Here, import options were set to re-create the PSD layers in the Flash Timeline.) Flash adds a folder to the library to hold the assets created by importing the PSD files (bottom).

5. To override PSD Import Preference settings for individual layers, click the layer name to select it in the Layers pane and choose new settings in the Options pane **M**.

6. After selecting the layers that you want to import and adjusting the import settings as desired, click OK.

Flash imports all the selected items, places them on the Stage, and places the associated assets in the library **N**.

TIP If the source PSD file contains *layer comps* (a layer-management feature for quickly viewing various combinations of visible and hidden layers), a Select Photoshop Layer Comp pop-up menu appears at the top of the PSD Import dialog. When you select a comp version from the menu, Flash automatically selects the checkboxes of the visible layers in that version and deselects the checkboxes of layers that are hidden.

TIP You can Shift-click to select multiple contiguous PSD layers; the settings you choose in the right-hand pane apply to all the selected items.

TIP You can rename the layers during import. In the Layers pane, double-click the name of a layer to activate its text field; enter a new name, and press Enter to confirm the name. When Flash creates the layers and assets, it uses the new name.

Practice Session

- Try importing a digital photograph (JPEG) directly to the library of your current document. (See *Importing Bitmaps*.) Now drag the bitmap to the Stage.

Adding Sound and Video

Adobe Flash Professional CS5 lets you incorporate sound and video in your projects to create a full multimedia experience. Sound in Flash can be an ongoing background element or a synchronized element that matches a particular piece of action. To add a sound, you import a sound-clip file to the library and then place an instance of the sound on the Stage. To add video, you can import the video data and embed it into the Flash Timeline, or you can add a component that displays external video files. Advanced scripters can use Action-Script to add and control sounds during playback or to display encoded video files as streaming video in their Flash creations. (The scripting techniques, however, are beyond the scope of a *Visual QuickStart Guide*.) In all cases, the video data must be encoded in a format that's compatible with Flash; for embedded video, the file must be in FLV (Flash video) format. You can use Adobe Media Encoder CS5 (AME), which comes with Flash and is installed by default, to encode video files in an appropriate format.

Importing Sounds

There are two commands for importing sounds: File > Import > Import to Stage or File > Import > Import to Library. Both commands bring the sound file into the library for the current document. Neither actually places the sound, however. You must drag a copy of the sound from the Library panel to the Stage to make the sound available for assignment to a keyframe.

To import a sound file:

1. Open the file to which you want to add sounds.

2. Choose File > Import > Import to Stage or press Command-R (Mac) or Ctrl-R (Windows) **A**.

   You can also choose File > Import > Import to Library. The standard file-import dialog appears **B**. (The first time you choose an import command during a work session, a progress bar labeled Preparing to Import appears before the file-import dialog appears.)

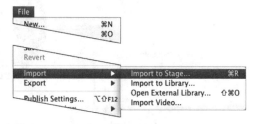

A Choose File > Import > Import to Stage (or Import to Library) to bring sounds into your Flash document.

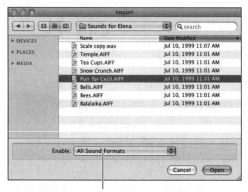

Choose file type

B The Import dialog lets you bring sound files into Flash. Choose a sound-file type that is appropriate for your platform from the pop-up menu of file types.

What Sound Formats Does Flash Import?

Flash deals only with *sampled sounds*—those that have been recorded digitally or converted to digital format. Flash imports files in AIFF format for the Mac OS and files in WAV format for Windows. For both platforms, Flash imports files in MP3 format and ASND format (a sound file format created by Adobe Soundbooth). In addition, with the combination of Flash CS5 and QuickTime 4 (or later versions), users on both platforms can import QuickTime movies containing just sounds (MOV, QT) and Sun AU files; Mac users can add import of WAV, Sound Designer II (SD2), and System 7 sounds (SND); and Windows users can add import of AIFF sounds. Any sounds you import or copy into a Flash document reside in the file's library.

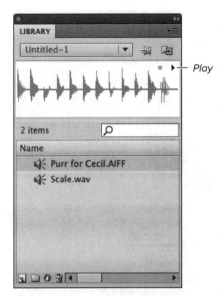

— Play

C Flash keeps sound files in the library. You can see the waveform for a selected sound in the preview window. Click the Play button to hear the sound.

Flashy Sounds

Flash CS5 comes with a common library of sound effects that you can use in your Flash movies. To access these sounds, choose Window > Common Libraries > Sounds. Flash opens a library containing 186 sounds. You use these sound assets just as you'd use sounds you imported to a document. Drag the sound asset from the Sounds common library to the Stage of your Flash document (see the next section, "Adding Sounds to Frames").

3. From the Enable pop-up menu (Mac) or the Files of Type pop-up menu (Windows), choose the format of the sound file you want to import.

   Choose All Sound Formats to see files in any sound format.

4. Navigate to the sound file on your system.

5. Select the file.

6. Click Import (Mac) or Open (Windows).

   Flash imports the sound file you selected, placing it in the library. When you select the sound in the library, the sound's waveform appears in the preview window **C**. Sound files can be quite large; as sounds import, a dialog named Importing appears, showing a progress bar. You can stop the import by clicking the Stop (Mac) or Cancel (Windows) button in the dialog.

TIP Despite the fact that one command choice is named Import to Stage, when you work with sounds, all imported assets wind up in the library. You must drag an instance of a sound clip to the Stage yourself to place it in a keyframe initially. Once the sound has been placed, you can assign it to other keyframes via the Property inspector.

TIP You can hear a sound without placing it in a movie. Select the sound in the Library panel. Flash displays the waveform in the preview window. To hear the sound, click the Play button in the preview window.

Adding Sounds to Frames

You can assign a sound to a keyframe the same way you place a symbol or bitmap: by selecting the keyframe and then dragging a copy of the sound from an open Library panel (either that document's or another's) to the Stage. You can also assign any sound that resides in a document's library to a selected keyframe in that document by choosing the sound from the Name pop-up menu in the Sound section of the Frame Property inspector.

To assign a sound to a keyframe:

1. Open a Flash document to which you want to add sound.

   The Ping-Pong animation you created in Chapter 12 makes a good practice file. The document contains a motion tween in which a ball connects with a paddle at four position keyframes. Adding sound can heighten the reality of that contact: you can make the sound realistic (say, a small *thwock*) or make it humorous, if the sound is unexpected (a *boing,* for example).

2. Add a new layer for the sounds in your document, name it Sound, and set its Layer Height Property to 200% 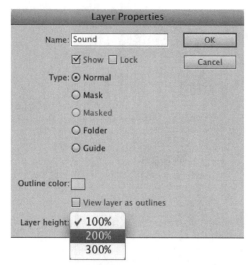.

   (For details on how to set up a sound layer, see the sidebar "Organizing Sounds," later in this chapter.)

3. In the Timeline, select the Sound layer, and add keyframes at Frames 5, 10, 15, and 20.

   These four keyframes match the position keyframes in which the ball hits one of the paddles in the motion tweens that make up the animation 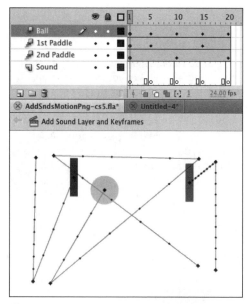.

A It's a good idea to enlarge sound layers to make viewing sound waves easier. Double-click the layer icon in the Timeline to access the Layer Properties dialog, then choose 200% or 300% for layer height.

B Create a separate layer for the sounds in your movie. In that layer, add a keyframe at each place where you want a sound to occur. Here, the keyframes in the Sound layer correspond to the position keyframes in the tween spans where the ball makes contact with a paddle.

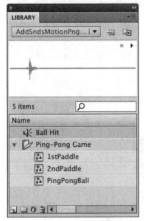

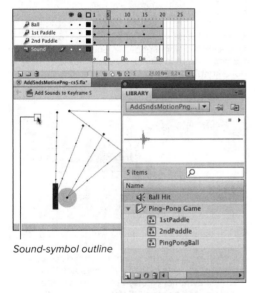

Sound-symbol outline

Waveform of the sound assigned to Keyframe 5

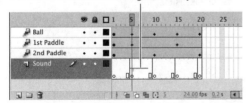

C After you've imported a sound, it appears in the Library panel. Select the sound, and drag it to a keyframe.

D When you drag a sound from the Library panel to the Stage, you see the symbol outline (top). A sound has no visible presence on the Stage, but Flash displays the sound's waveform in a keyframe span in the Timeline (bottom).

4. Import the sound you want to hear when the paddle connects with the ball.

5. In the Timeline, select Keyframe 5 of the Sound layer.

This is the first frame in which the ball and paddle connect.

6. Access the Library panel, and select your sound **C**.

Its waveform appears in the preview window.

7. Drag a copy of the sound from the Library panel to the Stage.

Although sounds have no visible presence on the Stage, you must drag the sound copy to the Stage. As you drag the sound, you see the outline of a box on the Stage. When you release the mouse button, Flash puts the sound in the selected keyframe and displays the waveform in that keyframe and any in-between frames associated with it **D**.

8. In the Timeline, select Keyframe 10 of the Sound layer.

This is the second frame in which the ball and paddle connect.

9. Access the Frame Property inspector.

continues on next page

10. In the Sound section, from the Name pop-up menu, choose your sound.

All the sounds in the document's library are available from the menu **E**. You don't have to drag a copy of the sound to the Stage each time you want to turn on that sound in a keyframe.

For now, leave the other Sound settings alone. You'll learn more about them in later tasks.

11. Repeat Steps 6 and 7 (or 8, 9, and 10) for Keyframes 15 and 20.

After adding the sound to the Sound layer's four keyframes, you're ready to play the movie and check out the sounds **F**. As each paddle strikes the ball, Flash plays the assigned sound, adding a level of realism to this simple Ping-Pong animation.

TIP Flash CS5's common library of sounds (see the sidebar "Flashy Sounds," earlier in this chapter) contains a nice sound effect for this task. It's called Sports Ball Ping Pong Ball Hit Table Single01.mp3.

E In the Sound section of the Frame Property inspector, the Name pop-up menu lists all the sounds that are in the library of the current document. From this menu, you can choose a sound that you want to assign to the keyframe that's selected in the Timeline.

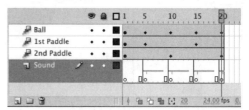

F For each spot in the movie where a sound should occur, add a sound to a keyframe in the Sound layer. A condensed image of the sound's waveform appears in the keyframe span. Within a single keyframe, you won't see much of the waveform; in Keyframe 20, for example, just the initial line is visible.

Organizing Sounds

Nothing prevents you from placing sounds in regular layers that contain other content, but your document will be easier to handle—and sounds will be easier to find for updating and editing—if you always put sounds in separate layers reserved for a soundtrack. You cannot place sounds in motion-tween spans or inverse kinematics (IK) pose spans. Here are some tips for working with layers for sounds:

- Name layers as a reminder of their content. For detailed instructions on working with layers, see Chapter 6.

- Place all the sound layers either at the bottom of the Timeline or at the top, so you can find them easily. The position of layers in the stacking order has no effect on the playback of sounds in the movie.

- Create a layer folder for sounds. Flash Player 8–10.1 can handle up to 32 sounds playing at one time; earlier Flash Player versions can handle up to 8 simultaneous sounds. (You'll learn about publishing for Flash Player in Chapter 18.) If you put each sound on a separate layer, that's a lot to track. If you'll be working with lots of sound layers, create a layer folder and name it Sound-Tracks. Placing all the sound layers in the SoundTracks folder makes it easier to work with the sounds 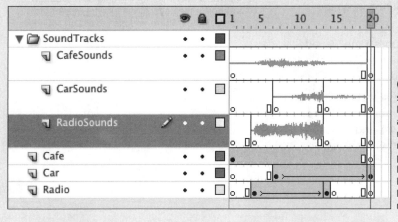.

- Increase the height for sound layers to make it easier to see the waveform (a graphic image of the sound) for that layer. Choose Modify > Timeline > Layer Properties (or double-click the layer icon of the selected layer) to access the Layer Properties dialog. From the Layer Height pop-up menu, choose 200% or 300% to make the layer taller. Click OK.

- After you've placed sounds in a layer, lock the layer—to prevent yourself from adding graphics to it accidentally—by clicking the bullet in the Lock column.

- To avoid adding sounds to the wrong layer, Option-click (Mac) or Alt-click (Windows) the bullet in the padlock column for the sound layer you want to work with. Flash locks all other layers.

G It's best to keep sounds in separate layers from the graphics and actions in your movie. To organize multiple sound layers, place them in a separate layer folder. Increase the layer height for sound layers to make more room for the waveforms.

Adding Sounds to Buttons

Auditory feedback helps people who view your Flash creation interact with buttons correctly. For buttons that look like real-world buttons, adding a click sound to the Down frame provides a more realistic feel. For more fanciful buttons or ones disguised as part of the scenery of your movie, adding sound to the Over frame lets users know they've discovered a hot spot.

To enhance buttons with auditory feedback:

1. Open a Flash document containing a button symbol to which you want to add sound.

   (To learn about working with button symbols, see Chapter 14.)

2. Open the file's Library panel (choose Window > Library), and select the button symbol you want to modify.

3. From the library's panel menu, choose Edit .

   Flash opens the button in symbol-editing mode.

4. In the button symbol's Timeline, add a new layer (click the New Layer button), and name it Sound.

5. In the Sound layer, select the Over and Down frames, Control-click (Mac) or right-click (Windows), and choose Convert to Blank Keyframes 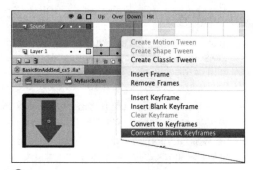.

Ⓐ To edit a symbol, you can select it in the Library panel and choose Edit from the panel menu.

Ⓑ Add a new layer for the sounds in a button symbol. In that layer, create keyframes for the button states where you plan to assign sounds.

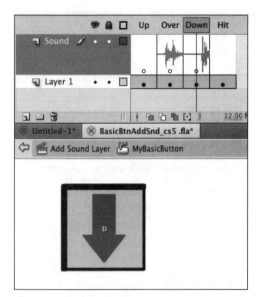

C Flash displays the waveform of the assigned sound in the keyframe. Unlike movie Timelines, button-symbol Timelines have no in-between frames that can contain part of the waveform. Increasing the layer height for a button symbol's Sound layer enlarges any waveforms in the button's frames, letting you see more detail.

6. Using the techniques described in "Adding Sounds to Frames," earlier in this chapter, assign a sound to the Over frame and a different sound to the Down frame.

   Flash displays as much of the waveform as possible in each frame. When you add sounds to buttons, it makes sense to increase the height of the layer that contains sounds **C**. Make sure that the sound's Sync property is set to Event (the default) in the Sound section of the Frame Property inspector. (You'll learn more about setting the Sync property in the next section.)

7. Return to document-editing mode.

   Every instance of the button symbol in the document now has sounds attached.

8. To hear the buttons in action, choose Control > Enable Simple Buttons.

   When you move the pointer over the button, Flash plays the sound you assigned to the Over frame. When you click the button, you hear the sound you assigned to the Down frame.

   TIP The most common frames to use for button feedback are the Over and Down frames, but you can add sounds to any of the button symbol's frames. Sounds added to the Up frame play when the pointer rolls out of the active button area. Sounds added to the Hit frame play when you release the mouse button within the active button area.

Using Event Sounds

One of the parameters available in the Sound section of the Frame Property inspector is Sync. Sync determines the way Flash synchronizes the sounds in your movie. Sync has four settings: Event, Start, Stop, and Stream. The default is Event.

Event sounds play independently of the main Timeline. Flash starts an event sound at a keyframe in a movie; the event sound plays until Flash reaches the end of the sound clip or encounters an instruction to stop playing that sound or all sounds. Long event sounds can continue to play after the playhead reaches the last frame in the movie. If your movie loops, every time the playhead passes a frame with an event sound, Flash starts another instance of that sound playing.

To understand how synchronization works, it's helpful to work in a file that has identifying text in keyframes.

To set up a file for testing sounds:

1. Create a 20-frame, three-layer Flash document.

2. Label the layers Objects, Sound 1, and Sound 2.

3. In all layers, insert keyframes into Frames 5, 10, 15, and 20 (Frame 1 has a keyframe by default).

4. In the Objects layer, place identifying text on the Stage for each keyframe.

5. Import several sounds of different lengths into the file's library.

   This example uses a 15.8-second sound clip of a musical-scale passage, a water-drop sound, a melodic passage, and some rhythm sounds.

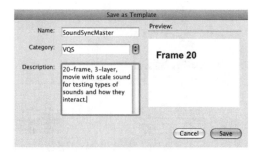

A After setting up a testing file for use in this chapter, choose File > Save As Template to access the Save As Template dialog. Save the file as SoundSyncMaster. Be sure to close the template document after creating it. For detailed instructions on saving documents as templates, see Chapter 1.

Independent Sounds vs. Synchronized Sounds

Unsynchronized sound clips play independently of the frames in a movie and can even continue playing after the playhead reaches the last frame in the movie. Flash starts these *event sounds* at a specific frame, but thereafter, event sounds play without relation to specific frames. On one viewer's computer, the sound may play over ten frames; on a slower setup, the sound may finish when only five frames have appeared.

Flash can also synchronize entire sound clips with specific frames. Flash breaks these *stream sounds* or *streaming sounds* into smaller pieces and attaches each piece to a specific frame. For streaming sounds, Flash forces the animation to keep up with the sounds. On slower setups, Flash draws fewer frames so important actions and sounds stay together.

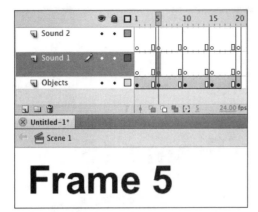

Frame 5

B Select the keyframe to which you want to assign a sound. Settings that you create in the Sound section of the Frame Property inspector are applied to the selected keyframe.

C In the Sound section of the Frame Property inspector, choose a sound from the Name pop-up menu.

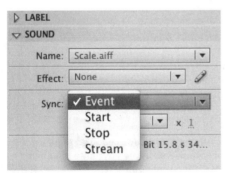

D From the Sync pop-up menu, choose Event to make the assigned sound start in the selected keyframe and play to the end of the sound, without synchronizing to any subsequent frames of the movie.

6. Save the document as a template for use throughout this chapter, and name it SoundSyncMaster **A**.

To make an assigned sound an event sound:

1. Open a new document using the SoundSyncMaster template you created in the preceding task.

2. In the Timeline, select Keyframe 5 of the Sound 1 layer **B**.

3. In the Sound section of the Frame Property inspector, from the Name pop-up menu, choose a long sound, such as the 15.8-second sound named Scale.aiff **C**.

4. From the Sync pop-up menu, choose Event **D**.

   The Scale.aiff sound is assigned to Keyframe 5 of the Sound 1 layer.

5. Position the playhead in Keyframe 1, and play your movie (choose Control > Play).

   In a movie that has a standard frame rate of 24 frames per second (fps), the 15.8-second Scale sound continues to play after the playhead reaches the last frame of the movie.

TIP To understand better how Flash handles event sounds, choose Control > Loop Playback. Now play the movie again, and let it loop through a couple of times. Each time the playhead enters Keyframe 5, Flash starts another instance of the Scale sound, and you begin to hear not one set of notes going up the scale, but a cacophony of bad harmonies. When you stop the playback, each sound instance plays out until its end—an effect sort of like people singing a round.

To play overlapping instances of the same sound:

1. Using the file you created in the preceding task, to assign a sound to a later point in the movie's Timeline, do either of the following:

   ▸ Select Keyframe 15 of the Sound 1 layer.

   ▸ Select Keyframe 15 of the Sound 2 layer.

   Because Flash starts a new instance of an event sound even if that sound is already playing, you have the choice of adding a second instance to the same layer as the first or adding it to a different layer.

2. In the Sound section of the Frame Property inspector, from the Name pop-up menu, choose the same sound (Scale.aiff).

3. From the Sync pop-up menu, choose Event.

   The Scale.aiff sound is assigned to Keyframe 15 of whichever layer you chose **E**.

4. Position the playhead in Keyframe 1, and play your movie one time.

   When the playhead reaches Keyframe 5, the Scale.aiff sound starts. When the playhead reaches Keyframe 15, another instance of the Scale.aiff sound starts, and the two sounds play together (you hear two voices). When the first instance ends, you again hear only one voice. Within a single layer, each frame can contain only one sound. To make Flash begin playing different sounds at the same point in a movie, you must put the sounds in separate layers.

5. Save this file for use in a later task; name it OverlapSnds.fla.

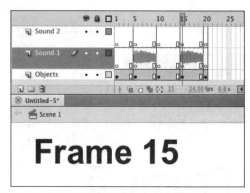

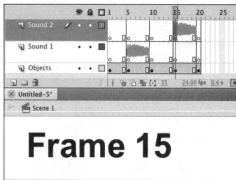

E You can add a second instance of your sound and make it play on top of the first. Event sounds play independent of the main Timeline, so you're free to add the second sound to the same layer as the first (top). Alternatively, you can add the second sound to its own layer (bottom).

TIP All the information required to play an event sound lives in the keyframe to which you assigned that sound. When you play the movie, Flash pauses at that keyframe until all the information has downloaded. It's best to reserve event syncing for short sound clips; otherwise, your movie may be interrupted by long pauses for downloading sounds.

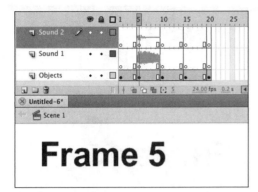

F To make two different sounds begin playing simultaneously, you must put each sound in a different layer in a keyframe at the same spot in the Timeline—for example, Keyframe 5.

To start different sounds simultaneously:

1. Open a new document using the SoundSyncMaster template you created earlier in this chapter.

2. In the Timeline, select Keyframe 5 of the Sound 1 layer.

3. In the Sound section of the Frame Property inspector, from the Name pop-up menu, choose the first sound (here, Scale.aiff).

4. From the Sync pop-up menu, choose Event.

5. In the Timeline, select Keyframe 5 of the Sound 2 layer.

6. In the Sound section of the Frame Property inspector, from the Name pop-up menu, choose a different sound (here, Rhythm.aiff).

   You can also import a new sound to your movie's library, or open the Sounds common library or the Library panel of another movie containing the sound you want to use, and then drag a copy of the sound to the Stage.

   Flash places the waveform for the second sound in Keyframe 5 of the Sound 2 layer **F**.

7. In the Sound section of the Frame Property inspector, from the Sync pop-up menu, choose Event.

8. Position the playhead in Keyframe 1, and play your movie one time.

   When the playhead reaches Keyframe 5, Flash starts playing the Scale.aiff and Melody.aiff sounds simultaneously.

Using Start Sounds

Start sounds behave just like event sounds, with one important difference: Flash doesn't play a new instance of a start sound if that sound is already playing.

To set an assigned sound's Sync parameter to Start:

1. Open OverlapSnds.fla, the file you created in "Using Event Sounds > To play overlapping instances of the same sound," earlier in this chapter.

   One instance of the Scale.aiff sound is in Keyframe 5; another is in Keyframe 15, in the Sound 1 or Sound 2 layer, depending on what you did in the earlier task.

2. In the Timeline, select Keyframe 15 containing Scale.aiff .

3. In the Sound section of the Frame Property inspector, from the Sync pop-up menu, choose Start **B**.

4. Position the playhead in Keyframe 1, and play your movie one time.

   When the playhead reaches Keyframe 5, the Scale.aiff sound starts. When the playhead reaches Keyframe 15, nothing changes; you continue to hear just one voice as the Scale.aiff sound continues playing. When a sound is playing and Flash encounters another instance of the same sound, the Sync setting determines whether Flash plays that sound. When Sync is set to Start, Flash doesn't play another instance of the sound.

TIP To avoid playing multiple instances of a sound when a movie loops, set the sound's Sync property to Start. If the sound is playing when the movie starts again, Flash adds no new sound. If the sound is done, Flash restarts the sound again when the playhead enters a keyframe containing the sound.

A To change a sound's Sync setting, first select the keyframe that contains the sound.

B To prevent Flash from playing another instance of a sound if that sound is already playing, choose Start from the Sync pop-up menu in the Sound section of the Frame Property inspector.

The Mystery of Streaming Sound

When you choose Stream as the Sync setting for a sound, Flash divides that sound clip into smaller subclips and embeds them in individual frames. The movie's frame rate determines the subclips' size. In a movie with a frame rate of 10 frames per second (fps), for example, Flash divides streaming sounds into subclips that are a tenth of a second long. For every 10 frames, Flash plays 1 second of the sound.

Flash synchronizes the start of each subclip with a specific frame of the movie. If the sound plays back faster than the computer can draw frames, Flash sacrifices some visuals (skips drawing some frames of the animation) so that sound and images match up as closely as possible. Setting a sound's Sync property to Stream ensures, for example, that you hear the door slam when you see it swing shut—not a few seconds before. If the discrepancy between sound-playback speed and frame-drawing speed is big enough, however, those dropped frames make the movie look jerky, just as it would if you set a low frame rate to begin with.

Using Stream Sounds

Stream sounds are specifically geared for playback over the web. When Sync is set to Stream, Flash breaks a sound into smaller sound clips. Flash synchronizes these subclips with specific frames of the movie—as many frames as are required to play the sound. Flash stops streaming sounds when playback reaches either a new keyframe in the sound's layer or an instruction to stop playing that specific sound or all sounds.

Unlike event sounds, which must download fully before they can play, stream sounds can start playing after a few frames have downloaded. This situation makes streaming the best choice for long sounds, especially if you'll be delivering your movie over the web.

To make an assigned sound a stream sound:

1. Open a new document using the SoundSyncMaster template you created earlier in this chapter.

2. In the Timeline, in the Sound 1 layer, remove keyframe status from Keyframe 10 (select it and choose Modify > Timeline > Clear Keyframe).

3. In the Timeline, in the Sound 1 layer, select Keyframe 5.

4. In the Sound section of the Frame Property inspector, from the Name pop-up menu, choose a long sound (here, Scale.aiff).

5. From the Sync pop-up menu, choose Stream **Ⓐ**.

continues on next page

6. To see how the sound fits into the available time in your movie, in the Sound section of the Frame Property inspector, click the Edit Sound Envelope button (the pencil icon).

The Edit Envelope dialog appears.

At 15.8 seconds, the Scale.aiff sound is too long to play completely in the frames between Keyframe 5 and Keyframe 15. When Sync is set to Stream, Flash plays only as much of the sound as can fit in the frames that are available to it—in this case, slightly less than a half second. In the Edit Envelope dialog, a vertical line indicates where Flash truncates this instance of the sound **B**.

7. To close the Edit Envelope dialog, click OK or Cancel.

The truncated waveform appears in the keyframe span **C**.

8. Position the playhead in Keyframe 1, and play your movie to hear the sound in action.

When the playhead reaches Keyframe 5, the Scale.aiff sound starts. When the playhead reaches Keyframe 15, the keyframe span ends, and Flash stops playback of the Scale.aiff sound.

9. Choose Control > Loop Playback, and then play the movie to hear the sound in looping mode.

Flash repeats the same snippet of sound, stopping it each time the playhead reaches Keyframe 15.

TIP You can hear streaming sounds play as you drag the playhead through the Timeline—a technique called *scrubbing*. As the playhead moves over the waveform, you can see how the images and sounds fit together. You can then add or delete frames to better synchronize the sounds with the images onscreen.

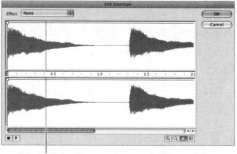

Sound will stop playing here

B When you set a sound's Sync to Stream, you can check how much of the sound will play, given the number of in-between frames there are for the sound to play in. In the Sound section of the Frame Property inspector, click the Edit Sound Envelope button (the pencil icon; top) to open the Edit Envelope dialog (bottom). The sound-editing window displays a sound's full waveform in relation to time or to frame numbers.

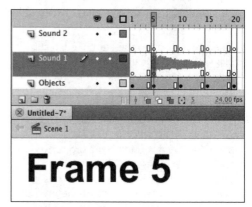

C There is time enough in the nine-frame keyframe span to play only the first note of the Scale sound. Flash displays just that much of the full 15.8-second waveform in the Timeline.

The Rhythm sound   *The Melody sound*

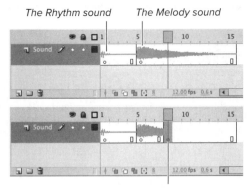

After adding blank keyframe

A Inserting a new keyframe cuts off your view of the preceding sound's waveform in the Timeline. If the sound is an event sound, however, it continues playing even when the playhead moves past the keyframe.

B To stop a sound's playback at a specific point in a movie, create and then select the keyframe where the sound should stop. In the Sound section of the Frame Property inspector, from the Name pop-up menu, choose the sound you want to stop. From the Sync pop-up menu, choose Stop. Here, the Stop instruction refers to the Rhythm sound.

Stopping Sounds

Although event sounds normally play to the end, you can force them to stop at a specific keyframe. To issue an instruction to stop a specific sound, set that sound's Sync property to Stop.

To stop playback of a sound:

1. Create a new single-layer 15-frame Flash document with two fairly long event sounds (at least 2 or 3 seconds each); place one sound in Keyframe 1 and the other in Keyframe 5.

   In this example, Keyframe 1 contains the sound Rhythm.aiff, and Keyframe 5 contains the sound Melody.aiff. Make sure that Sync is set to Event for both sounds.

2. In the Timeline, at Frame 8, insert a new blank keyframe **A**.

   The blank keyframe cuts off the waveform in the Timeline, but on playback, both event sounds continue to play after the playhead reaches Keyframe 8.

3. Select Keyframe 8.

4. In the Sound section of the Frame Property inspector, from the Name pop-up menu, choose Rhythm.aiff.

5. From the Sync pop-up menu, choose Stop **B**.

   Flash uses this instruction to stop playback of the Rhythm.aiff sound at Keyframe 8.

continues on next page

Flash places a small square in the middle of Keyframe 8 in the Timeline to indicate that the frame contains a stop-sound instruction 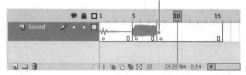.

6. Position the playhead in Keyframe 1, and play your movie to hear the sounds in action.

The Rhythm.aiff sound starts immediately; Melody.aiff kicks in at Keyframe 5. When the playhead reaches Keyframe 8, Rhythm.aiff cuts out, but Melody.aiff plays on even after the playhead reaches the end of the movie.

TIP The Stop setting and the sound that it stops can be in different layers. The Stop setting stops playback of all instances of the specified sound that are currently playing in any layer.

TIP To stop only one instance of a sound, set the Sync parameter of that instance to Stream; then, in the layer containing that instance, put a blank keyframe in the frame where you want that instance of the sound to stop.

Sync is set to Stop for this keyframe

C In the Timeline, a small square in the middle of a keyframe indicates the presence of the stop-sound instruction.

Using Buttons to Control Sounds

In this chapter, you learn to use sounds two ways. You create user-friendly buttons with audio feedback by adding sounds to keyframes in button symbols. You create soundtracks or sound effects for animation by adding and removing sound instances directly in the Timeline during authoring. A third way to work with sound is to use ActionScript (AS) to control sounds during playback—loading, playing, and stopping sounds as needed at runtime.

Two of Flash's predefined Code Snippets create frame scripts that let end users accomplish common sound-related tasks by clicking a button: one script sets up a button that stops all the sounds currently playing; the other script sets up a button that toggles a sound loaded from an external file on and off. Advanced scripters can also create their own sound-control objects, then add frame scripts that target those sound-control objects. When setting up buttons to control sounds, you must set the sound's Linkage properties. Scripting sounds is a complex task, beyond the scope of a *Visual QuickStart Guide*. To learn about creating basic frame scripts in ActionScript 3.0, see Chapter 15.

Editing Sounds

Flash lets you make limited changes in each instance of a sound in the Edit Envelope dialog. You can change the start point and end point of the sound (that is, cut a piece off the beginning or end of the waveform) and adjust the sound's volume.

Flash offers six predefined volume edits: Left Channel, Right Channel, Fade Left to Right, Fade Right to Left, Fade In, and Fade Out. These sound-editing templates create common sound effects, such as making a sound grow gradually louder (Fade In) or softer (Fade Out), or (for stereo sounds) making the sound move from one speaker channel to the other.

In addition to changing a sound's volume, you can make a sound shorter by instructing Flash to remove sound data from the beginning of the waveform, the end, or both.

To assign packaged volume effects:

1. Open a new document, and add a 20-frame soundtrack.

   Add a layer named Sounds, give it 20 defined frames, and place a sound in Keyframe 1 of that layer. For this task, use the sound Animal Dog Bark 26.mp3 from the Sounds common library. This sound clip is a recording of a dog that barks three times. If you like, add more defined frames to the Sounds layer to see more of the sound's waveform in the Timeline.

2. In the Timeline, select Keyframe 1 of the Sounds layer.

3. In the Sound section of the Frame Property inspector, click the Edit Sound Envelope button (the pencil icon).

   The Edit Envelope dialog appears, with a sound-editing window showing the waveform of the sound from Keyframe 1 **A**.

continues on next page

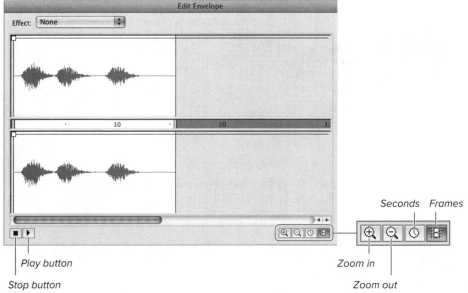

A Flash lets you perform simple sound editing—for length and volume—in the Edit Envelope dialog.

4. In the Edit Envelope dialog, click the Frames button.

The sound-editing window can measure the length of the sound in seconds or in frames. Clicking the filmstrip icon in the lower-right corner of the window sets the units to frames; clicking the clock icon sets the units to seconds.

5. From the Effect pop-up menu, choose Fade In **B**.

Flash adjusts the sound envelope **C**. When the envelope line is at the top of the sound-editing window, Flash plays 100 percent of the available sound. When the envelope line is at the bottom of the window, Flash plays 0 percent of the available sound.

6. Click the Play button to hear the sound with its fade-in effect.

The barking starts soft and grows louder.

7. Click OK.

Flash returns you to document-editing mode.

TIP If you don't need to look at your sound's waveform, you can bypass the Edit Envelope dialog. Just choose an effect from the Effect pop-up menu in the Sound section of the Frame Property inspector.

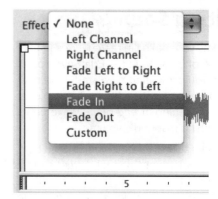

B The Effect pop-up menu in the Edit Envelope dialog offers six templates for common sound effects that deal with volume. Choose Fade In to make the sound start soft and grow in volume.

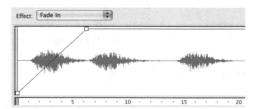

C The Fade In effect brings the sound's envelope down to 0 percent (the bottom of the sound-editing window) at the start of the sound and quickly raises it to 100 percent (the top of the sound-editing window).

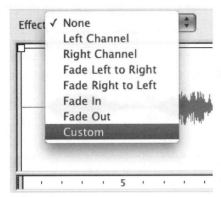

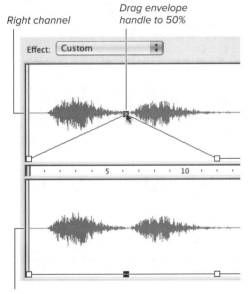

D To edit the volume of a sound yourself, from the Effect pop-up menu in the Edit Envelope dialog, choose Custom.

Right channel

Drag envelope handle to 50%

Left channel

E Click the waveform in the sound-editing window to add a handle. Drag the handle to adjust the sound envelope. You can make the sound envelope the same or different for both channels. For monaural sounds, both waveforms are identical.

To customize volume effects:

1. Follow Steps 1–3 in the preceding task.

2. From the Effect pop-up menu in the Edit Envelope dialog, choose Custom **D**.

3. In the sound-editing window, drag the square envelope handles that appear at the beginning of the sound in both channels down to 0 percent.

4. In the right channel (the top section of the window), click the waveform at three places to set a different level for different parts of the sound.

   For this example, click the waveform at Frames 6, 12, and 20. Flash adds envelope handles so both channels have four handles. Divide the sound roughly into thirds.

5. In the right-channel window, drag the second handle up to the 50 percent volume level **E**.

6. Repeat Step 5 for the left channel.

7. In both channels, drag the third handle to the 50 percent level and the fourth handle to the 100 percent level.

   You can use as many as eight handles to create a variety of volume changes within one sound.

8. Click the Play button to hear the sound with its fade-in effect.

   Flash fades in the dog's first bark, plays the second bark at half volume, and plays the last bark at full volume.

9. Click OK.

TIP To remove unwanted envelope handles, drag them out of the sound-editing window.

To edit sounds for length:

1. Using the movie you created in the preceding task, select Keyframe 1.

2. To access the Edit Envelope dialog, in the Sound section of the Frame Property inspector, click the Edit Sound Envelope button.

3. In the sound-editing window, drag the Time-out control (the bar on the right-hand side of the "Timeline" between the two channels) to the end of the sound where the waveform begins to go flat **F**. You may need to scroll to see the flat part of the wave.

   Flash shortens the sound in both channels **G**.

4. Click OK.

   Flash returns you to document-editing mode. Now the waveform of the entire sound is visible in the keyframe span in the Timeline **H**.

TIP If you don't see the Time-out control in the sound-editing window, scroll to the right to find the end of the waveform.

TIP To remove dead air from the beginning of a sound, drag the Time-in control. Flash places a light-gray background behind the initial portion of the sound's waveform to indicate that it won't play.

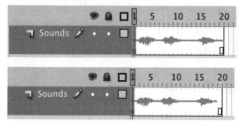

H The original sound is too long to fit within the keyframe span in the Timeline. After you shorten the sound, the shorter wave fits completely in the keyframe span.

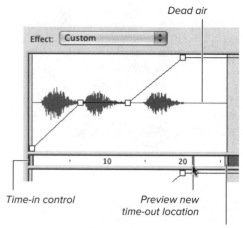

Dead air

Time-in control

Preview new time-out location

Time-out control

F Flash lets you trim the beginning and end of a sound in the Edit Envelope dialog's sound-editing window. Here, dragging the Time-out control clips off the end of the sound where the wave's amplitude is smaller, almost a flat line. (The small amplitude indicates a very soft sound or silence.)

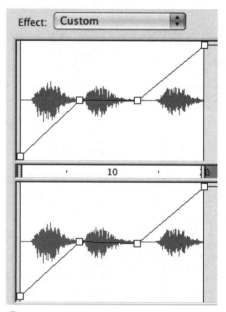

G After you reposition the Time-out control, the new, shorter waveform appears in the Edit Envelope dialog's sound-editing window.

About Encoding Video for Flash

Flash's Video Import Wizard can only handle files that have already been encoded in a Flash-compatible format (FLV and F4V are examples). When you choose to import for embedding, the wizard only allows files in FLV format. Flash includes a stand-alone video encoder—Adobe Media Encoder CS5—that lets you encode video data in the appropriate formats to work with Flash. AME lets you encode multiple files in batches. You create a list of files, then choose encoding options for video- and audio-compression, add filters, create cue points, and perform basic edits (cropping and resizing). Not sure if your video file is in a Flash-compatible format? Try importing it with the wizard. If the data is not encoded appropriately, the wizard notifies you. You can open up AME quickly by clicking the Launch Adobe Media button on the Select Video page of the wizard.

Adding Video to Flash

The process for adding video to Flash is similar to the process for adding sound. You start by choosing the Import Video command. This command accesses Flash's Video Import Wizard. The wizard asks you to locate an encoded video file and choose how you want to deliver the video. You can embed the video data to make it part of the FLA file during authoring; after you publish your movie for playback, the embedded video data becomes part of the SWF file (see Chapter 18). Alternatively, you can create a link to an encoded video file and use a component to display the video data at runtime. The Video Import Wizard ensures that the video data you select is encoded correctly. The wizard then imports the data or makes the appropriate link to it. The precise steps vary somewhat depending on the delivery method you choose.

Importing Video for Streaming or Progressive Download

Flash can stream video over the web or deliver video as a progressive download. Both methods allow you to work with larger amounts of video data and avoid delays in playback while video data downloads to the end user's system. To deploy the video as streaming or progressive download, you must use a playback component to link to the video data in an external file. Flash Player displays the video inside the component at runtime.

About the Video Import Wizard

Flash CS5's Video Import Wizard walks you through the process of importing video clips for use in Flash. The clips must already be encoded in a format that works with Flash, such as FLV (Flash video) or F4V. (F4V is a subset of the H.264 video-compression specification developed by the standards group known as the JVT [Joint Video Team]. Most video files encoded as MPEG-4—such as video podcasts in your Apple iTunes library—qualify as F4V.)

The biggest decision you have to make when using the wizard is how you want to deliver the video data to your viewers. You can embed the video data into the Flash document, or keep the data in an external file and display the video via a special Flash element—the FLVPlayback component.

Embedded video adds to the size of a published Flash movie, which may have a negative effect on your end users' experience as they wait for enough data to download to start viewing. Video displayed using the FLVPlayback component doesn't add to the size of the published movie. How long users must wait to see the video depends on whether you use progressive or streaming video and on the particulars of each user's computer setup.

You can have video displayed with the FLVPlayback component download progressively from a web server. In this method, Flash downloads the entire video file. You can start watching data as it downloads, but if download speed is slow, you may catch up to the downloaded video and have to wait for more to reach your system to continue watching. You can't skip ahead to start downloading a later section of the video.

You can have Flash stream video displayed with the FLVPlayback component, either from a Flash Video Streaming Service or from your own server using Flash Media Server. For streaming, Flash divides the video data into small segments. The video can start playing as soon as a few segments have downloaded. The server continues to download video data while the end user watches. Users can skip around to different segments of the video easily. Streaming video is also more efficient for longer videos; if users only watch a portion of the video, they don't need to download the whole thing. And the video streams don't wind up in the user's cache. To use streaming video, you must have access to a Flash Media Server, have a Flash Video Streaming Service account with your ISP, or use a dedicated streaming service, such as Limelight Networks.

In addition, Flash can deploy video for use with some mobile devices.

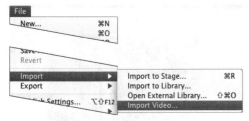

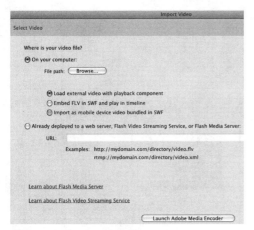

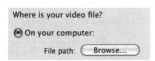

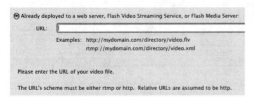

Ⓐ Choose File > Import > Import Video to open Flash's Video Import Wizard.

Ⓑ The Import Video dialog offers options for displaying encoded video in your Flash movie. The first step is locating the video file you want to display.

Ⓒ To locate video on your computer for import, select the On Your Computer radio button; then click the Browse button, navigate to the file, and select it.

Ⓓ To import video that's on an external server, select the "Already deployed to a web server" radio button and enter the video file's URL.

To import video for display in a playback component:

1. In a new Flash document, or a new layer, create a blank keyframe where you want the video to start playing.

   It's best to create a separate layer for the video component that Flash will add at the end of this task. Keeping the component on a separate layer helps you organize the Timeline.

2. To begin the import process, with the desired keyframe selected, choose File > Import > Import Video **Ⓐ**.

   The Select Video page of the Import Video dialog appears **Ⓑ**.

3. To use a file on your hard drive, select the On Your Computer radio button and click the Browse button in the File Path area **Ⓒ**. When the Open dialog appears, navigate to your file, select it, and click the Open button. The Video Import Wizard returns you to the Select Video page and displays the file's path.

   or

   To use a file that is located on a web server, select the "Already deployed to a web server" radio button **Ⓓ** and enter the file's address in the URL field.

continues on next page

4. Click Continue (Mac) or Next (Windows).

The Skinning page appears ⒠.

5. To create playback controls for end users, from the Skin pop-up menu, choose one of the following:

▸ To create a controller bar that that uses space efficiently, choose a skin whose name starts with the words *Minima*.

▸ To create a controller bar that floats on top of the image in the video-display window, choose a skin whose name starts with the words *SkinOver* ⒡.

▸ To create a controller bar that sits beneath the video-display window, choose a skin whose name starts with the words *SkinUnder*.

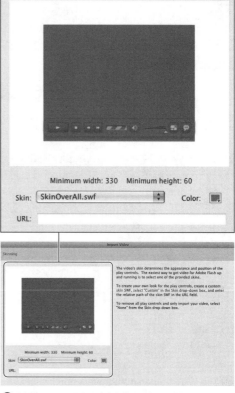

⒠ In the Skinning page of the Import Video dialog, you can choose a skin that creates user-interface controls for the progressive or streaming video displayed in your Flash movie.

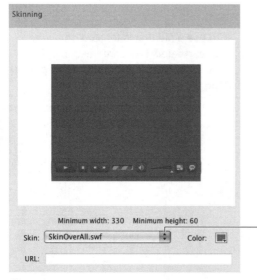

```
None
MinimaFlatCustomColorAll.swf
MinimaFlatCustomColorPlayBackSeekCounterVolMute.swf
MinimaFlatCustomColorPlayBackSeekCounterVolMuteFull.swf
MinimaFlatCustomColorPlayBackSeekMute.swf
MinimaSilverAll.swf
MinimaSilverPlayBackSeekCounterVolMute.swf
MinimaSilverPlayBackSeekCounterVolMuteFull.swf
MinimaSilverPlayBackSeekMute.swf
MinimaUnderPlayBackSeekCounterVolMuteFull.swf
MinimaUnderPlayBackSeekCounterVolMuteNoFull.swf
✓ SkinOverAll.swf
SkinOverAllNoCaption.swf
SkinOverAllNoFullNoCaption.swf
SkinOverAllNoFullscreen.swf
SkinOverAllNoVolNoCaptionNoFull.swf
```

⒡ Each skin in the pop-up menu uses a different set of elements to create the controller bar. Skins that contain the word *Minima* have small icons to save space; skins that contain the word *Over* get layered on top of the video image; skins that contain the word *Under* wind up just below the video-display window.

G The Finish Video Import page of the Import Video dialog provides information about how to work with the video files for publishing. To learn more, select the "After importing video, view video topics in Flash Help" checkbox.

H The imported video clip, along with any skin/controller you selected, appears on the Stage in the current keyframe.

6. Click Continue (Mac) or Next (Windows).

The Finish Video Import page appears **G**, describing the assets created by the wizard and giving a brief overview of how to use them (see the sidebar "Final Steps for Using FLVPlayback," later in this chapter).

7. Click Finish.

The Getting Metadata dialog with progress bar appears. To stop the import process, click the Cancel button. When loading has finished, Flash places an instance of the FLVPlayback component on the Stage in the keyframe you selected. The properties of the instance are already set to point to the source video file and to use the skin you chose in Step 5 **H**.

TIP In Step 5, to create a video clip with no controller bar, choose None from the Skin pop-up menu.

TIP You can select a color for any of the controller bar skins other than ones whose names start with *minimaSilver* or *MinimaUnder*. In the Video Import dialog's Skinning page, click the Color control and choose a new color from the pop-up swatch set.

TIP Best practice: Before importing the video, copy the encoded video file to the same folder as the FLA or SWF (or a subfolder in the same folder). The URL Flash creates as the Source parameter (see "Working with the FLVPlayback Component," later in this chapter) will be a relative path, ready to be put on a web server.

Importing Video for Embedding

When you choose to embed a video file, the video data becomes part of the FLA and SWF files. Embedded video must be in FLV format. When you import video for embedding, the Video Import Wizard has an extra page of settings.

To import and embed video:

1. Follow Steps 1–3 in the preceding task.

   You only need to select a keyframe if you want Flash to place the video in the Timeline for you.

2. Select the radio button labeled "Embed FLV in SWF and play in Timeline"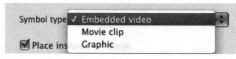

3. Click Continue (Mac) or Next (Windows).

   The Embedding page of the Import Video dialog appears, with options for working with embedded video clips **J**.

4. From the Symbol Type pop-up menu **K**, choose one of the following:

   Embedded Video places the video frames directly into the main Timeline of your movie.

   Movie Clip places the video frames into the Timeline of a movie-clip symbol.

   Graphic places the video frames into the Timeline of an animated graphic symbol.

5. To have Flash automatically place video frames in the Timeline (if you chose Embedded Video in Step 4) or place a symbol instance on the Stage (if you chose Movie Clip or Graphic in Step 4), select the "Place instance on Stage" checkbox.

   Upon completing the import process, Flash places the video or symbol instance in the currently selected keyframe.

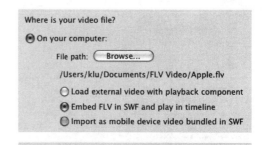

I When you choose embedding as the delivery method (top), Flash puts all of the video data into the published SWF file. This method has pluses and minuses, as indicated in the warning text that appears in the dialog when you choose to embed (bottom).

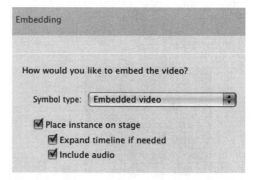

J You must choose settings for working with the embedded video. You can have Flash place an instance of the video clip on the Stage for you, expand the number of defined frames in the Timeline to display all the frames of the video, and include an audio track.

K The Symbol Type menu in the Embedding page of the Import Video dialog gives you the choice of turning the video clip into an animated graphic symbol or a movie-clip symbol, or placing the frames of the video directly into the main Timeline.

☑ Place instance on stage
☑ Expand timeline if needed
☑ Include audio

L With embedded video, you can include the soundtrack within the video itself or exclude it.

Finish Video Import

The video you are using is located at:
/Users/klu/Documents/FLV Video/Apple.flv

The video will be placed on the stage.

The timeline will be expanded to accommodate the playback length.

☐ After importing video, view video topics in Flash Help

M The Video Import Wizard summarizes the settings you chose for importing a video, telling you where the source video is. If you chose to have Flash place the video in your movie, or expand the Timeline to display the video, this window lets you know.

6. If you chose Embedded Video or Graphic in Step 4, to have Flash add enough frames to the selected keyframe span in the main Timeline to display all the video's frames, select the "Expand Timeline if needed" checkbox.

7. To include an audio track, select the Include Audio checkbox **L**.

8. Click Continue (Mac) or Next (Windows).

   The Finish Video Import window appears **M**.

9. Click Finish.

   Flash completes the import process. For details, see Step 7 of the preceding task.

TIP When you import video for embedding, do not attempt to place it in a tween span or pose span; Flash doesn't allow embedded video in these types of spans. If you continue the import process with these types of spans selected, Flash disables the option to place an instance on the Stage. Flash places the video clip (and movie-clip or graphic symbol if you chose to create one) in the library of your document but places nothing on the Stage or in the Timeline.

TIP Warning: Don't change the frame rate of your document (FLA) after you've imported video, as that all but guarantees synch issues during playback. If you must change the frame rate, reimport the video afterwards. It may also help to encode the video at the same frame rate as the FLA.

Working with Embedded Video

Depending on the settings you choose when you use the Video Import Wizard to create embedded video clips, Flash places an instance of the clip on the Stage or just places the embedded-video asset in the library. When automatically placing an instance on the Stage, Flash can create enough frames in the Timeline to show the full video, or allow the existing keyframe span to truncate the video. When you place an instance of an embedded clip into the Timeline yourself, you need to create a keyframe span that accommodates as much of the video as you want to show.

To place embedded video clips in the Timeline:

1. Open a Flash document and import the embedded video as described in "Importing Video for Embedding," earlier in this chapter.

   For this task, deselect the "Place instance on Stage" checkbox in Step 5.

2. In the Timeline, select the keyframe in which you want the embedded video to start playing.

   The keyframe must not be part of a motion tween's tween span or an IK pose span. Flash cannot use an embedded video clip as a tween target or an IK node.

3. From the Library panel, drag a copy of the embedded video clip to the Stage **Ⓐ**.

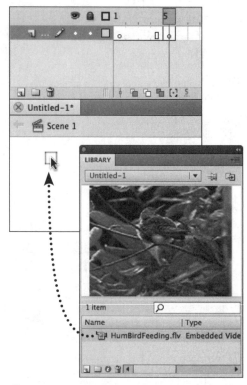

Ⓐ To place embedded video in a Flash movie, drag an instance of the embedded-video clip from the library to the Stage.

Previewing Embedded Video Clips

In Flash's authoring environment, embedded video clips display their images within the keyframe span that contains the clip. You can simply play the movie (choose Control > Play) or move the playhead through the Timeline to view the changing video frames. If the embedded clip has an audio track, however, you must use one of the test modes to preview the sound. You must also use one of the test modes to see the embedded video in context with interactive elements, such as movie clips or scripted buttons.

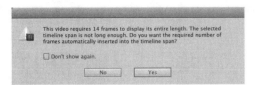

This video requires 14 frames to display its entire length. The selected timeline span is not long enough. Do you want the required number of frames automatically inserted into the timeline span?

☐ Don't show again.

No   Yes

B Flash alerts you when you attempt to add embedded video that has more frames than the current keyframe span where you are placing it.

Before adding embedded-video instance

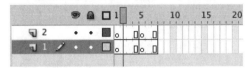

After adding embedded-video instance

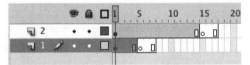

C Layer 2 in this Timeline shows the result of answering Yes in the dialog that warns that the current keyframe span is too short: Flash adds enough frames to display the full 14-frame clip. Layer 1 shows the result for answering No: the existing keyframe span truncates the video.

Unlike movie clips, which play in their own independent Timeline, embedded video clips need to fit their frames into the Timeline of the movie or movie clip containing them. Each time you drag an instance of an embedded video clip to the Stage, if the selected keyframe span contains fewer frames than the clip, a warning dialog asks whether you want to add enough frames to display the entire clip **B**.

4. To enlarge the keyframe span, click Yes.

   Flash adds enough frames to the span to reveal the entire video clip **C**.

   or

   To retain the current number of frames in the keyframe span, click No.

   Flash places the video clip on the Stage, but the keyframe span cuts off the end of the clip.

The Mystery of Embedded Video

Embedded video clips bear similarities to some Flash symbols, yet embedded video is a unique type of element. Like animated graphic symbols, embedded video clips play within—and must synchronize with—frames in the main movie Timeline. Embedded video clips can contain audio, although if you import the audio as an integrated track, you won't see the sound's waveform in the Timeline. As with any symbol, you place an instance of an embedded-video clip by dragging a copy from the library window to the Stage. The Property inspector gives you information about selected instances of embedded video clips. You can modify a selected instance of an embedded video clip in many of the ways that you modify other objects in Flash: you can use the free-transform tool, for example, to resize, rotate, or skew the video image. You can't use an embedded video clip as the tween target in a motion tween; you must put the embedded clip inside a Flash movie-clip symbol to tween the video. In addition, to give an embedded video clip an independent Timeline and to gain the same control over the clip's appearance that you have over movie clips (to be able to change the clip's brightness, tint, or alpha, for example), you must place the embedded video clip inside a Flash movie-clip symbol.

Working with the FLVPlayback Component

When you use Flash's Video Import Wizard to import video for use with a playback component, the wizard adds a component named FLVPlayback to the library and places an instance of it on the Stage. You can use the Property inspector to change the component's parameters, setting such things as the initial volume for the clip, the type of controller-bar skin and its color, and which video clip the component will display.

To choose source video for an FLVPlayback instance:

1. Select the FLVPlayback component instance on the Stage.

2. In the SWF Property inspector, access the Component Parameters section.

   The properties for the FLVPlayback component appear in a table consisting of two columns: Property and Value 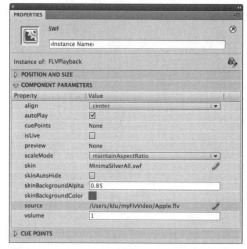. If the section is collapsed, click the triangle to the left of the section name to view the properties. The Source property displays the pathname of the video that appears in the selected FLVPlayback instance at runtime.

3. To choose a source video, in the Source row, click the pencil icon (or click the pathname directly).

   The Content Path dialog appears displaying a text field for the pathname of the current source.

4. To identify the source video file (it must be encoded in a Flash-compatible

Ⓐ The Component Parameters section of the SWF Property inspector panel contains settings for various modifiable properties of the selected FLVPlayback component instance.

Browse to locate file

Enter URL

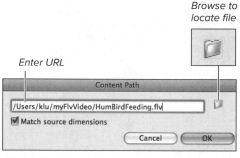

Ⓑ The Content Path dialog lets you choose an external video file for the FLVPlayback-component instance to display for the end user.

C The Source row of the Component Parameters section of the SWF Property inspector shows the pathname for the file that will play in the selected FLVPlayback-component instance in the finished movie.

TIP Instead of using the FLVPlayback component's prebuilt controller-bar skins, you can use other ActionScript 3.0 video components to create a user interface for controlling video that runs in the FLVPlayback window. Choose None as the skin for the FLVPlayback component instance on the Stage. Access the Components panel and expand the Video folder. You'll see a number of user-interface components: PlayButton, PauseButton, VolumeBar, and so on. Drag an instance of each element you want to use to the Stage. You can position the elements anywhere and modify them as you did with the button component (see Chapter 14).

TIP You can change the size of an FLVPlayback component instance on the Stage using the free-transform tool, the Transform or Info panel, or the Position and Size section of the Property inspector. But if you've chosen a controller-bar skin for your video, be careful. The controller bar must be wide enough to hold all the user-interface elements that are part of the skin (the Play, Pause, and Mute button; the volume slider; and so on). If you narrow the component instance too much, the controller bar may stick out over the edges of the video-display window.

format, such as FLV or F4V), do either of the following:

- ▸ Enter a URL for the source video in the Content Path field **B**.
- ▸ To find the file you want, click the folder icon on the right side of the field. In the Browse for Source File dialog that appears, navigate to the file you want, and click Open. Flash enters the URL in the Content Path dialog.

5. To determine how Flash sizes the FLVPlayback component instance, do either of the following:

- ▸ To resize the component to fit the source video, select the Match Source Dimensions checkbox.
- ▸ To resize the video to fit within the default FLVPlayback component (320 by 240 pixels), deselect the Match Source Dimensions checkbox.

6. Click OK.

The Getting Metadata dialog with progress bar appears. Once it's done, Flash updates the Source parameter with the file name **C**. Depending on what you chose in Step 5, Flash also resizes the FLVPlayback component instance on the Stage. The instance now points to the desired encoded video file.

TIP If the skin you've chosen for the FLVPlayback instance includes a volume-control slider, you can set its starting position at runtime. Enter a number in the Volume field: 1 sets the slider all the way to the right (full volume); values from 0.9 down to 0.1 set the slider farther to the left (lower volumes); a value of 0 sets the slider all the way to the left (no sound). You can enter values greater than 1, and those values create increasingly louder starting volumes, but the lever for the volume slider disappears. During playback, clicking anywhere in the slider brings the lever back, but end users may find this confusing.

About the FLVPlayback Component

Flash's Video Import Wizard imports encoded video files (such as FLV or F4V files) for use in your Flash movies. When you select the wizard's options to use the video with a playback component, the word *import* is a bit misleading. In fact, the data in the encoded file remains separate from your FLA and SWF files, but the wizard creates a link between your movie and the encoded video file via an element known as the *FLVPlayback component*. During the "import" process, the wizard places the FLVPlayback component in the library of your Flash document, places an instance of the component on the Stage, and sets the instance's source parameter to point to the file with the encoded video data. At runtime, the FLVPlayback component creates a video-display window within your Flash movie, and the video from the encoded source file appears in that window.

Components are a special type of Flash element. (You learned a bit about working with the button component in Chapter 14.) Components contain ActionScript that governs their behavior, but you can modify a component's behavior without actually doing any scripting; you simply change properties in the Component Parameters section of the Property inspector. ActionScript 3.0 user-interface components such as the button component are not fully compiled. You can modify the graphic elements that make up their look (their *skin*) the same way you'd modify any graphic element. The FLVPlayback component, however, is fully compiled; you cannot directly access its skin to modify it. The FLVPlayback component comes with a variety of packaged skins that create a controller bar for the video-display window. You can choose a new controller-bar style by setting the skin property for an FLVPlayback component instance. (Flash does allow you to create new skins for the FLVPlayback component, but that's beyond the scope of a *Visual QuickStart Guide*.)

Like other assets, the FLVPlayback component is reusable. To place another video-display window in your movie, drag a new instance of the FLVPlayback component to the Stage, then set the source property to point to the encoded video file you want to display. If you want, you can even bypass the Video Import Wizard. Access the Components panel (by choosing Window > Components, for example). Expand the panel's Video folder, then drag an instance of FLVPlayback to your document. The instance's source parameter is blank, but you can set it to point to an encoded video file as described in the task "To choose source video for an FLVPlayback instance."

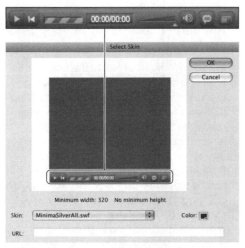

D Use the Select Skin dialog to change the user controls for video playback.

To change controller-bar skins:

1. Follow Steps 1 and 2 in the preceding task.

2. To choose the style of controller bar that appears with the video-display window during playback, in the Skin row, click the pencil icon (or click the skin name directly).

   The Select Skin dialog appears, showing the same items as in the Skinning page of the Import Video Wizard **D**.

3. From the Skin pop-up menu, select a new skin.

   For details, see Step 5 of the first task in "Importing Video for Streaming or Progressive Download," earlier in this chapter.

4. If desired, from the Color control, select a new background color for the controller bar.

   This option is not available for skins whose name starts with *MinimaSilver* or *MinimaUnder*.

continues on next page

Animating FLVPlayback Components

The FLVPlayback component has many similarities to a movie-clip symbol. The component is an asset that lives in the library, you can modify it using the free-transform tool, and you can mask its content using a mask layer. But there's an important difference: you can't use an FLVPlayback component instance in a motion tween, a classic tween, or an IK armature. Flash lets you set up a tween using the FLVPlayback component instance, but when you test the movie, it becomes clear that the tween doesn't work. The video-display window just sits in its original spot, and none of the changes you set up to animate occurs. The IK bone tool won't let you link FLVPlayback component instances into an armature; if you try, a warning dialog appears.

If you want to move the component's video-display window around the Stage (or create other animated effects) with motion or classic tweening, or create an IK armature out of video clips, first put the FLVPlayback component instance inside a movie-clip symbol. You can then animate the movie-clip symbol instance to get the tween effects you want. (To review the process of creating movie-clip symbols, see Chapter 12; to review classic tweening, see Chapter 9; to review motion tweening, see Chapter 11; to review IK animation, see Chapter 13.)

5. Click OK.

Flash updates the Skin property in the Component Parameters section of the SWF Property inspector and changes the controller bar in the FLVPlayback component instance on the Stage.

TIP In Step 3 of the preceding task, if you choose a skin whose name starts with *MinimaSilver* or *MinimaUnder,* the Select Skin dialog's color chip is disabled in Step 4. The underlying color for the controller bar of these skins is always silver-gray. The Color control associated with the SkinBackgroundColor property in the Property inspector always remains active, but using it to select a color has no effect on the *MinimaSilver* and *MinimaUnder,* skins. To use a different color for a *Minima* skin, choose one that has *FlatCustom-Color* as part of the name; then use the Color control in Step 4 or use the method outlined in the next tip.

TIP When you choose a skin whose name starts with *skinOver*, *skinUnder,* or *Minima-FlatCustomColor,* you can change the bar's color and transparency in the SWF Property inspector. Select the FLVPlayback component instance on the Stage and access the Component Parameters section of the SWF Property inspector. To change the color, click the SkinBackgroundColor control, and choose a new color from the pop-up swatch. To create transparency, in the SkinBackgroundAlpha field, enter a value between 1 and 0 (1 equals opaque, 0.5 equals 50 percent transparent, and 0 equals fully transparent).

TIP The style you choose for the FLVPlay-back component's skin is persistent. Change the skin property, and the next time you place an FLVPlayback component instance, it will be set to use that skin. The same is true for the skin's color and transparency settings.

Appearing Live Onstage: FLV Video

In earlier versions of Flash, the only type of video that would preview during authoring was embedded video. To see the way an external video clip would play inside the FLVPlayback instance, you needed to publish the movie or view it in one of the test modes. In CS5, the FLV-Playback component instance plays its source video live on the Stage. You can use any of the controls in the skin you've chosen—the Play/Pause button, the volume slider, and so on—to control the external video clip during authoring. You can also preview the video in an FLVPlay-back component by selecting it on the Stage and pressing the spacebar.

Final Steps for Using FLVPlayback

When you publish a Flash movie to make it available to your audience, you must place the resulting SWF file on the web server that hosts your creation. (You'll learn more about publishing in Chapter 18.) When you use the FLVPlayback component to deliver streaming video or progressive-download video, two other files must go on the server: the file containing the encoded video (for example, an FLV file), and a SWF file containing the controller-bar skin (if you use one for your video). When you publish your movie, including whenever you choose Control > Test Scene, Flash places the SWF file of your movie and the SWF file for the controller-bar skin in the folder with your FLA. The encoded video file remains at its original location.

You may publish your movie many times as you test it during the authoring phase. During that phase, all the pathnames Flash uses to locate these required files let you test without problems. Before you publish your movie for final delivery to your audience, make sure that the Source property for each instance of the FLVPlayback component shows the correct URL for the final location of the source video file on the hosting server. (For details about setting the source parameter, see "To choose source video for an FLVPlayback instance," earlier in this section.

Practice Session

In Chapter 9, you animated a symbol of a bird character moving along a path, getting dizzy and spinning, then flying off. Try adding sounds: add a background sound to create an environment; add a sound that occurs with the dizzy spin to enhance the humor. Use your own sounds or play with the sounds that come with CS5 in the Sounds common library (indicated below in parentheses).

- Open your practice file from Chapter 9 and save a copy.

- Add three new layers at the top of the Timeline; label them BackgroundSound, StartleSound, and DizzySound. (See Chapter 6.) Add blank keyframes at the points where you want the sounds to occur. (See Chapter 8.)

- In Keyframe 1 of the BackgroundSound layer, add a long-playing sound, to set the scene. (Try Weather Ambience Heavy Rain Downpour Splatty 01.mp3.) (See *Adding Sounds to Frames.*) Make this a streaming sound. (See *Using Stream Sounds.*)

- In the StartleSound layer, add a blank keyframe at a point just before your bird starts to spin. To this keyframe add a short sound that might startle the bird. (Try Weather Storm Lightning Bolt Crash Crack 01.mp3.) Make this a start sound. (See *Using Start Sounds.*)

- In the DizzySound layer, add a blank keyframe a few frames after the bird starts to spin. To this keyframe add a goofy sound to highlight the bird's dizziness. (Try Science Fiction Sci-Fi Electronic Laser 290.mp3.) Make this a start sound.

- Test your movie; adjust the position of your sound keyframes to improve the way the sounds fit the animation.

Save your file for further practice; name it BirdSoundscape.

Extra Credit

- In Chapter 12's Practice Session, you created a symbol containing a fully animated bird. Import a copy of that symbol to your practice document. Edit a copy of that symbol; name it something like noisyBird. In the symbol's Timeline (in symbol-editing mode), add sounds that accompany the flapping wings (Weapon Staff Whip Thin Fast 02.mp3), the moving beak (Cartoon Human Male Giggle 03.mp3; try editing this sound to make it shorter and more birdlike), and any other animated details you created. Now try swapping symbols to use noisyBird in the Bird-Soundscape file you created above.

- Open a new document and rename the initial layer Background. Import a short embedded video clip; allow Flash to add frames to display the entire video (or add frames yourself to show the desired amount of video after you import). Resize the video object to fill the entire Stage. Above the Background layer, add a layer named Bird. Place an instance of your noisyBird symbol in the layer. Use motion tweening or classic tweening to animate noisyBird to move across the Stage. Adjust the position and size of the symbol instance so that noisyBird seems to interact with whatever is happening in the video, for example, flying up over the head of a toddler playing on the swings, or swooping down to sniff a flower blowing in the wind.

Delivering Movies to Your Audience

When you finish creating graphics, animation, and interactivity in Adobe Flash Professional CS5, it's time to deliver the goods to your audience. You must publish or export the Flash document (FLA) to create a file in a format for playback. You have several formats to choose among. The one that guarantees viewers will see all your animations and take part in all your movie's interactivity is the Flash Player format (SWF). When you install Flash CS5, you can also install version 10.1 of the Flash Player application. You can view SWF files running directly in Flash Player on your computer. Other programs, such as web browsers, can also use Flash Player to display Flash content. You can export movies as a series of images in either bitmap format (GIF or PNG files, for example) or vector format (such as Adobe Illustrator files). Another option for movie delivery is a self-playing file called a *projector*. Users double-click the projector file to open and play the movie. And you can print your entire movie or individual frames, should you want to give someone a hardcopy version of the movie (for storyboarding, for example).

In This Chapter

Preparing Your Movie for Optimal Playback

When creating movies to show over the web, you face the issue of quality versus quantity. Higher quality increases file size, leading to longer download times and slower movies. You need to find a balance between the two (see the sidebar "Putting File Size into Perspective," later in this chapter). Things that add to a file's size include bitmaps (especially animated bitmaps), video clips (especially embedded video), sounds, multiple areas of simultaneous animation, embedded fonts, gradients, and the use of separate graphic elements instead of symbols and groups. Flash's simulated streaming helps you find out where your movie is bogging down. The Size Report and Bandwidth Profiler reveal which frames may cause download hang-ups.

To use the Bandwidth Profiler:

1. Open your Flash document.

2. Choose Control > Test Scene (or Test Movie > In Flash Professional).

   Flash exports the movie and opens it in Flash Player.

3. From Flash Player's View menu, choose Download Settings, and select the download speed you want to test.

   The menu lists eight speeds, all of which are customizable. To change them, choose View > Download Settings > Customize **Ⓐ**. By default, Flash lists five common connection speeds—14.4 Kbps, 28.8 Kbps, 56 Kbps, DSL, and T1—with settings that simulate real-world data-transfer rates. You can see the settings in the Custom Download Settings dialog **Ⓑ**. To create a custom setting, enter new values, and then click OK.

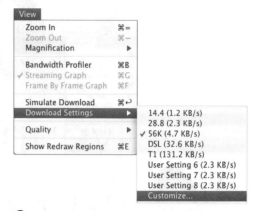

Ⓐ To create a custom connection speed for simulating playback over the web, from the test environment's View menu, choose Download Settings > Customize.

Name that appears in the menu

Speed to be simulated

Ⓑ At its default setting, Flash offers choices for simulating five standard connection speeds. You can change the names and rates for these speeds in the Custom Download Settings dialog.

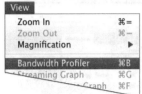

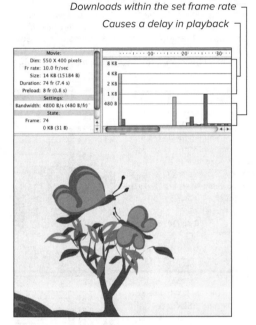

Downloads within the set frame rate
Causes a delay in playback

C To view a graph of the amount of data in each frame, choose View > Bandwidth Profiler when a Flash Player window is open.

D The Bandwidth Profiler graph at the top of the Flash Player window shows how much data each movie frame contains. Each bar in this version of the graph represents a frame of the movie.

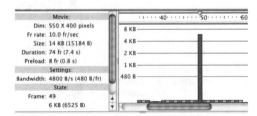

E In Frame by Frame Graph mode, the height of each bar indicates how much data the frame holds.

4. From Flash Player's View menu, choose Bandwidth Profiler **C**.

At the top of the Test Movie window, Flash graphs the amount of data that is being transmitted against the movie's Timeline **D**. The bars represent the number of bytes of data per frame. The bottom line (highlighted in red) represents the amount of data that will safely download fast enough to keep up with the movie's frame rate. Any frame that contains a greater amount of data forces the movie to pause while the data downloads.

To view the contents of each frame separately:

1. From the Flash Player's View menu, choose Frame by Frame Graph, or press Command-F (Mac) or Ctrl-F (Windows).

Flash presents a single bar for each frame in the Bandwidth Profiler graph. The numbers along the top of the graph represent frames **E**. The height of the bar represents the amount of data in that frame.

2. Select a bar.

Specifics about that frame and the movie in general appear in the profile window.

To see how frames stream:

1. From the Flash Player's View menu, choose Streaming Graph, or press Command-G (Mac) or Ctrl-G (Windows).

   Flash displays the frames as alternating bars of light and dark gray, sized to reflect the time each one takes to download 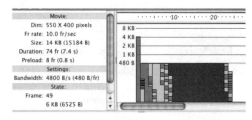. The numbers along the top of the streaming graph represent frames as a unit of time based on the frame rate. (In a 10-fps movie, for example, each number represents .1 second.) Where frames contain little data, several bars may appear in a single time unit. Frames that have lots of data may stretch out over several time units.

2. Select a bar.

   Specifics about that frame and the movie in general appear in the profile window .

F In Streaming Graph mode, the width of each bar indicates how long the frame takes to download at the given connection speed and frame rate. In this movie, Frame 49 contains 6 KBytes of data and takes about 1.3 seconds to download at a frame rate of 10 fps over a 56-Kbps modem.

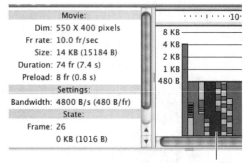

Frame 26

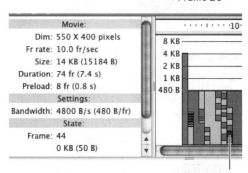

Frame 44

G The profile window to the left of the graph displays information about the movie. The State section identifies the selected frame (the frame highlighted in red) and indicates the amount of data in that frame. You can see that Frame 26 (top) has 1016 bytes of information, whereas Frame 44 (bottom) contains only 50 bytes.

About SWF History

Flash CS5's SWF History feature helps you track file size during authoring. When you publish a SWF by certain methods—choosing File > Publish, Control > Test Movie > In Flash Professoinal, or Control > Test Movie > Test— Flash enters the SWF size, and the date and time of publishing, into the current document's SWF History log. (Choosing Control > Test Scene does not update the log.) The three most recent entries appear in the SWF History section of the Document Property inspector. (If the Property inspector is not visible, choose Window > Properties; to have it display Document properties, click a blank area of the Stage.) If there are more entries, clicking the SWF History section's Log button displays the full log in the Output panel. Flash warns you about large increases in file size, flagging increases greater than 50 percent with a warning triangle in the Property inspector. To clear the log, click the SWF History section's Clear button.

To display a download-progress bar:

With Bandwidth Profiler active, from Flash Player's View menu, choose Simulate Download, or press Command-Return (Mac) or Ctrl-Enter (Windows).

As the animation plays in the test window, Flash highlights the numbers of the Timeline in green to show where you are in the download process.

To exit Bandwidth Profiler:

From Flash Player's View menu, choose Bandwidth Profiler again to deselect it.

TIP To get information about the amount of data in each frame in text form, choose Generate Size Report in the Advanced section of the Flash tab of the Publish Settings dialog. During the publishing process, Flash creates a file showing the number of bytes of data in each frame of the movie.

Putting File Size into Perspective

Throughout this book, you've seen notes about techniques that add to file size. You should pay attention to file size and its impact on the end user's experience, but it's also important to keep things in perspective. In Flash's early days, its ability to keep file sizes tiny was a boon to developers who wanted to create rich, interactive web content that people with slow dial-up connections could enjoy. Today, lots of people have fast Internet connections. The huge popularity of video sites like YouTube, live wildlife webcams, and streaming TV shows—complete with commercial advertisements—indicate that you need not be overly concerned about adding a few bitmaps, using frame-by-frame animation, even adding sound and video, if that's the best way to convey your message or fulfill your creative goals. If your main target audience is still dialing into the web using 14-Kbps modems, or you're developing for mobile devices using Adobe Flash Lite, then yes, minimizing file size is a high priority. Otherwise, allow yourself to take advantage of all the Flash techniques that help you create the content you envision.

A Note About Accessibility

As you think about the best ways to deliver Flash movies to your audience, also consider the fact that some members of the audience may have physical conditions that affect the way they interact with your site. As the web has become more visually interesting, it presents challenges to visually impaired users who want to take advantage of the many resources available online.

Our society is becoming more sensitive to the ways in which activities and resources exclude people with disabilities. Web designers need to use Flash to make not only eye-catching websites that dazzle with artwork, animation, interactivity, sound, and video, but also sites that convey information to a wide range of people. Remember that some of your users are unable to view or hear a site's content; some may not use a mouse, instead navigating and exploring the site by tabbing to each element in turn.

To address the issue of accessible websites, Flash lets you make content available to screen-reading software that uses Microsoft Active Accessibility (MSAA) technology. (At the time Flash CS5 was released, MSAA was available only for Windows.) Screen readers provide audio feedback about a variety of elements on a website, reading aloud the labels of buttons, for example, or reading the contents of text fields. Through Flash's accessibility features, you can create descriptions of objects for the screen reader; prevent the screen reader from attempting to describe certain objects (such as purely decorative movie clips); and assign keyboard commands that let the user manipulate objects by pressing keys or tabbing through text fields, for example.

In addition, Flash CS5 lets you create accessible video. Flash's FLVPlayback component (see Chapter 16) creates video controllers that respond to keyboard commands and screen readers. The FLVPlaybackCaptioning component allows you to create closed captions to provide a text version of audio content.

The considerations that go into making an effective, accessible site are too numerous and complex to cover in a *Visual QuickStart Guide*. But you can check out the tools for defining accessible objects in the Accessibility panel. Choose Window > Other Panels > Accessibility to open the panel. The accessibility parameters for selected objects appear in the panel ⓗ. You can also learn about best practices for accessibility from Adobe's Accessibility Resource Center (*http://www.adobe.com/accessibility/*).

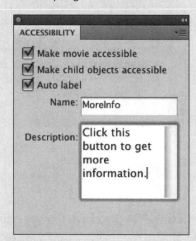

ⓗ The Accessibility panel contains settings for making selected objects in your movie available (or unavailable) to screen-reader software.

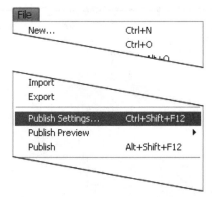

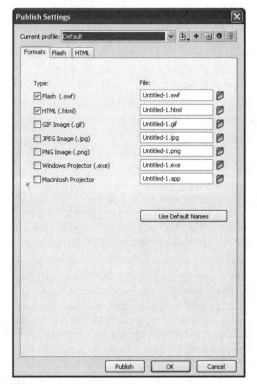

A To access the settings for publishing a movie, choose File > Publish Settings.

B The Formats section of the Publish Settings dialog lets you publish your Flash content in as many as six formats at the same time. A seventh format choice creates an HTML document for displaying the published files in a browser.

Publishing

To make your movie available to the public, you must publish or export it. Flash's Publish function is geared toward presenting material on the web and creating a range of formats for various viewers. The Export feature has similar settings but creates just one format at a time (see the sidebar "Publishing vs. Exporting").

To set the publishing format:

1. Open the Flash document you want to publish.

2. Choose File > Publish Settings, or press Option-Shift-F12 (Mac) or Ctrl-Shift-F12 (Windows) **A**.

   The Publish Settings dialog appears. The top of the dialog displays a Current Profile and buttons for working with profiles. If you're working in a new document and have never created a profile, Default is your only option. If you open a file made with a previous version of Flash, the profile name reflects that version. A profile is the compilation of settings for the various publishing options. You can save settings in new profiles. Leave the current profile in place.

3. Click the Formats button (Mac) or tab (Windows) **B**.

4. Choose one of the seven format options.

   The options are Flash (.swf), HTML (.html), GIF Image (.gif), JPEG Image (.jpg), PNG Image (.png), Windows Projector (.exe), and Macintosh Projector.

5. To set the options for a selected format, select the button (Mac) or tab (Windows) associated with that format (as outlined in separate tasks later in this chapter).

continues on next page

6. To save these settings with the current file, click OK.

Flash uses these settings each time you choose the Publish or Publish Preview command for this document. Flash also uses a file's current publish settings when you enter test mode (for example, by choosing Control > Test Scene).

TIP If the Document Property inspector is open, you can access the Publish Settings dialog quickly: in the Publish section, in the Profile area, click the Edit button.

Publishing vs. Exporting

Flash's Publish command uses a document's publish settings to create all the elements needed to display your Flash creation on the web. With default settings, publishing creates a Flash Player (SWF) file and an HTML file that includes JavaScript. The HTML and JavaScript work together, creating HTML code that displays the SWF (running in Flash Player) in a browser window. The JavaScript can also perform version detection, ensuring that end users have the right version of Flash Player to view your content. Depending on the content of your FLA, publishing may create additional files: For a FLA containing TLF text, default Publish Settings create a SWZ file with instructions for handling the text. For a FLA containing a compiled movie-clip component (SWC)—such as the FLVPlayback component for displaying video clips—publishing may create a SWF.

The Publish command can also create alternate file formats—GIF, JPEG, and PNG—and the HTML needed to display them in the browser window. Alternate formats let you make some of the animation and interactivity of your site available even to end users who lack the Flash Player plug-in. Finally, the Publishing command can create stand-alone projector files.

Flash's Export Movie command translates Flash content directly into a single format. You can export an entire movie as a SWF movie; as a QuickTime movie; as an animated GIF; or as a sequence of JPEG, GIF, or PNG images. You can export a single frame as an image in SWF, JPEG, GIF, PNG, or FXG format. You can select graphic objects on the Stage and export them in FXG format. (FXG is Adobe's graphics-exchange format, intended to make collaboration among designers and developers easier. Many Adobe applications in the CS5 suite, such as Fireworks, Photoshop, and Illustrator, can work with graphics in FXG format.)

In general, the options for exporting to GIF, JPEG, and PNG are the same as for publishing to those alternative formats. The arrangement of some options differs between the export and publish dialogs, and some formats have more options in the Publish Settings dialog. For example, the Publish Settings dialog offers the choice to remove gradients from GIFs (to keep the file size small), whereas the Export GIF dialog lacks that option. Another difference between publishing and exporting is that while Flash stores the Publish Settings with the FLA file for reuse, you must set export options each time you export a FLA file (even when you re-export the same FLA file to the same format).

When you export an entire movie, you have access to a delivery option that's unavailable when publishing: QuickTime. When you export to QuickTime, you lose any interactivity features in your Flash movie. QuickTime export works by playing back the SWF file in Flash Player, then capturing each frame of the animation (including animation generated by ActionScript) and writing it to a frame in a QuickTime MOV file.

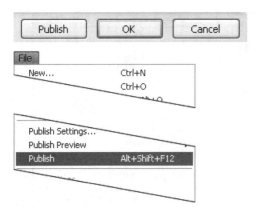

C Click the Publish button in the Publish Settings dialog (top) or choose File > Publish (bottom) to publish your Flash files.

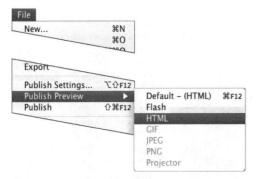

D To cancel the publishing process, click the Stop (Mac) or Cancel (Windows) button in the Publishing dialog. If you've published the file before, the dialog may appear only briefly, making it difficult to cancel the operation.

E The File > Publish Preview submenu displays all the formats selected in the Publish Settings dialog. Flash publishes your movie in the selected format and opens it in your browser.

To publish a movie:

1. Open the Flash file you want to publish.

2. To issue the Publish command, do either of the following:

   ▸ Choose File > Publish Settings.

     The Publish Settings dialog appears. You can follow the steps in the preceding task to set new format options or accept the current settings. Then click the Publish button **C**.

   ▸ Choose File > Publish, or press Shift-Command-F12 (Mac) or Alt-Shift-F12 (Windows).

     The Publishing dialog appears **D**. Flash uses the publish settings stored with your Flash document, creating a new file for each format selected in the Publish Settings dialog.

TIP By default, Flash places each published file in the same location as the original Flash file. You can choose a new location. In the Formats section of the Publish Settings dialog, click the folder icon to the right of the filename. The Select Publish Destination dialog appears, allowing you to choose a new location for the file.

TIP You can open your browser and preview a movie in one step. Choose File > Publish Preview. Flash offers a menu that contains all the formats selected in the Publish Settings dialog **E**. Choose a format. Flash publishes the file in that format, using the current settings, and opens the movie in a browser window. Note that if you're using Publish Preview to test SWF files that reside on your local system, and your Flash movie links to a URL on the network, you can run into security issues (see the sidebar "A Note About Flash Player 10's Security Settings," later in this chapter).

Working with Flash Player Settings

The stand-alone Flash Player is an application file that installs with Flash. The Player opens when you double-click the icon of a SWF file. (From within Flash Player, you can use the File > Open command to open and play SWF files.) To prepare a Flash movie for playing in the stand-alone Player, choose either the Publish or Export command in the Flash editor. The options are basically the same for both commands.

To publish a Flash Player (SWF) file:

1. From an open Flash document, choose File > Publish Settings.

   The Publish Settings dialog appears; choose a base publishing profile, or leave the current setting.

2. Click the Formats button (Mac) or tab (Windows).

3. In the Type section, select Flash (.swf).

   If you wish, type a new name in the File field for the Flash (SWF) file. Be sure to include the .swf extension.

4. Click the Flash button (Mac) or tab (Windows) 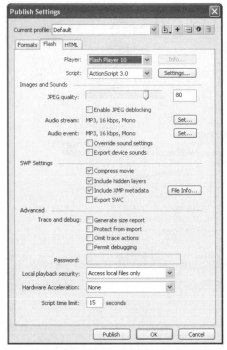.

5. Set Flash options as described in the following tasks.

6. Click Publish.

TIP To access the Flash section of the Publish Settings dialog quickly when the Property inspector is open, click a blank area of the Stage or the Pasteboard; access the Publish section of the Document Property inspector; then in the Profile area, click the Edit button **B**. The Publish Settings dialog opens displaying the Flash section.

A The Flash section of the Publish Settings dialog offers options for publishing your Flash movie as a Flash Player (SWF) file.

B The Document Property inspector's Publish section lets you quickly see which versions of Flash Player and ActionScript you're publishing to as well as what Profile is selected for publishing. To open the Publish Settings dialog quickly, click the Edit button in the Profile area.

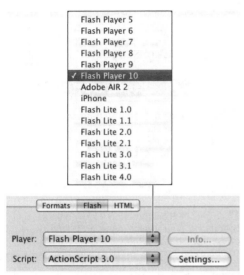

C Choose a version of Flash Player to publish to. Publishing to versions earlier than 10 makes some features of Flash CS5 unavailable, but ensures that a wider audience will have the correct player. Note that Flash CS5 can't publish to the earliest versions of Flash Player, only versions 5 and up.

To choose a Flash Player version:

In the Flash section of the Publish Settings dialog, from the Player pop-up menu, choose a version of Flash Player **C**.

Your options are Flash Player 5 through 10; Adobe AIR 2, a development platform that enables Internet applications to run on an end user's system without an Internet connection; iPhone, a method of converting Flash content into a native iPhone application, for possible use on Apple's iPhone; and Flash Lite 1.0, 1.1, 2.0, 2.1, 3.0, 3.1, and 4.0—players that work in devices such as mobile phones. If you publish your file to a Flash Player version earlier than 10, you lose some features specific to Flash CS5.

TIP At the time this book was in production, Apple was not accepting iPhone applications created with Flash's conversion tool.

TIP Before you start scripting with ActionScript, in the Flash section of the Publish Settings dialog, select the earliest version of Flash Player you plan to use to deliver content to your audience. The Actions Toolbox in the Actions panel highlights actions that won't work in the selected player version.

TIP When you choose Flash Player 6, 7, 8, 9, or 10, the Compress Movie checkbox becomes active. Compressing a file that has lots of text or ActionScript helps keep the file size down.

To choose the version of ActionScript used (Flash Player 6–10):

In the Flash section of the Publish Settings dialog, from the Script pop-up menu, choose ActionScript version 1.0, 2.0, or 3.0 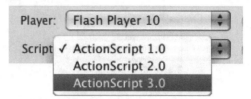.

This setting tells Flash which version of the scripting language your document uses so the compiler treats the code appropriately. The menu becomes active only when you've chosen Player 6, 7, 8, 9, or 10.

TIP Flash's components rely on Action-Script. It's crucial that the ActionScript version selected in the Publish Settings dialog match the components used in the FLA. If the FLA contains components from one ActionScript version and you publish to another, the components may not work or may not even appear in the published movie.

TIP During authoring, the Components panel displays only components that work with the version of ActionScript currently selected in Publish Settings. To have the panel show ActionScript 3.0 components, for example, you must choose ActionScript 3.0 for publishing.

To apply JPEG compression to bitmaps:

In the Flash section of the Publish Settings dialog, in the Images and Sounds area, do either of the following:

- Adjust the JPEG Quality slider.

  or

- Enter a specific value in the JPEG Quality field **E**.

  This setting controls how Flash applies JPEG compression as it exports the bitmaps in your movie.

D ActionScript 1.0, 2.0, and 3.0 present different tasks for the compiler when Flash publishes a SWF file. Be sure to select the version you used (or plan to use) for scripting.

E To set JPEG compression for any bitmaps in your movie, type a value in the JPEG Quality field or use the slider. A setting of 0 provides the most compression (and the lowest quality, because that compression leads to loss of data); a setting of 100 results in the least compression (the highest quality).

TIP Flash doesn't apply JPEG compression to GIF images that you've imported into your movie, because Flash defaults to using loss-less compression for GIFs.

TIP You can set compression for individual bitmaps in the library of your Flash document. Select the bitmap in the Library panel. From the panel menu, choose Properties to access the Bitmap Properties dialog. A Compression pop-up menu offers two choices: Photo (JPEG) and Lossless (PNG/GIF). The Photo option creates lossy compression.

TIP When you apply high levels of JPEG compression (low values in the JPEG Quality field), you can wind up with artifacts—areas that look blurry or blocky— in the published images. To smooth out blocky artifacts, select the Enable JPEG Deblocking checkbox just under the JPEG Quality slider.

Advanced ActionScript Settings and TLF

When you select ActionScript 3.0 in the Flash tab of the Publish Settings dialog, the Settings button to the right of the menu activates. Click the button to access the Advanced ActionScript 3.0 Settings dialog. Most of these settings come into play for movies that use advanced scripting techniques, beyond the basic tasks you learn in this book. But a few settings relate to the publishing and playback of TLF text; these you may want to adjust **F**.

Runtime shared library settings

When you use default Publish Settings for a movie that contains TLF text, Flash Player needs to access the TLF SWZ file, which contains ActionScript code needed for displaying TLF text at runtime. With default settings, Flash creates the TLF SWZ as a *runtime shared library* (RSL) in the same folder as the published SWF. (An RSL acts a bit like a public storage locker; it's a place to store assets and code outside your main movie SWF. Flash Player caches RSLs the first time they're downloaded, which can help keep SWF files lean for faster download. RSLs can also make reusable assets available to multiple movies.) Depending on how you plan to deploy your movie, you may relocate the folder containing your SWF and the TLF SWZ; if you do, you'll need to change the pathname. Default publishing also sets up links to Adobe's site as the primary location for accessing the TLF SWZ file. When you select the Library Path button (Mac) or tab (Windows) of the Advanced ActionScript Settings dialog, those links and pathnames appear in a scrolling window. Buttons above the window let you modify the settings, adding and removing items, and/or changing pathnames.

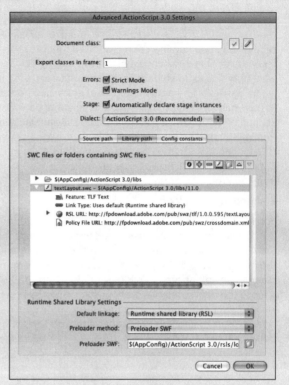

F Use the Advanced ActionScript 3.0 Settings dialog to determine how Flash Player accesses the TLF SWZ containing code needed to display TLF text at runtime. With default Publish settings (shown), the TLF SWZ works as a runtime shared library (RSL).

continues on next page

Advanced ActionScript Settings and TLF *continued*

About the preloader

Unless the TLF SWZ is already in the end user's Flash Player cache, default Publish Settings require downloading the entire TLF SWZ runtime shared library before playback can begin. That means with default settings a movie containing TLF text cannot stream, and users may need to wait for things to download. To make sure users don't just sit there with nothing onscreen as they wait, Flash links to a default preloader animation (found in the Configuration folder). If you prefer to use your own external preloader animation, you can. In the Runtime Shared Library Settings section of the Advanced ActionScript 3.0 Settings dialog, from the Default Linkage menu, choose Runtime Shared Library. From the Preloader Method menu, choose Preloader SWF and enter the URL for your SWF in the Preloader SWF field. If you prefer to use ActionScript to monitor loading from within the SWF and display an internal preloader animation, choose Custom Preloader Loop from the Preloader Method menu.

Embedding TLF SWZ code

You have the option to embed the TLF SWZ's code in your movie. One way to do that is to embed the code of all shared runtime libraries. Select the Library Path button (Mac) or tab (Windows) in the Advanced ActionScript 3.0 Settings dialog. In the Runtime Shared Library Settings section at the bottom of the dialog, from the Default Linkage menu, choose Merged into Code. You can also change the settings for individual libraries. Choose the library in the scrolling list (for the TLF SWZ, choose the item named textLayout.swc), click the first button above the window (the one with the *i* icon), then change settings in the Library Path Item Options dialog (for example, deselect the "Use default shared library linkage" checkbox and choose Merged into Code from the Link Type pop-up menu).

Options for Publishing Digitally Recorded Sounds

As motion pictures are to movement, digital recordings are to sound. Both media capture slices of a continuous event. By playing the captured slices back in order, you re-create the event. In a movie, the slices are frames of film; in a digital recording, they're snippets of sound.

You can think of the recording process as capturing a sound wave by laying a grid over it and copying a piece of the wave at each intersection on the grid. The lines across the horizontal axis are the *sample rate*—how often you capture the sound. The lines up and down the vertical axis are the *bit rate*—how much detail you capture about the sound wave's amplitude. The greater the frequency and bit rate (the finer the mesh of your recording grid), the greater the realism of your recording during playback. This greater realism translates into larger files.

The options in the Images and Sounds section of the Publish Settings dialog give you the flexibility to create different versions of your movie with different sample rates and bit rates without actually changing the sounds embedded in the movie. You might allow yourself larger file sizes and higher-quality sounds for a version being delivered on CD-ROM than for a version being distributed on the web. As you try different sound options, be sure to listen to your published sounds to determine the best balance between sound quality and file size.

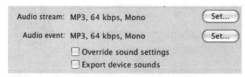

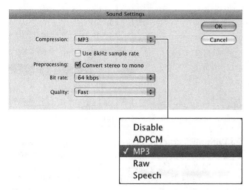

G You must set the sample rate and compression options for stream sounds and event sounds separately. Click the Set button to access the options for each type of sound.

H Choose a compression method from the Compression pop-up menu. Other options appropriate to the selected method appear. Choose Disable to turn off sound.

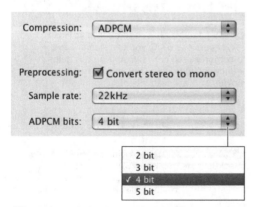

I The ADPCM Bits pop-up menu lets you control the amount of compression applied to the sounds in your movie. Choose 2-Bit for the greatest degree of compression (resulting in the lowest-quality sound); choose 5-Bit for the least compression (resulting in the highest-quality sound).

To control compression and sample rate for all movie sounds:

1. In the Flash section of the Publish Settings dialog, in the Images and Sounds area, for the Audio Stream option (or the Audio Event option), click the Set button **G**.

   The Sound Settings dialog appears. Flash divides sounds into two types: stream and event (for more details, see Chapter 17). You must set the compression for each type separately, but the process and options are similar for both.

2. From the Compression pop-up menu **H**, choose one of the following options:

   Disable removes sound from the published file.

   ADPCM compression works best for movies containing mostly short event sounds, such as hand claps or button clicks. (Generally, you'll use this setting in the Audio Event section for sounds other than MP3's.) The ADPCM options appear. From the ADPCM Bits pop-up menu, choose one of the four bit rates to determine the degree of compression applied to the sounds **I**. With the ADPCM setting, you can also set a sample rate and convert stereo sound to mono.

   continues on next page

Sample-Rate Rule of Thumb

Sample rates are measured in kHz or frequency. Flash works with 8-bit or 16-bit sounds at sample rates of 11 kHz, 22 kHz, or 44 kHz. Recording for music CDs is done at 44 kHz. For multimedia CD-ROMs, 22 kHz is a standard rate. For music clips in Flash movies played on the web, 11 kHz is often sufficient.

MP3 compression (the default setting) works best for movies containing mostly longer stream sounds. (Generally, you'll use this setting in the Audio Stream section.) The MP3 options appear. From the Bit Rate pop-up menu, choose one of 12 bit rates for the published sounds 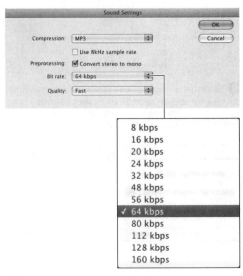. From the Quality pop-up menu, choose Fast when you are testing your movie; choose Medium or Best when you publish for your target audience, as they provide better quality.

Raw omits sound compression. Raw does let you control file size by choosing a sample rate and converting stereo sound to mono.

Speech sets compression for sounds consisting of spoken words. Choose a sample rate from the pop-up menu that appears.

To compress the SWF file (Flash Player 6–10):

1. In the Flash section of the Publish Settings dialog, from the Player pop-up menu, choose Flash Player 6, 7, 8, 9, or 10.

2. In the SWF Settings area of the dialog, select the Compress Movie checkbox **K**.

   Compress Movie is an option only when you publish for Flash Player versions 6–10. The setting has no effect on the JPEG-quality and audio-compression settings you chose in the preceding tasks.

To include XMP metadata:

In the Flash section of the Publish Settings dialog, in the SWF Settings area, select the Include XMP Metadata checkbox **L**.

J With MP3 compression and a bit-rate setting of less than 20 Kbps, Flash converts sounds from stereo to mono. At settings of 20 Kbps and above, you can publish stereo sounds or convert them to mono sounds.

Select to compress

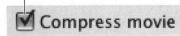

K When you've chosen to publish to Flash Player versions 6–10, you can also choose to compress the movie. Compression helps reduce the file size, especially for text-heavy movies or those with lots of ActionScript.

L When you select the Include XMP Metadata checkbox, the published SWF file includes information—such as titles, descriptions, copyright notice—that you've entered into the XMP info dialog.

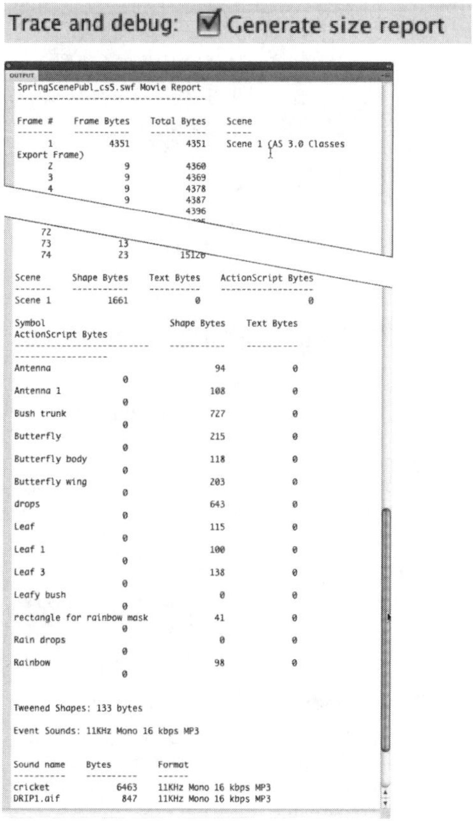

Trace and debug: ☑ Generate size report

```
OUTPUT
SpringScenePubl_cs5.swf Movie Report
---------------------------------------------

Frame #    Frame Bytes    Total Bytes    Scene
-------    -----------    -----------    -----
    1          4351           4351       Scene 1 (AS 3.0 Classes
Export Frame)
    2             9           4360
    3             9           4369
    4             9           4378
                  9           4387
                              4396

   72
   73            13
   74            23          15120

Scene      Shape Bytes    Text Bytes    ActionScript Bytes
-------    -----------    ----------    ------------------
Scene 1        1661            0                    0

Symbol                        Shape Bytes    Text Bytes
ActionScript Bytes
-------------------           -----------    ----------
------------------
Antenna                            94            0
             0
Antenna 1                         108            0
             0
Bush trunk                        727            0
             0
Butterfly                         215            0
             0
Butterfly body                    118            0
             0
Butterfly wing                    203            0
             0
drops                             643            0
             0
Leaf                              115            0
             0
Leaf 1                            100            0
             0
Leaf 3                            138            0
             0
Leafy bush                          0            0
             0
rectangle for rainbow mask         41            0
             0
Rain drops                          0            0
             0
Rainbow                            98            0
             0

Tweened Shapes: 133 bytes

Event Sounds: 11KHz Mono 16 kbps MP3

Sound name    Bytes       Format
----------    ------      ------
cricket       6463        11KHz Mono 16 kbps MP3
DRIP1.aif      847        11KHz Mono 16 kbps MP3
```

Ⓜ When you choose Generate Size Report (top), Flash uses the Output panel to list the amount of data in your movie (bottom).

To list the amount of data in the movie by frame:

In the Flash section of the Publish Settings dialog, in the Advanced area, select the Generate Size Report checkbox Ⓜ.

Flash lists the frames of the movie and how much data each frame contains in the Output panel. This data—known as the *Size Report*—helps you find frames that bog down the movie's playback. You can then optimize or eliminate some of the content in those frames.

TIP In addition to displaying the Size Report in the Output panel, Flash creates a text file containing the Size Report.

TIP The Size Report details how much data is in each symbol used in the movie. Symbols that aren't used appear in the report, but they contain 0 bytes of data. The Size Report also shows you the size of every sound, bitmap and font exported.

TIP Depending on how you've sized the Output window, and the specific data generated by the Size Report, you may see only white space in the Output window. Resize the window or scroll up to view the Size Report data.

About XMP File Info

Flash CS5 lets you include XMP (Extensible Metadata Platform) information in your FLA file. Adding XMP data can be helpful when you work collaboratively, sharing the file with others and using multiple Adobe products to create content. You can also include XMP metadata as a part of a published SWF file. You can use XMP metadata to create titles, descriptions, copyright notices, and so on. When you include XMP metadata with a SWF, the data becomes available to Internet search engines for indexing. To create the XMP metadata, during authoring choose File > File Info. The File Info dialog that appears offers 13 categories of information. To choose a category, click its tab at the top of the dialog window. For example, click the Description tab to enter information about your Flash document, including title, author, description, rating, keywords, and copyright notice. Once you've entered information into all the categories you want, click OK. When you select the Include XMP Metadata checkbox in the Flash section of the Publish Settings dialog, the data you entered into the File Info dialog becomes part of the published SWF file.

To protect your work:

In the Flash section of the Publish Settings dialog, in the Advanced area, under Trace and Debug, select the Protect from Import checkbox **N**.

This setting prevents viewers from obtaining the SWF file and converting it back to a Flash document (FLA).

TIP You can make the Protect from Import setting selective. Enter a password in the Password field. Only those who enter the correct password can import the SWF file.

To set trace and debug options:

In the Flash section of the Publish Settings dialog, in the Advanced area, under Trace and Debug, select either of the following checkboxes:

Omit Trace Actions prevents `trace` actions from appearing in the Output window during debugging **O**.

Permit Debugging allows remote debugging of ActionScripts **P**. You or other users running the debug version of Flash Player can debug a Flash Player (SWF) file as it plays over the Internet.

TIP When the Permit Debugging option is selected, you should always select Protect from Import and enter a password in the Password field **P**. This password prohibits unauthorized individuals from accessing your script, but allows authorized personnel to debug the file remotely.

Trace and debug: ☑ Generate size report ☑ Protect from import ☐ Omit trace actions ☑ Permit debugging Password:

N Select the Protect from Import checkbox to prevent viewers from converting a SWF file back into a FLA file.

☑ Omit trace actions

O When you select the Omit Trace Actions option, the Flash compiler strips all `trace` actions from the SWF file, allowing you to view only non-`trace` debugging items in the Output window. Omitting `trace` actions also reduces file size slightly if your scripts contain lots of `trace` actions.

Trace and debug: ☐ Generate size report ☑ Protect from import ☐ Omit trace actions ☑ Permit debugging Password: myPasswordHere

P When you select the Permit Debugging option, you should also select Protect from Import and enter a password to protect movies that are open to remote debugging.

Local playback security [✓ Access local files only ▲▼]
　　　　　　　　　　　Access network only

Q Flash CS5 provides security by restricting SWF files from manipulating data on different systems. With Access Local Files Only as the setting, the published SWF file can copy or write data only to files on the local system. With Access Network Only, the SWF file can copy or write data only to files on the Internet and not on the local system.

To control access to local and network files for security:

To determine which types of files the SWF file can copy data from or write data to, in the Flash section of the Publish Settings dialog, in the Advanced section, from the Local Playback Security pop-up menu **Q**, choose either of the following options:

Access Local Files Only. With local-only access, the SWF file can share information with files on the local system where the SWF file resides, but not with files located on the Internet. Local-only access prevents a SWF file from loading XML files from the Internet or posting data from an entry form to the Internet, for example.

Access Network Only. With network-only access, the SWF file can share information only with files located on the Internet, not with local files.

Advanced Sound Handling

Flash applies the sound-compression settings in the Publish Settings dialog to all sound assets that have no specific settings of their own. By assigning higher quality to some sounds, you can keep file size reasonable and have high-quality sound where needed.

To set compression options for sounds individually, select a sound asset in the Library panel; then click the Properties button (the *i* icon) at the bottom of the panel or choose Properties from the panel menu. The Sound Properties dialog appears. Its Compression pop-up menu gives you access to the same sound-export settings you find in the settings for Audio in the Images and Sounds area of the Flash section of the Publish Settings dialog.

If you apply individual sound-export settings to some sound assets, Flash uses those settings for those sounds when you publish the movie. For all other sounds in the movie, Flash uses the current sound settings in the Publish Settings dialog.

You can force Flash to ignore the individual sound settings and publish all sounds with the sound-export settings currently selected in the Publish Settings dialog. In the Images and Sounds area of the Flash section of the Publish Settings dialog, select the Override Sound Settings checkbox. You might use this feature to make a lower-quality web version of a movie you created for CD-ROM.

A Note About Flash Player 10's Security Settings

Flash CS5 and Flash Player versions 8–10 let you create content that uploads and/or downloads files at runtime; this capability gives Flash more power than it had with earlier player versions, but with that power comes the potential to do harm. Flash Player versions 8–10 use a security feature that ensures that SWF files can't perform malicious deeds on the systems of your target audience. Flash's default local-security settings prohibit SWF files running locally (on a single computer) from communicating with files being served on the Internet (and vice versa); to allow such communication, you must give Flash Player specific permissions.

When you choose Flash Player version 8, 9, or 10 in Publish Settings, the security model comes into play. When you publish your Flash creation locally before deploying it to a server and you try out the movie in a browser, clicking a button or link in the movie that connects to the Internet may trigger a warning that Flash Player has stopped an operation that might be unsafe.

If the SWF you're testing doesn't need to communicate with both the local system and the Internet, you can solve the problem by changing your Publish Settings. In the Flash section of the Publish Settings dialog, under Local Playback Security, choose Access Network Only. (Note that if you try out your movie using one of the testing modes, the security alert does not appear. In test mode, Flash automatically trusts all local files being accessed.)

If, after changing the Local Playback Security setting, you still get the warning, you need to give your SWF file special permission to communicate with the Internet. When the Adobe Flash Player Security dialog appears ⓡ, click the Settings button. Flash opens a browser window and directs you to a page of the Flash Player documentation on the Adobe site (http:// www.macromedia.com/ support/documentation/en/flashplayer/help/settings_manager04a.html). This page gives you access to the Adobe Flash Player Settings Manager ⓢ.

Global Security Settings tab

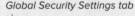

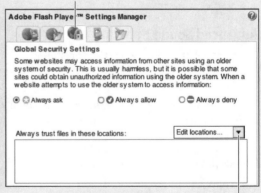

Click to add trusted files and/or folders

ⓡ When a SWF file on a local computer attempts to access a file on the Internet, Flash Player 10 won't allow it to, unless you've set the proper security settings. You'll see a warning dialog to alert you to the fact that your settings don't allow this communication.

ⓢ The Global Security Settings tab of the Adobe Flash Player Settings Manager lets you create a list of trusted files and/or folders for Flash Player 10 security. Any SWF files in locations covered by this list can communicate with Internet files.

Use the Global Security Settings tab of the manager to create a list of trusted items. Flash Player always allows SWF files from the Global Security Settings list to communicate with the Internet, even if they're being run locally. Use the Edit Locations pop-up menu to add individual SWF files or folders to the trusted list or remove them from the list ❶. If you'll be doing lots of this type of testing, it makes sense to set up a special Trusted folder where you keep only your own SWF files you need to test. Don't allow Flash Player to trust folders on your system that might include SWF files downloaded from other sources. Such files have the potential to do something dangerous, such as copying information from your system and sending it to an outside location.

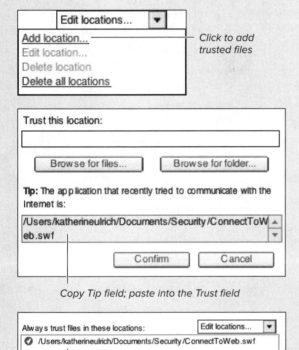

Click to add trusted files

Copy Tip field; paste into the Trust field

List of confirmed trusted files

❶ Click the Edit Locations pop-up menu to manage a list of trusted files (top). Click Add Location to open a window where you can add a new file or folder to a trusted list (middle). If you opened the Global Security Settings Manager by clicking the Settings button of the security warning dialog ❺, the window's Tip field shows the pathname for the file you were working on. Copy and paste that name to the Trusted field (or use a Browse button to find a file); click Confirm to add the trusted file to the trusted list (bottom).

Publishing HTML for Flash Player Files

An *HTML document* is a master set of instructions that tells a browser how to display web content. The Publish function of Flash creates an HTML document that tells the browser how to display the published files for your document (these files can be in SWF, GIF, JPEG, and/or PNG format—whatever you choose in the Formats section of the Publish Settings dialog). The Publish command creates the required HTML by filling in blanks in a template document. Flash comes with ten templates; you can also create your own.

To publish HTML for displaying a Flash file:

1. In the Flash document you want to publish for the web, choose File > Publish Settings.

   The Publish Settings dialog appears; choose a new publishing profile, or leave the current setting.

2. Click the Formats button (Mac) or tab (Windows).

3. In the Type section, select the HTML (.html) checkbox.

   When you choose HTML, Flash automatically selects the Flash checkbox (.swf) as well.

4. Click the HTML button (Mac) or tab (Windows).

   The options for displaying your Flash movie in the browser window appear in the dialog **Ⓐ**. When you publish the current file, Flash feeds your choices into the appropriate HTML tags and parameters in the template of your choice.

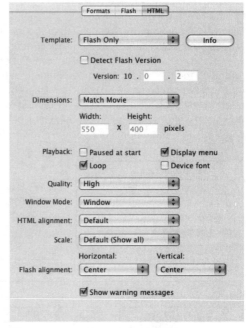

Ⓐ The HTML section of the Publish Settings dialog contains options for displaying your Flash movie in the browser window.

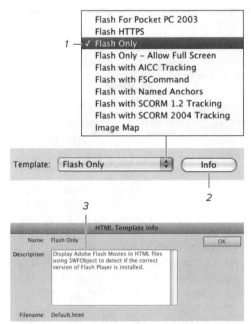

B Choose Flash Only (1) as the template when you want to create HTML for displaying only a Flash movie with no other options for alternate images. Click the Info button (2) to see a description of what the template does (3).

To create HTML for Flash only:

From the Template pop-up menu, choose Flash Only **B**.

This template is the simplest one. It uses HTML to display your Flash content for viewers who are properly equipped with the Flash Player version that you select in the Flash section of the Publish Settings dialog. To allow viewers to install or upgrade their Flash Player, select the "Detect Flash Version" checkbox below the Template pop-up menu. Flash fills in the Player version based on your current setting in the Flash settings. (Other template choices create HTML that performs other tasks; for example, the Image Map template creates HTML that displays alternate images or files when the viewer lacks the proper Flash Player plug-in.)

TIP If you can't remember what one of the included HTML templates does, select it from the Template pop-up menu in the HTML tab of the Publish Settings dialog, and then click the Info button next to the menu. Flash displays a brief description, including instructions about choosing alternate formats, if necessary.

TIP The companion website to this book (www.peachpit.com/flashcs5vqs) contains more information on settings for publishing. There you'll find tasks for setting the dimensions of your Flash movie in the browser; tasks for using alternate image formats, and for version detection (checking the end user's version of Flash Player and offering access the latest version if they need it).

The Mystery of HTML Templates

The traditional HTML codes (called *tags*) required for displaying a SWF file in a browser window are **<object>** for Microsoft Internet Explorer (Windows) and **<embed>** for other browsers. (In addition, Flash can use the **<img>** tag to display a file in another format, such as a JPEG image or an animated GIF.)

Flash's Publish command works hand in hand with HTML templates—which are fill-in-the-blank recipes—and JavaScript to define the parameters of the **<object>** and **<embed>** tags. These parameters include the width and height of the movie window, the quality of the images (the amount of antialiasing to provide), and the way the movie window aligns with the browser window.

Each option and parameter in the HTML section of the Publish Settings dialog has an equivalent template variable. The template variable is a code word that starts with the dollar sign (**$**). When you choose an option in the Publish Settings dialog, Flash enters your choice as an HTML tag that replaces the variable in the template document. If you set the width of your movie as 500 pixels in the Publish Settings dialog for HTML, for example, Flash replaces the template variable for width (**$WI**) with the proper coding to display the movie in a window 500 pixels wide. To get a bit more technical, the template variables are actually parameters in a JavaScript function. When you publish, Flash creates an HTML file that calls the JavaScript function to write out the **<object>** and **<embed>** tags dynamically at runtime.

Flash's HTML templates contain coding not only for displaying your Flash movie, but also for showing the JPEG, GIF, or PNG version of your movie that you want to make available to viewers who don't have the proper browser player to view Flash.

During the publishing process, Flash saves a copy of the HTML template for your movie, giving it the name of your movie file and adding whatever extension the template file has. (The template files that come with Flash use the extension .html, for example.) You can go into a template file as you would any other text file and modify the HTML coding.

You can extend the Publish command's capacity for creating HTML documents by setting up your own HTML templates. To be available to Flash's template menu, the HTML file must include a title (use the code **$TT**). The HTML file must be inside the HTML folder, which lives in the Configuration Folder. For more details on locating this folder, see the sidebar "The Mystery of the Configuration Folder," in Chapter 1.

A Background of a Different Color

The default HTML template automatically sets the background color of your web page to the background color of your movie. If you want to use a different color, try creating a modified template. Open the default template, and save a copy with a new name. In the first line of code—**$TTFlash Only**—change the title to something like **$TTFlash Only (BlackBackground)**, so Flash recognizes and adds the template to the Template menu. In the tag **<BODY bgcolor="$BG">**, replace **$BG** with the HTML code for a specific hex color (**000000** for a black background, for example). Be sure to place the new template in Flash's HTML folder inside the Configuration folder (for more details about locating this folder, see the sidebar "The Mystery of the Configuration Folder," in Chapter 1).

Practice Session

When creating Flash movies for delivery to a real-world audience, many factors will influence the precise methods you use for deploying Flash content, among them your target audience's systems and your own resources. The variety of issues makes it hard to tell you how to practice working with the Publish Settings meaningfully. But, for a taste of publishing, try creating a movie that combines some of the practice items you've created in earlier chapters. Then publish it for Flash and HTML. View it in Flash Player with the Bandwidth Profiler and preview it in your browser locally.

- Start by creating a new document—save it as MyPublishTest. Open the Publish Settings dialog and make sure the document is set to use ActionScript 3.0 and Flash Player 10. (See *Working with Flash Player Settings.*)

- Add layers, and bring in some of the items you created earlier. Name the layers to indicate what content they hold. (See Chapter 6.) Include some frame-by-frame animation along with classic, shape, and motion tweens. (See Chapters 8–12.) Try using some inverse kinematics (IK) animation, some set to simply play as animation, some set to runtime IK that you can manipulate at playback. (See Chapter 13.) Include some TLF text, symbols, sounds, and video. (See Chapters 3, 7, and 17.) Add buttons, and script them to control playback and Timeline navigation. (See Chapters 14 and 15.)

- In the Publish Settings dialog, choose Flash and HTML as the publishing format. (See *Publishing > To set the publishing format.*)

- Choose the desired Flash and HTML settings. (See *Working with Flash Player Settings* and *Publishing HTML for Flash Player Files.*)

- Use the Bandwidth Profiler and Size Report to analyze the content of your movie. Add more items, new sounds, symbols, and video; see how the additions increase your download times.

- Use the Publish Preview command to view the SWF in a browser. Or use the Publish command to create the files necessary to display your movie, locate the HTML file created by the Publish command, and drag a copy to your browser window. (See *Publishing.*) Try interacting with your content.

Extra Credit

- Save a few copies of MyPublishTest, use different Publish settings for each one and compare the effects on playback of your movie. Try different settings for audio compression, for example, to get a feel for the difference in sound quality and file size.

- Try embedding the TLF SWZ code in your published SWF instead of having the SWF access the code from the runtime shared library.

Index

descenders, 99
Designer workspace, 9
Developer workspace, 9
device fonts, 92, 93
diamond icon, 292, 302
DIB files, 492
digitally recorded sounds, 550
Disabled state, 426, 427, 474
Disney, Walt, 215
Distort modifier, 123–125
docking panels, 1, 11
document-level undo, 210
Document Property inspector
    accessing Publish Settings dialog from, 544, 546
    purpose of, 15, 16
    setting frame rate in, 19, 241
    shortcut to Document Setting dialog, 16
    Stage color control, 19
    SWF History section, 541
Document Settings dialog, 16–19
    opening, 16
    purpose of, 16
    saving default settings in, 19
    setting background color in, 19
    setting frame rate in, 19, 241
    setting size of Stage in, 17–18
dot pattern, 107, 164–166
dot syntax, 441
doubleClick event, 466
double-clicking, 107, 140, 159
double slash, 428
Down keyframe, 414
download-progress bar, 541
Down state, 412, 415–416
drawing
    with pencil tool, 54
    with pen tool, 55–57
drawing aids, 21, 53
Drawing Effect options, 164, 166, 169
drawing-object containers, 159
drawing-objects
    changing fills/strokes for multiple, 125
    combining multiple, 162–163
    converting shape type, 150–151
    converting TLF text into, 150–151
    editing, on inactive layers, 180–181
    modifying, 133, 159
    removing part of another object with, 163
    resizing, 115
    selecting, 107, 108
    and shape tweening, 273
    undoing changes to, 121
    vs. other types, 48
drawing preferences, 2, 53, 374
drawing tools, 29, 30, 53–62
Duplicate Symbol button, 213
Duplicate Symbol dialog, 206
DXF files, 492
Dynamic text, 70

E

easing, 364–368
    applying to spans, 365–366

in classic tweening, 255
    custom, 364, 367–368
    in IK animation, 407
    in motion tweening, 293, 295
    purpose of, 364
Editable TLF text fields, 69, 70, 73
Edit bar, 20
Edit Envelope dialog, 514, 517–520
Edit Grid command, 22
Edit Guides command, 23
Edit in Place command, 159, 208
Edit Multiple Frames mode, 246–247
Edit Selected command, 158, 159
Edit Snapping dialog, 27
Edit Stroke Style button, 45
embedded fonts, 93
embedded video, 522, 526–529, 534
EMF files, 492
encoding options, 521
End Angle field, 52
end-link pointer, 82
end margin, 96, 97
Enhanced Windows Metafile format, 492
Erase Lines setting, 148
Erase Normal setting, 153
Eraser Mode menu, 148
eraser tool, 148, 153
Essentials workspace, 9
event handlers, 451, 457–458, 470–471
events
    defined, 451
    handling multiple, 470–471
    mouse, 448, 466
    rollover, 463–465
event sounds, 508–511
exporting movies, 543, 544

F

F4V files, 521, 522, 532
fade effects, 38, 269, 517–518, 519
Faucet mode, 148
feedback, auditory, 506
file formats
    and ActionScript versions, 4
    choosing, 4
    for images/graphics, 492
    for movies, 543
    for sounds, 500
Fill Color control, 40–42, 126
fill paths, 136, 155
fills
    adding to shapes, 63–67
    changing, for multiple selections, 125
    changing center point for, 129
    choosing colors for, 33
    converting strokes to, 149
    defined, 31
    editing across layers, 181
    interaction of merge-shapes and, 155
    interaction of strokes and, 156
    intersecting, 155
    modifying, 126–132
    rotating, 132

Hit keyframe, 414
Hit state, 412, 416, 427
hollow bullet, 216
Horizontal Scale property, 263
Horizontal Spacing option, 167
hot text, 14
HSB values, 35
HTML
    documents, 558–559
    tags, 560
    templates, 559, 560, 561
HTML section, Publish Settings dialog, 558–559
hyphenation, 100

I

identifiers, 450
if statements, 452
IK. *See also* inverse kinematics
    animation, 373, 377, 389
    author-time *vs.* runtime, 390
    drawing preferences, 374
    instance naming, 379
    meaning of acronym, 373
    shapes, 381–383, 402–403
    tools, 388
IK Armature Property inspector, 390
Illustrator, 489, 491, 492
images. *See also* graphics
    bitmap (*See* bitmaps)
    flowing text around, 76
    for frame-by-frame animation, 235
    inline, 76, 100
    for traditional animation, 215
Import command, 489
importing, 490–497
    bitmaps, 490–491
    to Library *vs.* Stage, 491
    Photoshop files, 492–497
    series of graphics files, 491
    sounds, 500–501
    video, 521–527
import statement, 450
Import to Library command, 490, 491
Import to Stage command, 490, 491, 497
Import Video dialog, 523, 524, 525, 526
in-betweeners, 224
in-between frames
    creating, 223, 224
    extending tween spans with, 326
    varying animation speed by adding, 242–243
    vs. keyframes, 224
inches, 18
indents, 97
Info panel, 116, 200
ink-bottle tool, 63–64, 125, 128
inline graphics, 76, 100
Input text, 70
Insert commands, 223
Insert Frame command, 243
Insert > Keyframe command, 332
Insert Target Path button, 481
instances, 195, 450. *See also* symbol instances
interactive buttons, 409, 430

interactive environments, 409
interactive objects, 466
interactive pattern brushes, 169
interactive websites, 431
interactivity
    best way to create, in Flash, 431
    defined, 436
    practice session, 487–488
    scripting for, 451, 468–469
    using ActionScript to create, 431 (*See also* ActionScript)
international typography, 92
Internet connection speeds, 538, 541
Internet Explorer, 560. *See also* web browsers
Intersect command, 163
intersecting fills, 155
inverse kinematics, 373–408
    author-time *vs.* runtime, 390
    constraining IK motion, 391–400
    creating IK shapes, 381–383
    defined, 373
    and easing, 367, 407
    editing IK elements, 401–407
    incorporating into symbols, 389
    and instance naming, 379
    and motion tweens, 355
    and pose layers, 380
    practice session, 408
    saving as symbols, 389
    using armatures to connect symbols, 374–377
    vs. shape tweening, 273
    when to use, 388
    working with poses, 384–389
iPhone applications, 547

J

join styles, 43, 44, 45
joints, 378
JPEG compression, 494, 548
JPEG files, 492
justified text, 90, 96, 101
Justify button, 101
JVT, 522

K

kerning, 91
keyboard shortcuts, 31, 143
Keyframe command, 219, 221, 222, 332
keyframes
    adding to classic tweens, 256
    assigning sounds to, 502–504
    blank, 216, 219–220, 221, 222
    for bouncing-ball animation, 235–236
    creating, 219–220, 236
    defined, 215
    duplicating, 221, 332
    editing multiple, 246–247
    how Timeline displays, 216
    inserting *vs.* adding, 221
    inserting *vs.* converting, 222
    position, 292, 302, 314–316
    removing, 232
    rotation, 292, 319

N

naming/renaming
    components, 420
    frame labels, 429
    instances, 379, 450
    layer folders, 175
    layers, 175, 497
nested objects, 477
network-only access, 555, 556
New Document dialog, 4
New Document option, 2
New Folder button/command, 210
New From Template dialog, 7
New Symbol button/command, 201
New Workspace dialog, 9
nodes, 379
No Document option, 2
non-contact-sensitive selection rectangles, 111–112
numeric values, 14

O

Object Drawing mode, 29, 47, 48, 62
object-level undo, 210
Omit Trace Actions option, 554
onion skinning, 244–245, 247, 255, 303, 348
On Launch options, 2
Open As Library dialog, 196
open-link icon, 82
OpenType fonts, 11, 70, 98
operators, 452
Orient to Path mode, 262
Oval Options section, Property inspector, 52
oval-primitives, shape tweening, 285
oval-primitive tool, 144, 146–147
ovals, transforming rectangles into, 275–276
oval tool, 50–51
Over keyframe, 414
overlapping
    fills, 155, 162
    graphics, 171
    images, 213
    shapes, 59, 150, 162–163
    sounds, 510, 512
Over state, 411, 415–416, 426

P

padding, 102
paint-bucket tool, 63, 65–66, 125, 126, 132
painting
    with gradients, 60–62
    random dot pattern, 164–166
Paint Normal setting, 153
Paint Over Edge checkbox, 168
panels, 11–15. See also specific panels
    accessing, 11
    modifying fills/strokes in, 127
    opening/closing, 12
    purpose of, 11
    resizing, 13
panel windows, 12
paragraph attributes, 95–97

paragraphs
    creating space between, 97
    indenting, 97
    setting alignment for, 95–96
    setting margins for, 97
Paragraph settings, Text Edit mode, 84, 85
parameter hints, 444
parameters
    for button components, 422, 423, 424
    for button states, 420
    for events, 446
    for FLVPlayback component, 530
    for functions, 453
    for grids/guides, 22–23
    for patterns, 164, 167
    for snapping to grids/guides, 26
    for sounds, 508
    for Stage, 16
parent bones, 375, 378
parentheses (( )), 441
parent object, 477
Particle System pattern, 169
Password behavior, 102
password fields, 102
Pasteboard, 17
Paste Frames command, 228, 330, 337, 338
Paste in Center command, 182
Paste in Place command, 183–184
Paste Motion command, 369, 371
Paste Pose command, 389
pasting modes, 183
paths
    adding points to, 143, 301
    closing, 140
    copying and pasting, 306
    creating open, 56
    defined, 58
    extending, 140, 143
    math for creating, 58
    modifying, 105, 144–147
    moving symbols along, 259–261
    orienting tween target to curved, 303
    removing points from, 301
    repositioning, 297
    reshaping, 299
    resizing, 298
    swapping, 306–307
    target, 477–478, 481
    viewing, 136
pattern brushes, interactive, 169
patterns, creating/customizing, 164–169
Pattern Scale option, 167, 168
pattern tools, 67, 164
pencil tool, 53, 54
pen tool, 53, 55–57, 140
Permit Debugging option, 554
perspective, 124
Photoshop, 489, 491, 492–497
Ping-Pong game, 339–348
pixels, 18
playback, preparing movies for optimal, 538–541
Play command, 239

Streaming Graph mode, 540
stream sounds, 513–514
Strength value, 395
strikethrough text, 94
Stroke Color control, 43–45, 126
stroke height, 43
strokes. *See also* lines
    adding to shapes, 63–67
    changing, for multiple selections, 125
    choosing colors for, 33
    constraining scaling of, 45
    converting to fills, 149
    defined, 31
    interactions between fills and, 156
    modifying, 126–132
    setting properties for, 43–45
    setting style for, 44
    shape-tweening fills with, 277–278
    and TLF border colors, 104
    transforming, 275–276
Stroke Style dialog, 45
stroke styles, 44, 45
Style menu, 88
subscripts, 94
subselection tool, 133, 136, 143, 147
Sun AU files, 500
superscripts, 94
Swap button, 212
Swap Symbol dialog, 212–213
Swatches panel, 38, 39, 127
.swf extension, 239, 456
SWF files
    compressing, 552
    controlling access to, 554, 555
    embedding fonts in, 93
    embedding video in, 521
    extension for, 239
    how Flash stores, 239
    password-protecting, 554
    publishing, 449, 546
    viewing in Flash Player, 537
SWF History feature, 541
SWZ files, 17, 240
symbol-editing mode, 201, 202, 203, 208
symbol instances, 203–213. *See also* symbols
    breaking link to, 211
    converting to graphics, 211
    defined, 203
    and IK animation, 377
    linking in linear armatures, 375–377
    modifying, 204–207
    placing in movies, 203
    swapping one for another, 212–213
symbols, 197–202. *See also* symbol instances
    animating change in size of, 263–264
    changing color over time, 268–269
    and classic tweening, 252
    converting animations to, 357–358
    converting graphics to, 197–199
    creating from scratch, 201–202
    defined, 195
    and Distort Modifier, 125
    duplicating, 206, 213

editing, 202, 208
moving along paths, 259–261
moving in straight lines, 257–258
positioning tweened, 253
practice session, 214
reducing layer buildup with, 359
registration point for, 200, 202
rotating/spinning, 265–267
swapping, 305
switching, 212–213
testing interactivity of, 456
transformation point for, 200
transforming, 204
and tweening types, 250
types of, 199
using IK armatures to connect, 374–377
symbol types, 199, 206, 414, 526
Symmetry Brush pattern, 169
synchronized sounds, 508
Sync setting, 512, 513, 515
syntax, ActionScript, 441, 454–455
System 7 sounds, 500
System Color Picker, 42

T

Tab bar, 13
tail, of bone, 378
tangent handles, 58
targeting frame labels, 461
target instances, 287
target paths, 477–478, 481
template documents, 6–7, 28
template variables, 560
test modes, 454
Test Movie command, 239, 240, 456
Test Scene command, 240, 243, 363, 456
text, 69–104. *See also* text fields
    anti-aliasing, 87, 92
    breaking apart, 151
    converting TLF to Classic, 83
    flowing, 70, 83
    highlighted, 94
    images amid, 76
    justified, 90, 101
    links, 482–483
    multicolumn, 70, 100, 102
    multidirectional, 92
    multinational, 92
    non-wrapping, 72–73
    point *vs.* area, 71
    preferences, 2
    ragged, 95, 96
    selecting, 86
    setting character attributes for, 84–94
    setting paragraph attributes for, 95–97
    strikethrough, 94
    threaded, 76, 86
    underlined, 94
    vertical *vs.* horizontal, 92
    wrapping, 74–75
text-alignment methods, 96
text color, 91, 94
Text Edit mode, 84

WATCH
READ
CREATE

Meet Creative Edge.

A new resource of unlimited books, videos and tutorials for creatives from the world's leading experts.

Creative Edge is your one stop for inspiration, answers to technical questions and ways to stay at the top of your game so you can focus on what you do best—being creative.

All for only $24.99 per month for access—any day any time you need it.

creativeedge.com